Everything's a Text

Everything's a Text
Readings for Composition

Dan Melzer
California State University, Sacramento

Deborah Coxwell-Teague
Florida State University

Longman

Boston Columbus Indianapolis New York San Francisco Upper Saddle River
Amsterdam Cape Town Dubai London Madrid Milan Munich Paris Montreal
Toronto Delhi Mexico City São Paulo Sydney Hong Kong Seoul Singapore Taipei Tokyo

Publisher: Joseph Opiela
Senior Acquisitions Editor: Lauren A. Finn
Development Manager: Mary Ellen Curley
Senior Development Editor: Anne Brunell Ehrenworth
Senior Supplements Editor: Donna Campion
Senior Media Producer: Stefanie Liebman
Senior Marketing Manager: Sandra McGuire
Production Manager: Eric Jorgensen
Project Coordination, Text Design, and Electronic Page Makeup: Electronic Publishing
    Services Inc., NYC
Cover Design Manager: Wendy Ann Fredericks
Cover Designer: Kay Petronio
Cover Photo: © Gavin Hellier/Getty Images
Photo Researcher: Poyee Oster
Senior Manufacturing Buyer: Dennis J. Para
Printer and Binder: Courier Companies, Inc.
Cover Printer: Courier Companies, Inc.

For permission to use copyrighted material, grateful acknowledgment is made to the copyright holders on pp. 557–563, which are hereby made part of this copyright page.

Copyright © 2011 by Pearson Education, Inc.

Library of Congress Cataloging-in-Publication Data

Everything's a text : readings for composition/[compiled by] Dan Melzer, Deborah Coxwell-Teague.
    p. cm.
Includes bibliographical references and index.
ISBN 978-0-205-63954-0
1. College readers.   2. English language—Rhetoric.   3. Report writing.   4. Culture.
I. Melzer, Dan.   II. Coxwell-Teague, Deborah.   III. Title.

PE1417.E895 2011
808′.0427—dc22   2010038982

5 6 7 8 9 10 V092 16 15

Longman
is an imprint of

www.pearsonhighered.com

ISBN-13: 978-0-205-63954-0
ISBN-10:   0-205-63954-2

Brief Contents

Contents

Contents

PART II   Readings for Situating Multiple Literacies

Preface

In every aspect of life, from home to school to work, the way we interact with the world is becoming more complex—more multifaceted. The idea that the world is becoming more complex is true of literacy as well. Literacy has traditionally been defined as the quality of being educated or having knowledge, and a literate person as one with the ability to read and write. What has always been implied in this definition is the ability to read and write *print texts*. But today, to be literate, we must be able to read and write print texts, visual texts, digital texts, and those that combine these mediums. In fact, wider definitions of literacy might include cultural literacy, academic literacy, literacy about civic issues—even numeric and financial literacy.

Everything's a Text doesn't encourage a simple definition of what literacy is or focus on a single type of literacy. It offers readings and projects that help the reader explore the concept of literacy in many contexts, from oral to visual to digital and more. "Context" is a key idea because every act of literacy, whether it's composing a text message to a friend or a research paper for a political science class or a speech for a wedding, presents writers with different situations. *Everything's a Text* encourages practice in analyzing and composing in a variety of situations, for a variety of purposes and audiences, and in a variety of genres. For this reason, the texts explored range from songs to personal narratives to blogs to graphic novels to academic essays.

Not only does this approach reflect the range of reading and composing situations we encounter every day, but it's also based on current scholarly theories of literacy, which emphasize the teaching of reading and composing in multiliterate ways. Current scholarship in Composition Studies argues that the focus of composition courses should be literacy itself. *Everything's a Text* draws on all of this research to help college students explore and develop twenty-first–century literacies that will serve them in their college courses, their personal lives, and in their careers beyond college.

Pedagogical Features

Contemporary Readings in Varied Genres

The anthology features contemporary readings that range in genres from essays and articles to blogs, photos, lyrics, editorials, graffiti, paintings, posters, and more. The range of authors includes academics, college students, newspaper reporters, fiction writers, and more. While some texts mix genres, all are organized into chapters that focus on a broad type of literacy, including personal, oral, visual, digital, cultural, academic, and civic literacies. Students explore many rhetorical contexts, practice a variety of literacies, and reflect critically on their own reading and composing processes. Teachers can use the readings to organize their class either by type of literacy or by theme.

A Rhetoric of Reading and Writing Instruction

Chapters 1 and 2 establish a foundation for reading *Everything's a Text*, including a framework and common language for definitions and key concepts. Chapter 1 asks the question "What is literacy?" and not only explores varied definitions, but also encourages students to investigate their own assumptions. The aim of Chapter 1 is to foster a broader and deeper understanding of what it means to be literate in the twenty-first century. Chapter 2 builds on this discussion and provides strategies for reading and composing by providing information that will help students learn to think carefully about purpose, audience, persona, medium, genre, and context. Students will revisit these concepts throughout the text both in the questions that follow each reading and the questions that close each anthology chapter.

Topical Reading Clusters within Chapters

Some readings within each chapter appear in topical clusters so that they "speak" to each other in conversation, such as several readings in the civic literacies chapter that explore whether the United States should be "English only." Rather than provide simple pro/con arguments, these challenge readers to consider a variety of perspectives on challenging issues. Writers can use them as a jumping-off place for researched writing, and teachers can use them to facilitate synthesis assignments.

Commissioned Readings Investigate Different Kinds of Literacy

Each of Chapters 3–9 opens with a reading authored for *Everything's a Text* that explores different definitions of the literacy that is the chapter's focus (visual, digital, oral, etc.). While the chapter's readings are typically *examples* of each chapter's broad literacy, this opening reading takes on the chapter's literacy as its *topic*, often offering a brief history, inquiring into definitions, and investigating variations so that students and instructors can use the reading as a foundation for analyzing the texts that follow.

Literacy Connections and Before You Read Questions

Bookending each reading are Before You Read and Literacy Connection questions. Literacy Connections follow each reading. The first few questions help students recognize and understand important or nuanced ideas, the next encourage reading response and analysis, and the last question fosters connections between the reading and other readings in the chapter. Before each reading, a Before You Read thinking and writing prompt engages students in a reading's subject matter. By contextualizing what they are about to read, students associate a reading's topic with an idea or experience familiar to them, leading to a fuller understanding of the text.

Literacy Projects

Closing each of Chapters 3–9 are several Literacy Projects that often involve extended research and always involve more formal composing tasks. Some projects encourage textual analysis or writing a researched argument paper, but others propose new media projects such as creating a documentary film, composing a poster campaign, recording an audio script, and so on. Students will create examples of a certain type of literacy (e.g., a text that demonstrates visual literacy) as well as critically reflect on their experiences working within and developing that literacy.

Student Case Studies

Immediately after the commissioned reading in each anthology chapter follows a case study of a college student's work. For example, the digital literacies chapter features a student's work creating a Web site, while the chapter on civic literacies boasts a student composing a report for a government agency. Student work is treated like that of professional writers and offers strategies for composing.

Model Papers in MLA, APA, and CSE Styles

While several texts throughout the book are researched and cited, three student texts are specifically presented as models for formatting in common academic styles that students will encounter in their general education curriculum. In Chapter 8, Situating Academic Literacies, students can refer to Nancy Alkema's "Emotional Disturbances: The Effects of Parental Neglect Types on Children" for a model of APA style, Harshjit Sethi's "Constitutionality v. Morality: San Antonio School District v. Rodriguez" for a model of MLA style, and Ashley Nicole Phares's "Mechanistic and

Genetic Causes of Depression and the Effect of SSRIs on the Serotonergic Pathway" for a model of CSE style.

Freewrites

Within Chapters 1 and 2 students will find Freewrites: informal writing activities that encourage reflection on literacy experiences; analytic thinking about different kinds of literacy; and practice thinking critically about purpose, audience, persona, medium, genre, and context. These Freewrites offer opportunities to explore topics that are emphasized throughout each chapter's readings.

Supplements

Instructor's Manual

The *Instructor's Manual* includes an analysis of each reading, additional writing projects and readings, and ideas for syllabi. The sample syllabi and additional writing projects offer a variety of teaching alternatives, and we hope they further emphasize the flexibility of *Everything's a Text*. Each semester an instructor can try a different approach, whether that means focusing on different literacy contexts, a different theme, or different mediums and genres.

The only online application to integrate a writing environment with proven resources for grammar, writing, and research, *MyCompLab* gives students help at their fingertips as they draft and revise. Instructors have access to a variety of assessment tools, including commenting capabilities, diagnostics and study plans, and an ePortfolio. Created after years of extensive research and in partnership with faculty and students across the country, *MyCompLab* offers a seamless and flexible teaching and learning environment built specifically for writers.

How Students Might Use *Everything's a Text*

Many of us grew up thinking of literacy as the ability to read and write print texts, so the idea that literacy is a much broader concept and can include personal, oral, visual, digital, popular culture, academic, and civic literacies is both exciting and challenging. If you take a few minutes to think about it, you might reach the conclusion that we "read" all kinds of texts every day—not just traditional texts such as books, newspapers, and magazines, but also billboards, Web sites, posters, *Facebook* pages, and even radio programs, television shows, movies, and online videos.

In the past most of us didn't think of reading in terms of what we do when we *hear* a story, *listen* to a radio program, or *watch* a movie, an online video, or a television show. But if you consider what it is that you do when you listen to or watch these "texts," you might realize that you take in information, interpret it, and react to it much as you do when you read traditional print texts.

Allow yourself to think about literacy in new and various ways. When you broaden your ideas about what it means to be literate in the twenty-first century, you'll be more likely to appreciate the importance of learning how to read, interpret, and analyze the full range of texts that bombard you every day—whether those texts are political campaign ads, reality TV shows, or lyrics from your favorite musician.

Chapters 1 and 2 introduce key ideas and terms used throughout the readings, questions, and projects in Chapters 3–9. In these chapters you will find excerpts from Malcolm X speeches and *The Lord of the Rings* novel and film script; song lyrics from Mos Def; a cartoon by Lynda Barry; a poem by Billy Collins; essays composed by students and professional writers; an excerpt from a graphic novel by Joe Hill; and readings about blogging, online identities, and the nature of community in video games.

While the selections are interesting and engaging, you are likely to find that some of them challenge you as a reader and perhaps require not only active and critical reading, but also more than one reading. For example, Billy Collins's poem "Marginalia" includes several references that may be unfamiliar to you, and you'll need to take time to check out those references and re-read the poem in order to fully enjoy and appreciate it. Gloria Anzaldúa incorporates two languages—both English and Spanish—in "How to Tame a Wild Tongue," and reading her bilingual essay may require extra time. As you read these texts, react to them, question them, agree or disagree with the authors, make personal connections with the readings, and think about how you can use the ideas presented in the various texts to enrich your own life.

Equally relevant and challenging are literacy projects at the end of each chapter that range from snapshots essays, radical revision projects, and digital literacy narratives to political blogs, audio script group projects, and poster campaigns. Whether you work on projects in the book or others, think of ways you can approach the assignment so that you are spending your time on something that interests you and matters to you as an individual—something you want to share with others and receive feedback on, something you want to work on and revise until you have done your best work.

Facebook

Join us at www.facebook.com/EverythingsaText for additional activities and links. Correspond with fellow users of *Everything's a Text* to exchange ideas or just become a fan of the book!

Acknowledgments

We would like to thank our mentors and colleagues at Florida State University, present and past, especially Wendy Bishop, Richard Straub, Carrie Leverenz, Ruth Mirtz, and Kathleen Yancey. We are also grateful to the instructors who reviewed our book at various points in its development and helped us shape it:

Cheryl E. Ball, Illinois State University; Jo Ann M. Bamdas, Palm Beach State College; Felicia Campbell, University of Nevada, Las Vegas; Jonikka Charlton, The University of Texas—Pan American; Andrea Davis, Michigan State University; Dominic DelliCarpini, York College of Pennsylvania; Julie Douberly, Georgia Southern University; Denise Frusciante, Palm Beach Atlantic University; Susanmarie Harrington, University of Vermont; Barbara Heifferon, Rochester Institute of Technology; Pam Hollander, Nichols College; David A. Jolliffe, University of Arkansas; Bonnie Lenore Kyburz, Utah Valley University; Kimberly Lacey, Wayne State University; Heidi McKee, Miami University; Susan Miller-Cochran, North Carolina State University; Shannon R. Mortimore, Shippensburg University; Alyssa J. O'Brien, Stanford University; Darin Payne, University of Hawaii-Manoa; Randy Phillis, Mesa State College; Anna C. Priebe, Ball State University; Deborah Scaggs, Texas A&M International University; Bob Schwegler, University of Rhode Island; Stacia Watkins, Middle Tennessee State University; Casey White, Iowa State University; Carl Whithaus, University of California, Davis.

We would like to thank the editorial team at Pearson Longman, especially Lauren Finn and Anne Brunell Ehrenworth. Finally, thanks to the authors of our commissioned essays, Amy Hodges Hamilton, Alexis Davidson, Pavel Zemliansky, Dustin Anderson, Stacey Suver, Fiona Glade, and Catherine Gabor. And thanks to our fine photographer, Claire Smith.

DAN MELZER

DEBORAH COXWELL-TEAGUE

1

What Is Literacy?

Today information about the world around us comes to us not only by words on a piece of paper, but also more and more through the powerful images and sounds of our multimedia culture. . . . If our children are to be able to navigate their lives through this multimedia culture, they need to be fluent in "reading" and "writing" the language of images and sounds just as we have always taught them to "read" and "write" the language of printed communications.

—*Center for Media Literacy*

Meaning is made in ways that are increasingly multimodal—in which written-linguistic modes of meaning are part and parcel of visual, audio, and spatial patterns of meaning. Take for instance the multimodal ways in which meanings are made on the World Wide Web, or in video capturing, or in interactive multimedia, or in desktop publishing, or in the use of written texts in a shopping mall. To find our way around this emerging world of meaning requires a new, multimodal literacy.

—Professors Bill Cope and Mary Kalantzis, *Multiliteracies*

Twenty-first-century readers and writers need to

- Develop proficiency with the tools of technology
- Build relationships with others to pose and solve problems collaboratively and cross-culturally
- Design and share information for global communities to meet a variety of purposes
- Manage, analyze, and synthesize multiple streams of simultaneous information

- Create, critique, analyze, and evaluate multimedia texts
- Attend to the ethical responsibilities required by these complex environments

—from *Toward a Definition of 21st Century Literacies*
by the National Council of Teachers of English

Freewrite Definitions of Literacy

A *freewrite* is a kind of informal, in-class writing that focuses on using writing to think about and explore ideas. The goal of a freewrite is *not* to create finely crafted paragraphs or grammatically correct sentences, but to just keep your pen moving (or keep typing on the keyboard) and let the ideas flow. Some of the freewrites in this book will ask you to make a list, some will ask you to reflect on your experiences, and some will ask you to talk and write in groups. The goal of this freewrite is to get you thinking about the definition of *literacy*. What do you think it means to be *literate*? Are there different definitions for literacy in different time periods, cultures, and countries?

Definitions of Literacy

When you hear the word *literacy*, the first thing you might think of is print literacy—reading words in books, magazines, and newspapers, or writing essays for a class. Maybe you associate being literate with knowing Standard English or with having read the novels that are required reading in high school literature courses, like *The Scarlet Letter*, *The Catcher in the Rye*, or *Pride and Prejudice*. Traditional ideas about what it means to be literate are reflected in grammar handbooks and in composition textbooks that provide universal rules for good writing and in books such as E. D. Hirsch's *Cultural Literacy*, which makes the argument for a single, standard English language and a set of texts that all educated Americans should read.

These traditional ideas about literacy have been challenged by rapid transformations in America and around the world. You've probably heard terms like *multimedia, multiple intelligences, multiculturalism,* and *multilingual.* The traditional idea that there should be one standard way of writing and speaking in America is being questioned by educators who think of literacy as "multiple." Because of the increasing ethnic diversity of America and the variety of global Englishes being used around the world, a literate person needs to know how to cross linguistic boundaries and how to respect language and cultural diversity. In his book *Critical Literacy*, Eugene Provenzo argues that being literate means having knowledge of "complexity and diversity." Educators such as Provenzo, Paulo Freire, and Ira Shor argue that one aspect of this complexity and diversity is political and cultural conflict. Critical literacy educators argue that an important part of being literate is being aware of the relationship between language and power, and they ask who is left out and why one group gets to decide what the rules of communication are and who gets to speak. Being literate means being able to evaluate what you read and being able to reflect critically on your own reading and writing processes. This means being able to understand how economic, social, and political factors have shaped your own literacy history.

Writers such as Cynthia Selfe, James Paul Gee, and John Seely Brown argue that because of the explosion of digital communications, a literate person needs to be skilled in more than just print literacy. Many new types of communications—blogs, graphic novels, streaming video, PowerPoint, text messaging, e-mail, virtual reality—require skills that are different than the skills needed to compose in traditional print literacies. These new media literacies often combine print literacy with digital, visual, and oral literacies. These channels of communication—print, digital, visual, and oral—are what communication theorists call *modes*. The term *multimodal* is used to refer to literacies that combine these different channels of communication. Traditional print literacies like books, magazines, and newspapers are still important forms of literacy, but the ability to read and compose in digital, visual, and oral modes is also critical to being a literate person in the twenty-first century. It's just as important that you learn to "read" a photo, song, or television show as it is to learn to read words on the page or the screen.

One of the kinds of literacies we'll focus on throughout this book is *academic literacies*. But academic literacy is only one kind of literacy, and even academic literacy is not a universal standard or a unified set of rules. What we value in academic writing in America is not necessarily what is valued in academic writing in other countries. Even in your own college, each field (the natural sciences, the social sciences, the humanities) will present you with a different version of what it means to be literate. You might find conflicts and connections with the writing you do in school and the writing you do for yourself, or the kinds of literacies that are valued by your family or your community.

You will encounter many kinds of literacies in your public life outside of school, whether they are political speeches, newspaper editorials, or pop culture magazines. Academic literacies, personal literacies, pop culture literacies, and civic literacies are all contexts for literacy that will present you with different purposes, audiences, and forms of writing that will shape your reading and writing processes. All acts of literacy are *situated*—they are constructed by the specific situation you find yourself in as a reader or composer. This literacy situation includes the role you play as the composer of a message, the form you compose in, your audience, and the social and cultural contexts for you and your audience. Rather than talking about a single, unified concept of literacy or the writing process, this book talks about multiple and situated literacies and composing processes. We use the term *compose* instead of *write* because literacy involves the creation of not just printed words but also photos, speeches, songs, artwork, videos, and so forth.

To help us think about this concept of multiple literacies, consider these literacy examples:

> The Mexican music group Molotov combines heavy metal and hip-hop, English and Spanish, and rap beats and traditional Mexican music to create a new "hybrid" form of rap music that has an audience in Mexico, the United States, and around the world.

> A student in a history class at San Antonio Community College creates an informative Internet resource site about the feminist movement that includes JPEG images, an essay about feminism, links to other Web sites, audio clips of an interview with a professor on campus who was part of the feminist movements of the 1970s, and a link to a video about the feminist Betty Friedan.

> In 1998, Joan Blades and Wes Boyd, two Silicon Valley entrepreneurs, start an online petition to "Censure President Clinton and Move On to Pressing Issues Facing the Nation." Within days, hundreds of thousands sign the petition, and Blades and Boyd form a Political Action Committee, MoveOn.org, with ad campaigns, marches, civic events, petitions, book publishing, and a Web site.

> Magic Bean Café in Michigan creates a page on *Facebook* to share photos and advertise their menu, music events, poetry readings, and newsletter. The page has 295 friends. The *Facebook* page is linked from Magic Bean Café's Web site.

In the four examples above, composers work in oral modes (creating music or clips of interviews), in digital modes (creating Web sites and online petitions), in visual modes (adding JPEG images and photo galleries to a Web site), and in multimodal literacies (creating a *Facebook* site that includes print text, images, and hyperlinks). In order to be literate, the composers in our examples needed the agility to compose for multiple purposes and audiences. The composers in our examples gathered information about feminism for a college class and for a global audience on the Internet, started a petition in order to affect political change, and advertised a business while creating a sense of community among the people who frequented the business.

New audiences and contexts mean new forms of writing that evolve to meet the demands of new literacy situations—new *genres*. Genres such as the online petition or the social networking Web site (such as *Facebook*) are new forms that have evolved as useful ways of communicating—new genres of communicating. The composers in our examples work in multiple genres.

MoveOn.org communicates through books, news articles, press releases, ads, letters, e-mails, petitions, and so forth. Some of these genres have been around for a long time (such as the press release), and others have evolved with new technologies (such as e-mails or online petitions). In addition to being able to communicate in a variety of genres, the ability to combine genres to create hybrid forms is a valuable skill for twenty-first-century literacy.

Molotov combines hip-hop, heavy metal, and traditional Mexican music genres to create a new genre of hip-hop. Molotov also combines Spanish and English, adding even more language variety to a genre—hip-hop—that constantly adds new expressions to the English language. As the United States becomes more diverse and global communications become faster and easier, composers who can speak and write in multiple languages and dialects will have an advantage over those who are monolingual and can use only the standardized version of English found in grammar handbooks.

Freewrite Your Literacy Experiences

In this freewrite, you will see just how many different literacies you read and compose. Make a list of everything you read and composed in the last week. How many different modes did you compose in (print, visual, digital, oral)? How many different types of compositions (genres) did you read and compose? How many different audiences did you compose for?

At this point you might be thinking that all of this talk about literacies doesn't connect to you, a student in college. But consider what a student in one of our first-year writing courses read and composed in a single week.

Composed:

- A research paper for a history class
- E-mails to friends and family
- An Evite invitation to a party
- Lyrics for a song for her band
- A blog entry about her literacy history for her composition class
- A job application

- Text messages to friends
- A PowerPoint presentation in a marketing class
- Reading responses posted to an electronic discussion board for a sociology class

Read:

- Articles from an academic journal for the history research paper
- *Spin* magazine
- Other students' blog entries from her composition class
- Strips of the Webcomic *Achewood*
- The student newspaper
- Textbook chapters for her sociology and chemistry classes
- The TV show *The Office*
- Mail from her bank about an account she just opened up
- Songs on her iPod
- A yoga video on *YouTube*

Each of these composing and reading situations presented our student with different audiences, different purposes for reading and composing, and different kinds of texts (including digital, visual, and oral texts). The purposes, audiences, and texts shaped her reading and composing processes, and she needed the flexibility to adjust her approach for each new literacy situation she encountered. Each act of reading and composing was situated in a specific purpose, genre, audience, and context. When you stop and think about all of the different kinds of texts you compose and read, in school and out of school, it's clear that the way we define literacy—and what it means to be a literate person—is multiple.

When we use the term *multiple literacies*, then, we mean that a literate person in the twenty-first century needs to be able to:

- Compose in multiple modes (print, oral, visual, digital)
- Compose for multiple purposes and audiences, including audiences with diverse cultural, ethnic, and linguistic backgrounds
- Compose in multiple contexts, including school, home, work, and civic contexts
- Compose in multiple genres, including new media genres such as blogs or text messages
- Read multiple kinds of texts, including visual texts such as ads, billboards, films, and so forth.

Even though a key word you will see throughout this book is *multiple*, there are features of any literacy situation that composers need to be aware of in order to communicate effectively. We've already touched on some of these features, such as purpose and audience and genre. In this next section, we'll look at some of these factors in any literacy situation

Situating Literacy

Even though there is no single definition of literacy or of the composing process, there are factors that a reader or composer needs to consider in any literacy situation, whether it's writing an essay for a sociology class, viewing a video on *YouTube*, or putting together a PowerPoint presentation. In the rest of this chapter, we'll look at some of the major factors you'll need to consider in any literacy situation: purpose, audience, persona, medium, genre, and context. Even though twenty-first-century literacies are complex and demanding, being aware of these different rhetorical factors in literacy situations can help you analyze any kind of text and compose in any kind of literacy situation.

Freewrite Defining the Factors in Literacy Situations

The goal of this freewrite is to find out what you already know about some of the key factors in any literacy situation that we're going to discuss in the rest of this chapter. Write for a total of ten minutes about how you would define each of the key terms below. If you're not sure of a definition, write down words you associate with the term. Be prepared to share your thoughts with the class.

purpose	persona	genre
audience	medium	context

Literacy Purposes

Everything we compose has a purpose: to persuade someone to buy a product, to make someone laugh or cry, to get an "A" on a test, to remind yourself what you need at the grocery store, to brainstorm a topic for a research paper. The composing we do both in and out of school calls on us to read and write for multiple purposes, and the literacy situation will play a role in constructing our purposes. For example, if you're taking an essay exam for a college class, your purposes will be shaped by the exam questions, the teacher as your audience, the genre of the essay exam, and even the amount of time you have to complete the exam.

To talk in more detail about composing purposes, let's look at a letter written by former President Bill Clinton. This letter of apology was sent to Japanese Americans who were interned during World War II, and it was part of the
Civil Liberties Act of 1988, which gave reparation checks of $20,000 to Japan-
ese Americans who were forced to live in prison camps when the United
States went to war with Japan.

THE WHITE HOUSE

WASHINGTON

October 1, 1993

Over fifty years ago, the United States
Government unjustly interned, evacuated, or
relocated you and many other Japanese Americans.
Today, on behalf of your fellow Americans, I
offer a sincere apology to you for the actions
that unfairly denied Japanese Americans and
their families fundamental liberties during
World War II.

In passing the Civil Liberties Act of
1988, we acknowledged the wrongs of the past
and offered redress to those who endured such
grave injustice. In retrospect, we understand
that the nation's actions were rooted deeply in
racial prejudice, wartime hysteria, and a lack
of political leadership. We must learn from
the past and dedicate ourselves as a nation to
renewing the spirit of equality and our love of
freedom. Together, we can guarantee a future
with liberty and justice for all. You and your
family have my best wishes for the future.

Bill Clinton

Let's take a close look at former President Bill Clinton's letter of apology to Japanese American victims of internment camps to think about the way composers' purposes affect what they compose. The first paragraph reveals that one purpose of the letter is to admit that the United States had acted unjustly. President Clinton's primary audience, the Japanese Americans who were held in internment camps, is fully aware of the injustice of the government's behavior during World War II, but up until this point the government had not officially acknowledged that it was wrong. One purpose of Clinton's letter, then, is to finally acknowledge that the U.S. government had seriously wronged Japanese Americans. Because this is such an important purpose, it's the focus of the first paragraph. To clearly signal this intent, President Clinton uses words such as *unjustly, sincere apology,* and *unfairly denied.*

Another purpose for writing the letter is to outline why the United States acted unjustly and how we can learn from past mistakes. President Clinton argues that "the nation's actions were rooted deeply in racial prejudice, wartime hysteria, and a lack of political leadership," and he says that we must learn from these mistakes. Clinton ends his letter with words such as *equality, freedom,* and *liberty and justice for all.* These words could be aimed at both the primary audience (Japanese Americans) and a broader secondary audience (Americans in general).

Even though President Clinton states that this is a letter of apology, a close look at the language he uses could reveal other purposes. For example, notice that he begins the letter with the phrase "Over fifty years ago." This phrase gives readers a sense of distant events—the first sentence might have had a different effect on readers if he would have written, "It was only fifty years ago . . . ." The language he uses to describe the internment is much different from the language that a Japanese American who was interned might use to describe his or her experiences. Words such as *evacuated* or *relocated* can have positive connotations, as when people in danger are evacuated by the government to a safer location, or when people relocate for a better job. Even the word *interned* has fewer negative meanings than the word *imprisoned.*

Ending with familiar patriotic words and phrases such as "liberty and justice for all," President Clinton further distances himself and the current government from past injustices and ends his apology on an optimistic note rather than a note of regret. You could argue that even though his primary purpose was to acknowledge and apologize for past injustices, his language reveals that he is also distancing himself and the current government from these injustices, and trying to put a positive spin on his apology by aligning his own values with patriotism. As you read the texts in this book and analyze composers' purposes, think about both what composers state as their purposes and what other, unstated purposes their language might reveal.

Freewrite Literacy Purposes

Read President Barack Obama's inaugural address on page 152. As you read President Obama's address, think about the ways that his purposes affect his voice and style, the tone he takes, the way he organizes his address, the kind of arguments he makes, and the type of evidence he uses. In small groups, discuss your analysis of President Obama's address.

Take notes on the group's analysis of the composer's stated and unstated purposes, and how his purpose (or purposes) affected his voice, style, tone, word choice, organization, arguments, evidence, and so forth. Be prepared to report out to the class.

Literacy Audiences

Composers always have both a purpose for composing and an audience or audiences to receive their message. Sometimes the primary audience for what you compose is you—for example, when you're writing in your diary or making a to–do list. In school the teacher is often the primary audience, but teachers can play different roles. A teacher might play the audience of an "examiner," testing you to see whether you've understood ideas from a class text or a lecture. A teacher might play the role of representative of her academic field, asking you to learn to write like a chemist, a historian, or an anthropologist in order to initiate you to her field. A teacher could simply play the role of an interested reader, asking you to tell her about your literacy history or your personal opinions on a subject.

Beyond school, the audiences we compose for become even more diverse: friends, family, Web surfers, government officials, companies—the list is endless. Often we compose for both primary and secondary audiences: We send an e-mail to a friend and "cc" other friends, we create an electronic portfolio of our work for a capstone course that will also be used when we enter the job market, and we write a poem to a loved one but then decide to publish it in a school journal, and so forth. Some writing situations ask us to create an audience through the words we use—to invoke an audience. Other writing situations present us with a very real audience that we need to address directly to be persuasive—for example, a speech at a public event. Every time someone sits down to compose, he or she imagines audiences they're writing to, and they're shaped by the audience they're imagining.

Freewrite Audience Contexts

The purpose of this freewrite is to give you some context for the three speeches by Malcolm X that we'll discuss in the section below. If you're in a computer classroom with Internet access, choose a search engine and enter the term *Malcolm X*. Browse a few Web sites to find out more about Malcolm X, the Civil Rights movement, and the Nation of Islam. If you're not in a computer classroom, form small groups and have the group compose a list of facts they already know about Malcolm X, the Civil Rights movement, and the Nation of Islam, and then share their list with the class.

Let's look at a concrete example to see how an audience shapes a composer's message. The speeches of the Civil Rights leader Malcolm X reveal how composer's adjust their arguments, tone, style, and evidence for different audiences. Read the passages that follow from three speeches by Malcolm X, each given to a different audience. The first speech was to a Civil Rights group in Detroit, the second speech was given to the Harvard Law School, and the third speech was given to the Nation of Islam. As you read the speeches, think about the different voice and style that Malcolm X takes on for each audience and the different kinds of examples that he uses to make his arguments.

Excerpt from a Malcolm X speech to a Detroit Civil Rights group:

Just as the slavemaster of that day used Tom, the house Negro, to keep the field Negroes in check, the same old slavemaster today has Negroes who are nothing but modern Uncle Toms, 20th century Uncle Toms, to keep you and me in check, keep us under control, keep us passive and peaceful and nonviolent. That's Tom making you nonviolent. It's like when you go to the dentist, and the man's going to take your tooth. You're going to fight him when he starts pulling. So he squirts some stuff in your jaw called novocaine, to make you think they're not doing anything to you. So you sit there and 'cause you've got all of that novocaine in your jaw, you suffer peacefully. Blood running all down your jaw, and you don't know what's happening. 'Cause someone has taught you to suffer—peacefully.

Excerpt from a Malcolm X speech to Harvard Law School:

There was another man back in history whom I read about once, an old friend of mine whose name was Hamlet, who confronted, in a sense, the same thing our people are confronting here in America. Hamlet was debating whether

"To be or not to be"—that was the question. He was trying to decide whether it was "nobler in the mind to suffer (peacefully) the slings and arrows of outrageous fortune" or whether it was nobler "to take up arms" and oppose them. I think his little soliloquy answers itself. As long as you sit around suffering the slings and arrows and are afraid to use some slings and arrows yourself, you'll continue to suffer.

Excerpt from a Malcolm X speech to the Nation of Islam:

The Honorable Elijah Muhammad teaches us that as it was divine will in the case of the destruction of the slave empires of the ancient and modern past, America's judgement and destruction will also be brought about by divine will and divine power. Just as ancient nations paid for their sins against humanity, White America must now pay for her sins against twenty-two million "Negroes." White America's worst crimes are her hypocrisy and her deceit. White America pretends to ask herself: "What do these Negroes want?" White America knows that four hundred years of cruel bondage has made these twenty-two million ex-slaves too (mentally) blind to see what they really want.

White America should be asking herself: "What does God want for these twenty-two million ex-slaves?" Who will make White America know what God wants? Who will present God's plan to White America? What is God's solution to the problem caused by the presence of twenty-two million unwanted slaves here in America? And who will present God's solution? We, the Muslims who follow The Honorable Elijah Muhammad, believe wholeheartedly in the God of justice.

When Malcolm X spoke to the Civil Rights group in the blue-collar town of Detroit, he used informal, conversational language, with words such as *stuff* and *cause* and sentences such as *Blood running all down your jaw*. Malcolm X also used images that were effective for persuading his audience who was not sure whether to follow Martin Luther King's nonviolent approach or Malcolm X's more militant approach. The African American Civil Rights group in Detroit would have had a strong negative reaction to the image of an "Uncle Tom," and none of them would have wanted to be associated with that image.

Notice that Malcolm X adjusted his language when he addressed the Harvard Law School audience, which at that time was made up almost exclusively of upper-class Caucasian males. For the Harvard audience, Malcolm X used a formal dialect of English, with words such as *whom* and quotes from Shakespeare. The example of Shakespeare not only struck a chord with the audience, but also caused them to perceive Malcolm X as being aware of white European cultural traditions and able to draw on those traditions. Making a parallel between Hamlet and the suffering of African Americans at the hands of those in power in America helped Malcolm X persuade a skeptical audience to sympathize with his cause.

Malcolm X delivering a speech

When Malcolm X spoke before the Nation of Islam, his language, tone, and delivery was in the style of a preacher speaking a sermon, with techniques such as repetition (for example, repeating the phrase *White America*) and asking the audience a series of questions. He used images and ways of thinking that appealed to his religious audience, such as the idea of sin and divine will. Because his audience was receptive to his message, Malcolm X was more forceful in his language and stance. He talked about White America paying for its sins, hypocrisy, and deceit—language he wouldn't have used in front of the Harvard audience.

The ability to move effectively between different audiences and adjust your language and delivery is what linguists call *code switching*. In a sense we're all code-switchers, whether we're moving between the language of our school and our home or the different composing expectations of our biology class and our English class.

When you compose in college and beyond, your audience will always influence the way you compose and what you say. Sometimes you'll have an immediate and very "real" audience, such as when you give a speech or conduct a phone interview. Sometimes you'll be able to imagine your audience but they will be more distant, such as when you write an editorial for the campus newspaper or post a video to *YouTube*. At other times you will shape the audience you want to receive your message: for example, if you were to create a political blog to attract College Republicans or Democrats. Often we write only for ourselves as an audience, whether it's a to-do list in a PDA or an entry in a diary. Audiences can be encouraging or hostile, diverse or monolithic, inspiring or debilitating. As you analyze and respond to the readings in this book, think carefully about how the composers' audiences have shaped their texts.

Freewrite Analyzing Audience

The goal of this freewrite is to practice analyzing the ways an audience shapes a composition. Find a magazine ad that does an effective job of appealing to its target audience. Write about whom you think the target audience is, how the target audience shapes the ad, and why you think the ad is effective in appealing to the target audience. Be prepared to share your ads in small groups and discuss the ads with the class.

Literacy Personas

A composer's persona includes the stance she takes, her tone, the vocabulary she uses, her voice and style—everything that makes up the image she portrays in her text. A composer's persona is influenced by the previous texts she has read, the audience she's composing for, and the purpose, medium, and genre of what she's composing. Writing teachers such as David Bartholomae and Patricia Bizzell argue that a writer's persona is *socially constructed*, which means that the literacy situation shapes the composer's persona. For example, when you write an essay for a college class, your persona will be influenced by what you think is the appropriate style for academic writing, and that may or may not conflict with the persona you take on when you're writing for yourself or to friends and family. Your idea of what the appropriate persona is for a particular academic essay will also be shaped by what your high school teachers told you about college writing, the writing expectations of the teacher who assigned the essay, the academic field of the class, the genre of the essay, and so forth.

Let's look at an example of the way a composer's persona is shaped by the writing situation. In Chapter 8, which focuses on academic literacies, there is a case study of a student writing in a sociology class. Greg Calabrese was a junior at Albion College when he wrote a research report for Social Psychology, a course for sociology majors. Greg's persona in his research report was shaped by the writing assignment, Greg's prior experiences writing in his major of sociology, the expectations of the teacher, and the genre of the sociology research report. Below is an excerpt from the part of Greg's report that describes his research methods. As you read it, think about the persona that comes across in Greg's text.

> For the purpose of this essay, I decided that my research would be two-fold. First, I felt that I would gain a better insight to men's views of how they interact with each other and by themselves if I conducted some form of semi-structured interviews. I chose to interview three college aged men (Alex, David, and Jim), all from a small Midwest college and all who grew up in middle-class families. I asked them a series of questions about their experiences in bathrooms as well as their feelings about certain common occurrences in bathrooms throughout their lives. I also will be discussing what observations I have made in my countless experiences in male bathrooms over the past twenty-one years. These observations are intended to supplement my interviews with the three participants as well as add to the discussion of how men interact with each other and by themselves in a restroom or locker-room setting. I feel that it will be interesting to consider not only what interactions are like in a normal bathroom or locker-room, but also to examine these events through a gendered lens to a certain extent.

Greg is composing in the genre of the sociology research report, which is often published in sociology journals and is read and reviewed by other sociologists. Although Greg is not planning to publish his report, he knows that his teacher is going to play the role of an expert sociologist helping Greg gain access to the field of sociology by learning how to write, think, and talk like a sociologist.

Typically sociologists don't use informal language in research reports, and some of Greg's choices of words (for example, *two-fold* or *certain common occurrences* or *supplement*) would sound overly formal in a casual conversation about men's behavior in bathrooms or a stand-up comedy performance about men and bathrooms. Greg is taking on a persona that will be effective for the literacy situation. Part of the persona that Greg establishes through his writing involves the use of specific jargon terms that sociologists use, such as *semi-structured interviews* or *gendered lens*. Greg is consciously creating his persona to sound like a sociologist, but that persona is constructed by the genre of the sociological research report and the conventions of sociology as a field (the ways of researching and writing that are considered acceptable by the community of sociologists). As you read and analyze the selections in this book, think about the ways that authors' personas are shaped by their purpose, audience, and genre.

Freewrite Changing Personas

The goal of this freewrite is to get you to reflect on how your persona changes depending on the context of what you're composing. First, think of something interesting that happened to you since you've started college. Pretend you're writing an e-mail to a friend and describe the experience. Then, pretend you're writing an e-mail to a parent or grandparent and describe the same experience. Finally, describe the same experience in an e-mail to a former high school teacher. Read your three e-mails to a writing partner and discuss the ways that your persona changed depending on your audience and purpose.

Literacy Mediums

Mediums and modes are closely related. If a mode is a channel of communication—oral, visual, digital, print—then a medium is the tool that the composer uses within that channel to deliver his or her message. For example, composers working in a visual mode might use mediums such as photographs, painting, or billboards. Composers working in a print mode might use mediums such as books, magazines, newsletters, or fliers. Understanding the way that the medium of a composition affects its content can help you understand and analyze any type of text, whether the medium is a sculpture, Web site, or poster. The medium that a composer uses to deliver her message affects every aspect of the content of a message. For a concrete example of how medium affects composing, let's look at a composition in different mediums. Read the following passage from the third book in J. R. R. Tolkien's *Lord of the Rings* series, *The Return of the King*, and then read the version from the script of *The Lord of the Rings: The Return of the King*. As you read these two excerpts, think about how the different mediums affect the composition.

> **Excerpt from J. R. R. Tolkien's novel *The Return of the King*:**
>
> The light sprang up again, and there on the brink of the chasm, at the very Crack of Doom, stood Frodo, black against the glare, tense, erect, but still as if he had been turned to stone.
>
> "Master!" cried Sam.
>
> Then Frodo stirred and spoke with a clear voice, indeed with a voice clearer and more powerful than Sam had ever heard him use, and it rose above the throb and turmoil of Mount Doom, ringing in the roof and walls.
>
> "I have come," he said. "But I do not choose now to do what I came to do. I will not do this deed. The Ring is mine!" And suddenly, as he set it on his finger, he vanished from Sam's sight. Sam gasped, but he had no chance to cry out, for at that moment many things happened.

Something struck Sam violently in the back, his legs were knocked out from under him and he was flung aside, striking his head against the stony floor, as a dark shape sprang over him. He lay still and for a moment all went black.

Excerpt from the script for *The Lord of the Rings: The Return of the King*:

INT. CRACK OF DOOM - DAY

The HEAT is almost UNBEARABLE . . . SAM sees FRODO in the DISTANCE . . .

FRODO

I'm here, Sam.

ANGLE ON: FRODO is standing on the EDGE of the CRACK OF DOOM . . . a deep LAVA FILLED CHASM, in the very heart of ancient SAURON'S FORGES, the greatest in Middle-earth.

The RAGING ORANGE GLARE from the CHASM turns FRODO into a BLACK SILHOUETTE . . . standing TENSE and STILL.

FRODO holds the RING in his HAND . . . he RAISES IT, holding it over the BUBBLING LAVA far below.

SAM
(yelling)

Destroy it — go on! Throw it in the
fire!

CLOSE ON: FRODO . . . a STRANGE EXPRESSION on his face . . .

SAM

What are you waiting for? Just let
it go!

ON THE SOUNDTRACK: The HUM of the RING grows louder and louder! FRODO PULLS the RING close to his body as he turns to SAM.

FRODO looks at SAM, the RING has finally taken him.

FRODO

The Ring is mine.

SAM SCREAMS as . . .

. . . FRODO PUTS THE RING ON! He VANISHES!

SAM

No!

CUT TO:

EXT. BLACK GATES OF MORDOR - DAY

With a storm of wings, the NAZGUL wheel around and hurtle towards MOUNT DOOM!

In the midst of the BATTLE — GANDALF . . . realising FRODO has been seen . . .

INTERCUT WITH:

INT. CRACK OF DOOM - DAY

CLOSE ON: SAM is SCREAMING for FRODO . . .

ANGLE ON: FOOTPRINTS moving across the ASH COVERED CAVERN FLOOR!

SUDDENLY! GOLLUM smashes a ROCK down on SAM'S HEAD, knocking him to the GROUND!

GOLLUM LEAPS on to the INVISIBLE FRODO!

CLOSE ON: FRODO'S FOOTPRINTS . . . staggering about under GOLLUM'S WEIGHT!

ANGLE ON: GOLLUM clawing FRANTICALLY, riding on the BACK of the INVISIBLE FRODO . . .

INTERCUT WITH:

EXT. BLACK GATES OF MORDOR - DAY

ARAGORN turns and is confronted by an ARMOURED TROLL, wielding an ENORMOUS MALLET . . .

Composing in the medium of the book, Tolkien relies on vivid and detailed description to create the scene. The words he chooses, the length and tone of his sentences, his character descriptions—all of these matters of language and style are critical to the composition, and each sentence and paragraph must be carefully shaped.

The visual medium of film relies much more heavily on visual motion and camera angles to tell a story, with brief directions for close-ups, sound, and specific camera angles. The medium of film lends itself to "intercuts," and the script breaks away from one scene and goes to another (the gates of Mordor) and then returns to the scene with Sam and Frodo and Gollum. If Tolkien had gone back and forth between scenes in such a short span, the passage would have felt choppy, but in the medium of film intercuts can be an effective way to build tension and interest. The conventions of what makes for an effective composition vary from medium to medium, and awareness of the conventions associated with the different mediums that you'll encounter in 21st century literacies will make you a more effective reader and composer.

Freewrite Changing Mediums

The purpose of this freewrite is to consider how a change in mediums affects a composition. Think of a text that you've read in two different mediums: a book that was made into a film, a comic strip that was made into a video game, a play that was made into a film, a book that was made into a television show, and so forth. How did the change in medium affect the content of the composition (think about composing features we've been discussing like purpose, audience, and persona)?

Literacy Genres

If a mode is a channel of communication, and a medium is a tool for delivering a message within that channel of communication, then a genre is a form of that tool that is appropriate for specific literacy situations. For example, within the oral mode of communication, there is the medium of the speech, and within the medium of the speech, there are genres such as wedding toasts, political acceptance speeches, graduation speeches, and so forth. Each genre of a speech is appropriate in a specific kind of situation (a political rally, a graduation, a wedding, and so forth). In the example from the freewrite below, the mode is oral and the medium is music. Genres of music include country, hip-hop, reggae, jazz, and so forth. Within each genre there may be subgenres as well. For example, within the genre of jazz, there are swing, Dixieland, bop, acid jazz, and so forth.

Freewrite Music Genres

The purpose of this freewrite is to help you understand the concept of genre by thinking about genres you're familiar with: music genres. As a class, come up with a list of genres of music. Then choose a genre from the list and write for five minutes, exploring the following questions:

- What kinds of personas do musicians tend to take on in their songs in the genre?
- Who are the primary audiences for the genre, and how do those audiences affect the subject of the music and persona of the composers?
- What social contexts influence artists in the genre (for example, race, class, gender, politics)?
- If you're familiar with the history of the genre, how has the genre changed and evolved over time?

A genre is much more than a format. Genres—such as the scientific experimental report, the newspaper editorial, the poetry slam, the baseball box score—all have evolved as useful responses to literacy situations. Genres shape and are shaped by composers' purposes, audiences, mediums, and contexts. Genres are complex; a genre such as comedy in film can have many subgenres (romantic comedy, parody, dark comedy, slapstick, and so forth).

To get a better sense of this idea of genres as complex responses to literacy situations, let's look at a genre of music you might be familiar with: hip-hop. Hip-hop developed out of communities of urban MCs sampling records and rapping over the beats during parties. The genre of hip-hop developed from social action—a community of composers with similar purposes and interests, all trying to communicate in similar ways. Hip-hop has many subgenres, such as trip-hop, gangsta rap, alternative, and so forth.

Following is an example of one subgenre of hip-hop, message rap. We'll look at the rapper Mos Def's "Dollar Day," which is a response to the aftermath of Hurricane Katrina in New Orleans. As you look at Mos Def's song, think about the form, style, and social context for message rap as a genre. You can also watch the video of this song by doing a Google video search of "Mos Def Dollar Day."

Excerpt from Mos Def's "Dollar Day":

Listen, homie, it's Dollar Day in New Orleans
It's water water everywhere and people dead in the streets
And Mr. President he bout that cash
He got a policy for handlin the niggaz and trash
And if you poor you black
I laugh a laugh they won't give when you ask
You better off on crack
Dead or in jail, or with a gun in Iraq
And it's as simple as that
No opinion my man it's mathematical fact
Listen, a million poor since 2004
And they got-illions and killions to waste on the war
And make you question what the taxes is for
Or the cost to reinforce, the broke levee wall
Tell the boss, he shouldn't be the boss anymore
Y'all pray amen

God save these streets
One dollar per every human being
Feel that Katrina clap
See that Katrina clap
God save these streets
Quit bein' cheap nigga freedom ain't free
Feel that Katrina clap
See that Katrina clap

Lord have mercy
Lord God God save our soul
A God save our soul, a God
A God save our souls
Lord God God save our soul
A God save our soul soul soul
Soul survivor

If a genre is a response to a recurring literacy situation, then one way to analyze a genre such as message rap is to think about some of the factors in literacy situations that we've been discussing: purpose, audience, persona, medium, and context.

The purpose of some genres of hip-hop is focused on getting people to dance and relax and have fun, but message rap has a more serious purpose. The primary purposes of songs in the subgenre of message rap are to make a political statement by exposing injustices and to persuade the audience to take action. Mos Def's purpose is to make a strong political message about then-President Bush and the war in Iraq, and his language reflects his purpose ("Mr. President he bout that cash" and "killions to waste on the war"). Mos Def is aware of his primary audience (teenagers and young adults, primarily from urban areas), and he is trying to get his audience to understand the injustice he perceives and take action against it. At the end of the video of "Dollar Day," Mos Def says to his audience, "Don't talk about it be about it."

Purpose and audience affect the personas that artists take on when they compose message rap. In his performance Mos Def gradually takes on an angrier and louder tone, and by the end of the song he's shouting—and because he's working in an oral medium, his tone of voice is an important way to establish his persona. In message rap, this persona of anger is shaped by the social context. Most message rap is composed by people who grew up poor and who experienced firsthand racism and inequality. Message rap is a good example of genre as social action—a useful and repeated response to events such as Katrina and the Iraq war that expose inequalities of class and race in America.

Freewrite College Writing Genres

The purpose of this freewrite is to help you make a connection between the discussion of genre in this section of Chapter 1 and the kinds of genres you're going to be writing in your college classes. Review the syllabi and any assignment descriptions your college teachers have given you this semester. Make a list of the genres of writing you're going to be asked to compose in. Then, choose one writing assignment and analyze it as a genre. What is the purpose and audience of the genre? What are the conventions of the genre, including conventions of form and style? What is the social context of the genre?

Literacy Contexts

Every factor of a literacy situation that we've been discussing—purpose, audience, persona, medium, genre—is influenced by social contexts. An audience's ethnicity, social class, political beliefs, and so forth influences its response to a text, and a composer's persona is shaped by her personal history and values and the language communities she belongs to. Consider the ways these advertising campaigns failed because the advertisers didn't consider the social context of their situation:

> When Gerber started selling baby food in Africa, they used the same packaging as in the U.S., with the baby on the label. Later they learned that in Africa, companies often put pictures on the label of what's inside, because many African consumers can't read English.

> In a joint advertising campaign with Hummer, McDonald's gave away toy plastic Hummers in Happy Meals. Environmental groups raised an outcry, and McDonald's ended the promotion because of the negative response from the environmental groups and from consumers concerned about the message McDonald's was giving kids.

> A British brewery had to cancel a multimillion-dollar TV advertising campaign for an alcoholic fruit drink after protests from the New Zealand government. The ad featured eight British women in bikinis on a beach performing a version of the haka, a ceremony performed by the indigenous New Zealand Maori. The haka is a revered ceremony, and the Maori were offended that it is was being performed by British women in a commercial selling alcohol.

In each of these literacy situations, the composers' message failed to be persuasive because the composers were insensitive to cultural and social contexts.

Freewrite Composing Contexts

The purpose of this freewrite is to help you think about the importance of context for literacy situations by analyzing the context of a recent literacy situation you responded to. Choose something you've composed recently, and write for five minutes about the ways the broader social context of the situation influenced your composing processes and the final product. This might include your own social contexts as a composer (your literacy history, your gender, your ethnicity, and so forth), the values and attitudes of the audience you were composing for, or the social context of the genre you were composing in.

Every composition is situated in a social context. For example, take a close look at the following advertisements from Coca-Cola, each one from a different social/historical context.

Coca-Cola advertisement from 1905

This ad is a reflection of—and is shaped by—its social context. The way the woman is portrayed in the ad, from her elaborate clothing to the delicate way she is posed, reveals the social context of gender roles in the early 1900s.

The following Coca-Cola ad from the 1950s is also shaped by the context of women's strict gender roles at the time.

Coca-Cola advertisement from 1950s

To understand why this ad was effective at reaching its target audience, you need to understand the social context of women's roles in the 1950s, with the husband going off to work and the wife focused on serving her husband. Compare the ad from the 1950s to a Coca-Cola ad from the 1980s on the following page:

Coca-Cola advertisement from 1980s

Analyzing this ad would require some consideration of race relations in the 1980s, which would also require a knowledge of the history of race relations between African Americans and whites in America.

As you analyze and respond to the selections in this book, think about the composers' purposes, the audiences they are writing for, the way purposes and audiences affect the persona they take on, the mode and genre of the texts they're composing, and the social context. Throughout your college career, you will explore a variety of modes and genres of texts, written in a variety of social contexts, but these factors of any literacy situation can be a tool for you no matter what kind of text you read or compose.

Freewrite Reflecting on Literacy

The purpose of this freewrite is to get you to reflect on what you learned about literacy in this chapter. How did your definition of literacy change after reading this chapter?

2

Reading and Composing Processes

In Chapter 1, we focused on the
ways in which literacy is multiple, with multiple mediums
and genres, multiple audiences
and purposes for composers,
and multiple social and cultural
contexts for literacy situations. Today, just as there's no
single kind of literacy, there's no single process for reading or for composing. Each medium, genre, and context
you encounter, in school and out of school, will require
a different set of reading strategies. Each literacy situation you respond to will ask you to engage in different

composing processes. In this chapter, we're not going to present you with
one standard reading process or one universal composing process. Rather,
we'll talk about multiple reading and composing processes for multiple
purposes, mediums, genres, and contexts.

Freewrite Your Multiple Reading and Composing Processes

The purpose of this freewrite is to connect your own experiences as a reader and
composer with the reading and composing processes we're going to talk about in
this chapter. Think of two things you've read recently in two different mediums
and describe your reading processes for each medium. How did your reading
processes differ in the two mediums? Next, choose two things that you composed
recently in two different genres and describe your composing processes for each
genre. How did your composing processes differ for each genre?

Reading Processes

In the introduction to this chapter, we talked about the need to adapt different reading processes to different purposes for reading and for different genres of texts, but no matter what medium or genre you're reading in or what your purpose or context is for reading, your literacy will improve if you think of reading as a process and if you are an active and critical reader.

Freewrite Reading Quiz

To get you thinking about your own beliefs about reading and your own reading processes, take this reading quiz and discuss it in small groups and/or with the class.

1. I like to read. True ___ False ___

2. I do a lot of reading. True ___ False ___

3. If I don't understand something I've read, I read it more than once. True ___ False ___

4. I use different reading strategies depending on why I'm reading and what I'm reading. True ___ False ___

5. I think you can "read" an ad or a video or an event just like you read a book. True ___ False ___

6. Good readers are fast readers. True ___ False ___

7. Good readers understand what they're reading the first time. True ___ False ___

8. If you read something from a book or a Web site, it's probably true. True ___ False ___

9. I'm an active, not a passive, reader. True ___ False ___

10. Reading a lot can help you become a better writer. True ___ False ___

To think about reading as a process, let's take a look at a hypothetical example of an assignment for a college film studies class that has you "read" a film and write a critical analysis. Here's a typical assignment you might get in a film class:

> Write a three to five page essay analyzing the cinematography of the film *Trainspotting*. Consider how the cinematography influences plot, character development, mood, and theme.

If you were given this assignment, you might begin your reading process by "prereading" to get ready to view *Trainspotting*—especially if you haven't seen the film before. To preread, you might get on the Web and browse through reviews of *Trainspotting*. After reading four or five reviews, you'd get a sense of some themes from the movie: drug use as a mental escape from gritty surroundings, the horrors of drug addiction, and drugs as both a rush and a destructive force.

Once you've prepared yourself to "read" *Trainspotting*, it would be a good idea to come up with a strategy for being an active and not a passive viewer when it's time to watch the film. You might reread the assignment to make sure you have a good understanding of its purpose. Because you need to "analyze" the film, you know you'll need to do more than just summarize the plot. You'll need to watch the film carefully and closely and break down the role of cinematography in the film, and especially how cinematography influences plot, character development, mood, and theme. To help you be an active reader and focus on your primary purpose, you might keep a double-entry reading log as you view the movie. On one side of your log you can list "plot," "character development," "mood," and "theme." On the other side of the log you can leave space for your observations and responses on each of these topics as you view the film. Here's what an excerpt from a double-entry log on *Trainspotting* might look like:

Scene where the main character is in his bed with drug withdrawal

Theme	The bedroom looks like a prison, with bare walls and only one small window. Connects to the theme of drugs as a kind of prison.
	The character is hallucinating that a baby is crawling on the ceiling and crying. Contrast of innocence versus world of drug use.
	The character also hallucinates that his parents are on a cheesy game show talking about his drug problem. This connects to the theme of drugs as an escape from a fake modern world. The drug world is more "real" but also scarier.
Mood	The lighting is dark, especially the character is under the sheets. The darkness and shadows set a mood of fear and despair.
	It looks like the bed sheets are suffocating the main character as he gets panicky, and the odd camera angle from under the sheet adds to this effect.
	Music you might hear at a techno club is playing in the background. This adds to the tension because it's the kind of music the character would listen to when he's doing drugs at a club, but instead of being relaxed and dancing he's going through withdrawal and hallucinating.

Once you reach the end of your "reading" of *Trainspotting*, you might use the "scene selection" link on the root menu of the DVD and, using your reading log as a guide, return and "reread" key scenes, adding to your reading log. Even after you've reviewed key scenes, there will probably be aspects of the film you didn't understand. To help you get a better understanding, you might visit the teacher during his or her office hours to talk about your questions, chat with some of your peers in class, or look up some critical responses to *Trainspotting* by searching for articles about it in film journals. Your reading process won't be done when you begin writing your essay. As you draft the essay you will probably want to review parts of the movie, and as you draft you might discover new things you want to say about the film, which might require more "rereading" of *Trainspotting*.

The example of this film assignment shows that there are some general aspects of reading processes that you should consider no matter what you are reading—aspects such as prereading, using writing to help you read, rereading, and seeking feedback on what you're reading. But there are also aspects of the reading process needed to successfully complete the film assignment that relate specifically to the purpose and medium of the task. For example, if you were asked to summarize the film or give your personal response to the acting, your reading process would be different. If you were

A still shot from the film *Trainspotting*

asked to read the book *Trainspotting* by Irvine Welsh, your reading process wouldn't involve drawing on visual and oral literacies or navigating a DVD menu.

Despite the fact that your reading process is always situated—that it always depends on the purpose, genre, medium, and context—it's possible to make some generalizations about good readers. Good readers don't expect to perfectly understand what they're reading the first time they read it, and they know that responding to and analyzing texts requires rereading. Effective readers are active, not passive, readers. They interact with the text, highlighting key words and ideas, writing comments and questions in the margins, and thinking about ways the text is similar to and different than prior texts they've read. Active reading means critical reading—questioning assumptions authors make and thinking about your own responses to ideas and arguments authors present in their texts. Successful readers see reading as a social process. That means that they're open to revising their understanding of and responses to a text after they've talked about the text with others.

Advice for Improving Your Reading Processes

Following is advice for improving your reading processes:

Use "prereading" strategies to activate prior knowledge before you read.
Being literate in the twenty-first century means having to read and respond to new genres, hybrid texts, and texts from cultural contexts you aren't familiar with. Before you read a textbook or watch a film or interpret an event, reflect on what you already know about the subject and genre of what you're reading and what questions you know you'll have. You can do some freewriting about what you already know about a topic before you read, or create a list of questions you have before watching a film or observing an event. Prereading can also include skimming a text before you read. This might mean browsing through the table of contents of a textbook for a class, reading an abstract of an article in a journal before reading the article, viewing a movie trailer on *YouTube* before seeing the film, or listening to a sample of a CD on *Amazon.com* before purchasing it.

Read texts more than once.
Don't think that because you need to read a text multiple times, you're a bad reader. Even experienced and successful readers need to reread passages or entire texts to understand and fully engage with what they're reading. The willingness to reread a text is an important quality of being a successful reader. The more difficult the text, the more you will need to reread. Just as words on a page can have deeper meanings that

you can't get from one quick read, images in a movie or the way instruments are played in a song can be significant in ways that you will miss the first time you watch or listen.

Annotate texts as you read.   To be a successful reader of twenty-first-century texts, you'll need to develop an active reading process. Being an active reader means interacting with texts as you read them by annotating. This could mean highlighting key words and concepts in a textbook, writing notes and questions in the margins of an article, taking field notes when you observe a place or an event, writing your personal responses to a television show in a fan blog, and so forth. Annotating as you read keeps your mind active, helps you retain information, and gives you ideas for responding. We looked at one strategy for annotating—the double-entry log—in the example reading process for the *Trainspotting* assignment. You can also annotate directly on a text—even an electronic text. For example, let's say you're surfing the Internet for reviews of *Trainspotting* and you find a review you want to annotate. You might capture a screen shot of the online review by pressing the "Print Scrn" key of your computer, save it as a PDF file, and then annotate it using the Adobe Acrobat commenting tools.

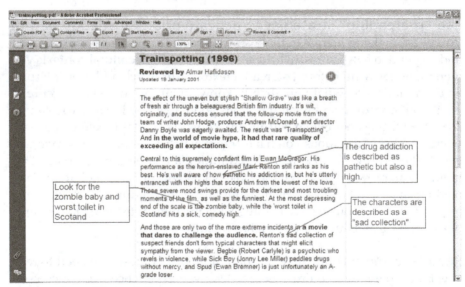

Online review with annotations

Annotating could mean writing notes in the margin, like in the PDF file above, or it could mean underlining, highlighting, circling, and so forth.

Think critically about the assumptions, arguments, and evidence the author presents.   Many of the messages we're bombarded with are meant to try to sell us products or win our vote or promote a person or company. It's important to be a critical and not a passive reader when you're confronted with messages from campaign commercials, billboard ads, charts and graphs in a newspaper, mass e-mails, and so forth. Being a critical reader means asking questions:

> What assumptions does the composer make in his or her arguments?
> What is the composer's background?
> Who is the intended audience?
> Does the composer consider more than one perspective?
> Are there social/cultural/political aspects of the issue that the composer doesn't consider?
> What does the composer's language or imagery reveal about his or her position?
> What kind of evidence (written or visual or oral) does the composer use to support his or her argument?
> Does the composer use reliable evidence?
> What is your position on the issue, and how is it similar to or different from the composer's position?

Talk about what you've read with others.   When you go to a movie with friends, the first thing you probably do afterward is ask your friends what they thought of the movie. If there was a scene you didn't understand, you might ask them how they interpreted it. If you're trying to evaluate how good the movie was, it helps to hear what other people thought of it. When you get home, you might search the Web for some reviews of the movie to see what critics said. Reading is an individual *and* a social process. If you're struggling with a difficult text for a college class, ask questions of your teacher and of your classmates. You can also do some research and find out what others have said about the text you're struggling with.

Reading for Multiple Purposes

In the introduction to this chapter, we mentioned that there's no single reading process that successful readers go through. Just as you compose for multiple purposes, you read for multiple purposes. If you read *People* magazine while you're stuck in a long line at the grocery store, you're not going to annotate or reread, and you probably aren't going to worry about whether you retain the information you're reading. If you're reading a dense philosophy book that you'll be tested on in a college class, you'll expect to reread and use a pencil or highlighter to mark up the book as you read, underlining key concepts and writing comments and questions in the margins. Your purpose for reading shapes your process.

Freewrite Reading Purposes and Processes

The purpose of this freewrite is for you to reflect on how different purposes for reading affect reading processes. Think of something you read recently for pleasure, something you read to get information, and something you read to support an argument you were making in an essay for college. Write for five minutes about how your reading processes differed for each different purpose for reading.

To think about how your reading purpose affects your reading processes, we'll look at three purposes for reading the same text. Below is an article from the opinion section of a college newspaper, the *Arizona Daily Wildcat*. The article was written by Allison Dumka, a senior at the University of Arizona. Try reading this article three times, with a different purpose each time. First, pretend that you've picked up a copy of the *Wildcat* between classes, and you're just reading the article casually on your own. Then, read the article as though you've been assigned to read it for a class and to summarize and analyze the author's main arguments. Finally, read the article as though you're the editor of the *Wildcat*. Pretend that Allison has submitted the article to you as a draft, and you're going to give her feedback for revising it.

Mascot ban about abuse, not political correctness

This isn't a debate about political correctness. The NCAA was right to decide that schools with hostile American Indian symbols must abandon their mascots to be eligible for lucrative post-season games. They were right because the inconvenience of changing a college sports team's mascot is negligible, compared to the injustices of colonization forced on hundreds of indigenous groups in the U.S.

The Indian Removal Act of 1830 forced five major tribes east of the Mississippi River to relocate to Indian Territory, or what is now Oklahoma, so that Southerners could take over the land these tribes had lived on.

You get where I'm going with this. The manipulation of indigenous groups in the United States, along with the general disrespect our government has shown for tribal sovereignty, has been clearly documented.

In 1838, the U.S. government forced the Cherokee Nation to relocate to the West, under part of the Indian Removal Act. Cherokee leaders never agreed to this treaty, but federal troops forced 17,000 Cherokee to leave their land.

Cherokee Nation v. Georgia, decided in 1831, effectively provided no protection of the basic human rights of the Cherokee people. It allowed Georgia to violently "encourage" Cherokee to leave. Approximately 4,000 Cherokee died along the 2,200-mile journey, which is now called the Trail of Tears.

Not only has the NCAA decided that mascots based on Native American symbols are unacceptable, but some students agree. University of Illinois student Stephen Naranjo became a plaintiff in a lawsuit brought by the Illinois Native American Bar Association with intent to retire the mascot. A Native American, Naranjo says: "If the people you think you're honoring say you're not, that should be case closed."

The Chief Illiniwek mascot has performed dances thought to be offensive exaggerations of American Indian sacred rituals.

A team's success is not contingent upon its mascot. Therefore, when a mascot is offensive to the groups of indigenous people it is based upon, it's time to change it.

Now, I'm not a sports person. So I wondered how important a mascot is to athletes.

Marcus Tyus, a political science junior and a sprinter for the UA men's track and field team, said, "Using a tribe to represent a student body isn't really fair. Most of them aren't members of a tribe, so they shouldn't be able to use that as their mascot. It's crossing a line. A symbol that can be offensive shouldn't be a mascot. Racism is racism."

If a mascot were loosely based on stereotypes of any other ethnic, religious or gender identity, it would be obvious how tasteless and potentially racist these mascots would be. Imagine a NCAA team called the Meatheads, the Fairies or the Whities.

Ultimately, it's up to the NCAA to set these standards of respect, and teams that want to participate in lucrative postseason play will have to comply. Compliance with demonstrating respect to indigenous groups should be a fairly basic concept. Students or players who disagree need to take a class about colonization, and then they can come argue about political correctness.

Freewrite Your Multiple Reading and Composing Processes

In what ways did your reading processes differ for each different purpose for reading the mascot ban article above? Talk about your different reading processes in small groups and/or with the class.

Reading in Multiple Mediums

Throughout this book, we've defined *reading* broadly, as much more than just reading books and magazines. Reading in the twenty-first century means interpreting and analyzing not just printed texts, but also visual images, speeches, Web sites, performances, architecture, and so forth. This means that the medium of a text—the kind of tool that is used to deliver the message—shapes our reading process. For an example of how a medium can dictate what kind of reading process we go through, take a look at the following excerpts from the book *Understanding Comics* by Scott McCloud. McCloud talks about the ways that the medium of the comic affects the way we read and understand comics.

Scott McCloud, from *Understanding Comics*

Scott McCloud, from *Understanding Comics* (continued)

Now that you've read McCloud's ideas about how the medium can shape your reading process, try reading a similar "message" in three mediums. Following is a newspaper editorial, a poster, and a link to a television commercial that are all from an advertising campaign by the Ad Council and Stop Impaired Driving. The campaign is focused on stopping drunk driving. First, read the newspaper editorial and think about your reading process.

"Drunk Driving. Over the Limit. Under Arrest."
Aggressive Impaired Driving Crackdown Seeks to Save Lives

Drunk driving is one of America's deadliest crimes. In 2005, nearly 13,000 people were killed in highway crashes involving a driver or motorcycle operator with an illegal blood alcohol concentration (BAC) of .08 or higher. The picture for motorcycle operators is particularly bleak. Forty-one percent of the 1,878 motorcycle operators who died in single-vehicle crashes in 2005 had BAC levels of .08 or higher.

That's why local law enforcement officials will join with thousands of other law enforcement and highway safety agencies across the nation from August 15 and throughout the Labor Day holiday to take part in the *Drunk Driving. Over the Limit. Under Arrest.* crackdown on impaired driving.

Our message is simple. No matter what you drive—a passenger car, pickup, sport utility vehicle or motorcycle—if we catch you driving impaired, we will arrest you. No exceptions. No excuses. We will be out in force conducting sobriety checkpoints, saturation patrols, and using undercover officers to get more drunk drivers off the road—and save lives that might otherwise be lost.

Driving with a BAC of .08 or higher is illegal in every state. Yet we continue to see far too many people suffer debilitating injuries and loss of their loved ones as a result of impaired driving. This careless disregard for human life must stop. To help ensure that happens, our local law enforcement officers are dedicated to arresting impaired drivers wherever and whenever they find them.

To further prevent people from driving while impaired, many judges sentence drunk drivers not only to jail time, but also require certain convicted impaired drivers to install ignition interlock devices on their vehicles. Ignition interlocks can detect when an offender has been drinking and prevent a vehicle from starting, thus helping reduce the chances that offenders might again take to the road while impaired. Other technologies prescribed by judges include transdermal devices that detect alcohol through a person's skin and are used in combination with a treatment plan.

It's important to remember, however, that much of the tragedy that comes from drunk driving could be prevented if everyone would take these few simple precautions:

- If you are planning to drink alcohol with friends, designate a sober driver before going out and give that person your keys.
- If you're impaired, call a taxi, use mass transit or call a sober friend or family member to get you home safely.
- Use your community's Sober Rides program.
- Promptly report to law enforcement drunk drivers you see on the roadways.

- Wear your seat belt while in a car or use a helmet and protective gear when on a motorcycle as these are your best defenses against an impaired driver.
- Finally, remember, if you know someone who is about to drive or ride while impaired, take their keys and help them safely make other arrangements to get to where they are going.

Drunk driving is simply not worth the risk. Not only do you risk killing yourself or someone else, but also the trauma and financial costs of a crash or an arrest for impaired driving can be significant. Violators often face jail time, the loss of their driver's license, higher insurance rates, attorney fees, time away from work, and dozens of other expenses.

Don't take the chance. Drunk driving is a serious crime. Remember: *Drunk Driving. Over the Limit. Under Arrest.*

For more information, visit www.StopImpairedDriving.org.

Now, "read" the poster that was also part of the anti–drunk-driving campaign, and think about the ways that the process of reading the medium of the poster differs from the process of reading the editorial.

Drunk-driving poster

For the same message in the medium of a television commercial, visit the Ad Council Web site http://www.adcouncil.org/default.aspx?id=49 and click "Ambulance" under the heading "Television."

Freewrite Reading in Different Mediums

The purpose of this freewrite is for you to reflect on your reading of the three mediums of the anti-drunk-driving advertising campaign. Write for five minutes about the ways your reading processes differed for each medium. Be prepared to share your freewrite in small groups or with the class.

Reading in Multiple Genres

In Chapter 1, we defined a genre as much more than just a template or a set of rules for a composition. We said that genres are common and useful responses to literacy situations—they are a form of social action within a community of readers and composers. Understanding the genre you're reading and the conventions and purposes of that genre can help you develop more effective reading processes.

Freewrite Genre and Reading Processes

Review the discussions of genre in Chapter 1, and in your own words, write a definition of *genre*. Then, think of a genre you've read recently (for example, a textbook, Web site, lab report, or horror movie). Write for five minutes about the ways in which the genre of what you read affected your reading process.

Let's take a look at a genre you might encounter in one of your college classes, the scientific experimental report. The experimental report in the sciences is a response to a common literacy situation: scientists needing to report the results of their research in an organized and clear way to other scientists. As it evolved, the scientific experimental report developed conventions of form that helped the science community read and write about scientific research. One convention of the scientific experimental report is a summary of the purpose, research methods, and results of the experiment in a single paragraph at the beginning of the report—an "abstract." Here's an example of an abstract from a scientific experimental report of a study of chimpanzees published in the science journal *Behavioural Processes*:

Abstract

The majority of studies on self-recognition in animals have been conducted using a mirror as the test device; little is known, however, about the responses of non human primates toward their own images in media other than mirrors. This study provides preliminary data on the reactions of 10 chimpanzees to live self-images projected on 2 television monitors, each connected to a different video camera. Chimpanzees could see live images of their own faces, which were approximately life-sized, on one monitor. On the other monitor, they could see live images of their whole body, which were approximately one-fifth life-size, viewed diagonally from behind. In addition, several objects were introduced into the test situation. Out of 10 chimpanzees tested, 2 individuals performed self-exploratory behaviors while watching their own images on the monitors. One of these 2 chimpanzees successively picked up 2 of the provided objects in front of a monitor and watched the images of these objects on the monitor. The results indicate that these chimpanzees were able to immediately recognize live images of themselves or objects on the monitors, even though several features of these images differed from those of their previous experience with mirrors.

Abstracts became a common convention of the genre of the experimental report because, as more and more scientific studies and scientific journals were published, the community of scientists found it useful for writers to include a brief summary of their study and findings that other scientists could read first to decide whether they wanted to read the entire study. If you were asked to read the study of chimpanzees, you'd want to read the abstract as a form of *prereading*. The abstract will give you a good sense of the most important aspects of the research you're about to read, which can help focus your reading.

Most scientific reports are divided into specific and clearly labeled sections: an introduction, a section on research methods, a section reporting the results, and a discussion section in which the researcher reflects on the significance of the results. Knowing that the genre of the scientific report is structured this way can help improve your reading process. For example, let's say you've come across this article on chimpanzees as part of a research paper you're writing for a biology class. If you know that it's a convention of the "Introduction" section of an experimental report to include a review of previous research on the topic—a *literature review*—you can find other sources for your research paper by looking carefully at the literature review. Here's one paragraph from the literature review in the "Introduction" section of the chimpanzee research report:

Another study showed that chimpanzees can use the live image on a video monitor to locate an otherwise hidden object (Menzel et al., 1985). Poss and Rochat (2003) also showed, in a slightly different experiment, that chimpanzees and one orangutan were successful in finding a reward hidden in one of two areas when they were able to view the hiding event on a video monitor. Eddy et al. (1996) described that chimpanzees responded differently to a self-image in a mirror versus a videotaped image of other chimpanzees.

If you know that scientists usually include a literature review in the "Introduction" section of the genre of the experimental research report, you can focus your reading on finding more sources for your own research paper.

In the genre of the scientific research report, it's a convention that writers summarize the most important findings of their experiment in the "Discussion" section. If you were reading the chimpanzee article and having trouble understanding the study and the results, you could skip ahead to the discussion section, read the writer's discussion of his results, and then go back and reread the results section, armed with more information and a better understanding. Here are the first few sentences of the "Discussion" section of the chimpanzee article:

Discussion

This experiment showed that two chimpanzees with experience of mirrors used live-video images to investigate their own body. They inspected parts of their face not otherwise visible, although the orientation of left and right was the reverse of that of their previous experience with a mirror. They also explored the back of their body while looking at the monitor; the absolute size of the image was much reduced from life-size. In addition, the object-directed behavior shown by one individual indicates that this chimpanzee not only recognized self, but also environmental objects.

The major findings of the study are clearly explained in the discussion section, and if you were having trouble understanding what the most important findings of the study are, you could adjust your reading process and skip right to the "Discussion" section.

Whatever you're reading—a music video, a bumper sticker, a play, a novel—your reading process will be shaped by the genre you're reading, and an awareness of the conventions of the genre you're reading will help improve your reading process.

Freewrite Television Genres

The purpose of this freewrite is to connect our discussion of the way genre affects reading process to genres you're probably familiar with—television show genres. First, think of a genre of television shows that you like (for example, sitcoms, reality shows, sketch comedy shows, soap operas, talk shows, and so forth.). Next, list some conventions of the genre you've chosen. Write for five minutes about the ways in which your "reading" of that genre (your viewing of those kinds of shows) is affected by the conventions of the genre.

Reading in Multiple Contexts

Freewrite Context Questions

The purpose of this freewrite is to get you thinking about how your personal context affects the way you read a text. Reread the song by Mos Def, "Dollar Day," on page 20. How did your knowledge of Hurricane Katrina affect your reading? How did your own attitudes about the government's reaction to Hurricane Katrina affect your reading? How did your knowledge of and attitudes about rap music affect your reading?

If you completed the freewrite above, you probably found that your reading process and the way you responded to Mos Def's song "Dollar Day" depended on your personal context. If you were a supporter of former President Bush and the Iraq War, your experience of reading "Dollar Day" was different than someone who did not favor the Bush government or the war. If you're a fan of Mos Def, that probably influenced the way you responded to his message. If you don't listen to rap as a genre and aren't familiar with it, then you probably went through a different reading process than someone who listens to rap all of the time. Personal context plays an important role in reading processes, and so do social and cultural contexts. You couldn't read and respond to "Dollar Day" without some knowledge of its historical and social context.

The act of reading always involves a complex and dynamic personal and social context for the reader and the text. Readers' processes and the way they interpret and respond to texts are influenced by factors such as:

Their ethnicity	Their economic background
Their gender	Their age
Their personal beliefs	Their prior experiences with the kind of text they're reading

In addition to the reader's personal and social context, the social and cultural context surrounding the text is also important. Factors that help shape a text include:

The author's race, gender, economic class, and so forth

The historical period of the text

The culture in which the text was produced

The history of the genre and medium of a text

The ways people have responded to the text

Let's look at a poem about the war in Iraq to help us think about the ways social and cultural factors shape how we read a text. First, read the poem

"Eulogy," and think about how your own personal knowledge and experiences shape your reading of the text.

Eulogy

Brian Turner

It happens on a Monday, at 11:20 A.M.,
as tower guards eat sandwiches
and seagulls drift by on the Tigris River.
Prisoners tilt their heads to the west
though burlap sacks and duct tape blind them.
The sound reverberates down concertina coils
the way piano wire thrums when given slack.
And it happens like this, on a blue day of sun,
when Private Miller pulls the trigger
to take brass and fire into his mouth:
the sound lifts the birds up off the water,
a mongoose pauses under the orange trees,
and nothing can stop it now, no matter what
blur of motion surrounds him, no matter what voices
crackle over the radio in static confusion,
because if only for this moment the earth is stilled,
and Private Miller has found what low hush there is
down in the eucalyptus shade, there by the river.
PFC B. Miller
(1980–March 22, 2004)

Freewrite Context and "Eulogy"

In small groups or with the class, talk about how your own personal knowledge and experiences shaped your reading of "Eulogy." Then do an Internet search for information about the problem of soldiers committing suicide in the war in Iraq, and after you've explored some Web sites about this problem, reread "Eulogy." How did your further knowledge of the problem of soldiers committing suicide in the Iraq war shape your second reading? Explore this question in groups or with the class. Next, do an Internet search for reviews of Brian Turner's book of poems, *Here, Bullet.* Once you've browsed some review of the book, read "Eulogy" again and discuss the ways your knowledge of the author and the book affected your reading. How do you think Turner's experiences shaped his poem?

Composing Processes in Multiple Literacies

Freewrite Your Composing Processes

The purpose of this freewrite is to encourage you to think about your own composing processes and compare your composing processes with your peers'. Draw a cartoon or some other visual image (for example, a flowchart) that describes your composing processes. Share your cartoons or visual images in small groups and compare the similarities and differences among your processes and your peers' processes. Be prepared to discuss these differences with the class.

In the rest of Chapter 2, we'll explore the ways that purpose, medium, genre, and context shape your composing processes. But before we talk about the ways composing processes will differ in different literacy situations, let's talk about some general features of composing processes. To do this, let's take a look at the composing process of an artist, M. C. Escher, as he composed a lithograph (a print). First, take a look at the final version of M. C. Escher's lithograph *High and Low* on page 46.

High and Low is a complex and detailed work of art, and it would be a mistake to think that Escher composed it in one sitting, or that he created it the night before an exhibition—just as you can't write a research paper for a class in one sitting, or the night before it's due. Escher engaged in a lengthy composing process that involved drafting, revising, and editing. When Escher began to compose *High and Low*, he did some first-draft sketches of the drawing. Take a look at the first draft of *High and Low* on page 47.

If you compare this first version of *High and Low* to the final version on page 46 you'll get a sense of how different even an expert composer's first draft and final draft are. Although the basic concepts in the first draft and final draft of *High and Low* are similar, every aspect of the composition changed dramatically from the first draft to the final draft: the perspective, the shape and style of the buildings, the trees, and the addition of human figures. You can see some of these changes in the second version of *High and Low* on page 47.

M. C. Escher's *High and Low* (final version)

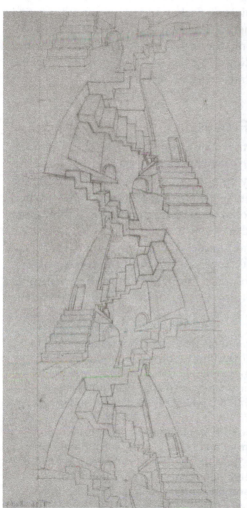

M. C. Escher's *High and Low*
(preliminary work 1)

M. C. Escher's *High and Low*
(preliminary work 2)

Escher made significant changes between the first and second drafts of *High and Low*. He changed the perspective, and completely revised the structure and style of the buildings. But even this second draft was rough, and between the second draft and the final draft, Escher added human figures and went through many more major changes. Consider all of the details he developed as he drafted, such as the shading, the added stairways and arches and banisters, and the background buildings. In each draft of *High and Low*, the content, style, mood, and surface details changed significantly.

One Student's Composing Process

For an example of a composer's process in a print medium, let's look at parts of an early draft and a final draft of an essay by a college student writer. Lauren Kiser was a first-semester, first-year student enrolled in ENC 1101, the first of two required composition courses at Florida State University, when she composed "Unearthing," a personal literacy narrative. We'll look more closely at Lauren's essay drafts and her composing processes in the case study in Chapter 3: Situating Personal Literacies, but for now we'll focus on some specific revisions Lauren made. To get a sense of how a composition changes as composers revise, let's compare the first draft of the opening of Lauren's essay to the final draft. Following is Lauren's first draft of the opening paragraphs:

> My life began with a backdrop of what some may consider paradise: a small, cozy home sitting on the side of a hill, the Blue Ridge Mountains on the horizon, and all of the solitude that comes with living in a town set in a frame made of pine, maple, and coal. Unfortunately for me, I never found my paradise in this small coalmining town, but it is where my life began, and so it is also where my story begins.
>
> The wooded scenery provided me with ample opportunity to explore the natural world as a child. My grandfather and I spent hours walking through what we called the "Bernstein Bear" trail in my backyard. There I learned about moss and ferns and rollie-pollie bugs that we found under rocks. I learned that pine trees are green year round and if you light pine needles on fire, the smoke keeps the gnats away.

Lauren received feedback from her peers and her teacher and took her essay through multiple drafts. In the process memo she wrote to describe her composing processes, Lauren said:

> My rough draft was a starting point. When I first sat down to write, I had no idea how I was going to approach the topic and began with an entirely different tone and storyline. One day after that I was in the mood to write and

sat down and completely rewrote the first part of my paper to what it is now (excluding some revisions). My second draft includes more details and a better flow.

For Lauren, the drafting and revising process involved more than just editing sentences. She relied on feedback to help add details that made her essay more descriptive and well developed. You can see the kind of revising she did by comparing the first draft of her opening paragraphs with the opening paragraphs of her final draft:

My life began with a backdrop of what some may consider paradise: a small, cozy home sitting on the side of a hill, the Blue Ridge Mountains on the horizon, and all of the solitude that comes with living in a town set in a frame made of pine, maple, and coal. Unfortunately for me, I never found my paradise in this small coalmining town, but it is where my life began, and also where my story begins.

The wooded scenery provided me with ample opportunity to explore the natural world as a child. From the time I could walk, I was interested in bugs, flowers, and leaves. The boundless forest in my backyard encouraged exploration. My grandfather and I spent hours walking through what we called the "Bernstein Bear" trail, named after my favorite series of books at the time. There I learned about moss and ferns and rollie-pollie bugs that we found under rocks. I learned that pine trees are green year round and if you light pine needles on fire, the smoke keeps the gnats away. My grandfather was part Native American and taught me that we should never take more than we need, and to always give back to nature. I learned many lessons that I did not realize until later in life. Most of all, he taught me to be observant of my surroundings and to appreciate seemingly insignificant things.

In addition to developing ideas and adding examples and details, revising could also mean changing the focus of your composition and adding and deleting entire sections. As Lauren drafted and revised, she deleted her entire closing paragraph and wrote a completely different ending. Following is Lauren's original closing paragraph:

Once I reached kindergarten, I was faced with my first major educational obstacle—my teacher Mrs. Nancy. Kindergarten teachers are typically perceived as kind, generous, and___. Mrs. Nancy, however, was exceptional at inhibiting my learning. When going through exercises that taught my classmates and I how to write our names, I was scolded because this was a skill that I had already acquired. I quickly lost interest in the monotony of writing my name, so my perfectly sculpted chicken scratch became more and more difficult to decipher and then again I was scolded for my sloppiness.

This was a major setback for me as far as my interest in school went. My teacher often sent notes home to my mother, complaining about everything from my brilliantly colored sky that had every color in the crayon box in it—except blue, to my lack of interest in playing kitchen with my classmates.

As Lauren drafted and revised her essay, she began to focus more and more on the influence of her mother on her literacy. She decided to delete the details about Mrs. Nancy and close her essay with a greater focus on her mother. She deleted most of the closing paragraph above and added these closing paragraphs:

My "home schooling" of sorts put me ahead of my peers when I began attending public school. It was difficult for me, given that my mother, not being a local, was already disliked by many, and that I had already been provided the education that was required for pre-k and kindergarten. I was scorned by teachers and administrators for being ahead and was left in a class that was not engaging and monotonous for my young and growing mind.

My mother, however, supplied me with a steady stream of activities to keep me interested in school-related subjects. Besides my extraordinary library of books, she encouraged me to be creative and supplied a limitless stock of glue, glitter, paint, and my favorite—Crayola crayons. In school, when my classmates were learning their colors and shapes, I was discovering new and innovative ways to incorporate them into whatever medium was available. Our refrigerator proudly displayed layer upon layer of colorful construction paper, tempera paint, and a rainbow of glitter. Often, my mother received notes from my teachers complaining about my excessive use of art supplies.

I also spent much time outdoors helping my mom do yard work. She taught me the names of flowers and the secret formula of sun, water, and love that makes them grow. I saw many of the things that I read put into action. I collected caterpillars and put them in a terrarium, hoping they would turn into butterflies like in *Where Butterflies Grow*. Seeing a bird's nest or a bunny transformed my literary knowledge into a hands-on experience.

The foundation of my education was made concrete by my mother and grandfather. They allowed me to explore the world around me with few boundaries. My youthful curiosity was satisfied not only with published texts, but also with many hands-on experiences. Because I was neither forced nor restricted in my education, my drive to obtain a better understanding of all subjects has been fueled by my intrinsic motivation.

Hopefully, the examples of M. C. Escher and Lauren will help you see that successful composers engage in an extensive process of drafting and revising and editing. In a moment, we'll think about the ways in which the mediums

Escher and Lauren were composing in shaped their processes, but first, let's look at some general strategies for composing processes that can apply in almost any literacy situation.

Don't pressure yourself to get the composition right in the first few drafts.
Even a famous artist such as M. C. Escher used early sketches to explore ideas and play with composition and perspective. Lauren wrote entire paragraphs that she later wound up deleting. In the early stages of composing processes, don't pressure yourself to create perfect designs or finely crafted and edited sentences. Try freewriting or sketching to generate ideas, and don't worry about editing sentences or perfecting visual designs in early drafts.

Separate revising from editing and proofreading.
When M. C. Escher revised his first version of *High and Low*, he didn't just change a few small details. He completely rethought the design and perspective of his composition, and added significantly to the content of the lithograph from the first version to the final version. Successful composers aren't afraid to revise the content of their compositions as they draft. They might change focus, add evidence, delete entire pages or paragraphs, change their voice and style, and so forth. Composing is thinking, and as you compose you'll think of new ideas that will change your first draft in significant ways—you'll revise. When you have a final draft of your composition, you're ready to edit. Editing means reshaping sentences and focusing on strategies like word choice and design formatting to improve your composition. After you've revised and edited, it's a good idea to proofread. Proofreading means looking closely and carefully at your final draft to catch typos, misspelled words, grammatical errors, and so forth.

Give yourself time to engage in the composing process.
The kinds of complex literacy situations you'll encounter in and out of school demand time for drafting, revising, and editing. Beginning your composing process just before an essay is due for a class won't give you time to explore your initial ideas, rethink your first drafts, or edit your final draft. Lauren began writing her literacy essay shortly after she received the assignment, and she took the essay through multiple drafts. You will also want to give yourself time to get feedback from an outside reader or readers. With feedback from her classmates and her teacher, Lauren was able to focus her essay and find out where she needed more details.

Composing is a social process; composers benefit from feedback throughout the process.
You might have a romantic vision of artists such as M. C. Escher in which they work alone in their studios, creating art from

inspiration. But the reality is that successful composers treat composing as a social process. Even before he began composing, an artist such as Escher sought out models from fellow artists to give him ideas: he looked for models of the genre he composed in and he explored what other composers had done. Artists also get feedback from fellow artists as they sketch and paint. To seek feedback in college, you could make appointments to talk about your drafts with your college teachers, form writing groups or partners with peers in your classes, or visit your school's writing (or tutoring) center. Getting feedback on drafts of your compositions can help you see different perspectives and develop your ideas and examples.

In the rest of this chapter, we'll explore the ways composing processes are "situated." This means that composing processes are shaped by the literacy situation: the purpose, audience, medium, genre, and so forth. For example, because Escher was working in the visual medium of drawing, his drafts consisted of sketches, and his revision strategy focused on perspective and the visual design of the composition. Lauren's revision process was influenced by the conventions of the genre of the literacy essay, with its emphasis on telling stories and providing descriptive details to help draw readers into the narrative. Both Escher and Lauren's processes were influenced by their own histories as composers—for example, their awareness of what kind of processes worked best for them. Prior "texts" were also an influence on both Escher and Lauren—In Escher's case, other painters whose work influenced him, and in Lauren's case, the example literacy narratives she was reading in class as well as her peers' literacy narratives that she read during peer-response workshops. Your composing process will always be shaped by the literacy situation, and you'll need the flexibility to adjust your processes for the multiple literacy situations you'll encounter both in school and out of school.

Composing for Multiple Purposes

Every aspect of your composing process will be shaped by your purposes for writing. If you're writing an e-mail to a friend with the purpose of planning a party, you're not going to do much revising and editing—and you may not even bother to use spell check. If you're writing an e-mail to a teacher for the purpose of asking to do an independent study, you'll probably draft and revise your request and take the time to edit your sentences. If you're writing an e-mail to a parent or grandparent for the purpose of explaining how to program his or her TiVo, you'll probably focus on choosing your words carefully and making sure the information is clear as you reread what you've written. To think about how purposes for composing shape composing processes, let's look at three assignments from three first-year writing classes. Read the assignments and think about the primary purpose for the writer in each.

First-year writing assignment from Professor Sylvia Morales of California State University, Sacramento

Write an essay that *analyzes* the ways in which the university uses language and prescribes language use. Some questions to consider are: (1) What does the university teach students about language use? (2) Why does it teach students these things? (3) What should the university teach students about language use, specifically writing? (4) Should the university change with the times, cultures, and so forth or should it maintain and/or teach some standard of spoken and written English? (5) How much of an influence does the university have on language use in America?

The length of this assignment will make it difficult to cover all of the above questions or all of the ways in which the university influences language use in adequate depth. Therefore, you should focus your essay on one or two aspects. For example, you may compare and contrast the academic discourse community with another discourse community. You may focus on just spoken language or on just written language. It is also possible to focus on certain conventions of language use, as many of our readings have done, such as grammar or word choice. Finally, you may analyze the influence that the university has on our language use versus other influences such as the media or family and friends. The focus and purpose of your essay is up to you; however, the essay must analyze in some way the university's role in determining and/or influencing language use.

First-year writing assignment from Professor Linda Haines of Purdue University

Comprehensive Annotated Bibliography
Annotated bibliographies provide brief overviews or summaries of articles related to a specific topic. Often they are compiled in order to demonstrate what sources are available on a topic that a scholar is considering studying.

For this assignment, you will find, read, and create annotations for scholarly articles and Web sites related to your semester-long research. We'll begin this assignment with the Convos Essay, in which you will research something that relates to the Kevin Locke Convocations performance. You will add to your bibliography when you research someone on Purdue's campus for your profile assignment and again when you work with a group on the Public Service Announcement assignment, and once again when you work on your final research report. By the end of the semester, you will have a detailed record of your research.

First-year writing assignment from Professor Robert Lamm of Arkansas State University

Each student will keep a writing journal that will act as a record of development as a reader, writer, and arguer. The student will follow these procedures:

A. Use a thin binder or a spiral notebook.
B. Write in the journal at least five days a week.
C. Label each entry with the day's date. Bind them sequentially.
D. Freewrite the journal, but focus on the subject of writing. Freewriting, also called automatic or stream of consciousness writing, involves never stopping your pen, even if you can't think of anything to write; but focused freewriting limits the subject of your journal. Freewrite for 5 minutes each session to produce entries of at least 100 words each session.
E. Scoring: Sixty complete entries will be an "A"; 50, a "B"; 40, a "C"; 30, a "D"; 20 or fewer, an "F."
F. Your journal must always be on some aspect of writing: your experiences, especially your reactions to reading or writing assignments in this class this semester.
G. You may label an entry "Don't Read" or "Don't Share" if you don't want the teacher to read a particular entry. You keep your journal at the end of the semester.
H. You shouldn't worry about grammar, punctuation, or spelling in your journal. Its grade will be based on the number of words, not upon quality. That is because the chief purpose of this kind of journal is to develop flow.

For each of these three assignments, the writer's purposes will affect the composing processes he or she engages in. For the first assignment, the composer needs to carefully analyze university language. This is not the kind of assignment that can be written at the last minute, and the writer would need to give himself or herself time to decide on a focus and engage in an extensive composing process. Because the assignment asks for an in-depth analysis, the writer will need to go through multiple drafts.

The second assignment asks the writer to read and summarize texts over an entire semester. Reading and writing are closely connected in this annotated bibliography assignment, and the composer would need to find the main ideas of texts and highlight those main ideas as he or she reads. Although writing brief summaries of texts won't require the kind of revising necessary for the first assignment, a composer completing the annotated bibliography assignment might find herself revising earlier annotations as her knowledge of her topic grows over the course of the semester.

The purposes of the first two assignments call for structured and organized thinking, whether it's analyzing or summarizing. Assignment number three is far less structured because the purpose is to explore ideas informally, and the writer's process wouldn't require revision or editing.

Freewrite Purpose and Process

Now that you've looked at the way the purpose of a writing assignment can shape a writer's process, think about the purposes of the writing assignments for the writing class you're in now. Write for five minutes about the purpose of each writing assignment for the class and how that purpose (or purposes) might shape your composing processes.

Composing in Multiple Mediums

Consider the ways that the medium an author is composing in shapes the author's composing process in these examples:

> A Web designer creates a flowchart of all of the pages she intends to include in a Web site so she can decide how many links to create on her index page and how she can keep the number of linked pages to a minimum so she doesn't overwhelm Web surfers visiting her site.

> A stand-up comic always reads his routines aloud after he has a first draft and then reads aloud again after each revision, trying to improve the timing of the routine and his choice of words.

> A photographer visits the same mountain at different times of the day and evening to create a series of photographs capturing the changes to a landscape based on shadows and the quality of light.

> A rock musician never writes her lyrics until after she's arranged the music because she feels that the music should set the tone and theme of the content of the song.

In each of these examples, the tool of communication the author is using to create his or her composition—the medium—plays a significant role in the kind of composing process the author engages in. To get some insight into how a composing process is shaped by the medium, we'll focus on the medium in the last example from above—a musician composing songs. Read the excerpts below from different interviews with the musician and songwriter Beck (Beck Hansen). In these interview excerpts, Beck discusses his composing processes for creating music.

From an interview with *Pitchfork.com:*

BH: With modern recording techniques and living in the Pro Tools era, the process gets really drawn-out, and it can become painstaking. There's an infinite amount of possibilities and detours and things that can distract you from actually just performing the song and having whatever emotion that's invested into the song come through in the recording. Basically, what I'm saying is there is such a technical aspect now, whereas they used to just set up mics and record it, and there weren't a lot of options. That is something that I think musicians routinely complain about or comment on. There's nothing new about that, but I thought it would be interesting to try it the old way. But on *Mutations* and *Sea Change*, a lot of those songs were recorded live. It's something that I've always been interested in, even though I *am* interested in the more modern recording techniques as well.

Pitchfork: Which technique would you say you enjoy more?

BH: I enjoy recording live better, but I think by the nature of it you are going to end up with something that's a little bit more traditional. When you use some of the more modern recording devices and Pro Tools, when you get into the technology, you are aching to get into some territory.

Pitchfork: A record like *Odelay* is almost the antithesis of the old way. That record is so full of information. Listening to it, it sounded like it must have taken forever.

BH: It *did* take forever, which in a way was good. I think we were using a very early version of Pro Tools. Compared to what we have now; it was digital, but it was very primitive, so it took forever. I remember you would record a guitar part, and we would have to sit there for 15 or 20 minutes waiting for the computer to process it. You'd see the little wheel spinning on the computer, and you'd be praying that the hard drive didn't crash and you didn't lose the performance. There were all kinds of limitations with how we did that record, but I think that's what made it more interesting and made us try more interesting things. Back then, Pro Tools only had four or eight tracks, so we couldn't actually hear all the tracks. We could only hear eight at a time, so if a song had 25 or 30 tracks, we wouldn't be able to hear it until we went into the studio and put it all on tape. The process was a little bit backwards.

From an interview with *Paste Magazine:*

Of "Guerolito" Beck says; "I was listening to a lot of Miles Davis records from the early '70s where he would do multiple versions of one song. There was this idea in rock that there was only one definitive version of a song. On "Guerolito," we did all the remixes and then I went into the studio and—for our own amusement—started doing a calypso version of "Scarecrow" and then all these other strange versions. A song is just a skeleton and you can just do whatever you want on top. That was the idea I was exploring."

While each album is united by feel, Beck has never worked to a theme. His method is to go into the studio with some beats and start improvising vocals over them. He has no lyrics prepared on paper. As he puts it, he just gets on the microphone and "lets it fly." When something magical happens, he keeps it. This process was made easier on The Information because it was the first record he and Godrich used computers on. "It afforded us the ability to experiment," he says. "We could try a lot of things and waste a lot of ideas. There are almost too many options. You can drive yourself crazy with options."

Often, Beck's best lines will come up when he's not even aware he's being recorded. It happened that way with the chorus of The *Information*'s lead track, "Elevator Music." He describes the state of mind he has to get into to do this as being almost like that of someone meditating. He has to ignore his surroundings and forget that close friends are listening in the control room. He can't afford to be self-conscious. "There are so many internal rhythms and rhymes," he says. "If I was to sit down right now and write out a couple of stanzas and tried to rap them, they wouldn't flow. The rhymes come out of the beat. They come from a conversation with the beat. Rhythmically, the process is closer to jazz improvisation."

It's tempting to describe this method of composition as stream-of-consciousness, but it's not quite as soul-baring because he has the opportunity to revise and erase. "It's like a conversation with another person," he explains. "Both people willfully talk about what they want to talk about, but it's not scripted. There are times when I go up on the mic when it is just stream-of-consciousness because I don't know what's coming next, but anyone who writes has to have some kernel of an agenda or plan. But we're all ultimately talking out of our necks. We're all making it up as we go along."

From an interview with *Interview Magazine*:

Interviewer: Your songs are such a hodgepodge of musical styles that somehow perfectly fit the evocative narratives. What comes first?
Beck: Usually the music inspires the lyrics. The lyrics just sort of fall off like a bunch of crumbs from the melody. That's all I want them to be—crumbs I don't want to work any kind of fabricated message. Sometimes I'll have an idea for a story or have a subject and that will inspire lyrics, but most of the time, hopefully, they already exist somewhere else.
Interviewer: When recording an album, how involved are you in what the other musicians are playing?
Beck: Well, my first few albums, I was playing most of the instruments myself. But I have been known to sit in front of a musician, singing to him what he needs to play.

Freewrite Medium and Composing Processes

The purpose of this freewrite is to help you think about the idea that the medium you compose in shapes your composing processes. Think of a composition you created that was in a medium other than print text (for example, a Web site or a speech or a photo). How were your composing processes different from your processes for composing in print? How did the medium you were composing in affect your composing processes?

Composing in Multiple Genres

Your composing process for writing an e-mail to a friend may involve one draft and no revising or editing, whereas your composing process for a book review for a history class may involve finding model book reviews to emulate, writing multiple drafts, and visiting the writing center to get some feedback from a tutor. Composing a job application will involve careful editing and proofreading, and composing a Web site will require attention to visual design and hyperlinks. Each different genre demands a different composing process.

Let's look at examples of student writers composing in two genres to help us think about the ways the genre you're composing in shapes your composing processes. Gopi Pitcher was a student at James Madison University when she composed a slide show for an assignment in a first-year writing course. We'll take a closer look at Gopi's slide show in the student case study in Chapter 5: "Situating Visual Literacies," but for now, we'll focus on what Gopi had to say about how composing in the genre of the slide show affected her processes:

> *I felt that composing the slide show was harder than I thought. Unlike the essay I have no words to explain everything I want to or had explained within the essay. Everything had to be shown. . . . Finding the pictures started to get difficult when trying to find those specific photos that capture the very emotions that I wanted to show my audience, so they too could evoke some emotion or reaction. With an essay, I could just ramble on then clean it up later with editing; you can't do that with a visual argument. Then there is the worry that the argument won't come through. It has to be a strong argument so anyone on any given day can view it and say, "Hey I know what she's trying to tell me."*

Composing in the genre of a slide show required Gopi to focus her process not on freewriting or revising words but on finding photos and then deciding which photos would be most effective. In the genre of the slide show, the convention is to focus on images rather than words to get your message across. As Gopi mentioned, she wasn't able to "ramble on and then clean it up later," like she could with a print genre such as an essay or research paper, so her process was more focused and limited.

The genre you're composing in will affect not just the way you brainstorm and revise but also the specific choices you make as you fine-tune your composition. Maria Correa was a student in a first-year writing course at Florida State University when she created a Web site about the communities with the worst poverty in Brazil (the "Favelas"). We'll look more closely at Maria's Web site in Chapter 6: "Situating Digital Literacies," but for now we'll focus on what Maria had to say about some specific choices she made about the design of her Web site:

> *As for the structure of the Web site, I chose to have the big banner on the top of the page with the title,* Favelas of Brazil. *I wanted the words* Favelas

and Brazil *to stand out, so I made that font larger than* of. *Then, I placed the links on the left side of the page. For the rough drafts and process memos, since there are three of each, I wanted to have a heading that stood out and each link to the rough drafts and memos as a sub-link to their headings. Then, I wanted to have my movie in the middle of my home page. I wanted the video itself to be bigger, but I tried changing it in several ways and it didn't work out. I didn't want to include anything else in my home page so it wouldn't distract from my movie.*

Because Maria was composing in the genre of the Web site, an important part of her process involved making choices about design: the size of the banner, the placement of links, the appearance of the video, and the overall look of the page. Banners, links, and embedded videos are all conventions of the genre of the Web site. These kinds of choices about the design of her composition would have been less important if Maria were composing in the genre of an e-mail or an editorial or a book report. Genre affects all aspects of composing processes, from finding a topic to drafting and revising to document design and editing.

Freewrite Genre Interview

Think of a specific genre you've composed in recently, whether for a course or on your own. Then, get into pairs and interview a peer about the ways in which the genre he or she composed in shaped the composing process. Here are some things you can consider in your questions:

    The conventions of the genre

    The composer's familiarity with the genre

    The purposes and audiences for the genre

    The social and cultural contexts of the genre

Be prepared to report to the class what you found in your interview.

Freewrite Literacy History

The purpose of this freewrite is to help you think about the ways your personal context will shape the writing you do in college. Write for ten minutes about your high school literacy history. Consider your personal background and how it influenced you as a writer and reader, the influence of your teachers, and the kinds of texts you read and composed.

Composing in Multiple Contexts

When we began drafting this textbook, our composing processes were shaped by many personal and social contexts: our experiences as teachers of writing, our prior experiences using textbooks in our classes, our attitudes about reading and writing, the trends in our field, the kinds of reading and writing that are becoming more and more influential in the wider culture, and so forth. If you completed the freewrite at the bottom of page 59, you probably found that the personal and social contexts you were composing in had a major influence on the way you composed. Let's look at some examples of how personal and social contexts affected composers' attitudes and processes. Read the following excerpts from three essays from Chapter 3: "Situating Personal Literacies." All of the excerpts focus on the ways that personal and social contexts influenced three writers.

Excerpt from Sherman Alexie's "Superman and Me":

My father, who is one of the few Indians who went to Catholic school on purpose, was an avid reader of westerns, spy thrillers, murder mysteries, gangster epics, basketball player biographies, and anything else he could find. He bought his books by the pound at Dutch's Pawn Shop, Goodwill, Salvation Army, and Value Village. When he had extra money, he bought new novels at supermarkets, convenience stores, and hospital gift shops. Our house was filled with books. They were stacked in crazy piles in the bathroom, bedrooms, and living room. In a fit of unemployment-inspired creative energy, my father built a set of bookshelves and soon filled them with a random assortment of books about the Kennedy assassination, Watergate, the Vietnam War, and the entire 23-book series of the Apache westerns. My father loved books, and since I loved my father with an aching devotion, I decided to love books as well.

Excerpt from Paule Marshall's "From the Poets in the Kitchen":

My mother and her friends were after all the female counterparts of Ralph Ellison's *Invisible Man.* Indeed, you might say they suffered a triple invisibility, being black, female and foreigners. They really didn't count in American society except as a source of cheap labor. But given the kind of women they were, they couldn't tolerate the fact of their invisibility, their powerlessness. And they fought back, using the only weapon at their command: the spoken word.

Those late afternoon conversations on a wide range of topics were a way for them to feel they exercised some measure of control over their lives and the events that shaped them. "Soully-gal, talk yuh talk!" they were always exhorting each other. "In this man world you got to take yuh mouth and make a gun!" They were in control, if only verbally and if only for the two hours or so that they remained in our house.

Excerpt from Gloria Anzaldúa's "How to Tame a Wild Tongue":

I remember being caught speaking Spanish at recess—that was good for three licks on the knuckles with a sharp ruler. I remember being sent to the corner of the classroom for "talking back" to the Anglo teacher when all I was trying to do was tell her how to pronounce my name. "If you want to be American, speak 'American.' If you don't like it, go back to Mexico where you belong."

Freewrite Responding to the Reading

Go to Chapter 3 and read the entire text of one of the three essays excerpted previously. Make a list of the personal and social/cultural factors that influenced the author. What factors were a positive influence? What factors were a negative influence? Next, write for five minutes about both the positive and negative personal and social/cultural contexts that influence you as a composer.

In every example of composing in this chapter, from Brian Turner's poem to M. C. Escher's lithographs to the essays by Alexie, Marshall, and Anzaldúa, factors such as purpose, medium, genre, and context shaped composers processes, and each composing process was different. Twenty-first–century readers and composers need the rhetorical agility to adapt their reading and composing processes to multiple literacy situations and to avoid using the same process for each literacy situation they face. As you read the texts in this book, think about what reading strategies will be most effective for your purposes for reading and for the medium and genre of the text. Before you begin to engage in the writing projects, consider what composing processes will best suit the kind of text you're composing and the context of the assignment. In this class and in all of the composing you do in and out of school, remember that the literacy situation will shape your composing processes.

3

Situating Personal Literacies

This chapter on personal literacies will help you better understand what is meant by the term *personal literacies*. It will also encourage you to explore the factors in your own life that have shaped you as a user of language.

While this chapter focuses on personal literacies, it's important to realize that there is a lot of overlap among the various types of literacies that are discussed in this text. For example, many of us heard stories while we were growing up that played a role in shaping our personal literacies—stories that affected our development as readers and writers, stories of young people who didn't take school seriously, dropped out, and messed up their lives, and stories of underprivileged individuals with a thirst for knowledge and a drive to excel who overcame huge obstacles and went on to become successful adults. While such stories are part of our personal literacies, they are also a part of oral literacies—of stories we have heard. In addition, they're part of our academic literacies in that they played a role in shaping us as students. Similarly, teachers who had a positive influence on us as students are a part of both our personal and academic literacies. They played an important role in shaping us as users of language and as members of academic communities. Internet sites such as *Facebook* and *MySpace*, along with technologies such as text messaging and e-mail, can play a role in shaping our personal literacies, but they can also be a huge part of our digital literacies. So while there is no denying the overlap among various types of literacies, the readings, case study, and various questions in this chapter will focus on helping you explore personal literacies.

As you read this chapter, you'll have the opportunity to—

- Read an essay in which a composition teacher explores the meaning of personal literacy and the place of the personal in the writing classroom
- Read a case study that includes a process memo and two drafts of a first-year student's personal literacy essay
- Become familiar with a statement titled "On Students' Right to Their Own Language," issued by an organization of writing teachers that felt compelled to take a stand for personal literacy and the rights of students to use their own dialects
- Find out about one first-year student's "Most Spectacular Failure" as you read her personal literacy narrative
- Read essays, poetry, a cartoon, and a video about Superman, about a Chinese mother and a Japanese American graduate student who wishes she could get rid of her accent, about sleeping with books, marginalia, wild tongues, poets from Barbados, and more.

But you won't just read stories of personal literacies; you'll also compose and use writing to explore your own personal literacies. If you respond to the personal literacy projects described at the end of the chapter, you might—

- Write a personal literacy narrative and reflection about your history as a reader and writer
- Write a position shift essay about an experience that altered how you thought or felt about an aspect of your personal literacy
- Create a snapshots essay in which you use words and images to create captured moments of select times in your life
- Write an analysis of your own personal language(s)
- Create a radical revision project in which you turn one of your earlier essays into a film, photo album, Web site, collage, poem, skit, short graphic novel—the possibilities go on and on
- Work with a group of your peers to collaboratively write an essay in which you compare your personal literacies.

And now, on to the exploration of personal literacies. . . .

What Are Personal Literacies?

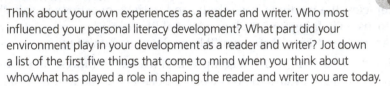

Before You Read

Think about your own experiences as a reader and writer. Who most influenced your personal literacy development? What part did your environment play in your development as a reader and writer? Jot down a list of the first five things that come to mind when you think about who/what has played a role in shaping the reader and writer you are today.

What's I Got to Do with It? Personal Literacies in the Writing Classroom

Amy Hodges Hamilton

Amy Hodges Hamilton is a Professor of English at Belmont University in Nashville, Tennessee. She earned a Ph.D. in Rhetoric and Composition from Florida State University, where she worked closely with the late Wendy Bishop. Amy's area of specialization is writing as therapy.

1 When asked to reflect on their earliest memories with language, one writing student, Linda, responded:

2   I can't remember when I learned to read. It would be like recalling when I first tasted food or when I first noticed that I was breathing. But I do remember being tortured by cursive writing exercises. Our teacher made us trace large slanted script in workbooks with a special yellow marker. At that age I wanted to write straight, not at an angle. Being a good girl, I did my assignments as asked, but, in private, I immediately reverted to my way.

3   What comes to mind when you think about your earliest memories of language? What experiences have you had with others—parents, siblings, teachers—that have shaped your language use? How does your personal literacy inform and define who you are as a writer, speaker, and thinker? In order to become personally literate, you must consider your attitude toward language and how it has been affected.

4   You might be asking yourself, is there really room for my personal literacy in the writing classroom and/or the larger academy? Richard Courage in "The Interaction of Public and Private Literacies" reminds us that declaring allegiance to either personal literacies or academic literacies is unnecessary and counterproductive. Writing is a complex, multi-layered process that can include both the personal and the academic. In fact, all

writing should. Through this introductory essay and the personal literacies chapter, you will develop new understandings of literacy by exploring the ways you, your peers, and acclaimed authors use language and
experience to help visualize the self as a writer, "open to revising even
deeply held beliefs" (Newkirk 23).

Exploring Personal Literacy History

5 Mina Shaugnessy, a pioneer in the teaching of writing, explores the ways
in which students' personal literacies inform their entrance into the university:

6 . . .They have nonetheless had their own worlds to grow up in and they arrive
on our campuses as young adults, with opinions and languages and plans
already in their minds. College both beckons and threatens them, offering to
teach them useful ways of thinking and talking about the world, promising even
to improve the quality of their lives, but threatening at the same time to take away
from their distinctive ways of interpreting the world, to assimilate them into the
culture of academic without acknowledging their experiences as outsiders. (292)

7 In order to most effectively enter the academy, all students should be
invited to consider their individual experiences with language. This might
happen in the writing classroom through exploring your literacy history.
Wendy Bishop defines personal literacy as "the story of coming into language, of learning how to read and write, of learning what reading and
writing mean in one's life" (52). Exploring your personal literacy histories
can help you challenge your education, your beliefs, your communities,
and your experiences with cultural and racial diversity. This process can
also help you understand the literature you read, create public voices and
identities, as well as explore your own writing and reading processes.

8 For example, one of my writing students, Janelle, explores how her relationship with her mother affected her personal literacy:

9 The best word, I guess, would be jealous. I wanted to capture the attention of
my mother the way that books did. She would forsake any and everything for
a good book . . . I started my own obsession with books by reading everything
she read. She read historical novels and had a particular fascination with World
War II. As you can imagine, this made for an interesting knowledge store for a
fourth grader. This would also explain why I had a good understanding of
German politics from 1933–1945 and why I had a bad habit of calling people
fops, milquetoasts, and hellions when I was angry.

10 Through writing this essay, Janelle was able to focus on specific
moments in her language and personal development, and her literacy history became a site "of self-translation where writers can articulate the meanings and consequences of passages between language worlds" (Soliday 511).

11   As Janelle's writing demonstrates, we each have individual histories as readers and writers. For example, what was your first word? What language did you speak as a child? What is the first thing you remember writing? Through drafting your literacy history, you can begin thinking about yourself as a writer and reader. In *On Writing: A Process Reader*, Wendy Bishop asks: "What do you remember about learning to read and write? In what way are you the same or a different reader than you were back then?" (116). Here are some other important questions to consider as you reflect on what it means to be personally literate:

1. What are some of the earliest encounters you remember with language, written or verbal? Why do you think you remember them?

2. Think of a time you were proud of or embarrassed by your ability to communicate. Why? Who was involved?

3. Did you ever say or write something and later wished you hadn't? Explain the circumstances and the outcome.

4. Who's the storyteller in your family? Relate a story frequently told. How has that person/story influenced you?

5. What are some of the "rules" of language that you've learned? How have they been helpful or harmful? Who taught them to you?

6. Who has helped shape you as the speaker, reader, or writer that you are today? How?

7. Think of a time when language (written or spoken) got you something you wanted. How did you accomplish this task? What did you learn?

8. What has someone ever written to you that you treasure? What have you ever written to someone that the receiver kept as a "treasure"?

9. Do you consider your literacy skills better/worse than those of others? Whose? Why?

10. Have you ever used your literacy to judge somebody else in a negative way? How? Why? Was it a conscious decision?

11. Do you think your literacy skills will develop/change? How? Why? (Bishop)

Personal Experiences and How They Shape Our Literacies

12 How do your personal experiences construct you as a literate individual? I have found when students begin by writing about their lives and language use, they begin to see and understand themselves and their place within culture in new and interesting ways. Bishop reminds us that "writing is a transformative act . . . we can make crossings into new intellectual and emotional territories" (53). This is well demonstrated in Lauren's essay featured in this chapter, "Unearthing," where through her analysis of her language use, she discovers that her literacy not only involved ". . . the published text, but also many hands-on experiences." She goes on to conclude, "Because I was

neither forced, nor restricted in my education, my drive to obtain a better understanding of all subjects has been fueled by my intrinsic motivation."

13   As you examine your life and personal literacy, can you think of life experiences that have been shaped specifically by language? Another writing student, Lee, does this well while reflecting on her first encounters with reading and writing:

14   I can't tell you for sure what the first thing I wrote was. Maybe it was that stupid book for the Young Author's Conference, *Mary Thankful*. I was in fourth grade and all I could produce when challenged was a dumb story about a dumb girl who liked Thanksgiving, printed on paper we laminated ourselves and bound in cardboard. I think we were supposed to be proud of the effort we made, but I felt disappointed. I knew I could do better. I can still see it in my mind's eye, poor illustration with cheap contact paper as the cover. Maybe that is why I put off writing for a long time after that.

15   Lee's personal voice and experience are strong here, and I would invite you to think about what experiences, both positive and negative, have shaped your understanding or misunderstanding of literacy. Mary Soliday argues, "An author of a successful literacy story goes beyond recounting 'what happened' to foreground the distance between an earlier and present self conscious of living in time, a distinction familiar to those who have studied autobiographical writing and literacy narratives" (514).

The Public Side of Personal Literacies

16 Stories appear in every culture and have appeared since the earliest recorded human cultures where people used oral storytelling to transmit information like hunting and migration patterns and family genealogies. As evidenced in the student examples so far in this essay, we all have important stories to tell. But how do these personal experiences and literacies intersect with others? As Bishop reminds us, we do not experience life as a single, unified consciousness. Instead, we are constructed through our family, various communities we are part of, cultural affiliations, and our racial and ethnic backgrounds (53).

17   So keep in mind when you are constructing your personal literacies that your experiences are automatically linked to a larger social and cultural reality. This writing approach is sometimes referred to as entering a contact zone, where cultures and people meet, clash, and grapple with each other. As you consider the public side of your personal literacy, remember the power of your experiences in both language and life and how those words and experiences might affect change. For example, In Gloria Anzaldúa's "How to Tame a Wild Tongue," she writes about the importance of embracing cultural diversity: "So, if you want to really hurt me, talk badly about my language. Ethnic identity is twin skin to linguistic identity. I am my language." Anzaldúa goes on to detail her literacy history, with its merging of Tex/Mex, English, and Spanish. Anzaldúa's examination of how various cultures and

languages come together is especially important in an academy where students come from widely varying cultural and language backgrounds.

18   As you begin to connect your language and life experiences to broader social constructs, consider sharing your "linguistic identity" like Anzaldúa suggests. It is important to move outside of your experience as you explore your personal literacies. You might do this through conducting primary research—perhaps by interviewing a parent or teacher about your early language use, by conducting a survey or questionnaire about your culture's dialect or jargon, or by completing an ethnographic study.

Putting Pen to Paper

19 As part of reading this chapter and exploring your personal literacies, your teacher might ask you to compose a personal literacy narrative. So how do you begin? Consider one of the following exercises to get started:

- Read the following excerpt from Terry Tempest Williams' "Why I Write" and then make a list of reasons why you write:

20   I write to make peace with the things I cannot control. I write to create fabric in a world that often appears black and white. I write to discover. I write to uncover. I write to meet my ghosts. I write to begin a dialogue. I write to imagine things differently and in imagining things differently perhaps the world will change . . . I write because as a child I spoke a different language (Williams).

- Open a blank document and freewrite for 20 minutes without stopping your pen or keypad, sharing the story of your personal literacy history—what did you read as a child? What are your earliest memories of reading and writing? What personal experiences have affected your attitudes about reading, writing, thinking, and learning?

- Talk it out. Try sharing the story of your literacy history with a friend, roommate, or classmate by answering the following questions:

  1. Where do you write most effectively? How? About what? When? Do you eat? Procrastinate?

  2. What do you enjoy writing most? Least?

  3. Recall your best writing experience, your best reading experience.

  4. Recall your worst writing experience, your worst reading experience.

  5. What writing or reading experience stands out as the most significant?

21   As you draft your own literacy narratives, remember to look at the powerful examples provided in this chapter of your textbook. For example, Amy Tan's "Mother Tongue" considers the effects of language on her life and how her Chinese American heritage informs her personal and

writing life. Be sure to ask yourself how you might emulate writing techniques such as Tan's in your own writing.

So I Has a Lot to Do with It

22 By writing about your own lives and literacies, you should both build confidence as a writer and be more willing to explore what you think and feel about yourself and the world around you. In turn, this should encourage you to take greater risks in your writing and language use. You will also learn how to adapt your personal literacies to various literacy situations. As Soliday reminds us:

23   Students' stories of everyday life enhance their personal success as writers in the university; these stories can also deepen their teachers' understanding of difference and shape their responses to today's competing versions of multiculturalism. In this way, literacy narratives contribute to the broader goal of building a more dialogical, multicultural curriculum that includes—indeed that both respects and responds to—the voices and stories of individual writers. (521)

24   Throughout this chapter, you will gain a greater sense of personal literacies as you write your own literacy narratives and as you read well-known authors such as Sherman Alexie and Amy Tan who explore theirs. Remember to ask yourself how both the personal and public sides of your literacy histories shape who you are as a writer, speaker, and thinker.

Works Cited

Anzaldúa, Gloria. "How to Tame a Wild Tongue." *Borderlands/La Frontera*. San Francisco: Aunt Lute Books, 1999. Print.

Bishop, Wendy, ed. *On Writing*. Boston: McGraw Hill, 2004. Print.

Courage, Richard. "The Interaction of Public and Private Literacies." *College Composition and Communication* 44.4 (1993): 484–496. Print.

Newkirk, Thomas. *The Performance of Self in Student Writing*. Portsmouth: Boynton/Cook, 1997. Print.

Shaugnessy, Mina. *Errors and Expectations: A Guide for the Teacher of Basic Writing*. Oxford: Oxford University Press, 1979. Print.

Soliday, Mary. "Translating Self and Difference through Literacy Narratives." *College English* 56.5 (1994): 511–526. Print.

Williams, Terry Tempest. "Why I Write." *Red: Passion and Patience in the Desert*. New York: Vintage, 2002. Print.

Literacy Connections

1. Now that you've finished reading Amy Hodges Hamilton's essay on personal literacies and started doing some thinking of your own about what the term means to you, in your own words define *personal literacies.*

2. Based on what Hamilton says in her essay regarding the place of the personal in the classroom, how do you think she would respond to someone who says that writing about the personal has no place in a composition class?

3. Hamilton is clearly convinced of the value and importance of allowing students to write about the personal in the composition classroom. What is your opinion on this issue and why? What experiences have you had with personal writing in academia?

4. Early in her essay, Hamilton poses the question: "What comes to mind when you think about your earliest memories of language?" To help you begin to explore your own personal literacy, freewrite for ten minutes on this topic. Don't worry about matters of grammar and correctness. Simply write nonstop for ten minutes, jotting down whatever comes to your mind when you think about your earliest memories involving language.

5. Hamilton says, ". . . we are constructed through our family, various communities we are part of, cultural affiliations, and our racial and ethnic backgrounds." Choose one of the personal essays in this chapter and discuss the ways the author was "constructed" by his or her family, communities, cultural affiliations, and racial and ethnic backgrounds.

Before You Read

You're about to read a case study of a student whose teacher asked her to write a personal literacy narrative—an essay that explores an individual's development as a reader and writer. If you were told to write a personal literacy narrative, what factors, people, and/or situations would you be likely to include in your essay?

Student Case Study: Composing a Personal Literacy Narrative

Lauren Kiser was a first-semester, first-year student enrolled in ENC 1101, the first of two required composition courses at Florida State University, when she composed "Unearthing," a personal literacy narrative.

Included in this case study of Lauren's composing processes are her process memo and two drafts of her essay—the first and the last, along with additional input she provided to give readers some extra insight into how she went about composing this personal literacies essay and the rhetorical choices she made. By taking a close look at Lauren's writing processes for her personal literacy narrative, you'll gain a better awareness of composing in personal literacy contexts.

Lauren's assignment for the first composition of the semester was to write a personal literacy narrative. Here's the assignment:

ASSIGNMENT: PERSONAL LITERACY NARRATIVE

For this essay, I'd like to learn about your history as a reader and writer. I'd like you to think about the factors, people, and situations in your life that played a major role in making you the reader and writer you are today. Think about the schools you attended, the people who taught you, and the situations you found yourself in that shaped you as a reader and writer. Reflect upon both positive and negative influences, how you reacted to those influences, and how they played a role in shaping you as a student.

There's no one way to approach or structure this essay or any of the other essays you write in this class. What you say in this paper and how you say it will depend on the ideas you want to communicate to your readers—the other students in this class, your teacher, and individuals who might access your ePortfolio site.

Expected essay length: 4–5 double-spaced pages.

Lauren shared her first and second drafts with her peer response group and received feedback from them as she worked on her essay. The day her third draft was due, she submitted it to her teacher in a folder that contained the earlier drafts with peer review comments, as well as the draft to which the teacher responded. At the end of the semester, Lauren posted the final draft of her essay to her *ePortfolio* site.

Lauren's process memo (written the day she submitted her third draft), rough draft, and final draft are included below.

PROCESS MEMO

My approach to my paper was obvious to me. The people that have influenced my life the most are my mother and my grandfather. My mother has always pushed me to do well in school, but most of my drive is self-initiated because of my early interest in exploring things around me.

My rough draft was a starting point. When I first sat down to write, I had no idea how I was going to approach the topic and began with an entirely different tone and storyline. One day after that I was in the mood to write and sat down and completely rewrote the first part of my paper to what it is now (excluding some revisions). My second draft includes more details and a better flow. That was also an inspired day. My third draft is not all that different from my second. I added a few details and corrected a few mistakes, but besides changing my ending, I did not do anything major to it.

My peer response group made me feel better about my paper. I am always cautious about whether others like what I write or not. They pointed out a few things that I had looked over and suggested corrections. Their positive comments were honest and helpful as well.

I am generally content with the way my paper is right now. I know there are a few things that might need to be smoothed out, but I think I have accomplished my goal of communicating my story.

Lauren shares in her process memo above that when she first started working on her rough draft, she "had no idea how [she] was going to approach the topic and began with an entirely different tone and storyline." She goes on to say that later, "when [she] was in the mood to write," she went back to her rough draft "and completely rewrote the first part of [her] paper." Although we don't have those original lines that Lauren knew she didn't want to keep, we do have the first draft that Lauren saved. Let's take a look at this early draft.

August 30

Draft 1

My life began with a backdrop of what some may consider paradise: a small, cozy home sitting on the side of a hill, the Blue Ridge Mountains on the horizon, and all of the solitude that comes with living in a town set in a frame made of pine, maple, and coal. Unfortunately for me, I never found my paradise in this small coalmining town, but it is where my life began, and so it is also where my story begins.

The wooded scenery provided me with ample opportunity to explore the natural world as a child. My grandfather and I spent hours walking through what we called the "Bernstein Bear" trail in my backyard. There I learned about moss and ferns and rollie-pollie bugs that we found under rocks. I learned that pine trees are green year round and if you light pine needles on fire, the smoke keeps the gnats away.

As we wore down the earth and left our trail as a mark, my grandfather also made his mark on me. He told me stories of growing up in Louisiana and catching alligators and practical jokes he and his brothers played on the neighbors. He told me fictional stories about adventurers not so different from us, traveling along, making impressions on the world. I learned some of life's most valuable lessons on those summer afternoons from my old companion dressed in a flannel shirt and khaki pants.

My grandfather and I were inseparable from day one, and though he passed away when I was seven, nothing has changed. I still learn from him. He has taught me much without speaking a single word.

Growing up in Southwest Virginia, I encountered a lot of very colorful language at an early age. By colorful, I do not mean profane, but language saturated with deep southern and Appalachian dialect typical of a small, mostly uneducated, town in the armpit of the state. It was not uncommon for outsiders to have some difficulty in deciphering certain words. For example, when one used the word "tar," they were not referring to the black sticky substance used in paving roads, but to the round rubber tubes known as "tires."

My mother, an incredible woman in my eyes for many reasons, saw quickly that her children were doomed for a lifetime of speaking the language of the locals and invested in the "Hooked-on-Phonics" program. I dreaded the yellow box filled with tapes and flash cards and never understood why the children in the picture on the label looked like they were having so much fun reading. I always put up a fight when my parents went out of town and left my grandmother with instructions to teach me ten flashcards and listen to one tape. I put my money on the fact that my grandmother, like most, spoiled me and I didn't have to complete my lessons.

My mother, however, was aware that I disliked the flashcards and found other ways to encourage me to read. I had the most magnificent library of children's books. I was attracted to the vivid images in "Grossamer." My mom tricked me into learning how to read. I loved it, and still do.

Had my mother been a math major, I probably would love numbers, but she was an English major and passed on her love and knowledge of words. Because of her early involvement in my literacy, I find it much more natural to analyze poetry than statistics and to write sentences than equations.

Because of my "home schooling" of sorts, I was significantly ahead of my peers when I began attending public school. It was difficult for me, given that my mother, not being a local was already disliked by many, and that I had already been provided the education that was required for Pre-K and Kindergarten children to learn. I was scorned by teachers and administration for being ahead and was left in a class that was unengaging and monotonous for my young and growing mind.

My mother took it upon herself to provide a means by which I could learn and still stay interested in my formal schooling. When at home, I was surrounded with interesting books filled with stories that never got old. My active imagination allowed me to transfer the fictional plots to my own personal microcosm, providing hours upon hours of entertainment.

Instead of learning at school, I created artistic masterpieces. While my classmates were learning their colors and shapes, I was discovering new and innovative ways to incorporate them into whatever medium was available. Often, my mother received notes from my teacher complaining about my excessive use of glue, paint, and glitter.

Once I reached kindergarten, I was faced with my first major educational obstacle—my teacher Mrs. Nancy. Kindergarten teachers are typically perceived as kind and generous. Mrs. Nancy, however, was exceptional at inhibiting my learning. When going through exercises that taught my classmates and I how to write our names, I was scolded because this was a skill that I had already acquired. I quickly lost interest in the monotony of writing my name, so my perfectly sculpted chicken scratch became more and more difficult to decipher and then again I was scolded for my sloppiness. This was a major setback for me as far as my interest in school went. My teacher often sent notes home to my mother, complaining about everything from my brilliantly colored sky that had every color in the crayon box in it—except blue, to my lack of interest in playing kitchen with my classmates.

Lauren tells us in her process memo that the day she wrote her rough draft was "an inspired day." The ideas came easily and she wrote them down quickly. In this draft she tells her readers about growing up against "a backdrop of what some may consider paradise: a small, cozy home sitting on the side of a hill, the Blue Ridge Mountains on the horizon, and all of the solitude that comes with living in a town set in a frame made of pine, maple, and coal." She goes on to tell us a little about the treasured times she spent with her grandfather, about the "colorful language" that surrounded her, and about her mother's influence. Then she moves on to kindergarten and the obstacles she faced there. The draft ends rather abruptly in the midst of a description of her not-so-happy experiences with Mrs. Nancy and "playing kitchen" with her classmates.

Lauren mentions her second draft (not included here) in her process memo. She tells us the day she worked on that draft "was also an inspired day"—that she included more details in that draft and worked on making the paper have "a better flow."

Next, she worked on her final draft, which appears below. Let's take a look at what she wrote.

Final Draft
December 12

Unearthing

by Lauren Kiser

My life began with a backdrop of what some may consider paradise: a small, cozy home sitting on the side of a hill, the Blue Ridge Mountains on the horizon, and all of the solitude that comes with living in a town set in a frame made of pine, maple, and coal. Unfortunately for me, I never found my paradise in this small coalmining town, but it is where my life began, and also where my story begins.

The wooded scenery provided me with ample opportunity to explore the natural world as a child. From the time I could walk, I was interested in bugs, flowers, and leaves. The boundless forest in my backyard encouraged exploration. My grandfather and I spent hours walking through what we called the "Bernstein Bear" trail, named after my favorite series of books at the time. There I learned about moss and ferns and rollie-pollie bugs that we found under rocks. I learned that pine trees are green year round and if you light pine needles on fire, the smoke keeps the gnats away. My grandfather was part Native American and taught me that we should never take more than we need, and to always give back to nature. I learned many lessons that I did not realize until later in life. Most of all, he taught me to be observant of my surroundings and to appreciate seemingly insignificant things.

As we wore down the earth and left our trail as a mark, my grandfather also made his mark on me. He told me stories of growing up in Louisiana and catching alligators and practical jokes he and his brothers played on the neighbors. He told me fictional stories about adventurers not so different from us, traveling along, making impressions on the world.

My grandparents moved away when I got a little older and I was introduced to a new side of nature. My summers spent on the York River allowed me to explore the habitats of Mallard ducks, Canadian geese, Fiddler crabs, and Rockfish. At night I would sit on the porch with my grandfather, drink milk with ice, eat sardines, and listen to his stories. I watched the lights of the passing boats as he explained that the red and green triangles were channel markers and boats had to go between them. The ospreys made residence on top of these markers and we watched them gracefully scoop fish out of the water to feed their young.

My slight maturity allowed me to grasp new concepts like the changes of the tide and the cycles of the moon. Occasionally, he would tell me stories of fighting in World War II. At the time, I had no concept of war and did not know what World War II was, but his stories fascinated me.

My grandfather and I were inseparable from day one, and though he passed away when I was seven, nothing has changed. He sparked my interest in the natural world and encouraged me to learn from my surroundings. I watch the Discovery Channel instead of Cartoon Network, and my favorite movies and books are about bold adventurers like John Wayne and Robinson Crusoe. I learned some of life's most valuable lessons on those summer afternoons from my old companion dressed in a flannel shirt and khaki pants.

There was a point, however, at which my exploration of the world had to move indoors. During the cold months of the year, I spent my days in a small room with white cinderblock walls and harsh white tile floors. The fluorescent electric lights replaced the sunshine that I was used to and my formal education began. The Wise County public school system had guidelines by which students were to be taught. My mother went to great lengths to enhance my basic education. She supplemented what I was taught in school with a multitude of extracurricular media.

Growing up in Southwest Virginia, I encountered much very colorful language at an early age. By colorful, I do not mean profane, but language saturated with deep southern and Appalachian dialect typical of a small, mostly uneducated, town in the armpit of the state. It was not uncommon for outsiders to have some difficulty in deciphering certain words. For example, when one used the word "tar," they were not referring to the black sticky substance used in paving roads, but to a round rubber tube known as a "tire."

My mother, an incredible woman in my eyes for many reasons, saw quickly that her children were doomed for a lifetime of speaking the language of the locals and invested in the "Hooked-on-Phonics" program. I dreaded the yellow box filled with tapes and flash cards and never understood why the children in the picture on the label looked like they were having so much fun reading. I always put up a fight when my parents went out of town and left my grandmother with instructions to teach me ten flashcards and listen to one tape. I put my money on the fact that my grandmother, like most, spoiled me and I didn't have to complete my lessons.

My mother, however, was aware that I disliked the flashcards and found other ways to encourage me to read. I had the most magnificent library of children's books. I was attracted to the vivid images in *Gossamer*. I learned moral lessons from *Aesop's Fables* and *The Giving Tree*. I loved the books that I read so much that I didn't realize that I had been tricked into reading.

Had my mother been a math major, I probably would love numbers, but she was an English major and passed on her love and knowledge of words. Because of her early involvement in my literacy, I find it much more natural to analyze poetry than statistics and to write sentences than equations.

My "home schooling" of sorts put me ahead of my peers when I began attending public school. It was difficult for me, given that my mother, not being a local, was already disliked by many, and that I had already been provided the education that was required for pre-k and kindergarten. I was scorned by teachers and administrators for being ahead and was left in a class that was not engaging and monotonous for my young and growing mind.

My mother, however, supplied me with a steady stream of activities to keep me interested in school-related subjects. Besides my extraordinary library of books, she encouraged me to be creative and supplied a limitless stock of glue, glitter, paint, and my favorite—Crayola crayons. In school, when my classmates were learning their colors and shapes, I was discovering new and innovative ways to incorporate them into whatever medium was available. Our refrigerator proudly displayed layer upon layer of colorful construction paper, tempera paint, and a rainbow of glitter. Often, my mother received notes from my teachers complaining about my excessive use of art supplies.

I also spent much time outdoors helping my mom do yard work. She taught me the names of flowers and the secret formula of sun, water, and love that makes them grow. I saw many of the things that I read put into action. I collected caterpillars and put them in a terrarium, hoping they would turn into butterflies like in *Where Butterflies Grow*. Seeing a bird's nest or a bunny transformed my literary knowledge into a hands-on experience.

The foundation of my education was made concrete by my mother and grandfather. They allowed me to explore the world around me with few boundaries. My youthful curiosity was satisfied not only with published texts, but also with many hands-on experiences. Because I was neither forced nor restricted in my education, my drive to obtain a better understanding of all subjects has been fueled by my intrinsic motivation.

In her final draft Lauren made some significant changes/additions/deletions. She kept the opening paragraph from her earlier draft, but then in the second paragraph adds wonderful details about her interests in the outdoors and about her grandfather. We learn that he "was part Native American and taught [her] that we should never take more than we need, and to always give back to nature." She uses words as a medium to draw a clearer picture for us of her relationship with her grandfather and all that she learned from him.

Lauren goes on to add more details that bring her writing to life. She tells us about exploring "the habitats of Mallard ducks, Canadian geese, Fiddler crabs, and Rockfish." She paints a picture for us of sitting at night "on the porch with [her] grandfather, drink[ing] milk with ice, eat[ing] sardines, and listen[ing] to his stories." She allows us to "see" ospreys as they "gracefully scoop fish out of the water to feed their young" and she gives us a glimpse of how she "learned some of life's most valuable lessons on those summer afternoons from [her] old companion dressed in a flannel shirt and khaki pants."

In her final draft, Lauren adds a transition paragraph that takes us—her audience—from a focus on her grandfather's influence on her literacy history to the influence of her mother. She keeps the section on the "home schooling of sorts" and how she "was scorned by teachers and administrators for being ahead," but she gets rid of Mrs. Nancy and her lack of interest in "playing kitchen," and instead, focuses on her mother's positive influence. She keeps the section on the "colorful language" that surrounded her in Southwest Virginia, and the "Hooked-on-Phonics" program that did not interest her, and then she adds details about the books she loved that captured her young mind. We learn that she "collected caterpillars and put them in a terrarium, hoping they would turn into butterflies like in *Where Butterflies Grow*." And to bring her essay to closure, Lauren adds a paragraph in which she reflects on how "the foundation of [her] education was made concrete by [her] mother and grandfather."

Lauren's Strategies for Composing

To give us more insight into Lauren's strategies for composing this personal literacy narrative, we asked her to tell us a little about the kinds of brainstorming activities she usually does to help her come up with ideas for her essays. She told us:

> *When I sit down to write, usually I have a pretty clear idea about what I want to write. When I am not so sure about the direction I want to go in, I start my paper with the first idea I have. If I decide I don't like it, then I move on to my next idea and try that one out but don't totally neglect the first. It usually is a process of jotting down what I want to say, and then finding some way to make it all fit together.*

Unlike many of us who sit down to write without a clue where we might be headed, Lauren usually does a lot of thinking before she starts writing. For her, much of her brainstorming actually does go on in her head, so that when she begins to write, she already has ideas about what she wants to say and how she wants to say it. While this strategy usually works for her, many of us need to freewrite, cluster, share ideas with others, and/or make a list to help us generate ideas.

Next, we asked Lauren to share with us whom she considered as her audience as she composed this personal literacy narrative. We thought she would probably tell us that she considered her classmates and her teacher to be her audience, but we were wrong:

> I wrote this paper as though my mom and my grandfather were telling the story through me. I like to share what I write with my mom, so I tend to write for her. Since this paper was about her and her father, I wanted to make sure that both of them were represented accurately and truthfully. My mom actually printed out this paper and let my uncles and my grandmother read it. They all called me and told me how much my limited memory of my grandfather meant to them. THAT is what makes me proud of what I write or do in any aspect of life.

So Lauren was not writing for her classmates or for her teacher; she was writing for her mom—her mom was her intended audience, even though her classmates, teacher, uncles, and grandmother read it.

We also learn from her response to the previous question about audience that as Lauren wrote she attempted to take on the persona of her mom and grandfather. She wanted to write her essay "as though [her] mom and grandfather were telling the story through [her]." She "wanted to make sure that both of them were represented accurately and truthfully."

Personal literacy contexts typically ask us to write about our own experiences in our own language, often to audiences with whom we already have a personal relationship. But this idea of writing in our own language is often complicated, as it was for Lauren, when we try to take on someone else's persona. Lauren's composing processes were shaped by the voices she had in mind as she wrote, the storytelling structure that is typical of the genre of the literacy narrative, her own habits as a composer, and the audience that she imagined as readers of her narrative.

Literacy Connections

1. In her personal literacy narrative, Lauren includes lots of specific details. Jot down five details from her essay that stand out in your mind. How does her use of specific details enhance her essay?

2. Many writers consider nothing they have written to ever be truly finished; many of us feel that we could always return to what we've written and work on another draft. If you were part of Lauren's peer response group and you were responding to the final draft she wrote of "Unearthing," what would you tell her that you liked about her essay? Point out specific passages that provide examples of what you liked. What parts of the essay would you tell her were unclear to you? Point those out. What other questions would you ask her?

3. What ideas would you offer Lauren that might help her write an even stronger next draft?

4. Lauren shares in her process memo that when she first started working on the rough draft of her paper, she had no idea how she

was going to structure her paper. She simply started typing to discover how she wanted to tell the story of her literacy development. How do you typically go about getting started on your first draft? Do you typically brainstorm, freewrite, develop an outline, or use some other invention technique to help you figure out how to get started, or do you dive in the way Lauren did when she began this paper? Which techniques/strategies typically work best for you?

5. Later in this chapter, you'll find a statement titled "On Students' Right to Their Own Language," issued by an organization of writing teachers who felt compelled to take a stand for personal literacy and the rights of students to use their own dialects. How would you describe Lauren's dialect and use of language?

Personal Literacy Readings

Before You Read

Following is a statement issued by an organization of composition and communication teachers—a statement in which they take a stand for students' right to use their own language. Think about the various ways you use language. How would you describe your dialect?

Position Statement on Students' Right to Their Own Language

Conference on College Composition and Communication

The Conference on College Composition and Communication (CCCC), an organization made up of thousands of composition and communication teachers, made the decision more than 30 years ago to take a stand for personal literacy. In the Fall 1974 issue of *College Composition and Communication (CCC)*, the organization's leading journal, Richard Larson, chair of the organization at that time, states that "dedicated members of CCCC" worked for two years "toward a position statement on a major problem confronting teachers of composition and communication: how to respond to the variety in their students' dialects."

To access this statement and learn more about the context in which it was composed and adopted, go to http://www.csus.edu/wac/WAC/ PositionStatements/NewSRTOL.pdf.

We affirm the students' right to their own patterns and varieties of language—the dialects of their nurture or whatever dialects in which they find their own identity and style. Language scholars long ago denied that the myth of a standard American dialect has any validity. The claim that any one dialect is unacceptable amounts to an attempt of one social group to exert its dominance over another. Such a claim leads to false advice for speakers and writers and immoral advice for humans. A nation proud of its diverse heritage and its cultural and racial variety will preserve its heritage of dialects. We affirm strongly that teachers must have the experiences and training that will enable them to respect diversity and uphold the right of students to their own language.

Literacy Connections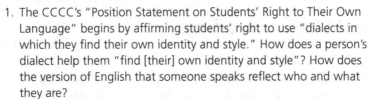

1. The CCCC's "Position Statement on Students' Right to Their Own Language" begins by affirming students' right to use "dialects in which they find their own identity and style." How does a person's dialect help them "find [their] own identity and style"? How does the version of English that someone speaks reflect who and what they are?
2. The CCCC's position statement makes the point that "language scholars long ago denied that the myth of a standard American dialect has any validity." If there is no standard American dialect, can there be any such thing as standard written English? Why or why not?
3. Think about what might have prompted the members of CCCC to take a stand for students to have the right to use their own language. What might have been going on in classrooms across our nation that would have prompted the members of this organization to take such a stand?
4. What is your position on the issue of students' right to their own language? Do you think students should be allowed to, or encouraged to, use their dialects in the writing they do in college? Why or why not?
5. Later in this chapter you'll find an essay by Gloria Anzaldúa titled "How to Tame a Wild Tongue." Take a few minutes to skim Anzaldúa's essay, and then consider how she would be likely to react to the CCCC's position statement.

Before You Read

Take a few minutes to think about difficult situations you encountered in elementary, middle, and high schools that influenced you as a student. Was there a particular subject that was especially difficult for you, a teacher whose class you thought you would never do well in, a test you knew you had to pass in order to go on, a move to a new school that presented difficult circumstances? Write for 15 minutes or so about that difficult situation and how it affected your growth as a student.

My Most Spectacular Failure

Claras Leandre

Claras Leandre was a first-semester college student at Florida State University when she wrote the following essay for her first-year composition course. She missed the first day of class because on the morning when the class first met, she was being sworn in as a citizen of the United States.

1   When I was in the fourth grade, socializing was paramount. Recess was my favorite part of the day because I could congregate with my friends, reminisce about the previous day's happenings, and play to my heart's content. Day after day I anticipated the moment when my classmates and I would stomp out of the classrooms and make our way to what seemed like a haven from the rigors of fourth grade. Nevertheless, I completed my homework assignments and class work, in a less enthusiastic manner, but on time. My sole purpose was to stay focused long enough to get the work done, but not to learn the concepts being taught. Tests as well were completed in much the same manner, lightheartedly. Needless to say, education was not my priority and I had no drive for success, achievement, or focus. But there was nothing wrong with my lack of drive in my eyes because that philosophy made my life simplistic and carefree.

2   That academic year I failed the Florida Comprehension Assessment Test (FCAT). I was crushed. Students who failed could not move onto the fifth grade. The next year I had to watch my former classmates go on, without me, and eventually watch as they graduated from elementary school, leaving me behind. This pivotal experience was forever imprinted in my memory and haunted me throughout my secondary education. I had failed myself, my family, and everyone who had ever believed in me and my abilities as a scholar. With this "failure" I began to realize the importance of an education and how it could help me reach my future goals, not yet known to me. So I resolved to change. That next year, homework became something I did to learn, not merely to get by. I paid attention to what all my teachers said and did. I asked questions each and every time I didn't understand something. Learning became a desired and obtainable venture. With that newly formed outlook I believed success was possible. What was once stressful became a challenge which I was determined to overcome. When I took the FCAT again, with a newfound determination, I felt more

confident. But as time went by, I wondered if I would find myself in the fourth grade yet again. However, when I reported to school the next year, I was delighted to find that I was placed in the fifth grade. I had passed! This was a great accomplishment for me because I had recently immigrated to America just a year prior.

3   Raised in Port-au-Prince, Haiti, with a strong value on education, my parents were preparing me to achieve something they could not. So they made a tough decision. I was about five years of age when my dad left for the United States, leaving the family behind. The plan was that my dad would work and send money back to Haiti to fund his daughters' education. After seeing what the United States could offer our family, he decided to turn his mission into bringing the whole family to the United States. So three years later I entered the United States, knowing neither English nor the country and its culture. Although we were positive about this endeavor, nothing came easy for either my family or me. With just high school diplomas and some vocational training, my parents worked to provide for four girls with high ambitions.

4   Having been born in another country meant that I was already a step behind the rest. Although I knew how to speak and write both French and Creole almost fluently, I had just moved to the United States, which meant I had to learn the English language and its style of writing just as fluently or even better. Facing the FCAT reminded me that I still had a long way to go. Also it allowed me to see what I was still struggling with, which happened to be both syntax and reading comprehension. My struggle was also evident, later on, in my Scholastic Aptitude Test (SAT) and American College Testing (ACT) scores. What made me exceptional is that I refused to let the fact that English is not my first language be an excuse for low performance. So in high school I challenged myself with Advanced Placement (AP) Literature and Composition and Honors English courses, which facilitated my continual improvement in reading and English syntax.

5   For two of my high school years I was fortunate enough to be guided to success by Mrs. Pinckney, who was both my English II and AP Literature and Composition teacher. The most profound aspect of both courses was that most people in the class had her as their English teacher for three years in high school. She knew all our strengths and weaknesses as well as our potential and our goals. Once senior year came around, senioritis left no one untouched. Those who had the drive and were willing to excel before lost their tenacity. Others who had never grasped the drive to succeed reconfirmed their attitudes. Although Mrs. Pinckney realized that the class did not believe in their abilities and was not willing to do the work it would take to pass both the course and the AP exam, she was determined. Her convictions were unwavering. She would not tolerate blatant laziness.

6   That year she presented her senior class with what we thought would be an insurmountable assignment. Our school district had a program they referred to as the Laureate Program. Only students with unquestionable drive braved to enter the grueling requirements to complete the program and gain the prestigious Laureate Diploma. Even though this was an optional program she decided to present us with the challenge. The class was in every way capable; we all met the criteria to start the program and, therefore, had no reason not to pursue the recognition it entailed. Many were not willing to challenge themselves and cracked, dropping the course as soon as possible. Others, like me, took on the challenge, with great reservations. The assignment included a 5,000-word research paper on a topic of our choice; because I had a strong desire to expand my knowledge of the medical field, I chose the topic "The Effects of Long-term Antibiotic Usage on the Immune System." Upon completing the paper we had to prepare a PowerPoint presentation of our topics and present them to a group of teachers, faculty members, and a portion of the student body. After the presentation we would be asked challenging questions regarding our topic and research. This was an arduous task; however, upon completing this project, very successfully, I was convinced that there was now nothing that I could not do if I dedicated myself. I not only overcame my crippling fear of public speaking but also a fear of putting my work out there to be judged by others.

7   My purpose in life is to help others thrive and prosper. Steered in the right direction by my experiences and mentored by a dedicated and motivational teacher, I have seen the impact that one can make on another's life. My goals are now known to me. I am attending a major university and pursuing a passion of mine, which happens to be the arduous field of medicine. With that aspiration in mind I will major in biology, while minoring in chemistry, on a pre-medicine track in hopes of later attending my university's school of medicine. I aspire to become a general surgeon. Once well into my practice field I would like to join Médecins Sans Frontières (Doctors Without Borders) or another similar goal oriented organization and travel the world providing medical aid to people in need.

8   Does this all seem impossible? I mean, less than nine years ago I did not know where I was headed or wanted to go educationally. However, the experiences I have gained and the confidence I have obtained have forever changed me as a scholar. I do not think my goals are impossible because sometimes life teaches us our most important lessons, not by our successes but by our failures. Many aspects of life change over time. While some aspects of life move down the hierarchy of life pyramid, others move up. My search for knowledge has increased in importance over socializing, which was at one time essential. One life-changing event led me to contemplate this switch in priorities. Through failing the FCAT, my perception of schooling has now been greatly altered. Currently, I value

education as a search for knowledge, which has and can lead to continued successes. Only when I was held back did I realize the serious side of school, along with the importance of an education. In the nine years since my most spectacular "failure," I have continued to improve my listening, reading, writing, and study skills. Maintaining a very stringent work ethic, I am now diligent and meticulous at all I undertake. As a result, I graduated third in my class, successfully completed eight AP courses in addition to completing the grueling Laureate Presentation, although I did not receive the diploma. I am grateful for my novel characteristics, which have helped me set my priorities straight. I value knowledge, the thrill of overcoming challenges, and the payoff of diligence. Knowledge . . . I crave it.

Literacy Connections

1. Claras Leandre wrote her essay in response to a writing prompt in her first-year composition course. As she wrote, she knew that both her classmates and her teacher would be her primary audience. How might her essay have been different had she been writing for a school newspaper? Consider ways in which this new genre and audience might have affected her persona and the material she included.

2. How might Leandre's writing be different if she chooses to write about this topic in her personal statement when applying to medical school? How might this new genre and audience affect her persona and the information she decides to include?

3. How was your reaction to Leandre's failure of the FCAT and her subsequent forced repetition of the fourth grade affected when you later discovered that she did not move to the U.S. until she was eight years old and that on arriving in the U.S. she spoke and wrote in both French and Creole? How did this new knowledge change the way you read the initial failure?

4. Many critics claim that standardized tests such as the FCAT discriminate against multilingual students, and others maintain that all students, no matter what their backgrounds, should be held to the same standards. Do you think standardized tests such as Florida's FCAT with its section that requires timed, in-class writing on an assigned topic is fair to students like Leandre who are multilingual. Why or why not?

5. In this chapter's opening essay, "What's I Got to Do with It? Personal Literacies in the Writing Classroom," Amy Hodges Hamilton discusses the importance of considering how our ". . . experiences are automatically linked to a larger social and cultural reality." In what ways is Leandre's personal literacy linked to the social and cultural reality of her life?

Before You Read

Before you begin reading Sherman Alexie's essay, think about what you might already know or think you know about life on what Alexie calls "Indian reservations." Do an Internet search and see what you can discover about these reservations. When were they first established? Why were they established? How many existed 100 years ago? Fifty years ago? Currently? How many Native Americans still live on reservations? What are the typical living conditions on these reservations? Why might Native Americans today choose to live on them? What are the schools like? How are the living conditions on these reservations similar to living conditions in your early years? How are they different?

Superman and Me

Sherman Alexie

Sherman Alexie, a Spokane/Coeur d'Alene Indian, grew up on the Spokane Indian Reservation in Wellpinit, Washington. According to the "Official Sherman Alexie Web site" (http://fallsapart.com/biography .html), when Alexie enrolled in college, he "planned to be a doctor and enrolled in pre-med courses . . . but after fainting numerous times in human anatomy class realized he needed to change his career path. That change was fueled when he stumbled into a poetry workshop at Washington State University."

Since then Alexie has become widely recognized as an outstanding poet, short story writer, and novelist, and has won numerous awards. His publications include *First Indian on the Moon,* a collection of poetry (1993); *Reservation Blues*, a novel (1995); *Indian Killer*, a novel (1996); *The Toughest Indian in the World*, a collection of short stories (2000); and *The Absolutely True Diary of a Part-Time Indian,* a novel (2007).

The following essay appeared in the *Los Angeles Times*, April 19, 1998, as part of a series, "The Joy of Reading and Writing." This essay is also printed in *The Most Wonderful Books: Writers on Discovering the Pleasures of Reading*.

1   I learned to read with a Superman comic book. Simple enough, I suppose. I cannot recall which particular Superman comic book I read, nor can I remember which villain he fought in that issue. I cannot remember the plot, nor the means by which I obtained the comic book. What I can remember is this: I was 3 years old, a Spokane Indian boy living with his family on the Spokane Indian Reservation in eastern Washington state. We were poor by most standards, but one of my parents usually managed to find

some minimum-wage job or another, which made us middle-class by reservation standards. I had a brother and three sisters. We lived on a combination of irregular paychecks, hope, fear, and government surplus food.

2   My father, who is one of the few Indians who went to Catholic school on purpose, was an avid reader of westerns, spy thrillers, murder mysteries, gangster epics, basketball player biographies, and anything else he could find. He bought his books by the pound at Dutch's Pawn Shop, Goodwill, Salvation Army, and Value Village. When he had extra money, he bought new novels at supermarkets, convenience stores, and hospital gift shops. Our house was filled with books. They were stacked in crazy piles in the bathroom, bedrooms, and living room. In a fit of unemployment-inspired creative energy, my father built a set of bookshelves and soon filled them with a random assortment of books about the Kennedy assassination, Watergate, the Vietnam War and the entire 23-book series of the Apache westerns. My father loved books, and since I loved my father with an aching devotion, I decided to love books as well.

3   I can remember picking up my father's books before I could read. The words themselves were mostly foreign, but I still remember the exact moment when I first understood, with a sudden clarity, the purpose of a paragraph. I didn't have the vocabulary to say "paragraph," but I realized that a paragraph was a fence that held words. The words inside a paragraph worked together for a common purpose. They had some specific reason for being inside the same fence. This knowledge delighted me. I began to think of everything in terms of paragraphs. Our reservation was a small paragraph within the United States. My family's house was a paragraph, distinct from the other paragraphs of the LeBrets to the north, the Fords to our south, and the Tribal School to the west. Inside our house, each family member existed as a separate paragraph but still had genetics and common experiences to link us. Now, using this logic, I can see my changed family as an essay of seven paragraphs: mother, father, older brother, the deceased sister, my younger twin sisters, and our adopted little brother.

4   At the same time I was seeing the world in paragraphs, I also picked up that Superman comic book. Each panel, complete with picture, dialogue, and narrative was a three-dimensional paragraph. In one panel, Superman breaks through a door. His suit is red, blue, and yellow. The brown door shatters into many pieces. I look at the narrative above the picture. I cannot read the words, but I assume it tells me that "Superman is breaking down the door." Aloud, I pretend to read the words and say, "Superman is breaking down the door." Words, dialogue, also float out of Superman's mouth. Because he is breaking down the door, I assume he says, "I am breaking down the door." Once again, I pretend to read the words and say aloud, "I am breaking down the door." In this way, I learned to read.

5   This might be an interesting story all by itself. A little Indian boy teaches himself to read at an early age and advances quickly. He reads *Grapes of*

Wrath in kindergarten when other children are struggling through "Dick and Jane." If he'd been anything but an Indian boy living on the reservation, he might have been called a prodigy. But he is an Indian boy living on the reservation and is simply an oddity. He grows into a man who often speaks of his childhood in the third-person, as if it will somehow dull the pain and make him sound more modest about his talents.

6   A smart Indian is a dangerous person, widely feared and ridiculed by Indians and non-Indians alike. I fought with my classmates on a daily basis. They wanted me to stay quiet when the non-Indian teacher asked for answers, for volunteers, for help. We were Indian children who were expected to be stupid. Most lived up to those expectations inside the classroom but subverted them on the outside.

> **"I refused to fail. I was smart. I was arrogant. I was lucky."**

They struggled with basic reading in school but could remember how to sing a few dozen powwow songs. They were monosyllabic in front of their non-Indian teachers but could tell complicated stories and jokes at the dinner table. They submissively ducked their heads when confronted by a non-Indian adult but would slug it out with the Indian bully who was 10 years older. As Indian children, we were expected to fail in the non-Indian world. Those who failed were ceremonially accepted by other Indians and appropriately pitied by non-Indians.

7   I refused to fail. I was smart. I was arrogant. I was lucky. I read books late into the night, until I could barely keep my eyes open. I read books at recess, then during lunch, and in the few minutes left after I had finished my classroom assignments. I read books in the car when my family traveled to powwows or basketball games. In shopping malls, I ran to the bookstores and read bits and pieces of as many books as I could. I read the books my father brought home from the pawnshops and secondhand. I read the books I borrowed from the library. I read the backs of cereal boxes. I read the newspaper. I read the bulletins posted on the walls of the school, the clinic, the tribal offices, the post office. I read junk mail. I read auto-repair manuals. I read magazines. I read anything that had words and paragraphs. I read with equal parts joy and desperation. I loved those books, but I also knew that love had only one purpose. I was trying to save my life.

8   Despite all the books I read, I am still surprised I became a writer. I was going to be a pediatrician. These days, I write novels, short stories, and poems. I visit schools and teach creative writing to Indian kids. In all my years in the reservation school system, I was never taught how to write poetry, short stories, or novels. I was certainly never taught that Indians wrote poetry, short stories, and novels. Writing was something beyond Indians. I cannot recall a single time that a guest teacher visited the reservation. There must have been visiting teachers. Who were they? Where are they now? Do they exist? I visit the schools as often as possible. The Indian kids crowd the classroom. Many are writing their own poems, short

stories, and novels. They have read my books. They have read many other books. They look at me with bright eyes and arrogant wonder. They are trying to save their lives. Then there are the sullen and already defeated Indian kids who sit in the back rows and ignore me with theatrical precision. The pages of their notebooks are empty. They carry neither pencil nor pen. They stare out the window. They refuse and resist. "Books," I say to them. "Books," I say. I throw my weight against their locked doors. The door holds. I am smart. I am arrogant. I am lucky. I am trying to save our lives.

Literacy Connections

1. Sherman Alexie's essay first appeared in the April 19, 1998 publication of *The Los Angeles Times*. What kinds of issues must a writer consider when writing for a daily newspaper? How might this essay differ had it been written for a different audience—say a group of Native American students whose classroom Alexie was visiting? How might the essay differ had it been written for publication in a magazine such as *The New Yorker?*
2. How might Alexie's cultural context have shaped his persona in this essay?
3. Take a few minutes to skim back over Alexie's essay and think about the way your mind wandered while you first read it. What experiences of your own came to mind as you were reading? How are your experiences similar to Alexie's? How do they differ?
4. Alexie begins "Superman and Me" with the statement: "I learned to read with a Superman comic book." How did you learn to read? Are there particular books that come to mind?
5. Compare Alexie's early personal literacy experiences with Lauren Kiser's as described in her case study essay "Unearthing" and with Claras Leandre's in "My Most Spectacular Failure." What similarities do the three share? What differences?

Before You Read

Like Sherman Alexie, Ellen Wade Beals, author of "Between the Sheets," clearly loves books. She begins her poem with the words "I confess, to sleeping with books . . ." and goes on to speak of them as if they were lovers who have passed through her life.

Take ten minutes to freewrite about a book (or perhaps a collection of books by a single author) that you truly enjoyed reading. You might write about a book or collection you read as a young child or something you read more recently. What was the book about? What was there about the book that made you enjoy it so much? What sort of need did the book fill in your life?

Between the Sheets

Ellen Wade Beals

Ellen Wade Beals started writing as soon as she could hold a pencil. She has been a featured poet at Women Made Gallery in Chicago, Illinois, and her work has appeared in literary anthologies, journals, and college publications, including *Willow Review*, which first published the following poem in 2004. Beals likes various types of writing so much that she is launching a publishing imprint called *Weighed Words*, which will publish poems, stories, and essays by many authors in themed collections. The first book, *Solace in So Many Words*, is due out in Fall 2010 (www.womanmade.org/pdfs/experience_poetry_reading-07_08).

I confess,
to sleeping with books,
covers spread open and waiting—
they beckon,
a fluttering of leaves
like lapping tongues.
Oh, their smooth embossed spines.

The tawdry ones are good for a night.
Rumpled, smelling of smoke,
usually borrowed and broken.
They're anybody's book,
sorry, sticky maybe,
used and returned.

The worldly wise leave an exotic taste,
others have the common language
of guttersnipes but
provide good tale.
Some disappoint—
summer flings, read
and dismissed,
important as the sand
shaken from my shoe.

I can't help but embrace them all,
stroking the ones I love,
smelling their words.

After a good read, I'm bushed.
Lying across my chest,
The latest listens to my heartbeat
while I take in what else it says.

Literacy Connections

1. In what ways is the genre of poetry more conducive to the message the author is trying to convey than another genre such as the essay or short story might be?
2. How would you describe the author's persona in this poem?
3. Ellen Wade Beals likes all kinds of books—"tawdry ones . . . good for a night," "worldly wise" books that "leave an exotic taste," others that use "the common language of guttersnipes." What kinds of books do you like? Is your taste in books as broad as hers or do you prefer to read only certain types?
4. Using Beal's poem as a model, write a poem about your relationship with books or about a favorite book or book series.
5. Compare what you know of the role of books in Ellen Wade Beals' life with the role of books in the life of Sherman Alexie, as described in his essay "Superman and Me."

Before You Read

To help you better appreciate Billy Collins' "Marginalia," conduct an Internet search and see what you can discover about the following:

- Soren Kierkegaard
- Conor Cruise O'Brien
- T. S. Eliot
- *A Modest Proposal*
- Duns Scotus
- James Baldwin
- Joshua Reynolds
- William Blake
- Holden Caulfield

Marginalia

Billy Collins

Billy Collins was the U.S. Poet Laureate 2001–2003 and was selected as the New York State Poet for 2005. On the "Meet the Writers" section of the Barnes & Nobles Web site (http://barnesandnoble.com/writers/), Billy Collins is described as a poet ". . . whose laid-back name suits his open-collar-and-blue-jeans appearance, as well as his unpretentious writing style." The site goes on to state, "For Collins, anything from the barking of a neighbor's dog to the egg-salad stain on a copy of *The Catcher in the Rye* can be a fit subject for a poem." See how those stains move you as you read "Marginalia," included in Collins' 2001 collection, *Sailing Alone Around the Room.*

Sometimes the notes are ferocious,
skirmishes against the author
raging along the borders of every page
in tiny black script.
If I could just get my hands on you,
Kierkegaard, or Conor Cruise O'Brien,
they seem to say,
I would bolt the door and beat some logic into your head.
Other comments are more offhand, dismissive—
"Nonsense." "Please!" "HA!!"—
that kind of thing.
I remember once looking up from my reading,
my thumb as a bookmark,
trying to imagine what the person must look like
who wrote "Don't be a ninny"
alongside a paragraph in *The Life of Emily Dickinson.*

Students are more modest
needing to leave only their splayed footprints
along the shore of the page.
One scrawls "Metaphor" next to a stanza of Eliot's.
Another notes the presence of "Irony"
fifty times outside the paragraphs of *A Modest Proposal.*

Or they are fans who cheer from the empty bleachers,
Hands cupped around their mouths.
"Absolutely," they shout
to Duns Scotus and James Baldwin.
"Yes." "Bull's-eye." "My man!"
Check marks, asterisks, and exclamation points
rain down along the sidelines.
And if you have managed to graduate from college
without ever having written "Man vs. Nature"
in a margin, perhaps now
is the time to take one step forward.

We have all seized the white perimeter as our own
and reached for a pen if only to show
we did not just laze in an armchair turning pages;
we pressed a thought into the wayside,
planted an impression along the verge.

Even Irish monks in their cold scriptoria
jotted along the borders of the Gospels
brief asides about the pains of copying,
a bird singing near their window,
or the sunlight that illuminated their page—
anonymous men catching a ride into the future
on a vessel more lasting than themselves.

And you have not read Joshua Reynolds,
they say, until you have read him
enwreathed with Blake's furious scribbling.
Yet the one I think of most often,
the one that dangles from me like a locket,
was written in the copy of *Catcher in the Rye*
I borrowed from the local library
one slow, hot summer.
I was just beginning high school then,
reading books on a davenport in my parents' living room,
and I cannot tell you
how vastly my loneliness was deepened,
how poignant and amplified the world before me seemed,
when I found on one page

A few greasy looking smears
and next to them, written in soft pencil
by a beautiful girl, I could tell,
whom I would never meet—
"Pardon the egg salad stains, but I'm in love."

Literacy Connections
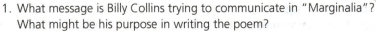

1. What message is Billy Collins trying to communicate in "Marginalia"?
   What might be his purpose in writing the poem?
2. In what ways does the genre of poetry allow Collins to communicate
   his ideas more effectively than he might be able to communicate

them, if he were, say, writing an essay? What are the advantages of communicating his ideas through poetry rather than through another genre?

3. If you were assigned the "Before You Read" that preceded "Marginalia," you performed an Internet search and became familiar with various names and titles included in the poem. How did your increased knowledge of these names and titles affect your reading of the poem? How would your reading of the poem have been different had you not taken the time to familiarize yourself with these names and titles?

4. Are you an advocate of "marginalia"? Do you typically write in the margins as you read? Why or why not?

5. Imagine a conversation among Billy Collins, Sherman Alexie (author of "Superman and Me"), and Ellen Wade Beals (author of "Between the Sheets,") in which they discuss their love for books. Work with two of your classmates and write a script of the conversation that you can perform for your class.

Before You Read

Following is a cartoon by Lynda Barry in which she explores why she lost her passion for drawing and writing and tries to figure out how to get that passion back.

As you read her cartoon, think about your attitudes regarding drawing and writing when you were a small child and how those attitudes have changed over the years.

Two Questions

Lynda Barry

Cartoonist, novelist, and playwright Lynda Barry is the creator of the syndicated strip *Ernie Pook's Comeek* and author of several illustrated novels, including *Cruddy* (2001), *One Hundred Demons* (2002), and *What It Is* (2008). Her 2002 novel *The Good Times Are Killing Me* was adapted into an off-Broadway play.

"Two Questions" originally appeared in a 2004 issue of the literary journal *McSweeney's Quarterly.*

Literacy Connections

1. What are the two questions Lynda Barry references in her title, and how does focusing on those questions affect her attitude toward drawing and writing?
2. Describe the persona Barry creates of herself in her cartoon.
3. Barry's cartoon is included in the 2008 edition of *The Best American Essays* (Houghton Mifflin). Why do you think it might have been chosen for inclusion in this collection?
4. Take a few minutes to think about how your attitudes toward drawing and writing have changed over the years, and draw a cartoon that tells your story.
5. Compare Barry's passion for drawing and writing to Ellen Wade Beal's passion for books as described in her poem "Between the Sheets" that appears earlier in this chapter on situating personal literacies.

Before You Read

Paule Marshall was born in 1929 to parents who immigrated to the U.S. from Barbados. What do you know about Barbados? Do an Internet search and see what you can find out. Jot down five interesting details regarding this island and its culture.

Excerpts from "From the Poets in the Kitchen"

Paule Marshall

Paule Marshall was born in 1929, in Brooklyn, New York, to parents who had recently emigrated from Barbados, and much of her writing reflects her West Indian ancestry. She is highly regarded for her journalism, short fiction, novels, and essays. Marshall's novels and fiction collections include *Brown Girl, Brownstones* (1959), *Soul Clap Hands and Sing* (1961), *Reena and Other Stories* (1983), *Daughters* (1991), and *The Fisher King: A Novel* (2001).

"From the Poets in the Kitchen" first appeared in "The Making of a Writer," a series published in the *New York Times Book Review* (January 9, 1983), and is the first selection in *Reena and Other Stories* (1983), a collection of her early fiction.

1   Some years ago, when I was teaching a graduate seminar in fiction at Columbia University, a well-known male novelist visited my class to speak

on his development as a writer. In discussing his formative years, he didn't realize it but he seriously endangered his life by remarking that women writers are luckier than those of his sex because they usually spend so much time as children around their mothers and their mothers' friends in the kitchen.

2   What did he say that for? The women students immediately forgot about being in awe of him and began readying their attack for the question and answer period later on. Even I bristled. There again was that awful image of women locked away from the world in the kitchen with only each other to talk to, and their daughters locked in with them.

3   But my guest wasn't really being sexist or trying to be provocative or even spoiling for a fight. What he meant—when he got around to explaining himself more fully—was that, given the way children are (or were) raised in our society, with little girls kept closer to home and their mothers, the woman writer stands a better chance of being exposed, while growing up, to the kind of talk that goes on among women, more often than not in the kitchen; and that this experience gives her an edge over her male counterpart by instilling in her an appreciation for ordinary speech.

. . .

4   "If you say what's on your mind in the language that comes to you from your parents and your street and friends you'll probably say something beautiful." Grace Paley tells this, she says, to her students at the beginning of every writing course. It's all a matter of exposure and a training of the ear for the would-be writer in those early years of apprenticeship. And, according to my guest lecturer, this training, the best of it, often takes place in as unglamorous a setting as the kitchen.

5   He didn't know it, but he was essentially describing my experience as a little girl. I grew up among poets. Now they didn't look like poets—whatever that breed is supposed to look like. Nothing about them suggested that poetry was their calling. They were just a group of ordinary housewives and mothers, my mother included, who dressed in a way (shapeless house dresses, dowdy felt hats and long, dark, solemn coats) that made it impossible for me to imagine they had ever been young.

6   Nor did they do what poets were supposed to do—spend their days in an attic room writing verses. They never put pen to paper except to write occasionally to their relatives in Barbados. "I take my pen in hand hoping these few lines will find you in health as they leave me fair for the time being," was the way their letters invariably began. Rather, their day was spent "scrubbing floor," as they described the work they did.

7   Several mornings a week these unknown bards would put an apron and a pair of old house shoes in a shopping bag and take the train or streetcar from our section of Brooklyn out to Flatbush. There, those who didn't have steady jobs would wait on certain designated corners for the white housewives in the neighborhood to come along and bargain with them over pay for a day's work cleaning their houses. This was the ritual even in the winter.

8   Later, armed with the few dollars they had earned, which in their vocabulary became "a few raw-mouth pennies," they made their way back to our neighborhood, where they would sometimes stop off to have a cup of tea or cocoa together before going home to cook dinner for their husbands and children.

9   The basement kitchen of the brownstone house where my family lived was the usual gathering place. Once inside the warm safety of its walls the women threw off the drab coats and hats, seated themselves at the large center table, drank their cups of tea or cocoa, and talked. While my sister and I sat at a smaller table over in a corner doing our homework, they talked endlessly, passionately, poetically, and with impressive range. No subject was beyond them. True, they would indulge in the usual gossip: whose husband was running with whom, whose daughter looked slightly "in the way" (pregnant) under her bridal gown as she walked down the aisle. That sort of thing. But they also tackled the great issues of the time. They were always, for example, discussing the state of the economy. It was the mid and late 1930s then, and the aftershock of the Depression, with its soup lines and suicides on Wall Street, was still being felt.

> "... they talked endlessly, passionately, poetically, and with impressive range. No subject was beyond them."

10   Some people, they declared, didn't know how to deal with adversity. They didn't know that you had to "tie up your belly" (hold in the pain, that is) when things got rough and go on with life. They took their image from the bellyband that is tied around the stomach of a newborn baby to keep the navel pressed in. They talked politics. Roosevelt was their hero. He had come along and rescued the country with relief and jobs, and in gratitude they christened their sons Franklin and Delano and hoped they would live up to the names.

11   If F.D.R. was their hero, Marcus Garvey was their God. The name of the fiery, Jamaican-born black nationalist of the 1920s was constantly invoked around the table. For he had been their leader when they first came to the United States from the West Indies shortly after World War I. They had contributed to his organization, the United Negro Improvement Association (UNIA), out of their meager salaries, bought shares in his ill-fated Black Star Shipping Line, and at the height of the movement they had marched as members of his "nurses' brigade" in their white uniforms up Seventh Avenue in Harlem during the great Garvey Day parades. Garvey: He lived on through the power of their memories.

12   And their talk was of war and rumors of wars. They raged against World War II when it broke out in Europe, blaming it on the politicians. "It's these politicians. They're the ones always starting up all this lot of war. But what they care? It's the poor people got to suffer and mothers with their sons." If it was their sons, they swore they would keep them out of the Army by giving them soap to eat each day to make their hearts sound defective. Hitler? He was for them "the devil incarnate."

13   Then there was home. They reminisced often and at length about home. The old country. Barbados—or Bimshire, as they affectionately called it. The little Caribbean island in the sun they loved but had to leave. "Poor—poor but sweet" was the way they remembered it.

14   And naturally they discussed their adopted home. America came in for both good and bad marks. They lashed out at it for the racism they encountered. They took to task some of the people they worked for, especially those who gave them only a hard-boiled egg and a few spoonfuls of cottage cheese for lunch.

15   "As if anybody can scrub floor on an egg and some cheese that don't have no taste to it!"

16   Yet although they caught H in "this man country," as they called America, it was nonetheless a place where "you could at least see your way to make a dollar." That much they acknowledged. They might even one day accumulate enough dollars, with both them and their husbands working, to buy the brownstone houses which, like my family, they were only leasing at that period. This was their consuming ambition: to "buy house" and to see the children through.

17   There was no way for me to understand it at the time, but the talk that filled the kitchen those afternoons was highly functional. It served as therapy, the cheapest kind available to my mother and her friends. Not only did it help them recover from the long wait on the corner that morning and the bargaining over their labor, it restored them to a sense of themselves and reaffirmed their self-worth. Through language they were able to overcome the humiliations of the workday.

18   But more than therapy, that freewheeling, wide-ranging, exuberant talk functioned as an outlet for the tremendous creative energy they possessed. They were women in whom the need for self-expression was strong, and since language was the only vehicle readily available to them they made of it an art form that—in keeping with the African tradition in which art and life are one—was an integral part of their lives.

19   And their talk was a refuge. They never really ceased being baffled and overwhelmed by America—its vastness, complexity, and power. Its strange customs and laws. At a level beyond words they remained fearful and in awe. Their uneasiness and fear were even reflected in their attitude toward the children they had given birth to in this country. They referred to those like myself, the little Brooklyn-born Bajans (Barbadians), as "these New York children" and complained that they couldn't discipline us properly because of the laws here. "You can't beat these children as you would like, you know, because the authorities in this place will dash you in jail for them. After all, these is New York children." Not only were we different, American, we had, as they saw it, escaped their ultimate authority.

20   Confronted therefore by a world they could not encompass, which even limited their rights as parents, and at the same time finding themselves per-

manently separated from the world they had known, they took refuge in language. "Language is the only homeland," Czeslaw Milosz, the émigré Polish writer and Nobel Laureate, said. This is what it became for the women at the kitchen table.

21   It served another purpose also, I suspect. My mother and her friends were after all the female counterpart of Ralph Ellison's *Invisible Man*. Indeed, you might say they suffered a triple invisibility, being black, female, and foreigners. They really didn't count in American society except as a source of cheap labor. But given the kind of women they were, they couldn't tolerate the fact of their invisibility, their powerlessness. And they fought back, using the only weapon at their command: the spoken word.

22   Those late afternoon conversations on a wide range of topics were a way for them to feel they exercised some measure of control over their lives and the events that shaped them. "Soully-gal, talk yuh talk!" they were always exhorting each other. "In this man world you got to take yuh mouth and make a gun!" They were in control, if only verbally and if only for the two hours or so that they remained in our house.

· · ·

23   By the time I was 8 or 9, I graduated from the corner of the kitchen to the neighborhood library, and thus from the spoken to the written word. The Macon Street Branch of the Brooklyn Public Library was an imposing half block long edifice of heavy gray masonry, with glass-paneled doors at the front and two tall metal torches symbolizing the light that comes of learning flanking the wide steps outside.

· · ·

24   I was sheltered from the storm of adolescence in the Macon Street library, reading voraciously, indiscriminately, everything from Jane Austen to Zane Grey, but with a special passion for the long, full-blown, richly detailed 18th- and 19th-century picaresque tales: *Tom Jones, Great Expectations, Vanity Fair*.

25   But although I loved nearly everything I read and would enter fully into the lives of the characters—indeed, would cease being myself and become them—I sensed a lack after a time. Something I couldn't quite define was missing. And then one day, browsing in the poetry section, I came across a book by someone called Paul Laurence Dunbar, and opening it I found the photograph of a wistful, sad-eyed poet who to my surprise was black. I turned to a poem at random. "Little brown-baby wif spa'klin'/eyes /Come to yo' pappy an' set on his knee." Although I had a little difficulty at first with the words in dialect, the poem spoke to me as nothing I had read before of the closeness, the special relationship I had had with my father, who by then had become an ardent believer in Father Divine and gone to live in Father's "kingdom" in Harlem. Reading it helped to ease somewhat the tight knot of sorrow and longing I carried around in my chest that refused to go away. I read another poem. "'Lias! 'Lias! Bless de Lawd!/Don' you know de day's/ erbroad?/Ef you don' get up, you scamp/Dey'll be trouble in dis

camp." I laughed. It reminded me of the way my mother sometimes yelled at my sister and me to get out of bed in the mornings.

26   And another; "Seen my lady home las' night/Jump back, honey, jump back./Hel' huh han' an' sque'z it tight . . ." About love between a black man and a black woman. I had never seen that written about before and it roused in me all kinds of delicious feelings and hopes.

27   And I began to search then for books and stories and poems about "The Race" (as it was put back then), about my people. While not abandoning Thackeray, Fielding, Dickens and the others, I started asking the reference librarian, who was white, for books by Negro writers, although I must admit I did so at first with a feeling of shame—the shame I and many others used to experience in those days whenever the word "Negro" or "colored" came up.

> **"True, I am indebted to those writers, white and black, whom I read during my formative years . . ."**

28   No grade school literature teacher of mine had ever mentioned Dunbar or James Weldon Johnson or Langston Hughes. I didn't know that Zora Neale Hurston existed and was busy writing and being published during those years. Nor was I made aware of people like Frederick Douglass and Harriet Tubman—their spirit and example—or the great 19th-century abolitionist and feminist Sojourner Truth. There wasn't even Negro History Week when I attended P.S. 35 on Decatur Street!

29   What I needed, what all the kids—West Indian and native black American alike—with whom I grew up needed, was an equivalent of the Jewish shul, someplace where we could go after school—the schools that were shortchanging us—and read works by those like ourselves and learn about our history.

30   It was around that time also that I began harboring the dangerous thought of someday trying to write myself. Perhaps a poem about an apple tree, although I had never seen one. Or the story of a girl who could magically transplant herself to wherever she wanted to be in the world—such as Father Divine's kingdom in Harlem. Dunbar—his dark, eloquent face, his large volume of poems—permitted me to dream that I might someday write, and with something of the power with words my mother and her friends possessed.

31   When people at readings and writers' conferences ask me who my major influences were, they are sometimes a little disappointed when I don't immediately name the usual literary giants. True, I am indebted to those writers, white and black, whom I read during my formative years and still read for instruction and pleasure. But they were preceded in my life by another set of giants whom I always acknowledge before all others: the group of women around the table long ago. They taught me my first lessons in the narrative art. They trained my ear. They set a standard of excellence. This is why the best of my work must be attributed to them; it stands as testimony to the rich legacy of language and culture they so freely passed on to me in the wordshop of the kitchen.

Literacy Connections

1. What do we learn about Paule Marshall's personal literacy through her writing? Make a list of five of the most interesting things you learned about Marshall's personal literacy history as you read her essay.
2. Who is Marshall's audience in this essay? For what kind of audience do you think she was writing? Support your answer with details from the essay.
3. As a reader, what characteristics of Marshall's essay made it interesting for you?
4. How do you and your friends use language in fun ways? In the unabridged version of this essay, Marshall tells us that her mother and her mother's friends ". . . had taken the standard English taught them in the primary schools of Barbados and transformed it into an idiom, an instrument that more adequately described them—changing around the syntax and imposing their own rhythm and accent so that the sentences were more pleasing to their ears." Give several examples of ways you play with language—ways you make it your own.
5. In what ways does Marshall's essay exemplify the importance of the "CCCC's Position Statement on Students' Right to Their Own Language" that appears earlier in this chapter?

Before You Read

In "Mother Tongue" Amy Tan reveals that there were times in her life when she was embarrassed by her mother's use of "broken" English. Take a few minutes to think about an incident when you were embarrassed by your own or someone else's use of language. Write a paragraph in which you describe the incident and reflect upon it.

Mother Tongue

Amy Tan

Amy Tan's homepage *(http://amytan.net/)* tells readers that Tan was "born in the U.S. to immigrant parents from China," and that she "failed her mother's expectations that she become a doctor and concert pianist" and "settled on writing fiction." Tan's novels include *The Joy Luck Club* (1989), *The Kitchen God's Wife* (1991), *The Hundred Secret Senses* (1995), *The Bonesetter's Daughter* (2001), and *Saving Fish from Drowning* (2005), all *New York Times* bestsellers and the recipient of various awards. She is also the author of a memoir, *The Opposite of Fate*, two children's books, *The Moon Lady* and *Sagwa*, and numerous articles for magazines, including *the New Yorker*, *Harper's Bazaar*, and *National Geographic*. Her work has been translated into 35 languages, from Spanish, French, and Finnish to Chinese, Arabic, and Hebrew.

"Mother Tongue" was first published in *Three Penny Review* (1990).

1   I am not a scholar of English or literature. I cannot give you much more than personal opinions on the English language and its variations in this country or others.

2   I am a writer. And by that definition, I am someone who has always loved language. I am fascinated by language in daily life. I spend a great deal of my time thinking about the power of language—the way it can evoke an emotion, a visual image, a complex idea, or a simple truth. Language is the tool of my trade. And I use them all—all the Englishes I grew up with.

3   Recently, I was made keenly aware of the different Englishes I do use. I was giving a talk to a large group of people, the same talk I had already given to half a dozen other groups. The nature of the talk was about my writing, my life, and my book, *The Joy Luck Club*. The talk was going along well enough, until I remembered one major difference that made the whole talk sound wrong. My mother was in the room. And it was perhaps the first time she had heard me give a lengthy speech, using the kind of English I have never used with her. I was saying things like, "The intersection of memory upon imagination" and "There is an aspect of my fiction that relates to thus-and-thus"—a speech filled with carefully wrought grammatical phrases, burdened, it suddenly seemed to me, with nominalized forms, past perfect tenses, conditional phrases, all the forms of standard English that I had learned in school and through books, the forms of English I did not use at home with my mother.

4   Just last week, I was walking down the street with my mother, and I again found myself conscious of the English I was using, the English I do use with her. We were talking about the price of new and used furniture and I heard myself saying this: "Not waste money that way." My husband was with us as well, and he didn't notice any switch in my English. And then I realized why. It's because over the twenty years we've been together I've often used that same kind of English with him, and sometimes he even uses it with me. It has become our language of intimacy, a different sort of English that relates to family talk, the language I grew up with.

5   So you'll have some idea of what this family talk I heard sounds like, I'll quote what my mother said during a recent conversation which I videotaped and then transcribed. During this conversation, my mother was talking about a political gangster in Shanghai who had the same last name as her family's, Du, and how the gangster in his early years wanted to be adopted by her family, which was rich by comparison. Later, the gangster became more powerful, far richer than my mother's family, and one day showed up at my mother's wedding to pay his respects. Here's what she said in part:

6   "Du Yusong having business like fruit stand. Like off the street kind. He is Du like Du Zong-but not Tsung-ming Island people. The local people call putong, the river east side, he belong to that side local people. That man want to ask Du Zong father take him in like become own family. Du Zong father wasn't look down on him, but didn't take seriously, until that man big like become a mafia. Now important person, very hard to inviting him. Chinese way, came only to show respect, don't stay for dinner. Respect for making big celebration, he shows up. Mean gives lots of respect. Chinese custom. Chinese social life that way. If too important won't have to stay too long. He come to my wedding. I didn't see, I heard it. I gone to boy's side, they have YMCA dinner. Chinese age I was nineteen."

> "Her language, as I hear it, is vivid, direct, full of observation and imagery. That was the language that helped shape the way I saw things . . ."

7   You should know that my mother's expressive command of English belies how much she actually understands. She reads the *Forbes* report, listens to *Wall Street Week*, converses daily with her stockbroker, reads all of Shirley MacLaine's books with ease—all kinds of things I can't begin to understand. Yet some of my friends tell me they understand 50 percent of what my mother says. Some say they understand 80 to 90 percent. Some say they understand none of it, as if she were speaking pure Chinese. But to me, my mother's English is perfectly clear, perfectly natural. It's my mother tongue. Her language, as I hear it, is vivid, direct, full of observation and imagery. That was the language that helped shape the way I saw things, expressed things, made sense of the world.

8   Lately, I've been giving more thought to the kind of English my mother speaks. Like others, I have described it to people as "broken" or "fractured" English. But I wince when I say that. It has always bothered me that I can think of no way to describe it other than "broken," as if it were damaged and needed to be fixed, as if it lacked a certain wholeness and soundness. I've heard other terms used, "limited English," for example. But they seem just as bad, as if everything is limited, including people's perceptions of the limited English speaker.

9   I know this for a fact, because when I was growing up, my mother's "limited" English limited *my* perception of her. I was ashamed of her English. I believed that her English reflected the quality of what she had to say. That is, because she expressed them imperfectly her thoughts were imperfect. And I had plenty of empirical evidence to support me: the fact that people in department stores, at banks, and at restaurants did not take her seriously, did not give her good service, pretended not to understand her, or even acted as if they did not hear her.

10   My mother has long realized the limitations of her English as well. When I was fifteen, she used to have me call people on the phone to pretend I was she. In this guise, I was forced to ask for information or even to complain and yell at people who had been rude to her. One time it was

a call to her stockbroker in New York. She had cashed out her small portfolio and it just so happened we were going to go to New York the next week, our very first trip outside California. I had to get on the phone and say in an adolescent voice that was not very convincing, "This is Mrs. Tan."

11   And my mother was standing in the back whispering loudly, "Why he don't send me check, already two weeks late. So mad he lie to me, losing me money."

12   And then I said in perfect English, "Yes, I'm getting rather concerned. You had agreed to send the check two weeks ago, but it hasn't arrived."

13   Then she began to talk more loudly. "What he want, I come to New York tell him front of his boss, you cheating me?" And I was trying to calm her down, make her be quiet, while telling the stockbroker, "I can't tolerate any more excuses. If I don't receive the check immediately, I am going to have to speak to your manager when I'm in New York next week." And sure enough, the following week there we were in front of this astonished stockbroker, and I was sitting there red-faced and quiet, and my mother, the real Mrs. Tan, was shouting at his boss in her impeccable broken English.

14   We used a similar routine just five days ago, for a situation that was far less humorous. My mother had gone to the hospital for an appointment, to find out about a benign brain tumor a CAT scan had revealed a month ago. She said she had spoken very good English, her best English, no mistakes. Still, she said, the hospital did not apologize when they said they had lost the CAT scan and she had come for nothing. She said they did not seem to have any sympathy when she told them she was anxious to know the exact diagnosis, since her husband and son had both died of brain tumors. She said they would not give her any more information until the next time and she would have to make another appointment for that. So she said she would not leave until the doctor called her daughter. She wouldn't budge. And when the doctor finally called her daughter, me, who spoke in perfect English—lo and behold—we had assurances the CAT scan would be found, promises that a conference call on Monday would be held, and apologies for any suffering my mother had gone through for a most regrettable mistake.

15   I think my mother's English almost had an effect on limiting my possibilities in life as well. Sociologists and linguists probably will tell you that a person's developing language skills are more influenced by peers. But I do think that the language spoken in the family, especially in immigrant families which are more insular, plays a large role in shaping the language of the child. And I believe that it affected my results on achievement tests, IQ tests, and the SAT. While my English skills were never judged as poor, compared to math, English could not be considered my strong suit. In grade school I did moderately well, getting perhaps B's, sometimes B-pluses, in English and scoring perhaps in the sixtieth or seventieth percentile on achievement tests. But those scores were not good enough to override the opinion that my true abilities lay in math and science, because in those areas I achieved A's and scored in the ninetieth percentile or higher.

16   This was understandable. Math is precise; there is only one correct answer. Whereas, for me at least, the answers on English tests were always a judgment call, a matter of opinion and personal experience. Those tests were constructed around items like fill-in-the-blank sentence completion, such as, "Even though Tom was _____, Mary thought he was _____:" And the correct answer always seemed to be the most bland combinations of thoughts, for example, "Even though Tom was shy, Mary thought he was charming;" with the grammatical structure "even though" limiting the correct answer to some sort of semantic opposites, so you wouldn't get answers like, "Even though Tom was foolish, Mary thought he was ridiculous." Well, according to my mother, there were very few limitations as to what Tom could have been and what Mary might have thought of him. So I never did well on tests like that.

17   The same was true with word analogies, pairs of words in which you were supposed to find some sort of logical, semantic relationship—for example, "*Sunset* is to *nightfall* as _____is to _____." And here you would be presented with a list of four possible pairs, one of which showed the same kind of relationship: *red* is to *stoplight, bus* is to *arrival, chills* is to *fever, yawn* is to *boring*. Well, I could never think that way. I knew what the tests were asking, but I could not block out of my mind the images already created by the first pair, "*sunset* is to *nightfall*"—and I would see a burst of colors against a darkening sky, the moon rising, the lowering of a curtain of stars. And all the other pairs of words—*red, bus, stoplight, boring*—just threw up a mass of confusing images, making it impossible for me to sort out something as logical as saying: "A sunset precedes nightfall" is the same as "a chill precedes a fever:" The only way I would have gotten that answer right would have been to imagine an associative situation, for example, my being disobedient and staying out past sunset, catching a chill at night, which turns into feverish pneumonia as punishment, which indeed did happen to me.

18   I have been thinking about all this lately, about my mother's English, about achievement tests. Because lately I've been asked, as a writer, why there are not more Asian Americans represented in American literature. Why are there few Asian Americans enrolled in creative writing programs? Why do so many Chinese students go into engineering? Well, these are broad sociological questions I can't begin to answer. But I have noticed in surveys—in fact, just last week—that Asian students, as a whole, always do significantly better on math achievement tests than in English. And this makes me think that there are other Asian-American students whose English spoken in the home might also be described as "broken" or "limited": And perhaps they also have teachers who are steering them away from writing and into math and science, which is what happened to me.

19   Fortunately, I happen to be rebellious in nature and enjoy the challenge of disproving assumptions made about me. I became an English major my first year in college, after being enrolled as pre-med. I started writing nonfiction as a freelancer the week after I was told by my former boss that writing was my worst skill and I should hone my talents toward account management.

20   But it wasn't until 1985 that I finally began to write fiction. And at first I wrote using what I thought to be wittily crafted sentences, sentences that would finally prove I had mastery over the English language. Here's an example from the first draft of a story that later made its way into *The Joy Luck Club*, but without this line: "That was my mental quandary in its nascent state." A terrible line, which I can barely pronounce.

21   Fortunately, for reasons I won't get into today, I later decided I should envision a reader for the stories I would write. And the reader I decided upon was my mother, because these were stories about mothers. So with this reader in mind—and in fact she did read my early drafts—I began to write stories using all the Englishes I grew up with: the English I spoke to my mother, which for lack of a better term might be described as "simple"; the English she used with me, which for lack of a better term might be described as "broken"; my translation of her Chinese, which could certainly be described as "watered down"; and what I imagined to be her translation of her Chinese if she could speak in perfect English, her internal language, and for that I sought to preserve the essence, but neither an English nor a Chinese structure. I wanted to capture what language ability tests can never reveal: her intent, her passion, her imagery, the rhythms of her speech and the nature of her thoughts.

22   Apart from what any critic had to say about my writing, I knew I had succeeded where it counted when my mother finished reading my book and gave me her verdict: "So easy to read."

Literacy Connections

1. In her opening lines, Amy Tan tells us, her readers, "I am not a scholar of English or literature. I cannot give you much more than personal opinions on the English language and its variations in this country or others." What does she accomplish by beginning her essay with these lines? How do these lines affect her persona and the way we read her text?

2. What are Tan's primary messages for her readers in this essay? What ideas does she communicate? Of the many ideas she communicates, what might be the main one?

3. Later in her essay, Tan tells us that she decided she "should envision a reader for [her] stories." Why do we need to picture a reader as we compose? What purpose does that serve? When you are working on a composition for one of your classes, how does envisioning a reader affect your writing process?

4. Tan writes about how many Asian American students come from homes like the one in which she grew up where "English spoken in the home might also be described as 'broken' or 'limited'" and whose teachers "are steering them away from writing and into math and

science." Describe a time when you were the subject of stereotyping—a time when someone made an assumption about you based on some characteristic of yours—perhaps your language use, or maybe an assumption based on the color of your skin or some other aspect of your appearance or background. How did the stereotyping make you feel? How did you react? How did you want to react?

5. Look back over the stories about personal literacies you've read in this chapter—"Unearthing" by Lauren Kiser, "My Most Spectacular Failure" by Claras Leandre, "Superman and Me" by Sherman Alexie, "Two Questions" by Lynda Barry, "From The Poets in the Kitchen" by Paule Marshall, and the one you just read, "Mother Tongue" by Amy Tan. With which author do you think Amy Tan could most closely relate if they were discussing their personal literacies? Why? What do they share?

Before You Read

While Amy Tan's essay focuses on her mother's English, Miku Rager uses a documentary assignment in her advanced composition class to explore the cultural stereotypes associated with the Asian female voice. Take a few minutes to think about various accents and the cultural stereotypes often associated with them. Which accents do you find appealing? To which accents do you react negatively? Think about the factors that figure into why you respond positively to some accents and negatively to others.

"Why I Don't Like My Accent"

Miku Rager

Miku Rager grew up in Nagasaki, Japan, and moved to the U.S. after finishing high school. She was a student in Michelle Comstock's advanced composition class at the University of Colorado at Denver when she composed the documentary "Why I Don't Like My Accent." Miku went on to earn a Bachelor of Fine Arts in Photography.

Rager's documentary is included on the Web site *Voice and the Cultural Soundscape: Sonic Literacy in Composition Studies,* created by professors Michelle Comstock and Mary E. Hocks. In their discussion of Rager's documentary they state:

> The articulation of accented voices and dialects can become even more radical in a culture that privileges Standard American English. One of Michelle's advanced composition students, Miku Rager,

use[s] her documentary assignment to explore the cultural assumptions and dissonance around the "accented voice"—in her case, a woman's voice speaking English with a Japanese accent.

Comstock and Hocks go on to explain—

> In "Why I Don't Like My Accent," Miku powerfully contextualize[s] her own voice over and her "paranoid" (her words) self-consciousness of it within the larger cultural production of the Asian female voice. Using clips from *Kill Bill* and *Full Metal Jacket*, Miku demonstrate[s] the synthesization and fetishization of the Asian female voice in the U.S. popular cultural soundscape, a voice attached to an eroticized, infantilized, and in the case of *Kill Bill's* O-Ren Ishii (Lucy Liu), lethal body. Throughout the composition, Miku takes issue with Professor Higgins of *My Fair Lady*, claiming that certain individuals cannot "conquer" or tame their own voices:

>> I came to the U.S. when I was eighteen, so no matter how hard I try, how motivated I am, how great my teachers and their methods are, I cannot speak English without an accent so far. In fact, I've been trying for eight years, and I don't see significant improvement in my accent.

In their discussion of Miku Rager's documentary, Comstock and Hocks further explain that

> Miku's piece points to the material effects of voice in our culture, where particular accents continue to possess more earning power than others: "How much accent am I allowed to have?" In the end, Miku decides to take on the cultural stereotypes and not her own voice. She chooses to resonate (and work) with her own voice as it is and teach others to do so, too. She concludes her documentary with brief portraits of Japanese women in the fields of astronomy and art. This is just the beginning, she suggests, of a "lifelong re-education project." These counter-images become part of Miku's own voice in the piece. They give her voice and voice-over narration a social and cultural capital and credibility that is missing in the stereotypes.

Please view Miku Rager's documentary on Comstock and Hocks' Web site by going to http://www.bgsu.edu/cconline/comstock_hocks/cultureand-voice.htm and clicking on the "Why I Don't Like My Accent" Video Clip.

Literacy Connections

1. Miku Rager states that "an accent reflects an individual's originality, so embrace your accent." But then she goes on to negate that statement by revealing that she has tried for years to get rid of her accent and

cannot. Why does she so dislike her accent? What does she reveal to us regarding why she wishes she could get rid of her accent?

2. Near the end of her documentary, Rager tells us, "I cannot master the standard accent, and I cannot take advantage of the stereotypes available to me." Once she has come to these conclusions, what does she decide to do that will help her feel better about speaking accented English?

3. Rager shares that *My Fair Lady* is her favorite movie. She tell us that she identifies with Eliza Doolittle and her quest to learn to speak the version of English spoken by the very proper Professor Higgens. While Professor Higgens' goal is to help Eliza conquer her accent, he also speaks with an accent—one that is, perhaps, considered more preferred. Do we all speak with an accent? What do you think and why?

4. Rager uses the movies *Kill Bill* and *Full Metal Jacket* as examples of movies that encourage negative stereotypes of Asian women. Think about movies or TV shows you're familiar with that encourage stereotypes of various groups. Make a list of four or five and describe the ways in which they stereotype specific groups.

5. Compare Rager's concerns regarding her accent with Amy Tan's statements in "Mother Tongue" regarding her mother's accent.

Before You Read

What comes to your mind when you hear the phrase "a wild tongue"? What kind of behavior might result in someone being accused of having "a wild tongue"? Jot down a list of possible reasons why someone might be told she has "a wild tongue."

How to Tame a Wild Tongue

Gloria Anzaldúa

Gloria Anzaldúa (1942–2004) was a Mexican American lesbian feminist writer and activist who was born in Jesus Maria of the Valley, Texas. Her family members were Mexican immigrants. Upon graduation from college, she taught the children of migrant families before going on to teach courses in feminism, Chicano studies, and creative writing at various colleges and universities.

Anzaldúa is well known for several edited collections, including *This Bridge Called My Back: Writings by Radical Women of Color* (1981), *Making Face, Making Soul/Haciendo Caras: Creative and Critical Perspectives by Women of Color* (1990), and *This Bridge We Call Home: Radical Visions for Transformation* (2002). She is also the author of children's books, including *Prietita Has a Friend* (1991) and *Friends from the Other Side—Amigos del Otro Lado* (1993).

Her best known collection of writings is *Borderlands/La Frontera: The New Mestiza* (1987), which was chosen as one of the 38 Best Books of 1987 by *Library Journal*. The selection that follows is an essay from that award-winning book.

1 "We're going to have to control your tongue," the dentist says, pulling out all the metal from my mouth. Silver bits plop and tinkle into the basin. My mouth is a mother lode.

2   The dentist is cleaning out my roots. I get a whiff of the stench when I gasp. "I can't cap that tooth yet, you're still draining," he says.

3   "We're going to have to do something about your tongue," I hear the anger rising in his voice. My tongue keeps pushing out the wads of cotton, pushing back the drills, the long thin needles. "I've never seen anything as strong or as stubborn," he says. And I think, how do you tame a wild tongue, train it to be quiet, how do you bridle and saddle it? How do you make it lie down?

4   "Who is to say that robbing a people of its language is less violent than war?"

—Ray Gwyn Smith[1]

5   I remember being caught speaking Spanish at recess—that was good for three licks on the knuckles with a sharp ruler. I remember being sent to the corner of the classroom for "talking back" to the Anglo teacher when all I was trying to do was tell her how to pronounce my name. "If you want to be American, speak 'American.' If you don't like it, go back to Mexico where you belong."

6   "I want you to speak English. *Pa'hallar buen trabajo tienes que saber hablar el inglés bien. Qué vale toda tu educación si todavía hablas inglés con un* 'accent,'" my mother would say, mortified that I spoke English like a Mexican. At Pan American University, I, and all Chicano students were required to take two speech classes. Their purpose: to get rid of our accents.

7   Attacks on one's form of expression with the intent to censor are a violation of the First Amendment. *El Anglo con cara de inocente nos arrancó la lengua.* Wild tongues can't be tamed, they can only be cut out.

Overcoming the Tradition of Silence

8   *Ahogadas, escupimos el oscuro.*
Peleando con nuestra propia sombra
el silencio nos sepulta.

9   *En boca cerrada no entran moscas.* "Flies don't enter a closed mouth" is a saying I kept hearing when I was a child. *Ser habladora* was to be a gossip and

---

[1]Ray Gwyn Smith, *Moorland Is Cold Country*, unpublished book.

a liar, to talk too much. *Muchachitas bien criadas,* well-bred girls don't answer back. *Es una falta de respeto* to talk back to one's mother or father. I remember one of the sins I'd recite to the priest in the confession box the few times I went to the confession: talking back to my mother, *hablar pa' 'trás, repelar. Hoci cona, repelona, chismosa,* having a big mouth, questioning, carrying tales are all signs of being *mal criada.* In my culture they are all words that are derogatory if applied to women—I've never heard them applied to men.

10 The first time I heard two women, a Puerto Rican and a Cuban, say the word "*nosotras*," I was shocked. I had not known the word existed. Chicanas use *nosotros* whether we're male or female. We are robbed of our female being by the masculine plural. Language is a male discourse.

And our tongues have become
dry the wilderness has
dried out our tongues and
we have forgotten speech.

—*Irena Klepfisz*[2]

11 Even our own people, other Spanish speakers *nos quieren poner candados en la boca.* They would hold us back with their bag of *reglas de academia.*

Oyé como ladra: el lenguaje de la frontera

Quien tiene boca se equivoca.

—*Mexican saying*

12 "*Pocho,* cultural traitor, you're speaking the oppressor's language by speaking English, you're ruining the Spanish language," I have been accused by various Latinos and Latinas. Chicano Spanish is considered by the purist and by most Latinos deficient, a mutilation of Spanish.

13 But Chicano Spanish is a border tongue which developed naturally. Change, *evolución, enriquecimiento de palabras nuevas por invención o adopción* have created variants of Chicano Spanish, *un nuevo lenguaje. Un lenguaje que corresponde a un modo de vivir.* Chicano Spanish is not incorrect, it is a living language.

14 For a people who are neither Spanish nor live in a country in which Spanish is the first language; for a people who live in a country in which English is the reigning tongue but who are not Anglo; for a people who cannot entirely identify with either standard (formal, Castillian) Spanish nor standard English, what recourse is left to them but to create their own language? A language which they can connect their identity to, one capable of communicating the realities and values true to themselves—a

---

[2]Irena Klepfisz, "*Di rayze aheym*/The Journey Home," in *The Tribe of Dina: A Jewish Women's Anthology,* Melanie Kaye/Kantrowitz and Irena Klepfisz, eds. (Montpelier, VT: Sinister Wisdom Books, 1986), 49.

language with terms that are neither *español ni inglés,* but both. We speak a patois, a forked tongue, a variation of two languages.

15   Chicano Spanish sprang out of the Chicanos' need to identify ourselves as a distinct people. We needed a language with which we could communicate with ourselves, a secret language. For some of us, language is a homeland closer than the Southwest—for many Chicanos today live in the Midwest and the East. And because we are a complex, heterogeneous people, we speak many languages. Some of the languages we speak are:

1. Standard English

2. Working class and slang English

3. Standard Spanish

4. Standard Mexican Spanish

5. North Mexican Spanish dialect

6. Chicano Spanish (Texas, New Mexico, Arizona, and California have regional variations)

7. Tex-Mex

8. *Pachuco* (called *caló*)

16   My "home" tongues are the languages I speak with my sister and brothers, with my friends. They are the last five listed, with 6 and 7 being closest to my heart. From school, the media and job situations, I've picked up standard and working class English. From Mamagrande Locha and from reading Spanish and Mexican literature, I've picked up Standard Spanish and Standard Mexican Spanish. From *los recién llegados,* Mexican immigrants, and *braceros,* I learned the North Mexican dialect. With Mexicans I'll try to speak either Standard Mexican Spanish or the North Mexican dialect. From my parents and Chicanos living in the Valley, I picked up Chicano Texas Spanish, and I speak it with my mom, younger brother (who married a Mexican and who rarely mixes Spanish with English), aunts, and older relatives.

17   With Chicanas from *Nuevo México* or *Arizona* I will speak Chicano Spanish a little, but often they don't understand what I'm saying. With most California Chicanas I speak entirely in English (unless I forget). When I first moved to San Francisco, I'd rattle off something in Spanish, unintentionally embarrassing them. Often it is only with another Chicana *tejana* that I can talk freely.

18   Words distorted by English are known as anglicisms or *pochismos.* The *pocho is* an anglicized Mexican or American of Mexican origin who speaks Spanish with an accent characteristic of North Americans and who distorts and reconstructs the language according to the influence of English.[3] Tex-Mex, or Spanglish, comes most naturally to me. I may switch back and

---

[3]R. C. Ortega, *Dialectología Del Barrio,* trans. Hortencia S. Alwan (Los Angeles, CA: R. C. Ortega Publisher & Bookseller, 1977), 132.

forth from English to Spanish in the same sentence or in the same word. With my sister and my brother Nune and with Chicano *tejano* contemporaries I speak in Tex-Mex.

19   From kids and people my own age I picked up *Pachuco. Pachuco* (the language of the zoot suiters) is a language of rebellion, both against Standard Spanish and Standard English. It is a secret language. Adults of the culture and outsiders cannot understand it. It is made up of slang words from both English and Spanish. *Ruca* means girl or woman, *vato* means guy or dude, *chale* means no, *simón* means yes, *churo* is sure, talk is *periquiar, pigionear* means petting, *que gacho* means how nerdy, *ponte águila* means watch out, death is called *la pelona*. Through lack of practice and not having others who can speak it, I've lost most of the *Pachuco* tongue.

Chicano Spanish

20   Chicanos, after 250 years of Spanish/Anglo colonization have developed significant differences in the Spanish we speak. We collapse two adjacent vowels into a single syllable and sometimes shift the stress in certain words such as *maíz/maiz, cohete/cuete*. We leave out certain consonants when they appear between vowels: *lado/lao, mojado/mojao*. Chicanos from South Texas pronounced *f* as *j* as in *jue (fue)*. Chicanos use "archaisms," words that are no longer in the Spanish language, words that have been evolved out. We say *semos, truje, haiga, ansina*, and *naiden*. We retain the "archaic" *j*, as in *jalar*, that derives from an earlier *h* (the French *halar* or the Germanic *halon* which was lost to standard Spanish in the 16th century), but which is still found in several regional dialects such as the one spoken in South Texas. (Due to geography, Chicanos from the Valley of South Texas were cut off linguistically from other Spanish speakers. We tend to use words that the Spaniards brought over from Medieval Spain. The majority of the Spanish colonizers in Mexico and the Southwest came from Extremadura—Hernán Cortés was one of them— and Andalucía. Andalucians pronounce *ll* like a *y*, and their *d's* tend to be absorbed by adjacent vowels: *tirado* becomes *tirao*. They brought *el lenguaje popular, dialectos y regionalismos*.[4])

21   Chicanos and other Spanish speakers also shift *ll* to *y* and *z* to *s*.[5] We leave out initial syllables, saying *tar* for *estar, toy* for *estoy, hora* for *ahora* (*cubanos* and *puertorriqueños* also leave out initial letters of some words). We also leave out the final syllable such as *pa* for *para*. The intervocalic *y*, the *ll* as in *tortilla, ella, botella*, gets replaced by *tortia* or *tortiya, ea, botea*. We add an additional syllable at the beginning of certain words: *atocar* for *tocar*,

---

[4]Eduardo Hernandéz-Chávez, Andrew D. Cohen, and Anthony F. Beltramo, *El Lenguaje de los Chicanos: Regional and Social Characteristics of Language Used By Mexican Americans* (Arlington, VA: Center for Applied Linguistics, 1975), 39.
[5]Hernandéz-Chávez, xvii.

agastar for *gastar*. Sometimes we'll say *lavaste las vacijas,* other times *lavates* (substituting the *ates* verb endings for the *aste*).

22   We use anglicisms, words borrowed from English: *bola* from ball, *carpeta* from carpet, *máchina de lavar* (instead of *lavadora)* from washing machine. Tex-Mex argot, created by adding a Spanish sound at the beginning or end of an English word such as *cookiar* for cook, *watchar* for watch, *parkiar* for park, and *rapiar* for rape, is the result of the pressures on Spanish speakers to adapt to English.

23   We don't use the word *vosotros/as* or its accompanying verb form. We don't say *claro* (to mean yes), *imagínate,* or *me emociona,* unless we picked up Spanish from Latinas, out of a book, or in a classroom. Other Spanish-speaking groups are going through the same, or similar, development in their Spanish.

Linguistic Terrorism

24   *Deslenguadas. Somos los del español deficiente.* We are your linguistic nightmare, your linguistic aberration, your linguistic *mestizaje,* the subject of your *burla.* Because we speak with tongues of fire we are culturally crucified. Racially, culturally, and linguistically *somos huérfanos*—we speak an orphan tongue.

25   Chicanas who grew up speaking Chicano Spanish have internalized the belief that we speak poor Spanish. It is illegitimate, a bastard language. And because we internalize how our language has been used against us by the dominant culture, we use our language differences against each other.

26   Chicana feminists often skirt around each other with suspicion and hesitation. For the longest time I couldn't figure it out. Then it dawned on me. To be close to another Chicana is like looking into the mirror. We are afraid of what we'll see there. *Pena.* Shame. Low estimation of self. In childhood we are told that our language is wrong. Repeated attacks on our native tongue diminish our sense of self. The attacks continue throughout our lives.

27   Chicanas feel uncomfortable talking in Spanish to Latinas, afraid of their censure. Their language was not outlawed in their countries. They had a whole lifetime of being immersed in their native tongue; generations, centuries in which Spanish was a first language, taught in school, heard on radio and TV, and read in the newspaper.

28   If a person, Chicana or Latina, has a low estimation of my native tongue, she also has a low estimation of me. Often with *mexicanas y latinas* we'll speak English as a neutral language. Even among Chicanas we tend to speak English at parties or conferences. Yet, at the same time, we're afraid the other will think we're *agringadas* because we don't speak Chicano Spanish. We oppress each other trying to out-Chicano each other, vying to be the "real" Chicanas, to speak like Chicanos. There is no one Chicano language just as there is no one Chicano experience. A monolingual Chicana whose first language is English or Spanish is just as much a Chicana as one who speaks several variants of Spanish. A Chicana from

Michigan or Chicago or Detroit is just as much a Chicana as one from the Southwest. Chicano Spanish is as diverse linguistically as it is regionally.

29   By the end of this century, Spanish speakers will comprise the biggest minority group in the U.S., a country where students in high schools and colleges are encouraged to take French classes because French is considered more "cultured." But for a language to remain alive it must be used.[6] By the end of this century, English, and not Spanish, will be the mother tongue of most Chicanos and Latinos.

30   So, if you want to really hurt me, talk badly about my language. Ethnic identity is twin skin to linguistic identity—I am my language. Until I can take pride in my language, I cannot take pride in myself. Until I can accept as legitimate Chicano Texas Spanish, Tex-Mex and all the other languages I speak, I cannot accept the legitimacy of myself. Until I am free to write bilingually and to switch codes without having always to translate, while I still have to speak English or Spanish when I would rather speak Spanglish, and as long as I have to accommodate the English speakers rather than having them accommodate me, my tongue will be illegitimate.

31   I will no longer be made to feel ashamed of existing. I will have my voice: Indian, Spanish, white. I will have my serpent's tongue—my woman's voice, my sexual voice, my poet's voice. I will overcome the tradition of silence.

> My fingers
> move sly against your palm
> Like women everywhere, we speak in code . . . .
>
> —*Melanie Kaye/Kantrowitz*[7]

"Vistas," corridos, y comida: My Native Tongue

32   In the 1960s, I read my first Chicano novel. It was *City of Night* by John Rechy, a gay Texan, son of a Scottish father and a Mexican mother. For days I walked around in stunned amazement that a Chicano could write and could get published. When I read *I Am Joaquín*[8] I was surprised to see a bilingual book by a Chicano in print. When I saw poetry written in Tex-Mex for the first time, a feeling of pure joy flashed through me. I felt like we really existed as a people. In 1971, when I started teaching High School English to Chicano students, I tried to supplement the required texts with works by Chicanos, only to be reprimanded and forbidden to do so by the principal. He claimed that I was supposed to teach "American" and English literature. At the risk of being fired, I swore my students to secrecy and slipped in Chicano short stories,

---

[6]Irena Klepfisz, "Secular Jewish Identity: Yidishkayt in America," in *The Tribe of Dina*, Kaye/Kantrowitz and Klepfisz, eds., 43.

[7]Melanie Kaye/Kantrowitz, "Sign," in *We Speak in Code: Poems and Other Writings* (Pittsburgh, PA: Motheroot Publications, Inc., 1980), 85.

[8]Rodolfo Gonzales, *I Am Joaquín/Yo Soy Joaquín* (New York, NY: Bantam Books, 1972). It was first published in 1967.

poems, a play. In graduate school, while working toward a Ph.D., I had to "argue" with one advisor after the other, semester after semester, before I was allowed to make Chicano literature an area of focus.

33   Even before I read books by Chicanos or Mexicans, it was the Mexican movies I saw at the drive-in—the Thursday night special of $1.00 a carload—that gave me a sense of belonging. *Vámonos a las vistas,* my mother would call out and we'd all—grandmother, brothers, sister and cousins—squeeze into the car. We'd wolf down cheese and bologna white bread sandwiches while watching Pedro Infante in melodramatic tear-jerkers like *Nosotros los pobres,* the first "real" Mexican movie (that was not an imitation of European movies). I remember seeing *Cuando los hijos se van* and surmising that all Mexican movies played up the love a mother has for her children and what ungrateful sons and daughters suffer when they are not devoted to their mothers. I remember the singing-type "westerns" of Jorge Negrete and Miguel Aceves Mejía. When watching Mexican movies, I felt a sense of homecoming as well as alienation. People who were to amount to something didn't go to Mexican movies, or *bailes* or tune their radios to *bolero, rancherita,* and corrido music.

"**The rhythms of Tex-Mex music are those of the polka, also adapted from the Germans, who in turn had borrowed the polka from the Czechs and Bohemians.**"

34   The whole time I was growing up, there was *norteño* music, sometimes called North Mexican border music, or Tex-Mex music, or Chicano music, or *cantina* (bar) music. I grew up listening to *conjuntos,* three- or four-piece bands made up of folk musicians playing guitar, *bajo sexto,* drums and button accordion, which Chicanos had borrowed from the German immigrants who had come to Central Texas and Mexico to farm and build breweries. In the Rio Grande Valley, Steve Jordan and Little Joe Hernández were popular, and Flaco Jiménez was the accordion king. The rhythms of Tex-Mex music are those of the polka, also adapted from the Germans, who in turn had borrowed the polka from the Czechs and Bohemians.

35   I remember the hot, sultry evenings when *corridos*—songs of love and death on the Texas-Mexican borderlands—reverberated out of cheap amplifiers from the local *cantinas* and wafted in through my bedroom window.

36   *Corridos* first became widely used along the South Texas/Mexican border during the early conflict between Chicanos and Anglos. The *corridos* are usually about Mexican heroes who do valiant deeds against the Anglo oppressors. Pancho Villa's song, *La cucaracha,* is the most famous one. *Corridos* of John F. Kennedy and his death are still very popular in the Valley. Older Chicanos remember Lydia Mendoza, one of the great border *corrido* singers who was called *la Gloria de Tejas.* Her *El tango negro,* sung during the Great Depression, made her a singer of the people. The everpresent *corridos* narrated one hundred years of border history, bringing news of events as well as entertaining. These folk musicians and folk songs are our chief cultural mythmakers, and they made our hard lives seem bearable.

37   I grew up feeling ambivalent about our music. Country-western and rock-and-roll had more status. In the 50s and 60s, for the slightly educated and *agringado* Chicanos, there existed a sense of shame at being caught listening to our music. Yet I couldn't stop my feet from thumping to the music, could not stop humming the words, nor hide from myself the exhilaration I felt when I heard it.

38   There are more subtle ways that we internalize identification, especially in the forms of images and emotions. For me food and certain smells are tied to my identity, to my homeland. Woodsmoke curling up to an immense blue sky; woodsmoke perfuming my grandmother's clothes, her skin. The stench of cow manure and the yellow patches on the ground; the crack of a .22 rifle and the reek of cordite. Homemade white cheese sizzling in a pan, melting inside a folded *tortilla.* My sister Hilda's hot, spicy *menudo, chile Colorado* making it deep red, pieces of *panza* and hominy floating on top. My brother Carito barbecuing *fajitas* in the backyard. Even now and 3,000 miles away, I can see my mother spicing the ground beef, pork, and venison with *chile.* My mouth salivates at the thought of the hot steaming *tamales* I would be eating if I were home.

Si le preguntas a mi mamá, "¿Qué eres?"

> "Identity is the essential core of who we are as individuals, the conscious experience of the self inside."
>
> —*Kaufman*[9]

39   *Nosotros los* Chicanos straddle the borderlands. On one side of us, we are constantly exposed to the Spanish of the Mexicans, on the other side we hear the Anglos' incessant clamoring so that we forget our language. Among ourselves we don't say *nosotros los americanos, o nosotros los españoles, o nosotros los hispanos.* We say *nosotros los mexicanos* (by *mexicanos* we do not mean citizens of Mexico; we do not mean a national identity, but a racial one). We distinguish between *mexicanos del otro lado* and *mexicanos de este lodo.* Deep in our hearts we believe that being Mexican has nothing to do with which country one lives in. Being Mexican is a state of soul—not one of mind, not one of citizenship. Neither eagle nor serpent, but both. And like the ocean, neither animal respects borders.

> *Dime con quien andas y te diré quien eres.*
> (Tell me who your friends are and I'll tell you who you are.)
>
> —*Mexican saying*

40   *Si le preguntas a mi mamá, "¿Qué eres?" te dirá, "Soy Mexicana."* My brothers and sister say the same. I sometimes will answer *"soy mexicana"* and at

---

[9]Kaufman, 68.

others will say *"soy Chicana" o "soy tejana."* But I identified as *"Raza"* before I ever identified as *"Mexicana"* or "Chicana."

41 As a culture, we call ourselves Spanish when referring to ourselves as a linguistic group and when copping out. It is then that we forget our predominant Indian genes. We are 70% to 80% Indian.[10] We call ourselves Hispanic[11] or Spanish American or Latin American or Latin when linking ourselves to other Spanish-speaking peoples of the Western hemisphere and when copping out. We call ourselves Mexican American[12] to signify we are neither Mexican nor American, but more the noun *American* than the adjective *Mexican* (and when copping out).

42 Chicanos and other people of color suffer economically for not acculturating. This voluntary (yet forced) alienation makes for psychological conflict, a kind of dual identity—we don't identify with the Anglo-American cultural values and we don't totally identify with the Mexican cultural values. We are a synergy of two cultures with various degrees of Mexicanness or Angloness. I have so internalized the borderland conflict that sometimes I feel like one cancels out the other and we are zero, nothing, no one. *A veces no soy nada ni nadie. Pero hasta cuando no lo soy, lo soy.*

43 When not copping out, when we know we are more than nothing, we call ourselves *Mexican*, referring to race and ancestry; *mestizo* when affirming both our Indian and Spanish (but we hardly ever own our Black ancestry); *Chicano* when referring to a politically aware people born and/or raised in the U.S.; *Raza* when referring to Chicanos; *tejanos* when we are Chicanos from Texas.

44 Chicanos did not know we were a people until 1965 when Cesar Chavez and the farmworkers united and *I Am Joaquín* was published and *la Raza Unida* party was formed in Texas. With that recognition, we became a distinct people. Something momentous happened to the Chicano soul—we became aware of our reality and acquired a name and a language (Chicano Spanish) that reflected that reality. Now that we had a name, some of the fragmented pieces began to fall together—who we were, what we were, how we had evolved. We began to get glimpses of what we might eventually become.

45 Yet the struggle of identities continues, the struggle of borders is our reality still. One day the inner struggle will cease and a true integration will take place. In the meantime, *tenemos que hacerla lucha. ¿Quién está protegiendo los ranchos de mi gente? ¿Quién está tratando de cerrar la fisura entre la india y el blanco en nuestra sangre? El Chicano, sí, el Chicano que anda como un ladrón en su propia casa.*

---

[10]Chávez, 88–90.

[11]"Hispanic" is derived from *Hispanis* (*España,* a name given to the Iberian Peninsula in ancient times when it was a part of the Roman Empire) and is a term designated by the U.S. government to make it easier to handle us on paper.

[12]The Treaty of Guadalupe Hidalgo created the Mexican-American in 1848.

46   *Los Chicanos,* how patient we seem, how very patient. There is the quiet of the Indian about us.[13] We know how to survive. When other races have given up their tongue, we've kept ours. We know what it is to live under the hammer blow of the dominant *norteamericano* culture. But more than we count the blows, we count the days the weeks the years the centuries the eons until the white laws and commerce and customs will rot in the deserts they've created, lie bleached. *Humildes* yet proud, *quietos* yet wild, *nosotros los mexicanos*-Chicanos will walk by the crumbling ashes as we go about our business. Stubborn, persevering, impenetrable as stone, yet possessing a malleability that renders us unbreakable, we, the *mestizas* and *mestizos,* will remain.

Literacy Connections

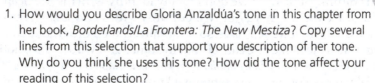

1. How would you describe Gloria Anzaldúa's tone in this chapter from her book, *Borderlands/La Frontera: The New Mestiza*? Copy several lines from this selection that support your description of her tone. Why do you think she uses this tone? How did the tone affect your reading of this selection?

2. Unlike many authors who write in English but include words, phrases, or sentences from another language, Anzaldúa does not always reveal to her English-only readers the meanings of the foreign words. Why might she have decided not to include translations of non-English words? What effect does her decision not to translate have on her persona in this essay?

3. How did Anzaldúa's decision not to translate affect your reading of the essay?

4. Each of us speaks many languages, even though we might think of ourselves as speaking only one. In "How to Tame a Wild Tongue," Anzaldúa lists eight languages she speaks. Look over her list, and then make your own list of the languages you speak and the context in which you use each one.

5. In the introductory essay of this chapter, Amy Hodges Hamilton says, "Anzaldúa's examination of how various cultures and languages come together is especially important in an academy where students come from widely varying cultural and language backgrounds." In what ways do you feel that Anzaldua's ideas are relevant for college writing?

---

[13]Anglos, in order to alleviate their guilt for dispossessing the Chicano, stressed the Spanish part of us and perpetrated the myth of the Spanish Southwest. We have accepted the fiction that we are Hispanic, that is Spanish, in order to accommodate ourselves to the dominant culture and its abhorrence of Indians. Chávez, 88–91.

Personal Literacy Projects

Personal Literacy Narrative and Reflection

In this essay, you'll share your history as a reader and writer. Reflecting on your literacy history will not only help you more clearly understand your attitudes regarding reading and writing, but also will allow your teacher to know more about your literacy history and more effectively respond to your writing.

Think about the factors, people, and situations in your life that played a major role in making you the reader and writer you are today. Think about the schools you attended, the people who taught you, and the situations you found yourself in that shaped you as a reader and writer. As you get ready to write, reflect upon both positive and negative influences, and on how you reacted to those influences.

In your essay, you should tell your story, but you should go beyond storytelling to reflect on the experiences you share and the role they played in shaping you as a user of language.

Position Shift Essay

This essay asks you to focus on a single experience or set of experiences in your life. The focus of the essay should revolve around a personal experience that altered how you thought or felt about an issue, idea, or belief involving your personal literacy.

Reflection on the experience and what it means to you should play as strong a role as memory. By focusing on one event, you can begin to acclimate yourself to examining your life through writing.

You should write about some time in your life when you had a *shift* (change in position or way of thinking) involving some aspect of your personal literacy. For example, you might write about a time when a teacher, parent, grandparent, or friend encouraged you by giving you positive feedback that altered your attitudes regarding yourself as a user of language. You might write about how you were a confident reader and/or writer until someone said or did something that destroyed your confidence as a user of language. You might write about an experience with a speech, an essay, a Web design, a PowerPoint presentation, or a poetry contest that affected your personal literacy or a book you read that changed your attitude about reading. What you write about will depend on your experiences as a user of language.

Snapshots Essay

For this project, you'll consider how the stories that make up your life have been shaped, and then you will "shape" a small cross section of this story for your peers. These stories will be conveyed in two types of snapshots—written text and visual text. You will paint a picture with words while also including images that reflect each story. The framing of narratives and images can drastically alter the meaning of the text; thus, you will need to think about the social and cultural contexts that have affected your opinions of yourself as well as others' perceptions of you.

In order to discover the many facets of your personality, each snapshot will be based on a different person's perspective of you. That is, one snapshot will capture how you see yourself, and the others will emerge from the opinions of those around you. You will gain varying insights about yourself by interviewing three or four people from different parts of your life.

You will write four or five "word" snapshots. Your snapshots will not be transcripts of your interviews, but rather, they will focus on specific traits or experiences important to the way each interviewee sees you. One may tell a story in which you and the other person are characters, and another may describe a certain trait that you can translate into an extended metaphor. You can also jump right into your interviewee's head and convey her thoughts in a fairly associative manner, or maybe you will use dialogue to show how you and the interviewee interact.

These snapshots are just that—individual pictures a reader might find in a photo album. Do not feel the need to make word transitions between the snapshots. You will shape your overall message through the selection, depiction, and organization of the snapshots.

Each of your written snapshots will be connected to a specific image chosen by you or the interviewee. The image does not have to be a personal photo but should represent in some way the written snapshot you have created. When completed, you will have both a textual collage as well as a visual collage. The images should be integrated into the written text, which requires that you make choices as far as the visual design of your piece.

Remember who your audience will be: the students sitting in your classroom with you. Choose those snapshots that they will be interested in and will want to read.

Along with your final draft, you will submit a one- to two-page cover letter in which you discuss the specific choices you made in creating each snapshot and how you decided to incorporate the images into the written text. This reflection will help you see the connection between the written and the visual.

Personal Language Analysis

The goal of this essay is to get you to think critically about your own personal language(s). Make a list of the personal contexts for your own language use: for example, your list might include your language when you talk to friends, your language when you talk to family members, your language when you compose in personal genres like a diary or blog or song. Choose three of these personal literacy contexts and analyze the language you use in these contexts, giving specific examples of the kinds of personas you take on in each situation. As you analyze your personal uses of language in the three situations you choose, consider literacy factors like purpose, audience, medium, and genre. How do these literacy factors shape your personal language use in each of the three situations?

Radical Revision Project

For this project you will radically revise your previous personal literacy project. You will take your earlier project and revise it in a different genre or medium that maintains your central focus. For example, if you wrote the "Personal Literacy Narrative and Reflection," you might radically revise that essay into a song or a skit. If you wrote the "Position Shift Essay," you might revise that essay into a short graphic novel or a film. If you wrote the "Snapshots Essay," you might revise that paper into a photo album, poem, or collage. These are just a few of many examples to get you thinking about your own radical revision.

This project will include several components:

- A process narrative in which you recount what you chose to do, why, how it worked, what you learned, and how composing in one genre or medium was different from composing in another
- All drafts/notes/peer review sheets that encouraged your revision
- The final revision
- Class presentation or reading/explanation of your revision.

Group Project: Peer Personal Literacy Questions

In this project, you're going to interview your classroom peers and ask them questions about their personal literacies. This project is an opportunity to better get to know your peers and their literacy backgrounds which will help you be a better responder to their writing. This project will also give your teacher some insight into you and your peers' personal literacies. As a class, brainstorm some questions you'd like to ask about your peers' personal literacies. For example, you might ask how many languages they speak, how their cultural background has shaped their language, what kinds of composing they do outside of school, etc. Once you have possible personal literacy questions, form groups of three to four and choose five questions for the group to answer. Have each group member discuss their answer to each question, and have another group member take notes to summarize each answer. You can rotate the person taking notes to allow everyone to answer each question and everyone to take notes for one other person's answer. When each group member has answered all five questions, write a collaboratively written essay comparing the personal literacies of the group members. This essay can be in whatever form you want it to be—as long as it gives readers a good sense of how the group members answered each of the five questions and makes some comparisons among the group members' personal literacies.

4

Situating Oral Literacies

This chapter on oral literacies will help you come to terms with what is meant by the term *oral literacies* and the role oral literacies play in your life. You might be wondering how oral performances and interpretation of those performances can be thought of as a type of literacy,

but if you think about it, you'll realize that, like digital and print literacies, oral performances present a rhetorical situation involving a speaker, a text, and an audience.

Sometimes oral literacies are practiced for civic purposes, such as political speeches, and sometimes oral literacies are combined with other literacies, such as digital literacies in multimodal genres, as on a streaming video Web site. But in this chapter, the readings, the student case study, and the literacy connection questions are primarily focused on defining/exploring oral literacies.

As you read this chapter, you'll have the opportunity to become familiar with selections that will help expand your vision of what is meant by the term *oral literacies* and also enable you to better read, interpret, and analyze oral texts. The selections that are included will give you the opportunity to—

- Read an essay by Professor Alexis Davidson, a university speech and communications instructor, in which she explores what the term *oral literacies* means to her

- Take a close look at the composing processes Alexandra Giang used as she went about preparing and presenting a speech for Professor Davidson's class

- Closely read President Barack Obama's historical 2009 inaugural address
- Read an essay by a student about his "rock-and-roll baptism"
- Enjoy some slam poetry from HBO's Def Poetry Jam
- Understand more about the history of oral literacy in African American communities
- Enjoy folktales that offer an explanation for "Why We Have Gophers" and provide a "Ritual to Get a Man"
- Read an essay that will help you learn more about oral history
- Read the oral history narrative of a Vietnam War veteran who went to war with a scout dog named Marty, and learn something about what life was like for them.

But you won't just read these selections and think about how they help us understand what the term *oral literacies* means; you'll also compose. If you use the oral literacy projects described at the end of the chapter, you might—

- Complete a project in which you explore you own family stories
- Compose a music history narrative
- Conduct an oral history interview
- Participate in a classroom slam
- Compose and present a researched speech
- Take part in an audio script group project.

And now, let's start exploring oral literacies.

What Are Oral Literacies?

Before You Read

What comes to your mind when you hear or read the term *oral literacies*? Most of us connect the word *oral* to spoken, and the word *literacy* to reading and writing. So what could possibly be meant by *oral literacies*? Write for five minutes and explore these questions.

In the essay you're about to read, Alexis Davidson tries to come to terms with what she thinks is meant by the term *oral literacies*. As you read this selection, keep a pen in hand and underline or highlight sentences or phrases that help you have a clearer understanding of this term.

Oral Literacies—Finding Your Voice

Alexis Davidson

Alexis Davidson completed her graduate work in communications studies and currently teaches a variety of speech and communications
courses at California State University, Sacramento. Her oral performance
experience includes radio, theater, singing, public speaking, and debate.
Her essay that follows explores the meaning of the term *oral literacies*
and will help you develop your own definition of the term.

**If you know what you want to say but just can't express it,
you *don't* know what you want to say.**

1 How do you react to that statement? Do you squirm nervously? Do you
firmly disagree? Do you think, "Wow! That's true!" Most of us have said
at some point in our life, "I know what I want to say, but I just can't express
it." When I was a student and a classmate stated this during a class discussion, my English professor responded, "If you can't express it, you *don't*
know what you want to say." When I began teaching public speaking, that
exchange came to mind. Some people react against it with surprising intensity, but I believe there is a core of truth. Whether we are presenting a
speech to a classroom or a group, or we are having a private conversation,
or talking to our boss, or telling a story, or reading a poem aloud, or performing a song: we need to know what we want to say and be able to
express it. In his book *The Art of Winning Conversation*, Morey Stettner
states, "You need to have a clear, precise idea of what you want to accomplish: what you want to say and why you want to say it" (111). Part of the
"art" includes knowing *how* we want to say it. As we explore the concept
of oral literacies, it must include the ability to form our thoughts in a way
that can be expressed clearly to others.

2 Oral *performance* is a broad field that includes choral reading, debate,
drama, interpretations, oral reading, poetry slams, etc. Oral communication *requirements* vary among institutions. The requirement among colleges
and universities most often is synonymous with public speaking. However, this requirement is sometimes met through group discussion and performance, debate, or other oral performance courses. Regardless of the
format, the purpose is to help us become competent communicators who
can express our own thoughts or appropriately interpret someone else's
thoughts when we perform them.

3   Oral competence includes the ability to construct a message worth hearing. In *Communication Incompetencies*, Gerald Phillips describes the competent (rhetorically sensitive) speaker as someone who "can put ideas together in an intelligible pattern and select and arrange words to make the ideas intelligible to the listener" (223). In this essay I will define oral literacy, discuss the importance of the audience in oral performance, and describe how literacy helps contribute to performer competence. I will also address some similarities and differences between written and oral literacy, and finally suggest ways to become orally literate.

Oral Literacy

4   In public speaking and other communication courses, we most often speak of oral competence. The two features of competence are effectiveness and appropriateness. Effectiveness is how well the message was understood: did the audience "get it"? There are three primary purposes for public speaking, and perhaps for any form of oral performance: to entertain, to inform, or to persuade. If the audience does not understand the message, they will not be entertained or informed or persuaded. Appropriateness is the degree to which the message and delivery fit the occasion and audience: was the message acceptable for the time, place, and audience? Gerald Philips says that competent oral discourse is that which accomplishes the goal without generating any negative responses that undermine the message (36). He asserts that literacy is gained through formal instruction and what we learn in life, and it is literacy that gives us the ability to assess situations to select the best topics and ideas (130). To be literate is to be "well-educated; having or showing extensive knowledge, learning, or culture" (*Webster's* 838). Culture is made up of many things, including a group's values, beliefs, traditions, art forms, and communication patterns. The values and practices determine what is appropriate for the culture, and being aware of cultural standards and expectations is an important part of literacy.

5   Public speaking textbooks highlight the importance of understanding the audience when constructing a message. The audience and occasion determine the nature of the situation, or context, for a speech. Understanding the audience is also a factor in selecting performance pieces such as poetry, readings or recitations, or songs. What is the audience expecting to hear in this situation? Some long-time musicians have encountered a conflict when they want to play their new music at a concert but the audience has come to hear its (old) favorites. Some performers have learned that the audience is there for the music or scheduled performance and not interested in a political statement. Oral literacy means understanding the

audience, being aware of the range of options available for the audience and the occasion, selecting the one most fitting for the situation, and using the kind of language that best conveys the message to the audience. Thus, literacy includes fluency with language, whether it be framing our own message or giving interpretive voice to the language of others in reading a story or poem or singing a song or selecting a scene from a play. Regardless of our point of view and what we want to say, to be successful we must present a message the audience can understand and will pay attention to.

The Audience

6 Whether writing or speaking, the three key ingredients are the writer or speaker (also known as the *sender*), the audience, and the message (content). These elements are known as the rhetorical triangle. Each element is important, but many argue that the audience is the primary component. Textbooks refer to being audience-centered; and as noted previously, competence is determined by the ability to understand what is effective and appropriate for a given audience. Bob Boylan, a leadership and presentation coach for senior and middle management, gives maximum importance to the audience: "It's the only reason you are speaking" (15). We can add for other formats, "It's the only reason you are performing."

7   Understanding your audience influences several aspects of a speech or performance. Knowing the audience will help you decide which topics are appropriate or if special consideration needs to be given to the *way* the topic is presented. There are as many ways to approach audience analysis as there are authors writing on the topic. Most people agree that the basic necessary information is the audience's level of interest and level of knowledge on your topic. You can give a speech on almost any topic by keeping the audience in mind. Think about ways to make them interested in the topic and how to present it in terms that fit their level of knowledge, neither too technical nor too simplistic. Similarly, other oral performances should be aimed at audience in degree of formality, complexity, and fit for the occasion.

8   You have a goal in your presentation, which is to convey your message and convince the audience to accept it. Your audience also has a goal of finding out what's in it for them. In a class where audience analysis was not assigned, one of my students did an informal survey of her classmates on each of her speech topics. By knowing the audience's attitude toward and knowledge about her subject, she was able to relate her speeches to them. The students looked forward to her speeches to learn what she did with the information they gave her, and she was always successful at getting their attention. Stettner says, "The best goals are those that you and

your audience share. Strive to portray our goals and theirs as the same" (116). Understanding the audience will help you align your goal with theirs to maximize the likelihood of the audience accepting your message.

Speaker Literacy and the Audience

9   The two main components of a message are content and delivery. Content is the substance of the message, the point you are trying to convey to the audience. Delivery is the way in which you convey the message. We have all heard speakers who have good content but are not interesting or who have distracting mannerisms or vocal characteristics. On the other hand, we have sometimes listened to speakers who are entertaining and expressive without making a clear point. Oral literacy encompasses meaningful content and engaging delivery. Content is the point of the presentation; delivery influences the degree to which the audience pays attention and stays interested. I often compare a speech to an athletic performance: content is the technical merit and delivery is the artistic merit.

10   Boylan refers to focused content (centered, clear, and concise) and correct content—that which meets the audience's needs (77). The literate speaker researches the topic, narrows it to fit the time frame and the interest and knowledge of the audience, and supports the points with relevant and credible sources. Written literacy assists the speaker in finding topics and supporting materials for speeches and debate; it also provides the background knowledge for selecting poetry, stories, readings, or songs that will interest a particular audience.

11   A speaker's style can have a strong influence on the audience. Vocabulary, grammar, and pronunciation are part of style. Vocabulary—language choices—can be considered with content, but those choices also affect delivery. Audiences are tuned into whether language choices and style are appropriate for them and the situation. Consider the example of Malcolm X and the excerpts from his three speeches from Chapter 1. The core of his message is the same in all three situations: should the fight for civil rights be passive, with people waiting for what will be granted them by those in power, or should it be managed by those who believe they have waited long enough and must now take action to bring about change? Malcolm X did not change the core content or purpose of his message; he did change the way he delivered it to each audience. He chose language, images, and a delivery style that was typical of the experience and traditions of each audience. Malcolm X not only understood the cultural background of his audience but also gauged their position on the issue. The Nation of Islam was already convinced; Malcolm X reinforced their position and rallied them to the cause. The Detroit audience was uncertain about how to proceed in the struggle, and they were encouraged to take a proactive

stance. The Harvard audience needed to be told why civil rights advocates were upset and why it was no longer an option to sit quietly and suffer. Malcolm X chose both his content emphases and his delivery style to match the expectations of each audience.

12   Cargile and Bradac did a review of research on how attitudes toward language influence audience evaluations of speakers. According to Cargile and Bradac, audiences know that different situations demand different forms of discourse and linguistic styles (353). The audience has a sense of appropriate language choices and diversity of vocabulary for the occasion, and they expect a speaker to fit her or his speech to the occasion. The standards and expectations will vary among audiences and cultures. Learning about the audience allows the speaker to make the appropriate language choices to meet its standards as has been noted in the Malcolm X examples. For the Detroit workers, the language and style was consistent with what they heard on a regular basis in their churches. To the Harvard audience, Malcolm X demonstrated his knowledge of the classics and his ability to speak in a traditionally educated fashion. The images, slogans, and intense manner of speaking were those that were customary in Nation of Islam gatherings.

> "Good speakers know that the audience will remain interested when the speech content is matched by variety in pace, volume, and expression."

13   Language choice and style is one part of delivery. Vocal expression, movement, and gestures are also important in delivery. If literacy means a broad range of knowledge, then orally literate speakers understand the options available for vocal expression, movement, and gestures, and they know how to apply them appropriately for the situation. Phillips reminds us that a competent speaker can keep the listeners' attention (36). The audience stays more engaged when a speaker can be easily understood through clear articulation, good pacing, and volume that allow the message to be heard. Good speakers know that the audience will remain interested when the speech content is matched by variety in pace, volume, and expression. The Roman rhetorician Quintilian is widely quoted as saying, "It is feeling and force of imagination that make us eloquent." Speakers who convey excitement about their topic and point of view are more likely to keep the audience engaged to the end of the speech. Performers who convey the soul of their selections will likewise keep the audience interested and feeling they have experienced the essence of the writer/originator of the material.

Written Literacy and Oral Literacy

14 After in-class discussions about structure, organizational strategies, introductions, and conclusions for effective speeches, students will sometimes say, "So it's just like writing an essay!" Well, not exactly. The same planning

and care is needed to construct the content, but language is generally less formal in a speech. With all oral presentations, the audience also hears and sees the sender. This can be a problem if body language becomes a distraction or poor pronunciation and unclear speech make the words hard to understand. In an oral presentation there are no re-writes or do-overs. You have only one chance to communicate your message. However, presenting your message orally is an advantage when you are comfortable; you can emphasize and add expression that clarifies meaning and keeps the audience's attention in a way that may not happen when they are reading.

15   Literacy has common features regardless of the medium: written, oral, visual, digital, or musical. All have a message to be conveyed, an audience to be reached, and the sender of the message, whether it is a writer, a speaker, a visual artist, graphic designer, or musician. The success of the communication depends on the sender understanding the audience and framing the message in the way that is most likely to be understood and accepted. In all formats, the sender has the opportunity and responsibility to plan and organize the message and to determine which delivery methods will be appropriate and effective with the specific audience. A person who is familiar with literature, art, music, and other aspects of the audience culture will have a broader base of knowledge to draw upon when deciding what examples to use, where to find information, and how to gain the audience's attention.

16   Earlier, culture was explained in terms of values, beliefs, traditions, etc. There are other aspects to understanding the audience, such as demographics. These factors include age, gender, sexual orientation, religion, group memberships, educational level, and economic status. As far back as 2000 years ago, Aristotle said that a person is most affected by his or her age, and research has confirmed this (Lucas 117). Age information may be important in cultural references in a presentation: will the audience know the "line" from a movie, television show, book, or song? Will the audience members recognize names of current or past celebrities or politicians? When selecting a reading, play scene, poem to perform, or song to sing, will the audience know the artist and work? Will the audience understand and appreciate the topic or point of view presented in the selection? In considering the audience, you may decide that a topic or approach is not the best way to gain interest or keep the audience engaged or convey your message.

Becoming Orally Literate

17 To perform well, one needs to also recognize good performance. A literate person is able to evaluate the quality of another's performance, whether it is written, spoken, musical, or visual. Exposure to literature,

art, good non-fiction writing, and conversation will build a base of knowledge. Recall Gerald Phillips's statement that literacy comes from both formal instruction and life learning. You can read user-friendly books on public speaking such as Bob Boylan's *What's Your Point?* and *Getting There: Functional Public Speaking*, which use the metaphor of a journey and road map to explain how to get where you want to go in a speech. As you watch people around you, pay attention to classmates' presentations, read famous speeches, or view them on line, and you will become aware of your options. You will see what works well and where improvements can be made. Select aspects of organization or delivery that you want to practice. To build your appreciation and experience in other forms of oral performance, support your campus theater productions, debate team, or recitals.

18   Keep in mind that, as a student, one of your primary audience members will be your instructor. He or she will tell you the requirements of the speech content and structure or of the particular oral performance assignment. You will also be given feedback on your content and delivery skills. Pay attention to comments and suggestions, and practice them for your next speech, recitation, or musical performance. You can observe your classmates and discuss your performance with them or ask about their strategies. You can select readings, poems, or songs that are not familiar and experiment with interpreting them through vocal expression, movement, and gestures. Practice does increase skill and comfort, and as you become more comfortable, you will become increasingly competent. With your expanding vocabulary and ability to organize, awareness of your audience in selecting or formulating content, and development of delivery skills, when you know what you want to say, you *will* be able to express it.

Works Cited

Agnes, Michael, ed. *Webster's New World College Dictionary*. 4th ed. Cleveland: Wiley Publishing, Inc., 2005. 838. Print.

Bostrm, Robert N., Enid S. Waldhart, Michael W. Shelton, and Sissy Bertino. *Getting There: Functional Public Speaking*. Prospect Heights: Waveland Press, Inc., 1997. Print.

Boylan, Bob. *What's Your Point?* Holbrook, MA: Adams Media Corporation, 2001. Print.

Cargile, Aaron Castelan, and James J. Bradac. "Attitudes Toward Language: A Review of Speaker-Evaluation Research and a General Process Model." *Communication Yearbook 25*. Willam B. Gudykunst, ed. Mahwah: Lawrence Earlbaum Associates, 2001. 347-382. Print.

Lucas, Stephen E. *The Art of Public Speaking*. 9th ed. New York: McGraw-Hill, 2004. Print.

Phillips, Gerald M. *Communication Incompetencies: A Theory of Training Oral Performance Behavior*. Carbondale: Southern Illinois University Press, 1991. Print.

Stettner, Morey. *The Art of Winning Conversation*. Englewood Cliffs: Prentice Hall, 1995. Print.

Literacy Connections

1. Take a few minutes to jot down and review the sentences and phrases you underlined or highlighted as you read Professor Davidson's essay—sentences and phrases that you thought might help you more clearly understand what is meant by the term *oral literacies*.

2. Now, form a group with two or three of your classmates and share your lists. Make a compiled list that includes what each of you have, and discuss the ideas you've noted as you read. Share your ideas with each other and talk about what you think it means to be orally literate. As a group, work on coming up with a definition for *oral literacies* that you can share with the class. Share your group's definition with the class, and talk with the class about how you decided on your particular definition. Then, listen carefully to the definitions the other groups came up with and how they arrived at their definition. After each group has shared its definition and talked with the class, work on developing a definition the whole class can agree on.

3. Jot down several occasions when you have needed to be "orally literate" both inside and outside of school.

4. In her essay on oral literacies, Professor Davidson explains, "Whether writing or speaking, the three key ingredients are the writer or speaker (also known as the *sender*), the audience, and the message (content). These elements are known as the rhetorical triangle." How is your focus on audience different when you are writing a speech as compared to when you are composing an essay?

5. Later in this chapter, you'll have the opportunity to read President Barack Obama's inaugural address. Think about how President Obama likely envisioned the rhetorical triangle to which Professor Davidon refers in her essay. How do you imagine he envisioned his audience, and in what ways would that image of his audience have played a role in shaping his message?

Before You Read

The following selection is a case study that will allow you to see the composing process Alexandra Giang used as she completed an assignment for her communications class. As you read the selection, think about speeches that you have written and how the composing process you used while writing a speech differed from the process you usually use when composing an essay.

Student Case Study: Composing and Delivering a Speech

Alexandra Giang was a student in Professor Alexis Davidson's communications class at California State University Sacramento when she completed the assignment described below. Alexandra later transferred to San Jose State University where she is pursuing a major in accounting.

As you read this case study, you'll see how Alexandra decided on a topic for her speech and how she went about composing it, and you'll learn something about her perception of how her speech was received by her audience.

Following is the assignment Professor Davidson gave to her students, followed by Alexandra's outline, the typed version of her speech, and a section in which she shares her strategies for composing her speech.

Assignment: Informative Speech

Format

Five to six minutes in length. Points are deducted for presentations that are too short or too long.

At least one visual aid is required—overhead transparency, poster, object, model, or etc.; no PowerPoint or videos. Visual aides must be large enough to be visible to everyone in the audience. For typed overheads, use at least 20-point font or larger. For posters, lines should be thick, dark, and at least 1½ inches high. Visual aids need to be high quality. You may make your own charts and graphs, but write neatly and make sure lines are clean. Use visual aid(s) wisely to illustrate statistics or concepts that may need clarification. Practice working with it/them.

At least three oral citations are required. Signpost these with "According to . . ." or "In a Newsweek article, George Will said . . .," or some similar phrase. If I don't hear it, it isn't there, even if it's in your outline. Five points per citation will be deducted if fewer than three citations are used.

A full outline, containing an introduction, a body, a conclusion, transitions, and a bibliography, is required. You submit an outline in advance for feedback and a revised outline when you give the speech. An outline is required. Your presentation generally reflects the quality of your outline. Outlines are not accepted after the speech date; turning in your outline after you make your speech indicates that you did not prepare an outline for the speech. The speech grade includes 5 points for submitting your final outline.

Follow the guidelines and handouts discussed in class and the worksheet provided for gathering your speech ideas. Remember that the outline is not the starting point; it is the "blueprint" of your completed speech that will help you deliver your speech extemporaneously.

1. Establish your credibility by stating your experience, expertise or research on the topic.
2. Use key words or phrases that will indicate exactly what you wish to say on a given point.
3. Put your main points in the order that will be most effective for your topic and goal.
4. Write out transition sentences to move through your points.
5. Note in the outline your oral citations and what your visual aid is and how it will be used.
6. A bibliography in MLA or APA format must be attached to the outline.

Content

Your presentation must be appropriate to this audience. What may they already know or need to learn about your topic? Inform or explain, but do not attempt to persuade us. Tell us something that you know about, have studied or are interested in; the topic does not need to be "heavy" or controversial but should be worth our time and your effort. Creativity/interest value: You will enjoy preparing and presenting something that interests you, and your audience will be more attentive if you are enthusiastic in your presentation.

This speech is to be delivered extemporaneously—you know it well but have not memorized it word for word and are not reading it. I will check your speaking notes. These notes, whether on pages or note cards, must not be a full script of your speech. You may use three index cards if you prefer them for speaking notes. In addition to any points lost for eye contact, points will be deducted for reading. Practice your speech, especially new names or vocabulary.

Contact me by phone or e-mail, or come to office hours, if you have questions. If you have any doubt about your topic, outline, or sources for your bibliography, I will be happy to help you.

Following is the required outline Alexandra submitted to her teacher.

Topic: Human Trafficking
I. Intro
(Put up sign)
A. What industry brings in 9 billion dollars a year? (usinfo.state.gov). (Take 3 guesses)
B. Define Human Trafficking (UNESCAP)
1. The recruitment, transportation, transfer, harboring or receipt of persons, by means of the threat or use of force or other forms of coercion, of abduction, of fraud, of deception, of the abuse of power or of a position of vulnerability or of the giving or receiving of

payments or benefits to achieve the consent of a person having control over another person, for the purpose of exploitation.

    2. Different from prostitution for prostitution is more of a choice.

II. Who are the victims?
   A. 600,000 to 820,000 (usinfo.state.gov)
   B. Women (put up picture)
   C. Men
   D. Children (put up picture)

III. How people get stuck in human trafficking
   A. Sold
       1. Pay family debt. (UN Chronicle)
   C. Punishment
       1. Ghanna (equalitynow.org)
   D. Tricked and lured (UN Chronicle)
       1. Jobs
       2. Education
       3. Citizenship

IV. Where does trafficking occur? (humantrafficking.org)
   A. Poor countries
   B. Asia
       1. Japan is one of the main
   C. Africa
   D. Europe
       1. Prime destination (natcatch.com)
   E. America
       1. 50,000 a year (natcatch.com)

V. Conclusion
   A. Is illegal.
       1. Violates every form of human rights
       2. Brothels (restaurants, nail shops, massage parlors, etc.)
   B. For more information.
       1. Humantrafficking.org

Now, let's take a look at the typed version of Alexandra's speech.

"Not for Sale"

Alexandra Giang

1 It is an industry that brings in 9 billion dollars a year and has over 800,000 workers which is rapidly increasing. What is this industry? It is human trafficking (usinfo.state.gov). According to United Nations Economic and

Social Commission for Asia and the Pacific (UNESCAP), human trafficking is "the recruitment, transportation, transfer, harboring or receipt of persons, by means of the threat or use of force or other forms of coercion, of abduction, of fraud, of deception, of the abuse of power or of a position of vulnerability or of the giving or receiving of payments or benefits to achieve the consent of a person having control over another person, for the purpose of exploitation." Thousands of people are taken into human trafficking each year. Those people include women, men, and a growing favorite in the trafficking world, children.

2   These people get caught into the world of human trafficking for many reasons. According to *UN Chronicles,* poverty is a big reason why women and children are being sold as sex slaves. Traffickers tend to stay in local villages and prey on poor families. Traffickers usually lure in victims by promising a better life for the victim and their families and promising them a job. Or in the case of children, traffickers promise the parents that their child will get an education which will lead to a better life. However, not all the families are tricked. Some families who cannot make ends meet sell their own family members or friends to traffickers for a profit, knowing very well what will happen to the person being sold. In other cases money has nothing to do with why a person is given up to trafficking. As stated in equalitynow.org, in Ghana a virgin daughter is usually given to the priest as a way to appease the gods for crimes committed by her family. Then there is a factor that nobody can really control and that is kidnap. Children are kidnapped and sold everyday, and in many poor countries when a child goes missing they are believed to never return for the trafficking business is growing so rapidly.

3   Trafficking is a huge industry that is growing around the world. It is very common around poor countries as well as some not so poor countries. Trafficking occurs every where whether we choose to acknowledge it or not. In Asia trafficking is happening in countries like Thailand, Cambodia, Hong Kong, and according to humantrafficking.org, a huge trafficking destination is Japan. Sex brothels can also be found in Europe, in Africa, in South America, and the list wouldn't be complete unless we added of course the United States of America. 50,000 people are smuggled into the US borders each year. That is 50,000 people from all over the world of all sexes and ages.

4   Human trafficking violates every human right possible and it is illegal especially when it comes to children. For more information go to www. humantrafficking.org.

Alexandra's Strategies for Composing

5 We asked Alexandra to answer a few questions that would help us better understand how she went about composing her speech. First, we wanted

to know how she decided on her topic—human trafficking—and what she saw as the purpose of her speech.

6   *I decided to write on human trafficking because I had watched a movie on it on Lifetime and it really affected me. I was shocked by all the things those girls have to go through. As for the purpose of my speech, I wanted to inform my peers about the things going on in our own backyards.*

7   Alexandra was smart to find a topic that truly interested her and to think about the effect she wanted her presentation to have on her audience. No matter what the type of literacy in which you're composing, it's important to choose a topic you find engaging and to carefully consider your audience and purpose.

8   Next, we asked her how she went about gathering information to include in her speech.

9   *To get some information, I just went online and typed in "human trafficking." Because it is such a huge issue in the world, I knew there would be lots of sites for it or about it.*

10   While this method of finding information worked O.K. for Alexandra, it's important to remember that not all sites provide reliable, appropriate information. Writers and researchers at all levels need to know how to locate trustworthy sources and how to evaluate the sources they are thinking about using.

11   Next, we asked Alexandra to talk about drafting the speech and the outline. We specifically wanted to know whether she completed the outline first and then wrote the speech, wrote the speech and then made up the outline based on what she had written, or did them simultaneously.

12   *I actually did do the outline first because up until I finished it I didn't know how to write my paper.*

13   Many writers who are required to complete outlines find that they don't know what they want to write or how they want to organize their material until they are actually involved in the composing process. These composers complete their writing assignment and then put together an outline to satisfy the requirements for the assignment. However, coming up with the outline first worked well for Alexandra and helped her figure out what she wanted to cover in her presentation and how to present it to her audience.

14   Next, we asked Alexandra to tell us about the typed version of the speech she allowed us to use in this chapter. We noted that in the assignment, her teacher specified that the speech was to be delivered extemporaneously—not read word for word. We wondered whether the version she gave us to use in this case study was what the assignment referred to as "speaking notes."

15   *The typed version of the speech I gave you is what I typed out so I would know how I wanted to word everything, but when I spoke I used my outline, so the wording was probably a little different when I actually presented the speech in our class.*

16   So the typed version of Alexandra's speech wasn't really her final draft; the actual performance of the speech was the final version. With an oral performance, the revision process continues as the speaker makes her presentation to an audience.

17   Then, we asked Alexandra to comment on how the composing process she used as she went about preparing her speech on human trafficking differed from the composing process she typically goes through when composing an essay. Here's what she told us:

18   *I pretty much use the same type of composing process whether I'm writing a speech or an essay. The only difference is that when I'm working on a speech, I get to make my writing more personal and actually make it sound like I sound when I'm speaking.*

19   So Alexandra's composing process typically begins with choosing a topic, then gathering information she can use, then developing an outline to help her get her information organized, and, finally, composing her drafts and revising. Even though the situation will influence the composing process, the kinds of suggestions you read about in Chapter 2 (consider your audience and purpose, be aware of your genre, find an effective persona, etc.) are useful considerations in any kind of composing situation.

20   We also wanted to know more about the visual aids she used in her presentation. We saw in her outline that she used a sign and two pictures, but we asked her to tell us more about the visual aids, how she went about choosing them, and what she hoped to accomplish by using them.

21   *All of the visuals I used were pictures of children and girls being trafficked that I just found on Google. I used children because I wanted my peers to understand that children are trapped in the harsh world of trafficking and all the awful things they hear about human trafficking is really true—it's not made up.*

22   Alexandra's use of visuals in her speech illustrates the way oral literacies can overlap with other types of literacies, such as visual. As she presented her speech, Alexandra made use of multiple literacies, and this combination helped her create a more persuasive composition.

23   Next, we asked Alexandra to tell us about her audience, how the audience affected her choice of a topic, and how she thought they received her

speech—her perception of how her classmates and teacher received her speech. Here's what she told us:

24   *I chose human trafficking for the topic of my speech because a lot of the people being trafficked are usually around the ages of first-year college students and I thought it would move them as much as it did me. They seemed interested in the topic and listened to what I had to say.*

25 Finally, we asked Alexandra to think about changes she would make if she could go back and compose and present her speech over again. She shared:

26   *If I could go back and present my speech all over again, I think I would show a clip from the Lifetime movie that motivated me to write the speech in the first place. I think the movie clip would have had more effect than the pictures did.*

27 Alexandra realizes the important role visuals play in a presentation. The next time she presents a speech, she'll be likely to spend more time considering effective visuals.

Literacy Connections

1. Now that you've closely read Alexandra's speech on human trafficking, what do you think is the main point she is trying to make?
2. In the guidelines for the assignment, Professor Davidson states that students should "establish [their] credibility by stating [their] experience, expertise, or research on the topic." How does Alexandra fulfill this part of the assignment?
3. When asked about how she gathered information to use in her speech, Alexandra told us that she just typed her topic into her search engine and found plenty of material. Most of us have done this at one time or another when we were trying to gather information. What are the dangers of this kind of search? How do you determine which sites are reliable and appropriate?
4. There is an increasing focus on the inclusion of visuals in the college composition classroom. More and more teachers are encouraging or requiring their students to make their compositions more effective by using visuals—even in essays and research papers. What experience have you had when including visuals in your written texts? How can the inclusion of visuals make compositions more effective?
5. In her essay that opens this chapter, Professor Davidson states that "Oral literacy means understanding the audience, being aware of the range of options available for the audience and the occasion, selecting the one most fitting for the situation, and using the kind of

language that best conveys the message to the audience." How does Alexandra's speech reflect her oral literacy skills? In what ways does her speech reflect her understanding of her audience?

Oral Literacy Readings

Before You Read

In this chapter on situating oral literacies you'll be reading various kinds of texts—a speech, traditional essays, slam poetry, folktales, an oral history, and more. Take a few minutes to think about these various kinds of texts. Write for ten minutes and explore which two or three of these various texts are your favorites and why you are drawn to these genres.

The first selection included in this section is a print copy of President Barack Obama's inaugural address. While millions of individuals around the world listened to his historic speech, not nearly as many have carefully read the words he spoke on the morning of January 20, 2009. As you read his text, think about how reading the print text differs from listening to the text presented orally.

Inaugural Address

President Barack Hussein Obama
January 20, 2009

Barack Hussein Obama, born August 1, 1961, the son of a father from Kenya and a mother from Kansas, is the 44th President of the United States of America. Following is his inaugural address, which he presented on January 20, 2009, to a crowd of more than one million individuals. As you read his historic speech, think about the important role oral literacies play in our lives and in the way we perceive our world.

1   My fellow citizens: I stand here today humbled by the task before us, grateful for the trust you've bestowed, mindful of the sacrifices borne by our ancestors.

2   I thank President Bush for his service to our nation, as well as the generosity and cooperation he has shown throughout this transition.

3   Forty-four Americans have now taken the presidential oath. The words have been spoken during rising tides of prosperity and the still waters of

peace. Yet, every so often, the oath is taken amidst gathering clouds and raging storms. At these moments, America has carried on not simply because of the skill or vision of those in high office, but because we, the people, have remained faithful to the ideals of our forebearers and true to our founding documents.

4 So it has been; so it must be with this generation of Americans.

5 That we are in the midst of crisis is now well understood. Our nation is at war against a far-reaching network of violence and hatred. Our economy is badly weakened, a consequence of greed and irresponsibility on the part of some, but also our collective failure to make hard choices and prepare the nation for a new age. Homes have been lost, jobs shed, businesses shuttered. Our health care is too costly, our schools fail too many—and each day brings further evidence that the ways we use energy strengthen our adversaries and threaten our planet.

6 These are the indicators of crisis, subject to data and statistics. Less measurable, but no less profound, is a sapping of confidence across our land; a nagging fear that America's decline is inevitable, that the next generation must lower its sights.

7 Today I say to you that the challenges we face are real. They are serious and they are many. They will not be met easily or in a short span of time. But know this America: They will be met.

8 On this day, we gather because we have chosen hope over fear, unity of purpose over conflict and discord. On this day, we come to proclaim an end to the petty grievances and false promises, the recriminations and worn-out dogmas that for far too long have strangled our politics. We remain a young nation. But in the words of Scripture, the time has come to set aside childish things. The time has come to reaffirm our enduring spirit; to choose our better history; to carry forward that precious gift, that noble idea passed on from generation to generation: the God-given promise that all are equal, all are free, and all deserve a chance to pursue their full measure of happiness.

9 In reaffirming the greatness of our nation we understand that greatness is never a given. It must be earned. Our journey has never been one of short-cuts or settling for less. It has not been the path for the faint-hearted, for those that prefer leisure over work, or seek only the pleasures of riches and fame. Rather, it has been the risk-takers, the doers, the makers of things—some celebrated, but more often men and women obscure in their labor—who have carried us up the long rugged path toward prosperity and freedom.

10 For us, they packed up their few worldly possessions and traveled across oceans in search of a new life. For us, they toiled in sweatshops, and settled the West, endured the lash of the whip, and plowed the hard earth.

For us, they fought and died in places like Concord and Gettysburg, Normandy and Khe Sanh.

11   Time and again these men and women struggled and sacrificed and worked till their hands were raw so that we might live a better life. They saw America as bigger than the sum of our individual ambitions, greater than all the differences of birth or wealth or faction.

12   This is the journey we continue today. We remain the most prosperous, powerful nation on Earth. Our workers are no less productive than when this crisis began. Our minds are no less inventive, our goods and services no less needed than they were last week, or last month, or last year. Our capacity remains undiminished. But our time of standing pat, of protecting narrow interests and putting off unpleasant decisions—that time has surely passed. Starting today, we must pick ourselves up, dust ourselves off, and begin again the work of remaking America.

13   For everywhere we look, there is work to be done. The state of our economy calls for action, bold and swift. And we will act, not only to create new jobs, but to lay a new foundation for growth. We will build the roads and bridges, the electric grids and digital lines that feed our commerce and bind us together. We'll restore science to its rightful place, and wield technology's wonders to raise health care's quality and lower its cost. We will harness the sun and the winds and the soil to fuel our cars and run our factories. And we will transform our schools and colleges and universities to meet the demands of a new age. All this we can do. All this we will do.

14   Now, there are some who question the scale of our ambitions, who suggest that our system cannot tolerate too many big plans. Their memories are short, for they have forgotten what this country has already done, what free men and women can achieve when imagination is joined to common purpose, and necessity to courage. What the cynics fail to understand is that the ground has shifted beneath them, that the stale political arguments that have consumed us for so long no longer apply.

15   The question we ask today is not whether our government is too big or too small, but whether it works—whether it helps families find jobs at a decent wage, care they can afford, a retirement that is dignified. Where the answer is yes, we intend to move forward. Where the answer is no, programs will end. And those of us who manage the public's dollars will be held to account, to spend wisely, reform bad habits, and do our business in the light of day, because only then can we restore the vital trust between a people and their government.

16   Nor is the question before us whether the market is a force for good or ill. Its power to generate wealth and expand freedom is unmatched. But this crisis has reminded us that without a watchful eye, the market can spin out of control. The nation cannot prosper long when it favors only the

prosperous. The success of our economy has always depended not just on the size of our gross domestic product, but on the reach of our prosperity, on the ability to extend opportunity to every willing heart—not out of charity, but because it is the surest route to our common good.

17 As for our common defense, we reject as false the choice between our safety and our ideals. Our Founding Fathers, faced with perils that we can scarcely imagine, drafted a charter to assure the rule of law and the rights of man—a charter expanded by the blood of generations. Those ideals still light the world, and we will not give them up for expedience sake.

> **"With old friends and former foes, we'll work tirelessly to lessen the nuclear threat, and roll back the specter of a warming planet."**

18 And so, to all the other peoples and governments who are watching today, from the grandest capitals to the small village where my father was born, know that America is a friend of each nation, and every man, woman and child who seeks a future of peace and dignity. And we are ready to lead once more.

19 Recall that earlier generations faced down fascism and communism not just with missiles and tanks, but with the sturdy alliances and enduring convictions. They understood that our power alone cannot protect us, nor does it entitle us to do as we please. Instead they knew that our power grows through its prudent use; our security emanates from the justness of our cause, the force of our example, the tempering qualities of humility and restraint.

20 We are the keepers of this legacy. Guided by these principles once more we can meet those new threats that demand even greater effort, even greater cooperation and understanding between nations. We will begin to responsibly leave Iraq to its people and forge a hard-earned peace in Afghanistan. With old friends and former foes, we'll work tirelessly to lessen the nuclear threat, and roll back the specter of a warming planet.

21 We will not apologize for our way of life, nor will we waver in its defense. And for those who seek to advance their aims by inducing terror and slaughtering innocents, we say to you now that our spirit is stronger and cannot be broken—you cannot outlast us, and we will defeat you.

22 For we know that our patchwork heritage is a strength, not a weakness. We are a nation of Christians and Muslims, Jews and Hindus, and nonbelievers. We are shaped by every language and culture, drawn from every end of this Earth; and because we have tasted the bitter swill of civil war and segregation, and emerged from that dark chapter stronger and more united, we cannot help but believe that the old hatreds shall someday pass; that the lines of tribe shall soon dissolve; that as the world grows smaller, our common humanity shall reveal itself; and that America must play its role in ushering in a new era of peace.

23   To the Muslim world, we seek a new way forward, based on mutual interest and mutual respect. To those leaders around the globe who seek to sow conflict, or blame their society's ills on the West, know that your people will judge you on what you can build, not what you destroy.

24   To those who cling to power through corruption and deceit and the silencing of dissent, know that you are on the wrong side of history, but that we will extend a hand if you are willing to unclench your fist.

25   To the people of poor nations, we pledge to work alongside you to make your farms flourish and let clean waters flow; to nourish starved bodies and feed hungry minds. And to those nations like ours that enjoy relative plenty, we say we can no longer afford indifference to the suffering outside our borders, nor can we consume the world's resources without regard to effect. For the world has changed, and we must change with it.

26   As we consider the role that unfolds before us, we remember with humble gratitude those brave Americans who at this very hour patrol far-off deserts and distant mountains. They have something to tell us, just as the fallen heroes who lie in Arlington whisper through the ages.

27   We honor them not only because they are the guardians of our liberty, but because they embody the spirit of service—a willingness to find meaning in something greater than themselves.

28   And yet at this moment, a moment that will define a generation, it is precisely this spirit that must inhabit us all. For as much as government can do, and must do, it is ultimately the faith and determination of the American people upon which this nation relies. It is the kindness to take in a stranger when the levees break, the selflessness of workers who would rather cut their hours than see a friend lose their job which sees us through our darkest hours. It is the firefighter's courage to storm a stairway filled with smoke, but also a parent's willingness to nurture a child that finally decides our fate.

29   Our challenges may be new. The instruments with which we meet them may be new. But those values upon which our success depends—honesty and hard work, courage and fair play, tolerance and curiosity, loyalty and patriotism—these things are old. These things are true. They have been the quiet force of progress throughout our history.

30   What is demanded, then, is a return to these truths. What is required of us now is a new era of responsibility—a recognition on the part of every American that we have duties to ourselves, our nation and the world; duties that we do not grudgingly accept, but rather seize gladly, firm in the knowledge that there is nothing so satisfying to the spirit, so defining of our character than giving our all to a difficult task.

31   This is the price and the promise of citizenship. This is the source of our confidence—the knowledge that God calls on us to shape an uncertain destiny. This is the meaning of our liberty and our creed, why men and women and children of every race and every faith can join in celebration across this magnificent mall; and why a man whose father less than 60 years ago might not have been served in a local restaurant can now stand before you to take a most sacred oath.

32   So let us mark this day with remembrance of who we are and how far we have traveled. In the year of America's birth, in the coldest of months, a small band of patriots huddled by dying campfires on the shores of an icy river. The capital was abandoned. The enemy was advancing. The snow was stained with blood. At the moment when the outcome of our revolution was most in doubt, the father of our nation ordered these words to be read to the people:

33   "Let it be told to the future world . . . that in the depth of winter, when nothing but hope and virtue could survive . . . that the city and the country, alarmed at one common danger, came forth to meet [it]."

34   America: In the face of our common dangers, in this winter of our hardship, let us remember these timeless words. With hope and virtue, let us brave once more the icy currents, and endure what storms may come. Let it be said by our children's children that when we were tested we refused to let this journey end, that we did not turn back nor did we falter; and with eyes fixed on the horizon and God's grace upon us, we carried forth that great gift of freedom and delivered it safely to future generations.

35   Thank you. God bless you. And God bless the United States of America.

Literacy Connections

1. What three or four adjectives would you use to describe the voice that comes through loud and clear, even in the written text of President Obama's speech?

2. Make a list of several ways in which President Obama appeals to the huge group of diverse individuals that made up his audience for this inaugural address. Refer to specific passages from the text to back up your assertions.

3. What about this speech works for you? What doesn't work so well for you? Why?

4. Go to an online site such as *YouTube* and watch President Obama as he delivers his inaugural address. In what ways does the experience of watching the oral performance differ from the experience of reading the written text? In what ways is the oral performance

superior to the written text? In what ways is the written text more effective?

5. In her essay that opens this chapter, Alexis Davidson states that "the two main components of a message are content and delivery. Content is the substance of the message, the point you are trying to convey to the audience. Delivery is the way in which you convey the message." What do you think is the primary content of President Obama's speech—the point he is trying to convey to his audience? How would you describe his delivery style? Is it effective? Why or why not?

Before You Read

Before you begin reading "The Boss in Common," think about the role of music in your life. Why do you listen to music? What purpose does it play in your life? How would your life be different if there was no music in it?

The Boss in Common

Andrew Burgess

Andrew Burgess was an undergraduate in ENC 4311—Advanced Article and Essay Workshop—when he wrote this essay in which he shares what he calls his "rock-and-roll baptism" and discusses the "healing power of music." Burgess is a creative writing major at Florida State University and plans to go on to graduate school on completing his bachelor's degree.

1   Nothing before this matters. It must not anyway—I can't remember much of it. My childhood comes to me sometimes like movie clips. My memories are quick little scenes and the kid in them rarely resembles me. Nothing traumatic happened to me to make me block out my childhood, but I guess I just wasn't as observant in the '80s and early '90s as I could have been. No, my memories start with a specific moment in my sixteenth year.

2   I vaguely remember being very much interested in *Star Wars* throughout junior high. Before that, it was climbing trees and before that, riding bikes. A haze surrounds all of these interests like the blurred edges of a very old Polaroid. When I turned sixteen, though, my dad gave me his old stereo and his record collection. Now I know that this must have taken a lot of trust on his part. Now that I understand how much time and money and

energy he must have invested in collecting all these records, I wonder if I would have handed them over so easily were I in his place.

3   One afternoon, just after we moved into a new house (our second after a decade or more of apartment living), my dad came into my room and told me that the milk crates with his records in them were in the garage. He set the record player down on my bed and told me if I needed any help to let him know, but he thought I could probably figure it out. And I did, but it took a while. The archaic meshing of tangled speaker wires, twisting rats' nests into straight lines, the splicing and the sheer weight of the receiver unit, dense as it was with electronics, tubes and switches were all totally foreign to me. Before this, I had only known my walkman and the all-in-one boom boxes I had seen at my friends' houses. I hadn't known that sound could be so big as it was coming through the waist-high speakers which I wrestled into place on either side of my bookshelf.

4   I spent a half hour or so—it may as well have been an eternity—deciding which record to play first. I flipped through the huge cardboard sleeves, looking at the pictures and searching for names I knew. I finally settled on Bruce Springsteen's *Born to Run,* with its stark white cover, the photo of a little white guy with a scruffy beard and a Fender Telecaster leaning on a huge black man's shoulder. The black man looked to me like a tribal warrior from a different time and place. Only his saxophone and wide-brimmed hat set him apart in my mind from the aborigines. I didn't know it then, but the little guy was Bruce and the saxophone wielding terror (the image of the devastating white of his eyes peering out of the blackness around them will never leave me) was the "Big Man," Clarence Clemons.

5   I dropped the needle on the record, swinging the arm out over the outer edge of it. The hissing and popping which were then so strange to me have become over the last decade welcome friends. The soft piano introduction to "Thunder Road" came out of the speakers and as the harmonica came in over it, I lay down on the carpet of my room with the record's huge gatefold liner notes draped over my chest like a tent. I closed my eyes and listened to the whole first side of the record that way. There was something in Springsteen's voice that I had never heard in any of my punk rock. There was real pain and agony there. Later, I learned that *Born to Run* was Springsteen's last chance to produce a hit record before CBS dropped him from the label. At the time of its release in 1975, Springsteen didn't even have an address to which CBS could send his royalty checks. The album was the last chance effort of a desperate man. That's why, when Springsteen sings of "pulling out of here to win," and "hiding on the back streets," you can tell he knows what he's talking about. I could tell he'd been there, and for that matter, as he sang at the recording sessions for this album, he still was

there. I felt for a moment, even though I didn't know anything about Springsteen as I listened that first time, that I had something in common with this guy. I felt like maybe he knew something about me, too.

6   This was the beginning of a new life for me. I can't equate rock and roll with religion, but the feeling of being born again was so powerful as I stood up from the place where I lay on the carpet, I could almost feel the healing power of the music washing over me, and I'm surprised I've never claimed to have heard voices. The sound coming from those speakers as the E Street Band played through first one side then the other were so big and loud that I imagined the walls toppling, papers fluttering across the floor, my hair blowing in the wind of them. This was my rock and roll baptism.

> "... I could almost feel the healing power of the music washing over me, and I'm surprised I've never claimed to have heard voices."

7   At dinner the next night, my dad asked me if I had listened to any of those old records. I told him that I had been through all the Springsteen he had. He kind of grinned a half grin like he knew exactly what had happened to me. He didn't have to ask me how I liked it, and I don't remember ever discussing it further, but I could tell that in his eyes, I had become a man.

8   My dad and I never had an intimate emotional relationship. He was always distant and silent when it came to his problems (I never remember him discussing work or money or anything like that at dinner), and I always went to my mom with mine. Before rock and roll, my dad and I never really had anything to talk about. I've just realized recently that throughout my childhood, I can't remember any serious conversation I ever had with him. But as I sifted through his record collection, and as I talked to him about rock and roll, I realized that he was once a mixed up kid like me. My problems were mostly academic and social and so were his three decades before me. He had turned to rock and roll the same way I had. He told me about the way he used to sit with his guitar and try to play along with guitar solos on Springsteen's "Darkness on the Edge of Town." I tried to show off to him as I sat with my Les Paul and played the solo from "Prove It All Night" for him. (This same solo, on CD later played a major role in my first car crash. I got so lost in the music that I didn't notice the minivan stuck in the middle of an intersection.) He didn't say anything, but he smiled and that was enough.

9   As an adult, I still don't feel like I know my dad that well on an emotional level. I don't ever talk about my marriage or my money problems with him. Instead, I still go to my mom. But we've still got rock and roll. I've primarily discussed Springsteen here, but my dad and I have sat through countless hours of music together, talking and laughing and listening together. Pink Floyd, Elvis Costello, Talking Heads, Led Zeppelin,

the Beatles—this is where our bond surfaces, but it's deeper than that. Our relationship seems to have evolved over the years to not need words. A friendship without communication seems problematic, but my dad and I have this in common: the ideas that we can't express in words are always hidden between the grooves somewhere, and if you listen long enough, our language will come through the music.

Literacy Connections
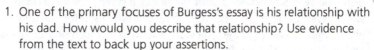

1. One of the primary focuses of Burgess's essay is his relationship with his dad. How would you describe that relationship? Use evidence from the text to back up your assertions.
2. Burgess closes his essay with the following: "A friendship without communication seems problematic, but my dad and I have this in common: the ideas that we can't express in words are always hidden between the grooves somewhere, and if you listen long enough, our language will come through the music." What do you think Burgess means when he writes "language . . . come[s] through the music"? Explore this idea.
3. Burgess states, "There was something in Springsteen's voice that I had never heard in any of my punk rock." The music in the albums his dad gave him was different, and he immediately connected with the artists, their messages, their methods, and their medium. How have your musical tastes evolved over the years? Take a few minutes to explore how and why your preferences have changed as you've grown older.
4. Andrew Burgess shares that his most important memories—the ones that are more than a recollection of some vague interests in *Star Wars* or climbing trees or riding bikes—began in his sixteenth year, and these important memories are related to music. What are your earliest musical memories? What particular song, artist, or group stands out in your mind? Take a few minutes to jot down your story.
5. Earlier in this chapter you read another work by a student—Alexandra Giang's speech "Not for Sale." What are some of the differences between the rhetorical situations the writer must consider when composing in these two genres—songs and speeches? What are some of the similarities between the two?

Before You Read

What do you know about slam poetry? Have you ever heard of the term? Have you ever participated in a slam? Share what you know (or don't know) with a small group of your classmates. See what you can learn about slam poetry from each other before you read the following selections.

Slam Poetry from HBO's Def Poetry Jam

Slam poetry, a movement that began in the late 1980s, is described by *poets.org* as "one of the most vital and energetic movements in poetry" that has "revitalized interest in poetry in performance" (www.poets. org). The Web site defines a *slam* as "simply a poetry competition in which poets perform original work alone or in teams before an audience, which serves as judge. The work is judged as much on the manner and enthusiasm of its performance as its content or style, and many slam poems are not intended to be read silently from the page."

Poets.org goes on to remind us that poetry began as part of an oral tradition. The site explains that:

> . . . movements like the Beats and the poets of Negritude were devoted to the spoken and performed aspects of their poems. This interest was reborn through the rise of poetry slams across America; while many poets in academia found fault with the movement, slam was well received among young poets and poets of diverse backgrounds as a democratizing force. This generation of spoken word poetry is often highly politicized, drawing upon racial, economic, and gender injustices as well as current events for subject matter.

And now let's take a look at some material from HBO's Def Poetry site (http://hbo.com/defpoetry/about/index.html) and see what we can learn about an ongoing, televised poetry slam:

> The audacious, uncensored late-night series Russell Simmons Presents Def Poetry returns to HBO for a sixth season Fridays at midnight. This year the seminal spoken word series presents seasoned and up-and-coming poets performing their work onstage before a live audience, interspersed with a big-ticket lineup of celebrities also trying their hand at poetry.
>
> Russell Simmons Presents Def Poetry features a spectrum of voices, from struggling urban poets who've cut their teeth in speakeasies and small clubs across the country, to the icons of the form, to celebrated actors, singers, dancers, and comedians writing and sharing poems for the first time. This season's special guests include DMX, Big Mike, Red Storm, Jill Scott, Talib Kweli, Carole King, Black Ice, Beau Sia, Poetri, Suheir Hammad, George Clinton, Lemon, Steve Coleman, and many others.
>
> Each installment of Russell Simmons Presents Def Poetry is hosted by the highly regarded hip-hop artist and actor Mos Def. The series is directed by Stan Lathan, who, along with Simmons, executive produced the long-running hit series Russell Simmons' Def Comedy Jam, which was also directed by Lathan.
>
> Recognizing the power of urban poetry on modern culture, top rap music impresario Simmons, whose Def Jam Records launched the careers of artists such as LL Cool J and Jay-Z, teamed up with HBO to create Russell Simmons

Presents Def Poetry in 2001, turning the spotlight on the freshest and most fearless voices in America today.

Previous seasons have featured performances by special guests ranging from Dave Chappelle, Common, Savion Glover, Lauryn Hill, Wyclef Jean, Alicia Keyes, Eve Ensler, John Legend, Phylicia Rashad, Smokey Robinson, Kanye West to many others.

Co-Dead Language

Saul Williams

Whereas, break-beats have been the
missing link connecting the diasporic
community to its drum-woven past.

Whereas, the quantized drum has
allowed the whirling mathematicians
to calculate the ever-changing distance
between rock and stardom.

Whereas, the velocity of spinning vinyl,
Cross-faded, spun backwards, and re-released
at the same given moment of recorded history,
yet, at a different moment in time's continuum
has allowed history to catch up with the present.

We do hereby declare reality unkempt
by the changing standards of dialogue.

Statements such as, "keep it real," especially
when punctuating or articulating modes of
ultra-violence inflicted psychologically or
physically or depicting an unchanging rule
of events, will henceforth be seen as retroactive
and not representative of the individually
determined IS.

Furthermore, as determined by the collective
consciousness of this state of being and the
lessened distance between thought patterns
and their secular manifestations, the role of
men as listening receptacles is to be increased

by a number no less than 70 percent of the
current enlisted as vocal aggressors.
MTHRFCKRs better realize, now is the time
to self-actualize. We have found evidence that
Hip-hop's standard 85 RPM when increased
by a number at least half the rate of the standard
or decreased by 3/4's of its speed may be a
determining factor in heightening consciousness.
Studies show that when a given norm is changed
in the face of the unchanging the remaining
contradictions will parallel the truth.

Equate rhyme with reason. Sun with season.
Our cyclical relationship to phenomena has
encouraged scholars to erase the centers of
periods thus symbolizing the non-linear
character of cause and effect.

Reject mediocrity. Your current frequencies
of understanding outweigh that which has
been given for you to understand. The current
standard is the equivalent of an adolescent
restricted to the diet of an infant. The rapidly
changing body would acquire dysfunctional
and deformative symptoms and could not properly
mature on a diet of applesauce and crushed pears.

Light years are interchangeable with years of living
in darkness. The role of darkness is not to be seen
as or equated with ignorance but with the unknown
and the mysteries of the unseen.

Thus, in the name of: Robeson,
God's son, Hurston, Akhenaton,
Hatshepsut, Blackfoot, Helen,
Lennon, Kahlo, Kali, The Three
Marias, Tara, Lilith, Lourde,
Whitman, Baldwin, Ginsberg,
Kaufman, Lumumba, Gandhi,
Gibran, Shabazz, Shabazz,
Siddhartha, Medusa, Guevara,
Gurdjieff, Rand, Wright, Banneker,

Tubman, Hamer, Holiday, Davis,
Coltrane, Morrison, Joplin, Du Bois,
Clarke, Shakespeare, Rachmaninoff,
Ellington, Carter, Gaye, Hathaway,
Hendrix, Kuti, Dickerson, Ripperton,
Mary, Isis, Theresa, Plath, Rumi,
Fellini, Michaux, Nostradamus,
Neferttiti, La Rock, Shiva, Ganesha,
Yemaja, Oshun, Obatala, Ogun,
Kennedy, King, four little girls,
Hiroshima, Nagasaki, Keller, Biko,
Perón, Marley, Shakur, Those who
burned. Those still aflame. And the
countless un-named.

We claim the present as the pre-sent as the
hereafter. We are unraveling our navels so
that we may ingest the sun. We are not afraid
of the darkness. We trust that the moon shall
guide us. We are determining the future at this
very moment. We now know that the heart is
the philosopher's stone.

Our music is our alchemy. We stand as the
manifested equivalent of three buckets of water
and a handful of minerals, thus, realizing that
those very buckets turned upside down supply
the percussive factor of forever. If you must
count to keep the beat then count. Find your
mantra and awaken your subconscious. Carve
your circles counter-clockwise. Use your cipher
to decipher coded language, man-made laws. Climb
waterfalls and trees. Commune with nature snakes
and bees.

Let your children name themselves and claim
themselves as the new day for today we are
determined to be the channelers of these
changing frequencies into songs, paintings,
writings, dance, drama, photography, carpentry,
crafts, love, and love.

We enlist every instrument: acoustic, electronic,
every so-called race, gender, sexual preference
every per-son as beings of sound to acknowledge
their responsibility to uplift the consciousness
of the entire f*cking world!

Any utterance un-aimed will be disclaimed,
will be maimed. Two rappers slain!

From Beau Sia, "An Open Letter to the Entertainment Industry"

Let me be honest.
If there's anyone in the entertainment industry watching me perform,
I want you to keep in mind,
that regardless how you feel about the content or performance of my work,
that if you're casting any films,
and you need a Korean grocery store owner,
a computer expert,
or the random thug of the Aguza gang,
then I'm your man.
If you need some martial arts-like stuff,
or 1-800 collect, the Gap, or Rolaids,
I can be believable.
If you need a Chinese Jay-Z,
A Japanese Eminem, yo,
Or a Vietnamese N Sync,
please consider me, because I am all those things and more.
I come from the house that Stepin Fetchit built,
and I'll wield broken English my way to sidekick status if that's what's
    expected of me.
Make an Asian *Different Strokes*, I'll walk around on my knees going,
"Ooohh, what you talk about a Willis."
Cause it's been twenty three months and fourteen days since my art has done
    anything for me,
and I would be noble and toil on, I swear I would,
live for the art and the art alone and all that crap a*s,
but college loans are monthly up my a*s,
my salmon teriyaki habit is getting way out of control,
and I want some mother f*cking cable.

So you can understand where I'm coming from,
when our culture rejoices in its pretty, packaged boy group talentless jerks,
sent from Florida to make me puke.
But I'm not preaching.
I cannot stress how ready I am to sell out . . . .
If you need a voiceover artist,
Just tell me where you want the "Hellos" to go.
And I will be there.
Because I'm all that and more.
I'm a pop culture whore.
I'm a co-sponsored world tour.
And I'm an appropriated culture at my core.
I've been noticed, acclaimed, and funny,
And now all I want is a beach front house to paint in,
and a Range Rover to listen to my music in,
cause struggling f*cking sucks hard
After the ninth baggage of Ramen noodle soup,
I'm Beau Sia
Give me a chance and I'll change the world.

Literacy Connections

1. Now that you've read (and re-read) the two selections from *Def Poetry Jam*, what kinds of connections can you make between the messages Saul Williams and Beau Sia are trying to convey to their audiences?

2. Take a few minutes to watch the two performances on *YouTube*. Which performance do you think is most effective? Why? What factors might make one of the performances more effective than the other?

3. Compare your reaction to the reading of the print text of each poem with your reaction to the live performances. What advantages, if any, did you find to reading the print texts as compared to watching the live performances? What advantages, if any, did you find to watching the live performances as compared to reading the print texts?

4. The language used in these two poems would be considered by many to be raw and even offensive. What is your opinion of the language? Is it appropriate for the intended audience? Does the use of raw language help the composers more effectively communicate their ideas to their audience? Why or why not?

5. Compare the messages Saul Williams and Beau Sia are communicating to their audiences with the message being conveyed in President Obama's inaugural address. What similarities do you see? What differences?

Before You Read

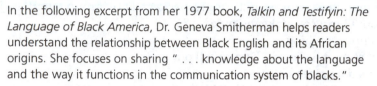

In the following excerpt from her 1977 book, *Talkin and Testifyin: The Language of Black America*, Dr. Geneva Smitherman helps readers understand the relationship between Black English and its African origins. She focuses on sharing " . . . knowledge about the language and the way it functions in the communication system of blacks."

Take a few minutes to think about your experiences with what Smitherman calls "Black English." Do you speak it? Do some of your friends? If you don't speak it but your friends do, do they use this version of English around you? If they do, can you easily understand what they're saying? If they don't use Black English around you, why do you suppose they don't?

Excerpt from *Talkin and Testifyin: The Language of Black America*

Geneva Smitherman

On her Web site, Dr. Geneva Smitherman is described as "University Distinguished Professor, Director of the African American Language and Literacy Program, Michigan State University (www.msu.edu/~smither4/)." Her bio at that same site states:

> A linguist and educational activist, she has been at the forefront of the struggle for language rights for over 25 years. She has forged a writing style which combines academic discourse and African American Language that has become widely celebrated for efficacy in making the medium the message. (About Me)

Dr. Smitherman's 1977 publication had quite an impact across the United States and beyond. Not only did it gain almost instant attention in academic circles, its publication drew national media attention. In the "Afterword" to the book, Dr. Smitherman states:

> . . . within a week after the book was put on sale, I found myself, to my astonishment, discussing the language of Black America on NBC's Today program! This turned out to be only the first of a succession of national and local media appearances and interviews . . . From that point on, I became "the author." (243)

Wayne State University Press offers the following succinct review of her 1977 publication, *Talkin and Testifyin: The Language of Black America*:

> In her book, Geneva Smitherman makes a substantial contribution to an understanding of Black English by setting it in the larger context of Black

culture and lifestyle. In addition to defining Black English by its distinctive structure and special lexicon, Smitherman argues that the Black dialect is set apart from traditional English by a rhetorical style which reflects its African origins. Smitherman also tackles the issue of Black and White attitudes toward Black English, particularly as they affect educational policy. Documenting her insights with quotes from notable Black historical, literary and popular figures, Smitherman makes clear that Black English is as legitimate a form of speech as British, American, or Australian English. (http://wsupress.wayne.edu/africana/afrlanguage/smithermantt.htm)

And now, read an excerpt from Chapter 1, "From Africa to the New World and into the Space Age: Introduction and History of Black English Structure."

1   "WHAT IT IS! What it is!"

2   "That cat name Shaft is a bad mother—" "Hush yo mouf!"

3   "Can't nobody never do nothin in Mr. Smith class."

4   "Least my momma don't buy her furniture from the Good Will!"

5   "I come here today to testify what the Lord done did for me."

6   "It bees dat way sometime."

7   What it is! What is it? It is the voice of Black America, variously labeled Black English, Black Dialect, Black Idiom, or recently, Ebonics. Black writer Claude Brown, author of *Manchild in the Promised Land,* called it the "language of soul." White writer Norman Mailer named it the "language of hip." Some folk, like black poet Nikki Giovanni, refer to it as just plain "black talk."

8   Before about 1959 (when the first study was done to change black speech patterns), Black English had been primarily the interest of university academics, particularly the historical linguists and cultural anthropologists. In recent years, though, the issue has become a very hot controversy, and there have been articles on Black Dialect in the national press as well as in the educational research literature. We have had pronouncements on black speech from the NAACP and the Black Panthers, from highly publicized scholars of the Arthur Jensen–William Shockley bent, from executives of national corporations such as Greyhound, and from housewives and community folk. I mean, really, it seem like everybody and they momma done had something to say on the subject!

9   Now, concern over the speech of blacks and educational programs to bring about dialect change has been generated by two major forces. The first major force was the social change movements (or upheavals—depending on where you comin from) of the sixties, spearheaded by the 1954 Supreme Court school desegregation decision, followed by the 1955 refusal of black Rosa Parks to move to the back of the bus, and the emergence of Martin Luther King, Jr., and the civil rights thrust, followed by

black power and the black cultural consciousness movement. The second major force was embodied in White America's attempt to deal with this newly released black energy by the implementation of poverty programs, educational and linguistic remediation projects, sociolinguistic research programs, and various other up-from-the-ghetto and "Great Society" efforts. As well all know, these two forces have not acted in concert. While blacks were shouting "I'm black and I'm proud," Anglos were admonishing them to "be like us" and enter the mainstream. While you had black orators, creative artists, and yes, even scholars rappin in the Black Thang, educators (some of them black, to be sure) were preaching the Gospel that Black English speakers must learn to talk like White English speakers in order to "make it."

10   Much that you hear nowadays about Black Dialect tends to be general and to focus on global concerns over social policy and political matters, with insufficient attention to elements of the language itself and the historical background and sociocultural development of that language (aside from the special academics mentioned earlier). That has been unfortunate because we need much more knowledge about the language and the way it functions in the communication system of blacks. Therefore, let us get off this global trip and get down to the nitty-gritty of answering the questions, just what is Black English, where did it come from and what are the implications for black-white interaction and teaching black children?

11   In a nutshell: Black Dialect is an Africanized form of English reflecting Black America's linguistic-cultural African heritage and the conditions of servitude, oppression and life in America. Black Language is Euro-American speech with an Afro-American meaning, nuance, tone, and gesture. The Black Idiom is used by 80 to 90 percent of American blacks, at least some of the time. It has allowed blacks to create a culture of survival in an alien land, and as a by-product has served to enrich the language of all Americans.

12   Think of black speech as having two dimensions: language and style. Though we will separate the two for purposes of analysis, they are often overlapping. This is an important point, frequently overlooked in discussions of Black English. Consider two examples. Nina Simone sing: "It bees dat way sometime." Here the language aspect is the use of the verb *be* to indicate a recurring event or habitual condition, rather than a one-time-only occurrence. But the total expression—"It bees dat way" suggests a point of view, a way of looking at life, and a method of adapting to life's realities. To live by the philosophy of "It bees dat way sometimes" is to come to grips with the changes that life bees puttin us through, and to accept the changes and bad times as a constant, ever-present reality.

13   Reverend Jesse Jackson preach: "Africa would if Africa could. America could if America would. But Africa cain't and America ain't." Now here Reverend Jesse is using the language of Black Dialect when he says "ain't" and when he pronounces *can't* as "cain't." But the total expression, using black rhythmic speech, is the more powerful because the Reb has plugged into the style of Black Dialect. The statement thus depends for full communication on what black poet Eugene Redmond calls "songified" pattern and on an Afro-American cultural belief set. That belief holds that White America has always failed blacks and will continue to do so; and that going back to Africa or getting any help from African countries is neither feasible nor realistic because newly emerging African nations must grapple first with problems of independence (economic and otherwise) inherited from centuries of European colonization.

"Black English, then, is a language mixture, adapted to the conditions of slavery and discrimination . . ."

14   These two very eloquent examples of Black English illustrate that the beauty and power of the idiom lies in its succinctness: saying the same thing in standard written English has taken more than ten times as many words. Black English, then, is a language mixture, adapted to the conditions of slavery and discrimination, a combination of language and style interwoven with and inextricable from Afro-American culture.

15   Where did this black language and style come from? To answer this question, we have to begin at least as far back as 1619 when a Dutch vessel landed in Jamestown with a cargo of twenty Africans. The arrival of this slaveship marked the beginning of slavery in Colonial America. What kind of language did these and immediately succeeding generations of slaves speak? Was it Ibo, Yoruba, Hausa, some other West African language, Pidgin English? We know that these "new Negroes" (as they were often described in Colonial America) did not jump fresh off the boat doing the Bump and speaking White English! Yet we don't have any tape or phono recordings, nor any other actual direct speech samples of early Black American English. Thus we have to rely on reconstructions of black talk based on indirect evidence, such as representations of Black Dialect in White and Black American literature, written reproductions of the dialect in journals, letters, and diaries by whites, and generalized commentary about slave speech, usually also from whites. Another important source of evidence is based on analogies of Black American speech characteristics with those of other English-based pidgins and creoles found in the Caribbean and in parts of Africa. Language systems such as Jamaican Creole or Nigerian Pidgin English are still in active use today and provide a kind of linguistic mirror image of Black American (Pidgin and Creole) English in its early stages of development.

16   What this image suggests is as follows. African slaves in America initially developed a pidgin, a language of transaction, that was used in communication between themselves and whites. Over the years, the pidgin gradually became widespread among slaves and evolved into a creole. Developed without benefit of any formal instruction (not even a language lab!) this lingo involved the substitution of English for West African words, but within the same basic structure and idiom that characterized West African language patterns. For example, West African languages allow for the construction of sentences without a form of the verb *to be*. Thus we get a typical African-English Pidgin sentence such as "He tell me he God," used by Tituba, a slave from the island of Barbados in the British West Indies, and recorded by Justice Hathorne at the Salem witch trial in 1692. In Tituba's *he God* statement, the words are English, but the grammar or structure is West African. Such sentence patterns, without any form of the verb *be*, can frequently be heard in virtually any modern-day black community.

17   Now, as anyone learning a foreign tongue knows, the vocabulary of the new language is fairly easy to master; to some extent, sounds are also. But syntactical structure and idiomatic rules require considerable time and practice to master. Moreover, the one item of a language that remains relatively rigid and fixed over time is its structure. The formation of this Black American English Pidgin demonstrates, then, simply what any learner of a new language does. They* attempt to fit the words and sounds of the new language into the basic idiomatic mold and structure of their native tongue. For example, when I used to teach English to foreign students at the university, I once had a German student render Patrick Henry's famous motto as "Give me the liberty or the death." He was generalizing from the German rule which dictates that definite articles must accompany nouns. Similarly, when I used to teach high school Latin, I'd get native English speakers (whites) who would insist on using the apostrophe rather than the proper case ending to indicate possession, producing, for instance, *agricola's filia* (or sometimes even worse, *agricolae's filia*) for *the farmer's daughter*. And then there is the typical error of the English speaker learning French who forms the compound *paille-chapeau* on the model of *straw hat*.

18   Below are a few of the West African language rules that were grafted onto early Black English, and which still operate in Black English today.

---

*In traditional usage, this sentence would have begun with the masculine pronoun "he," since it refers to "any learner," which is singular. However, due to the public's increased awareness of sexist uses of the English language, plural pronouns have now become acceptable substitutes for the masculine singular. I will continue to follow this procedure throughout, along with using "his or her." For an excellent set of guidelines for avoiding sexist language use, see "Guideline for Nonsexist Use of Language in NCTE Publications," National Council of Teachers of English.

GRAMMAR AND STRUCTURE RULE

IN WEST AFRICAN LANGUAGES	BLACK ENGLISH
Repetition of noun subject with pronoun	My father, he work there.
Question patterns without *do*	What is come to?
Same form of noun for singular and plural	one boy; five boy
No tense indicated in verb; emphasis on manner or character of action	I know it good when he ask me
Same verb form for all subjects	I know; you know; he know; we know; they know

SOUND RULE IN

WEST AFRICAN LANGUAGES	BLACK ENGLISH
No consonant pairs	*jus* (for *just*); *men* (for *mend*)
Few long vowels or two-part vowels (diphthongs)	*rat* or *raht* (for *right*); *tahm* (for *time*)
No /r/ sound	*mow* (for *more*)
No /th/ sound	Black English speaker substitutes /d/ or /f/ for /th/; thus *souf* (for *south*) and *dis* (for *this*)

19   The slave's application of his or her intuitive knowledge of West African rules to English helped bridge the communications gap between slave and master. However, the slaves also had the problem of communicating with each other. It was the practice of slavers to mix up Africans from different tribes, so in any slave community there would be various tribal languages such as Ibo, Yoruba, Hausa. Even though these African language systems shared general structure commonalities, still they differed in vocabulary. Thus the same English-African language mixture that was used between slave and master had also to be used between slave and slave. All this notwithstanding, it is only logical to assume that the newly arrived Africans were, for a time at least, bilingual, having command of both their native African tongue and the English pidgin as well. However, there was no opportunity to speak and thus reinforce their native language, and as new generations of slaves were born in the New World, the native African speech was heard and used less and less, and the English pidgin and creole varieties more and more. Needless to say, didn't nobody sit down and decide, consciously and deliberately, that this was the way it was gon be—languages, pidgins, creoles, dialects was all like Topsy: they jes grew.

20   Unfortunately, we have little empirical record of this growth in what we may call its incubation period, that is, for the period from the arrival of the first slaves in 1619 up until the Revolutionary War in 1776. In point of fact, not until 1771 do we get an actual recorded sample of Black American speech *from a black*. (Slightly before this time, there are a few recorded instances of *whites* trying to speak "Negro" in addressing both slaves and Indians.) In the comedy *Trial of Atticus Before Justice Beau, for a Rape,* written in 1771, a Massachusetts Negro named Caesar is given a bit part in the play—two short lines—in which he says:

21   *Yesa, Master, he tell me that Atticus he went to bus [kiss] 'em one day, and a shilde [child] cry, and so he let 'em alone . . . Cause, Master, I bus him myself.*

22   Though scant, this speech sample is striking for its parallel to modern-day black speech forms. For example, note the lack of *-s* on the verb in *he tell* and the repetition of the subject in *Atticus he*. Contemporary Black English examples are found in sentences like "The teacher, he say I can't go" and "My brother, he know how to fix it."

. . .

23   It is true that a number of early Black American English forms have survived until the present day, but it is also true that the distance between contemporary Black and White American English is not as great as it once was. And certainly it is not as great as the distance between, say, contemporary Jamaican Creole English and the English of White American and Britain. How have time and circumstance affected the African element in Black American English? The answer to this question lies in the impact of mainstream American language and culture on Black America, and in the sheer fact of the smaller ratio of blacks to whites in this country (as compared to overwhelmingly huge black populations in the Caribbean and in Africa). With such close linguistic-cultural contact, the influence of the majority culture and language on its minorities is powerful indeed, and there is great pressure on the minorities to assimilate and adopt the culture and language of the majority.

24   In the early period of American history, the African experience was very immediate and real to the slaves and many yearned to escape back to Africa. As time progressed, though, the African slave became rather firmly entrenched in the New World, and hopes of returning to the motherland began to seem more like unattainable fantasies. Having thus resigned themselves to a future in the New World, many slaves began to take on what Langston Hughes has termed the "ways of white folks"—their religion, culture, customs, and, of course, language. At the same time, though, there were strong resistance movements against enslavement and the oppressive ways of white folks. Thus, from the very beginning, we have the "push-pull" syndrome in Black America, that is, *pushing* toward White American culture while simultaneously *pulling* away from it. (W. E. B.

DuBois used the term "double consciousness" to refer to this ambivalence among blacks.) A striking example of the phenomenon is the case of the ex-slave Absalom Jones, founder of one of the first separate black church movements within white Protestant denominations. Jones took on the white man's religion, and proceeded to practice it. (The "push.") Yet when he attempted to pray in a white church in Philadelphia in 1787, an usher pulled him from his knees and ousted him from the church. Thereupon, Jones, along with another ex-slave, Richard Allen, established the African Methodist Episcopal Church. (The "pull.")

25   The "push-pull" momentum is evidenced in the historical development of Black English in the push toward Americanization of Black English counter-balanced by the pull of retaining its Africanization. **"Talkin proper (trying to sound white) just ain considered cool."** We may use the term "de-creolization" to refer to the push toward Americanizing of the language. As slaves became more American and less African, the Black English Creole also became less Africanized. It began to be leveled out in the direction of White English and to lose its distinctive African structural features—that is, the Black English Creole became de-creolized. This process was undoubtedly quite intense and extensive during the Abolitionist period and certainly following Emancipation. It was a primary tactic of Abolitionists (and, traditionally, all fighters for the black cause) to prove blacks equal to whites and therefore worthy of freedom and equality. How could blacks claim American equality if they were not speaking American lingo? Ay, but here we come to the rub or the pull. For blacks have never really been viewed or treated as equals, thus their rejection of White American culture and English—and hence today the process of de-creolization remains unfinished (not to mention various undercurrent and sporadic efforts at re-creolization, such as that among writers, artists, and black intellectuals of the 1960s, who deliberately wrote and rapped in the Black Idiom and sought to preserve its distinctiveness in the literature of the period).

26   The dynamics of push-pull can help to illuminate the complex sociolinguistic situation that continues to exist in Black America. That is, while some blacks speak very Black English, there are others who speak very White English, and still others who are competent in both linguistic systems. Historically, black speech has been demanded of those who wish to retain close affinities with the black community, and intrusions of White English are likely to be frowned upon and any black users thereof promptly ostracized by the group. Talkin proper (trying to sound white) just ain considered cool. On the other hand, White America has insisted upon White English as the price of admission into its economic and social mainstream. Moreover, there is a psychological factor operating here: people tend to feel more comfortable when they can relax and rap within the linguistic framework that has

been the dialect of their nurture, childhood, identity, and style. Hence, even when there is no compelling social pressure to use Black English, there may be an inner compulsion to "talk black."

27   Let us return to history for a minute to gain a broader understanding of these dynamics. Slaves continued to be imported into America at least up to 1808 when the African slave trade was outlawed by federal legislation. In a sense, we can extend the date even further since the Slave Trade Act was not rigidly enforced. (As late as 1858, just three years before the Civil War, over 400 slaves were brought direct from Africa to Georgia.) This constant influx of slaves made the black community one where there were always numbers of slaves who could speak no English at all. Some idea of the linguistic situation in Black America can be gleaned from newspaper advertisements about runaway slaves. These ads generally cited the slave's degree of competence in English as a method of identification. Judging from the advertisements, there were, linguistically speaking, three groups of African slaves in Colonial times.

28   The recent arrivals ("new" Negroes) knew practically no English at all. An ad in the *New York Evening Post* in 1774 read: "Ran away . . . a new Negro Fellow named Prince, he can't scarce speak a Word of English."

29   Then there were slaves who were not born in the U.S. but had been here some time and were still in the process of learning English; some of these were referred to as speakers of either "bad" English or only "tolerable" English. In 1760 the *North-Carolina Gazette* ran this ad: "Ran away from the Subscriber, living near Salisbury, North Carolina . . . a negro fellow named JACK, African born . . . came from Pennsylvania about two years since . . . He is about 30 years of age, and about 5 feet high, speaks bad English."

30   Those slaves who had successfully mastered English, most of whom, according to the ads, had been born and brought up in America, were referred to as speakers of "good" or "exceptional" English. In 1734 this ad appeared in the Philadelphia *American Weekly Mercury:* "Run away . . . a Negro Man named *Jo Cuffy*, about 20 Years of age . . .; he's *Pennsylvania* born and speaks good *English.*"

31   Recall that not all blacks in early America were slaves; many either were freed by their masters or bought themselves out of servitude. An important mark of the free person of color, and thus a survival necessity for runaway slaves, was linguistic competence in White English. Moreover, early black writers such as Phillis Wheatley, Jupiter Hammon, Frederick Douglass, and others wrote in the current White English dialect of their respective times. Clearly, from these very early years, there seemed to be one variety of English prevalent among unlettered blacks and those still bound to the plantation way of life, and another variety, quite like that of whites, used and acquired by those few blacks who were literate and free, as well as by those

who were more closely associated with Ole Massa. Furthermore, it is highly probable that the black speakers of White English, because of proximity and necessity, commanded the Black English Creole as well. In Beverly Tucker's 1836 novel, *The Partisan Leader*, this white Southerner distinguished two types of slave speech: field and house. Tucker asserted that the dialect of the house slave was highly similar to that of Ole Massa. Moreover, in the novel, the house slave Tom switches from the dialect acquired from his master to field speech to mislead Yankee invaders.

32   In short, there was a social pattern in early Black America where status—and even survival as a freeman—depended to a great extent on competence in White English (the "push"). Yet, then as now, the linguistic situation was complicated by other forces—the oppression and slavery associated with White English speakers; and the simple fact that there were more black speakers of Black English than black speakers of White English. Hence, both circumstance and psychology would propel blacks toward Black English (the "pull") and require that any black speaker of White English be fluent in Black English as well ("push" and "pull").

33   Our look at the history of Black English would be incomplete without attention to the special case of Gullah Creole. This dialect, also known as Geechee speech, is spoken by rural and urban blacks who live in the areas along the Atlantic coastal region of South Carolina and Georgia. While some Geechees inhabit the Sea Islands along the coast, many also live around Charleston and Beaufort. Most of the ancestors of these blacks were brought direct from Nigeria, Liberia, Gambia, Sierra Leone, and other places in West Africa were Ibo, Yoruba, Mandingo, Wolof, and other West African languages were and still are spoken. Today, Gullah people form a special Black American community because they have retained considerable African language and cultural patterns. Even the name Gullah and Geechee are African in origin—they refer to languages and tribes in Liberia. For decades, these people have lived in physical and cultural isolation from both mainstream Black and White America, and they bear living witness to the language and way of life that other American blacks have long since lost. (However, the African purity of the Geechee community has recently been threatened by the advent of American tourism attempting to capitalize on the "exotic, Old World charm" of the folk. Hotels, night spots, and other modern-day conveniences and tourist attractions are being constructed on the Sea Islands, thereby uprooting large numbers of blacks and disrupting their traditional African way of life.)

34   Despite a twentieth-century white writer's reference to Gullah speech as a "slovenly" approximation of English, issuing forth from "clumsy, jungle tongues and thick lips," anybody knowledgeable about African-English language mixtures can readily discern the systematic African element in

Gullah Creole. In black linguist Lorenzo Turner's fifteen-year study of this dialect, he found not only fundamental African survivals in sound and syntax, but nearly 6,000 West African words used in personal names and nicknames, in songs and stories, as well as in everyday conversation. It is important for our understanding of Black English to recognize that black speech outside of Geechee areas was undoubtedly once highly similar to Gullah and is now simply at a later stage in the de-creolization process. For example, both Gullah and non-Gullah blacks still use the West African pattern of introducing the subject and repeating it with a personal pronoun. Thus, the Gullah speaker says, " De man an his wife hang to de tree, they lik to pieces." (The man and his wife hanging to the tree, they were licked to pieces.) The non-Gullah speaker handles the subject in the same way: "Yesterday, the whole family, they move to the West Side." On the other hand, only Gullah blacks still use the West African pattern of placing the adjective after the noun: "day clean broad." Other speakers of Black English follow the same pattern as White English speakers: "broad daylight."

35   We can say, then, that contemporary Black English looks back to an African linguistic tradition which was modified on American soil. While historical records and documents reveal a good deal about the development and change of this Africanized English, there is much that the records don't tell us. As a former slave said, "Everything I tells you am the truth, but they's plenty I can't tell you."

Literacy Connections

1. How does Dr. Geneva Smitherman define "Black Dialect"? How does she define "Black Language"?
2. According to Dr. Smitherman, what are the two dimensions of black speech? Give an example of a phrase that makes use of each of these dimensions, and explain how each is used.
3. Dr. Smitherman discusses the "push-pull" syndrome in Black America. What does she mean when she uses this term?
4. Dr. Smitherman explains that when a person is trying to learn a new language, "they attempt to fit the words and sounds of the new language into the basic idiomatic mold and structure of their native tongue." Reflect on your experiences learning a new language, and give an example of a time when you tried to make the new language fit into the structure of your native language.
5. Near the end of Chapter 1, Dr. Smitherman makes the statement, ". . . people tend to feel more comfortable when they can relax and rap within the linguistic framework that has been the dialect of their nurture, childhood, identity, and style." How is the truth of her assertion exemplified in the slam poetry performances included earlier in this chapter on situating oral literacies?

Before You Read

In the following selections by Zora Neale Hurston, you'll learn about her arrival in Eatonville, Florida, where she went to collect folktales in the early 1930s, and you'll have the opportunity to enjoy two of the folktales that she records in *Mules and Men*: "Why We Have Gophers" and "Eulalia—Ritual to Get a Man." As you read and enjoy these selections, think about the role of folktales in our lives. What is their purpose? Why does virtually every culture have its own set of folktales?

Excerpts from *Mules and Men*

Zora Neale Hurston

Zora Neale Hurston, 1891–1960, a highly regarded American folklorist, is best known for her 1937 novel, *Their Eyes Were Watching God*. Hurston was born in Notasulga, Alabama, but moved to the all-African American community Eatonville, Florida, at the age of three and grew up there.

Hurston was especially interested in analyzing and affirming the oral literacy traditions of African Americans. Her works include *Jonah's Gourd Vine* (1934), *Mules and Men* (1935), *Their Eyes Were Watching God (1937)*, *Tell My Horse (1938),* and *Dust Tracks on a Road: An Autobiography (1942).*

From Part I—Chapter 1 Folk Tales

1   As I crossed the Maitland-Eatonville township line I could see a group on the store porch. I was delighted. The town had not changed. Same love of talk and song. So I drove on down there before I stopped. Yes, there was George Thomas, Calvin Daniels, Jack and Charlie Jones, Gene Brazzle, B. Moseley and "Seaboard." Deep in a game of Florida-flip. All of those who were not actually playing were giving advice—"bet straightening" they call it.

2   "Hello, boys," I hailed them as I went into neutral.

3   They looked up from the game and for a moment it looked as if they had forgotten me. Then B. Mosely said, "Well, if it ain't Zora Hurston!" Then everybody crowded around the car to help greet me.

4   "You gointer stay awhile, Zora?"

5   "Yep. Several months."

6   "Where you gointer stay, Zora?"

7   "With Mett and Ellis, I reckon."

8   "Mett" was Mrs. Armetta Jones, an intimate friend of mine since childhood and Ellis was her husband. Their house stands under the huge camphor tree on the front street.

9   "Hello, heart-string," Mayor Hiram Lester yelled as he hurried up the street. "We heard all about you up North. You back home for good, I hope."

10   "Nope, Ah come to collect some old stories and tales and Ah know y'all know a plenty of 'em and that's why Ah headed straight for home."

11   "What you mean, Zora, them big old lies we tell when we're jus' sittin' around here on the store porch doin' nothin'?" asked B. Moseley.

12   "Yeah, those same ones about Old Massa, and colored folks in heaven, and—oh, y'all know the kind I mean."

13   "Aw shucks," exclaimed George Thomas doubtfully. "Zora, don't you come here and tell de biggest lie first thing. Who you reckon want to read all them old-time tales about Brer Rabbit and Brer Bear?"

14   "Plenty of people, George. They are a lot more valuable than you might think. We want to set them down before it's too late."

15   "Too late for what?"

16   "Before everybody forgets all of 'em.". . .

And set them down is precisely what Zora Neale Hurston did. Following is a sampling of two of the stories included in *Mules and Men*.

"Why We Have Gophers"

18   God was sittin' down by de sea makin' sea fishes. He made de whale and throwed dat in and it swum off. He made a shark and throwed it in and then he made mullets and shad-fish and cats and trouts and they all swum on off.

19   De Devil was standin' behind him lookin' over his shoulder.

20   Way after while, God made a turtle and throwed it in de water and it swum on off. Devil says, "Ah kin make one of those things."

21   God said, "No, you can't neither."

22   Devil told him, "Aw, Ah kin so make one of those things. 'Tain't nothing to make nohow. Who couldn't do dat? Ah jus' can't blow de breath of life into it, but Ah sho kin make a turtle."

23   God said: "Devil, Ah know you can't make none, but if you think you kin make one go 'head and make it and Ah'll blow de breath of life into it for you."

24   You see, God was sittin' down by de sea, makin' de fish outa sea-mud. But de Devil went on up de hill so God couldn't watch him workin', and made his outa high land dirt. God waited nearly all day befo' de Devil come back wid his turtle.

25   As soon as God seen it, He said, "Devil, dat ain't no turtle you done made."

26   Devil flew hot right off. "Dat ain't no turtle? Who say dat ain't no turtle? Sho it's a turtle."

27   God shook his head, says, "Dat sho *ain't* no turtle, but Ah'll blow de breath of life into it like Ah promised."

28   Devil stood Him down dat dat was a turtle.

29   So God blowed de breath of life into what de Devil had done made, and throwed him into de water. He swum out. God throwed him in again. He come on out. Throwed him in de third time and he come out de third time.

30   God says: "See, Ah told you dat wasn't no turtle."

31   "Yes, suh dat *is* a turtle."

32   "Devil, don't you know dat all turtles loves de water? Don't you see whut you done made won't stay in there?"

33   Devil said, "Ah don't keer, dat's a turtle, Ah keep a tellin' you."

34   God disputed him down dat it wasn't no turtle. Devil looked it over and scratched his head. Then he says, "Well, anyhow it will go for one." And that's why we have gophers!

"Eulalia—Ritual to Get a Man"

35 So I went to study with Eulalia, who specialized in Man-and-woman cases. Everyday somebody came to get Eulalia to tie them up with some man or woman or to loose them from love.

36   Eulalia was average sized with very dark skin and bushy eyebrows. Her house was squatting among the palmettos and the mossy scrub oaks. Nothing pretty in the house nor outside. No paint and no flowers. So one day a woman came to get tied to a man.

37   "Who is dis man?" Eulalia wanted to know.

38   "Jerry Moore," the woman told her. "He wants me and Ah know it, but dat 'oman he got she got roots buried and he can't git shet of her—do we would of done been married."

39   Eulalia sat still and thought awile. Then she said, "Course Ah'm uh Christian woman and don't believe in partin' no husband and wife but since she done worked roots on him, to hold him where he don't want to be, it tain't no sin for me to loose him. Where they live at?"

40   "Down Young's Quarters. De third house from dis end."

41   "Do she ever go off from home and stays a good while durin' de time he ain't there neither?"

42   "Yas Ma'am! She all de time way from dat house—off fan-footin' whilst he workin' lak a dog! It's a shame!"

43   "Well you lemme know de next time she's off and Ah'll fix everything like you want it. Put that money back in yo' purse, Ah don't want a thing till de work is done."

44   Two or three days later her client was back with the news that the over-plus wife was gone fishing. Eulalia sent her away and put on her shoes.

45   "Git dat salt-bowl and a lemon," she said to me. "Now write Jerry's name and his wife's nine times on a piece of paper and cut a little hole in the stem end of that lemon and pour some of that gun-powder in de hole and roll that paper tight and shove it inside the lemon. Wrap de lemon and de bowl of salt up and less go."

46   In Jerry Moore's yard, Eulalia looked all around and looked up at the sun a great deal, then pointed out a spot.

47   "Dig a little hole right here and bury dat lemon. It's got to be buried with the bloom-end down and it's got to be where de settin' sun will shine on it."

48   So I buried the lemon and Eulalia walked around to the kitchen door. By the time I had the lemon buried the door was open and we went inside. She looked all about and found some red pepper.

49   "Lift dat stove-lid for me," she ordered, and I did. She threw some of the pepper into the stove and we went on into the other room which was the bedroom and living-room all in one. Then Eulalia took the bowl and went from corner to corner "salting" the room. She'd toss a sprinkling into a corner and say, "Just fuss and fuss till you part and go away." Under the bed was sprinkled also. It was all over in a minute or two. Then we went out and shut the kitchen door and hurried away. And Saturday night Eulalia got her pay and the next day she set the ceremony to bring about the marriage.

Literacy Connections

1. According to Hurston's folktale, why do we have gophers? What explanation does the folktale offer?

2. In the second folktale, "Eulalia—Ritual to Get a Man," the male being pursued, Jerry Morre, already has a wife. Even so, Eulalia is willing to "loose him" from his wife. What explanation does Hurston offer for this? Why is this "Christian woman" who "don't believe in partin' no husband and wife" willing to help, and how does she bring about the parting?

3. Think about the folktales Hurston shares and the folktales you grew up hearing. What are some of the conventions of the genre of the folktale? How do these conventions connect to the fact that the folktale as a genre is rooted in oral performance?

4. Choose one of your favorite folktales you grew up hearing. Write out the story in the dialect you remember hearing it told in, and share your folktale with a small group of students in your class.

5. How does the Black English that Hurston uses to tell her tales reflect the speech patterns described by Dr. Smitherman in the previous selection?

Before You Read

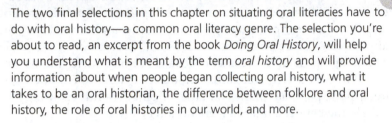

The two final selections in this chapter on situating oral literacies have to do with oral history—a common oral literacy genre. The selection you're about to read, an excerpt from the book *Doing Oral History*, will help you understand what is meant by the term *oral history* and will provide information about when people began collecting oral history, what it takes to be an oral historian, the difference between folklore and oral history, the role of oral histories in our world, and more.

As you read this excerpt from Chapter 1 of *Doing Oral History*, think about stories you've heard but never read, perhaps stories from older members of your family—grandparents, great grandparents, an aunt or uncle—stories that share a slice of history. Unless someone writes down these stories—these oral histories—there's a strong chance they won't survive. Perhaps you have a good reason for learning how to do oral history.

Excerpt from *Doing Oral History: A Practical Guide*

Donald Ritchie

According to Oxford Univeristy Press, publisher of Donald Ritchie's *Doing Oral History* (2003):

> Donald Ritchie is Associate Historian in the United States Senate Historical Office, where he conducts an oral history program. A former president of the Oral History Association he has served on the council of the American Historical Association and chaired the Organization of American Historians' committee on research and access to historical documentation. (www.oup.com/us/catalog/general/subject/HistoryOther/)

The following excerpt is from the first chapter of Ritchie's *Doing Oral History*.

What is oral history?

1 Memory is the core of oral history, from which meaning can be extracted and preserved. Simply put, oral history collects memories and personal commentaries of historical significance through recorded interviews. An

oral history interview generally consists of a well-prepared interviewer questioning an interviewee and recording their exchange in audio or video format. Recordings of the interview are transcribed, summarized, or indexed and then placed in a library or archives. These interviews may be used for research or excerpted in a publication, radio or video documentary, museum exhibition, dramatization or other form of public presentation. Recordings, transcripts, catalogs, photographs and related documentary materials can also be posted on the Internet. Oral history does not include random taping, such as President Richard Nixon's surreptitious recording of his White House conversations, nor does it refer to recorded speeches, wiretapping, personal diaries on tape, or other sound recordings that lack the dialogue between interviewer and interviewee.

2   To avoid repeating common mistakes, oral historians have created standards for doing interviews, and established principles for dealing ethically with their interviewees. But oral history is too dynamic and creative a field to be entirely captured by any single definition. For every rule, an exception has worked. Imaginative interviewers are constantly developing and sharing new methods and uses of oral history. Any definition of the oral history process, or any method of interviewing, must reflect the goals of the specific project, the resources available, and other practical considerations.

When did people begin collecting oral history?

3 As distinct from oral traditions—stories that societies have passed along in spoken form from generation to generation—oral history *interviewing* has been occurring since history was first recorded. Three thousand years ago, scribes of the Zhou dynasty in China collected the sayings of the people for the use of court historians, and several centuries later, Thucydides interviewed participants in the Peloponnesian wars. Skepticism of oral testimony dates back equally as far. Thucydides complained that "different eye-witnesses give different accounts of the same events, speaking out of partiality for one side or the other or else from imperfect memories."

4   During the European conquest of the Americas in the sixteenth century, Spanish chroniclers relied on oral sources to reconstruct the history of the indigenous people, from the Aztecs to the Incas. To assist in both colonization and conversion, they collected the testimony of survivors of these once great civilizations, concentrating on their social, economic, and religious traditions. Although strongly colored by the colonizers' cultural assumptions, these histories remain important sources for the new world's pre-Columbian history.

5   In 1773, when Samuel Johnson argued against the proposition that an impartial history could not be written in the lifetime of those who had

experienced the events, he reasoned that "a man, by talking with those of different sides, who were actors in it and putting down all that he hears, may in time collect the materials of a good narrative." Johnson admonished that "all history was at first oral" and noted that this was how Voltaire had prepared his histories of the French kings. Indeed, Voltaire wrote that he had questioned "old couriers, servants, great lords, and others" and recorded only "those facts about which they agree." Jules Michelet studied the French Revolution, a half century after it took place, by contrasting the official documents with the recollections of "peasants, townsfolk, old men, women, even children; which you can hear if you enter an evening into a village tavern."

> "Ironically, historians turned away from oral sources just as other professions and disciplines were embracing the interview."

6   Soon after the battles of Lexington and Concord launched the American Revolution in 1775, a Congregationalist minister named William Gordon interviewed the participants, among them Paul Revere. Gordon's recounting of Revere's elaborate preparations contradicted efforts to portray the battle as unprovoked attacks by the British, and revolutionary leaders managed to suppress the story. Two centuries later the historian David Hackett Fischer declared Gordon's essay drawn from Revere's interview "remarkably full and accurate." In the 1870s the California publisher Hubert Howe Bancroft compiled his seven-volume *History of California* (1884–90) by sending students out to collect the papers and the reminiscences of nineteenth-century Mexican military governors and *alcaldes* (civilian officials) and of the first American settlers.

7   It seemed reasonable to consult oral as well as written sources until the late nineteenth century, when the German school of scientific history promoted documentary research to the exclusion of other, less "objective" sources. Leopold von Ranke asserted that documents created at the time historical events occurred are the most reliable form of historical evidence; Ranke's followers helped turn history from a literary form into an academic discipline dependent on the rigorous use of evidence. They trained historians to scrutinize documents in their search for truth and dismissed oral sources as folklore and myth, prized only by well-meaning but naive amateurs and antiquarians. They deemed oral evidence too subjective; shoddy memories told from a biased point of view.

8   Ironically, historians turned away from oral sources just as other professions and disciplines were embracing the interview. Journalists made interviewing a main stay of their craft around the time of the American Civil War. In 1859, when New York *Tribune* editor Horace Greeley went west to conduct a highly publicized interview of Mormon patriarch Brigham Young in Salt Lake City, he launched a trend in newspaper interviews. By 1868,

President Andrew Johnson, facing impeachment by Congress, sought to present his side to the public by giving the first presidential interviews for attribution. "I want to give those fellows hell," Johnson told the reporter who was interviewing him, as he gestured towards the Capitol, "and I think I can do it better through your paper than through a message, because the people read the papers more than they do messages." Interviews quickly became so popular that clever politicians took to preparing their own question-and-answer dialogues, which obliging journalists published as news.

9   In the 1890s, the U.S. Bureau of Ethnography dispatched researchers to record on wax cylinders the songs and stories of Native Americans. During the Depression of the 1930s, the Works Progress Administration (WPA) hired unemployed writers to chronicle the lives of ordinary citizens. Especially valuable were the WPA's interviews with former slaves. Four decades later, when historians finally accepted these records—comprising more than 10,000 pages of interviews, they helped to alter fundamentally the historical interpretation of American slavery.

10   When the United States entered World War II, President Franklin D. Roosevelt ordered all military branches and civilian agencies of the government to prepare records of their wartime experiences. Planning not only a postwar history, but a series of moral-boosting "American Forces in Action" booklets, the U.S. Army dispatched historians into the battlefields, armed with heavy wire recorders. Directed by Lt. Col. S. L. A. Marshall, a World War I veteran and journalist turned army historian, they pioneered in the post-combat interview, debriefing soldiers immediately after the battle to reconstruct the events of the day. Sgt. Forrest Pogue spent D-Day interviewing wounded soldiers who had been evacuated to a hospital ship anchored off Normandy Beach. Recalling concerns that his bulky wire recorder might attract sniper fire, Pogue noted that the army wanted live history "and live historians."

11   Although the term had been used earlier, not until the 1940s did "oral history" attach itself to interviewing. A Harvard-educated Greenwich Village bohemian and flophouse denizen, Joseph Gould, otherwise known as "Professor Sea Gull," wandered around Manhattan collecting what he called "An Oral History of Our Time." Joseph Mitchell's profile of Gould that appeared in the *New Yorker* in 1942 drew attention to his crusade to record the stories of average people. "What people say is history," Gould insisted. "What we used to think was history—kings and queens, treaties, inventions, big battles, beheadings, Caesar, Napoleon, Pontius Pilate, Columbus, William Jennings Bryan—is only formal history and largely false. I'll put down the informal history of the shirt-sleeved multitude—what they had to say about their jobs, love affairs, vittles, sprees, scrapes, and sorrows—or I'll perish in the attempt." The

quest garnered many a free meal for Gould, but his oral history proved to be a figment of his imagination. When Gould died he left nothing behind but the name.

12   Another journalist-turned-historian, Allan Nevins, created the first modern oral history archives at Columbia University in 1948. A decade earlier, in his book *The Gateway to History*, Nevins had proposed to reinvigorate historical study in America by making "a systematic attempt to obtain from the lips and papers of living Americans who had led significant lives, a fuller record of their participation in the political, economic and cultural life of the last sixty years." Recognizing that modern communication and transportation were making letter-writing and diary-keeping obsolete, Nevins founded the Columbia Oral History Research Office. This new effort raised complaints from those who considered "Oral History" either too imprecise or too Freudian. But by the 1960s Nevins's successor, Louis Starr, could point out that the term had so worked its way into the language that newspapers were referring to it in the lower case. "Oral history, like it or not, is here to stay," Starr declared. "It's gone generic."

13   The University of California at Berkeley launched a similar oral history program in 1954, as did UCLA in 1958. The Harry S. Truman Library inaugurated the first presidential library oral history program in 1960. The John F. Kennedy Library began interviewing shortly after Kennedy's assassination, before the library was constructed. Oral history soon became standard practice for building presidential collections. By 1967 the Oral History Association was founded, gaining membership throughout the United States and abroad. Oral history projects developed on every continent, and national oral history organizations formed from Mexico to New Zealand. In 1972 the Imperial War Museum in London established a Department of Sound Records to collect and preserve oral testimony of those servicemen and women who "for lack of inclination, opportunity, or literary skill" would leave no other record for history. A 1987 meeting in Oxford, England, established the International Oral History Association, which meets biannually around the world.

14   Worldwide political and social changes during the last decades of the twentieth century confronted historians with the inadequacy of archival documentation, which often reflected a discredited government rather than the resistance against it. Newly emerging nations in Asia and Africa found that the written documents reflected the views of former colonial masters and used oral history to revive buried national identities. When the Soviet Union dissolved, Russian and Eastern European oral historians' efforts began immediately to reexamine and rewrite that region's discredited official history by collecting personal testimony suppressed under Communist regimes. In Brazil and Argentina, oral history projects have focused on

periods of military dictatorship to record the experiences of those brutalized by state terrorism. South Africans similarly turned to oral history in their search for truth and healing in the post-Apartheid era. Interviewers in many nations have found interviewing a critical tool when confronting issues of repression and reconciliation.

. . .

What does it take to become an oral historian?

15 Oral history has always been multi-disciplinary. While many professional historians conduct oral history, a degree in history has never been a prerequisite for entering the field. Well-established scholars sometimes make poor interviewers, and those who are part of the community or profession being interviewed, if properly trained in conducting oral history, have advantages in establishing rapport and in prior knowledge. Law students have interviewed judges, women coal miners have successfully interviewed other women coal miners, and members of a community have conducted oral histories with their neighbors. In Alaska, a portrait artist conducted interviews with the people she was painting to gain a deeper understanding of the personalities she was trying to capture on canvas. In Japan, a physician interviewed his elderly patients in a fishing community that was rapidly disappearing. He wrote the resulting book from his office overlooking a new expressway built on the riverbed. "That vanished river, that water's edge, once rang out with the shouts of men hauling in their net as couples on houseboats waited among the reeds for night to fall. It wasn't so very long ago, and yet that era, that scenery, and the life-breath of those people have all vanished liked phantoms," the doctor wrote. The oral histories he collected stood as a tribute "to the too-swift passing of time."

16   Saying that a Ph.D. in history is no requirement for doing oral history does not mean that anything anyone records is oral history. The Oral History Association has developed principles, standards, and guidelines to raise the consciousness and professional standards of all oral historians. There are interviewing skills to be learned. There are right and wrong ways to conduct an oral history. There are great differences between useable oral history and useless ones, and there are far too many of the latter.

17   Oral history has room for both the academic and the layperson. With reasonable training, through oral history courses, workshops, or manuals, anyone can conduct a useable oral history. Oral history conferences are notable for the variety of participants, among them radio and video documentary makers, museum curators, archivists, journalists, gerontologists, anthropologists, and folklorists. Regardless of their diverse objectives, they share many common methods of interviewing. "If an interview goes well, then we say it's magic," the Canadian investigative reporter John Sawatsky

commented. "But it's not magic. It happens for an understandable reason. It's rational. It's a skill. It's easy to teach someone skills."

How reliable is the information gathered by oral history?

18   "The most naive policeman knows that a witness should not always be taken at his word . . . ," wrote the French historian Marc Bloch. "Similarly, it has been many a day since men first took it into their heads not to accept all historical evidence blindly." Oral history is as reliable or unreliable as other research sources. No single piece of data of any sort should be trusted completely, and all sources need to be tested against other evidence. The historian James MacGregor Burns, who was trained under S. L. A. Marshall to interview American soldiers during World War II, found that the interviews generated some spurious information (about how frequently infantrymen fired their rifles in combat) and also some startling insights (about how many troops were killed by friendly fire). Burns concluded that "such interviews were a most valuable contribution to military history, but only if used in careful conjunction with more conventional sources, like documents and enemy records."

> "Oral history is as reliable or unreliable as other research sources."

19   Although archival documents have the advantage of not being influenced by later events or otherwise changing over time, as an interviewee might, documents are sometimes incomplete, inaccurate, and deceiving. For instance, researchers have found more than one occasion of a local newspaper ignoring an entire event, such as a strike against one of its major advertisers. Until the 1960s, most general circulation newspapers ignored news from black communities. As a result of such blind spots, oral history can develop information that might not have appeared in print. As the novelist Gore Vidal has commented: "Since I have been written about perhaps a bit more than most historians, I am not as impressed as they are by what I see in print, no matter how old and yellow the cutting."

20   Scholars have accepted correspondence, diaries, and autobiographies as legitimate documentation, although their authors may be biased or incorrect. Politicians have kept diaries with publication in mind, designing them to present themselves in the best possible light. Oral history interviews are often conducted years after the event, when memories have grown imprecise, but they have the advantage of being conducted by a trained interviewer who can raise questions and challenge dubious answers. As any researcher can attest, letter writers and diary keepers do not always address all the issues that scholars are researching. Autobiographers are often unaware of all the issues that interest researchers. Well-trained interviewers can coax interviewees into areas of concern to researchers that the interviewees might never have thought of discussing otherwise. . . .

Memory and Oral History

Isn't oral history limited by the fallibility of human memory?

21 Dealing with memory is risky business, and it is inescapably the interviewer's business. Every interviewer has a story about someone interviewed too late, when memory had lost its sharpness, begun to dim, or faded almost entirely. Such disappointments are balanced by experiences with interviewees who possess remarkable recall, who remember individuals and incidents clearly, and whose accounts can be corroborated in other evidence. As one of the interviewers who collected oral histories with immigrants for the Ellis Island museum noted, elderly interviewees "might not remember their daughter's phone number. But they do remember what it was like when they got off the boat."

22   Motivated by the death of baseball legend Ty Cobb in 1961, Lawrence Ritter set out to interview as many of the surviving pre-World War I baseball players as he could find. Traveling thousands of miles, he tracked down a group of elderly men who shared a remarkable storehouse of memories and an ability to articulate them vividly. "Many of the people I talked to had to think longer to get the names of all their great-grandchildren straight than they did to run down the batting order of the 1906 Chicago Cubs," he observed. But they were not garrulous old men chewing over oft-repeated stories. "Well, this is more than I've talked about in years, and it's good," said "Wahoo Sam" Crawford, who had played for the Detroit Tigers at the turn of the century. "I don't see many people, and even when I do I don't talk about baseball too much." As a skeptical researcher, Ritter went back to the old newspapers to verify the stories he heard, and almost without exception found that the events had occurred just as the old-time players had described them, embellished only occasionally "to dramatize a point, to emphasize a contrast, or to reveal a truth."

23   The study of memory by psychologists has concentrated largely on short-term memory rather than on the long-term recall of a life span. Short-term memory studies that evaluate the accuracy of an individual's perception of events are of little help in explaining the uncanny preciseness with which some interviewees recall events that took place decades ago, or in understanding how interviewees who had reached obvious senility—forgetful even that they had scheduled the interview—can still speak authentically about events far in the past. Long-term memory has been less thoroughly explored, although the phenomenon has often been commented upon. The Confederate leader Jefferson Davis, for instance, on his deathbed began recalling scenes from his youth as a West Point cadet. "I seem to remember more every day," Davis marveled.

24   The gerontologist Robert Butler has postulated that all people, as they grow older and perceive that they are approaching death, undergo a

mental process of life review accounting for depression and despair in some, and for candor, serenity, and wisdom in others. The past "marches in review," permitting the elderly to survey and reflect especially on moments of unresolved conflict. Older people will review their lives whether anyone asks them about their memories or not, either mulling over their thoughts silently, or regaling family, neighbors, and visitors. In this process, the elderly may reveal details of their lives, and characteristics about themselves, previously unknown to their families and friends. Butler concluded that memory "serves the sense of self and its continuity; it entertains us; it shames us; it pains us. Memory can tell our origins; it can be explanatory; and it can deceive."

25   Oral history is an active process in which interviewers seek out, record, and preserve such memories. Knowing that with age most people find it difficult to recall names and dates, oral historians conduct preparatory research to assist interviewees, give some context and structure to the dialogue through their questions, and mutually address any seeming misstatements and contradictions in the testimony. . . .

What's the difference between oral history and folklore?

26 Oral historians and folklorists both use interviews to collect information, but not necessarily the same type of information. The two practices have been described as opposite ends of a continuum: oral historians concentrate on recording the personal experiences of the interviewee, and folklorists collect the traditional stories, songs and other expressions of the community, fact or fiction. An oral historian would most likely interview a husband and wife separately, seeking to identify the unique perspective of each spouse. A folklorist, being as interested in the way a story is told as in its substance, would interview the couple together to observe the interplay as one begins a story and the other finishes it. The folklorist Barbara Allen has observed that historians "tend to see oral historical sources as mines of raw data from which historical evidence can be extracted," while folklorists are more concerned with "recognizing identifiable patterns" in the way people shape their narrative.

27   Sharing an interest in interviewing, oral historians, folklorists, ethnographers, cultural anthropologists, sociologists, and linguists each have different objectives that influence their methodology. "Field-oriented" disciplines rely on participant observation and may not even take notes in the presence of those they are studying, waiting to write up their notes later from memory. Unlike historians, who seek concrete evidence of what actually happened and to document it as fully as possible, folklorists, ethnographers, and anthropologists are often less interested in verification of facts and see folk tales and folklore as no less legitimate than other stories.

Linguists will often be more concerned with the manner of telling a story than in its substance. Despite the distinctive way that these assorted disciplines analyze and use interviews, the intersection of their methodological techniques has permitted collaborative, cross-disciplinary oral history projects on a range of community, racial, ethnic and immigration issues.

Can storytelling be considered oral history?

28   Diverse cultures depend on storytelling to pass along knowledge and understanding. The storyteller might be a parent teaching a child, a tribal elder recalling communal traditions, a preacher illustrating a point in a sermon, an Old Salt spinning a yarn, or anyone else able to recount past experiences in a manner entertaining enough to hold a crowd. Folklorists find that tales passed down, family lore, and community legends have value as much for their form (how they are told) as for their content. Such stories are often communal in nature, transcending the individual experiences they describe. Recurring stories within a community that emerge in oral history collections also reveal what people consider to be the key aspects of their historical experience.

29   In those cases where storytelling takes place without an interviewer who can pursue issues raised in the stories by questioning the narrator, it does not fit the standard definition of oral history, but its study illuminates some significant issues facing oral historians. Most storytellers aim not so much to preserve a permanent record as to inform and influence their immediate audience. Although the storyteller usually controls the performance, the particular setting and audience can affect the story's presentation. Telling a story in a new setting, to a new audience creates new meanings. Storytelling reminds us that all oral presentations involve a degree of performance, and that the audience (even an audience of one, as in the interviewer) can affect that performance. Stories told in an interview often involve a re-telling of something the interviewee heard from someone else or has previously told to others. As the "audience," the interviewer can affect in subtle or even striking ways the content of the story. The process continues even after the interview is completed. The oral historian William Schneider has pointed out that "once the narrator stops talking and the recorder leaves with the tape, the teller no longer knows who will hear it and how they will understand what he or she said." Some sensitivity to the nature of storytelling is therefore essential to the management of oral history collections. To be fair to participants, Schneider advises, "we have to be mindful of a wide range of considerations, not the least of which is the oral tradition from which the narrator may have built the telling and from which the audience derives its background for understanding what has been shared. . . ."

Public History and Oral History

What will future historians want from our oral histories?

30 Researchers will want to hear the first-person observations of events great and small, and to learn what sense those people made out of the events in their own lives. Motivations and objectives are especially important. Other sources can usually provide the who, what, when, and where of history; interviews can offer better insights into the how and why. The historian's job is to pull together a multitude of evidence from documents, objects, interviews, and other resources, weaving them together to create a narrative that makes sense of all of the often conflicting evidence.

31 Not all human activity is coherent and purposeful, the historian Elie Kedourie pointed out; it is more often a complex of choices producing unpredictable effects. Kedourie defined history as an account of people "in the peculiarity, idiosyncracy, and specificity of their personalities, out-

> **"Today's oral historians are doing the preliminary work of tomorrow's biographers and researchers, hoping they will not have to agonize too often over the questions we failed to ask."**

looks, capacities, and positions, confronting or dealing with other [people] differently placed in respect to these things, and confronting or dealing with them in situations different from one another at least in respect of time and place, initiating, originating, talking measures, parrying, responding, reacting; the vocabulary we use to describe all this amply indicating that here are present and involved purpose and choice, mind and will." Or, as Ecclesiastes 9:11 instructs, "The race is not to the swift, nor the battle to the strong . . . but time and chance happeneth to them all." Oral history records both the purposeful and the accidental. Interviewers who allow people a chance to assess why they did what they did will most likely capture the peculiarities and idiosyncracies of the history of our time.

32 Historians writing a dissertation or a book, planning an exhibit or scripting a documentary, will have their own set of questions they want to ask but may not have the opportunity to ask those questions personally. I first used oral history while writing a biography of a man who had died ten years earlier. Fortunately, he had given a lengthy oral history to Columbia University just months before he died. It was a thoroughly detailed, in-depth life history, amounting to seven hundred pages of transcripts. As I could no longer question the man, Columbia's interviewer served as my surrogate. Today's oral historians are doing the preliminary work of tomorrow's biographers and researchers, hoping they will not have to agonize too often over the questions we failed to ask.

33 Oral history is about asking questions. While researching the history of Methodist camp meeting in Southern Mississippi, Charles Sullivan sought to visit every campground still operating. One day he mentioned to a

student each of the camps that he had identified. "Yes, and Mt. Pleasant, too," the student responded, explaining that it was a black Methodist campground established after emancipation from slavery. Astonished, Sullivan wondered why no one had mentioned this camp before. "Probably because you never asked," came the reply. That is the reason for doing oral history: to ask the questions that have not been asked, and to collect the reminiscences that otherwise would be lost.

Literacy Connections

1. Now that you've read excerpts from Donald Ritchie's chapter, how would you define *oral history*?
2. What are some of the factors that figure into the reliability of information collected by oral history?
3. How would you define the difference between oral history and folklore?
4. Think of a piece of oral history that you're familiar with and that you believe is worth saving. Describe it. Share your response with others in your class.
5. What do folktales such as the ones recorded by Zora Neale Hurston have in common with the kinds of oral histories Ritchie is discussing in this chapter?

Before You Read

Following is an oral history interview with a Vietnam veteran, Jerry K. Walsh, a scout dog handler who was drafted into the war when he was 18 years old. As you read the transcript of his interview with Kelly Lamb, a student who conducted the study for her American Military History class, think about the kind of oral history project you would conduct if your composition teacher asked you to capture a slice of history in a similar project.

Oral History Interview with Jerry K. Walsh: A Transcript of a Veteran's Oral History

This interview was conducted by Kelly Lamb on November 5, 1998, for Professor Tom Forgey's class in American Military History at Southern Arkansas University. The interview took place in the McAlester Office at South Arkansas Youth Services (S.A.Y.S.) in Magnolia, Arkansas. The transcript below is an excerpt of this tape-recorded interview. The original audio tape is archived at Magale Library at Southern Arkansas University.

Jerry K. Walsh in Vietnam in 1965

His scout dog, Marty (Serial Number 5X31)

During the Vietnam era about 4,000 dogs served as scout dogs, combat trackers, or sentry dogs as part of the United States armed forces. Two hundred and eighty-one dogs were officially listed as killed in action and many more were wounded in action. It is impossible to accurately estimate the number of lives that these dogs saved.

It is clear that the use of canines by our forces in Vietnam is a significant part of the history of that conflict, but very little has been written about them. Even an Internet search resulted in only two Web sites related to the subject. See the Vietnam War Dog Handlers Association and its Memorial to Scout Dogs (www.vdhaonline.org/mem.html) and the Quartermaster's Foundation History of the U.S. Army's Use of Dogs from 1942 to the Present (www.qmfound.com/War_Dogs.htm).

Jerry Walsh served in Vietnam in the early years of the conflict as a scout dog handler. A few years after his return to the United States, he moved to southwest Arkansas. He completed undergraduate and graduate work at Southern Arkansas University and holds a master's degree in Agency Counseling. Jerry Walsh is the Chief Operating Officer of South Arkansas Youth Services, an agency dedicated to serving juveniles in need.

Lamb: When and where were you born?

Walsh: I was born in Connsville, Pennsylvania. June 16, 1946.

Lamb: How did you come to live in Arkansas?

Walsh: I was recruited by Rip Powell (of SAU) for track back in 1965. I graduated (high school) in '64. The smartest thing I ever did is not to go to college right out of high school. I had a basketball scholarship to go to Shippensburg University. I didn't take it because I listened to the admissions counselor who said that I would probably flunk out. The reason I bring that up is that it kind of plays into serving in Vietnam and getting out. What I did was that I went back around Pittsburgh and ran for the track club and worked. And then Rip Powell recruited me to come down (to SAU) in January of '65 and I got drafted in December of 1964. I told the draft board that I was accepted to Southern State College and, I think conveniently, they lost my confirmation letter. I think they were trying to meet their quota on the draft board so I was gone. I was in.

Lamb: Did a lot of other people your age from your area go to Vietnam?

Walsh: Oh yeah. In '65 no one was really stepping out of the line at the induction center and saying I'm not going to serve. Later on, some people did that but at that time, very few people did.

Lamb: Were you married back then? Or still single?

Walsh: I was single. I was sort of engaged. Getting ready to get engaged. In fact, I went into the Army, when I went to Vietnam, we were engaged.

Lamb: Is that the same lady that you later married?

Walsh: That's the one I am married to now.

Lamb: That's a long time.

Walsh: I never got any dear Jody letters from her when I was over there.

Lamb: So you got a notice and you were drafted?

Walsh: Yes. I was drafted. I went to Pittsburgh and I was inducted into the armed services there. Then I got on a train.

Lamb: Where did you go from there?

Walsh: Ft. Jackson, South Carolina. I went through basic training there. At that time, we got down South and we stopped someplace to get off the train and stretch our legs. Two cars were all draftees out of western Pennsylvania. I went to get a drink of water and they had "colored only" fountains. We kind of looked around and said (to ourselves) what are you going to do about it? They still had those signs up.

Lamb: It was a culture shock for you coming from Pennsylvania down South?

Walsh: It was not as much for me. It was a culture shock for a lot of guys but not for me. Number one, I went to a military school in Pennsylvania. I had six years of that kind of military structure behind me. Also, my mother was from Virginia and she was an unreconstructed rebel. She believed in the South. She wasn't racial or anything but she believed in the South. A lot of my relatives were from Virginia and Texas, so it wasn't a big cultural shock.

Lamb: You were a little better able to adapt?

Walsh: Yes. Some guys were quite shocked at the South and the military camps.

Lamb: You had basic training at Ft. Jackson?

Walsh: Yes. Advanced Infantry Training too. I never saw the inside of a barracks. There were so many people that they had to put big tents up. I never spent a day in a barracks, practically my whole two years of active duty. It was winter time. When I finished up Advanced Infantry Training, I got a ten day leave. Initially I had orders for sniper school. I pointed out that they were making a mistake because I was just average in qualifying with the usual infantry weapons. Like a dummy, I fired expert on a big heavy machine gun which was stupid because if you did real good then they could give it to you. Then you are lugging all that weight around.

I got those sniper orders changed. They realized they had made a mistake. I got orders for Scout Dog Handlers School at Ft. Benning, Georgia. I was assigned to the 40th Infantry Scout Dog Platoon. We were in a barracks for two days and then we were promptly moved out the barracks and into the field. We got our dogs and went through a six-month training program in three months. We were going 15- or 16-hour days.

Lamb: What were they training you to do with the dogs?

Walsh: We trained, the dog and the handler, to detect, to work out in front of a point man on a combat patrol. The point man is the lead person. We would actually work out in front of them with the dog. We would have a couple guys assigned to guarding us. We would utilize the dog's sense of smell to detect ambushes and trip wires and they used to dig these pits, put stakes in them and cover them up. What we tried to do was use the dog to keep our people safe.

Lamb: The dog that you got when you went to school, is that the dog that you went to Vietnam with?

Walsh: Yes. In fact, I got to pick him out because I went down to the airport. They flew the dogs from Lackland Air Force Base. I volunteered to go down and unload them off a C-130 transport plane. We staked them out and I saw the dog and he looked like Rin Tin Tin. I got a chance to lobby for him when they made the assignments. I got him assigned to me.

Lamb: How old was he?

Walsh: About 13 or 14 months old. I later found out that the people that had owned him were from San Pedro, California. They had a ranch out there and had retired into a condominium so they decided they would donate him to the United States Air Force. He came from a good family. He was a very good, well-adjusted dog.

Lamb: Did you name him?

Walsh: No. He was already named. His name was Marty. His serial number was 5X31. It was tattooed in his ear.

Lamb: You remember his serial number?

Walsh: Yes. Most service people remember their serial number. I remember his too.

Lamb: You two became good friends?

Walsh: Relationships with canines, whether military or non-military, are special. I think they are really special when they are military. That is your job, 24 hours a day, to take care of that dog. You become a team. You have feelings for him.

Lamb: You have to count on him?

Walsh: Yes. And he counts on you. I have tracker dogs now at the house that I use in my work here at South Arkansas Youth Services and the Wilderness Camp. We have a Black Mouth Cur and we have a mixed Bloodhound up at Mansfield, Arkansas. She's the most homely of all of our dogs but she has the biggest heart. I think she has the best heart. Our dogs work hard for us here and the dogs in the military worked hard for us. They didn't do it because we gave them treats. They did it because they wanted us to rub their head and tell them what a great job they did. That is what they worked for. It becomes a special relationship.

Lamb: You and Marty went from Fort Benning to . . . ?

Walsh: We went from Fort Benning, about 25 guys and 35 dogs, we had some extra dogs we carried with us. We went there as a unit. We went to Robbins Air Force Base in Georgia and flew from there to Anchorage, Alaska. Then we flew into Japan. It was cold in Anchorage. It was cold and wet in Japan.

Then we flew into Saigon. We got out at Tonsunu Air Force Base and unloaded the dogs and man you are in another world. It looks different. It smells different. You don't know what the hell to expect.

Lamb: Weather?

Walsh: It was hot.

We had to quarantine the dogs there for two weeks. I'll say this, when I got the hell out of Saigon, I was the happiest guy in the world. It was teeming with people. I could never tell the bad guys from the good guys.

We went with the 25th Infantry Division. We were very lucky because the 25th Infantry Division was a very experienced outfit. The Brigade Commander up there had our kennels built for us. They were really looking forward to us coming in there. Man, they treated us . . . anything we needed.

The best thing we did was as soon as we got there we went to work. We got into the jungle right away and when we made mistakes we brought that back to our unit and shared that information with each other. We got on a good rotation, getting out and working patrols and things like that.

Lamb: Was it common to have scout dogs in those units you were working with?

Walsh: No. They had never seen them. The 25th Infantry Division had never seen scout dogs. Of course we had to do some education because I'd show up out there and I have a dog that looks like Rin Tin Tin. They think that he is and he's not. He's a dog that if used in the right way, can help you. If you use him in the wrong way, he can get you killed. You cannot have false expectations. When the dog is tired, they may want you to stay on point. But you have to tell them, "No, he's tired, he's got to come off, he's got to rest." The 25th Infantry Division was real good. I don't think I can ever remember having any kind of hassle with them. When I told them something, they always listened to me. Anything I needed they got for me.

When you got up in the morning the first thing you always did was check your dog. Take him down off his feet, check his belly, under his legs, everything. I checked mine and we had hit some ants the day before and apparently they had bitten him and a fly had laid some eggs (in the bite) that had almost immediately hatched and he had a hole in his stomach. You could see the worms eating, trying to get into his stomach lining. I told the company commander. We were in thick jungle, you couldn't see two feet in front of you. They took all their C-4 explosives and they blew trees down left and right until they could get a chopper in there to take the dog back to the veterinarian. They would do anything.

Lamb: There was no help for Marty (the Dog) in the field?

Walsh: The handlers were trained. A lot of things with dogs you just treated like human beings. If they are wounded, you apply pressure. We were trained in first aid. I could do most of it. Marty had a bad deal, I think, one time with a vet and he would just go crazy anytime he would get a sniff of one. For most of his medical stuff, they just brought it all out to me outside the vet. If he needed a shot, I gave it to him. If he needed to get his teeth cleaned, generally, they would put a dog to sleep to clean his teeth. I would just open his mouth up, make him lay down and scrape all the tartar off. He would keep his mouth open for me. I could practically do everything myself because anytime I took him (to the vet) I would have to sedate him. If they needed blood, I took the blood. I learned how to do all that.

Lamb: Were you and Marty together the whole time you were in Vietnam?

Walsh: I was with him the whole time.

Lamb: How long were you over there?

Walsh: Thirteen months.

Lamb: What did Marty eat?

Walsh: We carried two types of dog food. We carried Hill's Horse Meat. I ate some of it myself one time. It wasn't bad. When we were out on patrol for seven or eight days, we carried kind of a dried food, in chunks. Then when we got back in the area, we would mix in the horsemeat. Anytime that we got hot food choppered in, if there was any meat, steak or porkchops, the cooks always had something for him. They would bring it up and ask if they could give it to him. He always ate good.

Lamb: Were you aware of the protests going on at home?

Walsh: Sure.

Lamb: How did you feel about them?

Walsh: I didn't feel anything about them. What went on over here, I couldn't care less. The only thing that I cared about was getting up every day and doing what I was supposed to do, taking care of my job and staying alive. I understood. You didn't have to be there very long to realize that we were not going to win that war. It didn't take too long, at least for me, to understand that we probably didn't need to be there. It's hard when you are 18 years old. You don't think in terms of Cold War, Asian politics. We hadn't had those opportunities to sit around in college and talk about containment policies and things like that. You just knew that was the policy to contain communism. You obviously could see that they were trying to unite the country. Good or bad, that is what they were trying to do.

Lamb: What was your rank when you got over there?

Walsh: I was nothing. I was an E-4 when I got over there. I made Sergeant later on.

Lamb: How did you feel about the leadership?

Walsh: We had good leadership. I was a squad leader myself. Even today, the things I do as the Chief Operating Officer of South Arkansas Youth Services, which we have 130 employees and 65 beds and we are probably going to get a little bigger, the thing I learned is to lead by example. Don't ask anyone to do what you won't do and when you are assigning guard duty, take the worst shift. When you do these things, people will work for you.

You develop bonds. You are really closer to those guys (that you served with) than you are to your wife or fiancée. None of these people were important on a day to day basis. The most important person in your life was your buddy, was the guy next to you because he did everything to watch out for you. And you needed to do everything you could to watch out for him.

Lamb: What was the best part of your experience?

Walsh: The best part for me was that we only lost a couple of guys in our whole platoon. We lost two men. Very early on, we lost a sergeant. He didn't really have to be out there. He was one of those guys who led by example. He could've stayed back. Then, one of my squad guys, we were on patrol together, both of our dogs were tired and another unit was going out. They needed a dog. Neither one of us should have gone but he went. He felt that they needed that dog. The fact that we only lost two guys was gratifying at the end of our tour.

The other thing is that personally, the dog I had, we never took anybody into an ambush. We saved some units from going into ambushes. We probably saved the legs of a couple guys and our legs too by picking up some trip wires.

This was an excellent dog. I spent all my time working with him. If I thought that he was getting weak in something, we would work on it. Anytime I came off patrol, he got two days in the kennel just to rest. I would visit with him, feed him, take care of him. The third day, I would take him out and just play with him. If I went to the PX or something, he just went with me. If I went to a movie, I would take him. They had an outdoor movie theater there at the base camp. He would sit there with me. Then the fourth day, we would do any corrective work. This is a dog that I could work off the leash 100 yards, just on hand signals. This is a dog that if I ran, he ran with me. If I hit the ground, he hit the ground. If I low crawled, he low crawled. He was beyond value. His initial training was $10,000. After he started working, he was invaluable. That's the kind of schedule I tried to keep him on.

Lamb: Were either of you seriously injured or was there a time that you thought you would be?

Walsh: The closest that he and I ever came, we were with a recon platoon down at Chu Lai. We were working up a mountain trail. We were going up a back route to reinforce a company up there. There was a firefight on top of the mountain. We took a break because it was really hot but every five minutes we would get a little breeze off the ocean which was about ten miles away. We sat down and took a break. We could hear our own artillery going over. One of the guys said it sounds like they are shooting good today. I don't think it was out of his mouth when a short round came in. A 105 round came in right in the middle of the platoon.

We were spread out and the concussion threw the dog over my head. I was sitting down and he was standing and it threw him completely over my head. It threw me down. He flew five or six feet. I was thinking that he was hit. Amazingly, he didn't sustain a thing. Everybody around us, we had 22 guys in that platoon, and we carried 17 to the Medevac choppers. We went down the hill and there was a rice paddy and we got the Medevacs in. We got everyone on the chopper and there is only four or five of us left. So we just hiked back to camp because we didn't have enough guys to go on up and help them.

That was the closest. Friendly fire. I'm sure we had thousands killed in Vietnam from friendly fire.

You were scared all the time but not scared to the point where you couldn't do your job. It was dirty, nasty work. We were out there chasing people through the jungle, trying to find them, trying to kill them. It was mostly in the mountains, it was not around populated areas. If you made a mistake, you got killed. That's the biggest difference between military canine work and civilian is that if you make a mistake you got killed. When my buddy got killed, he made a mistake. He went in with a tired dog.

At the same time that my buddy got killed, my cousin was killed over there. He was with the 173rd Airborne. My buddy got killed, two days later my cousin got killed.

I didn't know it for about a week. When I went to the wall a couple of years ago, my buddy was on one line and about ten lines below was my cousin from Houston.

You were in the jungle and it was beautiful and deadly. It was the third world. I did spend some time around villages. Near one village, they had some plague victims. I also saw people with leprosy. There are these people with leprosy and I guarantee you that movie *Ben Hur* didn't do any justice to it. It is absolutely terrible. People just rot and fall apart. I just felt good getting out of there.

Lamb: How did you leave?

Walsh: When a new platoon came over they went over to the 4th Infantry Division which is close to the 25th Infantry Division. I took my squad over there and they sent a new squad. We exchanged squads. What that gave them was six of us experienced dog handlers at the end of our tour. So what we did for a month or two, we carried our dogs over and trained them between what they learned back at scout dog school and what the realities were. Then we went on patrols with them. Then I turned my dog over to them. Since I was a squad leader, I got to choose who got assigned the dogs. I think I picked out the best kid to take my dog over.

Lamb: How did you feel about leaving him?

Walsh: Just terrible. I knew that we couldn't get him because this sergeant who was killed in my platoon, he wasn't killed immediately. He eventually died in a medical facility in Florida.

When he was at Walter Reed, his wife, who was a very tough lady, got in to see President Johnson. He (the sergeant) had woken up following his gunshot to the head and called for this dog. We got orders to take the dog back to Washington. One of our PFCs took the dog back to see him and the Army wouldn't even release that dog. The kid told them, "We don't want this dog."

When a handler got shot up, nobody else would work with that dog. We'd trade the dog to another platoon, because you couldn't make a guy work with that dog.

Even if it wasn't the dog's fault, everybody blamed the dog. It was rough. I had such a bond with that dog. Then two days before I left, it may have been the day before I left, I didn't know where they were training and apparently I got close to their training area and Marty saw me. I was maybe a half mile away. I'm walking somewhere and he saw me and took off. I hear this yelling and screaming and I turned around and there he was, running toward me. The kid, the handler, is behind him trying to catch him. I did the toughest thing I ever did in my life. When he was about 75 yards out, I gave him the hand signal to halt. He stopped on a dime and sat. The kid did the right thing. The kid put the leash on him and jerked him and scolded him and took him back to the training area. I never saw him after that. I wrote to him for about three or four months and we lost contact. That was it.

I went to Fort Benning to the 26th Infantry Scout Dog Platoon and I worked there for six months before I got out. So I got to work with guys who were going over there. Some guys were there from other units that served in Vietnam. We were really able to show these guys the realities.

Lamb: You separated at Fort Benning?

Walsh: Yes.

Lamb: What decorations?

Walsh: The only one that means anything to me is the Combat Infantryman's Badge. You get that when you are in the theater of war for three months in the infantry. It is a blue rifle with a crest. I got some bronze stars and stuff like that but I think they give those to everybody.

Lamb: After Fort Benning you went back to Pennsylvania?

Walsh: I went back to Pennsylvania. Worked in a glass factory. I got married and we had a baby. Worked in the factory. Boy, I hated that. I went down to get a puppy one day at the Animal Rescue League which is a big humane organization and I ended up going to work for them. They had 26 acres out in Penn Hills which is a plush suburb of Pittsburgh. They had a couple of kennels.

We got a house. There were two houses. The smaller house, we got that as part of the job. They were losing money. I took it over. I went down to the unemployment office and hired some veterans and trained them like we were trained at Fort Benning. That means if you dropped a candy bar on the floor, you wouldn't be afraid to pick it up and eat it. The floor would be that clean.

There may have been 40 dogs in that kennel but you weren't going to smell one of them. That place was immaculate. I made pretty good money for them. I got some promotions.

My wife's family wasn't too happy because she had two years of Catholic nursing school. They thought she was going to lose that. I really did want to go to college and we wanted to go out of state. I called Rip Powell at S.A.U.

We came down in 1970.

Lamb: What do you want people who are now the age you were then to know about Vietnam?

Walsh: The draft was unfair. I was against the draft. I was anti-draft. Still am anti-draft. I thank God for Norman Schwarzkopf and guys like that who understood and learned the lessons of Vietnam that soldier's lives are valuable and you can't squander those lives for reasons like trying to impose your political will.

If you are going to war there should be a consensus to do so. You should win it with the least amount of loss of life. I think that's the biggest lesson that we've learned. I was anti-war when I got back.

You might have thought the war was over. You might have thought you were cut of it, but it wasn't over for you really. I'm sure a lot of guys are proud of serving their country. I mean we just didn't get the good war. Some people got World War I or World War II. Korea was a dirty, nasty war and so was Vietnam.

I'll tell you one thing—you better vote and you had better be politically active and you had better be aware of what's going on. And if you're not, your son or daughter can get sent off to war real quick. Things can change real quick. You hear people talk about putting that draft back in. Everybody needs to be in the military. It won't make a man or a woman out of you. You either have that in you or you don't.

I am proud of having been in the military. I just didn't catch a popular war. It is a victory that neither of my sons were forced into the military.

Literacy Connections

1. As you read this oral history interview with Jerry Walsh, what did you learn that helped you appreciate the value of oral history projects?
2. How would you describe Jerry Walsh's persona as portrayed in the oral history interview?
3. Think about the genre of oral histories and the purpose they serve. In what ways do oral histories contribute to our culture?
4. If you were going to conduct an oral history project, what might your subject be? Make a list of five topics that you find interesting and that you think deserve to be documented.
5. Earlier in this chapter, in an excerpt from his book *Doing Oral History: A Practical Guide*, Donald Ritchie discusses factors that figure into the reliability of information collected by oral history. If you were conducting an oral history project such as this one that Kelly Lamb conducted for her American Military History class, what steps could you take to help ensure that the information you collected was reliable?

Oral Literacy Projects

Family Stories

For this project, you'll transcribe a family story—perhaps a story about a memorable experience someone in your family had, a story about a family experience you'll never forget, a story involving family members that is remembered differently depending on who is telling the story, etc. The possibilities for topics are as endless as are the stories that play a role in family histories. You're encouraged to talk to family members and hear the story told afresh.

While you might compose a paper that tells your family story, you might also consider presenting your story in another form such as a PowerPoint or Flickr slideshow with words and images, a Web site, an oral performance, or a comic strip.

Music History Narrative

Think about the role music has played in your life, and write an essay in which you explore your history with music and the influence music has had in shaping you into the person you are today. Be sure to include plenty of specific details, including titles of songs and names of artists/groups, what was going on in your life that made certain types of music resonate with you at particular times, etc.

Oral History Interview

For this project you'll interview someone who experienced a significant historical event, record the interview, and transcribe it. You'll also need to preface the interview with a biography of the interviewee so that your readers will have some background before jumping into the transcribed interview.

An important part of this project will be talking with the interviewee before the interview to find out a little about her or his experience. This information will help you as you are developing the interview questions you would like to ask during the recorded interview. You might also find that you'll need to schedule a follow-up interview, in case you find that you need to obtain additional information to complete your project.

Along with the biography and transcribed interview, you'll need to submit a reflective cover letter in which you comment on how you decided whom to interview, how you developed your interview questions, how you conducted the interview(s), and what you learned as a result of conducting the oral history project.

Classroom Slam

This is a full-class project in which each member of the class writes a poem and presents it to the class, much as you saw in the poetry slams included in this chapter. Be careful to consider your audience as you compose your poem and prepare to present it. Think about what kind of topic would interest your audience, what kind of language would be appropriate, and what sort of presentation would be most effective.

You'll need to write a poem that can be presented in two to three minutes, and you'll need to take your poem through at least three drafts. You should share at least two of those drafts in peer response groups. You'll also practice your oral performance with your group so they can give you feedback not only on your writing but also on your performance.

Along with writing a poem, working with your peer review group, and making an oral performance to the class, you'll also submit a cover letter in which you explore how composing for an oral performance was different from composing a text that's only in print and discuss the rhetorical choices you made (organization, persona, revising and editing, etc.) based on the fact that this was an oral performance.

Researched Speech

For this project you'll prepare and present a researched speech to your class. Your teacher will specify the various requirements, such as the number of sources you must include, whether an outline is required, how many visuals you need to include, time requirements, etc. Your teacher will either allow you to choose the purpose of your speech (to inform, argue a position on an issue, argue for solution to a problem, etc.) or will define a purpose for you.

Be careful to choose a topic for your speech that truly interests you. If you aren't engaged with the topic, you won't enjoy conducting the research or making your presentation.

In addition to the various requirements described above, you'll also submit a reflective cover letter in which you explore how composing for an oral performance was different from composing a text that's only in print, and discuss the rhetorical choices you made (organization, persona, revising and editing, etc.), based on the fact that this was an oral performance.

Group Project: Audio Script

In this project, groups of three to five students will write and produce an audio script in the style of the program *This American Life*. To get a sense of the genre of the *This American Life* audio script, the group will listen to three different audio scripts from *This American Life* and write a two- to three-page rhetorical analysis of the audio scripts, discussing the persona, conventions, organization, audience, etc. These audio scripts can be found on the *This American Life* Web site at www.thisamericanlife.org/.

Once the group decides on a theme, it will write and revise a script and record the script. Groups can use a cassette recorder, a microphone and a computer, or a cell phone or PDA voice recorder. Your teacher might ask you to play the recording to the class or Podcast it, using an RSS feed. Groups will include their rhetorical analysis, drafts of their script, and a cassette tape or audio file on a CD or flash drive in a portfolio.

5

Situating Visual Literacies

This chapter will explore a medium you're familiar with but might not have thought about in terms of "literacy": the medium of the visual. As Professor Pavel Zemliansky argues in the introductory essay of this chapter, "We live in a visual culture." From television to movies to the Internet to billboards, we're immersed in visual messages every day. Because of this, it's just as important to  understand visual messages as it is to understand written messages. This chapter will help you think of images as acts of persuasion, and you'll consider the rhetoric of visuals using the components of literacy situations we discussed in Chapters 1 and 2: purpose, audience, genre, context, etc. In addition to applying the approaches to literacy situations we discussed in Chapters 1 and 2, you'll learn key terms and principles that are specific to reading images. The authors of the readings in this chapter will encourage you to be active and critical readers of images, and you'll practice active and critical visual literacy by examining the images in this chapter as well as finding your own images to analyze. Many of the "readings" in this chapter are images, and in this chapter we'll define what it means to "read" images and discuss strategies for "reading" visual texts.

You'll find selections that will—

- Expand your idea of literacy to include images as well as words
- Help you consider the meaning of *visual literacies*
- Help you explore the idea of what it means to be immersed in a visual world

- Give you a look at the process that Gopi Pitcher, a first-year college student, went through as she composed a digital slide show in response to an assignment from a composition course
- Provide you with principles for reading pictures
- Help you understand the cultural and political contexts of visual messages and become an active and a critical reader of images
- Help you learn to more effectively compose your own visual images
- Give you practice "reading" paintings, photographs, graffiti, and other images.

If you use the visual literacy projects at the end of this chapter, you might—

- Analyze an image
- Create a photo essay
- Design your own poster campaign
- Do a visual revision of a previous essay
- Write a film or television review
- Participate in a group project in which you create a documentary.

Let's start exploring visual mediums.

What Are Visual Literacies?

Before You Read

Think of a powerful image you've viewed recently—an advertisement, an image from television, a painting, a photograph, a poster, etc. What kind of argument did the image make, and how did it make that argument? In what ways did you "read" the image in order to understand it?

Literacy Is Not Just Words Anymore

Pavel Zemliansky
James Madison University

Pavel Zemliansky is an associate professor in the School of Writing, Rhetoric, and Technical Communication at James Madison University, where he also coordinates the first-year writing program. He teaches a variety of writing and rhetoric classes, both face-to-face and online.

Many of those classes focus on digital and visual rhetoric. Pavel has published books and articles about the teaching of writing, computers and writing, and professional communication. He believes that in order to be literate in the information age, we need to learn to write not only with words, but also with images, video, and sound.

We Live in a Visual Culture

1 Images profoundly influence our lives. Here are some examples:

2   Between 2001 and 2004, The US Department of Defense refused to release to the public images of flag-draped caskets of US soldiers killed during the wars in Afghanistan and Iraq. According to George Washington University's National Security Archive, the images were finally released in 2005 after a series of lawsuits based on the Freedom of Information Act had been filed ("The Return of the Fallen"). The images can now be seen at the Archive's website and other online locations.

3   In September of 2007, the website of *Time* Magazine published a photo of three Democratic Party candidates for President of the United States at a political fundraising event in Iowa. The photo showed the three candidates against a backdrop of a large American flag, during the performance of the national anthem. One of the candidates neglected to place his hand on his heart for the performance of the anthem, thus breaking a long-standing patriotic tradition. Within hours of the image's publication, the Internet was abuzz with speculations about this candidate's "lack of patriotism" and therefore his unsuitability for the highest political office in the land.

4   In October of 2007, National Public Radio aired a story about the producer of *Redacted*, a film about the Iraq war, blocking "a horrifying montage of real photos of dead and wounded Iraqis" against the objections of the film's director Brian DePalma (McChesney). According to the story, DePalma was angry because he believed that the producer was trying to conceal the truth about the war.

5   These three stories demonstrate that visual messages can shape the opinions and actions of individuals, political parties, and governments. They also suggest that being visually literate is crucial for living in the 21st century and for participation in the civic society.

6   We live in a visual culture. According to some estimates, an average American may encounter up to a thousand visual messages in the course of a single day. Writing in the *New York Times* in 2005, author Sarah Boxer notes that famous visuals, such as the Nike "swoosh" logo, or the Campbell Soup can, have become more than commercial messages. According to Boxer, they are "cultural moments," and "if you don't know at least some of them, you've probably just arrived on Earth from another planet." These visual messages have become parts of the fabric of life in modern-day

America. Some scholars have even argued that, because of the constant presence in our lives of television, Internet, and other visually based media, understanding visual messages has become more important than understanding print ones. While this claim is certainly debatable (writing is not going away any time soon), it is hard to deny that visuals play an increasingly important role in our lives.

7   My purpose in this essay is to explore ways in which visual arguments, which include images, movies, visual elements of the Internet, and so on, inform us, persuade us, and affect us, and what we need to do to become educated and informed readers of visuals. I will also develop a working definition of the term "visual literacy" and suggest several ways by which such literacy can be developed. I will work from the assumption that visual messages are texts that deserve careful and deliberate readings.

Visual Messages Are Arguments

8 Most of us have heard the statement "A picture is worth a thousand words." This statement implies that images reflect and represent reality accurately and objectively and that they do it better than words, which are liable to be misread and misinterpreted. And if that is the case, this thinking goes, then arguing with and about images becomes impossible, since images depict objects, persons, or events that are real. They exist now or existed in the past, and therefore, according to this view, only one interpretation of each of these images is possible.

9   To some extent, this view is correct. After all, images, especially photos, often reflect people or objects that exist in real life. But they do more than that. Like verbal texts, images can argue or contain claims and provide evidence in support of those claims. Photographers, visual designers, and other authors of visual messages can and do compose those messages in ways that influence viewers.

10   The notion that visuals simply reflect existing reality positions viewers as uncritical and inert consumers who are not equipped to read, interpret, or critique visual messages actively. This way of positioning the viewer is beneficial for the creators of visual arguments because that allows them to press their claims and agendas on the viewer with less expectation of resistance to the image's message or its critique.

Key Elements of Persuasion

11 The first step towards developing visual literacy, then, may be learning to treat visual messages as texts and as arguments. That means treating photos and other visuals not as simply objective representations of reality, but as persuasive creations designed to influence specific audiences.

As receivers of visual messages, we need to become active readers of visual texts rather than just passive and uncritical observers.

12   The online Merriam-Webster Dictionary defines the word "argument" as "discourse intended to persuade." Arguments make explicit or implicit claims and offer evidence in support of those claims. According to classical rhetoric, a theory of persuasion developed in Ancient Greece, arguments have the following features:

- Purpose, or the awareness by the author of what the text is trying to accomplish and the ability to accomplish that purpose in an argument
- Audience, or the ability to identify and reach the people who are likely to be persuaded by the text
- Context or occasion, or the ability to recognize and use the social and other conditions in which a text is produced and will be read

13   In addition, to be effective, every author must reach the target audience at three levels:

- Logical, or the level of reason manifested in the use of credible and appropriate evidence, such as facts, statistics, and so on
- Emotional, or the level of emotional identification of the audience with the issues covered in the argument
- Ethical, or the author's ability to present him or herself as a credible and trustworthy person.

14   To illustrate these ideas briefly, let us consider the structure of a typical political campaign and the kinds of persuasive messages it produces. A political candidate's staff identifies the issues that are important for voters. Then they create messages (press releases, speeches, TV, radio, and Internet ads) designed to persuade voters that their candidate is the best one for the job. This is the reflection of the purpose in their arguments. These messages are also crafted to reach the voters who might be amenable to voting for this candidate. This is how the campaign tries to reach its audience. Finally, they take into account the social condition, or mood, in which these messages will be delivered and consumed by the audience. In order for the messages to be persuasive, the voters must consider the issues those messages address as important as the political campaign considers them. This is the reflection of the author's awareness of the context or occasion of the campaign. As they do all this, the campaign's staff also tries to include in their arguments evidence that would appeal to the audience logically, emotionally, and ethically.

15   Rhetorical theory originated more than two thousand years ago with the purpose of studying the persuasive power of spoken language. Later on, when writing replaced speech as the main medium of communication

and persuasion, rhetoric became primarily concerned with the persuasive power of writing. As visual persuasion became more prevalent and important in our highly technological society, it is only natural that rhetoric as a discipline has moved beyond spoken and written language and into the study of visual persuasion. In the next section of this essay, I consider ways in which these basics elements of rhetoric can be used for reading and understanding visual texts.

How to Read a Visual Text

16 The main difficulty with reading visual texts is that they rarely, if ever, present claims in the kind of overt and explicit form that verbal texts do. In other words, visual arguments usually do not contain the kind of succinct thesis statements, which we know to look for when analyzing verbal texts. Instead, the clues about such texts' argumentative nature are elsewhere: in the author's intentions, the context surrounding the photograph, in its composition, color-scheme, and so on.

17 Nevertheless, it is possible to apply the main principles of active and critical reading used with verbal texts to visual arguments. In order to examine how this might be done, let us look at a visual argument created by Christina Griffin, a student in one of my writing classes.

18 The photograph below was taken in Harrisonburg, Virginia, in response to the assignment to create visual arguments about the local community.

Downtown Harrisonburg, Virginia, by Christina Griffin

19   Like any other argument, verbal or visual, this photo can be read in many different ways. For example, a casual observer might conclude that Harrisonburg is a town with a cold climate, a gray sky, and some industrial plants. A more careful reader, however, will see it an argument about the dual identity of Harrisonburg, a changing town which is influenced by both industry and culture.

20   In the kind of reading of this image which I am about to undertake, I will attempt to go beyond the initial impressions or reactions one might get after looking at the photo casually. Instead, I will read the photo in a way similar to the one I'd apply to a complex verbal text. I will try to decide what the purpose of the photographer might have been, what audience Christina might have been trying to reach, and how the context in which the image was created and would be viewed might have contributed to my reading of this visual text.

Purpose

21   In order to read an image like an argument, it is important to think about its purpose. While doing that, it is important not to try to "guess" the author's intentions. Inexperienced readers often hesitate to make conclusions about the purpose of a text because they have no way of knowing what exactly the author wanted to convey. Remember, however, that the purpose of any critical reading is not to guess the author's intentions, but to create a reading which makes sense to the reader and which can be supported by the evidence presented in the text. Therefore, during my reading, I will look for evidence to support my reading of this photograph.

22   I am in a privileged position because I know what Christina's purpose was when she was taking the photograph. I know that she was trying to create a visual argument. This knowledge makes my reading of the photograph easier. Other readers, who do not have such "behind the scenes" knowledge, should nevertheless think about the purpose of this visual text. There are clues in the photograph which will help them in that.

23   Compositionally, the image clearly consists of two parts: the industrial side of Harrisonburg on the right and the cultural one on the left. The part of the photo which shows the "industrial side" of Harrisonburg is larger than the part representing the town's "cultural" side. This leads me to conclude that the industrial side still dominates local life. In addition, the cloudy skies over the "industrial" part of the image might suggest the somewhat depressed state of the local economy while the blue skies over the "culture" part might be telling us that culture in Harrisonburg has a bright future.

24   Translated into more familiar terms of an overt thesis or claim, then, we might say that this photograph advances the following argument: "Harrisonburg is a town whose life is influenced by both industry and culture. While industry plays an important part now, its future is uncertain as the

town tries to reinvent itself." Like all arguments, this one is, of course, open to debate and re-interpretation. It is not the final answer to the meaning of the photograph, but only one of many possible readings of it.

Target Audience

25 The next element of a rhetorical approach to reading images critically is audience. The immediate audience for Christina's project was the other members of the class. However, the argument presented in the photograph provides a new and interesting perspective on Harrisonburg to its inhabitants and visitors outside of the class. More broadly, we can see the photograph as an argument directed at anyone interested in issues of "small town America," urban revitalization, or other similar social issues.

26   Notice that while the target audience may not be particularly friendly or particularly hostile to the argument presented in the photograph, the photograph could lead to some interesting discussions about the past, present, and future of the town depicted in it as well as about larger issues that surround the image.

Context

27 Finally, as critical readers of visual arguments, we need to look at the context in which the image was created and in which it is likely to be read by its target audience. What we know about the circumstances in which the argument was created can significantly influence our reading of those arguments. Because I work in Harrisonburg and know it fairly well, when reading Christina's photograph, I mentally "fill in the blanks" around what is depicted in it, to include two university campuses located in the town, the rolling farmland around it, and other details. I also know that a major downtown revitalization project is under way in Harrisonburg and that some of the results of that revitalization are depicted on the photograph. All this knowledge changes my reading of the images and makes it different from that of someone who has never visited the place.

Rhetorical Appeals in Visual Arguments

28 Earlier in the essay, I stated that successful arguments must appeal to audiences in three ways: logically, emotionally, and ethically. The logical appeal of Christina's photograph is manifested in the evidence of the "dual" character of Harrisonburg which she noticed and conveyed to her readers. While most of us don't know her exact intentions when taking the photo, given the evidence presented to us in the image, it would be reasonable to conclude that this was the argument she had tried to create.

29   Christina also has the necessary credibility, or ethical appeal, to be persuasive. While she is not a world-famous photographer, as a resident of Harrisonburg, she knows the town well enough to create arguments about it. Her credibility is also bolstered by the fact that she took the photo as a member of a class that studied visual persuasion. To a certain extent, this makes her an expert in the creation of visual arguments.

30   Emotional appeal in the photograph is achieved through its color scheme which is dominated by gray tones. That color scheme creates a feeling of a cold late winter day.

Creating Visual Arguments

31 To be a visually literate person, it is important to not only read visual arguments but also to write them. Digital cameras and other modern technologies make the creation of visual arguments easier than ever, and in some of your classes you may be asked to argue not only with words but also with visuals. Such visual arguments range from single images and photo essays to documentary films and sophisticated multimedia presentations which combine images, film clips, audio, and text.

32   Throughout this essay, I have hoped to show how basic rhetorical principles can be applied to the reading of visual arguments. They can also be applied to their production. In their interactive CD-ROM *IX Visual Exercises*, writing teachers Cheryl Ball and Kristin Arola offer the following principles for composing visual arguments:

• Pay close attention to your purpose and audience. Just like in verbal arguments, having a clear sense of both will give your work the necessary direction and force.

• Be aware of the context in which you create the argument and in which it will be read. In photography, context is often provided through captions.

• Organize elements of the visual argument to present a coherent whole. When taking a photo, for example, "compose" it in the viewfinder of your camera to emphasize the elements which you consider to be the most important.

• Create coherence and emphasis through careful alignment, sequencing of visual elements, and color coordination or juxtaposition (Ball and Arola).

33   To rephrase Ball and Arola's advice, successful visual compositions tell a story or present an argument, much like an essay that consists only of words. A variety of computer programs can be used to create visual compositions. Some of these programs include Microsoft PowerPoint; Apple's

iLife software, which allows users to edit images, video, and sound; and such online tools as Google Picasa Albums, Flickr, YouTube, and others. Many of these tools are either low cost or free.

(Re)Defining Visual Literacy

34 We must read images and other visual compositions in the same manner in which we read verbal texts: critically, actively, and thoroughly. We must recognize that visual messages do not simply represent "objective reality," but rather tell stories and advance arguments, points of view, and agendas. Finally, we must recognize the power of visual compositions to influence the thinking, behavior, and decision-making of individuals, groups, and whole societies.

35   A visually literate person is able to recognize the basic rhetorical elements of visual arguments: purpose, target audience, and context or occasion. A visually literate person also understands how authors of visual arguments use logical, emotional, and ethical appeals to create their messages. Finally, a visually literate person has some proficiency with creating visual arguments using a variety of visual media.

36   Computers, the Internet, and other technological advancements of the late 20th century have changed our idea of what writing is. Now, the concept of "writing" is often meant to include not only verbal, but also visual elements. This change requires us to develop new forms of literacy if we are to remain active participants in society's intellectual and political life. Visual literacy is one of those new literacies required of any educated person in the 21st century.

Works Cited

Ball, Cheryl E. and Kristin L. Arola. *IX Visual Exercises*. Boston: Bedford St. Martin's, 2004. CD.

Boxer, Sarah. "Got Wit? Make It Visual in Ads Online." *New York Times*. 3 Oct. 2005. Web. 28 Nov. 2007.

Frazier, Danny Wilcox. "Senator Barack Obama, Governor Bill Richardson, Senator Hillary Clinton and Ruth Harkin Stand During the National Anthem." 17 Sept. 2007. Photograph. *Time Magazine*. 28 Nov. 2007.

Griffin, Christina. "Downtown Harrisonburg, Virginia." 22 Jan. 2007. Photograph. *Flickr*. 28 Nov. 2007.

McChesney, John. "'Redacted' Producer Blocks Real, Horrifying Images." *All Things Considered*. Nat. Public Radio. WBUR, New York, 23 Oct. 2007. Radio.

"Return of the Fallen." *The National Security Archive*. The George Washington University. Washington, DC, 28 Apr. 2005. Web. 28 Nov. 2007.

Literacy Connections

1. Do you agree with Zemliansky's assertion that visual messages are arguments? Why or why not?
2. What are the qualities that Zemliansky associates with a "visually literate person"?
3. Zemliansky suggests becoming an active reader of visual texts. In small groups, come up with some strategies for being an active and critical viewer, drawing on Professor Zemliansky's own reading of his student's photograph of Harrisonburg and your own strategies for reading visual texts.
4. Think of an image that represents a "cultural moment." Why is the image culturally significant? What is it about the image that gives it such a strong impact?
5. Compare Zemliansky's approach to reading images to the approach Sturken and Cartwright take in the excerpt from their book *Practices of Looking*. In what ways are the approaches similar?

Before You Read

Think of a time you used both words and images together to compose a message, either in school or out of school. How was composing with words and images different than composing in just words? Why did you choose the images that you used?

Student Case Study: Composing a Digital Slide Show

Gopi Pitcher was enrolled in a first-year composition course at James Madison University when she was given an assignment to revise an essay she'd written and turn it into a completely visual presentation. Included in this case study is Gopi's original essay, a *photo essay* that combined print and visual images, and her completely visual revision of the photo essay, a digital slide show.

A close look at Gopi's composing processes for her photo essay and her digital slide show will help you think about rhetorical choices that composers make when they work in visual mediums. Before we look at Gopi's digital slide show, let's take a look at the photo essay that inspired the slide show. Here's the assignment Gopi was given for the photo essay:

> *After reading and discussing Walker Evans' and James Agee's work "Let Us Now Praise Famous Men," compose a similar essay on a topic of your choice. Combine images with words, in a manner similar to Evans and Agee. When images and words are used together in this manner, images do not illustrate words and words do not describe images. Instead, they work interdependently to create and express meaning in various ways.*
> *Your final product will consist of two parts:*
>
> - *The first part will be a photo essay consisting of five to seven images;*
> - *The second part will be textual*
>
> *Your images may come from any source, either from your own collection or from external sources.*

Here's Gopi's response to the assignment, a photo essay about her experiences as an American immigrant:

> *Before you even begin to read this essay, consider the following. The images used in this work are to be looked at before reading the text. The images are taken independently from the actual words written on the page, then put together later during a second reading of the work. After looking at the pictures the first time, next read over the text. The purpose of the piece is to raise awareness on a subject, but not specifically and directly state our arguments so don't be confused when you don't find a main thesis. After reading the text the first time, go back over everything, even the pictures. Remember the pictures are a part of the work too and have as much importance in depicting what I am trying to say. After a second look at both parts of the essay, try to envision it as one piece of work: a photographic essay. Without pictures, the words are just a description, which allows readers freedom to picture the description. Without words, images aren't explained and can be interpreted in different ways, and sometimes interpreted so the artist's true meaning isn't clear. Both images and words are there so there is no guessing about our intentions or about the topic we want to push through, even without a direct thesis. It is actually an advantage to having a photographic essay, this or Agee and Evan's. With ours, both images and words are there, so there is no guessing about our intentions or about the topic we want to push through, even without a direct thesis.*

1   The other kids were loud and wouldn't sit still. I seemed to be the only one who wasn't moving around. Maybe it was because I was scared of my surroundings or maybe I was just trying to take in all of the commotion. Whatever the reason, I sat in silence, just looking around at all the people. I stuck out from the other children since my mom gave me a nice red, white and blue outfit to wear. After a long ceremony, my mom was given a certificate; I was legal.

2   My mother adopted me from India when I was about two years old. By the time my mother wanted to adopt a child and finished preparing a home study and other documents that needed to be approved, signed, notarized,

and certified by the state of Virginia, the U.S. State Department and the Indian Embassy, she waited for three years for a referral for a child. Then my mom waited for the phone call to tell her that a child (me) needed a family. Next my mother went on December 18 to the INS (Immigration and Naturalization Service) to file that I (who was an orphan) was now an immediate family member. On March 18, three months later, she received a notification from INS that the immediate family member application had been approved. Then on May 22, my mother went back to the INS to apply for an immigrant visa to bring me over. June 18, news arrived that my visa had been sent to Bombay. July 17, my mom received a call saying that I didn't have a visa, and it wasn't in Bombay. Going back to INS, my mother was furious and it turned out that INS didn't even have a record of a visa being sent to Bombay. However, my mom did have documentation showing it had. Needing to work fast because the arrival date was approaching, my mother called Congressman Jim Moran and India, trying to fix the situation. The next day Congressman Moran secured a visa to be sent to India. All of us, back in India, had to get a new flight to America since we had to wait for my visa. Finally, on July 24, I arrived in New York City. I arrived with my passport and a resident alien card that served as proof that I was allowed in the United States. We made another visit to INS to apply for citizenship. September 24, I was finally granted citizenship. My mother put in about four years and $18,000 just to get me here and legalized. She paid the adoption agencies here and in India, courts in India, fees every time she went to the INS, attorney fees, and fees for every piece of document that was certified and notarized.

3   As I looked upon the mass of people surrounding DC, and watching the news, I remembered that day. Mothers, fathers, sisters, brothers, young and old, everyone had come with signs and banners of all different colors. There were many flags waving in the air, as the hot sun beat down on the thousands of people. There were massive bulks of green, red, even blue and white parading down the city sidewalk. Foreign flags as well as American flags were swaying back and forth in the slight breeze, while many different people were cheering and chanting in several languages. They were all there for one purpose, to be heard.

4   Mothers were holding children, and families walking hand in hand, what a glorious sight to see. I was sure of it, I knew I too wanted to be heard, but was in awe at the demonstration to even open my mouth to talk. I asked my mother what exactly was happening, and she just pointed to a white building and said, "They are deciding these people's fate."

Border Security

5 **The Administration Will Continue to Strengthen Security at the Border with Additional Personnel and Infrastructure.** We are committed to implementing the following border security measures by December 31, 2008:

- 18,300 Border Patrol agents
- 370 miles of fencing
- 300 miles of vehicle barriers
- 105 camera and radar towers
- Three additional UAVs

6   I looked again at the crowd in the streets, then back at the television. I saw a woman in the crowd where the news channel was filming. She was dressed very casual, but had two flags pinned to her jacket, one of her home country and one of the United States. She was crying and reaching out towards that white building. As tears rolled down her cheeks she pulled out a photograph from her jacket. It was a picture of a younger girl, and two young boys, and finally an older man. She was balling almost uncontrollably, begging, in Spanish, for Congress to let her family come over the border.

7   *Naturalization Facts:*
    The applicant must lawfully enter the country and gain legal permanent resident
    status. After becoming a legal resident, a foreign national must reside in the
    United States continuously for five years (or three years for spouses of American
    citizens). During that period, he or she must be physically present in the country
    for at least fifty percent of the time. This "probationary" period allows the foreign
    national to become fully acclimated to American life and systems so that he or she
    can fully participate in the national community upon becoming a citizen.

8   *A naturalization applicant must be at least eighteen years old. The applicant*
    must possess the ability to understand, speak, read, and write basic English.
    Certain older applicants may receive an exemption from this requirement if their
    residence is of long standing. Applicants must also demonstrate knowledge of
    U.S. history, politics, and government. The Immigration and Naturalization
    Service (INS) administers an examination to applicants that they must pass to
    qualify for naturalization.

9   *The cost of naturalization soars from $330 to $595 for adult applicants and*
    from $355 to $460 for children. The fee for a green card application zooms from
    $325 to $900.

10 A little while later, my mom took me home, and during the whole ride
    back, I kept thinking about that sobbing woman. I thought to myself, "I know
    there are others just like her. Why won't anyone help her? Why won't any-
    one go over and comfort her?" Just then, I too started to cry. My mom looked
    over at me, and took my hand, and said "I know, we were very lucky."

11 **"You, Whoever You Are"**
    You, whoever you are!...
    All you continentals of Asia, Africa, Europe, Australia, indifferent of place!
    All you on the numberless islands of the archipelagoes of the sea!
    All you of centuries hence when you listen to me!
    All you each and everywhere whom I specify not, but include just the same!
    Health to you! good will to you all, from me and America sent!
    Each of us is inevitable,
    Each of us is limitless—each of us with his or her right upon the earth,
    Each of us allow'd the eternal purports of the earth,
    Each of us here as divinely as any is here.
    Walt Whitman

12 She said, "We all deserve an opportunity to better ourselves." Then she
    turned away and continued to drive. Every day of my life I think of how
    lucky I am and how wonderful my mother is.

Works Cited

Bland, Susikind Susser. "Price Tag: Immigration Fee Hikes and How We
    Should Respond; Guest Commentary by Gary Endelman." 2006. Web.
    13 Oct. 2007.

Hood, Michael. "Talk radio wins the immigration battle, the GOP loses the war." 28 June 2007. Web. 12 Oct. 2007.

"Immigration." *Library of Congress* 6 Apr. 2002. Web. 13 Oct. 2007.

"Immigrant DNA testing." 2007. Web. 12 Oct. 2007.

Lynn, Jane. "Destination: Washington." n.d. Web. 16 Oct. 2007.

"U.S. Citizenship & Naturalization Overview." *Find Law*. 2007. Web. 17 Oct. 2007.

White House. "Comprehensive Immigration Reform." 10 Aug. 2007. Web. 14 Oct. 2007.

Now that you've read Gopi's photo essay, take a look at the assignment she was given that inspired her digital slide show:

Revisit the image/text work you created following the Evans/Agee piece and revise it in a visual medium. As you revise, you may choose to keep your original message or to change it; you may choose to address the same or a different audience; you may choose to keep the original tone or change it.

Here are some options:
- *a photo essay*
- *a short movie clip, with or without sound*
- *a poster or collage*
- *a Web site*

Follow up your revision with a 500–600-word long reflection piece in which you discuss the revision process and the results you hope to achieve with this work.

Gopi chose to turn her essay into a digital slide show. Let's get a glimpse into Gopi's process for composing her digital slide show. In our interview with her, Gopi talked about the process of finding images for her slide show:

Since my whole argument was about immigration and its laws, I was trying to find pictures of immigrants. Where else better to find pictures than to type in "Ellis Island" on the Internet? Most of those pictures were black-and-white, but I wanted to add some color into the slide show. I also typed in "adoption," "Indian immigrants," "Hispanic immigrants," even "homeless children." All were an attempt to give me photos of people now, in this time, and decade, of people who want to immigrate or capture the idea that thousands of people want better lives, and need homes.

Gopi had another reason why she wanted both black-and-white and color images. Gopi said that "the images were supposed to show that this issue has occurred before (the black-and-white photos) and is still an issue today (color pictures)." Making decisions about what kinds of visuals you're including in your composition requires thoughtful reflection. Gopi had a rhetorical purpose for including both black-and-white and color images—her decisions about visual persuasion weren't made randomly.

Gopi found that the composing process for creating the slide show was more challenging than she thought it would be when she was first given the assignment. Here's what she had to say about the process of creating the slide show:

> *I felt that composing the slide show was harder than I thought. Unlike the essay I have no words to explain everything I want to or had explained within the essay. Everything had to be shown. . . . Finding the pictures started to get difficult when trying to find those specific photos that capture the very emotions that I wanted to show my audience, so they too could evoke some emotion or reaction. With an essay, I could just ramble on then clean it up later with editing; you can't do that with a visual argument. Then there is the worry that the argument won't come through. It has to be a strong argument so anyone on any given day can view it and say "hey I know what she's trying to tell me."*

Below are some images from Gopi's slide show, which combines music (the song "This Land Is Your Land" by Woody Guthrie) with a series of images:

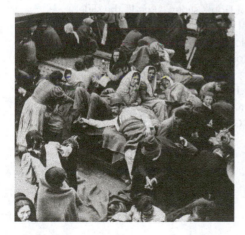

Gopi found out that composing in a visual medium is as challenging as composing in a verbal medium. She said that creating a visual composition "can take a while and it is a long and difficult process on deciding what clips or pictures to use to convey the message being sent out to the audience. A lot of thought is put into these types of works." But even though the processes of composing her photo essay and her digital slide show were more complex and challenging than she thought they would be, Gopi felt that the chance to present her argument about immigration in different formats was an advantage:

> *I feel that for this work to be a real success and for the argument to affect a broader range of viewers it should be presented in more than one way. Any story, essay, speech or argument can be told in many different ways and with a wide range of media. I also feel if we have the ability to use different types of media to present a topic or idea why not use them?*

Literacy Connections

1. Do an Internet search using the key term *photo essay* and find examples of photo essays. What are some of the conventions of the genre of the photo essay?
2. Compare Gopi's photo essay with the photo essay you found in question 1. How does Gopi's photo essay fulfill the expectations of the genre?
3. In her essay, Gopi says, "Without pictures, the words are just a description, which allows readers freedom to picture the description. Without words, images aren't explained and can be interpreted in different ways, and sometimes interpreted so the artist's true meaning isn't clear." Respond to Gopi's assertion. To what extent do you agree or disagree with Gopi?
4. Do a rhetorical analysis of one of Gopi's slides. "Read" the slide closely and discuss the rhetorical effects of the slide. Consider formal features of the slide, such as color, composition, perspective, tone, etc., as well as the political, historical, and cultural context of the image.
5. In his introductory essay to the chapter, Pavel Zemliansky discussed rhetorical appeals that images make. What rhetorical appeals does Gopi make in her photo essay? Give specific examples.

Visual Literacy Readings

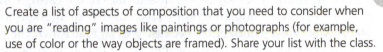

Before You Read

Create a list of aspects of composition that you need to consider when you are "reading" images like paintings or photographs (for example, use of color or the way objects are framed). Share your list with the class.

Excerpts from *Picture This: How Pictures Work*

by Molly Bang

In *Picture This,* Molly Bang uses examples of her own drawings to explore some principles for reading images. On her Web site, *www.mollybang.com,* Bang says *Picture This* "explains the structural principles that all artists use to make their pictures emotionally powerful." This excerpt from Bang's book will help give you some approaches to visual literacy that you can apply to any visual encounter—in the readings in the rest of this chapter and in your everyday life. In the first half of *Picture This,* Bang uses drawings of the children's story *Little Red Riding Hood* to illustrate her principles about the composition of pictures, and, in the second half, she explores those principles in more detail. The following excerpt is from the second half of *Picture This.* Bang is a writer and artist who has published numerous children's books in addition to *Picture This.*

The Principles

I can't remember the order in which these principles occurred to me. I had read a lot and thought a lot about what went on in pictures, but largely things seemed to either "work" or "not work" for unrelated reasons. I think the principles pretty much came to me all at once, while I was playing with the Little Red Riding Hood pictures. What has taken time is paring them down to the bone. I've ordered them not in any hierarchical order, because I don't feel there is a hierarchy here, but more in the order that seemed most logical. Was it when I tilted the trees that I saw how gravity affected pictures? Whatever the reason, the first principles have to do with gravity.

Gravity is the strongest physical force that we're consciously aware of, and we're subject to it all the time. The force of gravity affects our responses to horizontal, vertical, and diagonal shapes, and it affects our responses to the placement of shapes on the page.

This all sounds very abstract, but what does it mean in concrete terms?

1. **Smooth, flat, horizontal shapes give us a sense of stability and calm.**
   I associate horizontal shapes with the surface of the earth or the horizon line—with the floor, the prairie, a calm sea. We humans are most
   stable when we are horizontal, because we can't fall down. Shapes that
   lie horizontal look secure because they won't fall on us, either. Because
   of this, pictures that emphasize horizontal structure generally give an
   overall sense of stability and calm.

   But, also, smaller horizontal or horizontally oriented shapes within a
   picture can be felt as islands of calm. Part of the stability we felt in Little
   Red Riding Hood as a triangle was due to her wide, flat, horizontal base.
   [Bang is referring here to drawings of Little Red Riding Hood that appear
   in the first half of her book.]

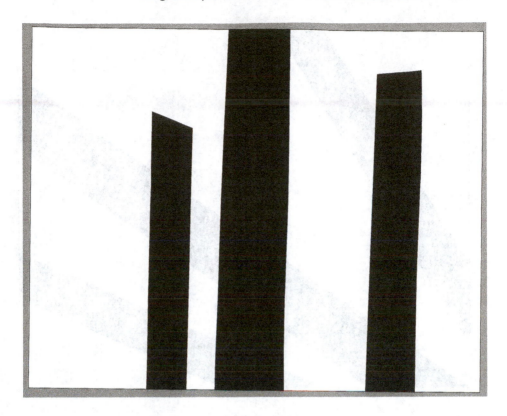

2. **Vertical shapes are more exciting and more active. Vertical shapes rebel against the earth's gravity. They imply energy and a reaching toward heights or the heavens.**
   Think of the things that grow or are built vertically: trees and plants grow up toward the sun; churches and skyscrapers reach toward the heavens as high as they can go. These structures require a great deal of energy to build—to become vertical. They will release a great deal of energy if they fall.
   Vertical structures are monuments to kinetic energy of the past and the future, and to potential energy of the present.

3. **Diagonal shapes are dynamic because they imply motion or tension.**
   Objects in nature that are on a diagonal are either in movement or in
   tension.

   Most of us see these diagonal lines as some sort of pillars falling.
   (I see them as flat bars of iron.) They could as easily be roof beams, supported by structures outside the picture, or parts of growing branches,
   pulled up toward the light of the sun but at the same time pulled down
   to the earth by gravity.

   We can also see these bars as leading us into the picture, leading
   us back into space. In an asymmetrical frame, diagonals give a sense
   of depth.

   But however we see the bars, they are felt to be in movement or in
   tension because they are on a diagonal.

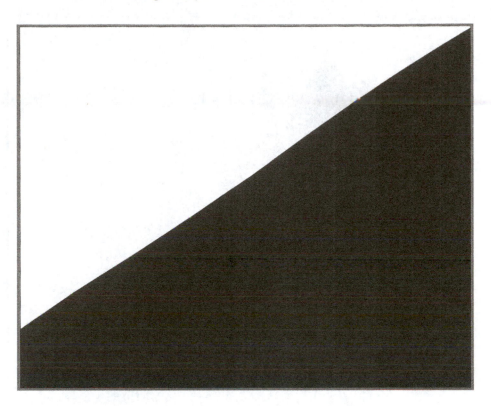

Mountains, sliding boards, waves: all of these are diagonals in movement or in tension. (Mountains are not visibly in motion, but they are gradually being worn down to flatness.) If we imagine an object on this surface, it has to move. Even our eyes can't help moving down and up it.

Notice how we tend to read diagonals from left to right, as though they are going up or descending.

Pictures are usually read as though there is an invisible, emotional horizon line stretching across the middle of the space and dividing it into top and bottom.

4. **The upper half of a picture is a place of freedom, happiness, and triumph; objects placed in the top half often feel more "spiritual."**
When we are high up, we are in a stronger tactical position: we can see our enemies and throw things down on them. Down low, we can't see very far; things might fall on us and crush us.

If we identify with an object that is in the upper half of a picture, we tend to feel lighter and gayer. If we want to show the spirituality of

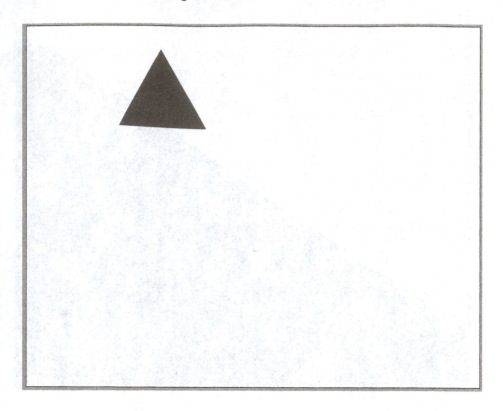

an object, we tend to place it high up. Again, this is due to the force of gravity: objects that are higher up give a sense of floating or flying or otherwise escaping the gravitational pull of the earth.

Think of some of the expressions we use every day to show that we're feeling happy or have done well: "Top o' the morning to you!" "She's at the top of the charts/the class/her form," "top man on the totem pole," "top gun," "top dog," "top-drawer," "top-notch," "Things are looking up," "I'm high as a kite," and so forth.

When people are said to be "high," however, it implies that they may eventually have a "terrible downer" when they "come back to earth."

The bottom half of a picture feels more threatened, heavier, sadder, or constrained; objects placed in the bottom half also feel more grounded.

Think of expressions that show sadness or failure: "down in the dumps," "feeling down," "feeling low," "low-down dirty dog," "living the low life," "lower than a snake's belly," and so on. We feel the same sorts of emotional responses to this lower position in pictures.

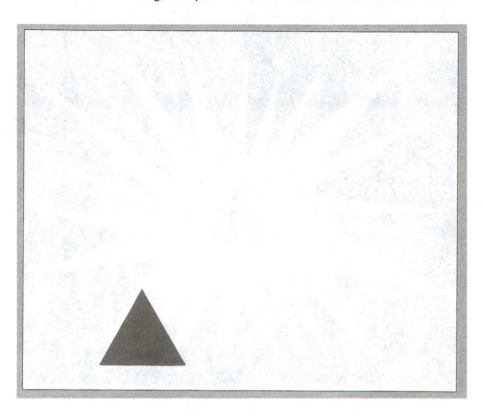

On the other hand, because we tend to see pictures as extensions of our world, thinking of the top half as "sky" and the bottom half as "ground," objects in the lower half of the picture feel more grounded—more attached to the earth and less mobile.

There is an odd corollary here, which at first seems contradictory: **an object placed higher up on the page has "greater pictorial weight."** This simply means that our attention is drawn to the same object more, or it feels more important, if it is higher up than if it is lower down. We must feel that most things truly "belong on the ground," and we are perturbed when this is not the case. All other things being equal, if we want to put more emphasis on an object, we tend to place it in the upper half of the page. It tends to feel freer, less attached to the earth, and lighter, but it also has greater pictorial weight.

5. **The center of the page is the most effective "center of attention." It is the point of greatest attraction.**
This picture can be read either as a jewel radiating light (or a heroine radiating triumph) or as a figure surrounded on all sides by attackers. Our emotional response depends on the context, but the fact remains that it is difficult to take our eyes from the center and move them around the page. They are trapped, pinned to the center.

What happens when the focus of attention is shifted away from the center of the page?

First of all, the picture is more dynamic. We feel that the triangle is moving now, on a diagonal path either down toward the lower right and out toward us or away from us and toward the upper left. This sense of movement comes about because our eyes are now encouraged to move. We can shift along the points to the darkness at the right, which has now become a focus on its own; we move from darkness to the triangle and back again.

Or we can move to the white space at the left—and clear off the page. Because the white area extends to the frame, the picture implies space outside itself. It breaks out into the world beyond.

But notice that with all of this moving around, the invisible lines of force are ever-present. We are aware of gravity as we move up and down and across the page. At the same time, we are very aware of the center as our eyes go back and forth across it; we are aware of the jagged lines dividing the page down the center. The center can be used as the hub of the picture, where more intense action takes place, as an empty area of calm or incompleteness, as a divider of left from right, as the area at which two equal elements join, and so forth. But whatever we do with the center, our eyes are drawn to it and our feelings are strongly affected by it.

We are also aware of "breaking out of" the rectangular frame. Whether or not we are conscious of these forces, we are aware of them. They encourage our eyes to move in certain directions, and they affect our emotional response to what is going on.

The next principle has to do with light and dark. We read light backgrounds as day and dark backgrounds as night, twilight, or storm.

6. **White or light backgrounds feel safer to us than dark backgrounds because we can see well during the day and only poorly at night.** As a result of our inability to see in the dark, black often symbolizes the unknown, and all our fears associated with the unknown, while white signifies brightness and hope.

There are, however, exceptions to every rule, usually due to context. Two obvious exceptions here are that we would feel safer if we were escaping from some danger "under cover of darkness," and we would feel terrified if we were deserted on a limitless expanse of ice.

7. **We feel more scared looking at pointed shapes; we feel more secure or comforted looking at rounded shapes or curves.**
   Our skin is thin. Pointed objects can easily pierce through to our innards and kill us. What do we know of that has sharp points? Most weapons are pointed: knives, arrows, spears, missiles, rockets; so are rocky mountains, the bows of boats that cut through the water, cutting tools like scissors and saw blades, bee stingers, teeth . . .

Curved shapes embrace us and protect us.

This picture of curves can't make us any safer than can the picture of points, and we know this, but the picture of curved surfaces makes us feel more secure than the one with sharp points, because of our associations with these shapes. What do we know of that is formed from curves? Rolling hills and rolling seas, boulders, rivers—but our earliest and strongest association is with bodies, especially our mothers' bodies, and when we were babies, there was no place more secure and full of comfort.

Because of these associations, pictures with curved shapes feel more secure and comforting than ones with sharp points, which feel scarier and more threatening.

8. **The larger an object is in a picture, the stronger it feels.**

We generally feel more secure physically when we are big than when we are little, because we're more capable of physically overpowering an enemy. One of the easiest ways to make a protagonist—or a threat—appear strong is to make it VERY large.

The same figure appears much more vulnerable if it is made very small. If we want to show a protagonist facing a terrible danger, the danger will seem much more threatening if it is huge and the protagonist is very small. We associate size with strength—strength of any sort.

This word *associate* is the key to the whole process of how picture structure affects our emotions. We know these pictures can't do us any more harm or make us any safer than a blank sheet of paper can, but we feel different looking at different pictures, because we associate the shapes, colors, and placement of the various picture elements with objects we have experienced in the "real" world outside the picture.

When we look at a picture, we know perfectly well that it's a picture and not the real thing, but we suspend disbelief. For a moment, the picture is "real." We associate pointed shapes with real, pointed objects. We associate red with real blood and fire. Specific elements such as points or color or size seem to call up the emotions we felt when we experienced actual sharp points or colors or noticeably large or small things. It is these "emotions attached to remembered experiences" that seem largely to determine our present responses.

However, notice what happens when we are given the same instructions for this collection of shapes.

Our eyes immediately associate the forms by color, regardless of their shapes. We can still make groups of triangles and circles, but we are forcing ourselves to do it; our strongest association is by color. (This is not necessarily the case for small children, however: they tend to make a stronger association with shape.)

9. **We associate the same or similar colors much more strongly than we associate the same or similar shapes.**

Our association of objects by color is immediate and very strong.

The association can be "positive," as with team players who all wear the same color uniform, or "negative," as with Little Red Riding Hood and the wolf's eye and tongue. But in both cases we associate entities of the same color, and we read a meaning into their association.

This page represents a situation that I'm not clear enough about to give a name to or call a principle, but that I can see working.

Repetition and confusion (regularity and irregularity? order and disorder?) are more difficult to talk about than the other elements because they involve patterns made by those other elements. Our eyes search for repetitive patterns, which enable us to make sense out of what we see. We notice repetition amid confusion, and the opposite, and we notice a break in a repetitive pattern. But how do these two sorts of patterns make us feel?

My question is hampered by the idea of "perfect" regularity and "perfect" chaos. Some repetition gives us a sense of security, in that we know what is coming next. We plant our hedges and beans in orderly rows and arrange our lives in largely repetitive schedules. Confusion is more frightening for most of us. We say we are "disoriented."

But "perfect" regularity—continual, relentless repetition—is perhaps even more horrifying in its monotony than confusion is. It implies a cold, unfeeling, mechanical mind, whether human or inhuman. Such patterns do not exist in nature; there are too many forces working against each other.

Either extreme is terrifying. I think of a remark made by the Japanese novelist Ryunosuke Akutagawa, that for him the worst hell would be an unending forest of cherry trees in full bloom.

Life needs a mixture. Our feelings seem to be elicited by the proportion and "perfection" of regularity and irregularity, as well as by what shapes and colors are chosen.

The last principle involves combinations of all the others and is perhaps the most basic to our survival and to our way of understanding the world—and pictures. It is simply that:

10. **We notice contrasts, or, put another way, contrast enables us to see.** The contrast can be between colors, shapes, sizes, placement, or combinations of these, but it is the contrast that enables us to see both patterns and elements. Pictures—and human perceptions—are based on contrasts.

Literacy Connections

1. List three things you learned about reading pictures that you didn't know before you read this excerpt from *Picture This*.
2. In your own words, write down the ways that Bang defines the following key terms and why they are so important to reading pictures:

   Movement   Pictorial weight
   Tension   Contrast

3. Choose a picture (a painting, photograph, billboard, poster, etc.) and do a "reading" of the picture, applying Bang's principles.
4. In *Picture This*, Bang is focused on the "formal" aspects of reading pictures—the formal features of the picture itself (contrast, movement, tension, etc.). Can you think of aspects of reading pictures that we need to consider that are outside of the formal features of the picture itself? Describe these aspects.
5. Use Bang's principles to do a close reading of the three Edward Hopper paintings in the color insert in this chapter.

Before You Read

Before you read about the relationships among images, culture, and power, practice exploring these issues. Find an image of a cover of a magazine you're interested in, either in print or online. In a five-minute freewrite, discuss what you think are the cultural beliefs the image reflects. Give evidence from the image to support your observation.

Excerpts from *Practices of Looking: An Introduction to Visual Culture*

Marita Sturken and Lisa Cartwright

Practices of Looking focuses on how we understand visual media and how we use images to communicate. The purpose of *Practices of Looking* is to introduce college students to visual literacy. The following excerpts are from Chapter 1, "Images, Power, and Politics." These excerpts will help you think about the way that culture and politics shape the way we use and read images. Marita Sturken is a professor at the University of Southern California, where she teaches cultural studies. Lisa Cartwright is a professor at the University of Rochester and director of the Susan B. Anthony Institute for Gender and Women's Studies.

Representation

1 *Representation* refers to the use of language and images to create meaning about the world around us. We use words to understand, describe, and define the world as we see it, and we also use images to do this. This process takes place through systems of representation, such as language and visual media, that have rules and conventions about how they are organized. A language like English has a set of rules about how to express and interpret meaning, and so, for instance, do the systems of representation of painting, photography, cinema, or television.

2 Throughout history, debates about representation have considered whether these systems of representation reflect the world as it is, such that they mirror it back to us as a form of *mimesis* or imitation, or whether in fact we construct the world and its meaning through the systems of representation we deploy. In this *social constructionist* approach, we only make meaning of the material world through specific cultural contexts. This takes place in part through the language systems (be they writing, speech, or images) that we use. Hence, the material world only has meaning, and only can be "seen" by us, through these systems of representation. This means that the world is not simply reflected back to us through systems of representation, but that we actually construct the meaning of the material world through these systems.

3 Over time, images have been used to represent, make meaning of, and convey various sentiments about nature, society, and culture as well as to represent imaginary worlds and abstract concepts. Throughout much of history, for example, images, most of them paintings, have been used by religions to convey religious myths, church doctrines, and historical dramas. Many images have been produced to depict seemingly accurate renditions of the world around us, while others have been created to express abstract concepts and feelings such as love. Language and systems of representation do not reflect an already existing reality so much as they organize, construct, and mediate our understanding of reality, emotion, and imagination.

Images and Ideology

4 To explore the meaning of images is to recognize that they are produced within dynamics of social power and *ideology*. Ideologies are systems of belief that exist within all cultures. Images are an important means through which ideologies are produced and onto which ideologies are projected. When people think of ideologies, they often think in terms of *propaganda*—the crude process of using false representations to lure people into holding beliefs that may compromise their own interests. This understanding of ideology assumes that to act ideologically is to act out of ignorance. In this particular sense, the term "ideology" carries a pejorative cast. However, ideology is a much more pervasive, mundane process in which we all engage, whether

we are aware of it or not. For our purposes, we define ideology as the broad but indispensable, shared set of values and beliefs through which individuals live out their complex relations to a range of social structures. Ideologies are widely varied and exist at all levels of all cultures. Our ideologies are diverse and ubiquitous; they inform our everyday lives in often subtle and barely noticeable forms. One could say that ideology is the means by which certain values, such as individual freedom, progress, and the importance of home, are made to seem like natural, inevitable aspects of everyday life. Ideology is manifested in widely shared social assumptions about not only the way things are but the way we all know things should be. Images and media representations are some of the forms through which we persuade others to share certain views or not, to hold certain values or not.

5   Practices of looking are intimately tied to ideology. The image culture in which we live is an arena of diverse and often conflicting ideologies. Images are elements of contemporary advertising and consumer culture through which assumptions about beauty, desire, glamour, and social value are both constructed and responded to. Film and television are media through which we see reinforced ideological constructions such as the value of romantic love, the norm of heterosexuality, nationalism, or traditional concepts of good and evil. The most important aspect of ideologies is that they appear to be natural or given, rather than part of a system of belief that a culture produces in order to function in a particular way. Ideologies are thus, like Barthes's concept of myth, connotations parading as denotations.

6   Visual culture is integral to ideologies and power relations. Ideologies are produced and affirmed through the social institutions in a given society, such as the family, education, medicine, the law, the government, and the entertainment industry, among others. Ideologies permeate the world of entertainment, and images are also used for regulation, categorization, identification, and evidence. Shortly after photography was developed in the early nineteenth century, private citizens began hiring photographers to make individual and family portraits. Portraits often marked important moments such as births, marriages, and even deaths (the funerary portrait was a popular convention). But photographs were also widely regarded as tools of science and of public surveillance. Astronomers spoke of using photographic film to mark the movements of the stars. Photographs were used in hospitals, mental institutions, and prisons to record, classify, and study populations. Indeed, in rapidly growing urban industrial centers, photographs quickly became an important way for police and public health officials to monitor urban populations perceived to be growing not only in numbers, but also in rates of crime and social deviance.

7   What is the legacy of this use of images as a means of controlling populations today? We live in a society in which portrait images are frequently used, like fingerprints, as personal identification—on passports, driver's

licenses, credit cards, and identification cards for schools, the welfare system, and many other institutions. Photographs are a primary medium for evidence in the criminal justice system. We are accustomed to the fact that most stores and banks are outfitted with surveillance cameras and that our daily lives are tracked not only through our credit records, but also through camera records. On a typical day of work, errands, and leisure, the activities of people in cities are recorded, often unbeknownst to them, by numerous cameras. Often these images stay within the realm of identification and surveillance, where they go unnoticed by most of us. But sometimes their venues change and they circulate in the public realm, where they acquire new meanings.

"Critics charge that *Time* was following the historical convention of using darker skin tones to connote evil and to imply guilt."

8   This happened in 1994, when the former football star O. J. Simpson was arrested as a suspect in a notorious murder case. Simpson's image had previously appeared only in sports media, advertising, and celebrity news media. He was rendered a different kind of public figure when his portrait, in the form of his police mug shot, was published on the covers of *Time* and *Newsweek* magazines. The mug shot is a common use of photography in the criminal justice system. Information about all arrested people, whether they are convicted or not, is entered into the system in the form of personal data, finger prints, and photographs. The conventions of the mug shot were presumably familiar to most people who saw the covers of *Time* and *Newsweek*. Frontal and side views of suspects' unsmiling, unadorned faces are shot. These conventions of framing and composition alone connote to viewers a sense of the subject's deviance and guilt, regardless of who is thus framed; the image format has the power to suggest the photographic subject's guilt. O. J. Simpson's mug shot seemed to be no different from any other in this regard.

9   Whereas *Newsweek* used the mug shot as it was, *Time* heightened the contrast and darkened Simpson's skin tone in its use of this image on the magazine's cover, reputedly for "aesthetic" reasons. Interestingly, the magazine's publishers do not allow this cover to be reproduced. What ideological assumption might be said to underlie this concept of aesthetics? Critics charged that *Time* was following the historical convention of using darker skin tones to connote evil and to imply guilt. In motion pictures made during the first half of this century, when black and Latino performers appeared, they were most often cast in the roles of villains and evil characters. This convention tied into the lingering ideologies of nineteenth-century racial science, in which it was proposed that certain bodily forms and attributes, including darker shades of skin, indicated a predisposition toward social deviance. Though this view was contested in the twentieth century, darker skin tones nonetheless continued to be used as literary, theatrical, and cinematic symbols of evil. Thus, darkness came to connote negative qualities. Hollywood studios even developed

special makeup to darken the skin tones of Anglo, European, and light-skinned black and Latino performers to emphasize a character's evil nature.

10   In this broader context, the darkening of Simpson's skin tone cannot be seen as a purely aesthetic choice but rather an ideological one. Although the magazine cover designers may not have intended to evoke this history of media representations, we live in a culture in which the association of dark tones with evil and the stereotype of black men as criminals still circulate. In addition, because of the codes of the mug shot, it could be said that by simply taking Simpson's image out of the context of the police file and placing it in the public eye, *Time* and *Newsweek* influenced the public to see Simpson as a criminal even before he had been placed on trial.

11   Like Simpson's mug shot, images often move across social arenas. Documentary images can appear in advertisements, amateur photographs and videotapes can become news images, and news images are sometimes incorporated into art works. Each change in context produces a change in meaning.

12   People use systems of representation to experience, interpret, and make sense of the conditions of their lives both as image-makers and as viewers. In essence, we construct ideological selves through a network of representations—many of them visual—that includes television, film, photography, popular magazines, art, and fashion. Media images and popular culture interpellate us as viewers, defining within their mode of address, style of presentation, and subject matter the ideological subjects to whom they speak, yet we also negotiate that process ourselves.

13   It is important, when thinking about ideologies and how they function, to keep in mind the complicated interactions of powerful systems of belief and the things that very different kinds of viewers bring to their experiences. If we give too much weight to the idea of a dominant ideology, we risk portraying viewers as cultural dupes who can be "force fed" ideas and values. At the same time, if we overemphasize the potential array of interpretations viewers can make of any given image, we can make it seem as if all viewers have the power to interpret images any way they want, and that these interpretations will be meaningful in their social world. In this perspective, we would lose any sense of dominant power and its attempt to organize our ways of looking. Meanings of images are created in a complex relationship among producer, viewer, image or text, and social context. Because meanings are produced out of this relationship, there are limits to the interpretive agency of any one member of this group.

Encoding and Decoding

14   Images present to viewers clues about their dominant meaning. A dominant meaning can be the interpretation that an image's producers intended viewers to make. More often, though, it can be the meaning that

most viewers within a given cultural setting will arrive at, regardless of the producers' intentions. All images are both *encoded* and *decoded*. An image or object is encoded with meaning in its creation or production; it is further encoded when it is placed in a given setting or context. It is then decoded by viewers when it is consumed by them. These processes work in tandem. So, for instance, a television show is encoded with meaning by the writers, producers, and the production apparatus that allows it to be made, and it is then decoded by television viewers according to their particular set of cultural assumptions and their viewing context.

15   Stuart Hall has written that there are three positions that viewers can take as decodes of cultural images and artifacts.

1. *Dominant-hegemonic reading.* They can identify with the hegemonic position and receive the dominant message of an image or text (such as a television show) in an unquestioning manner.

2. *Negotiated reading.* They can negotiate an interpretation from the image and its dominant meanings.

3. *Oppositional reading.* Finally, they can take an oppositional position, either by completely disagreeing with the ideological position embodied in an image or rejecting it altogether (for example, by ignoring it).

16   Viewers who take the dominant-hegemonic position can be said to decode images in a relatively passive manner. But it can be argued that few viewers actually consume images in this manner, because there is no mass culture that can satisfy all viewers' culturally specific experiences, memories, and desires. The second and third positions, negotiation and opposition, are more useful to us and deserve further explanation.

17   The term "negotiation" invokes the process of trade. We can think of it as a kind of bargaining over meaning that takes place among viewer, image, and context. We use the term "negotiation" in a metaphorical sense to say that we often "haggle" with the dominant meanings of an image when we interpret it. The process of deciphering an image always takes place at both the conscious and unconscious levels. It brings into play our own memories, knowledge, and cultural frameworks as well as the image itself and the dominant meanings that cling to it. Interpretation is thus a mental process of acceptance and rejection of the meanings and associations that adhere to a given image through the force of dominant ideologies. In this process, viewers actively struggle with dominant meanings, allowing culturally and personally specific meanings to transform and even override the meanings imposed by producers and broader social forces. The term "negotiation" allows us to see how cultural interpretation is a struggle in which consumers are active meaning-makers and not merely passive recipients in the process of decoding images.

18   Let us take, for example, the television show *Who Wants to Be a Millionaire,* which has versions in many countries and is based on the premise that any ordinary person can win large amounts of money with the proper amount of trivial knowledge and luck. The show stages a spectacle of both desire and greed, and is encoded by its producers with the meaning that we all desire large amounts of money. The show aims to create the fantasy for viewers that they too could win. A dominant hegemonic reading of the show would agree with its encoded values that money increases one's happiness and social status and that any viewer could potentially be on the show and win. However, the show has come under fire, even while it is immensely popular, for representing crass commercialism and the further debasement of mainstream popular culture. Many viewers have thus engaged in a negotiated reading of the show, so that even while they may enjoy watching it, they see it as an indicator of what's wrong with contemporary culture. Furthermore, the show has been criticized for equating knowledge with trivia. An oppositional reading might read the show critically as an example of how capitalism creates the impression that everyone has equal potential to succeed when in fact it is fundamental to the structure of capitalism that only some can accede to power and wealth. An oppositional reading might note, for instance, how the American version of the show has been criticized for having mostly white male contestants, thereby reflecting the structures of privilege in society.

19   To varying degrees, all cultures are in flux and constantly in the process of being reinvented through cultural representations. This is in part an effect of the economics and ideologies of the free market, which demand that participants negotiate not only to trade in goods, services, and capital, but to produce meaning and value in the objects and representations of cultural products. Hence conflicting ideologies coexist in tension. There is a constant reworking of hegemonic structures, which allows both for contradictory ideological messages and new, potentially subversive messages produced through culture products. At the same time, semiotics shows us that viewers create meaning from images, objects, and texts, and that meanings are not fixed within them. Most images we see are caught up in dominant ideologies; however, the value of negotiation as an analytic concept is that it allows space for the different subjectivities, identities, and pleasures of audiences.

Literacy Connections

1. Reread the excerpts from *Practices of Looking* and underline any words or sentences that confused you. Then, get into small groups and together try to come to a better understanding of the items you underlined.

2. What do you think Sturken and Cartwright mean when they say images "do not reflect an already existing reality so much as they organize, construct, and mediate our understanding of reality, emotion, and imagination"?

3. Think of an image you view in your everyday life—a billboard you pass frequently, a Web site you look at, a magazine cover you've seen lately in the grocery store. What ideology shapes the image (what set of values and beliefs does the image assume)? What clues in the image reveal its ideology?

4. Think of your own personal experiences with the images you encounter in your daily life. Would you say that you are primarily a passive reader of images or do you engage in negotiated or oppositional reading? Explain your answer.

5. Use Sturken and Cartwright's discussion of images and ideologies to think about Gopi Pitcher's photo essay from the student case study in the chapter. In what ways do Gopi's images reveal conflicting ideologies?

Before You Read

Before you read about images and American culture in Cameron Granger's essay, "Pictures in America," think of an image that represents America to you. Explain what the image is and why you think it represents America. Be prepared to discuss your response with the class.

Pictures in America: It Isn't Just About How Many Words They're Worth

Cameron Granger

Cameron Granger was a sophomore at James Madison University when he composed the photo essay, "Pictures in America," in Critical Reading and Writing. According to Cameron's instructor, the purpose of the photo essay assignment "is to help a reader (your classmates and instructor) appreciate the complexity of some idea or subject that is important to you and that cannot be adequately understood without the use of both text and image." Cameron's subject is the way money, space, and power influence images in American culture. Cameron's essay was published in e-*Vision,* a collection of outstanding essays from Critical Reading and Writing at JMU.

1   During my high school years my family hosted three different exchange students, for a year apiece. When I asked Sanna, a foreign exchange student from Finland who lived at my house during my junior year, what Europeans thought of when they thought of America, she said MTV and George Bush. "Greeeeeeeeeaaaat," I sarcastically thought, as I pictured the America someone would form based on only these two things. I know people have a better grasp of what America is like than just George Bush and MTV, but Sanna's comment made me start to ponder the question of how people's thinking, not just Europeans', is influenced by how the media presents America. And as I thought about this, the more I thought that perhaps even Americans aren't sure what America is like sometimes.

We may live in this country, but we are frequently exposed to media that attempts to tell us who we are. The visual media that we absorb is nothing more than pictures. Even video media is just a series of ordered, individual pictures being run through our televisions at a fast enough rate for our minds to perceive them as a fluid, working reality of motion. That "a picture is worth a thousand words" is a lie. They're worth more. We see pictures every day (on the front of a cereal box, on the front page of a newspaper, or on posters on the walls in our dorms) that hold more meaning than we can sometimes fathom, and sometimes we pick up on those messages without realizing it.

2   We know that there are messages in pictures that can affect our thinking, but rarely, if ever, do we consider the relationship between these messages and reality. Pictures are merely representations of real things, so someone who has not seen or experienced the actuality of what the picture conveys has nothing but the picture to judge that thing on. This idea may not seem like anything new, yet it is important to consider because images can misrepresent something important such as one's culture. The culture a person grows up in has a huge and lasting effect on the development of that particular person. Culture, in some ways, provides its members with a general way of thinking because the popular way of thinking (created by the culture) is generally accepted by the individual as the appropriate way to think. This acceptance of popular thinking is inevitable but also dangerous because our ways of thinking determine our actions, and actions have repercussions. With this worrying thought in mind, one must consider the dynamics of the relationship between the individual and his culture.

3   If I lived alone on an island somewhere, then the culture of that place is determined by what I carry about from day to day and by how I think about things. That is it. The culture of that island is a direct reflection of myself. However, let's say we add a guy named "Mike" into this island scenario. Now the culture of the island must change to incorporate how Mike acts and thinks. By adding another person, parts of the original culture are lost because Mike thinks and acts differently than I do (naturally, since he is a different

person). So, the culture of the island adjusts to encompass both Mike and me. With each person added, the gap between my culture and me grows greater.

4   The greater the number of people in a culture, the greater the distance between the individual and his culture. But what does this mean for people living in America? There are millions of people in America and only one culture for all of us. The culture of such a large population must become an "estimate" or "average" of what those people do and how they think because there is no way it could represent every individual. In fact, the individual in such a large population has very little hope of ever affecting his own culture unless he is able to make a substantially large portion of America think in the same way he does so that the "average" thinking of the country changes. By this logic, the number of people an individual can affect translates to how much capacity he has for shaping his culture. With this in mind, the people who produce the visual media (commercials, magazines, billboards, television, and so on) have a gargantuan capacity for affecting our culture because they reach out across all of America. While the media commands a powerful position, we, the individuals, have little-to-no capacity for affecting our culture and are left to be fed only a version of our culture from the spoon that is popular media.

> ". . . the people who produce the visual media (commercials, magazines, billboards, television, and so on) have a gargantuan capacity for affecting our culture because they reach out across all of America."

5   What do the images circulated in America have to say about our culture? In our country, ownership is a sign that we are successful. There are three things we try to own, and they are money, space, and power. How can a person own space and power when these things are merely concepts? The answer is that we can't truly own space or power, but we have created artificial ways to "buy" what can't be sold. We buy physical representations of concepts, and our culture accepts these representations as the actual thing. Images, then, can reflect, distort, and perpetuate culture as expressed in three dimensions of American culture: money, space, and power.

6   By analyzing some of the pictures circulated in America, we can begin to peer into the details of this idea that images reflect culture. Ludacris is a very famous and rich rapper whose image can be found anywhere from the pages of *Maxim* magazine to the televised images of MTV (Figure 1). Ludacris's newest album cover is an image that's placed across CD racks all over the world where millions of people are exposed to it. At first glance, one might not see anything to this picture, yet upon closer inspection and thought, we notice details such as how Ludacris's clothes speak of high price tags, and the only thing in the picture that isn't Ludacris himself is a crisp hundred-dollar bill. The bill is poised in his hand as he if he is about to slap it down on a table to spend on something; and his eyes say that he

doesn't care—he's got more where that came from. There could be anything in his hand, but what's in it is money; and the cool, calm look on his face says that's what he wants. The message conveyed in this image about American culture is that money is paramount, which might not be too far from the truth.

7   Just as the music culture circulates images that send messages about America's culture, so does the food aspect of our culture. It seems that size is the most important dynamic of our food here in America. Nearly every food commercial we see on television goes for the size appeal. The very names of some of these advertised foods is enough to clue you in: The Big Mac, Biggie fries, and the monster thick burger (Figure 2). This hulking mass of bacon, cheese, bread, and Angus beef is Hardee's newest burger. It is clear to the eye that this is not a weak burger. The beef alone weighs 2/3 of a pound! This burger's size is stressed as the most important aspect of this food: its size is the key marketing point, and the dominant thought in the mind of any viewer of this picture. The double-stacked beef just explodes out of the burger as the bacon sticks out of the sides like sleeves that dangle out the edge of an over-packed suitcase. The cheese looks as if it is attempting to cover the beef, but there is just far too much beef to be covered, and the sesame seed bun looks almost feeble trying to contain the contents of the burger. With the ingredients ready to burst into life, the image taunts Americans with an "I dare you to eat me" challenge, as if a person's ability to finish this burger decides if they are truly American or not. With its hugely commanding size, this burger conveys a sense of power. This image strikes a chord with me because it is a veritable monument to America's love of excess. Who needs this big a burger? A lumberjack who has been working all day, maybe. One thing is for sure: this burger is not suited for the average American. However, thousands of Americans see this image, with all of its underlying messages, daily (on decals pasted on Hardee's windows, in newspaper advertisements, on television commercials) and say, "Hey, that's what I need." With as many monster thick burger images as are out there, the "voice" of this visual media has made itself heard, and this voice is very loud.

8   It's not just burger places that try to harness America's love for power through size. We've all seen the Taco Bell commercial where a car pulls up to the pickup window, a man is handed a grilled, stuffed burrito, and the car tips over from its now immense weight. So what causes us Yankees to have such love for excess? Surely, it is partially because we are influenced by images shown in advertisements as with the Monster Thick Burger, but I think there is more going on here in the internal workings of our culture.

9   I see such emphasis on size everywhere in the messages popular media sends. Therefore, it was no surprise to me when I read a survey in *Men's Health* magazine concluding that men who take up more space (through

Continued on page 255, following Insert.

Before You Read

Before you explore an online, interactive chart of visualization methods, as a class, come up with a list of as many genres of visuals as you can (for example, photos, charts, paintings, etc.). Choose two of the visuals the class has come up with and write for five minutes about the different "reading" strategies you would use for the two types of visuals you've chosen.

A Periodic Table
of Visualization Methods

This interactive table, developed by Ralph Lengler and Martin J. Eppler, has examples of different types of visuals, from a pie chart to a concept map to a cartoon. The chart is published by *VisualLiteracy.Org* as part of a visual literacy tutorial that is designed to help students "evaluate, apply, or create conceptual visual representations." You can access the *Periodic Table of Visualization Methods* online at *www.visual-literacy.org/periodic_table/periodic_table.html*.

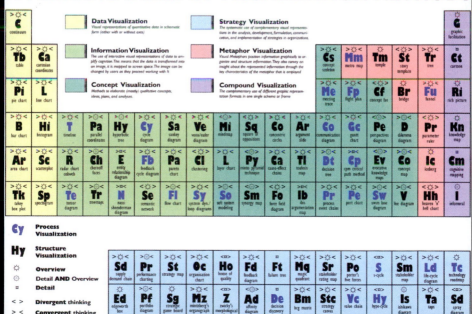

A Periodic Table of Visualization Methods

Literacy Connections

1. The table names six different types of visuals: data, information, concept visualization, strategy visualization, metaphor visualization, and compound visualization. In small groups, discuss the definition of each of these kinds of visualizations until everyone in the group has an understanding of each category. Then, come up with a list of specific example of visuals from each category that group members have used in their own composing, in school or out of school.

2. Why do you think Lengler and Eppler included the terms "divergent thinking" and "convergent thinking" in their table? What connections do you think these terms have to visual literacy?

3. Find an example of a visual from the table that you have used or are planning to use in your college composing processes or products this semester. What did you (or will you) need to consider when you compose in that visual?

4. Find three types of visualization strategies from the table that you might use to help you in your own composing processes for college writing (for example, clustering). How might you use the visuals to help you compose?

5. Read (or reread) Zemliansky, Bang, and Sturken and Cartwright, as well as this Table of Visualization Methods, keeping a double-entry notebook as you read. On one side of the notebook, make a list of key terms that the authors use to help understand and analyze visuals. On the other side of the notebook, write down a definition of the terms in your own words. Be prepared to share your notebooks with your peers and with the class.

Before You Read

Before you "read" the images of graffiti, think about your own attitude toward graffiti. Do you think graffiti is an artistic expression, an act of vandalism, or both? Explore your position on this question and explain why you feel the way you do.

Images of Graffiti

The following images of graffiti are from the streets of New York City. These images will help you explore questions of the connections between culture, politics, and visual literacy. Graffiti is one example of the ways that the kinds of literacies we explore in this book, such as visual, personal, and civic, can converge in a literacy situation.

www.coolchaser.com/graphics/tag/graffiti

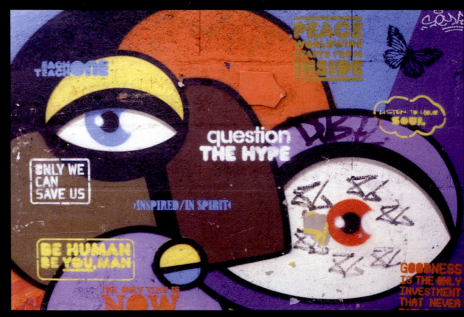

www.flickr.com/photos/15702350@N00/1318737291/

RIP MJ

OMEN514.COM

www.omen514.com

Literacy Connections

1. Use a pencil to annotate the four graffiti images, highlighting important aspects of the images and making notes on your response to and analysis of the images. Share and discuss your annotated images in small groups.
2. Read Cathy Gabor's introductory essay to the Civic Literacies chapter. What connections do you see between Gabor's definition of civic literacy and graffiti?
3. Choose either the reading by Zemliansky, Bang, or Sturken and Cartwright and use that author's approach to reading images to analyze one of the graffiti images.

4. Do an Internet search for images of graffiti and choose an image that you had a strong response to. Make a copy of the image and write a one-page response to the image, discussing why it had an effect on you and why it's effective as an act of visual communication.
5. What do you think are the purposes and audiences for these four works of graffiti?

Before You Read

Before you view some of the images of paintings that Mark Strand mentions in his essay about Edward Hopper's work, make a list of all of the terms that Strand uses to describe Hopper's paintings.

Paintings of Edward Hopper

Nighthawks

Approaching a City

Automat

Literacy Connections

1. Use a pencil to annotate the images of the Hopper paintings, highlighting important aspects of the images and making notes on your response to and analysis of the images. Share and discuss your annotated images in small groups.
2. Apply Mark Strand's discussion of "vanishing point" to the paintings by Edward Hopper.
3. Create your own image using Hopper's themes and style as a model. This could be a drawing, painting, photograph, etc. Then, write a paragraph describing how your image connects to Hopper's themes and style.
4. What kind of persona do Hopper's paintings project? Provide details from his paintings that show evidence of their persona.
5. Reread the excerpt from Molly Bang's *Picture This: How Pictures Work* and use Bang's suggestions for understanding how pictures work to describe how Hopper's pictures work.

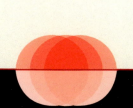

Figure 1   Figure 2

actions such as stretching one's legs out or throwing one's arms across the back of a bench when one is sitting) are perceived as commanding more power. It didn't surprise me because I have seen how our culture has had an influence on the meaning of space and size. This phenomenon starts with money. If you have money, then you have power. If you have money, then you spend that money on things that allow you more space (such as bigger houses and cars). After a time, society begins to associate amount of space with amount of power. Upon investigation of this association, one finds that boundless power equals, by American standards, boundless space.

10   If we want proof of this, all we need to do is look around us. We see a couple buy an enormous house and a single person driving a huge seven-passenger Suburban. Other countries see this too—the fat American, driving his road-hog vehicle with supersized drink in the double cup holder and supersized burger in hand. Why do we waste so much space? What causes us to think, consume, and act this way? Perhaps some of these answers can be found in the analysis of this next image (Figure 3). Here is the mammoth Chevy Colorado. The patriotic vibe is so strong in this advertisement that I can almost feel Abe Lincoln patting me on the shoulder as I peer at it. "AN AMERICAN REVOLUTION" is printed across the top with the dominant Chevy Colorado standing atop some mountain rocks along with the caption "CARPE MOUNTANIUM" on the left side of the truck. At the bottom of the advertisement is the slogan "Colorado: That's Latin for 'go wherever you darn well please.'" Clearly, the people who came up with this advertisement knew what they were

Figure 3

trying to accomplish. The bold print, the capitalized phrase, "AN AMERICAN REVOLUTION," yells out at the viewer. It tells the viewer that this product is not only American, but that it is so powerful that it can be called a revolution.

11   Similar to the marketing strategy style of the American food industry, the theme here is definitely size. The camera has been set at a low angle, making the Colorado look even bigger and taller than it otherwise would. Mountains loom in the background, and even the words are capitalized to increase their size! "Carpe Mountanium" it says, as if to imply that with the size of this truck, we can seize the day and conquer a mountain. With the sentence, "Colorado: That's Latin for 'go wherever you darn well please,'" the implication is that with this truck's size, we have enough power to go wherever we feel like going. The ad implies that, with this truck, we can drive on our neighbor's lawn or down the wrong way on a one-way street if we feel like it because we have the power to do so. This advertisement attempts to harness the American-man icon. It wants the viewer to see himself in this vehicle and see how the size of the vehicle can get anyone anywhere, so Chevy has capitalized on, and perpetuated by doing so, the American obsession with space and size and power to market its product.

12   Whatever the purpose of the photographer, or the people who present these images to the eyes of Americans, these images send messages about material wealth, space, and power. We can't stop the messages from being sent, but our minds can act as filters if we think about what we are being told and then decide if we agree with those messages or not.

13   Every human being is born into a culture. It is something we cannot control or pick. However, although we have been born into a particular culture, we can in time become an active, sovereign part of it. This means that as adults we can make decisions based on our own thinking rather than letting our culture do the thinking for us. This ability to function outside

of our culture's natural trends is what has allowed me to step aside for a moment to consider the workings of the culture I am a part of, and I encourage every person to do the same—for aren't we first individuals, cultural consumers, second?

Literacy Connections

1. Summarize Granger's arguments in your own words. What do you think are the most important points he is trying to make?
2. Find an image from a CD cover or a magazine ad and write a one-page rhetorical analysis of the image modeled on Granger's analysis in "Pictures in America" by focusing on money, space, and power.
3. Granger argues, "While the media commands a powerful position, we, the individuals, have little to no capacity for affecting our culture and are left to be fed only a version of our culture from the spoon that is popular media." What is your response to Granger's statement?
4. Reflect on the images that the class came up with for the "Before You Read." Do most of the images focus on money, space, or power? What other aspects of American culture were reflected in the images the class came up with?
5. What connections do you see between Granger's perspective on culture and images and the perspective of Sturken and Cartwright in the excerpts from *Practices of Looking*?

Before You Read

Before you read the essay by Mark Strand on painter Edward Hopper, do a quick Internet search on Hopper to find out about his style of painting and what critics have said about him. Then, do another Internet search to explore definitions of the following terms, which are used by Strand in his essay about Hopper's paintings:

Motif   Foreground
Vanishing point   Picture plane

Hopper: The Loneliness Factor

Mark Strand

Mark Strand's essay, "Hopper: The Loneliness Factor," is an analysis of the work of Edward Hopper. Strand approaches Hopper's paintings using many of the "practices of looking" that the authors in the readings in the chapter have been discussing. Three of the paintings that Strand discusses in his essay, *Nighthawks, Approaching a City,* and *Automat,* are included in the color insert for this chapter. Mark Strand is a poet whose books include *Dark Harbor, The Continuous Life,* and *The Late Hour,* among others. Strand was Poet Laureate of the United States in 1990. He has written a book about Edward Hopper (*Hopper*), and his essay below is from the book *Writers on Artists,* edited by Daniel Halpern.

1   It is often remarked that many of Edward Hopper's paintings engender feelings of loneliness. It is also assumed that such feelings are in response to narrative elements in the paintings, but in fact they are in response to certain repeated structural motifs. We often feel left behind, even abandoned, while something else in the painting, usually a road or tracks, continues. We feel caught in a wake that offers no possibility of catching up to whatever has departed. Likewise, if we have the impulse to linger, allowing ourselves to be taken into the painting's reduced ambience, we are resisted by a force within the painting that closes us out. It is this being left behind or left out that gives rise to our experience of alienation. And if there are figures in the paintings who suggest loneliness, they do so because they represent our situation as viewers. What we see in them is our own stillness in relation to powerful resistant forces in the painting. It is not the figures themselves, no matter how we wish to characterize the look on their faces, that establish the element of loneliness. It is something else, something in the formal disposition of the painting that does it, certain geometrical imperatives having to do with missing or sealed-off vanishing points. For example, the loneliness of *Nighthawks* (1942) does not depend on the few people gathered together in an all-night diner. What guarantee, after all, do we have that a few people gathered at night are lonely? Or, for that matter, why should it be assumed that a figure alone in a painting is lonely unless—as I've said—the viewer finds in it some confirmation of his own situation? In *Nighthawks* loneliness depends on the dominant form of an isosceles trapezoid. The trapezoid moves from the right-hand side of the painting and stops two-thirds the way across. It alone establishes the emphatic directional pull of the painting to a vanishing point that cannot be witnessed but must be imagined, for the simple reason that it is not situated on the canvas but beyond it in an unreal and unrealizable place from which the viewer is forever excluded. The long sides of the trapezoid slant towards each other, but never join, leaving him midway in their trajectory. It is this element of passage that is constantly emphasized by Hopper, contributing to the general condition of loneliness in his work. *Dawn in Pennsylvania,* painted the same year as *Nighthawks,* is structured the same way except that we look "out" instead of "in." The dominant isosceles

trapezoid, the periodic posting of verticals that frame and give momentary respite from the strong horizontal movement are in identical positions and of the same size. *Approaching the City* [sic] (1946), also composed around an isosceles trapezoid, provides the most unsettling example of the nonexistent vanishing point. The trapezoid is a bleak, featureless wall of concrete that gradually darkens as it heads underground. There are no verticals to slow its disappearance as it is hurried along by the foreground tracks. Above and behind the wall are some buildings whose windows suggest vertical movement, but these, along with two truncated smoke stacks that run through a patch of half-clouded sky, hardly relieve the picture's atmosphere of gloom, its determination to disappear into itself even before a geometrical vanishing point can be indicated. It is a work that invites the viewer in only to bury him. It is the most remorseless and sinister of Hopper's paintings.

2   Other well-known Hoppers that point to a resolution or ultimate stability which is beyond the picture plane and, consequently, not within the picture's power to satisfy, seem almost benign when compared to *Approaching the City* [sic], *Drug Store* (1927), and *Seven A.M.* (1948), whose trapezoidal storefronts are less acute and less extended, are, geometrically at least, mirror images of each other. They do not present the issue of psychological closure in so extreme a way. In *Drug Store* there is a mollifying frontality about the illuminated plate glass; and in *Seven A.M.* a counter-trapezoid, formed by light entering the store window, dissolves into the shadowy but relatively safe interior.

3   Hopper has another means of isolating the viewer from the resolution of strong geometrical structures within the canvas. He frequently establishes a vanishing point inside the picture plane only to hide it, making it unreachable. In early painting, *Stairway* (1925), we look down some stairs through an open door to an impenetrable clump of trees. Everything in the painting points to wilderness, a mass of dark trees that effectively prevents us from seeing anything. All that the painting's geometry prepares us for is darkly denied us. In *Chair Car* (1965) a progression of yellow blocks of light on the train-car floor, flanked by windows and chairs, leads to the end of the car, which in this picture seems unusually large. The high ceiling and closed door have the effect of immobilizing the painting, freezing it in an absolute present. If the people here are traveling, they are not going far. There is nothing outside the windows, nothing but the light that enters the car establishing the painting's air of immobility. Another painting that uses the same device is *Automat* (1927). A woman, near a door and in front of a plate-glass window, sits alone at a round table. The plate glass reflects only the twin receding rows of ceiling lights, reflects nothing else of the automat's interior, and allows nothing of the street to be seen. The painting suggests

many things, but most obviously that if the glass is to be believed the scene takes place in limbo and the seated woman is an illusion, not least because Hopper has invented her.

4   These are only a few examples of how the loneliness factor in Hopper operates in ways that are strictly formal. There are many more works in which isosceles trapezoids and occluded vanishing points work their depressing magic. But some paintings that are generally assumed to project loneliness in fact project another form of refusal. The viewer feels excluded from the scene in the painting, but feels, at the same time, no desire to enter. Two of the best known are *House by the Railroad* (1925) and *Early Sunday Morning* (1930). *House by the Railroad,* which seems so forthright in its frontality, is deeply mysterious. The harsh sunlight on the house walls is not conventionally descriptive. It illuminates secrecy without penetrating it. The house is really a tomb, a monument to the idea of enclosure, a stately emblem of withholding. It is like an elaborate coffin in sunlight; it shines with finality, and has no door. In its starkness it promises so little that its air of absolute denial cannot be taken personally and can only be trivialized by attempts to associate it with loneliness. True, it stands alone, but does so with rigid, disdainful insularity. The trapezoidal element is more than compensated for by the house's verticality and its strong position in the center of the painting. *Early Sunday Morning* also suffers from the misapplication of the term "loneliness." Though it is a scene devoid of people, the viewer is not made to feel isolated from anything, surely not from any suggested terminus or vanishing point. The absence of slanting trapezoids lends the painting a calming air. Though the street may be extended infinitely on either side, the viewer is made to feel that he is in the center, the true center, somewhere between the fire hydrant and the barber pole, that if the painting were to spread out it would offer only a repetition of the order he is already familiar with. There is no actual or implied progression in the shaded or open windows, none in the dark doorways and store fronts. The painting is utterly frontal. It is a quiet, peaceful scene that would inspire loneliness only in those who derive comfort from being able to shop seven days a week.

Literacy Connections

1. Strand does a sophisticated analysis of Hopper in this essay, and you may have found this essay to be challenging reading. Underline places where you were confused by Strand's ideas. In small groups, discuss these points of confusion and, as a group, try to come to the best understanding you can of Strand's ideas. Be prepared to share these points of confusion and the group's interpretation with the class.

2. At your school's library or on the Internet find a Hopper painting not discussed by Mark Strand and apply Strand's theory of why we feel loneliness in Hopper's paintings to the painting you've chosen. Use some of the key words discussed in the "Before You Read" such as vanishing point, foreground, etc.

3. Choose a work from your favorite painter and in one to two pages, compose the kind of close "reading" of the painting that Strand does with Hopper's paintings. Then, write a paragraph reflecting on the process of analyzing a painting. What key visual elements did you focus on? What did you learn about paintings from doing the analysis? What general strategies for analyzing images can you take away from your experience?

4. Do you agree with Strand's argument about why we feel a sense of loneliness when we look at Hopper's paintings? Look closely at *Nighthawks, Approaching* a *City*, and *Automat* and discuss any other factors that might cause the viewer to feel a sense of loneliness.

5. What are some strategies for looking at images that you learned from reading Strand's essay that weren't discussed in the previous readings from the chapter?

Visual Literacy Projects

Visual Rhetoric Analysis

In this project, you'll apply what you've been practicing in Chapter 5 and analyze the visual rhetoric of an image of your choosing. Choose an image that you feel has a strong impact (a photograph, a painting, a poster, an ad—whatever image you like) and do a critical analysis of the visual rhetoric of the image. In your analysis, consider both the formal aspects of the image (color, tone, perspective, composition, etc.) and the contexts for the image (purpose, audience, ideology, cultural context, etc.). Make sure you do a close and careful viewing of the image, and provide specific examples to support your analysis. You don't need to refer to outside sources, but you can bring in outside sources if they help further your analysis.

Photo Essay

This project asks you to combine words and images to create a photo essay. The purpose of the essay is up to you: you can make an argument, explore a topic you want to know more about, inform an audience, tell a story, etc. The most important aspect of the photo essay is to create a composition in which words and images work together effectively. Carefully consider the images you choose, the way you design your essay, and the way the words and images are integrated. You can use whatever computer software that you'd like to create the photo essay: word processing, PowerPoint, Adobe Photoshop, movie editing software, etc.

Poster Campaign

In this project you'll work individually or in small groups to create a poster campaign and write a one- to two-page reflection on your campaign. You'll create at least three different posters for your campaign. The purpose of the campaign is up to you. You might advertise a band, promote a political candidate, advocate your point of view on a social issue, or publicize a campus service or organization. You'll need to carefully consider the purpose and audience for your posters, as well as the visual design. After you've created the posters, your teacher might ask you to present them to the class and/or post them in appropriate public spaces. In addition to creating three posters, write a two- to three-page reflection discussing how you decided on your campaign topic, the purpose and audience for your campaign, and the decisions you made about the visual design of the posters.

Visual Revision

This project asks you to practice visual literacy by taking an essay you've already written for this class and turn it into a completely visual composition. For example, you could turn a personal literacy narrative into a photo album, a research paper or speech into a slide show, a position paper into a series of advertisements, etc. You'll also reflect on your revision in a two- to three-page process memo. In the process memo, discuss the ways that the visual revision made you rethink the subject and consider the advantages and disadvantages of the visual revision compared to the original work.

Film or Television Review

In this project, you'll practice "reading" the visual medium of film or television by writing a film or television review. The first step in this project is to choose a target publication for your review—for example, the local newspaper, an alternative weekly, a movie review Web site, a film or television studies journal, etc. Write a one- to two-page rhetorical analysis of some example reviews from your target publication. Discuss the tone and language of the reviews, as well as their organization, writing style, intended audience, etc. Then, choose a film or television show you've seen recently and write a review in the style of the target publication. As you compose your review, be sure to consider the visual rhetoric of the film or television show, as well as the plot and acting.

Group Project: Documentary

This group project requires access to a camcorder and video editing software, either through your school or from someone in your group. In this project, the class will divide into small groups and script and film a documentary. The group will decide the documentary topic and the process of composition. The group might begin by drafting a script; it might sketch out a storyboard with text and images, or it might choose to draft a script as it films. The group might divide the duties and give everyone a role (scriptwriter, cameraperson, editor, etc.), or it might have everyone share all the responsibilities. In addition to filming the documentary, the group should film a reflection piece where each group member talks about his or her role in the project, the purpose and audience of the documentary, and the significance of the visual composition of the documentary and the relationship between words and images. This filmed reflection by each group member should appear after the documentary. Another option for this reflection piece is to include a version of the film with a "director's commentary." As a culmination of this project, the documentaries can be shown in class or at a computer lab on campus.

6

Situating Digital Literacies

Digital literacies are redefining what it means to compose in the twenty-first century. As Dustin Anderson argues in the introductory essay of this chapter, digital literacy involves "our ability to read and compose in a culture that has seamlessly integrated technology into the ways we communicate." The digital mode of communication can include a variety of media (the Web, audio files, digital images, streaming video), and often digital literacy genres combine these media— for example, a *YouTube* page might include a  streaming video and posted text in response to the video, or a blog about Kanye West that includes audio file samples of his songs, written reviews of his CDs, and a gallery of images. In the chapter, you'll explore a variety of digital literacy genres, from Web sites to blogs to *MySpace* pages. The readings reflect the variety of purposes you encounter in digital literacy situations, from entertainment to social networking to education. The readings in the chapter will help you develop a clearer image of what we mean when we use the term *digital literacies* and will give you opportunities to explore your own ever evolving digital literacies.

You'll find selections that will—

- Start you thinking about the meaning of *digital literacies*
- Help you explore the idea of what it means to "grow up digital"
- Give you an inside look at what Maria, a first-year college student, came up with when her teacher told her to compose a mixed-media project

including an article, a video essay, and a Web site on a topic about which she was passionate

- Help you learn to write more effectively on the Web
- Get you thinking about what you're doing when you blog
- Encourage you to consider why so many of us can't get enough of *YouTube* and *MySpace* and *Facebook*
- Take you on a journey through the virtual world of *Second Life*
- Show you why some people think video games are "good for our souls"
- Help you think about the good and maybe not-so-good aspects of living in this digital age.

But you won't just read, write, and think about a variety of texts—Web sites, blogs, traditional essays, video essays, articles, and more—you'll also have the opportunity to create your own compositions. If you respond to the digital literacy projects at the end of the chapter, you might—

- Write a digital literacy narrative focused on your experiences with digital literacy
- Create a digital literacy project in which you decide who receives the best and worst Web site awards
- Create your own personal or political blog
- Transform one of your earlier writing projects into a digital medium
- Find out more about an area of digital literacy you're especially interested in and share what you learn with your peers
- Participate in a group project in which you work with your peers to study a digital community.

Let's get started.

What Are Digital Literacies?

Before You Read

What does the term *digital literacy* mean to you? Before you begin reading this chapter that explores digital literacies, jot down what the term means to you now. And then later, after you've read some of the selections in the chapter, come back to your original definition and think about how you might want to revise what you wrote.

Surfing, Searching, and Social Networking: Redefining Digital Literacy with *Facebook* and *Wikipedia*

Dustin Anderson

Dustin Anderson was a graduate student working on his Ph.D. at Florida State University when he wrote this essay exploring the definitions and features of digital literacies. He was also a graduate teaching assistant who taught a variety of literature and composition courses, including "Writing About Tolkien in the Digital Age," a course in which he and his students created online discourse communities about reimagining print texts as visual and digital texts. He has designed courses incorporating visual and media literacy, and he routinely incorporates nontraditional digital texts into class discussions and writing assignments in all of the courses he teaches.

> *Wikipedia is the best thing ever. Anyone in the world can write anything they want about any subject, so you know you are getting the best possible information.*

—Michael Scott, *The Office*

1 The first time I really started thinking about what digital literacy meant was when my mom used the word *Google* as a verb. She was doing research on our ancestry in her spare time. When I asked her how she was finding all of this information, she told me that she had "just googled it." I was shocked. This is something that my students should be doing, not my mother. Sure, I'd heard the term *digital literacy* before; of course, I knew what it meant. This was the first time, though, that I really considered all of its implications. I had always taken for granted that I could define digital literacy, but now, I didn't know if I could anymore.

2 Whether we use social sites like *MySpace* and *Facebook*, gaming sites like *World of Warcraft*, virtual worlds like *Second Life*, or informational sites like *Wikipedia*, they are *inarguably* part of our everyday world. You might hear about them from a friend or roommate, or referenced by popular television characters like Michael Scott from *The Office*. We need to be able to not only define or describe what digital literacy is, but also to consider what skills it requires and, perhaps most importantly, to examine how we are already using those skills on a daily basis.

What Is Digital Literacy?

3 Very simply, digital literacy is our ability to read and compose in a culture that has seamlessly integrated technology into the ways we communicate.

While it is obvious that we have moved beyond thinking about literacy as simply the ability to read and write in a single medium (printed texts for instance), do we really know what that means in the twenty-first century? Digital literacy, like textual literacy, requires the ability to analyze, evaluate, and then produce some type of communication. However, digital literacy is more than that. It is not only always developing, it requires that we communicate in a *variety* of media: we have to consider not just textual or visual, but critical aspects (the ethical, social, and cultural implications) of these media as well. That means to more fully understand it we have to examine how we use it.

4   Every generation has a new explanation of what it means to be "literate." Paul Gilster's 1997 book, *Digital Literacy*, attempts to explain what digital literacy was at this point in time. This type of literacy was limited to basically three things: evaluating content (from e-mail to various types of websites), mastering search engines, and setting up personal news feeds. Of course, we know that since then there have been huge developments in the digital world. Our everyday communication isn't limited to a desktop research computer. Think about all of the things that your cell phone does. It seems like we spend more time sending text messages and photos, playing MP3s, or checking e-mail on the phone than we do talking on it. For Gilster, this type of literacy could be limited to a single research medium, but for us digital technologies are part of our everyday lives.

5   In "The Medium Is Not the Literacy," Jamie McKenzie explains that literacy is an evolving concept that mirrors the expanding information needs of our society. As our need for and uses of information have grown and changed, so has the very definition of what it means to be a literate individual. That need, Victor Vitanza tells us, often times takes the form of images and icons, which allows us to economize the words we use. Print texts and plastic arts are, in some ways, limited—or to think of it another way, these mediums work in a single direction. The digital world, on the other hand, is unlimited and unrestricted; it works in multiple directions. It should be no surprise that we think of the Internet as a web. The biggest difference between digital and print literacy is that digital literacy allows for widespread and instantaneous distribution as we compose. We can now contribute and distribute as much as we consume.

6   To explain what I mean by contribution, distribution, and consumption, let's use *Facebook* as an example. *Facebook* revised a *very* old technology (the "commonplace book") and made it new again. The commonplace book was the bound volume in which aristocratic readers during the Renaissance would copy out their favorite poems from manuscript or lines from plays, and then share them with a friend. What we can see in our own contemporary online culture (especially with college students) is that social networking communities, like *Facebook*, are a kind of descendent of the commonplace book.

7 Think for a moment about how this works as a text. The default features of a *Facebook* profile are things like Interests, Favorite Music, Favorite TV Shows, Favorite Movies, Favorite Books, Favorite Quotes, etc. If it stopped there, then it would just be a digital version of a print text. As we know, it functions as an *interactive* text, allowing you to create a personal anthology (in the sense that it is a new work on its own). It also emphasizes the *active* role that you take as both a writer and a reader in the distribution process. The chief benefit here is that the text can be redrafted, amended, or modified and re-distributed—which, of course, allows for parallel versions of an *original*—as many times as you see fit.

8 What a site like *Facebook* encourages are three primary things: replication, original composition, and distribution. These three things work to promote aural, visual, and written discourse within a continuously growing community. The engine that the site runs on streams constant updates to any textual changes made by the people connected to your site; in *Facebook*'s case, that means your *friends*. That means anytime you make a change to your profile—especially in a textual area, like the interactive chat *wall* or your *personal descriptions* (such as a favorite quote or poem)—your friends are notified. Anytime you update your *status*, or join a common interest *group* or compose a *note*, the *minifeeds* on your *friends'* homepages reflect those changes. If you think of making these changes as composing new drafts of your site, everyone in your community is immediately notified of that new draft. By composing like this you are always already aware that you are actively writing for a public audience. Digital writing spaces like these, whether you realize it or not, encourage you to compose. Your new compositions are instantaneously distributed to the reading community you are part of. You can distribute all of your new written material available to your friends with the click of a button.

9 Sites like this provide an avenue for you to both emulate texts and compose in a space that is simultaneously your own and public. The public, or shared, nature of these types of sites means that the distribution and publicity of your work are automatic. The opportunity for you to instantly share your favorite viral clips or videos and quotations or sayings (personal and published) on a large scale is very different from any other type of composition.

So . . . Don't We Do This Already?

10 The last time you wanted to answer a question that popped up during a conversation, what did you do? Go to the library? I doubt it. Like my mom, you probably went to the Internet—*googled* it. What about the last time you sent a message to someone who lives in another city? Was it written on paper, and sent in an envelope? Or was the most recent way that you communicated with someone via e-mail or a text message?

11   Or was it in a different way entirely? The ways in which we can communicate in digital worlds are almost unlimited. Not only do we have a text-based virtual world to communicate in, we also have a visual representation of it. These virtual worlds are certainly not new. In her 1995 book, *Life on the Screen*, Sherry Turkle discusses some of the dangers that lurk in Multi User Dungeons (MUDs), from how they have come to replace real-world meeting places like coffee shops or bars to sexual harassment and stalking. Since then, virtual worlds have not only advanced technologically, but they are also much safer and better monitored. They have also expanded to almost unbelievable proportions. Some of these virtual worlds are larger than some real world countries. *World of Warcraft*'s developers, Blizzard Entertainment, announced that their virtual world had over nine million subscribers. Like I said before, whether you have an account or not, you have probably heard of *World of Warcraft* and *Second Life*. What gaming sites like these provide (in addition to hours and hours and hours of entertainment) is a digital space or virtual world to communicate and socialize in. And, of course, these interactions range from completely normal and mundane to bizarre and supernatural.

> "The ways in which we can communicate in digital worlds are almost unlimited."

12   On the "normal" end of the spectrum is something like *Second Life*. In this virtual world, you can be anyone you want; you can look any way you want; you can, to a great extent, say anything you want.

13   In an episode of *The Office*, "The Local Ad," the character Dwight explains *Second Life* to his co-worker Jim. He claims that *"Second Life* is not a game. It is a multi-user virtual environment. It doesn't have points or scores; it doesn't have winners or losers!" Without missing a beat, Jim replies "Oh, it has losers." Dwight then explains why he started *Second Life* to the camera crew: "I signed up for *Second Life* about a year ago. Back then, my life was so great that I literally wanted a second one. In my *Second Life* I was also a paper salesman, and I was also named Dwight. Absolutely everything was the same . . . except I could fly." While his description is unintentionally humorous, it is a pretty accurate description of what *Second Life* is. It allows for thousands of people to occupy the same virtual social space. *Second Life* is a virtual world that allows its users (called Residents) to interact with each other through avatars, and provides a rather advanced level of a social networking in a fictional universe. This virtual world allows its Residents to explore or wander, to meet and socialize with other Residents by participating in group activities, or to create and trade virtual property.

14   To communicate in *Second Life*, Residents can use a local chat function or a global instant messaging function. Local chatting is a public conversation

between two or more avatars, and can be "heard" by other users nearby. Instant messaging is generally used for private conversations between two avatars, or a private group. Like Dwight's character, avatars can be made to resemble the person whom they represent, or users might be very creative with appearance or gender. Even if the avatar's appearance resembles the user's real-world looks, the user's identity is still generally anonymous. However, unlike many other virtual worlds (like *Active Worlds* or *Kaneva*), *Second Life*'s servers register the user's avatar as the content creator of the design of anything they create. (This is done in an explicit virtual copyright notice that is part of any user-created virtual property.)

15   On the other end of the spectrum, *World of Warcraft* allows users to create their own avatars, but in a much more fantastic setting. This multi-user virtual environment is inhabited not only by elves, wizards, and trolls, but by celebrities as well. In 2007, *World of Warcraft* launched a series of television spots for the game featuring pop culture celebrities including Mr. T (from the *A-Team*), William Shatner (from *Star Trek*), and Verne Troyer (from *Austin Powers*), each explaining the character classes they play in the game—you can see all of these celebrities next to their digital avatars on YouTube's World of Warcraft channel (www.youtube.com/worldofwarcraft). These commercials reveal something much more interesting than simply demonstrating that celebrities play video games.

16   Each of these very subtly displays aspects of digital literacy—one composition and the other communication. Part of composing in the digital world is understanding the language that the digital environment uses. For most sites there is a minimal vocabulary that you have to be familiar with (such as links, blogs, and the like). For other sites the vocabulary is much more specified (like the different types of characters, or *classes*, such as William Shatner's "tauren" *Shaman* or Mr. T's "night elf" *Warrior* in *World of Warcraft*). Mr. T demonstrates a more specialized aspect of digital literacy, the technical aspect. His commercial explains how he is able to compose in this environment as he asserts his *coding* and *programming* prowess when he shouts: "Well, maybe Mr. T hacked the game and created a Mohawk class! Maybe, Mr. T's pretty handy with computers! Had that occurred to you, Mr. 'Condescending' Director?!" Shatner's commercial demonstrates how users communicate in that virtual environment, specifically as he answers a question another user asked him about hurling lightning from his hands. Sites like these allow for visual and textual communication, and, in some cases, even verbal communication or voice chatting as well.

17   There are still more *text-specific* ways to communicate and compose in the digital world. Sites like *Wikipedia* allow us to create and revise collaborative texts in an ongoing fashion. Of course, like Michael Scott's comment about *Wikipedia* points out, some readers understand how this works better than others. Some texts we have instantaneous access to

through our friends (or our friends at Napster). Some texts and media are distributed to us directly from the artists, like the *Chrome Children* album that adultswim.com made available for free. Some of these texts are interactive, like *World War Z* has become. This best-selling novel has its own website, but the fans of the novel have made it interactive. That is, you cannot only contribute your own tale of the "Zombie War," but you can also submit your work in contests for cash prizes. What digital literacy provides in this capacity is the opportunity to compose actual collaborative texts with both professional and amateur authors. In her essay "Digital Soup," Jessica Heland compares this type of interactive media with traditional storytelling, and explains how we read these texts differently than regular print texts. It is these types of differences that we must be aware of as we move into a more fully digital world. That is, we must understand where digital literacy came from to understand where it is going.

Telling the Good from the Bad and the Ugly

18 Since digital literacy is something that is so pervasive, it is important to establish ourselves as critical readers of digital texts. How do we know what is good, what is bad, and what is just plain ugly? Luckily there are a couple of practices that we can employ to make sorting through the digital world just a little easier. Let's break it down this way—there are really only three categories of websites: those that entertain us, those that include us, and those that educate us.

- Entertaining
- Inclusive
- Educational

19   Within each of those categories are many types of websites. And, of course, sometimes the types of websites might fit in a number of categories. Take these types for example:

- Entertaining
  - *YouTube*
  - *ESPN.com*
- Inclusive
  - *Facebook*
  - *MySpace*
- Educational or Informative
  - *Wikipedia*
  - *theWallStreetJournal.com*

20   Let's look specifically at the Inclusive category to see how we can sort these types of sites. *Facebook* is primarily an inclusive site, but it can also be entertaining. *Second Life* works the same way. Some social networking sites, like *LinkedIn.com* (a professional networking site) or *Match.com* (a dating service), are inclusive, but not entertaining. So, here is what types within categories would look like:

- Inclusive
  - . . . and entertaining
    - *Facebook*
    - *Second Life*
  - . . . and not entertaining
    - *LinkedIn*
    - *Match*

21   The trick in sorting out these sites is to understand their purpose. What is this site supposed to do? Provide a service for me? Connect me with other people? Entertain me? Once we understand the purpose of the site, then we can begin looking at the ways in which these sites operate—what their rules and customs are. Questions like these help us understand these *ethical* aspects of the sites we visit.

22   With educational sites, it is a little easier to tell the good from the bad. However, we must be constantly vigilant as we read these. Many times there are no editors or webmasters who approve what people post on their own educational/informational sites. Writers, like Gilster, have been explaining how to evaluate content for a long time, but we know a lot of this simply through practice. Take *Wikipedia*, for instance: a good *Wikipedia* entry has plenty of published sources and is linked to a number of other properly documented pages both within *Wikipedia* and outside of *Wikipedia*. A bad site, on the other hand, has little or no documentation, or doesn't connect to anything else. In a lot of ways, a bad educational site is like a bad research paper—without proper citations and support, it is really only an opinion piece. If its purpose is to inform me of something, can it do that without support that makes the information legitimate? Does it effectively meet its purpose of thoroughly and responsibly informing me of something?

23   Entertaining and inclusive sites are much more difficult to evaluate. Since educational sites are typically unidirectional (you only read what someone else writes), the ethical implications go only one way. The interactive nature of many entertaining and inclusive sites requires us to be aware of the social and cultural customs of each site that we participate in. Not only do we have to identify the purpose of each site, and evaluate how effectively it meets that purpose, we must also keep in mind the very subtle cultural and social influences that each site might have. With a site like *YouTube*, we focus on the funny or interesting video clips, but we also see

all of the advertisements situated around the video. We have to consider what impact having an advertisement for *Netflix* "pop up" while we are trying to watch Will Ferrell argue with a toddler in "the Landlord" or seeing an ad for Sylvan Learning centers right above the video window where Teen USA's poor Miss South Carolina tries to explain that "Americans can't locate the U.S. on a world map," because they "don't have maps . . . such as." Recognizing how we see these texts in instances like these says as much about our cultural awareness of the social events that are going on around us, as it says about the way we read—it's no longer left to right, top to bottom; it's everything, all at once.

24　　As you read through the essays in the chapter think about your own development as a technology user. What were your attitudes towards technology and literacy as you were growing up? What did these two words mean to you as a child? What do they mean now? Do you already think of yourself as digitally literate, and why? How has technology already coincided with your understanding of the digital world? How do you already contribute to the online world? How do you imagine it will affect your life, personally and professionally, in the future?

Literacy Connections

1. How does Anderson define *digital literacy*?
2. Anderson uses *Facebook* to explain what he means by "contribution, distribution, and consumption." Choose another type of digital literacy and describe the ways it reflects contribution, distribution, and consumption.
3. Write a one-page digital literacy narrative that uses a specific example or examples from your past to reveal your attitudes toward technology and literacy as you were growing up.
4. Anderson discusses three categories of Web sites: entertaining, inclusive, and educational. Think of a Web site you've visited recently that has an entertainment purpose and a site you've visited recently that has an educational purpose. In what ways do the different purposes of each site shape their design and content?
5. How does Anderson's definition of digital literacy connect to the definitions of literacy discussed in Chapter 1?

Before You Read

You're going to look at a case study of a student composing in print and digital literacies, so to get you to think about the differences between composing in print and composing online, reflect on your own experiences as a composer. If you've ever composed in a digital genre (a Web site, a blog, a *Facebook* page, an online photobook, etc.), compare the ways your composing process differed from composing in a print genre.

Student Case Study:
Composing a Web Site

Maria Correa was a first-year student enrolled in the first of two required composition courses at Florida State University when she composed "Favelas in Rio de Janeiro: A Hidden Crisis." Her mixed-media project includes a feature article, a video essay, and a Web site. In this case study, we'll take a close look at Maria's work and her composing processes to get a better sense of what it means to compose in digital literacy situations.

In this case study of Maria Correa's mixed-media project, "Favelas in Rio de Janeiro: A Hidden Crisis," we'll get a chance to compare composing processes in print and digital literacy situations. In her first-year composition class at Florida State University, Maria created a feature article, a video essay, and a Web site. Included in this case study are the final draft of the feature article, the process memos for the video essay and the Web site, and links to her video and Web site. In addition, you'll hear from Maria through extra information she provided to give readers more insight into how she went about composing this mixed-media project and the rhetorical choices she made. By taking a close look at Maria's composing processes for this project, you'll gain a better awareness of composing in digital literacy contexts.

Maria's teacher, Toby McCall, asked his students to complete a mixed-media project on a topic of their choice. Here's the assignment:

ASSIGNMENT: MIXED-MEDIA PROJECT

Choose a topic that is important to you and that you'd like to explore, and apply that central topic to three different types of media: a four-page feature article that you write, a five-minute video essay you compose using MS Moviemaker, and a webspace you design using Nvu. The webspace will host both the article and the video essay. You'll also write three process memos—one for the article, another for the video, and a third for the webspace—in which you explore the compositional differences, design opportunities, and rhetorical situations afforded by the different media types.

First, let's take a look at Maria's final draft of her feature article, so we can compare it to her video and Web site versions. The Word version of her feature article is available as a link from Maria's Web site at http://www.csus.edu/writingcenter/correamm. Visit the link and read her feature article.

In addition to working in the medium of print literacy and composing the feature article about the favelas in Rio de Janeiro, Maria focused on the same subject matter in digital mediums: she also composed a video essay and designed a Web site. Before you read the process memo Maria wrote describing how she went about composing her video essay and making the decisions she made, "read" her video essay at http://www.csus.edu/writingcenter/correamm/favelas.wmv.

Now that you are familiar with the video essay, read what Maria shares with us about her composing processes.

PROCESS MEMO—VIDEO

I chose to start out my movie with what is the first thing that comes to mind when people think of Brazil. The way I chose to do this was to start off with a slide saying "The following people were asked what they pictured when they thought of Brazil." I wanted this slide to be simple and plain, an introduction to the next slides. Then, I interviewed three people on what they thought about Brazil and had their voices play while I showed images of what they were saying. So when one of them answered soccer, as she was saying it I showed an image of a famous Brazilian soccer player. I used the "Fade" transition between these slides because I thought that was the best way to make the images flow as the people are talking.

When the interview is done, I use a "flip" transition onto another slide with text. I chose to do this because now that I have introduced one side of Brazil, the beautiful side, I want to flip to a more serious discussion about the favelas. I then include a fact about the favelas to show people what really goes on, and that maybe they've heard about Brazil but most people don't know about the favelas at all. Then, I added another slide just to tell people what I'm going to be talking about and how it involves suffering, tragedies, drugs and violence. I chose to start off my song on this slide because this is when I actually start talking about the favelas, so I wanted to show a transition between talking about the good things and now the bad side. Also, by starting off the song on this slide, the beat actually starts right after the title slide.

I chose this song in specific for my video essay for several reasons. First of all, it is a song made by "favelados," and the lyrics themselves talk about the struggles in the favelas and how hard their lives are. Even though the listener most likely won't understand the lyrics themselves, I thought it was very appropriate to include a type of music which is typical to the favelas. Besides this, in my essay I include a translation from the chorus of this song, so I felt like including it in my video essay might make it more relevant. After that, I thought that since the listener most likely won't understand the lyrics, it won't be distracting when they are attempting to read the other slides and won't interfere. I feel like the rhythm and the beats are strong and fit perfectly with the rest of the video essay.

I chose my background for all of my slides because I wanted a neutral color on all the slides, but I also wanted a serious color, because my subject matter is very serious. However, I also wanted to portray that even though the situation right now is horrible, something can be done, and these people can be helped. Therefore, I felt that this background was perfect because the slides are gray, but then light is coming through the upper left corner, sort of like hope breaking through the darkness.

For my title slide, I chose very specific features. First, I chose to use a "Bars" transition onto the slide, because I wanted to show that the favelas are like a prison, and the people are behind bars in their own lives. Then, I chose to use the font "Weltron Urban" because it gives a feeling of urban, jail-like, smudged out, and it fits the theme of the favela. I also chose to have the word Favelas bigger than the rest of the words, because it's the focus of my project, so I wanted it to stand out. Also, I wanted it to clash with the font used in the introductory slides, to emphasize the shift from talking about the good side of Brazil to the bad side. Then I included two images. The picture on the left is of two poor children standing in a doorway, which I believe makes an impact and conveys to the viewer a feeling of sadness. The picture on the right is a picture of a kid holding a gun, to convey the violence that goes on in the favelas.

The next slide is a picture of the favelas from above, which shows how big they are. I then defined the favelas in the next slide to explain to the viewer what this actually is. Then, I included three other pictures of different favelas, which show exactly how many there are and how big they are. For the picture of the favela on a hilltop, I chose to have the picture zoom out, because it emphasizes how big the favelas are.

Then, I talk about how people live, and how many live on the streets or in poorly built houses, and then included three pictures again, one of a small kid by his house which is made of wood but covered in graffiti, and the next two pictures of people who actually live on the streets. When I saw these pictures, they were very strong and powerful, and made me feel extremely sad. The third picture is of a pregnant lady living on a couch. I felt that by seeing these pictures, the viewers would understand the gravity of the situation. Then I include a slide talking about how many people don't even have electricity, and I used the flip transition to go on to the image of the tangled wires so people will understand what I just mentioned. After this, I fade into an image of a small child eating food from the floor to show how families barely have money to feed their children, and how the living conditions are horrible.

For the next slide, I chose the transition to be split vertically because I included the picture on one side, and the information about it on the side. When I saw this picture, I thought it was perfect to show how rich people live with the favela in their background and do nothing about it. Then, I included a blank slide to transition onto the subject of how poverty leads to violence, and I fade the slide out to black. After this, I included two pictures of cops in the favelas, because the police are involved with all the violence that goes on in the favelas. I chose to have the picture dissolve onto the next one because I think that it causes an effect of shattered glass, which reminded me of bullets. The second picture shows an armed cop overlooking the favelas, which shows that it is always a dangerous place. Then, I include two slides including a quote to show exactly how dangerous the favelas really are. I fade the slide with the quote to black, to end it on a very serious grieving note.

The next slide I included a picture and information about it on top, and the slide shows an image of an armed officer carrying away a dead body on a cart. The next picture is of police officers pointing their guns at something, and the people who live there in agony and pain. I chose to zoom in the image to their facial expressions to emphasize how scared they are. The next slide, I included two pictures of dead bodies to show that this happens very often, and it is very serious. I zoom in the picture slightly to make the viewer closer to the corpses. Then, I had a slide including the logo imprinted on the side of cop vehicles. I chose to include this image because it shows how brutal the police force is, and how violent and unhelpful they are. I also wanted this picture to be in my video because I described it in my video essay, so I wanted my readers to be able to visualize what I'm talking about.

In the end of my video essay I wanted to include a small clip from City of God *which is one of the movies that has been made recently which depicts exactly how the favelas are. I fade out the music during this slide so that it doesn't interfere with the sound from the movie. The excerpt from the movie shows the violence, and how many people are involved and dying, and how even young children are being handed guns, how these people are surrounded by death every day. I ended my movie with a slide telling people to help, because this is what I wanted my viewers to take out from my movie. I wanted to shock them so they are compelled to do something about it.*

Now, let's read what Maria has to share with us regarding how she went about designing her Web site and the decisions she made. Before you read Maria's process memo for her Web site, take a look at her site at http://www.csus.edu/writingcenter/corream.

PROCESS MEMO—WEB SITE

For the web site, I wanted to keep it simple, but still convey the same theme that I do in my video and my essay. I wanted the background to be black, since my topic is sad and serious, and I wanted my text to be white. However, although my topic is sad, I am also hopeful that something can be done to fix this problem, so I wanted to show an idea of hope in the theme. Because of that, I made the colors of the title banner green and yellow, because those are the colors of the Brazilian flag. I also chose to make the headings "Rough Drafts" and "Process Memos" green and yellow to differentiate them from the white links, and again to represent Brazil.

As for the structure of the website, I chose to have the big banner on the top of the page with the title, Favelas of Brazil. I wanted the words "Favelas" and "Brazil" to stand out, so I made that font larger than "of." Then, I placed the links on the left side of the page. For the rough drafts and process memos, since there are three of each, I wanted to have a heading that stood out and each link to the rough drafts and memos as a sub-link to their headings. Then, I wanted to have my movie in the middle of my home page. I wanted the video itself to be bigger, but I tried changing it in several ways and it didn't work out. I didn't want to include anything else in my home page so it wouldn't distract from my movie.

Next, I wanted to have my essay on my website. Since it would be too inconvenient and long to have the entire essay on one page, I decided to break it up into four pages. When you click on the link "Essay" on the home page, it takes you to the first page of the essay. I didn't want to include links to all the pages of my essay because I want my reader to read it in order because I wrote it in a specific order, so that it makes more sense if you read it page by page instead of skipping around. So I put the first page of my essay, and then in the bottom I put a link saying "Next" to take you to the next page. Since it was also a requirement to have the final copy of the essay in word format, I included a link for that underneath each page of my essay on the website. I chose to have the links underneath the essay in green and yellow again, to contrast from the serious, white font of the rest of the essay.

For each page of the essay, I wanted to include a picture. For the first page, I included a picture of a favela from above. I wanted to use the pictures from my movie to connect both pieces. In the second page, when I begin to talk about violence and the police in my essay, I chose to include a picture of the police carrying a dead body, which is also in my video. Then, later in the same page I included a picture of sad children from the title page of my video when I begin to talk about how hard it must be to raise a family in the favelas. I wanted the pictures that I included to tie in with whatever I was mentioning in the essay where I placed the picture. In the third page, next to a paragraph where I talk about how wealthier people ignore the favelas, I placed the picture from my video that shows the expensive buildings, and in the background it shows the favelas. In the last page of my essay, I included a picture that wasn't in my video, because I didn't talk about the same subject in my video. In my essay, I begin to talk about the things that are being done to help the favelas, and in my video I didn't have enough time so I chose to only talk about the problem itself. So to coincide with the topic in the essay, I included a picture of the singer that sings the song that I talk about in that paragraph. The last touch that I included in my essay on the website was to link the MLA citations to the websites where I got the information from, instead of including a Works Cited on my website itself.

Maria's Strategies for Composing

To give us additional insight into Maria's strategies for composing this mixed-media project, we asked her to talk with us about her composing strategies. First, we asked her to tell us a little about the kinds of brainstorming activities she usually does to help her come up with ideas for her essays. She told us:

> *Usually when I'm writing an essay, I create some form of an outline, with a broad idea first, and then more specific aspects of that topic that I want to pinpoint with my essay. If it is a research paper, I usually read some information on the topic and maybe look at some articles on it in order to come up with more specific ideas.*

When we asked her if she used those same kinds of brainstorming activities to help her come up with ideas for this digital essay, she shared with us:

> *With this specific essay, I already knew I wanted to talk about the Favelas, and how there isn't a lot of awareness about them. I watched the movie* City of God, *and picked certain clips that inspired me and gave me ideas to talk about specifically in the essay. One of these clips was included in my video. Besides that, I googled "Favelas" to see what kind of information popped up, in order to illustrate the main problems and how they are depicted in the media. When I came up with enough points to talk about, I started thinking about the best way to put them together and began writing.*

Next, we asked her to talk with us about her concept of an audience for her mixed-media project by telling us for whom she was composing the project and for what audience she was writing. She told us:

> *Obviously, since it was a class assignment, I was mainly writing for my teacher and my peers, as an informational essay. However, I was also writing to all the people who haven't heard about the Favelas, in order to maybe make the problem more known across the world, hopefully to find a solution. I don't think that my 5-page*

digital essay will solve a problem going on for almost a century, but I just wanted more people to know what's going on.

Then, we asked Maria to tell us whether writing for a Web site and the conventions that go with that affected the way she went about composing the essay.

Definitely. Because this essay was digital, I knew that it had the capacity to reach more people, and it could be something interesting where I could link words to images, and the font and background and everything could be used in unison to create the mood that I wanted for my essay. I was able to talk about things more clearly in the essay because I knew that I could include a picture to explain it better next to it.

Finally, we asked her to talk about whether writing for a Web site affected her persona—the way she came across to her readers and the voice she used.

I wanted my voice to be directed to any kind of person that might come across my Web site, and to keep it interesting. Because it was on a Web site, I felt like most people on the web aren't looking for too many facts or too much information, because there is such a clutter of Web sites that they would probably just go somewhere else. Therefore I wanted my voice to not be too personal or harsh, but to convey an image to the readers.

Maria's answers to our questions make it clear that composing in a digital medium requires many of the same composing strategies as composing in print text alone, but this type of composing calls upon us to expand our repertoire of composing strategies as we consider all kinds of new factors—a worldwide audience and an appropriate persona for this huge audience; effective placement and use of links, images, and movie clips; effective color selections; etc. Working in a digital medium often requires composers to consider how print text, sound, video, digital images, and hyperlinks can work together to create an effective composition.

Literacy Connections

1. Working with a small group of your classmates, make a list of how the kinds of rhetorical decisions Maria had to make as she went about composing her Web site differed from those she made as she wrote her article and designed her video essay on the same subject. You can use Maria's process memos to help you understand her rhetorical decisions.
2. In what ways does Maria's print text differ from her digital texts?
3. What do you think are the advantages of composing in more than one medium—in, for example, both print and visual media? How

does composing in a variety of media push our thinking and broaden our vision?

4. If Maria were going to do another revision of her project (the feature article, Web site, and video), what suggestions would you have for her?

5. In what ways does Maria's project reflect Dustin Anderson's definition of digital literacy in the introductory essay of the chapter?

Digital Literacy Readings

Before You Read

In order to connect John Seely Brown's article about writing online to your own experiences, take a few minutes to think about your prior experiences writing online. What types of online writing have you done? How has the online writing you've done been similar to and different from writing in print?

Excerpt from "Growing Up Digital"

John Seely Brown

John Seely Brown is the former Chief Scientist of Xerox Corporation and the director of its Palo Alto Research Center (PARC). Today, he refers to himself as "The Chief of Confusion." He says that he is "helping people ask the *right questions,* trying to make a difference through [his] work—speaking, writing, teaching" (www.johnseelybrown.com/). His article "Growing Up Digital" appeared in an academic journal, the *United States Distance Learning Journal,* in 2002. In this excerpt Seely Brown focuses on the Web, and the generation that grew up using the Web, to discuss features of Web literacies. Seely Brown's article will give you another perspective on the definition of digital literacy.

1   In 1831 Michael Faraday built a small generator that produced electricity, but a generation passed before an industrial version was built, then another 25 years before all the necessary accoutrements for electrification came into place-power companies, neighborhood wiring, appliances (like light bulbs) that required electricity, and so on. But when that infrastructure finally took hold, everything changed—homes, work places, transportation, entertainment, architecture, what we ate, even when we went to bed. Worldwide, electricity became a transformative medium for social practices.

WEB⁺ AS A TRANSFORMATIVE LEARNING TECHNOLOGY

- INTERNET/WEB AS A   ⟶   INTERNET/WEB AS A
  NETWORK OF COMPUTERS   MEDIUM

- A MEDIUM THAT HONORS MULTIPLE FORMS OF INTELLIGENCE

- A MEDIUM THAT LEVERAGES THE SMALL EFFORTS OF THE MANY
  AND THE LARGE EFFORTS OF THE FEW

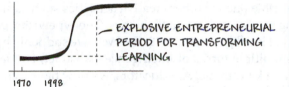

- VALUE OF
  COMPUTERS
  FOR LEARNING

— EXPLOSIVE ENTREPRENEURIAL
PERIOD FOR TRANSFORMING
LEARNING

1970 1998

COPYRIGHT JSB & SEH

2 In quite the same way, the World Wide Web will be a transformative medium, as important as electricity. Here again we have a story of gradual development followed by an exploding impact. The Web's antecedents trace back to a U.S. Department of Defense project begun in the late 1960s, then to the innovations of Tim Berners-Lee and others at the Center for European Nuclear Research in the late 1980s, followed by rapid adoption in the mid- and late 1990s. Suddenly we had e-mail available, then a new way to look up information, then a remarkable way to do our shopping—but that's barely the start. The tremendous range of transformations wrought by electricity, so barely sensed by our grandparents a century ago, lie ahead of us through the Web.

3   No one fully knows what those transformations will be, but what we do know is that initial uses of new media have tended to mimic what came before: early photography imitated painting, the first movies the stage, etc. It took 10 to 20 years for filmmakers to discover the inherent capabilities of their new medium. They were to develop techniques now commonplace in movies, such as "fades," "dissolves," "flashbacks," "time and space folds," and "special effects," all radically different from what had been possible in the theater. So it will be for the Web. What we initially saw as an intriguing network of computers is now evolving its own genres from a mix of technological possibilities and social and market needs.

A New Medium

4 The first thing to notice is that the media we're all familiar with—from books to television—are one-way propositions: they push their content *at* us. The Web is two-way, push *and pull*. In finer point, it combines the one-way reach of broadcast with the two-way reciprocity of a mid-cast. Indeed, its user can at once be a receiver and sender of "broadcast"—a confusing property, but mind-stretching!

5 A second aspect of the Web is that it is the first medium that honors the notion of multiple intelligences. This past century's concept of "literacy" grew out of our intense belief in text, a focus enhanced by the power of one particular technology—the typewriter. It became a great tool for writers but a terrible one for other creative activities such as sketching, painting, notating music, or even mathematics. The typewriter prized one particular kind of intelligence, but with the Web, we suddenly have a medium that honors multiple forms of intelligence—abstract, textual, visual, musical, social, and kinesthetic. As educators, we now have a chance to construct a medium that enables all young people to become engaged in their ideal way of learning. The Web affords the match we need between a medium and how a particular person learns.

6 A third and unusual aspect of the Web is that it leverages the small efforts of the many with the large efforts of the few. For example, researchers in the Maricopa County Community College system in Phoenix have found a way to link a set of senior citizens with pupils in the

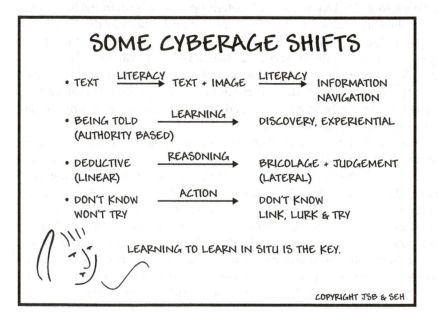

Longview Elementary School, as helper-mentors. It's wonderful to see—kids listen to these "grandparents" better than they do to their own parents, the mentoring really helps their teachers, and the seniors create a sense of meaning for themselves. Thus, the small efforts of the many—the seniors—complement the large efforts of the few—the teachers.

7   The same thing can be found in operation at Hewlett-Packard, where engineers use the Web to help kids with science or math problems. Both of these examples barely scratch the surface as we think about what's possible when we start interlacing resources with needs across a whole region.

8   The Web has just begun to have an impact on our lives. As fascinated as we are with it today, we're still seeing it in its early forms. We've yet to see the full motion video and audio possibilities that await the bandwidth we'll soon have through cable modems and DSL; also to come are the new Web appliances, such as the portable Web in a phone, and a host of wireless technologies. As important as any of these is the imagination, competitive drive, and capital behind a thousand companies—chased by a swelling list of dot-coms—rushing to bring new content, services, and "solutions" to offices and homes.

9   My belief is that not only will the Web be as fundamental to society as electrification, but that it will be subject to many of the same diffusion and absorption dynamics as that earlier medium. We're just at the bottom of the S-curve of this innovation, a curve that will have about the same shape as with electrification, but a much steeper slope than before. As this S-curve takes off, it creates huge opportunities for entrepreneurs. It will be entrepreneurs, corporate or academic, who will drive this chaotic, transformative phenomenon, who will see things differently, challenge background assumptions, and bring new possibilities into being. Our challenge and opportunity, then, is to foster an entrepreneurial spirit toward creating new *learning* environments—a spirit that will use the unique capabilities of the Web to leverage the natural ways that humans learn.

Digital Learners

10 Let's turn to today's youth, growing up digital. How are they different? This subject matters, because our young boys and girls are today's customers for schools and colleges and tomorrow's for lifelong learning. Approximately four years ago, we at Xerox's Palo Alto Research Center started hiring 15-year-olds to join us as researchers. We gave them two jobs. First, they were to design the "workscape" of the future—one they'd want to work in; second, they were to design the school or "learningscape" of the future—again, with the same condition. We had an excellent opportunity to watch these adolescents, and what we saw—the ways they think, the designs they came up with—really shook us up.

11   For example, today's kids are always "multiprocessing"—they do several things simultaneously—listen to music, talk on the cell phone, and use the computer, all at the same time. Recently I was with a young twenty-something who had actually wired a Web browser into his eyeglasses. As he talked with me, he had his left hand in his pocket to cord in keystrokes to bring up my Web page and read about me, all the while carrying on with his part of the conversation! I was astonished that he could do all this in parallel and so unobtrusively.

12   People my age tend to think that kids who are multiprocessing can't be concentrating. That may not be true. Indeed, one of the things we noticed **"The ability to 'read'** is that the attention span of the teens at PARC— **multimedia texts and** often between 30 seconds and five minutes—par- **to feel comfortable** allels that of top managers, who operate in a world **with new, multiple-** of fast context-switching. So the short attention **media genres is** spans of today's kids may turn out to be far from **decidedly nontrivial."** dysfunctional for future work worlds.

13   Let me bring together our findings by presenting a set of dimensions, and shifts along them, that describe kids in the digital age. We present these dimensions in turn, but they actually fold in on each other, creating a complex of intertwined cognitive skills.

14   The first dimensional shift has to do with literacy and how it is evolving. Literacy today involves not only text, but also image and screen literacy. The ability to "read" multimedia texts and to feel comfortable with new, multiple-media genres is decidedly nontrivial. We've long downplayed this ability; we tend to think that watching a movie, for example, requires no particular skill. If, however, you'd been left out of society for 10 years and then came back and saw a movie, you'd find it a very confusing, even jarring, experience. The network news shows—even the front page of your daily newspaper—are all very different from 10 years ago. Yet Web genres change in a period of *months*.

15   The new literacy, beyond text and image, is one of information navigation. The real literacy of tomorrow entails the ability to be your own personal reference librarian—to know how to navigate through confusing, complex information spaces and feel comfortable doing so. "Navigation" may well be the main form of literacy for the 21st century.

16   The next dimension, and shift, concerns learning. Most of us experienced formal learning in an authority-based, lecture-oriented school. Now, with incredible amounts of information available through the Web, we find a "new" kind of learning assuming pre-eminence—learning that's discovery based. We are constantly discovering new things as we browse through the emergent digital "libraries." Indeed, Web surfing fuses learning and entertainment, creating "infotainment."

17   But discovery-based learning, even when combined with our notion of navigation, is not so great a change, until we add a third, more subtle shift, one that pertains to forms of reasoning. Classically, reasoning has been concerned

with the deductive and abstract. But our observation of kids working with digital media suggests *bricolage* to us more than abstract logic. *Bricolage*, a concept studied by Claude Levi-Strauss more than a generation ago, relates to the concrete. It has to do with abilities to find something—an object, tool, document, a piece of code—and to use it to build something you deem important. *Judgment* is inherently critical to becoming an effective digital *bricoleur*.

18   How do we make good judgments? Socially, in terms of recommendations from people we trust? Cognitively, based on rational argumentation? On the reputation of a sponsoring institution? What's the mixture of ways and warrants that you end up using to decide and act? With the Web, the sheer scope and variety of resources befuddles the non-digital adult. But Web-smart kids learn to become *bricoleurs.*

19   The final dimension has to do with a bias toward action. It's interesting to watch how new systems get absorbed by society; with the Web, this absorption, or learning process, by young people has been quite different from the process in times past. My generation tends not to want to try things unless or until we already know how to use them. If we don't know how to use some appliance or software, our instinct is to reach for a manual or take a course or call up an expert. Believe me, hand a manual or suggest a course to 15-year-olds and they think you are a dinosaur. They want to turn the thing on, get in there, muck around, and see what works. Today's kids get on the Web and link, lurk, and watch how other people are doing things, then try it themselves. This tendency toward "action" brings us back into the same loop in which navigation, discovery, and judgment all come into play *in situ*. When, for example, have we lurked enough to try something ourselves? Once we fold action into the other dimensions, we necessarily shift our focus toward learning *in situ* with and from each other. Learning becomes situated in action; it becomes as much social as cognitive, it is concrete rather than abstract, and it becomes intertwined with judgment and exploration. As such, the Web becomes not only an informational and social resource but a learning *medium* where understandings are socially constructed and shared. In that medium, learning becomes a part of action and knowledge creation.

Literacy Connections

1. Individually or in small groups, make a list of the ways that literacy changes when we move from print to digital, according to John Seely Brown.
2. Because it was published in an academic journal, Brown's article contains some complex concepts and language you might be unfamiliar with. Reread the article and circle places where you were confused, and then work in small groups to discuss these points of confusion and try to get a better understanding of the article as a group.

3. Does Brown's idea of "multiprocessing" connect to your own experiences with digital literacy? Do you "multiprocess" when you're on the computer?

4. Do you agree with Brown's argument about the differences between print and digital literacy? Are there other features of digital literacy that he doesn't mention?

5. How is Brown's definition of digital literacy similar to Dustin Anderson's definition of digital literacy in the introductory essay of the chapter?

Before You Read

In the following essay, Crawford Kilian discusses characteristics of effective Web writing. Before you read his essay, think about your own experiences surfing the Internet. Individually or in small groups, come up with a list of the qualities of an effective Web site.

Effective Web Writing

Crawford Kilian

Crawford Kilian, born in 1941, is a novelist and college professor. His works include *Wonders, Inc.* (1968), *Brother Jonathan* (1985), *2020 Visions: The Future of Canadian Education* (1995), and *Writing for the Web* (2006). "Effective Web Writing" appeared on the Web site *New Architect*. Kilian's article uses some of the features we discussed in Chapters 1 and 2, such as purpose, audience, and organization, and applies them to composing for the Web. Hopefully, Kilian's advice will help you become a more effective composer on the Web.

1   Several years ago, I stood in a university bookstore and counted at least 170 shelf-feet of books about the Web: books about HTML, CGI, and Java; books about Perl and Web site administration. Not one book was about the text that all those tools were supposed to display. And although every one of those books could have been archived on a Web site, in practice the Web-creator market wanted print on paper.

2   That made sense. The Web is a pretty lousy way to transmit information—especially the text that gives the Web its chief reason for existence. But you can use writing techniques to exploit the Web's strengths while avoiding its weaknesses.

3   Let's start with the weaknesses. Reading text on a monitor is physically tiring and unpleasant. Intellectually, it's truly dangerous. Computers rev us up and dumb us down, leaving us in no frame of mind for logical thought or analysis.

4   They rev us up by conditioning us for jolts. A jolt is a sensory and emotional reward that follows a prescribed action. Turn on the machine and it boings at you. Click on an icon and a window opens up, delivering a jolt. Type a flame to your favorite adversary, and he'll send you back a jolt as repayment.

5   Like Pavlov's dogs, we're now conditioned to expect such stimuli. Addicted, we develop a tolerance and soon need more and bigger jolts to feed our habit. We grow impatient if a site loads slowly, or if we can't find what we're looking for—the jolt of useful information, a pretty graphic, or a funny noise. We demand faster connections because we need faster jolts.

6   At the same time, computer monitors dumb us down by their awful resolution. Jakob Nielsen, the usability guru who's been studying computer communications since the 1980s, warns that low-res text slows reading speed by up to 25 percent. It also destroys our ability to proofread accurately, which explains why so many students hand in beautifully laser-printed garbage—and why so many Web sites look as if they've been written by a 12-year-old in a hurry.

7   It gets worse. As people have swarmed into this new medium, they've brought all their bad habits from other media—especially from TV and its obsession with moving images. Simple, boring text just doesn't seem to cut it, except as something to keep the animated GIFs from bumping into each other. Emigrés from print media aren't much better because they still think in terms of long columns of closely-packed text.

8   So people from other media are trying to impose their habits on this new medium without even troubling to see what their audiences want, or how they behave on a Web site.

Understanding Web Visitors

9 Web designer Jeffrey Zeldman makes a crucial distinction about those who use this medium. He says there are three very separate groups with different goals and attitudes:

- **Viewers who would rather be watching TV.** This group goes to the Web in search of eye candy and other audiovisual jolts. They use text only as directions to the next surprise.

- **Users who want information they can apply to their own work.** They want your stats for their report, or your business plan as a model for their own. They love "hit and run" retrieval, they hate to scroll, and no one has ever built a site that they find really sticky.

- **Readers (a rare breed).** They will actually scroll through long documents, even whole books. Or they'll download what they find, print it out, and read it in an armchair like any other print document.

10   A new but growing fourth group is the listeners. Whether sight-impaired or not, they use programs that read text off the screen. As voice programs improve in quality, more people will adopt them.

11   Each of these groups needs a particular kind of text, and if they don't find it on your site, they'll move elsewhere.

12   Viewers and users both prefer chunks—stand-alone blocks of information, filling the screen with 100 words or less, requiring little or no scrolling. For viewers, chunks should contain very brief text excerpts with clear directions to the next big audiovisual jolt. Users need concise, well-organized, and well-mapped sites so they can go straight to what they want.

> **"Viewers and users both prefer chunks—stand-alone blocks of information . . . requiring little or no scrolling."**

13   In the early days, some Web content developers worried that jumping from chunk to chunk would be unpopular because of the lag time. Better to scroll, they argued, than make visitors wait. One technical writer, Michael Hoffman, makes a strong case for putting a Web site on a single page of scrolling text, but with a detailed, linked table of contents and numerous internal links.

14   But machines and connections are much faster now, and surfers routinely jump from page to page. Jakob Nielsen recently reported on a Poynter Institute study that found people on the Web now engage in "interlaced browsing," switching back and forth, for example, between CNN.com and MSNBC.com, comparing coverage of breaking news.

15   Nielsen found the Poynter study supported his own earlier investigation of the ways people read Web text. One key discovery was that people ignore graphics in the first three "eye fixations" they make on a page. Eight times out of ten they look for text—particularly headlines, summaries, and captions. Because only a third of a site's visitors read a whole article, simple headlines and concise summaries are critical.

16   So on sites like CNN and MSNBC, the top stories are designed pretty well, at least for users: headline, summaries, and full story—if only the site builders wouldn't add those slow-loading graphics. They rarely add value to the text, and viewers won't bother to stick around for them. Readers, who are in less of a hurry, aren't as interested in chunked text. They like archives—complete texts, written for print on paper and shoveled onto a site. They may well prefer text adapted for screen display, such as that with lines running only halfway across the screen, and with blank lines between

paragraphs. But they're often quite content to scroll through annual reports, long articles, and whole books.

17   When listeners become a significant group, they'll want writing that can be spoken clearly, even by a voice program, and understood at one hearing. Otherwise, their Web experience will resemble being trapped in an infinite voicemail system inhabited by robots.

Stepping into Your Visitors' Shoes

18 One of the sweetest ironies of Web culture is that it operates on a very modern constructivist communication model, while most of its creators are still stuck with an old-fashioned instrumental model that should have gone out with vacuum tubes.

19   In the instrumental model, your information is a tool operating on a passive receiver, intended to get the receiver to do as you wish. Instrumental communication likes ballistic and postal metaphors: Marketers "target" consumers, advertisers yearn for "penetration," and voters "send a message" to politicians, who in turn combine the metaphors with "bomb-o-grams"—launching cruise missiles to send a message to their enemies. The implicit message in this model is "Do what I say."

20   Instrumental communication is OK for radio, TV, and movies, and for print on paper, because users of those media really are targets who can't effectively reply. But Web surfers sure can, and most of the time the reply is "Goodbye forever."

21   And why not? They came looking for something and you didn't provide it.

22   The constructivist, interactive communication model isn't concerned with firing an information bullet between anyone's eyes. It wants to start and maintain a conversation. In any conversation, those who take part are both sending and receiving, changing each message in light of the latest response. They may be amazed at where the conversation leads them. The implicit message here is: "Is this what you want?"—which presumes a very different social relationship from the instrumental model: a relationship of equals.

Three Basic Principles

23 Once you understand the people for whom you've designed your site, your text should reflect three basic principles of Web writing: orientation, information, and action.

24   Visitors have two questions on arrival: they want to know where they are in the site and how to move around within it. Because visitors may arrive via search engine at a page buried deep in your site, you need to provide those answers everywhere—not just on your front page. Your site

name should be self-explanatory, stating its purpose, and every page should provide links to other pages, showing how the site is organized and how to navigate it.

25 The links themselves should also be self-explanatory, though a blurb is sometimes helpful. As a navigation aid, blurbs prepare visitors for what they can expect, and help save time. Suppose your organization has departments called Information Services and Information Management. The blurb for the first might be: "Public Relations, Newsletter, Technical Editing, Advertising Purchases." The blurb for the second might be: "Webmaster, Intranet, Staff Training, Computer Support." This makes it easier for visitors to go to the appropriate destination, especially if the terms in the blurbs are links themselves.

Molding Information to the Web

26 Information is what your visitors are here for, but unless they're all readers who are content to scroll, you need to adapt your text by cutting, hooking, and organizing.

27 Cutting is essential for text adapted from print. Even if you're archiving huge documents, you should also include summaries of them. Because visitors are reading at 75 percent of normal speed, and are impatient for those jolts of gratified inquiry, Nielsen suggests you should cut any given text by 50 percent—especially if you're adapting from print, which relies heavily on transitional phrases that don't belong in hypertext.

28 Even if you're creating original text, writing long and cutting short will keep your text tightly focused. If the writing still makes sense when cut in half, great; leave it short. If you need more text, add it word by word until you have just enough.

29 Don't be tender with your text, but be tender with visitors who read it. That means writing "use" instead of "utilize," which is identical in meaning but has two more syllables. It means writing "decided" instead of "made a decision." And cutting whole paragraphs of non-essential information. Every word and phrase should have to fight for its life.

30 Hooking an impatient visitor is vital. Your readers are skimming and scanning, so use both headlines and text to grab them. Headlines should be simple and informative. Text can exploit gimmicks long known to magazine writers for catching readers' interest.

31 "For example," he said, "use quotation marks because people seem to prefer reading what someone actually said." Other hooks include:

- questions—they make us seek the answer,
- unusual statements—we love surprises,

- promise of conflict—we love fights,
- news pegs—to tie content to the coattails of some big current event, and
- direct address—we love personal attention.

32   Organizing Web text isn't always as easy as cutting and hooking. Print on paper can be narrative, logical argument, or categorical. Narrative order, which relies on chronology, imposes a sequence that Web users may not want or need. Logical argument tends to be too long and sequential for impatient users.

33   Web writing, being hypertext, thrives best under categorical organization: "The Five Signs of Cancer," "Golf's Greatest Players," "The Best Beaches in Mendocino County." When users can jump from chunk to chunk, they get to their destinations much faster.

34   You should organize even within a chunk. A hundred words in one solid block of text is a symptom of paragraphosis, in which the eye becomes unable to focus or track through a mass of type. A chunk could have two or three short paragraphs, each with a subhead, all surrounded by lots of white space.

35   Organization can also mean junking declarative sentences and offering just fragments. Sometimes. Not always. Bulleted lists? Great!

36   Your site needs to welcome action by your visitors, even provoke it. If all you want is for them to click through to another page, the link title and blurb should make it seem worth their time. If you want them to join your movement, fill out your form, or buy your software, you need to make it appear to be in their interest to do so, and to make it effortless. Yes, as in the instrumental model, you still want them to do what you say, but you're also prepared to do what they say.

37   To achieve all this—orientation, information, action—demands much more than technical expertise with Flash or XML. It demands that you put the visitor's needs first. On the Web, the customer really is always right, and vanishes the moment you indicate otherwise. So you need to make a leap of empathy to put yourself in the visitor's shoes, and write your text accordingly. Your own team members may not be willing to make that leap unless you persuade them to. Judging from the experiences of my Web writing colleagues, many corporate and governmental Web sponsors still think text should be like an armor-piercing bullet, penetrating the reader's thick skull with a one-way message. This is why it's said that most commercial Web sites actually harm their sponsors by driving away customers.

38   Politically, the interactivity of the Web is as explosive as Gutenberg's printing press, creating a highly egalitarian society. No person or idea can count on origins to enforce respect or attention. The Web is literally a free market in information, and anyone who still dreams of a captive market is

dreaming, indeed. Your toughest job as a Web writer may be to wake up some of your own colleagues to that reality.

Review Yourself

39 You've written the text for your site. Short of hiring focus groups to test the usability and hospitality of your text, how can you evaluate it? Well, when I run into trouble writing a novel, I critique it in a letter to myself—a kind of autoreview. Detailing the story's failures leads quickly to ideas for solutions. So if knowledgeable critics aren't available, review your own and comparable sites.

40 You can do this by several standards—those of gurus like Nielsen, of sites like Web Pages That Suck, or of your competitors' sites. You may decide to set your own standards using some or all of the following:

- **Purpose.** Is the site for entertainment, marketing, information, education? Purpose achieved? How? Not achieved? Why not?

- **Audience**. Are your intended visitors veterans, experts, or novices? Are they young or old, male or female?

- **Content.** Is it information rich or just a jump page? Do you have adequate chunking and archiving? Is the text clean, clear, well-organized, and suited to the purpose and audience?

- **Appearance.** Do graphics enhance text or distract from it? Does text invite reading thanks to short paragraphs, legible fonts, relatively narrow columns, and white space between paragraphs?

- **Accessibility.** Does the page load quickly? Does it require special plugins? Why?

- **Organization.** Is the site easily navigable even on the first visit? Does it require a lot of scrolling? Can you get anywhere from anywhere else on the site?

Conclusion

41 As we Web creators and visitors learn more about the nature of this new medium, we also learn more about ourselves. It's not always good news: Many of us turn out to be jolt-addicted, impatient, and impulsive.

42 But as more and more people adopt the Web as a major venue for exchanging information, the jolts will become less important—or at least more sophisticated. As new Web writing genres evolve, some will become extremely subtle and nuanced, while others will stay as crude as graffiti. I think we're a very lucky generation, the first to use the Web and to learn what it has to teach us.

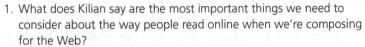

Literacy Connections

1. What does Kilian say are the most important things we need to consider about the way people read online when we're composing for the Web?
2. Kilian presents two models of delivering information—instrumental and constructivist. Look up both of these terms on the Web and use what you've found about these two models to create a list of the defining features of each model.
3. Kilian cites Jeffrey Zeldman's descriptions of four types of Web users: viewers, users, readers, and listeners. Think of the last time you surfed the Web and used Zeldman's categories to describe what type of user you were. How did your purpose for reading on the Web affect your reading process?
4. Choose one of your favorite Web sites and use Kilian's advice for Web writing to discuss whether or not the Web site you've chosen is rhetorically effective. Does your Web site apply any of the advice for effective Web writing outlined by Kilian? Would Kilian point out anything ineffective about the writing on the Web site you've chosen?
5. Kilian's description of using the Web in his opening paragraphs is much different than John Seely Brown's description of Web literacies. What is your own response to these two different positions on digital literacy?

Before You Read

You're about to read about the features of blogs, but before you do, share your experiences with blogs in small groups. Have you ever participated in blogs? What draws you to them? What purpose do they serve? What kinds of social interactions do you think they encourage? Have one group member make a summary of the group's blog experiences.

What We're Doing When We Blog

Meg Hourihan

Meg Hourihan is the cofounder of Pyra Labs, the company that launched Blogger, a blog publishing system at www.blogger.com. She is a co-author of the book *We Blog: Publishing Online with Weblogs*. She was named a Young Innovator Who Will Create the Future in 2003 by MIT's *Technology Review* magazine. In "What We're Doing When We

Blog," Hourihan discusses strategies for composing in one of the most popular digital genres, the weblog or "blog."

1 Every day it seems another article about weblogs appears in the press. At first, most of these stories seemed content to cover the personal nature of blogging. But more and more I'm seeing articles that attempt to examine the journalistic and punditry aspects of weblogs prominent in many of the so-called "warblogs," or sites that began in response to the events of September 11th.

2 The articles' authors are rarely webloggers themselves, which places them in the unenviable position of describing and defining weblogs based on observation, not experience. Given the vast number of blogs, it can be very difficult to understand the breadth and scope of blogging when an editor wants 750 words in 48 hours.

3 I've noticed this has resulted in a variety of ideas about and definitions of the weblogs—from statements that blogs are personal journals filled with the (often dull or trivial) minutiae of daily life to a belief that blogs are right-wing responses to the liberal media establishment. Witness the recent article "Online Uprising" by Catherine Seipp in the *American Journalism Review*:

4 *In general, "blog" used to mean a personal online diary, typically concerned with boyfriend problems or techie news. But after September 11, a slew of new or refocused media junkie/political sites reshaped the entire Internet media landscape. Blog now refers to a Web journal that comments on the news—often by criticizing the media and usually in rudely clever tones—with links to stories that back up the commentary with evidence.*

5 In her article, Catherine forgoes the more traditional weblogs-are-links-plus-commentary definition to carve out a new meaning for the word, limited to the type of blogs she reads. But Catherine's analysis misses some of the very subtleties that distinguish weblogs from other writing. Rather than rant that Catherine just "doesn't get it," it seems to me that her article, and others that are similar, are perfect opportunities for the blogging community to talk about our own evolution.

Our Commonality

6 If we look beneath the content of weblogs, we can observe the common ground all bloggers share—the format. The weblog format provides a framework for our universal blog experiences, enabling the social interactions we associate with blogging. Without it, there is no differentiation between the myriad content produced for the Web.

7   Whether you're a warblogger who works by day as a professional journalist or you're a teenage high school student worried about your final exams, you do the same thing: you use your blog to link to your friends and rivals and comment on what they're doing. Blog posts are short, informal, sometimes controversial, and sometimes deeply personal, no matter what topic they approach. They can be characterized by their conversational tone and unlike a more formal essay or speech, a blog post is often an opening to a discussion, rather than a full-fledged argument already arrived at.

8   As bloggers, we update our sites frequently on the content that matters to us. Depending on the blogger, the content varies. But because it's a weblog, formatted reverse-chronologically and time-stamped, a reader can expect it will be updated regularly. By placing our email addresses on our sites, or including features to allow readers to comment directly on a specific post, we allow our readers to join the conversation. Emails are often rapidly incorporated back into the site's content, creating a nearly real-time communication channel between the blog's primary author (its creator) and its secondary authors (the readers who email and comment).

9   And we're united by tools, whether we use Blogger, LiveJournal, Radio UserLand, Movable Type, or a custom job that's a labor of love. Webloggers often use tools to facilitate the publication of their sites. These tools spit out our varied content in the same format—archives, permalinks, time stamps, and date headers.

A Native Format

10 When the Web began, the page was the *de facto* unit of measurement, and content was formatted accordingly. Online we don't need to produce content of a certain length to meet physical page-size requirements. And as the Web has matured, we've developed our own native format for writing online, a format that moves beyond the page paradigm: The *weblog*, with its smaller, more concise, unit of measurement; and the *post*, which utilizes the medium to its best advantage by proffering frequent updates and richly hyperlinked text.

11 While a page usually contains one topic, or a portion of a single-topic item spans several pages (an opinion piece, an essay or column, a technical document, or press release), the weblog post is a self-contained topical unit. It can be as short as one sentence, or run for several paragraphs. And it's the amalgamation of multiple posts—on varying topics—on a single page that distinguishes the weblog from its online ancestor, the home page. Freed from the constraints of the printed page (or any concept of "page"), an author can

now blog a short thought that previously would have gone unwritten. *The weblog's post unit liberates the writer from word count.*

The Posts Collection

12   What distinguishes a collection of posts from a traditional home page or Web page? Primarily it's the reverse-chronological order in which posts appear. When a reader visits a weblog, she is always confronted with the newest information at the top of the page.

13   Having the freshest information at the top of the page does a few things: as readers, it gives a sense of immediacy with no effort on our part. We don't have to scan the page, looking for what's new or what's been changed. If content has been added since our last visit, it's easy to see as soon as the page loads.

14   Additionally, the newest information at the top (coupled with its time stamps and sense of immediacy) sets the expectation of updates, an expectation reinforced by our return visits to see if there's something new. Weblogs demonstrate that time is important by the very nature in which they present their information. As weblog readers, we respond with frequent visits, and we are rewarded with fresh content.

The Anatomy of a Post

15   A weblog post can be identified by the following distinguishing characteristics: a date header, a time stamp, and a permalink. Oftentimes the author's name appears beneath each post as well, especially if multiple authors are contributing to one blog. If commenting is enabled (giving the reader a form to respond to a specific post), a link to comment will also appear.

The Links

16   Links, and the accompanying commentary, have often been hailed as the distinguishing characteristic of a weblog. The linking that happens through blogging creates the connections that bind us. Commentary alone is the province of journals, diaries, and editorial pieces.

The Time Stamp

17   By its very presence, the time stamp connotes the sense of timely content; the implicit value of time to the weblog itself is apparent because the time is overtly stated on each post. Without the time stamp, the reader is unable to discern the author's update pattern, or experience a moment of shared experience.

18   But if I visit your site at 4:02 p.m. and see you just updated at 3:55 p.m., it's as if our packets crossed in the ether. You, the author, and I, the reader, were "there" at the same time—and this can create a powerful connection between us.

19   Moments of shared experience can be powerful connectors. They happen in the offline world when two strangers on the subway chuckle at the same funny billboard, and make eye contact as they do so. In the online world, they happen when I'm thinking about buying an iBook and I read on your blog that you've just bought one, at the same time.

The Permalink

20 The permalink (the link to the permanent location of the post in the blog's archive) plays a critical role in how authors participate in distributed conversations across weblogs. The permalink allows for precise references, creating a way for authors to link to the specific piece of information to which they're responding.

A Communication Evolution

21 When we talk about weblogs, we're talking about a way of organizing information, independent of its topic. What we write about does not define us as bloggers; it's how we write about it (frequently, ad nauseam, peppered with links).

22   Weblogs simply provide the framework, as haiku imposes order on words. The structure of the documents we're creating enable us to build our social networks on top of it—the distributed conversations, the blogrolling lists, and the friendships that begin online and are solidified over a "bloggers dinner" in the real world.

23   As bloggers, we're in the middle of, and enjoying, an evolution of communication. The traits of weblogs mentioned above will likely change and advance as our tools improve and our technology matures. What's important is that we've embraced a medium free of the physical limitations of pages, intrusions of editors, and delays of tedious publishing systems. As with free speech itself, what we say isn't as important as the system that enables us to say it.

Literacy Connections

1. In small groups, make a list of what Hourihan says are the features of the genre of the blog.
2. Why does Hourihan feel that blogs are a communication revolution?

3. Visit Meg Hourihan's blog at www.megnut.com/. When you read her blog, how did your reading process differ from the process you used while reading her article?

4. Hourihan argues that the genre of the weblog liberates the writer and provides freedom from editors. What's your perspective on Hourihan's argument? Are there any disadvantages to writing in the genre of the weblog?

5. In what ways does Hourihan's description of blogging connect to the definitions of digital literacy presented by Dustin Anderson and John Seely Brown in the previous readings?

Before You Read

You're about to read an article about the video-sharing Web site *YouTube* and the social networking site *MySpace*. Before you read about them, go online and visit *YouTube* (www.youtube.com) or *MySpace* (www.myspace.com). How would you describe the purpose of the site? Who do you think is the target audience for the site? Describe the visual design of the site. Is it difficult to navigate? Why or why not?

A Grand Unified Theory of *YouTube* and *MySpace*: Point-and-Click Sites That Don't Tell You What to Do

Paul Boutin

Paul Boutin, senior editor of *Wired Magazine*, says of himself at http://paulboutin.weblooger.com/, "I went to MIT. I didn't graduate. I grew up in working-class Maine, but live in upper-class San Francisco. 20 years of information technology experience and an overlapping 12 years writing for national publications. This explains everything about me you need to know." Boutin's article, "A Grand Unified Theory of *YouTube* and *MySpace*," was published in the online magazine *Slate* in 2006. Boutin considers an important aspect of digital literacies we haven't yet considered in the chapter—accessibility and ease of use.

1 I was skeptical when I heard how huge video-sharing hub YouTube and social-networking hotspot MySpace have become. YouTube claims 40 million plays a day, up from 35 million just a week ago. *The Washington Post* recently reported that MySpace pulls more monthly visitors than Amazon

and is closing in on AOL and eBay. Both sites are vague about their traffic details, though, so I ran them through Alexa, the traffic report generator favored by techies who don't trust press releases. I nearly fell out of my chair. On Alexa's charts, MySpace is an order of magnitude bigger than Friendster. YouTube will pass CNN any day now.

2   Both YouTube and MySpace fit the textbook definition of Web 2.0, that hypothetical next-generation Internet where people contribute as easily as they consume. Even self-described late adopters like New York's Kurt Andersen recognize that that by letting everyone contribute, these sites have reached a critical mass where "a real network effect has kicked in."

3   But the focus on the collaborative nature of these sites has been nagging at me. Sites like Friendster and Blogger that promote sharing and friend-making have been around for years with nowhere near the mainstream success. I've got a different theory. YouTube and MySpace are runaway hits because they combine two attributes rarely found together in tech products. They're easy to use, and they don't tell you what to do.

4   There are two design requirements for technology meant for the masses. First, you need to automate all the techie parts so people can just press Play. To watch television online, I shouldn't have to install extra video software, figure out my bandwidth setting (100K? 300K?), and sign up for an account with the player's maker. Second, Web moguls shouldn't presume to foresee what 100 million people will want to do with their site. I'm one of many who stopped using Google's Orkut social network because its hardwired page designs made everyone look like they were there to find a date and/or a job.

5   The guys behind YouTube hit the sweet spot. Most important, they made it head-slappingly easy to publish and play video clips by handling the tricky parts automatically. Given up on BitTorrent because it feels like launching a mission to Mars? If you've sent an e-mail attachment, you've got the tech skills to publish on YouTube.

6   To post your own video, sign up for a free account and go to the Upload page. Select your file, click the Upload Video button, and you're done! YouTube's servers convert your vid to a standardized format, but you don't need to know what that format is. If you send the URL to your aunt, it'll play in her browser without spraying the screen with pop-ups and errors.

7   You don't have to upload video to use YouTube. If you just like to watch, it's even easier. There's no software to install, no settings to muck with. The video auto-plays as soon as you load the page, without launching more windows—why can't CNN do that?

8   Three months ago, I predicted Google Video would become the hottest thing on the Net. I was wrong, and I think Google has failed to take off for the simple reason that it's more annoying to use than YouTube. To begin with, you have to install Google's special uploading application. When I tried to upload

the same clips I'd posted to YouTube, Google's app wouldn't let me. I combed through the FAQ and found this: "While we also support other digital formats such as QuickTime, Windows Media, and RealVideo . . . submitting your files in these formats may significantly delay us from using them on Google Video." Come on, guys. Whatever happened to "I'm Feeling Lucky?"

9   Google Video lets you google videos (of course) by their titles and a brief description of each. Each page links to other matches. That's OK, but predictable. YouTube lets posters tag each clip themselves. For example, I tagged this clip of my 12 seconds on *Good Morning America* with "boutin wired slate gma." Whenever you play a YouTube clip, the page shows a half-dozen potential matches. A tag like "slate" could mean all sorts of things, so each page mixes perfect matches with what-the-huh results. A documentary on Scientology links to a *South Park* episode, which links to comedian Pablo Francisco. A few clicks later I'm watching some merry prankster get an unexpected smackdown. In Web 2.0-speak, this is a "folksonomy." In English, it means YouTube is a mix of every video genre imaginable.

> ". . . it's fair to say that YouTube's warnings not to post copyrighted material aren't much of a deterrent."

10   Judging by the number of *South Park* episodes and music videos available for viewing, it's fair to say that YouTube's warnings not to post copyrighted material aren't much of a deterrent. The site removes porn much more aggressively than they do copyright violations. That makes a lot of sense: There are more than enough places to browse for porn online, but the presence of easily downloadable mainstream fare among YouTube's home movies is a huge draw. I hope the site's budding deals with Hollywood work out and the networks don't launch their own sites. If they do, it's a sure bet they won't be user-friendly. Just look at CNN's recent redesign, which just now threw a giant "PLUGIN WARNING!" onto my screen.

11   When trying to rope in the movie and TV studios, YouTube should point to MySpace, where A-listers like Eminem peddle their wares alongside unsigned bands and lip syncers. MySpace makes it easy for musicians, kids, and grandparents to post their own pages by removing the technical hurdles. I created a profile page in three minutes, complete with an autoplay jingle. I'd planned to upload an MP3 of a band I used to play in, until I found they already have their own MySpace page. Clicking "Add" instantly copied the song from their page onto mine. Another one-click tool imported my Gmail and Hotmail address books so I could mass-invite everyone to join me.

12   MySpace isn't that much easier to use than Friendster, or than other shared-user-content sites like Flickr (photo sharing), del.icio.us (bookmarks), or Digg (tech news). But it mixes multiple publishing models—

blogs, photos, music, videos, friend networks—into one personal space. Most important, it doesn't presume to know what your goals are. The site's management ditched their early focus as a home for musicians when they realized Margaret Cho and my crazy friend Kenny wanted spaces of their own. Next, MySpace may let marketers set up profiles for brands. That's a great idea—the same people who'll bitch about Snickers having a page will add Wikipedia as their friend.

13   I think MySpace's popularity has to do with its puppylike accessibility. A typical page looks like something a Web-enthralled high schooler might have put up in 1996, but with more pics and a soundtrack. I agree with design guru Jesse James Garrett, who says the site's untrained layout sends a "we're just like you" message to newcomers. That encourages them to experiment with content genres the site's designers didn't build into templates. If tech builders want to hand the controls over to their users, shouldn't they presume they haven't thought of everything? Apple's iWeb publishing system is easy to use and way more attractive than MySpace, but we'd have gotten old waiting for Apple to invent a Lip Sync Video template.

14   The secret to success is to make everything one-button easy, then get out of the way. If you think collaborative architecture matters more, click the charts: The same Alexa plots that show MySpace and YouTube obliterating top sites reveal that Flickr, Digg, and del.icio.us have plateaued with audiences barely bigger than *Slate's*. Photos, news, and other people's bookmarks just aren't as interesting as bootleg TV and checking out the hotties. The easier it gets to use, the less geeky the Net becomes, and the more it starts to look like real life.

Literacy Connections

1. Look up the term *Web 2.0* in an Internet search engine such as *Google* or *Yahoo*. How is the term being defined online? How does Boutin define *Web 2.0*?

2. Visit the *Slate* magazine Web site at www.slate.com and browse through the latest issue. Then consider how Boutin's persona connects to the target audience for *Slate*. How would you describe his persona, and do you think it's effective for his purpose and audience?

3. What's your perspective on Boutin's theory that *YouTube* and *MySpace* are so popular because they're "easy to use, and they don't tell you what to do"? Can you think of other reasons why these two sites might be so popular?

4. To make Boutin's arguments more concrete, try posting a video to *YouTube* or creating a *MySpace* page. After participating in these Web 2.0 sites, what is your reaction to Boutin's "Grand Unified Theory"?

5. Imagine a conversation among Boutin, Brown, Anderson, and you at a coffee house, a chat room, or some other location. Choose a topic all three authors are interested in and write a script of a conversation, including yourself in the discussion.

Before You Read

Before you read about the online virtual world *Second Life*, browse the *Second Life* Web site at http://secondlife.com. What are the features that make *Second Life* unique?

Living the Virtual Life: A Second Life

Peter Hall

Peter Hall was a student in a first-year writing course at Florida State University when he wrote the following essay about his experiences with the online virtual world *Second Life*. Peter's essay is both a firsthand account of *Second Life* and an analysis of the similarities and differences between the virtual world and the real world.

1   Imagine a life entirely independent of your real life, a life in which you are the one who gets to freely design your own appearance and lifestyle—even your own birth—a life in which anyone can transcend the societal and physical constraints they feel are unavoidable in reality, a simple life of manifested dreams. Such fantasy is the virtual reality of Second Life, a massively multiplayer online game created and freely released to the public by software entrepreneurs Linden Lab. However, Second Life isn't a game, not in the conventional sense at least. There are no levels to gain or beat, there are no bosses to fight, no magic mushrooms to jump on or any fashion of a linear structure one would normally associate with a computer game. The game is entirely what you make of it. One should think of Second Life as a universe in which you have the divine power to alter the world and yourself to whatever you desire. The laws of physics that apply to our world don't apply to the SL-world. Matter can be created out of thin air in an instant and destroyed equally as fast. In fact, all of the content in the game is created solely by the people who play it, not by the game's creators themselves. The game's website, SecondLife.com, presents a rather textbook picture of Second Life as a "3-D virtual world entirely built and owned by its residents." While that is certainly an accurate definition, I'd like to think of the game as a complex reflecting pool. What a

player puts into Second Life (and inversely expects to get out of SL) becomes a reflection of that person's inner desires.

2   So if the "game" has no single objective, why bother to play it at all? Over the past two or so years I had heard stories of the insane and creative things people do "in world" (a term the game's players use to refer to anything that happens while playing), but I had no personal experience with it so I decided to find out for myself why creating/living this virtual life was such an acclaimed experience. I signed up, downloaded the free client (available at SecondLife.com), created my virtual person (with the appropriately nerdy name of Intar Webb) and connected to the server.

3   Initially, Second Life looks no different than any other modern computer game. You go through the standard tutorial process in which the game teaches you how to move about in the world. Everything looks normal on the tutorial island and for a minute it appears just like a standard digitization of our own world. Birds chirp, trees are blown about in the wind, a stream trickles down a hill. But then you learn how to fly, a fun and effortless function of transportation in the game. With the simple pressing of a button, your character can lunge into the air with all the ease of a superhero. Following that, you teleport to a welcome center and from that point on you leave the real world behind.

4   Nothing prepares the uninformed, which I was at the time, for the mind boggling appearances of the SL-ites who openly great you at your destination. Back on the tutorial's plot of land, the people around you looked like regular people with regular body types, sporting a simple pair of jeans and a white t-shirt. This wasn't the case at the Second Life Welcome Center 4. I was surrounded by dozens of SL denizens, many of whom didn't resemble anything human. I stared in awe as I wandered around the island and gawked at what these players had created. Some were normal humans, just with outlandish costumes or hairstyles. Others were humanoid animals, such as cats or foxes. I stood in front of a giant robot for over a minute before I realized that it was actually a complete recreation of the RoboSapien, a recent robotic kid's toy. One person even wore a 3-D rendering of the depiction of the religious figure Mohammed from the European newspaper cartoons which had caused such a global controversy a few weeks prior. I couldn't believe it. He had the bomb on top of his head and everything. My brain could barely correlate it all. Each figure in front of me was actively walking around or chatting and each avatar represented a real person somewhere on earth. These people had gone through such extreme lengths to painstakingly design and create their SL avatars. I became slack jawed in the face of the technical mastery I was seeing before me. I couldn't imagine the hours and hours someone

had to invest to recreate, to the tiniest detail, a three-dimensional copy of a two-dimensional political cartoon. It takes me ages to try to draw a detailed, and yet still horrible, picture on a piece of paper. Transferring that picture onto a computer while adding an entirely new dimension to it is a task that seems so daunting I'd rather not think about how it was done and just assume it was pure magic.

5   Back on the tutorial island I was taught the basics of how to alter my body shape, my skin color, or my hair type, and I thought I had done a pretty decent job of making someone who looked relatively like me (though obviously with a better build), but what I was seeing before me was worlds beyond the simple sliding of a tick mark down a gradient bar to change the size of my nose. I had only been in the game itself a matter of minutes, but I already knew that the people who played this game played it seriously. They were willing to dedicate hours and hours of their real lives to enhancing their virtual lives. I soon learned that not everything I was seeing was created by each individual player, but that custom clothing and avatars could readily be purchased using the in-world currency called the Linden Dollar (L$). Game specific currencies are nothing new to MMOs, any game has them, but Second Life has revolutionized the function of their own virtual dollar. Actually, Linden Dollars can legally be converted to real American dollars at the player's discretion and vice versa. This means that any money earned in-world can be cashed out for real, tangible currency. A person can spend money they've earned at their real job and buy fake money for a virtual world. From a technical standpoint, I love this and respect the ability of the game developers to create a real, fully functional economy, but at the same time I was a little confused as to who would exchange the real for the fake. I wouldn't understand this until I had a little more experience under my belt.

6   After fiddling around with the in-game user interface for a while, I eventually brought up a map of the entire SL world. Made up of one large continent and over a dozen of islands, it was an intimidating view of a world I didn't fully understand yet. This 2-D view of the world around me was peppered with countless pink and blue stars, each representing an event scheduled by someone somewhere. Just taking a look at the titles of some of the pink events was even more confusing. Many were self-explanatory ("High Stakes Texas Hold 'Em"), but my innocence began to show as I had no clue as to what some of these events could possibly be: "Tringo With Prizes!!!," "Slingo at the Ranch!" It wasn't until I started browsing the blue stars (representing "mature events") that I began to see the much more adult side to the game; "Naked Skydiving Prizes," "Submissive's/Slave's Retreat," "Des Les (Gay Girls Club)—Live DJ!" I eventually found an event that sounded too hilarious to pass up,

"'80s Hair-band Night w/Live DJ @ Club EXPOSé!" With a title like that, I had to teleport in.

7   I don't know what I was expecting when I walked into the club. I was so naïve that I didn't think it actually would be exactly what the event title said (the strippers dancing on the poles were certainly a surprise), but of course I was met by some classic Warrant pumping through my speakers as I crossed through the velvet curtains. There were probably a dozen or so people inside. Some were standing idle on the side while others were bumping and grinding (literally) on the dance floor. The club's owner welcomed me along with the rest of the patrons. I'm a pretty steadfast nerd and have played a myriad of online games, but on top of the utterly bizarre, user-created visuals I was seeing all over the place, nothing could have prepared me for how nice everyone in Second Life is. Log into any other game and chances are high that any conversation going on will consist of only a string of juvenile insults, but not in SL. Every single person in the bar welcomed me with rapid typing and was actually eager to help me out and answer the countless questions I had as to how this whole world turned, so to speak. I was given some free clothes (by one of the strippers, of all people) that made me look like a rock star. I chatted on and off with everyone for an hour or so before I realized that in addition to the event's "'80s Hair-band" label being true, that there actually was a real DJ and not just some preprogrammed list of songs. I hadn't really been paying that much attention to the music until I heard my own name over the speakers. The DJ had dedicated the next song to "the newbie, Intar Webb" and it was a song that practically knocked me out of my chair.

> "If it can exist, if you look deep enough into the reaches of the SL-verse, you'll find it."

8   I had never, ever in my life expected to hear the titular song of 1987's *A Nightmare on Elm Street III: Dream Warriors* outside of the credits to that cinematic milestone and yet there I was in a virtual bar filled with virtual representations of real people and having that very song played in my honor. I was stunned, thanks in no small part to the fact that I had just watched that film days earlier and was equally stunned that that cheesy song even existed in the first place. It was this singular incident that convinced me beyond the shadow of a doubt that if someone has ever thought of it, it has occurred in Second Life. I was instantly reminded of the astronomical theory of multiple universes. The theory loosely postulates that if our universe is indeed infinite in size then anything that has a finite possibility of occurring will inevitably occur somewhere in the unlimited expanse of the night sky (Masters). That may or not be true of our reality (the jury is still out as to the size of our universe), but it certainly applies to Second Life. If it can exist, if you look deep enough into the reaches of the SL-verse, you'll find it.

9   If one needs any confirmation of this, one need look no further than SL's sexual freedoms which make up an entirely new universe within this virtual world. Strippers in an '80s bar are only the tip of the iceberg regarding as to what people do in this fantasy land. Pornography is rampant as you fly about the world. It can actually be a challenge to find areas that are free of any kind of sexual content. People have actually made thousands from in-game sexual addictions. Apparently, there is a big enough market for digital porn that a magazine called *Slustler* has pushed out two hot selling issues. However, instead of featuring photographs of the real people behind the keyboard, the publication consists entirely of the shirtless avatars themselves (Ruberg).

10   If simple pixilated nudity on a virtual page doesn't do it for an excitable SL resident, there is a sea of sexual services from which to partake. Signs for lap dances can be seen in any of the many raunchy establishments. Any player can readily pay for cyber sex, be it a simple chat in a private location or fully animated intercourse with a virtual prostitute. This last profession, however, isn't limited just to Second Life. Back in December 2003, a Sims-centric weblog called Alphaville posted an interview with a Sims Online player, Evangeline. According to that interview, Evangeline, who was a legal minor at the time, "claims to have worked as a cyber-prostitute and then to have been a madam for various cyber-brothels under the guise of her sims . . . claiming that at times she made the equivalent of $50 U.S. per trick from her customers" (Urizenus).

11   If that doesn't prove that if someone has thought of it, it exists in Second Life, a billboard I passed while flying about should dispel any doubt that remains. On the billboard was a snap shot of a naked virtual crotch; however, unlike the default body type which is round, this was anatomically correct. The advertisement was for a fully functional penis that one could purchase and attach to his/her person. The ad boasted that it came in any color desired, that it could go from flaccid to erect in seconds and, to my complete shock, it could actually ejaculate. At this point in my adventures, I wasn't surprised that someone had crafted an anatomically (if generous) correct bit of manhood for sale, but I was in complete awe of what someone had to go through to make that. Not only did they have to actually detail the penis, they took the time to make it fully functional. I laughed out loud, thinking of the hours someone spent staring at a digital penis until its arousal animations satisfied the artist's primal needs. That's a level of dedication to one's art that has to be respected.

12   I'm sure whoever manufactured that memorable piece of equipment was making a fortune from its sale. Unique, player-crafted items are truly treasured and will sell like hotcakes. Everyone respects individuality and will do whatever it takes to personalize their avatar to perfection, no matter the price. It was on an island specializing in the sale of custom avatars

that I got my first taste of this addiction. I had been brought there by a friend who told me it was the best place to find a Freddy Kruger costume, and, sure enough, it was. I browsed the horror section, which featured everything from one of the gremlins in Joe Dante's film of the same name all the way to Pennywise, the clown from *IT*. The price of the Freddy avatar was a bit more than I wanted to spend, so I ran around the island checking out everything it had to offer. I could have purchased anything from Harry Potter to Jack Sparrow to Bono, but I eventu-

> "I ended up not doing it because I realized how silly of a concept it was; paying real money for fake money . . ."

ally returned to the loveable Freddy (how could I ignore the fated *Dream Warriors* sign) and forked over the L$500. It was a pretty faithful recreation: fedora, claws and all. But now I had only a couple bucks left and wanted to earn more simply so I could buy more avatars.

13   I had learned that creating and selling items wasn't the only way to make some Linden, so I found my way to a casino. Casinos have, in addition to playable games like poker and blackjack, a money making system called camping chairs. All you have to do is sit in one of these chairs for a period of time and you'll slowly earn a payout (usually at the rate of 3L$ every 10 minutes). So I began camping out in these chairs whenever I wasn't actually playing the game. Eventually I earned enough money to go buy random items that interested me. And then the slot machine addiction hit and I promptly lost all the money I had earned (on more than one occasion). There was a 1000L$ avatar of a skeletal dragon that I had my eye on, so after having bankrupted myself for the last time I entertained the notion of buying Linden using real dollars. I ended up not doing it because I realized how silly of a concept it was; paying real money for fake money just so I could buy something that would make my fake guy look like something out of a nightmare. I began to question the very nature of Second Life.

14   I was almost disgusted by the perverse nature of consumerism that was on display here. People login to SL with the potential promise of freedom from the pressures of the capitalistic nature of the real world only to become obsessed with a mirrored, yet virtual, system of capital. It made some degree of sense to me because subjectively I had experienced these same thoughts, but objectively who would ever want to take such a silly, fabricated reality so seriously? A man who goes by the SL name of Bushi-doBrown Hightower explained it all to me through an interview we did.

15   BushidoBrown, who I found out shares the views of many typical Second Lifers, is a normal man leading a normal married life, he just happens to spend about 30 hours a week logged into this virtual world. When I first met Bushido, the cynic in me took over and I just assumed he was a bit on the odd side. He was a far more involved member of the SL community than I. He

rents a house and actually budgets about $40 a month to be cashed in for Linden Dollars and spent on virtual commodities. In our interview I learned that the roots of Bushido's habits don't lie in some perverted sense of consumerism, but the simple desire to make his in world life more enjoyable, "Just like in reality, you want to obtain things to make your time in world comfortable; your look, your environment, etc. For me to enjoy my immersion in this part of my reality, I try to make things as comfortable as possible."

16   He broke my ideology that the more dedicated players were simply using SL as a role playing medium so that they could escape their real lives. When asked about what Second Life means to him, he explained that, "SL is an extension of my reality format. Jacked into this metaverse, Bushido-Brown is an extension of Me. I don't role play; for me, SL is a consolidation of things like email/myspace/IM, [but] with a visual representation; [allowing] for even more interaction." To people like Bushido, Second Life is less a game and more a vast array of communication tools.

17   However, this doesn't explain the behavior of those who do treat Second Life as a method for escaping the real world. But before labeling these individuals as anomalies in the SL universe, it's important to realize that Second Life is a new frontier of the digital age, just like the Internet was in its startup days. Second Life merely provides a new way for people to escape their day to day life, if that is indeed what they want to get out of it. Though written over a century before Second Life's conception, Friedrich Nietzsche wrote a line in his famous work *Beyond Good and Evil* that can readily be related to how each individual takes in Second Life, "And if thou gaze long into an abyss, the abyss will also gaze into thee." The longer one's time spent in Second Life, the more their virtual identities begin to reflect their inner desires. If someone wants to escape their real life, there are countless ways they can shape their character's role. They can join any number of groups consisting of people just like them. Or, if they're more like BushidoBrown Hightower, they can use SL as an extension of their own real world identity to further their communication networks. Either way, it doesn't matter what path you take in Second Life as long as it's the path you *want* to take.

18   Though the game allows players to defy reality, what actually ends up happening in world is really no different than what happens in the real world. I've spent hours logged into this virtual world trying to discover that one thing that defines it all and in the end I've realized that just as with real life a singular meaning is indefinable. Now after having experienced the game for myself, whenever I think of Second Life I can't help but think of a quote from David Cronenberg's cult classic (and personal favorite) film, *eXistenZ*. In the film, eXistenZ is the name of a virtual reality game that mirrors the real world in appearance, but whose events are shaped by the inner desires of its players. There is a great exchange between the film's two main characters (Allegra Geller, the game's designer, and Ted Pikul, a

low-level employee for the game's publisher) that occurs when they both question the purpose of the game they're playing:

> **Ted:** We're both stumbling around together in this unformed world, whose rules and objectives are largely unknown, seemingly indecipherable or even possibly nonexistent, always on the verge of being killed by forces that we don't understand.
> **Allegra:** That sounds like my game, all right.
> **Ted:** That sounds like a game that's not gonna be easy to market.
> **Allegra:** But it's a game everybody's already playing.

19   It may just be a few lines of dialogue from a science fiction film, but it's a perfect presentation of the little difference that exists between how we go about living our real lives as well as our virtual ones.

Works Cited

eXistenZ. Dir. David Cronenberg. Perf. Jennifer Jason Leigh, Jude Law, Ian Holm, and Willem Dafoe. Dimension Films, 1999. Film.

Hightower, BushidoBrown. Online interview. 2 Apr. 2006.

Masters, Karen. "Curious About Astronomy: If the Universe Is Infinite Does That Mean There Is an Infinite Number of 'Me's?" *Ask an Astronomer*. July 2000. Cornell University. Web. 21 Mar. 2006.

Nietzsche, Friedrich. *Beyond Good and Evil*. Trans. Helen Zimmern. *Project Gutenberg*. 1 Aug. 2003. Web. 2 Apr. 2006.

Ruberg, Bonnie. "Cyberporn Sells in Virtual World." *Wired News*. Wired.com. 19 Dec. 2005. Web. 21 Mar. 2006.

Urizenus. "Evangeline: Interview with a Child Cyber-Prostitute in TSO." *Alphaville Herald*. Alphaville Herald. 8 Dec. 2003. Web. 21 Mar. 2006.

"What Is Second Life?" *SecondLife.com*. Linden Lab. 21 Mar. 2006.

Literacy Connections

1. In what ways does Hall feel that *Second Life* is similar to real life, and in what ways does he feel that it's different?

2. Do a close reading of the excerpt from the film *eXistenZ* that appears at the end of Hall's essay. Consider the ways that the lines from the film have significance for *Second Life* and for Hall's experience in a virtual world.

3. Use Hall's essay as a starting point to explore the concepts of "real" and "fake" as they apply to *Second Life*.

4. Visit *Second Life* at http://secondlife.com and sign up for a membership. Explore *Second Life* and write a brief essay about your experiences, modeled after Hall's essay.

5. Apply James Paul Gee's concept of "distributive learning" in the next reading from *What Video Games Have to Teach Us About Learning and Literacy* to *Second Life* and discuss the ways *Second Life* is a distributive learning environment.

Before You Read

James Paul Gee, author of the selection below, titled his 2005 book *Why Video Games Are Good for Your Soul: Pleasure and Learning*. Do you agree with Gee that video games are good? In what ways could playing video games be "good for your soul"? In what ways might playing them not be so "good for your soul"?

Excerpt from *What Video Games Have to Teach Us About Learning and Literacy*

James Paul Gee

James Paul Gee, a professor at the University of Wisconsin of Madison, earned degrees in philosophy and linguistics. His research focuses on discourse analysis, sociolinguistics, and applications of linguistics to literacy and education. His books include *What Video Games Have to Teach Us About Learning and Literacy* (2003) and *Why Video Games Are Good for Your Soul: Pleasure and Learning* (2005). In this excerpt, Gee focuses on playing video games as social learning.

1   So far I have talked about video games in terms of one individual playing the game alone because I wanted to concentrate on learning principles that primarily had to do with the individual mind and body as it confronts the world of experience. Nonetheless, I have shown that learning, even in these individualistic terms, is very much a matter of being situated in a material, social, and cultural world.

2   When I and my research assistants interview game players (because of our interest in schools, they are mostly young, between the ages of 5 and 19), we find that most play video games not alone but with others in three ways. (Younger players usually do only the first, while teens and above engage in all three modes.)

1. Players can hook multiple controllers into one video-game platform.

2. Players can network a number of computers into a local area network, so that they can play against each other without having to be in the same place.

3. The most popular option is for players to log on to special Internet sites and play certain games with and against sometimes thousands of other players allover the world.

3   Some games can only be played online, while many others can be played in single-player mode or online. (In fact, reviews tend to criticize games that can only be played in single-player mode.)

4   When online play first began, players moved through dungeons role-playing as different types of characters, but the universe through which they moved was composed entirely of text. Each player read text that told him or her what was there to be seen or done or what the effects were of various actions the player had taken. There were no pictures, only words. Now players move through fully realized, graphically beautiful, three-dimensional worlds. They can talk to each other by typing in words, though the technology now exists and is spreading where they can speak their words into a headset and be heard on the other people's computers. Players can talk to each other in their roles as fantasy virtual characters (their "avatars") or in terms of their real-world identities or switch between the two.

5   *EverQuest* is one of the most popular online games. More than 375,000 players have subscribed to play the game, and servers host more than 90,000 users playing at one time during peak game hours. (A game called *Lineage*, now available in the United States, has more than two million subscribers in South Korea.) *EverQuest* consists of multiple continents and numerous cities in which players carry out, alone or in groups, various quests. They run into other players who can help or, in some circumstances, hurt them (e.g., kill their fantasy virtual character). Sony Corporation now owns *EverQuest*, which was developed and is still run by a company named Verdant. Sony and Verdant put out new expansions (with new continents and cities) to *EverQuest* from time to time.

6   In the game you can choose to play in an ideal world where the monsters (not real people, but characters controlled by the computer and endowed with artificial intelligence) are the only bad guys and other players cannot kill you (and you can't kill them). Or you can choose to play in a world where you can kill and be killed by other players as well as the creatures that inhabit the countryside. If you make the latter choice, you become a "player-killer" and open yourself up to attack by other player-killers.

7   When you start playing *EverQuest*, you have to create your character, as in any role-playing game. There are a nearly endless combination of

races, classes, skills, and abilities with which to create your character. However, character creation basically breaks down into 14 professions (Bard, Cleric, Druid, Enchanter, Magician, Monk, Necromancer, Paladin, Ranger, Rogue, Shadowknight, Shaman, Warrior, or Wizard) and 12 "races" composed of three human cultures, three cultures of elves, and six others. Each race is limited in which professions it may choose, so, for example, you cannot be an Ogre Monk.

8   Depending on your race, you are given a number of ability points to distribute among your seven main statistics (strength, stamina, agility, dexterity, wisdom, intelligence, and charisma). Then you name your character, pick your sex, and decide which deity (religion) you wish to follow. Your race, gender, class, and religion will decide how people deal with you in the *EverQuest* world. You can also join a guild, an organization of sometimes hundreds or thousands of (real) people that support each other and cooperate in the game (e.g., to kill particularly powerful gods). Your guild membership also affects how other people react to you in the game.

9   The *EverQuest* world is a very complex place with its own economic structure based on supply and demand. When a certain item becomes scarce (e.g., a certain piece of armor or certain type of sword), the price goes up. When something is common, the price drops. In some cases, players of games like *EverQuest* and *Diablo* 2 have gone online to auction sites such as eBay and bought and sold virtual items in these games (things like gloves that endow the character with special powers or special sorts of swords) for real money. Someone recently bought a virtual item to use in *Diablo* 2 for over $2,000.

10   *EverQuest* is different from any single-player game in that it never ends. The player cannot "beat" the game. There is no final goal other than the one you set for yourself. *EverQuest* is a persistent world and a game you can, if you like, play forever (as long as you pay the fee). You can log into the game, via the Internet, whenever you like and pick up wherever you left off. In most cases, over 1,000 other people will be playing with you. Indeed, certain places where there are particularly interesting monsters or valuable items to find can get quite crowded.

11   In games like *EverQuest,* sometimes players "flame" each other (say insulting things to each other) and otherwise do regrettable things. For example, a more powerful player may intrude on a battle between a less powerful one and a monster where the less powerful one is attempting to get the valuable items the monster owns. The powerful player can use a spell to give the monster more life, thereby saving it from the less powerful player's attacks, then kill it him—or herself—and take the good stuff, leaving the less powerful player with nothing and having to spend time healing from wounds sustained in the now-wasted battle. Some players try to hack into the program and find a way to "cheat" and give themselves more (virtual)

money. At times, this sort of behavior has led to gross inflation in the virtual worlds the players are playing in, rendering money nearly worthless.

12   When people started games like *EverQuest*, they thought the players would police themselves and create an ideal world of good behavior. However, the players created virtual worlds that contained many of the same flaws our real human worlds do. Game designers have thought up lots of ways to stop players from ruining the experience for others, such as *EverQuest*'s world where you cannot kill or be killed by other players. And, of course, players who behave badly enough can be disallowed from logging on to the game. But the designers barely stay one step ahead of very human characteristics like greed, hunger for power, and the sheer desire to use one's intelligence to outwit other players, the game, and computer systems in general. They also face the fact that many game players get very good at programming, both to design new games themselves (using free software that often comes with games to build expansions or to build new games called mods) and to hack into Internet-based games to transform them in their favor.

> "You (your spirit) must get back to your corpse as quickly as possible, before it decays or other players take your possessions . . ."

13   As in all role-playing games, in *EverQuest*, the more you play and the more you have accomplished, the higher the level of your character in terms of his or her skills. Higher-level characters can do more and go more places than can lower-level ones.

14   In *EverQuest*, when your character is killed, your corpse drops to the ground spilling all the valuable objects he or she was carrying (e.g., weapons, money, potions, armor, magical spells, etc.). However, your character, in a weaker form and with worse armor and weapons, also comes back alive, but far away, at the beginning of the area in which you were killed. (Yes, this is odd; you are both dead and alive. Let's just say it's your spirit that has come back.) You (your spirit) must get back to your corpse as quickly as possible, before it decays or other players take your possessions (which, if you are at a fairly high level, are quite valuable).

15   It's not easy to get back, since you are far away and weaker and have worse weapons, and so you must avoid strong enemies who can kill you again. If you do not get back, you must begin playing again at your lower level (you go down a couple of levels), fighting monsters to return to your former level. There is also another way to get back your corpse. If you have a cleric in your party (remember, players can play in teams with others, each being different characters with different powers) with the power to resurrect corpses, the cleric can resurrect your corpse.

16   Now, to exemplify the centrally social nature of game play and some key issues in this chapter, let a young man whom I will call Adrian

(a pseudonym) tell you a story about playing *EverQuest* and other experiences he has had with video games. Adrian was 15 when the story took place and he had played *EverQuest* a great many hours. After having achieved a quite high level for his character, his character died.

17   *My character was at a very high level: 46 out of a possible 50 levels. We have a clan [a small group that plays together and who are part of a much larger guild] made up of people from across the United States. It takes lots of people to kill the gods, so that's what the guilds are for. I was playing the game with my clan and we actually found a gate to one of the alter planes, the Plane of Fear. To get into the Plane of Fear there is a level requirement; your character has to be at least at level 45. We busted into the Plane of Fear and everybody killed a God of Fear. We killed all these godly characters, and, then, this hunchback gorilla—the Plane of Fear is like a giant jungle—this giant gorilla came up behind me and swatted me like a fly and killed me with two hits. My friends didn't see it, so they couldn't protect me.*

18   *So I was killed. Whenever you die, you can come back to life, but you lose experience. I came back to life at level 44—so I lost two levels. It had taken me about 12 hours of playing the game to gain those two levels. It would take me 12 more to get them back. I was very upset. I was mad because I couldn't go back to the Plane of Fear, since I was now level 44 and you needed to be at least level 45 to get in.*

19   *There are clerics in the game, and when you play with clerics, they can actually resurrect you. When they resurrect you, you get back all your experience—so I'd be level 46 when I came back. I was talking [via the Internet] to people [who were clerics in my guild] and I gave them my home phone number. I'm like "When you guys finally find my corpse, resurrect it." But the game has a timer—if you're on the computer for three hours, it will wait for three hours and then it will say that your body is too old to get resurrected. I said to my father, "Dad, get the hell off the phone." [In other words: There are only three hours in which his corpse can be resurrected. It will take the clerics time to fight their way to the Corpse. Adrian needs to know the moment the clerics resurrect it, so he can immediately get back online and retrieve his character and possessions before the three hours are up. Thus, he is waiting for the crucial phone call, hoping it comes in time.] There was a limited window of time in which I could be resurrected. And, if I didn't get resurrected, then I'd be level 44 and I'd never get my equipment back. So, I was like "Oh, my god, no." And then I logged off and I was like pacing around the room, and I said, "I'm gonna die. I'm gonna die." I mean, I'd invested like tons of time in the character. "I'm gonna die, I'm gonna die, I'm gonna die." And then one of my partners—a guy in his 30s—in my guild called me long distance from Indiana. He called me at like 11:45 P.M. from Indiana, and he told me that they got my corpse. He resurrected me and then I was back level 46, and then I spent—I think I played until like four in the morning killing things in the Plane of Fear, and then I went to sleep. When I woke up, it was like three in the afternoon the next day.*

20   *I still talk to the guy from Indiana sometimes. All of us have websites and message boards to talk on, to keep in contact with each other. Even with all like the Internet security stuff, we try not to give out our personal information, but after you get to know the person for a while, it becomes like second nature. I mean, with my character in EverQuest whenever I have gotten on I would say, "Hey, everyone." And, then there would be like a stream of like 40 people saying "Hi" to me, using my login name.*

21   *I actually have a website that tells you how to exploit game tips. My site and sites like it have interesting stuff on them about hackers trying to create a world where people*

don't have to pay to play the game. Not as a way to avoid paying, but for the challenge. The people who make the game don't really like these people at all. But what these people are trying to do is they're trying to take EverQuest and manipulate the game, even though much of it has been heavily encrypted. They try to decrypt the files. They try to take the graphics, and try to take the game engine itself, manipulate it, and then put all that stuff on their own server, so people can play without pay.

22   *What they're trying to do is trying to take the game and trying to make it so everyday people can play it for free. What I try to do on my website is I try to take people who play on the Internet, and if they don't like spending—I told you to get from level 44 to 46 it takes you like 12 hours of work, and no one has that amount of time—I tell them how they can take shortcuts in the game to get higher levels, so they can play at the level that other people play it at. And the game company doesn't like it, because they want you to play a lot. They want you to play a lot, and they want your money.*

23   *My little brother plays EverQuest now. He spends more time playing the game, I spend more time trying to crack the game open. To see what makes it work using hex editors. You can download these off the Internet. What a hex editor does is it basically breaks up computer code into pretty much binary code, and on the left side it gives you a bunch of zeros and ones and, then, on the right side it tells you what the code actually does. And, so, if you go and look on the right side, you can actually edit it. You don't learn this stuff by taking a class on it. It's just like here and there you pick stuff up. You may not be able to learn it all from one place, there's many sources [e.g., other people, chat rooms, websites, texts, etc.].*

24   *Actually, the very first time I edited a game was when I was playing* Civilization. *I played* Civilization. *I beat* Civilization. *I was reading down the credits and I'm like "Okay, that's pretty cool." Then, I was like "Okay, that's kind of cool, now let's see— it'd be kinda cool if I was like to experiment. I wanna see what makes it tick."*

25   *So I went inside and found this like little data file that's like called* credits.dat. *I'm like "Okay, what does this do?" I double-click on it—and it asks what program I want to use to open it up with. And I click use Picture View [i.e., tells the computer to try to open the file* credits.dat *with the program named Picture View] and it came up with this jumble of stuff. I'm like "Okay, so I'm going to close that." I double-clicked on* credits.dat *again, and it asks again what program I want to use to open it with. And I try Internet Explorer this time, and it showed a bunch of jumbled code again. I'm like "Hmm. All-right."*

26   *And I try it again and then it's like, all right, "I'll use Notepad this time." And, I open it up in Notepad and right in front of me there are the credits for the game. And I was like "Hey that's kind of cool." It says "Civilization by Sid Meier." Okay, and I backspace, I typed in my name—by "Adrian Name" [his first and last name]. And then I saved the file, I beat the game again, and when the credits rolled, it said that I had created the game. I thought, "That's kinda cool."*

27   *I spend more time now tinkering with games and making games myself than I do actually playing them. Right now me and my friends aren't really playing. We're playing like* Diablo II *every now and then, we're just wasting time until* WarCraft III *comes out, and, then all of us are going to get it and we're gonna kill each other. When me and my friend talk about the games, we tell each other like what we think of new games that we've got. Essentially we tell each other what the strategy guides tell you.*

28   When Adrian, who is an excellent student, is asked how he likes school, he has this to say: "School is fine. I don't live and breathe school, but it's fine."

29   Adrian's remarks exemplify several themes we have found with a number of the players we have interviewed. First, play for him is inherently social, in several different ways. He plays in a team with others. His team is part of a much larger group to which he belongs. He communicates with these people both inside the game and outside of it: about the game, about games in general, and about a wide variety of other issues. Players have told us that the people they play with range in age from the early teens to their 30s. One U.S. 15-year-old regularly plays *StarCraft* with, among others, two mid-30s Canadian college professors, and a man and wife. The 15-year-old regularly chats with these professors, while playing, both in terms of their in-game fantasy roles and their real-world identities.

> **"He learns so much about computers and game design that . . . he has already mastered most of the material in many of the courses he will need to take."**

30   Second, the knowledge and skills Adrian has in regard to playing *EverQuest* is "distributed." It exists in his own head and body. But some of it exists in other people on whom he can call for help. The clerics who came to his rescue not only had powers in the game that Adrian's character did not have (they were clerics), they were also older and more advanced players who knew how to handle the situation. (I have left out of the story the fact the three-hour limit actually ran out and Adrian and his friends together worked out a cheat to forestall the clock.)

31   Third, Adrian's knowledge and skills are not only distributed across himself and other people; some actually reside in various tools and technologies, like the hex editors he can use to manipulate the code of a game. The knowledge built into the hex editor counts as Adrian's knowledge because he knows how to leverage this tool. The real thinking and acting unit become "Adrian plus tool."

32   Fourth, Adrian's attitude toward games and the computer is itself game-like and highly metareflective. He looks at the game, whether *Civilization* or *EverQuest*, as a space that can be explored and "played with." He brings to this metalevel process the same exploratory and reflective attitudes that are required to play the game well in the first place. As part of this process, he greatly extends his knowledge and social connections. He sets up a web page to help others get to higher levels more quickly in *EverQuest*. He connects with a group of hackers who seek to understand the underlying program of *EverQuest* so thoroughly that they can actually transfer the game to another site where people can play the game free. He learns so much about computers and game design that, a few years later, when he is on his way to major in computer science and game design in college, he has already mastered most of the material in many of the courses he will need to take.

33   When we asked Adrian why he was interested in how hackers could "undermine" the Verdant company's hold over *EverQuest*, his reply was that, as he inspected their programming for the game, especially how they fixed various bugs that arose from time to time, he found their programming "inelegant." They took shortcuts and built programs that worked but weren't, as far as Adrian was concerned, optimal, especially at an aesthetic level. Companies like Verdant don't know whether to arrest or hire young people like Adrian. And, indeed, company staff members regularly "lurk" on websites and chat rooms devoted to *EverQuest* and designed by players to learn new things and use them themselves.

34   So learning here is social, distributed, and part and parcel of a network composed of people, tools, technologies, and companies all interconnected together. Adrian is a node in such a network and much of his knowledge and skill flows from his being such a richly interconnected node. Yet schools still isolate children from such powerful networks—for example, a network built around some branch of science—and test and assess them as isolated individuals, apart from other people and apart from tools and technologies that they could leverage to powerful ends.

35   Adrian's story also reflects a view of the mind current in some important work in cognitive psychology—a view that we might label "the social mind" perspective. This is not necessarily the mainstream view, but it is a viewpoint that, in one guise or another, plays a central role in helping people to think about learning in our modem, high-tech world—learning in businesses, communities, and in cutting-edge schools though, sadly, not in many mainstream schools.

Literacy Connections

1. James Paul Gee's book was written for an academic audience and published by a scholarly press, so you may have struggled to understand some of his ideas and terms. Circle places in the excerpt where you were confused and any terms you didn't understand. Then work in small groups to discuss these points of confusion and come to a better understanding of Gee's ideas and language.
2. According to Gee, how is online gaming different from school?
3. Have you used the computer for any kind of gaming? If you have, did your online gaming involve social interaction? Did you use "distributive learning" when you played games online?
4. Gee argues that multiplayer games reflect a "social mind" perspective, but most schools isolate students from networks. Do you agree with Gee's point? To what extent does your college tap into social, distributed learning?

5. Think about the idea of community in Peter Hall's "Living the Virtual Life" and in Gee's essay. How are these online communities similar to and different from "real-life" communities?

Before You Read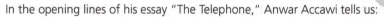

In the opening lines of his essay "The Telephone," Anwar Accawi tells us:

> When I was growing up in Magdaluna, a small Lebanese village in the terraced, rocky mountains east of Sidon, time didn't mean much to anybody, except maybe to those who were dying, or those waiting to appear in court because they had tampered with the boundary markers on their land. In those days, there was no real need for a calendar or a watch to keep track of the hours, days, months, and years.

How was the role of time in Accawi's early world different from the role of time for you as a child? Did time play an important role in your early life? Did it play an important role in the lives of adults in your early world? How has the role of time changed in your life as you've gotten older? Write a paragraph in which you explore these ideas.

The Telephone

Anwar Accawi

Anwar Accawi grew up in Lebanon and moved to the United States when he received a college scholarship to attend school here. He shares in an online interview that he started writing in the early 1980s. "My wife asked me to write something about my life and childhood for our children to read. A friend encouraged me to send these stories to a publisher. I did and one essay made it to the *Best American Essays* in 1998 ['The Telephone']." Accawi goes on to share that writing helped him become a better teacher: "The writing process has made me more aware of language, its beauty and its complexities" (www.outreach.utk.edu/ELI/highlights/default_accami.html-19k). Accawi's essay, which takes a skeptical look at technological progress, is a counterpoint to many of the other authors of the readings in the chapter who take a mostly positive attitude toward new technologies.

1   When I was growing up in Magdaluna, a small Lebanese village in the terraced, rocky mountains east of Sidon, time didn't mean much to anybody, except maybe to those who were dying, or those waiting to appear in court because they had tampered with the boundary markers on their land. In those days, there was no real need for a calendar or a watch to keep track

Continued on page 319, following Insert.

Before You Read

Before you look at some examples of effective Web sites, surf the Internet and find an example of an ineffective Web site. Save the URL of the site if you are in a computer classroom, or print a screen shot of the site using the "Print Scrn" function of your computer. Be prepared to share your site with the class and explain why it's an example of an ineffective Web composition.

Screen Shots from *Webby Award* Winners

The *Webby Awards* are international awards honoring excellence on the Internet. The *Webbys* are presented by The International Academy of Digital Arts and Sciences, a 550-member body of leading Web experts, business figures, luminaries, visionaries, and creative celebrities. The screen shots below are from *Webby* award winners—Greenpeace's "Green my Apple" site at *www.greenpeace.org/apple*, ASPCA's home page at *www.aspca.org*, and Twitter's home page at *twitter.com*. These examples of *Webby* award winners give you a concrete example of effective composing on the Web. For more information about the *Webbys*, visit *www.webbyawards.com*.

About | iPoison + iWaste | mAct | ProCreate | iPush

We love Apple. Apple knows more about "clean" design than anybody, right? So why do Macs, iPods, iBooks and the rest of their product range contain hazardous substances that other companies have abandoned? A cutting edge company shouldn't be cutting lives short by exposing children in China and India to dangerous chemicals. **That's why we Apple fans need to demand a new, cool product:** a greener Apple.

What's new NOW? It's all streaming in live at the iBuzz page.

Breaking News: Steve Jobs announces change in policy

WINNER
2007 WeBBY AWARDS

Green my Apple, to the core.

I love my iPod but can we lose the iWaste?

Take Action
Help make that green wish come true

view the best ProCreations

...all animals deserve to be as happy as DaVinci.

Every animal should be this carefree, but DaVinci suffered for two months before being rescued. Please take time to learn more about his story. When you do, you can also help the ASPCA rescue more animals in need. Together, we can provide happy and healthy lives for all of America's adoptable animals.

Donate Today!

ASPCA Rescues 11 Dogs from Overcrowded Home
On August 18, the ASPCA rescued 11 Pit Bull and Shepherd mixes from a cramped apartment in Brooklyn, NY. See our exclusive photo slideshow of the dogs being transported to safety. Read More »

Stay Connected Get Involved

Featured Highlights

Cat or Dog? Vote for Our 2011 Calendar Cover Model!
We want you to tell us which pet should grace the cover of the ASPCA's 2011 calendar! Cast your vote by Sept. 3. Read More »

Cast Your Vote for the ASPCA
The ASPCA is in the running for a Pepsi Refresh Grant, but we need your help! Find how to vote for us every day until August 31. Read More »

ASPCA Pet of the Week: Sabrina Speaks
Sabrina is a foster cat at our NYC offices, where her duties include napping and playing bottle cap hockey. Adopt her ASAP! Read More »

ASPCA Resources

Have an account? Sign in

Search for a keyword or phrase. **Search**

Discover what's happening right now, anywhere in the world

New to Twitter?
Twitter is a rich source of instant information. Stay updated. Keep others updated. It's a whole thing.

Give it a try ›

Customize Twitter by choosing who to follow. Then see tweets from those folks as soon as they're posted.

Using Twitter for a business? Check out Twitter 101

World Cup 2010 ›

See who's here

Friends and industry peers you know. Celebrities you watch. Businesses you frequent. Find them all on Twitter.

Top Tweets View all ›

nickjonas "Another foggy night in London town/all the dreamers are asleep/but know one understands what I have found/no not even me."
41 minutes ago

zackalltimelow some people just don't understand... sometimes its the nothing in your life you can be missing
31 minutes ago

SashaMallory alrighty... time to get ready... pushing and shoving not cool people... its all about love <3
26 minutes ago

Literacy Connections

1. Describe the use of visual rhetoric in these three sites (for example, use of color, font, images, contrast).
2. Who is the audience for each of these sites? How does the audience affect the visual rhetoric of the sites?
3. Visit the *Webby's* home page at www.webbyawards.com/ and click on the link "Winners" at the top of the page to view the most recent *Webby* award winners. Choose your favorite award-winning site and make a list of the reasons you thought the site you chose was most effective. Be prepared to share your list with the class.
4. If you were choosing a *Webby* award winner from the Web sites that you visit frequently, who would the winner be? Explain why the site you choose is effective.
5. Apply Crawford Kilian's criteria for effective Web writing in his essay earlier in the chapter to the *Webby* award-winning sites above. In what ways are the sites effective, based on Kilian's criteria for effective Web writing?

Before You Read

Go back to the definitions of *digital literacy* discussed in the earlier essays by Dustin Anderson and John Seely Brown. Write a summary of the ways the two authors define *digital literacy*, and think about these definitions as you look at the example screen shots from four blogs follow.

Screen Shots from Blogs

The following screen shots are from weblogs, or "blogs," written by college teachers and students. The first screen shot is from a writing course blog at Florida State University, the second screen shot is from a college student who publishes a movie review blog, the third screen shot is from a college student who publishes a blog about technology, and the fourth screen shot is from a student who blogs about her college experiences. These screen shots can give you a sense of the features of a blog that Meg Hourihan describes in "What We're Doing When We Blog."

Blog Post #10 November 29, 2009

Filed under: Blog Post #10 — jonjallen @ 4:09 pm

According to the California DMV, "The new Wireless Communications Device Law (effective January 1, 2009) makes it an infraction to write, send, or read text-based communication on an electronic wireless communications device, such as a cell phone, while driving a motor vehicle." (http://www.dmv.ca.gov /cellularphonelaws/) The website provides additional information and answers questions regarding the law—worth looking at.

Do you text while you are driving? How do you feel when your driver texts? Does it bother you or could you care less? Below is a video reenactment of what can happen as a result of texting while driving (Warning: this might be graphic for some people):

http://www.youtube.com/watch?v=DGE8LzRaySk&eurl

So, what are your thoughts? Should Florida enact a law similar to California? Why or why not?
Check out this solution. http://www.nbcsandiego.com/around-town/cars/New_Twist_for_Texting_While_Driving_San_Diego.html

Do you think this is a valid option?

💬 Comments (56)

Sunday, December 27, 2009

The Twilight Saga: New Moon (Review)
★★★☆☆

Weblog/Home
About Me
Screenshots
Schedule
DVD Movies

Friends

My aunt and I had postponed seeing this movie twice. We both were going to see it alone but since she was coming home for Christmas I suggested we should see it together and then we both got sick so had to postpone again. So on Christmas Day we decided to see it the next day. She has read all the books in the Twilight Saga and I have not expect since I was curious I did read the book synopsis on Wikipedia several weeks back. I got into Twilight on Black Friday when Wal-Mart had the first movie DVD for 5.00 so I decided to buy it since it is a Fad and wanted to see what it is all about.

New Moon picks up right after Twilight. Bella is turning 17 years old and wants her Vampire Boyfriend Edward to change her so she will not be older then him physically. He declines because he wants her to age and not have the burden of being a Vampire. Later on she is having a party with Edward and his Vampire Family and she opens her birthday card and gets a paper cut which causes Jasper to try to attack Bella, Edward stops and causes Bella to cut her arm even worse. Because he is afraid for Bella he decides to leave her and go live in Italy with the Volturi.

Meanwhile Bella is really depressed that she believe that she can see Edward if she does dangerous stuff. She convinces her friend Jacob to build BMX style bikes. She notices that he has bulked up and starts to fall for him. He is upset because his guy friends are acting weird and hanging around with a guy named Sam and never wear shirts and have a tattoo. Well Bella and Jacob mid movie are about to kiss at a movie theatre and Jacob leaves saying he is not feeling well. Later on we are told that it was mono. Bella goes to investigate and sees that Jacob is outside in the rain is shirtless and has cut his hair and also has the same tattoo that his friends have and is now friends with them again. Bella then discovers that Jacob is a Werewolf and that Vampires and Werewolf's don't get along. Bella is being hunted by Victoria from the first film and Jacob and his fellow wolves help to protect her. The movie then goes to Bella going to Italy to save Edward because he thinks she is dead.

The movie is ok, yes the big thing is Jacob is hot but that only applies if your a girl. I didn't care either way if he was shirtless for most of the film. The film also reminded me of a modern day of Romeo and Juliet and which Edward tries to kill himself because he thinks Bella is dead and Bella is not. The only thing was both didn't die. The special effects like changing Jacob to a wolf were good but the movie is all about love and being 2.1 hrs it could have been shorter, I would recommend for a couple to make out or if a teenage girl wanting to see a shirtless due in it but otherwise boring though most of it.

Labels: Movies

posted by Marcus @ 7:52 AM   0 comments

Recent Entries

*Avatar (Review)

*Inglourious Basterds (Worse Movie Ever)

*2012 (Review)

*Paladio 16 Theatre Review

*iPhone MMS Works

*Happy 4th of July

*My Loopt Journal

*Star Trek (Review)

*Happy New Year 2009

*Presidential Election Results

- Archives -

0 Comments:

Post a Comment

<< Home

Blog   About   Archives   Favorite Posts   Contact

About Me

Dustin Bachrach is a 20 year old Rice student and developer for both OS X and the web. He also deals a lot with design work and Photoshop. He blogs technology, Apple, programming, and life. Read more

Who I Read

- Paul Stamatiou
- Wil Shipley
- John Gruber
- Steven Frank
- Cabel Sasser
- Lorenz Sell
- Michael Whalen
- Keith Lang

DiggUpdate

BY FEEDBURNER

You!
Join My Community

10 Necessary Mac Apps for the College Student

September 17th, 2007 | Posted in: Applications, Mac, Tech | Save to del.icio.us

Going through the first few weeks of college, I've found a few apps that have made my university life so much easier. Some of these apps will be things you have heard of. Hopefully, some will be new to you. Most of the apps have been designed for a much larger audience, but greatly help college students in particular.

1. Caffeine

Quite simply, this app keeps your Mac from falling asleep or dimming your screen brightness. Although it is extremely useful for watching YouTube videos, this app is great for students. Just click the ZZZ's in the menu-bar when you go into class, and your computer won't go to sleep during the lecture. It can be very annoying to pause taking notes for a few minutes and to return to a sleeping Mac. Download here.

2. EtreTask

This is a super easy, super simple, to-do list program. It has all I want with none of the bloat. Its interface is stripped to the bare essentials. My only gripe with to-do list apps is that I rarely want to check an item off the list and still want to see it. Just get rid of it right then. Either way, this apps is nice to have running on your Mac to quickly add and remove things you need to do. Download here.

3. iFlash

This is by far the best flash card app I have seen. It works incredibly well and has beautiful transitions. It has a cool full screen study mode. I have to add this onto my list, because it helped me memorize everything perfectly for my Quiz in RELI 122. Download here.

4. iStumbler

Musings of a College Student

College Life – How it really is! :-)

Search

College   Goals   School Organization

Subscribe: Entries | Comments

Live & Learn (RANT Time)

I have been scarce the past few weeks...I know, so sad! School is kicking my butt! I'm so tired all of the time, so when I'm not in class, I'm sleep. lol. I'm working on that! Today's post is all about RANTS! Yes, I have some rants about my school! First off, as of right now, I don't know where I'll be living next semester! o_O I re-applied for my dorm, but since they are turning one of the dorms on campus into a "freshman only" residence, then other people got my room before me! Ugh! Sounds insane doesn't it? Well, I'm learning that that is how my school handles things, they don't warn you about anything until you ask. I applied in January for housing, and didn't find out until yesterday (March 29th) that I was S.O.L Naturally I went into complete panic mode! I was soooo upset! I'm trying not to worry to much, because I found another option and I'm going to see if it will work out. Its cheaper than a dorm, and way more spacious, so we will see.

THE PARKING AT MY SCHOOL IS RIDICULOUS! My school is predominantly a commuter campus, so you would think that they would have enough parking spots to go around, FALSE! I left campus for 20 minutes, came back, rode around for 10 minutes looking for a spot, and then had to park in some random spot to watch the parking lot like a stalker until someone left! UGH! And to top it all of, they are giving people tickets for parking in random spots when the parking lots and decks are full. UNBELIEVABLE!

In other news; 😊 The semester is almost over!!! My last final exam is on May 5th, and I'm going home for the summer!! My summer classes don't start until June 1st, and I will be making the 45-to an hour drive from my house to school twice a week so that I don't have to pay $1840 for summer housing, especially since they're going to kick me smooth out in August 😊

Share and Enjoy:

Digg   Facebook

This entry was posted on Tuesday, March 30th, 2010 at 5:40 pm and is filed under College. You can follow any responses to this entry through the RSS 2.0 feed. You can leave a response, or trackback from your own site.

Literacy Connections

1. What features do these four blogs have in common?
2. Based on the style and content of the four blogs, how would you describe the audience for each blog?
3. Go to the *Wordpress* blog at wordpress.com and surf the site. Based on your experiences, is this an effective blog? Why or why not?
4. Do a Web search for a blog that connects to one of your hobbies or areas of interest. Read the blog and then write about your experiences. What kind of information did you get from the blog? What made the blog unique as a digital genre? What kind of reading process did you engage in?
5. Read Meg Hourihan's article "What We're Doing When We Blog." Do you think Hourihan would find the four blogs above good examples of the genre of the blog? Why or why not?

Before You Read

Before you analyze the following screen shots closely from the online virtual world *Second Life*, do a quick "first reading" and view the screen shots. Write down any first impressions that come to mind about *Second Life* based on this quick reading of the screen shots.

Screen Shots from *Second Life*

The following screen shots are from the online virtual world *Second Life*. These screen shots can help you think about the ways that *Second Life* is similar to and different from real life. The first screen shot is of a virtual college classroom, the second screen shot is an avatar giving a presentation on technology and education, and the third screen shot is a cyber café for bloggers

Literacy Connections

1. Choose one of the screen shots and do a close "reading," writing down everything you notice about the visual rhetoric of the image.
2. What do you notice about *Second Life* participants' avatars in the screen shots?
3. Based on these screen shots, in what ways is *Second Life* similar to real life? In what ways is it different?
4. Find and print an interesting image from *Second Life* by doing a *Google* image search. Be prepared to share your image in small groups and discuss why you found the image interesting and what it reveals about the virtual world of *Second Life*.
5. In what ways do these images support or work against Peter Hall's view of *Second Life* in "Living the Virtual Life"?

of the hours, days, months, and years. We knew what to do and when to do it, just as the Iraqi geese knew when to fly north, driven by the hot wind that blew in from the desert, and the ewes knew when to give birth to wet lambs that stood on long, shaky legs in the chilly March wind and baaed hesitantly, because they were small and cold and did not know where they were or what to do now that they were here. The only time-piece we had need of then was the sun. It rose and set, and the seasons rolled by, and we sowed seed and harvested and ate and played and married our cousins and had babies who got whooping cough and chicken-pox—and those children who survived grew up and married *their* cousins and had babies who got whooping cough and chickenpox. We lived and loved and toiled and died without ever needing to know what year it was, or even the time of day.

2   It wasn't that we had no system for keeping track of time and of the important events in our lives. But ours was a natural—or, rather, a divine—calendar, because it was framed by acts of God. Allah himself set down the milestones with earthquakes and droughts and floods and locusts and pestilences. Simple as our calendar was, it worked just fine for us.

3   Take, for example, the birth date of Teta Im Khalil, the oldest woman in Magdaluna and all the surrounding villages. When I first met her, we had just returned home from Syria at the end of the Big War and were living with Grandma Mariam. Im Khalil came by to welcome my father home and to take a long, myopic look at his foreign-born wife, my mother. Im Khalil was so old that the skin of her cheeks looked like my father's grimy tobacco pouch, and when I kissed her (because Grandma insisted that I show her old friend affection), it was like kissing a soft suede glove that had been soaked with sweat and then left in a dark closet for a season. Im Khalil's face got me to wondering how old one had to be to look and taste the way she did. So, as soon as she had hobbled off on her cane, I asked Grandma, "How old is Teta Im Khalil?"

4   Grandma had to think for a moment; then she said, "I've been told that Teta was born shortly after the big snow that caused the roof on the mayor's house to cave in."

5   "And when was that?" I asked.

6   "Oh, about the time we had the big earthquake that cracked the wall in the east room."

7   Well, that was enough for me. You couldn't be more accurate than that, now, could you? Satisfied with her answer, I went back to playing with a ball made from an old sock stuffed with other, much older socks.

8   And that's the way it was in our little village for as far back as anybody could remember: people were born so many years before or after an earth-quake or a flood; they got married or died so many years before or after a

long drought or a big snow or some other disaster. One of the most unusual of these dates was when Antoinette the seamstress and Saeed the barber (and tooth puller) got married. That was the year of the whirlwind during which fish and oranges fell from the sky. Incredible as it may sound, the story of the fish and oranges was true, because men—respectable men, like Abu George the blacksmith and Abu Asaad the mule skinner, men who would not lie even to save their own souls—told and retold that story until it was incorporated into Magdaluna's calendar, just like the year of the black moon and the year of the locusts before it. My father, too, confirmed the story for me. He told me that he had been a small boy himself when it had rained fish and oranges from heaven. He'd gotten up one morning after a stormy night and walked out into the yard to find fish as long as his forearm still flopping here and there among the wet navel oranges.

9   The year of the fish-bearing twister, however, was not the last remarkable year. Many others followed in which strange and wonderful things happened: milestones added by the hand of Allah to Magdaluna's calendar. There was, for instance, the year of the drought, when the heavens were shut for months and the spring from which the entire village got its drinking water slowed to a trickle. The spring was about a mile from the village, in a ravine that opened at one end into a small, flat clearing covered with fine gray dust and hard, marble-sized goat droppings, because every afternoon the goatherds brought their flocks there to water them. In the year of the drought, that little clearing was always packed full of noisy kids with big brown eyes and sticky hands, and their mothers—sinewy, overworked young women with protruding collarbones and cracked, callused brown heels. The children ran around playing tag or hide-and-seek while the women talked, shooed flies, and awaited their turns to fill up their jars with drinking water to bring home to their napping men and wet babies. There were days when we had to wait from sunup until late afternoon just to fill a small clay jar with precious, cool water.

10   Sometimes, amid the long wait and the heat and the flies and the smell of goat dung, tempers flared, and the younger women, anxious about their babies, argued over whose turn it was to fill up her jar. And sometimes the arguments escalated into full-blown, knockdown-dragout fights; the women would grab each other by the hair and curse and scream and spit and call each other names that made my ears tingle. We little brown boys who went with our mothers to fetch water loved these fights, because we got to see the women's legs and their colored panties as they grappled and rolled around in the dust. Once in a while, we got lucky and saw much more, because some of the women wore nothing at all under their long dresses. God, how I used to look forward to those fights. I remember the rush, the excitement, the sun dancing on the dust clouds as a dress ripped

and a young white breast was revealed then quickly hidden. In my calendar, that year of drought will always be one of the best years of my childhood, because it was then, in a dusty clearing by a trickling mountain spring, I got my first glimpses of the wonders, the mysteries, and the promises hidden beneath the folds of a woman's dress. Fish and oranges from heaven . . . you can get over that.

> **"Every civilized village needed a telephone, he said, and Magdaluna was not going to get anywhere until it had one."**

11   But, in another way, the year of the drought was also one of the worst of my life, because that was the year that Abu Raja, the retired cook who used to entertain us kids by cracking walnuts on his forehead, decided it was time Magdaluna got its own telephone. Every civilized village needed a telephone, he said, and Magdaluna was not going to get anywhere until it had one. A telephone would link us with the outside world. At the time, I was too young to understand the debate, but a few men—like Shukri, the retired Turkish-army drill sergeant, and Abu Hanna the vineyard keeper—did all they could to talk Abu Raja out of having a telephone brought to the village. But they were outshouted and ignored and finally shunned by the other villagers for resisting progress and trying to keep a good thing from coming to Magdaluna.

12   One warm day in early fall, many of the villagers were out in their fields repairing walls or gathering wood for the winter when the shout went out that the telephone-company truck had arrived at Abu Raja's *dikkan*, or country store. There were no roads in those days, only footpaths and dry streambeds, so it took the telephone-company truck almost a day to work its way up the rocky terrain from Sidon—about the same time it took to walk. When the truck came into view, Abu George, who had a huge voice and, before the telephone, was Magdaluna's only long-distance communication system, bellowed the news from his front porch. Everybody dropped what they were doing and ran to Abu Raja's house to see what was happening. Some of the more dignified villagers, however, like Abu Habeeb and Abu Nazim, who had been to big cities like Beirut and Damascus and had seen things like telephones and telegraphs, did not run the way the rest did; they walked with their canes hanging from the crooks of their arms, as if on a Sunday afternoon stroll.

13   It did not take long for the whole village to assemble at Abu Raja's *dikkan*. Some of the rich villagers, like the widow Farha and the gendarme Abu Nadeem, walked right into the store and stood at the elbows of the two important-looking men from the telephone company, who proceeded with utmost gravity, like priests at Communion, to wire up the telephone. The poorer villagers stood outside and listened carefully to the details relayed to them by the not-so-poor people who stood in the doorway and could see inside.

14   "The bald man is cutting the blue wire," someone said.

15   "He is sticking the wire into the hole in the bottom of the black box," someone else added.

16   "The telephone man with the mustache is connecting two pieces of wire. Now he is twisting the ends together," a third voice chimed in.

17   Because I was small and unaware that I should have stood outside with the other poor folk to give the rich people inside more room (they seemed to need more of it than poor people did), I wriggled my way through the dense forest of legs to get a firsthand look at the action. I felt like the bare-foot Moses, sandals in hand, staring at the burning bush on Mount Sinai. Breathless, I watched as the men in blue, their shirt pockets adorned with fancy lettering in a foreign language, put together a black machine that supposedly would make it possible to talk with uncles, aunts, and cousins who lived more than two days' ride away.

18   It was shortly after sunset when the man with the mustache announced that the telephone was ready to use. He explained that all Abu Raja had to do was lift the receiver, turn the crank on the black box a few times, and wait for an operator to take his call. Abu Raja, who had once lived and worked in Sidon, was impatient with the telephone man for assuming that he was ignorant. He grabbed the receiver and turned the crank forcefully, as if trying to start a Model T Ford. Everybody was impressed that he knew what to do. He even called the operator by her first name: "Centralist." Within moments, Abu Raja was talking with his brother, a concierge in Beirut. He didn't even have to raise his voice or shout to be heard.

19   If I hadn't seen it with my own two eyes and heard it with my own two ears, I would not have believed it—and my friend Kameel didn't. He was away that day watching his father's goats, and when he came back to the village that evening, his cousin Habeeb and I told him about the telephone and how Abu Raja had used it to speak with his brother in Beirut. After he heard our report, Kameel made the sign of the cross, kissed his thumbnail, and warned us that lying was a bad sin and would surely land its in pur-gatory. Kameel believed in Jesus and Mary, and wanted to be a priest when he grew up. He always crossed himself when Habeeb, who was irrever-ent, and I, who was Presbyterian, were around, even when we were not bearing bad news.

20   And the telephone, as it turned out, was bad news. With its coming, the face of the village began to change. One of the first effects was the shifting of the village's center. Before the telephone's arrival, the men of the village used to gather regularly at the house of Im Kaleem, a short, middle-aged widow with jet-black hair and a raspy voice that could be heard all over the village, even when she was only whispering. She was a devout Catholic and also the village *shlikki*—whore. The men met at her house to argue about politics and

drink coffee and play cards or backgammon. Im Kaleem was not a true pros-titute, however, because she did not charge for her services—not even for the coffee and tea (and, occasionally, the strong liquor called arrack) that she served the men. She did not need the money; her son, who was overseas in Africa, sent her money regularly. (I knew this because my father used to read her son's letters to her and take down her replies, as Im Kaleem could not read and write.) Im Kaleem was no slut either—unlike some women in the village—because she loved all the men she entertained, and they loved her, every one of them. In a way, she was married to all the men in the village. Everybody knew it—the wives knew it; the itinerant Catholic priest knew it; the Presbyterian minister knew it—but nobody objected. Actually, I suspect the women (my mother included) did not mind their husbands' visits to Im Kaleem. Oh, they wrung their hands and complained to one another about their men's unfaithfulness, but secretly they were relieved, because Im Kaleem took some of the pressure off them and kept the men out of their hair while they attended to their endless chores. Im Kaleem was also a kind of confessor and troubleshooter, talking sense to those men who were having family problems, especially the younger ones.

> "And they were always looking up from their games and drinks and talk to glance at the phone in the corner, as if expecting it to ring any minute and bring news that would change their lives and deliver them from their aimless existence."

21   Before the telephone came to Magdaluna, Im Kaleem's house was bustling at just about any time of day, especially at night, when its win-dows were brightly lit with three large oil lamps, and the loud voices of the men talking, laughing, and arguing could be heard in the street below—a reassuring, homey sound. Her house was an island of comfort, an oasis for the weary village men, exhausted from having so little to do.

22   But it wasn't long before many of those men—the younger ones espe-cially—started spending more of their days and evenings at Abu Raja's *dikkan*. There, they would eat and drink and talk and play checkers and backgammon, and then lean their chairs back against the wall—the signal that they were ready to toss back and forth, like a ball, the latest rumors going around the village. And they were always looking up from their games and drinks and talk to glance at the phone in the corner, as if expect-ing it to ring any minute and bring news that would change their lives and deliver them from their aimless existence. In the meantime, they smoked cheap, hand-rolled cigarettes, dug dirt out from under their fingernails with big pocketknives, and drank lukewarm sodas that they called Kacula, Seffen-Ub, and Bebsi. Sometimes, especially when it was hot, the days dragged on so slowly that the men turned on Abu Saeed, a confirmed bach-elor who practically lived in Abu Raja's *dikkan*, and teased him for going

around barefoot and unshaven since the Virgin had appeared to him behind the olive press.

23   The telephone was also bad news for me personally. It took away my lucrative business—a source of much-needed income. Before the telephone came to Magdaluna, I used to hang around Im Kaleem's courtyard and play marbles with the other kids, waiting for some man to call down from a window and ask me to run to the store for cigarettes or arrack, or to deliver a message to his wife, such as what he wanted for supper. There was always something in it for me: a ten or even a twenty-five-piaster piece. On a good day, I ran nine or ten of those errands, which assured a steady supply of marbles that I usually lost to Sami or his cousin Hani, the basket weaver's boy. But as the days went by, fewer and fewer men came to Im Kaleem's, and more and more congregated at Abu Raja's to wait by the telephone. In the evenings, no light fell from her window on to the street below, and the laughter and noise of the men trailed off and finally stopped. Only Shukri, the retired Turkish-army drill sergeant, remained faithful to Im Kaleem after all the other men had deserted her; he was still seen going into or leaving her house from time to time. Early that winter, Im Kaleem's hair suddenly turned gray, and she got sick and old. Her legs started giving her trouble, making it hard for her to walk. By spring she hardly left her house anymore.

24   At Abu Raja's *dikkan*, the calls did eventually come, as expected, and men and women started leaving the village the way a hailstorm begins: first one, then two, then bunches. The army took them. Jobs in the cities lured them. And ships and airplanes carried them to such faraway places as Australia and Brazil and New Zealand. My friend Kameel, his cousin Habeeb, and their cousins and my cousins all went away to become ditch diggers and mechanics and butcher-shop boys and deli owners who wore dirty aprons sixteen hours a day, all looking for a better life than the one they had left behind. Within a year, only the sick, the old, and the maimed were left in the village. Magdaluna became a skeleton of its former self, desolate and forsaken, like the tombs, a place to get away from.

25   Finally, the telephone took my family away, too. My father got a call from an old army buddy who told him that an oil company in southern Lebanon was hiring interpreters and instructors. My father applied for a job and got it, and we moved to Sidon, where I went to a Presbyterian missionary school and graduated in 1962. Three years later, having won a scholarship, I left Lebanon for the United States. Like the others who left Magdaluna before me, I am still looking for that better life.

Literacy Connections

1. Accawi tells us that the year of the drought was one of the best and worse of his life. Why was it one of the best? Why was it one of the worst?

2. Underline or highlight passages in the essay that reference religion. In small groups, discuss the significance of these references to religion and compare the conflicts and connections between religion and technological progress in the essay.

3. Some of the villagers "did all they could to talk Abu Raja out of having a telephone brought to the village. But they were outshouted and ignored and finally shunned by other villagers for resisting progress and trying to keep a good thing from coming to Magdaluna." Think of a time in your life when you or someone close to you—perhaps a parent, a grandparent, a teacher—"resisted progress." Write the story and explore possible reasons for the resistance.

4. Think about the way the telephone changed life in Magdaluna, and write a paragraph in which you compare those changes to the changes new technology has brought to your own world.

5. Explore your response to the final words of Accawi's essay, "I am still looking for that better life," in light of the other authors you've read in this chapter of *Everything's a Text*.

Before You Read

In the following essay, Amanda Henderson uses the term *digital addictions* to describe the phase her mom went through when "she was completely addicted and taken over by the game *The Sims*." Think about your own digital addictions and write about the role they play in your life.

Flying Cars and Endless Playlists

Amanda Henderson

Amanda Henderson was a first-semester, first-year student at Florida State University when she wrote this digital literacy essay for her first-year composition class. She is a criminology major and plans to go on to law school and become a juvenile judge who makes a positive difference in children's lives. In "Flying Cars and Endless Playlists," Amanda reflects on digital obsessions and her and her family's history with technology.

1   It is obvious that our world and society today is completely submerged in and taken over by the digital. It takes innumerable forms and creates a plethora of obsessions. The reliance we have developed for the digital is sometimes quite evident, although at times you may not even realize your dependence on certain digital devices. Could you imagine your life without that cell phone you use to keep in touch with your family 500 miles away back home? That computer you spend hour after hour bound to checking emails, making business presentations and playing on MySpace, Facebook and YouTube? Or how about the countless hours you spend jamming away to personalized play lists on your iPod and other MP3 devices? No one is exempt. Everyone has their own preference; whether it be conscious or subconscious, we all have them.

2   My mom is not what you would call "computer savvy." She knows what she knows and that's about it. Even with her lack of in-depth knowledge of how computers work and all their gadgets and gizmos, my mom is addicted to her computer. She wakes up every morning, pours a hot cup of coffee in the kitchen and heads straight to the office. While everyone else in the house is still sound asleep, she spends her quiet mornings in her office checking emails, talking to the other early bird moms on AIM and reading up on the latest headlines. On road trips she is the DJ, through her laptop of course. She makes play list after play list for all of my family to enjoy. When she is not busy playing music, you can catch her playing Bejeweled, one of her more recent favorite computer games. A few years back my mom even went through a phase where she was completely addicted and taken over by the game: The Sims. It is yet another one of those virtual reality games where you get to control other characters' lives and have them live out your every dream and fantasy. She would spend countless hours feeding them, making them study and learn valuable skills to advance in their careers, send the children to school, bathe them, throw parties and even make new babies! Although she has moved away from such obvious digital addictions, she is still attached to her computer day after day.

3   My father is quite the opposite of my mother. He could tell you more about a computer than you could ever want to know and although he is quite knowledgeable on the subject, that is not his preference. My father is addicted to taking photographs. He used to be just a film photographer, that is until the digital took him over as well. He has all the hot new cameras, lenses and gadgets on the market. Now it is *only* digital cameras in my house. It must be the instant satisfaction of knowing whether or not he just shot the next best masterpiece, or if it is garbage. Either way, the digital captured him as well. My father doesn't like to sit back and take pictures of people or common subjects. He has quite a unique photographic hobby; he likes to chase lightning and photograph the strikes. I have

followed him along on these adventures and they can be quite dangerous, but his new digital cameras save him time and create more accuracy for capturing the strikes. It is clearly evident that the digital era has taken over and completely changed the way he views his photographs, the way he shoots pictures, and has even expanded his capabilities in the field.

4   At first glance I could not pick out my preference or obsession with anything digital. I figured yeah, of course I have a cell phone and use it a thousand times a day. Of course I have a hot, new trendy laptop that I am on every second I get a chance checking my MySpace page, Facebook, and email. Of course I have an iPod with literally 5000+ songs downloaded to it and take it with me everywhere I go. Whether it be walking to class, driving home for the weekend or flying to Colorado for Christmas, it is right by my side. Then I realized, I *am* taken over by the digital, in every way possible! So much that I don't even realize that everything I do has some sort of digital reliance.

5   My generation *is* the digital generation. We wake up every morning to our digital alarm clocks blaring in our ears, turn on the automatic coffee pots, flip on the television to catch the morning weather and then bounce right to our laptops. Our generation cannot get enough. We think only the geeky middle school boys who spend hour after hour attached to a PlayStation, Xbox, Wii, or some other video game console are the only ones affected and obsessed with the digital, but we are all wrong. I cannot walk down the street to class and not catch every other person clinging to their cell phones or jamming away to their iPods.

6   Socially we are heading for failure. Instead of having to make polite conversations to our friendly neighbors, we are stuck in our own worlds consumed by our digital preference of the moment. When was the last time you or I sat on the bus and actually made small talk with the person next to us? When was the last time you walked to class and made a new friend on the way? The truth is, we don't. Before iPods, text messaging, and cell phones people actually had to talk to the people around them. To not become a "hermit" or a complete social outcast, people actually had to make friends with people in person, not on the Internet, through text messages or over the phone. Our grandparents, great-great grandparents and generations prior did not rely on technology to create their memories and past times. They threw parties, had socials and went out of their way to approach someone new and make friends.

7   I rely so much on the digital I don't think I could choose just one digital device that I could not live without. I use my cell phone to keep in contact with my parents, boyfriend, and best friends from back home. I use my laptop to check homework deadlines, do research for classes, talk to friends online and even pay my bills. How ludicrous is it to think many

people in my generation have never even bought stamps! We click, and send. Then of course, there is my iPod. I got my first iPod for my fifteenth birthday and ever since, I have not gone a single day without using it. I use it when I am studying, working out at the gym, and jamming away in my car. Commercial free, personal preference music—how much better can it be? My generation doesn't have to *ever* listen to the same music as even the person right next to us in the backseat of our cars. We are entirely consumed by the digital.

8   Say goodbye to clunky, confusing PCs. So long to human tellers at the banks. Good riddance to checkout counters at the grocery store and say hello to the automated digital realm. Your wildest dreams of flying cars and keyless entries into your homes will soon be a reality. Everything will be voice automated or digitally designed. No more hand setting VCR clocks and having to actually step outside to check the weather. The only question is: are we ready to turn our world over to a complete reliance on digital technology and stop thinking for ourselves? Or is it already too late?

Literacy Connections

1. Write a one- or two-sentence summary of Henderson's central ideas. Then, get into small groups and compare summaries.
2. What evidence does Henderson present to support her assertion that the current generation is immersed in the digital?
3. Henderson tells us that "at first glance [she] could not pick out [her] preference or obsession with anything digital" and then she realized that she is completely "taken over by the digital, in every possible way." Are you taken over by the digital the way Henderson is? Make a quick list of the role of the digital in your life since you opened your eyes this morning.
4. Henderson believes that our reliance on everything digital is leading us into failure in our social lives. To what extent do you agree or disagree with her, and why?
5. Compare Henderson's perspective on technology with that presented by Anwar Accawi in his essay "The Telephone," which appears earlier in this chapter.

Digital Literacy Projects

Digital Literacy Narrative

In this project, you'll write a literacy narrative focused on your experiences with digital literacy (Web sites, blogs, e-mail, PowerPoint, etc.) You'll describe and reflect on significant experiences that have shaped your attitudes toward digital literacy. The purpose of the digital literacy narrative is to get you to reflect on your own experiences with digital literacy and to think about how those experiences have shaped your attitudes about digital literacy. The digital literacy narrative will also help you connect the readings in the chapter to your own experiences with digital literacy.

You can use a variety of media to reflect on your experiences and put them in the form of a narrative. You could write them in print form as an essay, or—because this is your *digital* literacy narrative, after all—you might want to experiment with creating a hypertext narrative.

The literacy narrative is a popular genre in school and out of school. Writers use the literacy narrative as a tool to reflect, and also to show readers how the writer's literacy was shaped. There are no "rules" for how a literacy narrative should be organized: some writers focus on their most important literacy experiences, some writers focus on a single experience. Some writers talk a lot about literacy influences, and some focus on important events. Some writers explore their struggles with reading and writing, whereas other writers focus more on their successes and turning points. You could focus on elementary school, high school, college—or talk about your experiences outside of school.

Best and Worst Web Sites Awards

In this project you're going to choose the best and the worst Web sites that you visit frequently and explain why you chose them (choose one ineffective Web site and one effective Web site). To evaluate them, you'll discuss features of Web sites mentioned in Crawford Kilian's "Effective Web Writing": purpose, audience, content, appearance, accessibility, and organization. The class may vote on the best and worst Web sites. If your classroom has Internet access and an LCD projector, you can project your Web sites and debate why they are the best and the worst. If you're not in a computer classroom, you can print screen shots of the home pages of your Web sites and the class can vote by exchanging these screen shots. The purpose of this project is to have you apply ideas about effective Web writing discussed in the chapter to Web sites that you're familiar with. Thinking about what's effective and what's ineffective in the Web sites you visit will help you better compose and design your own Web sites.

If your teacher asks you to write this project in print format, be sure to include a screen shot (or screen shots) of the Web sites you're evaluating. You can copy a screen shot by pressing the "Print Screen" key (usually it's on the top row of the computer keyboard), opening up a graphics editing tool (such as Microsoft Paint), pasting the image of the screen into the graphics editing tool, and saving it as an image file. You can then insert the image into your word processing document.

Personal or Political Blog

In this project, you'll create a personal or political blog and make posts to the blog until the end of the semester. You can create your own blog using the tools at blogger.com, or if you're familiar with a different blogging or social networking tool (such as *MySpace* or *LiveJournal* or *Facebook*), you may use that one. If you'd like, you can allow your peers to post comments to your blog. If you already have a blog, you can use this project to try blogging about something new.

You'll get to choose the primary audience for your blog. If you write a personal blog, you might want to make your family or your friends the target audience. If you create a political blog, you'll probably want to think in terms of a wider audience. (Because your blog will be published on the Internet, you might want to think of your readers as the general Internet-surfing public, or you might speak to a specific political group.)

Reread Meg Hourihan's article "What We're Doing When We Blog" to review some of the features of the genre of the blog, such as frequent posts, links, and time stamps. You might also surf the Web and try to find models of the kind of blog you're interested in creating. Because the genre of the blog focuses on posting frequently over a period of time, this won't be the kind of project where you draft and revise and then turn in a final draft. Instead, you'll make frequent posts and continue blogging until the semester ends (and you may want to continue blogging after the semester is over).

Digital Revision

In this project, you'll revise one of the writing projects you've already written in your class and put it in a digital medium. You could take an essay and turn it into a blog, a Web site, a PowerPoint presentation, a podcast, etc. You'll also write a two- to three-page process memo in which you reflect on the differences between composing in print and composing in a digital environment. The genre you compose in will be up to you, but keep in mind that the digital genre you choose will affect the way you revise the original essay. For example, an essay with a cause/effect or point/counterpoint type of linear organization would need to be rethought for a less linear form like a Web site or a blog. The purpose of this project is to give you experience composing in a digital environment and to get you thinking about the differences between composing digitally and composing in print.

As you compose your digital revision and write your process memo, keep in mind the context of the readings in the chapter. Think about what the authors in the chapter had to say about what it means to write in a digital environment and the differences between writing in print and composing digitally.

Digital Futures Researched Presentation

In this project, you'll explore the future of digital technologies by choosing a specific technology you're interested in (video games, the Internet, hypertext fiction, etc.) and researching what experts say is the future of the technology you've chosen. You'll also reflect on what types of literacies might be necessary in the future for the technology you've chosen. Your teacher might ask you to write up the results of your research in an essay or present your results to the class.

The purpose of this project is to encourage you to explore an area of digital literacy you're especially interested in and as a class to get a sense of the future of digital technologies and digital literacy. You will also get some practice researching a topic and using the library and online databases, and if you make a presentation to your peers, you'll get a chance to practice making a presentation to an audience.

If you're presenting the results of your research to the class, you can think of the genre as "classroom presentation." Because you're presenting to your peers and teacher, these audiences will help shape how you organize your presentation, the tone you take, the way you explain the technology, etc. Presentations that are engaging, well-organized, and informative tend to be more successful than presentations that aren't well thought out or that are presented in a dry, monotone style.

Group Project—Digital Discourse Community Study

In this project, you're going to collaborate with three or four of your peers to conduct an ethnographic study of a digital community, with a focus on the way the community communicates. The group will observe, analyze, and even take part in the community over an extended period of time. The digital community your group observes might be in *Second Life*, on a listserv, on a multi-player game, on an electronic bulletin board, etc. The group can play the role of a "participant observer" and take part in the digital community, or the group can play the role of "lurkers" in the community. To get more information about the community, the group will interview community members. The purpose of this project is for you to analyze digital literacy in an online community. You'll practice thinking skills that are important for any type of literacy: close and systematic observation, textual analysis, and interviewing. You'll also get some practice working in a group, which is a critical skill in college and in the workplace.

Ethnographic studies are a common genre in social science fields such as anthropology, sociology, and education. In ethnographic studies, researchers look for patterns in what they're observing and report the results of their research in an organized way. This means describing the community being observed; discussing what you learned about the community; giving examples from observation, participation, interviews, etc.; and drawing some conclusions based on the results of the research.

7

Situating Popular Culture Literacies

This chapter on popular culture literacies will help you understand what we mean when we talk about popular culture and popular culture literacies, and it will help make you more aware of the need to carefully read and analyze the popular culture  that surrounds you and the ways it affects your life.

There's no escaping pop culture, whether you claim that it doesn't interest you or whether you readily admit that you're intrigued by its many facets. Popular culture surrounds us. The music we listen to, the movies and TV shows we watch, the books and magazines we read, the video games we play, the Web sites we frequent (such as *Facebook*, *MySpace*, and *YouTube*), the celebrities whose lives many of us follow—each of these is part of our popular culture, and it's important to learn to critically read this culture. We need to carefully consider how popular culture affects who we are, what we think, and how we act. Instead of mindlessly being engulfed and influenced by pop culture, we need to be conscious of its possible effects on us. We need to become critical readers of popular culture, and the readings and composing activities in this chapter can help make that happen.

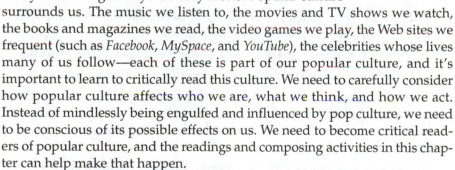

As you study this chapter you'll—

- Read an essay that will explain what we mean when we use the term *popular culture*, and discuss why it's important that you develop popular culture literacies

- Read a student case study that includes drafts of an essay on pop culture celebrity obsession, as well as inside information provided by the student (who admits to being obsessed with celebrities)
- Think about the terms *high culture* and *low culture* and the positive and negative connotations that accompany those terms
- Read an essay by a student who's concerned about the "dumbing down" of Americans by pop culture
- Critically consider four magazine covers that feature pop culture icons and think about the influence of celebrities on your life and on society at large
- Read an article written two days after Michael Jackson died and consider how the demands of celebrity culture affected the King of Pop
- Learn that Barbie was inspired by a porn doll and that she just might be both the most hated and the most loved of all toys
- Think about the place of heroes and role models in our lives
- Read a review of the comic book series *Locke & Key*, an interview with Joe Hill, author of the award-winning series, along with the cover and opening pages of the first installment in the series—*Locke & Key: Welcome to Lovecraft*
- Become more aware of the role popular culture plays in shaping your life and your personality
- Learn to more critically assess the popular culture that surrounds you.

But you won't just read essays and articles and think about your own popular culture literacies; you'll also compose. The popular culture literacy projects described at the end of the chapter give you the opportunity to—

- Write an essay in which you reflect upon particular elements of popular culture that have played a role in shaping who you are
- Analyze a pop culture event or artifact that particularly interests you
- Write a feature article for a pop culture magazine of your choice
- Conduct a television self-study in which you keep a record of everything you watch on television for a week and analyze why you watch the shows you watch, what you learn from them, and the role they play in making you who you are
- Compose a mini-ethnography of a pop culture subculture of your choice
- Work with a group of students to create a popular culture magazine.

Now, let's get started and see what we can learn about popular culture literacies.

What Are Popular Culture Literacies?

Before You Read

Before you begin reading Stacey Suver's essay "A Pop Life," in which he explores the many facets of popular culture and discusses the importance of developing popular culture literacies, think about the possible meaning of the term *popular culture literacies,* and jot down a definition.

A Pop Life

Stacey A. Suver

Stacey Suver was a graduate student working on his Ph.D. in Twentieth-Century American Literature when he wrote this essay. Composition courses Stacey has designed and enjoys teaching include "Writing about Representations of Addiction," in which he and his students look at ways addiction is presented in various types of literature, as well as how contemporary media (such as tabloids, nightly news programs, etc.) depict celebrity addictions. Another of his courses, "Writing About What If (Alternate History)," focuses on how contemporary culture might be different if particular events had happened—for example, how our world might be different if the South had won the Civil War or if John Kerry had become our President instead of George Bush, or how current body image issues might have been rewritten if pop stars such as Britney Spears and Christina Aguilera had been chubbier.

All objects, all phases of culture are alive. They have voices. They speak of their history and interrelatedness. And they are all talking at once!

—Camille Paglia

Popular Culture

1   If you perform an Internet search for Web sites dealing with popular culture, you're likely to find almost anything listed in your results: Jessica Simpson lunchboxes for sale, fansites dedicated to *Buffy the Vampire Slayer* and *Sex in the City,* nostalgia for early arcade games such as *Pac Man* and *Donkey Kong,* Web pages devoted to reporting movie production rumors while warning of "spoilers." You'll almost certainly find a seemingly endless roster of blogs dishing on the latest Britney Spears and Lindsay Lohan

gossip. As evidenced by the variety and sheer quantity of these Internet sites, popular culture is everywhere. We consume it, discuss it, wear it, watch it, reminisce about it, perpetuate it, and contribute to the creation of it. But what is it? Quite simply, popular culture is whatever is approved of or favored by a majority in society at any given time. Popular culture is just that—culture that is popular. In addition, the term is often used to refer to various forms of entertainment and public distraction. Because of this, it is not unusual to hear it spoken of as frivolous and accused of containing no actual substance or social value.

2   But is this true? How can something that is so integral to our cultural identity be valueless? Popular culture lies at the center of a debate concerning the relative worth of certain types of cultural artifacts. Some critics argue that these artifacts exist on a spectrum designated "high culture" at one end and "low culture" at the other. These critics are able to assign a hierarchical value to the type of culture according to where it falls on the spectrum. For instance, a live performance of a Puccini opera would land closer to the side marked high culture while a Justin Timberlake concert would be placed toward the low culture end. Comparing a supermarket romance novel to *Moby Dick* or a painting by Vincent Van Gogh to a Superman comic book are further examples of this. As you can see, popular culture routinely falls toward the low end of the spectrum. The problem with this assessment is that the division generally occurs along class lines. The artifacts designated high culture are those favored by the upper class while the popular culture artifacts, those enjoyed by the middle and lower classes, are routinely considered low. When you take into account that around 80% of Americans consider themselves middle class, the idea that popular culture is low culture sounds very misguided and elitist.

3   Simply by paying attention to your everyday environment, you're guaranteed to learn something about popular culture. Every time you watch a television program, visit the mall, shop for groceries, listen to the radio, or read a book you immerse yourself in it. But what does it mean to be truly knowledgeable? How do you achieve popular culture literacy? And why is acquiring something like this important?

Popular Entertainment

4   Popular culture literacy involves having at least passing familiarity with many forms of popular entertainment:

- **Film.** Being knowledgeable about movies consists of more than just frequenting the local multiplex. Literacy also includes familiarity with iconic moments from throughout the history of film. Even if you've never actually sat through the movie, you probably know the shower scene at the beginning of *Psycho* and the final scene in *Casablanca*, where Humphrey Bogart delivers one of the most quoted lines in all of cinema: "Louis, I think this is the beginning of a beautiful friendship." Familiarity with movies is necessary because film is the form of popular entertainment that is referenced most often by other types of popular entertainment and by popular culture in general. In addition, the medium can be self-referential. The Rob Reiner film, *When Harry Met Sally*, features a scene where the two main characters, played by Billy Crystal and Meg Ryan, have a lengthy conversation about *Casablanca* and the role it plays in their lives. Within the first five minutes of *Shrek 2*, we see references to at least three other films: *From Here to Eternity, Lord of the Rings,* and *Spiderman*. The scenes in *Shrek 2* are staged in such a way that they are funny even to those who haven't seen the original movies the references are borrowed from; however, the scenes contain a lot more meaning for those who have.

- **Television.** Americans spend almost as much time each week in front of the television as they do at work. Like film, television programs and the commercials that sponsor them provide popular culture with a constant supply of referents and catch phrases. *Seinfeld* is probably responsible for creating a couple dozen of these all by itself—"yada, yada, yada," "close talker," "re-gifter," etc. Unlike movies, however, television programs have the advantage of shorter running times and greater availability—it's broadcast directly into your home and onto your television screens. Also, television is capable of creating a "must see" event. In 1969, more than 600 million viewers watched the moon landing, and fourteen years later 125 million people tuned in to see the final episode of *M.A.S.H.*

- **Contemporary Music.** Pop music may be the form of popular culture with the greatest potential for emotionality. Since so much of what we do is accompanied by music, it has the ability to become associated with certain memories. This means that when we hear those songs, they have the ability to recall those memories along with the attendant emotions. This is one of the reasons why so many older pop songs show up in advertisements on television. The advertisers hope to invoke feelings of nostalgia and fondness for the past. While it's good to follow the current trends in music, the true popular culture literati know that previous generations' music contains just as much significance for their lives as their own music. That's one of the reasons seventies, eighties, and nineties nights are so popular. Venues promoting these themed evenings hope to attract not only young people searching for something retro and chic, but also the older crowd looking to re-experience the music they enjoyed when they were younger.

- **Books.** The general consensus is that people don't read as much as they should, although this sentiment is contradicted by the popularity of Oprah Winfrey's book club and the abundance of mega-chain book-sellers such as Borders and Barnes & Nobles. The furor surrounding J. K. Rowling's *Harry Potter* series and Dan Brown's *The Da Vinci Code*, and the magazine articles, movies, television specials, and social protests inspired by the books demonstrate that, now and then, litera-ture still has the ability to captivate the world of popular culture. How-ever, like film, the primary contribution of books to popular culture literacy lies, not in cultural shake-ups, but in the production of iconic images. Without ever reading Herman Melville's *Moby Dick*, nearly everyone knows the origin of the phrase "Thar she blows" and can rec-ognize Captain Ahab when he shows up in odd places like *Tom and Jerry* cartoons and *Saturday Night Live*.

- **Magazines.** The primary function of magazines is twofold. First, mag-azines inform; second, magazines entertain. Ideally, they do both at once by providing information in an entertaining way. This is the premise behind news magazines, like *Time Magazine* and *U.S. News and World Report*, and specialty magazines, such as *Rolling Stone, Sports Illustrated*, and *Discover Magazine*. Additionally, magazines are designed to be consumed in small portions. They typically contain plenty of pictures, and feature articles span only a few pages. This is why magazines are so plentiful in hospital waiting rooms and airport gift shops. They provide brief diversion and don't require the time commitment of books and novels. However, some magazines, instead of presenting information in an entertaining way, provide information on entertainment. This is the case with scandal sheets and supermar-ket tabloids. These magazines report on rumors surrounding the love life, night life, and deathbed confessions of celebrities and high profile police investigations that have managed to catch the public's attention. The American public generally acknowledges that you shouldn't take these types of magazines too seriously; however, they consistently sell thousands of copies week after week.

- **Video Games.** While home video game consoles have been available since the mid-seventies, they have never been more popular than they are right now. Platforms such as the Microsoft Xbox, the Sony PlaySta-tion, and the Nintendo Wii top the list of Christmas gifts every year. Popular games like *Halo* and *Madden NFL* have come a long way since the days when Mario was king. Games such as *Guitar Hero* and *Rock Band* have taken gaming beyond the traditional shoot 'em up and auto racing genres. With game controllers designed to look like musical instruments, players are able to simulate the experience of standing on a stage and performing their favorite rock song for a crowd of screaming fans. However, it's the multiplayer online role-playing computer games, such as *World of Warcraft,* that come the closest to supplying gamers with an alternate reality. In these games, players use an avatar to explore their virtual environment, interact with other players, undertake missions, and battle enemies. Since the game is played online and it's possible to face off against an opponent playing across town or on the other side of the planet, the virtual worlds created by these games succeed in socializing us in entirely new and unprecedented ways.

- **Web-based.** In 2006, *Time Magazine* gave the award for Person of the Year to "You," the general public. One of the reasons for this decision was the emphasis that Internet-based communities place on the individual. Sites like *MySpace, Facebook,* and *YouTube* take self-expression and networking with friends to a completely different level. *YouTube* allows users to upload, watch, and share videos with the rest of the *YouTube* community. The significant percentage of these video clips are homemade and run the gamut from mini semi-professional films— scripted, filmed, and directed by the user—to video diaries and editorials responding to current events. *MySpace* and *Facebook* allow users to create profile pages individualized to suit their personality by adding music, photos, and more. Members leave comments on one another's pages and keep their friends informed about their activities through updates to their status. Within a surprisingly short amount of time, it has become almost impossible to achieve literacy in popular culture without participating in some sort of online community.

Celebrity

5   In addition to engaging in the consumption of popular entertainment, popular culture literacy also involves participation in celebrity culture. Americans in general are endlessly fascinated by the lives of celebrities, and, consequently, we want to know everything about them. Luckily for us, we have plenty of opportunities to feed our addiction thanks to the efforts of tabloid journalism. Celebrity culture is simultaneously reported on and generated by supermarket tabloids with dubious reputations for accuracy like *The National Enquirer* or *The Sun,* semi-respectable publications like *People Magazine,* and television insider programs such as *Entertainment Tonight* or *TMZ.* Paris Hilton, who has been called the Marilyn Monroe of the twenty-first century, is famous simply for being famous. Hers is a form of self-perpetuating celebrity completely different from Britney Spears' (pop star) or Lindsay Lohan's (movie star).

6   The discussion over why we are so obsessed with celebrity culture is lively and often heated. One side argues that it matters if Britney Spears shaves her head or if Paris Hilton goes to jail for driving on a suspended license because celebrities serve as representatives for the entire culture. On the one hand they portray us in movie roles and speak for us in pop songs. On the other hand their faults are our faults. Mel Gibson can make *The Passion*, a film which millions of people describe as a deeply moving and spiritual movie going experience, and at the same time he can get arrested for drunk driving and verbally assaulting police officers. The two sides of Mel Gibson aren't mutually exclusive; he simultaneously represents the best and the worst of us. Additionally, the lives of celebrities are completely alien to the average American, and for that reason they're fascinating to us. Celebrity culture affords us the opportunity to experience, even if only vicariously, what it's like to run with the jet set crowd.

7   The other side argues that celebrity culture is frivolous and trite (a critique often applied to popular culture in general) and that it's dangerous to devote so much time to the study of celebrity culture because it draws our attention away from issues of real importance. When people know more about the personal lives of Angelina Jolie and Brad Pitt than they do about political issues or the war in Iraq, their priorities are out of order. Critics of celebrity culture also argue that celebrities are unacceptable role models, and by giving them our attention, we only encourage them to act out in order to attract more attention.

8   These critics also accuse the mainstream news media of assuming a negative role with regards to their coverage of celebrity culture. They argue that the news media feeds the American public's desire for celebrity gossip at the expense of straight news. During Paris Hilton's trial and subsequent jail time, professional cable news channels interrupted their regular news coverage with BREAKING NEWS about Hilton's situation. After a certain point, it becomes a question of whether the news media reports celebrity updates because the public is interested, or whether the public expresses interest because they are constantly being updated.

9   Regardless of what position you take concerning the merits of celebrity culture, one thing is absolutely certain—it is impossible to ignore, which is what makes it an essential component in the formation of popular culture literacy.

Language

10 One of the most interesting things about popular culture is its ability to contribute to the creation of language. Catch phrases, advertising slogans, and movie tag lines all enter the common vernacular through repetition or by striking a chord with the American public. Sometimes a phrase simply happens to be uttered at the right time and place for it to ignite our pop

cultural imaginations. Just days after footage of a Florida college student's arrest at a Q&A with former presidential candidate John Kerry flooded the Internet, the student's plea, "Don't tase me, bro," entered the cultural lexicon. T-shirts and bumper stickers bearing the catch phrase were widely available on the Web, late night talk show hosts used the phrase as a punchline for jokes, and video spoofs of the incident appeared on YouTube.com. A few weeks later the *Oxford American Dictionary* listed the word "tase" as a runner up for its word of the year. The incident became a pop culture event, and the student's phrase took on a life of its own.

"Film, television, literature, and nearly every other form of popular culture generate new terminology for the culturally literate."

11   Film, television, literature, and nearly every other form of popular culture generate new terminology for the culturally literate. Television commercials are especially adept at this. Verizon Wireless phones recently ran a series of commercials that feature a Verizon employee traveling to various exotic locations to test the strength of his phone signal. The dialogue in these commercials was always the same: "Can you hear me now?" This phrase has since become commonplace in regular conversation and is used to signify a breakdown in communication. Similarly, Wendy's iconic catch phrase from the 1980s, "Where's the beef?" entered everyday speech as a means of questioning the quality of a product or concept.

12   We probably adopt more new language and cultural catch phrases from the movies than from any other source. The popular culture literate will easily recognize Clark Gable's phrase, "Frankly, my dear, I don't give a damn," from *Gone with the Wind*, and the iconic lines, "Play it again, Sam" and "Here's looking at you, kid," from *Casablanca*. Even genre films have left their mark. The *Star Wars* franchise popularized "Use the force" as a way of offering encouragement and "Luke, I am your father," an expression indicating an incredibly melodramatic moment of revelation.

13   Catch phrases from popular culture enter the common vernacular for two reasons. The first reason is sheer repetition. Ed McMahon used the phrase "Heeeere's Johnny!" to introduce Johnny Carson on the *Tonight Show* for thirty years. So when Jack Nicholson's homicidal character in *The Shining* sticks his head through a hole he's hacked into a door with an axe and quotes, "Heeeere's Johnny!" we're easily able to identify the reference. The brilliance of this is that Nicholson is able to recast the phrase and make it his own. He anticipates the thrill we experience when we're able to recognize the everyday source of the quote, and then contrasts our pleasurable response to the phrase with the violence and horror of the scene. This endows McMahon's signature phrase with two completely different cultural connotations and our interpretation can change depending on the context in which the phrase is used. The other reason we adopt catch phrases

is that they strike a cord in the public imagination. This is what happened with "Don't tase me, bro." For whatever reason, the Florida student's words resonated with the rest of the culture, and they were subsequently adopted, commercialized, and inducted into the arena of popular culture.

Critical Literacy and Popular Culture

14   The most important thing to keep in mind about popular culture is to think about it critically. Since, as a phenomenon, it can be either spontaneously created or carefully crafted, it's necessary to try to discover exactly what any given artifact of popular culture has to say to you. Pop culture generally reflects American culture as a whole; however, the image it sends back tends to be more like an image from a funhouse mirror rather than an accurate representation. Popular culture overwhelmingly reinforces the hegemonic image of American society: patriarchal, white, middle class, heterosexual. This perception is exceedingly narrow and ignores the diversity and richness of the country as a whole.

15   Television is a prime example of this phenomenon. A complaint often lodged against the show *Friends* is that they don't have any non-white friends. The sitcom features almost no one of color over its ten year run, even in a peripheral capacity. Other shows, like *Scrubs* and *The King of Queens*, include non-white cast members in an effort to demonstrate diversity. However, these actors are often cast in the role of second banana, best friend to the white lead. Additionally, it's unusual for television programs to have a female lead character unless the show revolves around an ensemble cast. In these instances she's teamed with at least one other actor, usually male.

16   The women in these shows are typically thin and adhere to traditional notions of beauty. This is a common theme in popular culture. It is nearly impossible for a woman to become a pop culture icon if she has an average body type. Those that do are soon pressured to lose weight and some become dangerously thin. When Nicole Richie starred on *The Simple Life* as Paris Hilton's best friend, she had a realistic body type. However, after she became famous, her weight dropped significantly. It's not unusual to see supermarket tabloids with headlines celebrating a female pop star's weight gain. A paparazzo's unflattering photos of the star in a bathing suit at the beach or eating at a fast food restaurant always accompany the headlines. These headlines, along with the advertisements inside that depict women with body types smaller than average as the ideal, are often blamed for the rise in eating disorders among young women and teens.

17   Supermarket tabloids also frequently "out" celebrities in an effort to create a scandal and sell magazines. Celebrities fear that acknowledging

their homosexuality will negatively influence the public's perception of them and damage their careers. Increasingly this is not the case; it's becoming more and more common to hear of celebrities who reveal their sexual orientation to the media and come out without fear of reprisal. Famous personalities as diverse as talk show host Ellen DeGeneres, Elton John, Neil Patrick Harris, NBA star John Amaechi, *Frasier*'s David Hyde Pierce, Ian McKellen, who plays Gandolf in *The Lord of the Rings* movies, and even Rob Halford, singer for the heavy metal band Judas Priest, have all been open about their homosexuality and have discussed their orientation publicly.

The Importance of Popular Culture Literacy

18 Popular culture serves a very necessary function in society. It unifies people and supplies them with a common vocabulary and set of references that facilitate interaction with one another in ways that wouldn't be possible otherwise. Love it or hate it, you must be aware of it. It is necessary to understand what Marlon Brando really means in *The Godfather* when he decides to make an offer that can't be refused. It's also important to know the critical implications and cultural connotations of Britney Spears' song "Hit Me Baby One More Time" and that it was popularized by a teenager in a Catholic school girl outfit. And it's important to be aware of what someone is asking of you when they say they'll *Facebook* you. In a way, popular culture has taken the place of "the weather" as the one topic of conversation that everyone can be reasonably certain that everyone else has an opinion about. In a world where discussing politics with strangers in public places has become impolite and taboo, conversations about popular culture have become the norm.

Literacy Connections

1. How does Stacey Suver define the term *popular culture?*
2. What do you see as the main purpose of Suver's essay? What do you think is the main idea he is trying to communicate?
3. What role does popular culture play in your life?
4. Why is it important that we learn to think critically about the influence of popular culture on our lives?
5. Later in the chapter you'll have the opportunity to read "I'll Take My Stand: A Defense of Popular Culture," an article by Anthony DeCurtis in which he speaks out on the value of popular culture. How do you think Suver would react to DeCurtis's stance that popular culture plays an important and valuable role in our lives? Use references from Suver's text to substantiate your claims.

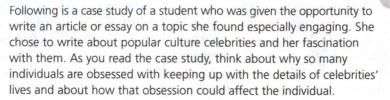

Following is a case study of a student who was given the opportunity to write an article or essay on a topic she found especially engaging. She chose to write about popular culture celebrities and her fascination with them. As you read the case study, think about why so many individuals are obsessed with keeping up with the details of celebrities' lives and about how that obsession could affect the individual.

Student Case Study: Composing an Essay About Pop Culture

Ali Maslaney was an undergraduate at Florida State University, enrolled in Advanced Article and Essay Workshop, when she composed "Check-out at Register 8," a composition in which she explores her fascination with popular culture celebrities. Included from Ali are an in-class response she wrote the day first drafts of the paper were due in class, her final ePortfolio draft, and insight into her composing process and why she made particular rhetorical choices.

Ali's assignment for the first composition of the semester was to write an essay on a topic she sincerely wanted to explore. Here's the assignment:

ASSIGNMENT: COMPOSITION #1

For this first assignment you may write any type of essay or article you choose—a reflective essay, an argument essay, an informative article, a newspaper or magazine feature, an editorial. Many of you will probably want to write reflective essays that focus on subjects that are close to your own experience and concerns and use your writing to explore and work through your ideas on the subject. The essay, in its original form, is a place to experiment; it is an act of thinking through writing. It records the writer's attempts to explore a problem or come to terms with an experience or deal with some issue or confusion. It is an open-ended form that allows digressions, encourages uncertainty, thrives on multiple perspectives, and looks to walk around, get underneath, and give breath to ideas and experience.

Probably most important for you to think about as you decide on a topic for this first assignment is that you write on a topic about which you are truly interested and want to explore.

Over the course of the semester you are expected to write for this class a total of 22–25 polished pages that you take through peer review and revision. The length of this first paper should depend on the topic about which you choose to write. However, a good idea might be to write around 5–6 polished pages for each of your four papers so that your total number of pages for the semester will be 22–25 pages.

The day rough drafts of the paper were due, Ali's teacher asked all of the students in the class to respond in class to the following prompt:

IN-CLASS WRITING #3

Take a few minutes to tell me about the first draft you wrote for today's class. What's it about? Do you like it? Do you think you'll stick with the topic or write something completely different for the next class?

In response to the prompt, Ali wrote the following:

For my last article and essay workshop, we mainly focused on memoirs/ personal essays. I enjoyed writing those, but I feel that to become a better writer, I need to try some new styles. For my first paper, I decided to write an opinion essay that was more closely related to an article. It is more based in the present, although I use some self-reflection as well. I thought to myself, what interested me the most, and I came up with "celebrities." They are not my only interest, but I find them fascinating. I especially love reading what occurs off the red carpet. They lead a glamorous life, filled with money, fame, and VIP status, yet they also seem to be the most unhappy human beings in America. When I read stories about affairs and the darker side of the media industry, they portray a sense of vulnerability. So the main purpose of my paper is to discover why regular people, like myself, are so obsessed with celebrities. I want to answer this question by reflecting on my own reasons why I enjoy reading about them as well.

Ali shared her ideas for her paper, along with her first and second drafts, with her peer response group and received feedback from them as she worked on her essay. When we asked her about the help she received from her group, she told us:

The peer review group I worked with on this paper was actually my favorite peer review group I worked with all semester. They were both females, and that made me a lot more comfortable sharing my paper with them. I was worried that because of the "fluff" topic I had chosen, the guys in the class wouldn't take it seriously, but later, after working with a few of them, I knew I shouldn't have worried about that.

The girls in my peer review group were very helpful with directing my essay. I was a little confused with the ending, and they helped me decide on keeping the story in scene. They were not intimidating and always had encouraging things to say. They also helped me with wording issues and grammatical errors. They were very helpful with editing my essay.

The day rough drafts were due, Ali posted the following and shared it with her peer review group:

DRAFT #1

"God, she is such a slut," a girl with chestnut brown hair swept up into a ponytail says to her friend.

The friend turns her peaches and cream complexion towards the US Weekly *magazine. A picture of a pregnant sixteen year-old celebrity graces the cover while the caption underneath reads "Pregnant and Scared." Peaches and Cream morphs her face into a look that looks as if she just shoved a handful of sour Jolly Ranchers into her mouth. The brunette removes the tabloid from its designated spot alongside the checkout line and thumbs through the rest of its glossy pages.*

As I wait in the lengthy line at Publix, with the harsh fluorescent lights casting down upon me, I eavesdrop into the rest of their conversation. It mostly consists of who is dating whom, who wore what where, and whose movie got pushed back. I glance over at the next register over, and another girl, probably college age, has picked up People *and is casually flipping to the cover story. I even see the muscular boy behind her secretively looking at the page over her shoulder.*

These magazines, thoughtfully placed in line at the checkout counter, entice the customers, such as me, into buying them. These magazines, so flimsily put together, with pages that might as well be scotch taped together, sell for four dollars a piece. These magazines that barely contain three consecutive sentences, gross over one billion dollars annually. This industry, whose idea of reporting accurate information contains quotes that someone who knows someone that used to work for someone anonymously reported is one of the highest grossing industries in the nation.

What is it about celebrities, or the entertainment industry in general, that captivates the human population? I admit to taking part in the hysteria by buying these tabloids and check my favorite blog website at least three times daily. What about these people interests me enough to the point that I choose to bookmark my favorite celebrity gossip websites over more intellectual ones like CNN *and* MSNBC*?*

Ali's first draft is a beginning—a start—and that was what it was supposed to be. Her teacher required only that students have something down on paper the day first drafts were due—ideas to share with their group so they could be ready to begin the real work of writing the paper.

As we discussed in Chapter 2, no matter what kind of literacy you're composing in, you shouldn't put pressure on yourself to "get it right" on the first draft.

At first glance, Ali's second draft looks identical to the first. The first page is the same. But then she picks up where she left off with "CNN and MSNBC," fleshes out the ideas in that paragraph, begins another body paragraph in which she explores the special challenges and problems that come with being a celebrity and how we can more easily relate to them because of the issues they have to try to deal with, and then skips to the end of the paper where she closes with a scene in the grocery store—the same setting with which she began the essay.

For her third draft, she keeps what she had, fleshes out the body of the paper with a specific example of the recent death of a star and an exploration of why so many celebrities are unhappy, and does some editing. Let's take a look at the final draft of her essay.

Checkout at Register 8

1   "God, she is such a slut," a girl with chestnut brown hair swept up into a messy ponytail says to her friend. The friend turns her peaches and cream complexion towards the *US Weekly* magazine. A picture of a pregnant sixteen-year-old celebrity graces the cover while the caption underneath reads "Pregnant and Scared." Peaches and Cream morphs her face into a look that appears as if she just shoved a handful of sour Jolly Ranchers into her mouth. The brunette removes the tabloid from its designated spot alongside the checkout line and thumbs through the rest of its glossy pages.

2   As I wait in the lengthy line at Publix, with the harsh fluorescent lights casting down upon me, I eavesdrop into the rest of their conversation. It mostly consists of who is dating whom, who wore what where, and whose movie got pushed back due to poor test audiences. I glance over at the next register, and another girl, probably college age, has picked up *People* and is casually flipping to the cover story. I even see the muscular boy behind her secretively looking at the page over her shoulder.

3   These magazines, thoughtfully placed in line at the checkout counter, entice the customers, such as me, into buying them. These magazines, so flimsily put together, with pages that might as well be scotch taped together, sell for four dollars each. These magazines that barely contain three consecutive sentences gross over one billion dollars annually. This industry, whose idea of reporting accurate information contains quotes that someone who knows someone that used to work for someone anonymously reported, is one of the highest grossing industries in the nation.

4   What is it about celebrities, or the entertainment industry in general, that captivates the human population? I admit to taking part in the hysteria by buying these tabloids and checking my favorite blog website, perezhilton.com, at least three times daily. What is it about these people that interests me enough to the point that I choose to bookmark my favorite celebrity gossip websites over more intellectual ones like CNN and MSNBC? Although I somewhat enjoy reading about the Iowa and New Hampshire caucuses, I am in utter bliss after reading headlines that contain words like SEX. DRUGS. MENTAL INSTABILITY. Perhaps it is because these celebrities provide scandal into my otherwise mediocre life. Their sordid love affairs and dramatic arguments ravish me. When I open the ink stained pages of my *US Weekly*, it is as if I am beginning a Harlequin Romance novel. Although they're set in different time frames, each follows a parallel plot: the poor maiden (i.e., struggling actor/actress) eventually becomes rich (makes a Blockbuster movie). They fall madly in love with a gorgeous member of nobility (their co-stars). Evil forces such as rogue kings and witches (managers and other co-stars) try to destroy their

holy union. But in the end, they overcome these obstacles and live happily ever after (divorced and married to their co-stars).

5   Throughout their intricate lives, celebrities endure obstacles average human beings would never have the chance to encounter. In 2010 alone, one Hollywood starlet received two DUIs, three stints in rehab, and served jail time. When scandalous stories are pasted across the weekly magazines and every broadcast television station's top story concerns them, the façade disappears. Their once seamless persona, now marred by allegations, has become a part of the mess. A few years back, one highly admired singer got caught lip-synching at a live performance and her credibility with her fans and critics suffered immensely. Although these superstars make eight figures a year and own four mansions, they possess a sense of vulnerability that tennis moms and adolescents can sympathize with, no matter how outlandish the charades they commit. Off the red velour lined carpet and away from the heavily scripted press conferences, yet never entirely inconspicuous due to the blinding shudder of flashbulbs, their normalcy is visible. The hurt that they experience when ending a committed relationship with their partner, the sadness they feel when their mother or father dies, the delight they get while pushing their children on a swing, this humble show of emotion and feeling connects Us to Them. Beneath their attention-grabbing antics, real emotions exist, deep and genuine ones. This past Tuesday, when a world-famous actor died mysteriously in his apartment, the paparazzi immediately hunted for other celebrities and their reaction to the tragedy. Many had already found out and prepared a scripted response. However, there were some who had not heard the news yet and when told their reactions were truly candid. They ranged from shocked and speechless to distraught and sobbing.

6   The untimely and tragic deaths of these celebrities raise another argument. Why are such wealthy and famous people unhappy? Celebrities live ridiculously well compared to the rest of the population. They get thousands of dollars worth of freebies every day, have a personal entourage cater to their every need, and millions of adoring fans. Could it be people like me who contribute to their downward spiral? People like me who have more than seven celebrity tabloids scattered across my coffee table. People like me who religiously check two or more gossip websites every few hours. I single-handedly support the media industry by indirectly funding aggressive paparazzi who stalk the celebrities. Is their source of sadness due to the fact that they can't even go to the grocery store without being stalked by paparazzi or bombarded by crowds of aggressive autograph seekers? In their lives, there is no such entity as privacy. Once an actor/actress/singer/reality show contestant becomes a certified star worthy of the public's interest, they become the prey of the paparazzi.

About seven or eight years ago, a very talented and well-known TV actress was sunbathing topless in her own backyard, but a paparazzo climbed her fence and took pictures of her naked top half. He then sold those pictures to magazines and the Internet for thousands of dollars. Even things that celebrities did before they became famous are now fair game, things that they thought no one else would ever find out about. One A-list actress posed for a few nude photos back in the early '90s for some much needed money. Unfortunately, over ten years later, the pictures were sent to various tabloids and the news of her scandalous photos spread throughout the U.S. The actress took the photographer and his agency to court, and the judge eventually ruled that the photos were to remain sealed, but the damage to her character was already done.

7   So I have to ask myself, am I the source of their unhappiness? Or did they sign up for this constant media frenzy themselves as a result of becoming famous? I struggle with the argument in my head.

8   "Um, Ma'am, are you ready to check out?" asks the confused looking teenager behind the register.

9   I glance upward toward the cashier and place my items onto the belt. "Sorry about that," I reply. I quickly grab the three closest celebrity gossip magazines and throw them onto the conveyor belt.

10   As she scans the miniscule barcode on each tabloid, she reads the bold headlines. "Can you believe she's pregnant?" the girl exclaims. "She's two years younger than I am."

11   I smile back at her, murmur in agreement, and carry my paper bag out the electronic door.

ALI'S STRATEGIES FOR COMPOSING

To gain more insight into Ali's strategies for composing her essay, we asked her to tell us a little about the kinds of brainstorming activities she usually does to help her come up with ideas. She told us:

> I almost always begin working on a paper by jotting down ideas in my notebook. Usually, the teacher gives us a topic or tells us what we're supposed to write about, but for this paper, we could write about whatever we wanted. I was excited to be able to write about anything I chose, but I was overwhelmed as well. I just jotted down a list of about five or six different topics that interested me.

In response to our question regarding how she decided on a topic for her essay, Ali told us:

> It wasn't until I was at the grocery store, flipping through the celebrity tabloids while standing in the checkout line that I actually committed to my topic. My vague idea was beginning to take direction and I knew I'd be able to form it into an actual essay.

When we asked Ali how she went about getting started on her essay she shared:

> After having chosen my specific topic, I wrote a handwritten, very rough, first draft in my notebook. The pages had half-complete sentences scattered across the pages, and other jot notes on the top and bottom. The notebook draft was very messy and disorganized.

So the first draft that Ali shared with her group wasn't really her first draft. The real first draft was handwritten.

Next, we asked Ali to tell us about the drafting process for this paper. She shared:

> When I actually began typing it up, I already had most of the sentences and structure formed. Generally my early typed drafts are very similar to my final drafts because I have been thinking about the sentences and the entire essay structure in my head. For this essay, with each draft, I read over what I had already written and just added onto what I had. I started out with about a page and a half, and then by the final draft, it added up to almost five pages.
>
> For a while I was confused about how to end the essay, but my peer group helped me with that, and I decided to end it by keeping the story in scene. My group gave me lots of encouragement and also helped me with editing and grammar.

While it might appear that Ali makes few changes from one draft to another, except for taking up where she left off in an earlier draft and adding a few paragraphs or a page or two to the next draft, her typed drafts are not her only drafts. She writes her essays in her head and drafts there, before she sits down to type.

Ali went on to tell us:

> Since I love pop culture, especially celebrities, I enjoyed writing this piece, especially after I had decided on the setting of the story. I knew how I wanted to begin the essay, and once I decided how I wanted to end it, the writing in the middle just naturally progressed.

Ali was given the opportunity to explore a topic in which she was truly interested, and she took advantage of that, decided on a topic that worked well for her, and enjoyed working on her essay.

When we asked her to tell us about the audience she envisioned as she wrote, she told us:

> To be honest, I never really have a specific audience in mind when I first start writing a piece. The further along I get, and the more drafts that I write, that's when I begin to picture a specific audience. For this piece, I was definitely envisioning it in a women's magazine like Glamour or Marie Claire. I also wrote it for other young females like me who are also addicted to celebrity gossip. Any person who reads magazines like People and US Weekly, or checks websites like PerezHilton or

TMZ could enjoy this article. They would notice the references I made about certain celebrities within my essay, celebrities that I didn't specifically name. I usually like to write pieces that can appeal to every group though. Maybe they won't get all of my pop culture terms, but if it's written well, they can still enjoy the writing.

So even though Ali didn't begin writing her essay with an audience in mind, she began to envision an audience as her essay was taking shape.

Literacy Connections

1. How does Ali Maslaney explain her fascination with celebrities? How does she account for it?
2. If you were a member of Ali's peer response group, what would you tell her you like about her essay? Be specific. Give examples. What parts of the essay would you tell her were unclear to you? Point those out.
3. When you first begin drafting an essay, do you take some time to think about the audience for whom you are writing—or are you likely to do like Ali does and wait until you are into the drafting process to envision an audience—or does your awareness of audience depend on what you are writing? Explain.
4. Near the end of her composition, Ali writes: "So I have to ask myself, am I the source of their unhappiness? Or did they sign up for this constant media frenzy themselves as a result of becoming famous? I struggle with the argument in my head." What do you think? Are those of us who are fascinated by or obsessed with the lives of pop culture celebrities in some way or to some extent responsible for the constant hounding of the paparazzi they endure? Explain your answer.
5. Later in the chapter you'll have the opportunity to read a student essay, "Don't Super Size Me . . . Dumbify Me" by Samantha Calarusse, in which she discusses her concern about the "dumbing down" of Americans by pop culture. Based on what you've read in Ali's essay, how do you think she would respond to Samantha's concerns?

Popular Culture Literacy Readings

Before You Read

In the following article, Anthony DeCurtis "takes a stand" for the value and legitimacy of popular culture. He discusses the "current climate of philistine defense of high culture" and the "cynical attacks on perfectly legitimate popular art."

Take a few minutes to think about what you think is usually meant by the terms *high culture* and *low culture*. Do you think of one of these types of culture as being superior to the other? Why?

I'll Take My Stand: A Defense of Popular Culture

Anthony DeCurtis

"I'll Take My Stand: A Defense of Popular Culture" is one of the articles Anthony DeCurtis chose to include in his book *Rocking My Life Away: Writing About Music and Other Matters* (Duke University Press, 1998). *Rocking My Life Away* is a collection of articles about music he began writing in 1978, when he was a graduate student in English at Indiana Universtiy. His other books include *In Other Words: Artists Talk About Life and Work* (Hal Leonard Publishing Company, 2005) and *Present Tense: Rock & Roll and Culture* (Duke University Press, 1992), which he edited. Each fall, DeCurtis teaches a course titled "The Arts and Popular Culture" in the writing program at the University of Pennsylvania, and he also directs the arts and culture concentration at the Graduate School of Journalism at the City University of New York.

1   One recent evening a writer who occasionally freelanced for *Rolling Stone,* where I edited the record review section for five years, dropped by my apartment to listen to music. To say that techno—a hyperkinetic, electronic dance music that had become hugely popular in Europe and that was beginning to develop a following in the United States—was his specialty would be to vastly diminish the extent of his commitment to that genre and the ecstatic "rave" scene that surrounds it. He played some hard-to-find techno tracks for me, discussed them with insight and passion, explained the social ramifications of the music, and gave me some recommendations for future listening.

2   Because of his growing interest in ambient techno—a much slower, and dreamier electronic music that ravers use to ease themselves down after their mad dancing—I put on some pieces by Erik Satie for him to hear. The idea was to connect Satie's notions about music that would mingle amiably with its environment and the intentionally atmospheric function of ambient techno. "Who is Erik Satie?" he asked.

3   I'll admit it: at first I was shocked. We'd touched on such a wide range of subjects that I assumed he'd be generally familiar with Satie, as I am; I just wasn't sure if he'd ever thought of him in this particular context. The evening had also included a viewing of *The Last Seduction* and a long talk about the history of film noir and the reasons for its current revival. We'd listened to Bob Dylan and Syd Barrett and rambled through a chat about the Beats and the intricacies of the most up-to-the-minute computer technology. How could this obviously intelligent, insatiably curious twenty-six-year-old product of a good university never have *heard of* Erik Satie?

4   For a moment, I found myself shedding my identity as an editor at a consumer magazine and reverting to my former role as a literature professor and, more or less by implication, ardent defender of academic "standards." What are they teaching these people nowadays?!?

5   That feeling, however, was quickly replaced by a more immediate delight. There was no question but that he would love Satie, and now I— while not an expert by the furthest stretch of the imagination—would have the pleasure of turning him on to that music. The antidote to my initial outrage seemed easy enough to achieve: I'll tell him, and then he'll know who Satie is. Somehow, that was a simple and fit end to a long evening of aesthetic exploration, sharing, and discovery.

6   Afterwards, at some remove from the actual event, I thought more seriously about whether or not my friend's ignorance of Satie constituted an indictment of our educational system—or even of him. I don't think it does at all—any more than I would like my ignorance of computer culture or the ramifications of techno to stand as an indictment of me. Somewhere my friend had learned how to be excited by knowledge and how to synthesize what he'd learned into fresh formulations. He'd learned how to listen, how to learn from someone else, and how to teach. His formal education must have played some role in all that, even if it wasn't an exclusive or even determinative one.

7   I also realized something else. Knowing about techno and not knowing much about classical music might be somebody else's very definition of dumbing down, but it certainly isn't mine. It's often struck me that many skeptics about popular culture succumb to one of its more obnoxious aspects—the reduction of complicated aesthetic issues to a hit parade—when setting forth what they think should or shouldn't be part of the curriculum or the canon, or even when just expressing their conviction about what is worth knowing. What is the point, though, of pitting one type of music, or one work of art, or one type of knowledge against another, as if in a popularity contest? That seems to me to betray even very traditional notions of the attitude an intellectual life should instill.

8   That type of thinking helps no one and really derives from issues that have little to do with aesthetic matters but everything to do with maintaining the cultural prerequisites of class privilege. I remember feeling bifurcated in my intellectual passions when I was in college in the late 1960s and early 1970s. I'd loved rock and roll since I was a child, and in the mid-1960s I was delighted to find that, at least in the underground press, a serious, powerful brand of criticism was developing in response to the increased ambition evident in the music itself. That development paralleled my own burgeoning interest in literature; in fact, many early rock critics had been trained in the New Criticism that dominated university English departments in the 1950s and early 1960s. These writers approached the music *as* literature, concentrating on close readings and lyrical exegesis to the virtual exclusion of musical analysis.

9   In many ways, both the bohemian world of rock criticism and the erudite, upper-crust world of the literary Great Tradition and its students were equally foreign to me. I grew up in a working-class Italian family—neither of my parents graduated from high school—and, because of that, it's important to consider the different routes through which popular music and literature came into my life. Music, of course, was readily accessible to me through the media—I could hear it on the radio and, somewhat less frequently, watch performances of it on television. Singles were inexpensive and, once I reached the age of ten or so, I could buy them nearly as often as I would like.

10   Critical writing about the music was almost as easy to come by. Underground newspapers were inexpensive; some were given away free. Because my family lived in Greenwich Village—which in those days was as much an Italian neighborhood as a bohemian enclave—I had as much access to that type of publication as I could have wanted.

11   The social process of learning about literature, unfortunately, was far more complex and problematic, as it no doubt continues to be for people from backgrounds like mine. Within the family itself, things were fine. Education was regarded as an important route to a better life. My older brother and sister encouraged me to read; their schoolbooks and other reading material were readily available around the house. My father read three newspapers a day and argued loudly with what he read in the sports and political columns; that was its own encouragement and no small contributor to my eventual career in journalism.

12   But penetrating the mysteries of literature required teachers and a formal education primarily because access to the world of such "high art" was almost exclusively a function of class. To learn about Dion and the Belmonts all I had to do was flip my radio or television on. To learn about Shakespeare, I would have to reorient my entire life and challenge the full spectrum of social expectations for someone like me.

13   Fortunately, at the time, the City University of New York offered an excellent education for free—I never could have afforded to go away to school, nor did I have any of the social skills or emotional wherewithal to survive in such an environment, even if my family could somehow have come up with the money. As for my teachers' occasional condescension toward popular music, one of them as recently as a year ago wrote to the *New York Times* complaining about a critic's characterization of rap lyrics as "poetry"—who cared? I knew that Bob Dylan, Muddy Waters, and the Rolling Stones would always be as sustaining to me as any literature I would ever read—they still are—and I didn't need professors to tell me why, or why they shouldn't be.

14   Moreover, it simply didn't seem important whether my professors cared about popular music or not. Whenever our teachers attempted to reach across the then-much-brooded-upon generation gap by discussing popular

music with us, my friends and I would laugh. As one exercise, the senior professor who taught my freshman honors seminar asked us to analyze the significance of *Abbey Road*, which had just come out, and I didn't even bother to write the paper. *He* was supposed to grade what I knew about the Beatles?" Get real. (I did, however, write a term paper in that course on the Rolling Stones—this was 1970, after all. After giving me an *A*, the professor, unconsciously substituting his own criterion for mine, asked me if I thought it would be pleasant to sit down and have dinner with the band.)

"A genuine education today must consist of providing people with the skills to engage and enter the enormous number of worlds . . . that will increasingly be open to them."

15   I can now see that what I set out to get from my teachers was two things—one obvious, one subtle, a kind of cultural secret. The first was a literary and critical training that would enable me to do the work I wanted to go on to do—my ambition at the time was to become an English professor. For the second, I wanted to crack a social code, a way of speaking, dressing, acting, and even thinking that disguised my class origins and made me seem like the sort of person who *could* go on to become a professor.

16   It's not that I intended to adopt all the mannerisms I learned, but I needed to know where the points of differentiation were. It was "upward mobility time," as a friend later described it, and I needed people to point out to me, intentionally or not, where the ladder was, because I didn't have a clue. All I knew, after having watched any number of my incredibly savvy neighborhood friends slide down the societal chute to dead-end lives, was that it wasn't exclusively about intelligence or merit by a long shot.

17   A good deal has changed in the last quarter-century, but the lessons of those years about the profound degree to which knowledge—types of knowledge, access to knowledge, validation of knowledge, uses of knowledge—functions in a social context, sometimes to very brutal ends, still shape my vision of things. Class issues are rarely discussed in relation to the subject of "dumbing down"—in fact, they're rarely discussed at all without prompting absurd charges of "inciting class warfare"—but they are crucial to it. A "pure" understanding of what it is essential to know cannot be attained—it simply does not exist. As has always been true—and, at least in this country, nearly always disguised—that question must be answered from a position within the rapidly shifting dynamics of our society.

18   If it was ever possible to establish a clear, pragmatic hierarchy among types of knowledge—and I don't think it ever was—it's no longer possible now. There are too many things to know and too many ways of knowing. A genuine education today must consist of providing people with the skills to engage and enter the enormous number of worlds—aesthetic, intellectual, technological, scientific—that will increasingly be open to them.

People must learn to converse across their differences, not learn the same rigidly defined things.

19   Despite reactionary arguments to the contrary, it is not content—opera as opposed to rock and roll, literature as opposed to film—but the nature of the critical approach that determines whether or not a specific discipline has been dumbed down. In the case of popular music, innumerable books, journal articles, newspapers, magazines, fanzines, documentaries, videos, and films address every issue of conceivable importance from every conceivable angle. Anyone who is interested enough to inquire will discover a level of cultural debate that is every bit as sophisticated and rich as that addressing any other subject.

20   Which is not to say that far too much popular music—not to mention much that is written or said about it—is not frighteningly stupid, and perhaps even dangerous. The escalating and overwhelming commercial imperatives of American culture dictate that only what is popular can survive. And what is popular will sometimes prove to be what is pandering.

21   That will be true as long as economics drives culture to the extent that we permit it to at this time, in this place. And that reality speaks to a paradox that the cultural Right in our country has yet to sort out. I debated Hilton Kramer at a college in Minnesota not too long ago, and he was attacking the Corporation for Public Broadcasting and National Public Radio, on the one hand, while espousing traditional American free-market values, on the other. So who will pay for symphonies, museums, and opera? I asked. Rock and roll does not require government grants, I pointed out; it does quite well on the open market. As clearly as I could see, his politics completely undermined his aesthetics.

22   It is apparent to me that leveling charges of "dumbing down" is simply a way of asserting particular aesthetic preferences and a desire for social privilege. And the reactionary political agenda such charges routinely advance makes it virtually impossible to address matters of genuine cultural concern in our society in a civilized manner—questions like, How do we increase literacy and educate people for the society that awaits them in the future?

23   Ever since rock and roll first exploded onto the cultural scene in the 1950s, criticizing it has had more to do with anxiety about burgeoning social movements than anything remotely to do with artistic criteria. Responding to such critiques in his recent book, *Rock and Roll: An Unruly, History,* critic Robert Palmer examines the musical sources of rock and roll and the aesthetic strictures of the Western classical tradition, and does not find a contrast between culture and decadence, but two different approaches to making music:

24   *In traditional West African cultures, a piece of music is held to be satisfying and complete if there is sufficient rhythmic interest; to oversimplify, rhythm is as fundamental to African music as harmony in European tradition and melodic sophistication in the music of India. Indian music has no harmony as such, and nobody*

complains; much European classical music is rhythmically one-dimensional—one is tempted to say "primitive"—and you don't hear symphony subscribers complaining about that. But when pop music begins moving away from tin pan alley song forms and musical values and embracing the aesthetics of its African origins, suddenly our culture is seen as adrift, endangered, riven by decadence and decay. Some pundits write books bemoaning "The Loss of Beauty and Meaning in American Popular Music." Others assert that heavy metal, or punk, or gangster rap—whatever the latest pop-music bogeyman happens to be—imperils the very fabric of civilization! . . . It would help if these gloom-and-doom mongers could see the history of this music as a matter of cycles within cycles, or as a developing idiom that periodically refreshes itself by drinking from its own deepest wellsprings.

25   Does it still really need to be asserted after all this time that art—*all* art, classical as well as popular—does not float unsullied above reality in some pure, eternal, universal realm, but is instead created and understood amid the gritty struggles and forced compromises of history? It is no less satisfying, and certainly no less challenging, for that.

26   Anyone yearning for cultural certainty at the present moment must face up to the curse of living in interesting times. Entire university programs are devoted to popular culture, and gangster rap is written about with great seriousness in the pages of the *New York Times*. At the same time, opera and theater are performed for free in Central Park and MTV underwrites speaking tours by young poets.

27   Culture is no less a battleground than it ever was, but now both sides have aesthetics in their armory. As someone who has grown comfortable moving from the art house to the club, from classic to contemporary literature, from rock and roll to a wide variety of other types of music, I'm saddened by the hardening of those lines, and I fight to break them down.

28   But I live in history, too. And against the current climate of philistine defense of high culture, cynical attacks on perfectly legitimate popular art, and reactionary longing for cultural privilege, I'll happily, eagerly, staunchly take my stand.

Literacy Connections

1. How does Anthony DeCurtis define *high culture* and *low culture*?
2. Close to the end of his article, DeCurtis states that "*all* art, classical as well as popular—does not float unsullied above reality in some pure, eternal, universal realm, but is instead created and understood amid the gritty struggles and forced compromises of history." Read over that statement a couple of times, and then write a paragraph in which you summarize what you think DeCurtis is saying.
3. De Curtis shares with us that Bob Dylan, Muddy Waters, and the Rolling Stones are "as sustaining to [him] as any literature [he] would ever read." How do you react to this statement? Are there musicians

who "sustain" you? Whose tunes and lyrics speak to your soul? What is it about their music that speaks to you?

4. What place do you think the study of popular culture plays in a college curriculum? Is it important that we think critically about the role of popular culture in our lives? Why or why not?

5. How do you think DeCurtis would respond to the claim that popular culture is "dumbing us down"—as Samantha Calarusse claims in her essay "Don't Super Size Me . . . Dumbify Me," that appears in the pages that follow?

Before You Read

In the following essay, Samantha Calarusse shares her concern that many Americans know more about the lives of our pop culture celebrities than they know about important historical figures and political issues. Do you think this concern is valid? Why or why not? Take five minutes to begin to explore your ideas on this subject.

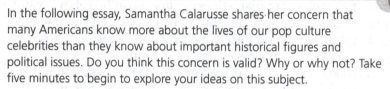

Don't Super Size Me . . . Dumbify Me

Samantha Calarusse

Samantha Calarusse was an undergraduate majoring in English at Florida State University when she wrote "Don't Super Size Me . . . Dumbify Me." She was given the opportunity to write an essay on a topic of her choice, and she says she chose this topic because she was so disillusioned by the widespread obsession with celebrity culture and wanted to explore her ideas on the subject.

1   In today's American Society, the content for breaking news deals with different issues than it did years ago. CNN no longer displays only domestic and international news, war on terrorism, or crisis situations around the world. The general public no longer desires constant updates about the presidential election or about strife in foreign countries. While traditional headlining news covers the latest stories about the national economy, crime, and issues within the government, a new trend has emerged. An increasing percentage of news which consumes the average American mind comes from the trivial aspects of life. A blurb at the bottom of CNN's screen reads, "Britney Spear's younger sister, Jamie-Lynn, is pregnant at sixteen."

2   While I feel sorry for any person who must undergo life-changing circumstances at such a young age, Jamie-Lynn's pregnancy will personally affect neither me nor the rest of the world. Pregnancy is a personal issue that shouldn't be discussed as the latest or juiciest gossip. Yet this sort of dribble consumes the interests of many people, all while we disregard the events that can shake a nation.

3   Many people overlook the issues that can affect them the most. The Presidential elections in the Middle East have affected many citizens. At a social gathering shortly after New Year's, the subject of politics or the war or something of the sort was brought to attention. Out of a college group of seniors, only three people out of the ten knew Bhutto had been assassinated. Only two of those three people knew the back story and its implications for Pakistan. Those who were unaware asked, "Who is Bhutto?"

4   To which the knowledgeable replied, "Benazir Bhutto."

5   "Running for political office in Pakistan," said another.

6   "First female Prime Minister of any Muslim country," I said.

7   While Bhutto's life and career should have been common knowledge after being in the news, many people in the United States still know more about our celebrities than our political leaders. Personally, I do not read, watch or seek out any awareness for celebrities, yet I seem to know about them anyway. In the line at the grocery store tabloids read:

8   "Angelina Jolie is pregnant with twins."

9   "Jennifer's jealous again."

10   During news break on the radio I hear, "Yes, twins. And she and Brad plan to adopt more as well."

11   These are tabloid headlines, phrases on the radio, blurbs on news stations, and gossip heard in the hallways.

12   One astounding radio conversation occurred on Martin Luther King Jr. Day. I was listening to Blazin' 102.3, a prominent rap station in my town. The DJ allowed callers to give shout-outs to their friends or request songs. A young girl, later established as being ten years old and African American, requested the newest song by Snoop Dogg. Because the girl sounded so young, the DJ asked her why she wasn't in school.

13   "We had the day off. Can I request my song now?" she asked.

14   "In a minute. Can you tell me why you don't have school today?"

15   She responded after a few seconds. "It's MLK day."

16   "Do you know who he was?" The DJ was obviously testing the girl's knowledge.

17   "I dunno." This response came after a few moments and whispers in the background with other people.

18   "But you do know who Snoop Dogg is though, right?"

19 "Duh, he's famous."

20 Astonished, I sat on my bed and wondered how a fourth grader could not identify one fact about MLK. If this child couldn't recognize any of his accomplishments while alive, what else did she not know? Was this the new America—dumbed down by pop culture instead of high culture?

21 This brings us to an interesting shift into the basics of knowledge. A name is simple. It identifies who we are, who we have been, and who we can be. I had a conversation with a friend recently; she is in tune with all aspects of politics and sports, yet doesn't pay much attention to the lives of celebrities. So, I asked her a few questions that I will ask you now. Let's play a game. I'll say a name and you tell me who it is.

22 "Britney." Yes, Britney Spears.

23 "Lindsey." Yes, Lindsey Lohan.

24 "George." Okay, let's say George Clooney, but what about George W. Bush, George Orwell, even Curious George? Society relates to celebrities as if they live next door; we have known them for years via television and blockbuster hits, yet they wouldn't recognize us from a can of tuna. Does watching a celebrity grow/prosper in the spotlight entitle us to the in's and out's of someone's life?

25 Britney Spears is the prime example at the moment. The limelight has taken Britney from the *Mickey Mouse Club* to psychotic breakdowns, the loss of her children, divorce, a harsh comeback, drunk driving and more. It has taken Whitney Houston from *I Will Always Love You* to her abusive relationship and cocaine addiction. From Mariah Carey singing *Butterfly* to jokes about her on sitcoms saying, "I just saw Mariah eating Ramon in her nighty." Even Mary-Kate and Ashley Olsen making the transition from *Full House* to anorexia. The list is endless.

26 The line between politics and celebrities is easy to see, yet a fine line is barely visible for what constitutes real news. For example, I was searching the Internet for movie times one evening. On the main page of Yahoo.com the featured items displayed "Miley Cyrus legally changes her name," in bold and larger font than the surrounding text. The small cramped box below this trivial celebrity formality discusses the news. In plain text, "Lebanese mourn Hezbollah militant and Hariri."

27 It seems more people living in the United States care about silly celebrity facts than a bill being passed in Congress; more about Hilary Clinton's masculine-turned-feminine appearance than the political issues she supports; more about Angelina Jolie's sex life than her humanitarian efforts. And while I write this essay, I wonder if anyone will remember the facts mentioned throughout a few months or even a year from now? It's something to think about.

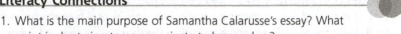

Literacy Connections

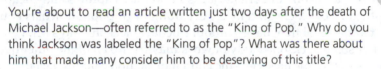

1. What is the main purpose of Samantha Calarusse's essay? What point is she trying to communicate to her readers?
2. How would you describe the tone Calarusse uses in her essay? Is her tone effective? Why or why not?
3. Calarusse wonders if we, the American people, are being "dumbed down by pop culture." What do you think? Explain your answer.
4. In the opening paragraph of her essay, Calarusse claims that news stations today are devoting an increased amount of coverage to popular culture icons and less to important breaking news. Do you think she's right? Watch a prime-time program on a news station of your choice and make a list of what's discussed. Then, analyze your list and sort it into various categories. Which category includes the most items?
5. Compare Ali Maslaney's view of popular culture in "Checkout at Register 8" (which is included earlier in the chapter) with the view Calarusse espouses in her essay. With which view do you most closely agree? Why?

Before You Read

You're about to read an article written just two days after the death of Michael Jackson—often referred to as the "King of Pop." Why do you think Jackson was labeled the "King of Pop"? What was there about him that made many consider him to be deserving of this title?

"Outpouring over Michael Jackson Unlike Anything Since Princess Di"

Daniel B. Wood

Daniel B. Wood was a staff writer for *The Christian Science Monitor* when he wrote the following article, which appeared in that publication on June 27, 2009, just two days after the death of Michael Jackson.

Since news of Michael Jackson's passing, there has been an emotional outpouring not seen perhaps since Princess Diana's death in 1997.

1 The 24-hour news cycle and social media are probably amplifying the reaction. But the response seems genuinely broad and intense—which may be surprising given the pop star's transformation into something of a bizarre and controversial recluse in his last 20 years.

2 If the death of a pop star was to be measured by tweets alone, Michael Jackson's would seem to be of monumental importance. About 15 percent of

Twitter posts mentioned Jackson when the news broke Thursday evening, noted Harvard researcher Ethan Zuckerman in one tweet, comparing that with hot topics such as Iran and swine flu that never crossed 5 percent.

3   By Friday afternoon, 9 of the top 10 albums selling on iTunes were Michael Jackson's, Amazon.com had sold out all of his CDs, and major retailers coast to coast were running out of his music. Online, *Facebook*, and news websites were swamped with tributes. And fans gathered across the world, from a mass moonwalk in London to tributes on the Walk of Fame in Los Angeles to vigils in Paris and Tokyo.

4   The overriding reason is his extraordinary musical influence.

5   "The reason you are seeing this global outpouring of interest is that Michael Jackson is singular in the history of pop culture. No one even comes close," says Professor James Peterson at Bucknell University in Lewisburg, Pa., who teaches hip-hop culture, African-American literature, and sociolinguistics. Mr. Peterson points out that Jackson's achievement of 750 million in global album sales will never again be equaled because of the absolute change in the music business caused by the Internet.

6   Besides having had a dramatic influence on such artists as Usher, Chris Brown, and Justin Timberlake, Jackson "at once captures and encapsulates the history of blacks in dance. Any number of popular artists could not exist at the level they have without Michael Jackson," says Mr. Peterson.

7   For some, Jackson's body of work may trump all of the other questionable aspects of his lifestyle—the child molestation charges, facial alteration, and reclusiveness.

8   "There have been at least three generations of listeners—one for each of his musical incarnations," Peterson notes, adding that he has a 10-year-old son who is now getting immersed in Jackson watching Peterson and his wife in mourning. "A fourth generation of followers is going to emerge because of this," he says.

9   Jackson was also one of the few musicians to transcend narrow ideas about how a black man should look and act and reach a global audience, says Professor Jeff Melnick, who teaches African American studies and popular culture at Babson College in Wellesley, Mass.

10   But the intense response to Jackson's death also reveals society's deep investment in celebrity culture worldwide, he says, adding that there is an acknowledgement that the demands of celebrity culture wounded Jackson from the moment he hit the scene as a boy in the late 1960s.

11   "The outpouring is partly guilt, then—it is a confession of sorts," says Mr. Melnick, "of the culpability of the fan in the premature death of the artist."

12   With virtually no offstage in his life, "Jackson became a canvas on which fans projected all kinds of fantasies—about proper gender behavior, about racial norms and what we should do with our bodies."

13   Jackson also gave more than $300 million over the course of his life to charities all over the world, which may have something to do with tributes coming from several world leaders, from Britain's Gordon Brown to former president of South Korea Kim Dae-jung, and South Africa's Nelson Mandela.

14   Other cultural anthropologists and researchers suggest the current economic downturn has accelerated global notions of nostalgia.

15   "We mourn the loss of ourselves through this pop icon," says Tracy Johnson, Research Director of Context-Based Research Group which studies consumer behavior.

> **"When an artist or performer is so well known and loved, the reaction to his or her passing is bound to be strong and widespread."**

16   "We recognize that we, particularly in America, have lost a little bit of what we were all about," she says. "Someone like Michael Jackson who so embodied the American Dream just makes that loss all that much more palpable."

17   Above all, it was his music and unique, energetic performance style that attracted fans around the world.

18   "One reason Michael Jackson's death is having such a wide impact is because his music had such a wide, and even sustained impact," says John Covach, a music historian at the University of Rochester. "Few artists have so completely saturated the market as Jackson did during the 1980s. It's comparable to the Beatles in the 60s or Elvis in the 50s. When an artist or performer is so well known and loved, the reaction to his or her passing is bound to be strong and widespread."

19   "One important difference between Jackson's career and those of many others is that he was a child star who became an adult star—a very difficult transition to pull off," says Professor Covach. "Even those who were too young to be fans of Jackson when he was a child have seen the clips of him performing with a mastery far beyond his years. The adult Michael Jackson that fans loved in the 1980s thus already had a bit of history—people felt like they knew him already."

20   And so, people from around the world continue to talk with friends and strangers about this musical legend, their voices spread more widely by new means of communication.

21   In the hours after Jackson's passing, AOL's instant messaging service was down for 40 minutes due to an increase in traffic. In a statement, AOL also noted that, "Today was a seminal moment in Internet history. We've never seen anything like it in terms of scope or depth."

22   As if to connect the two major icons of celebrity lost in recent years, the Telegraph in London reports that Harrods owner Mohamed Fayed has announced that he will erect a Michael Jackson Memorial at the store to join the one of his late son, Dodi, and Diana, Princess of Wales.

Literacy Connections

1. *The Christian Science Monitor* Web site describes its reporters as " . . . highly principled, professional journalists who look beyond the headlines to analyze how events affect individuals and communities around the globe and in our own backyards." In what ways does Daniel Wood's article on the death of Michael Jackson either substantiate or work against the validity of this claim?

2. Look back over the format of Wood's article. How does the format used here differ from that of a typical essay? What do you think accounts for the differences?

3. In his article, Wood quotes Professor James Peterson who says, "The reason you are seeing this global outpouring of interest is that Michael Jackson is singular in the history of pop culture. No one even comes close." To what extent do you agree or disagree with Peterson's assertion? Explain your response.

4. What are your memories of Michael Jackson and his music, his reputation, his style? Ask your parents to share with you their memories of the pop icon and compare your responses with theirs.

5. In his article, Wood refers to Jeff Melnick's claim that " . . . celebrity culture wounded Jackson from the moment he hit the scene as a boy in the late 1960s." How do you think Ali Maslaney, author of "Checkout at Register 8," the case study essay included earlier in this chapter, would respond to Melnick's assertion? What is your personal opinion regarding this issue?

Before You Read

The two essays that follow are included in Yona Zeldis McDonough's *The Barbie Chronicles: A Living Doll Turns Forty* (Simon and Schuster, 1999). McDonough's book includes essays that celebrate Barbie and others that promote driving a stake through her plastic heart. As you read these two essays, think about why this little doll evokes such strong reactions and whether or not you think the strong reactions are justifiable.

Barbie at 35

Anna Quindlen

Anna Quindlen, a Pulitzer Prize-winning journalist and best-selling author, is well known and highly acclaimed for her journalism as well as for her nonfiction, fiction, and children's books. Her works include *Black and Blue*

(Random House, 2000), *Being Perfect* (Random House, 2005) and *Good Dog. Stay* (2007). Quindlen's essay, "Barbie at 35," was originally published in the *New York Times* on September 10, 1994, and five years later was included in McDonough's collection of essays about Barbie.

1   My theory is that to get rid of Barbie you'd have to drive a silver stake through her plastic heart. Or a silver lame, stake, the sort of thing that might accompany Barbie's Dream Tent.

2   This is not simply because the original Barbie, launched lo these 35 years ago, was more than a little vampiric in appearance, more Natasha of "Rocky and Bullwinkle" than the "ultimate girl next door" Mattel describes in her press kit.

3   It's not only that Barbie, like Dracula, can appear in guises that mask her essential nature: Surgeon, Astronaut, UNICEF Ambassador. Or that she is untouched by time, still the same parody of the female form she's been since 1959. She's said by her manufacturers to be "eleven and one-half stylish inches" tall. If she were a real live woman she would not have enough body fat to menstruate regularly. Which may be why there's no PMS Barbie.

4   The silver stake is necessary because Barbie—the issue, not the doll— simply will not be put to rest.

5   "Mama, why can't I have Barbie?"

6   "Because I hate Barbie. She gives little girls the message that the only thing that's important is being tall and thin and having a big chest and lots of clothes. She's a terrible role model."

7   "Oh, Mama, don't be silly. She's just a toy."

8   It's an excellent comeback; if only it were accurate. But consider the recent study at the University of Arizona investigating the attitudes of white and black teen-age girls toward body image.

9   The attitudes of the white girls were a nightmare. Ninety percent expressed dissatisfaction with their own bodies and many said they saw dieting as a kind of all-purpose panacea. "I think the reason I would diet would be to gain self-confidence," said one. "I'd feel like it was a way of getting control," said another.

10   And they were curiously united in their description of the perfect girl. She's 5 feet 7 inches, weighs just over 100 pounds, has long legs and flowing hair. The researchers concluded, "The ideal girl was a living manifestation of the Barbie doll."

11   While the white girls described an impossible ideal, black teen-agers talked about appearance in terms of style, attitude, pride and personality. White respondents talked "thin," black ones "shapely." Seventy percent of the black teen-agers said they were satisfied with their weight, and there was little emphasis on dieting. "We're all brought up and taught to

be realistic about life," said one, "and we don't look at things the way you want them to be. You look at them the way they are."

13   There's a quiet irony in that. While black women correctly complain that they are not sufficiently represented in advertisements, commercials, movies, even dolls, perhaps the scarcity of those idealized and unrealistic models may help in some fashion to liberate black teen-agers from ridiculous standards of appearance. When the black teen-agers were asked about the ideal woman, many asked: Whose ideal? The perfect girl projected by the white world simply didn't apply to them or their community, which set beauty standards from within. "White girls," one black participant in the Arizona study wrote, "have to look like Barbie dolls."

14   There are lots of reasons teen-age girls have such a distorted fun-house mirror image of their own bodies, so distorted that one study found that 83 percent wanted to lose weight, although 62 percent were in the normal range. Fashion designers still showcase anorexia chic; last year the super-model Kate Moss was reduced to insisting that, yes, she did eat.

15   But long before Kate and Ultra Slimfast came along, hanging over the lives of every little girl born in the second half of the 20th century was the impossibly curvy shadow (40-18-32 in life-size terms) of Barbie. That preposterous physique, we learn as kids, is what a woman looks like with her clothes off. "Two Barbie dolls are sold every second," says Barbie's resume, which is more extensive than that of Hillary Rodham Clinton. "Barbie doll has had more than a billion pairs of shoes . . . has had over 500 professional makeovers . . . has become the most popular toy ever created."

16   Has been single-handedly responsible for the popularity of the silicone implant?

17   Maybe, as my daughter suggests while she whines in her Barbie-free zone, that's too much weight to put on something that's just a toy. Maybe not. Happy birthday, Babs. Have a piece of cake. Have two.

Literacy Connections

1. Anna Quindlen, quite clearly, does not care for Barbie. Why?
2. What effect might Barbie have on a little girl's (or a little boy's) dreams of what it means to be a beautiful, desirable female?
3. What do you think of Quindlen's statement that Barbie is a terrible role model? Do you agree? Why or why not?
4. Quindlen's essay was written in 1994, so the study to which she refers was conducted quite a few years ago. Do you think the findings of the study might differ if it were conducted today? How? Why?
5. Look over the selections you've read in this chapter. With which of the authors whose works you've read here do you think Quindlen's ideas have the most in common? Why and how?

Before You Read

Following are three magazine covers picturing various popular culture celebrities.

- Kim Kardashian and Britney Spears on the April 2010 cover of *OK!*
- Alicia Keys on the December 2009 cover of *Jet*
- Robert Pattinson on the December 2009 cover of *Vanity Fair.*

As you read each of these covers, think about the influence of popular culture icons in our society. What do you think accounts for their ever-growing influence in our society? What is it about our society that causes us to deify particular individuals?

Magazine Covers Featuring Pop Culture Icons

The following magazine cover photos featuring pop culture icons are from a variety of types of publications. The recently established *OK!* is a weekly British magazine first published in 1993, that proudly focuses on celebrity news. *Jet* began its circulation in 1951 as a weekly magazine targeting an African American audience, and the American version of *Vanity Fair*, first published in 1890, unashamedly touted itself as a magazine whose primary audience was "the vast, luxury-loving, money-spending multitude everywhere" (www.vanityfair.com/magazine/vintage/oneclickhistory).

SPRING BEAUTY SPECIAL!

OK!
WEEKLY

JESSE'S DAUGHTER BEGS SANDRA:
MOMMY COME HOME!

APRIL 5, 2010
ISSUE #14

BIKINI BODY COUNTDOWN

DIETS THAT WORK

Get your best body ever

Easy, delicious recipes

Sexy butt & flat tummy by summer

KIM: Mixes her own tasty shakes

$3.49

14>

0 75470 08966 4

WWW.OKMAGAZINE.COM

BRITNEY: Loves her fun dance workouts

April 2010 *OK!* cover

$1.99   DEC. 7, 2009

JET

**WHAT YOU NEED
TO KNOW ABOUT
THE HEALTH
CARE BILL**

FOCUSED
& FREE
ALICIA
KEYS
MAKES
IT HER
BUSINESS
TO INSPIRE

www.ebonyJET.com

4 9>

0 71486 64060 8

A JOHNSON PUBLICATION

December 2009 *Jet* cover

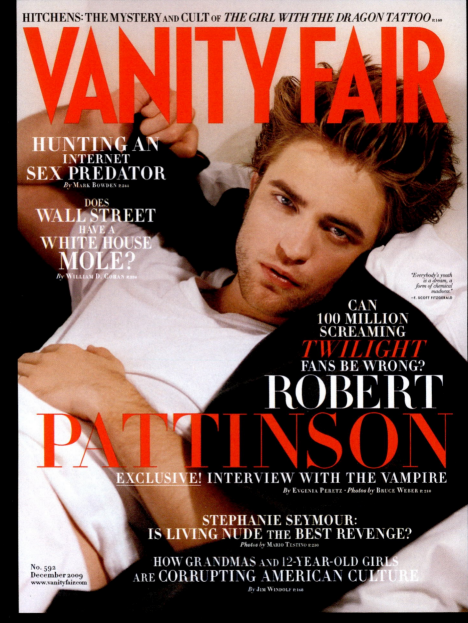

HITCHENS: THE MYSTERY AND CULT OF *THE GIRL WITH THE DRAGON TATTOO* P.140

VANITY FAIR

HUNTING AN
INTERNET
SEX PREDATOR
By MARK BOWDEN P.244

DOES
WALL STREET
HAVE A
WHITE HOUSE
MOLE?
By WILLIAM D. COHAN P.224

"Everybody's youth
is a dream, a
form of chemical
madness."
—F. SCOTT FITZGERALD

CAN
100 MILLION
SCREAMING
TWILIGHT
FANS BE WRONG?
ROBERT
PATTINSON
EXCLUSIVE! INTERVIEW WITH THE VAMPIRE
By EVGENIA PERETZ · *Photos by* BRUCE WEBER P.210

STEPHANIE SEYMOUR:
IS LIVING NUDE THE BEST REVENGE?
Photos by MARIO TESTINO P.230

HOW GRANDMAS AND 12-YEAR-OLD GIRLS
ARE CORRUPTING AMERICAN CULTURE
By JIM WINDOLF P.168

No. 592
December 2009
www.vanityfair.com

December 2009 *Vanity Fair* cover

Literacy Connections

1. Take a few minutes to study the layout and design of each of the three magazine covers. What similarities do you note? What differences?
2. Which of the three magazine covers do you find most appealing? Why?
3. Which magazines do you frequently read? Why do you read them? What kinds of articles do they feature? In what ways do these articles inform you?
4. How do the articles you read and the advertisements in these magazines affect your perception of our culture? How do they affect you as a consumer in our culture?
5. How do you think Anthony DeCurtis, author of "I'll Take My Stand: A Defense of Popular Culture," which you had the opportunity to read earlier in the chapter, would respond to the idea that popular magazines contribute to the dumbing down of Americans?

Before You Read

While many of us are fascinated by or even obsessed with pop culture celebrities, a huge number of us are intrigued by a sexy little plastic doll named *Barbie*. Following are five Barbie photos from across the decades. Before you take time to read the various images, take ten minutes to freewrite about your interactions with Barbie. It doesn't matter whether you are male or female, or whether you have ever owned or even played with a Barbie. She is ingrained in our popular culture and is virtually inescapable. Explore your history with her. If you have never encountered Barbie before, explore your initial reactions to the images below.

Barbie Photos

The first Barbie, created in 1959, was inspired by the German Lilli doll, who, according to Yona Zeldis McDonough, author of *The Barbie Chronicles*, was "a quasi-pornographic toy intended for men." In her introduction to *The Barbie Chronicles*, McDonough writes that the creators of Barbie "cleaned her up and toned her down before presenting her to the American market, but her inherent sexuality—so stunning in a world of baby dolls and little girl dolls—remained intact, just waiting for a generation of American children to discover her." And discover her they did. Today, over 40 years later, Barbie remains a popular doll who has undergone various transformations over the years to keep up new generations of little girls.

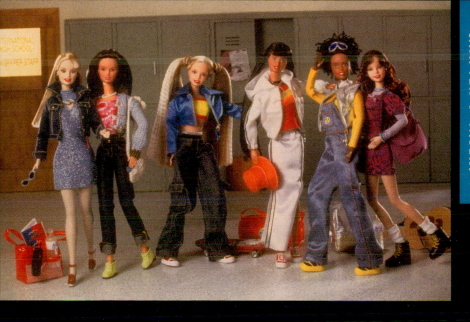

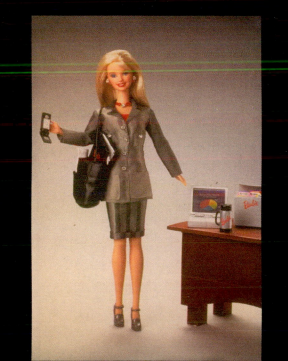

Literacy Connections

1. Compare the photos of the various Barbies. Write a paragraph in which you reflect on how Barbie has changed over the years.
2. What factors do you think account for the changes in Barbie over the decades?
3. Why do you think so many children—male and female—are attracted to plastic dolls? What need do the dolls satisfy?
4. What role did plastic dolls play in your life? Or, just in case you claim that you never played with dolls, what role did they play in the lives of your brothers, sisters, or friends?
5. This chapter includes Anna Quindlen's essay, "Barbie at 35," in which the author makes clear her disdain for the little plastic figure. Why do you think some individuals such as Quindlen have such a strong dislike for Barbie? What might account for their attitudes?

<u>**Before You Read**</u>

Yona Zeldis McDonough, author of *The Barbie Chronicles: A Living Doll Turns Forty,* included only one of her own essays in her collection—the essay you are about to read. As you read "Sex and the Single Doll," think about how McDonough's opinion of Barbie differs from Quindlen's, and about which opinion is closer to your own.

Sex and the Single Doll

Yona Zeldis McDonough

Yona Zeldis McDonough was born in Chadera, Israel, and grew up in Brooklyn, New York. Her novels include *The Four Temperaments* (Doubleday, 2002) and *In Dahlia's Wake* (Doubleday, 2005). Her collections of essays include *The Barbie Chronicles* (Touchstone, 1999) and *All the Available Light: A Marilyn Monroe Reader* (Touchstone, 2003). She is also the author of children's books designed to help young people learn about important historical figures, including Louis Armstrong, Anne Frank, John F. Kennedy, Nelson Mandela, Wolfgang Amadeus Mozart, and Harriet Tubman.

1   Now that my son is six and inextricably linked to the grade-school social circuit, he gets invited to birthday parties. Lots of them. Whenever I telephone to say he's coming, I always ask for hints on what might be a particularly coveted gift for the birthday child. And whenever that child is a girl, I secretly hope the answer will be the dirty little word I am longing to hear: *Barbie.*

2   No such luck. In the liberal Brooklyn neighborhood where we live, there is a definite bias against the poor doll, a veritable Barbie backlash. "My daughter loves her, but I can't stand her," laments one mother, "I won't let her in the house," asserts another. "Oh, please!" sniffs a third.

3   But I love Barbie. I loved her in 1963, when she made her entrance into my life. She was blond, with a Jackie Kennedy bouffant hairdo. Her thickly painted lids (carved out of plastic) and pouty, unsmiling mouth gave her a look both knowing and sullen. She belonged to a grown-up world of cocktail dresses, cigarette smoke, and perfume. I loved her in the years that followed, too, when she developed bendable joints; a twist-and-turn waist; long, silky ash-blond hair; and feathery, lifelike eyelashes. I never stopped loving her. I never will.

4   I've heard all of the arguments against her: She's a bimbo and an air-head; she's an insatiable consumer—for tarty clothes, a dream house filled with garish pink furniture, a pink Barbie-mobile—who teaches little girls that there is nothing in life quite so exciting as shopping. Her body, with its buoyant breasts, wasplike waist, and endless legs defies all human proportion. But at six, I inchoately understood Barbie's appeal: pure sex. My other dolls were either babies or little girls, with flat chests and chubby legs. Even the other so-called fashion dolls—Tammy, in her aqua-and-white playsuit, and Tressy, with that useless hank of hair, couldn't compete. Barbie was clearly a woman doll, and a woman was what I longed to be.

5   When I was eight, and had just learned about menstruation, I fashioned a small sanitary napkin for her out of neatly folded tissues. Rubber bands held it in place. "Oh, look," said my bemused mother, "Barbie's got her little period. Now she can have a baby." I was disappointed, but my girlfriends all snickered in a much more satisfying way. You see, I wanted Barbie to be, well, dirty. We all did.

6   Our Barbies had sex, at least our childish version of it. They hugged and kissed the few available boy dolls we had—clean-cut and oh-so-square Ken, the more relaxed and sexy Allan. They also danced, pranced, and strutted, but mostly they stripped, showing off their amazing, no-way-in-the-world human bodies. An adult friend tells me how she used to put her Barbie's low-backed bathing suit on backwards so the doll's breasts were exposed. I liked dressing mine in her pink-and-white candy-striped baby-sitter's apron—and nothing else.

7   I've also heard that Barbie is a poor role model for little girls. Is there such widespread contempt for the intelligence of children that we really imagine they are stupid enough to be shaped by a doll? Girls learn how to be women from the women around them. Most often this means Mom. My own was a march-to-a-different-drummer bohemian in the early sixties. She eschewed the beauty parlor, cards, and mah-jongg that the other moms in the neighborhood favored. Instead, she wore her long, black hair loose, her earrings big and dangling, and her lipstick dark. She made me a Paris bistro birthday party, with candles stuck in old wine bottles, red-and-white-checked tablecloths for decorations; she read the poetry of T.S. Eliot to the assembled group of enchanted ten-year-olds. She was, in those years, an aspiring painter, and her work graced not only the walls of our apartment, but also the shower curtain, bathroom mirror, and a chest of drawers in my room. She—not an eleven-and-a-half-a-inch doll—was the most powerful female role model in my life. What she thought of Barbie I really don't know, but she had the good sense to back off and let me use the doll my own way.

8   Barbie has become more politically correct over the years. She no longer looks so vixenish, and has traded the sultry expression I remember for one that is more wholesome and less covert. She now exists in a variety of "serious" incarnations: teacher, Olympic athlete, dentist. And Mattel recently introduced the Really Rad Barbie, a doll whose breasts and hips are smaller and whose waist is thicker, thus reflecting a more real (as if children wanted their toys to be real) female body. None of this matters one iota. Girls will still know the reason they love her, a reason that has nothing to do with new professions or a subtly amended figure.

9   Fortunately, my Barbie love will no longer have to content itself with buying gifts for my son's friends and the daughters of my own. I have a daughter now, and although she is just two, she already has half a dozen Barbies.

10   They are, along with various articles of clothing, furniture, and other essential accouterments, packed away like so many sleeping princesses in translucent pink plastic boxes that line my basement shelves. But the magic for which they wait is no longer the prince's gentle kiss. Instead, it is the heart and mind of my little girl as she picks them up and begins to play. I can hardly wait.

Literacy Connections

1. Based on the article you've read by McDonough, how do you think she would explain Barbie's role in our popular culture?
2. How does McDonough explain Barbie's appeal?
3. Do you agree with McDonough's explanation regarding Barbie's appeal? Why or why not?
4. McDonough asks: "Is there such widespread contempt for the intelligence of children that we really imagine they are stupid enough to be shaped by a doll?" Write a paragraph in which you respond to McDonough's question.
5. McDonough is as adamant in her praise of Barbie as Quindlen (the author of the preceding article, "Barbie Turns 35") is in her disdain of the little plastic figure. Their opinions are polar opposites, and yet, both are intelligent, respected, successful women. Consider both of their arguments and give your position.

Before You Read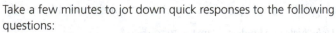

Take a few minutes to jot down quick responses to the following questions:

- How would you define the word *hero?*
- Who were the heroes of your childhood?

- Who are your heroes now?
- Do you think a pop culture celebrity can be a hero? Why or why not?
- In the following essay Jenny Lyn Bader discusses the changing role of heroes in our lives. She states: "Heroes are no longer in style"—that they went out of style in the 1970s and 1980s. What do you think of her assertion? Do you think she's right? Why or why not?

Larger Than Life

Jenny Lyn Bader

Jenny Lyn Bader is an essayist and playwright whose works include "Landing the Bachelor" (*New York Times*, May 5, 2002), "Ideas & Trends: The Necessity of Aimless Chitchat" (*New York Times*, January 6, 2002), and "In the Eye of the Beholder: When a Boom Begins" (*New York Times*, February 17, 2008). Bader's plays include *None of the Above*, first produced off-off Broadway in New York City in 2003 by the Obie-winning theater company New Georges, and published in the collection *Under 30: Plays for a New Generation* (Vintage).

"Larger Than Life" is the lead essay in the collection *Next: Young American Writers on the New Generation*, edited by Eric Liu (Norton, 1994).

1   When my grandmother was young, she would sometimes spot the emperor Franz Josef riding down the cobbled roads of the Austro-Hungarian Empire.

2   She came of age so long ago that the few surviving photographs are colored cream and chestnut. Early on, she saw cars replace horses and carriages. When she got older, she marveled at the first televisions. Near the end of her life, she grew accustomed to remote control and could spot prime ministers on color TV. By the time she died, the world was freshly populated by gadgetry and myth. Her generation bore witness to the rise of new machinery created by visionaries. My generation has seen machinery break down and visionaries come under fire.

3   As children, we enjoyed collecting visionaries, the way we collected toys or baseball cards. When I was a kid, I first met Patrick Henry and Eleanor Roosevelt, Abraham Lincoln and Albert Einstein. They could always be summoned by the imagination and so were never late for play dates. I thought heroes figured in any decent childhood. I knew their stats.

4   *Nathan Hale. Nelson Mandela. Heroes have guts.*

5   *Michelangelo. Shakespeare. Heroes have imagination.*

6   *They fight. Alexander the Great. Joan of Arc.*

7   *They fight for what they believe in. Susan B. Anthony. Martin Luther King.*

8   Heroes overcome massive obstacles. Beethoven, while deaf, still managed to carry an unforgettable tune. Homer, while blind, never failed to give an excellent description. Helen Keller, both deaf and blind, still spoke to the world. FDR, despite his polio, became president. Moses, despite his speech impediment, held productive discussions with God.

9   They inspire three-hour movies. They make us weepy. They do the right thing while enduring attractive amounts of suffering. They tend to be self-employed. They are often killed off. They sense the future. They lead lives that make us question our own. They are our ideals, but not our friends.

10   They don't have to be real. Some of them live in books and legends. They don't have to be famous. There are lower-profile heroes who get resurrected by ambitious biographers. There are collective heroes: firefighters and astronauts, unsung homemakers, persecuted peoples. There are those whose names we can't remember, only their deeds: "you know, that woman who swam the English Channel," "the guy who died running the first marathon," "the student who threw himself in front of the tank at Tiananmen Square." There are those whose names we'll never find out: the anonymous benefactor, the masked man, the undercover agent, the inventor of the wheel, the unknown soldier. The one who did the thing so gutsy and terrific that no one will ever know what it was.

11   Unlike icons (Marilyn, Elvis) heroes are not only sexy but noble, too. Unlike idols (Gretzky, Streisand), who vary from fan to fan, they are almost universally beloved. Unlike icons and idols, heroes lack irony. And unlike icons and idols, heroes are no longer in style.

12   As centuries end, so do visions of faith—maybe because the faithful get nervous as the double zeroes approach and question what they've been worshipping. Kings and queens got roughed up at the end of the eighteenth century; God took a beating at the end of the nineteenth; and as the twentieth century draws to a close, outstanding human beings are the casualties of the moment. In the 1970s and 1980s, Americans started feeling queasy about heroism. Those of us born in the sixties found ourselves on the cusp of that change. A sweep of new beliefs, priorities, and headlines has conspired to take our pantheon away from us.

13   Members of my generation believed in heroes when they were younger but now find themselves grasping for them. Even the word *hero* sounds awkward. I find myself embarrassed to ask people who their heroes are, because the word just doesn't trip off the tongue. My friend Katrin sounded irritated when I asked for hers. She said, "Oh, Jesus . . . Do people still have heroes?"

14   We don't. Certainly not in the traditional sense of adoring perfect people. Frequently not at all. "I'm sort of intrigued by the fact that I don't have heroes right off the top of my head," said a colleague, Peter. "Can I get back to you?"

15   Some of us are more upset about this than others. It's easy to tell which of us miss the heroic age. We are moved by schmaltzy political speeches, we warm up to stories of pets saving their owners, we even get misty-eyed watching the Olympics. We mope when model citizens fail us. My college roommate, Linda, remembers a seventh-grade class called "Heroes and She-roes." The first assignment was to write about a personal hero or she-ro. "I came home," Linda told me, "and cried and cried because I didn't have one . . . . Carter had screwed up in Iran and given the malaise speech. Gerald Ford was a nothing and Nixon was evil. My parents told me to write about Jane Fonda the political activist and I just kept crying."

16   Not everyone feels sentimental about it. A twentyish émigré raised in the former Soviet Union told me: "It's kind of anticlimactic to look for heroes when you've been brought up in a culture that insists on so many heroes . . . . What do you want me to say? Lenin? Trotsky?" Even though I grew up in the relatively propaganda-free United States, I understood. The America of my childhood insisted on heroes, too.

17   Of all the myths I happily ate for breakfast, the most powerful one was our story of revolution. I sang about it as early as kindergarten and read about it long after. The story goes, a few guys in wigs skipped town on some grumpy church leaders and spurned a loopy king to branch out on their own. The children who hear the story realize they don't have to believe in oldfangled clergy or a rusty crown—but they had better believe in those guys with the wigs.

18   I sure did. I loved a set of books known as the "Meet" series: *Meet George Washington*, *Meet Andrew Jackson*, *Meet the Men Who Sailed the Seas*, and many more. I remember one picture of an inspired Thomas Jefferson, his auburn ponytail tied in a black ribbon, penning words with a feather as a battle of banners and cannon fire raged behind him.

19   A favorite "Meet" book starred Christopher Columbus. His resistance to the flat-earth society of his day was engrossing, especially to a kid like me who had trouble trying new foods let alone seeking new land masses. I identified with his yearning for a new world and his difficulty with finding investors. Standing up to the king and queen of Spain was like convincing your parents to let you do stuff they thought was idiotic. Now, my allowance was only thirty-five cents a week, but that didn't mean I wasn't going to ask for three ships at some later date.

20   This is pretty embarrassing: I adored those guys. The ones in the white powder and ponytails, the voluptuous hats, the little breeches and cuffs. They were funny-looking, but lovable. They did outrageous things without asking for permission. They invented the pursuit of happiness.

21   I had a special fondness for Ben Franklin, statesman and eccentric inventor. Inventions, like heroes, made me feel as though I lived in a dull era. If I'd grown up at the end of the nineteenth century, I could have spoken on early telephones. A few decades later, I could have heard the new sounds of radio. In the sixties, I could have watched black-and-white TVs graduate to color.

22   Instead, I saw my colorful heroes demoted to black and white. Mostly white. By the time I finished high school, it was no longer hip to look up to the paternalistic dead white males who launched our country, kept slaves and mistresses, and massacred native peoples. Suddenly they weren't visionaries but oppressors, or worse—objects. Samuel Adams became a beer, John Hancock became a building, and the rest of the guys in wigs were knocked off one by one, in a whodunit that couldn't be explained away by the fact of growing up.

> **"By the time I finished high school, it was no longer hip to look up to the paternalistic dead white males who launched our country, kept slaves and mistresses, and massacred native peoples."**

23   The flag-waving of my youth, epitomized by America's bicentennial, was a more loving homage than I know today. The year 1976 rolled in while Washington was still reeling from Saigon, but the irony was lost on me and my second-grade classmates. The idea of losing seemed miles away. We celebrated July fourth with wide eyes and patriotic parties. Grown-ups had yet to tell themselves (so why should they tell us?) that the young nation on its birthday had suffered a tragic defeat.

24   Historians soon filled us in about that loss, and of others. Discovering America was nothing compared to discovering the flaws of its discoverers, now cast as imperialist sleaze, racist and sexist and genocidal. All things heroic—human potential, spiritual fervor, moral resplendence—soon became suspect. With the possible exception of bodybuilding, epic qualities went out of fashion. Some will remember 1992 as the year Superman died. Literally, the writers and illustrators at *D.C. Comics* decided the guy was too old to keep leaping buildings and rescuing an aging damsel in distress. When rumors circulated that he would be resurrected, readers protested via calls to radio shows, letters to editors, and complaints to stores that they were in no mood for such an event.

25   A monster named Doomsday killed Superman, overcoming him not with Kryptonite but with brute force. Who killed the others? I blame improved modes of character assassination, media hype artists, and scholars. The experts told me that Columbus had destroyed cultures and ravaged the environment. They also broke the news that the cowboys had brazenly taken land that wasn't theirs. In a way, I'm glad I didn't know that earlier; dressing up as a cowgirl for Halloween wouldn't have felt right. In a more urgent way, I wish I had known it then so I wouldn't have had to learn it later.

26   Just fifteen years after America's bicentennial came Columbus's quin-
centennial, when several towns canceled their annual parades in protest of
his sins. Soon other festivities started to feel funny. When my aunt served
corn pudding last Thanksgiving, my cousin took a spoonful, then said drily
that the dish was made in honor of the Indians who taught us to use corn
before we eliminated them. Uncomfortable chuckles followed. Actually,
neither "we" nor my personal ancestors had come to America in time to
kill any Native Americans. Yet the holiday put us in the same boat with the
pilgrims and anchored us in the white man's domain.

27   I am fascinated by how we become "we" and "they." It's as if siding with
the establishment is the Alka-Seltzer that helps us stomach the past. To swal-
low history lessons, we turn into "we": one nation under God of proud but
remorseful Indian killers. We also identify with people who look like us. For
example, white northerners studying the Civil War identify both with white
slaveholders and with northern abolitionists, aligning with both race and
place. Transsexuals empathize with men and women. Immigrants identify
with their homeland and their adopted country. Historians proposing a
black Athena and a black Jesus have inspired more of such bonding.

28   I'll admit that these empathies can be empowering. I always understood the idea of feeling stranded by unlikely role models but never emotionally grasped it until I watched Penny Marshall's movie *A League of
Their Own*. For the first time, I appreciated why so many women complain
that sports bore them. I had enjoyed baseball before but never as intensely
as I enjoyed the games in that film. The players were people like me. Lori
Petty, petite, chirpy, wearing a skirt, commanded the pitcher's mound with
such aplomb that I was moved. There's something to be said for identifying with people who remind us of ourselves, though Thomas Jefferson and
Lori Petty look more like each other than either of them looks like me. I'll
never know if I would've read the "Meet" books with more zeal if they'd
described our founding mothers. I liked them as they were.

31   Despite the thrill of dames batting something on the big screen besides
their eyelashes, the fixation on look-alike idols is disturbing for those who
get left out. In the movie *White Men Can't Jump*, Wesley Snipes tells Woody
Harrelson not to listen to Jimi Hendrix, because "White people can't hear
Jimi." Does this joke imply that black people can't hear Mozart? That I can
admire Geena Davis's batting but never appreciate Carlton Fisk? Besides
dividing us from one another, these emotional allegiances divide us from
potential heroes too, causing us to empathize with, say, General Custer and
his last stand instead of with Sitting Bull and the victorious Sioux.

32   Rejecting heroes for having the wrong ethnic credentials or sex organs
says less about our multicultural vision than our lack of imagination. By
focusing on what we are instead of who we can become, by typecasting

and miscasting our ideals—that's how we become "we" and "they." If heroes are those we'd like to emulate, it does make sense that they resemble us. But the focus on physical resemblance seems limited and racist.

33 Heroes should be judged on their deeds, and there are those with plenty in common heroically but not much in terms of ethnicity, nationality, or gender. Just look at Harriet Tubman and Moses; George Washington and Simón Bolívar; Mahatma Gandhi and Martin Luther King; Murasaki and Milton; Cicero and Ann Richards. Real paragons transcend nationality. It didn't matter to me that Robin Hood was English—as long as he did good, he was as American as a barbecue. It didn't matter to Queen Isabella that Columbus was Italian as

> "Oprah, Geraldo, and the rest turn their guests into heroes of the afternoon because they overcame abusive roommates, . . . cheerleading practice, or any sexual predilections."

long as he sailed for Spain and sprinkled her flags about. The British epic warrior Beowulf was actually Swedish. Both the German hero Etzel and the Scandinavian hero Atli were really Attila, king of the Huns. With all this borrowing going on, we shouldn't have to check the passports of our luminaries; the idea that we can be like them not literally but spiritually is what's uplifting in the first place.

34 The idea that we can never be like them has led to what I call jealousy journalism. You know, we're not remotely heroic so let's tear down anyone who is. It's become hard to remember which papers are tabloids. Tell-all articles promise us the "real story"—implying that greatness can't be real. The safe thing about *Meet George Washington* was that you couldn't actually meet him. Today's stories and pictures bring us closer. And actually meeting your heroes isn't the best idea. Who wants to learn that a favorite saint is really just an egomaniac with a publicist?

35 Media maestros have not only knocked public figures off their pedestals, they've also lowered heroism standards by idealizing just about everyone. Oprah, Geraldo, and the rest turn their guests into heroes of the afternoon because they overcame abusive roommates, childhood disfigurement, deranged spouses, multiple genitalia, cheerleading practice, or zany sexual predilections. In under an hour, a studio audience can hear their epic sagas told.

36 While TV and magazine producers helped lead heroes to their grave, the academic community gave the final push. Just as my peers and I made our way through college, curriculum reformers were promoting "P.C." agendas at the expense of humanistic absolutes. Scholars invented their own tabloidism, investigating and maligning both dead professors and trusty historical figures. Even literary theory helped, when deconstructionists made it trendy to look for questions instead of answers, for circular logic

instead of linear sense, for defects, contradictions, and the ironic instead of meaning, absolutes, and the heroic.

37   It was the generations that preceded ours who killed off our heroes. And like everyone who crucified a superstar, these people thought they were doing a good thing. The professors and journalists consciously moved in a positive direction—toward greater tolerance, openness, and realism—eliminating our inspirations in the process. The death of an era of hero worship was not the result of the cynical, clinical materialism too often identified with my generation. It was the side effect of a complicated cultural surgery, of an operation that may have been necessary and that many prescribed.

38   So with the best of intentions, these storytellers destroyed bedtime stories. Which is too bad for the kids, because stories make great teachers. Children glean by example. You can't tell a child "Be ingenious," or "Do productive things." You can tell them, "This Paul Revere person jumped on a horse at midnight, rode wildly through the dark, figured out where the mean British troops were coming to attack the warm, fuzzy, sweet, great-looking colonists, and sent messages by code, igniting our fight for freedom," and they'll get the idea. America's rugged values come gift wrapped in the frontier tales of Paul Bunyan, Daniel Boone, Davy Crockett—fables of independence and natural resources. Kids understand that Johnny Appleseed or Laura Ingalls Wilder would never need a Cuisinart. Pioneer and prairie stories convey the fun of roughing it, showing kids how to be self-reliant, or at least less spoiled.

39   Children catch on to the idea of imitating qualities, not literal feats. After returning his storybook to the shelf, little Billy doesn't look around for a dragon to slay. Far-off stories capture the imagination in an abstract but compelling way, different from, say, the more immediate action adventure flick. After watching a James Bond film festival, I might fantasize about killing the five people in front of in line at the supermarket, while legends are remote enough that Columbus might inspire one to be original, but not necessarily to study Portuguese or enlist in the navy. In tales about conquerors and cavaliers, I first flirted with the idea of ideas.

40   Even Saturday-morning cartoons served me as parables, when I woke up early enough to watch the classy Superfriends do good deeds. Sure, the gender ratio between Wonder Woman and the gaggle of men in capes seemed unfair, but I was rapt. I wonder whether I glued myself to my television and my high expectations with too much trust, and helped set my own heroes up for a fall.

41   Some heroes have literally been sentenced to death by their own followers. *Batman* subscribers, for example, were responsible for getting rid of Batman's sidekick, Robin. At the end of one issue, the Joker threatened to kill the Boy Wonder, and readers could decide whether Robin lived or died by calling one of two "900" numbers. The public voted overwhelmingly

for his murder. I understand the impulse of those who dialed for death. At a certain point, eternal invincibility grows as dull and predictable as wearing a yellow cape and red tights every day of the year. It's not human. We get fed up.

42   My generation helped kill off heroism as teenagers, with our language. We used heroic words that once described brave deeds—*excellent, amazing, awesome*—to describe a good slice of pizza or a sunny day. In our everyday speech, *bad* meant good. *Hot* meant cool. In the sarcastic slang of street gangs in Los Angeles, *hero* currently means traitor, specifically someone who snitches on a graffiti artist.

43   Even those of us who lived by them helped shatter our own myths, which wasn't all negative. We discovered that even the superhero meets his match. Every Achilles needs a podiatrist. Every rhapsodically handsome leader has a mistress or a moment of moral ambiguity. We injected a dose of reality into our expectations. We even saw a viable presidential candidate under a heap of slung mud, a few imperfections, an alleged tryst or two.

44   We're used to trysts in a way our elders aren't. Our parents and grandparents behave as if they miss the good old days when adulterers wore letter sweaters. They feign shock at the extramarital exploits of Thomas Jefferson, Frank Sinatra, JFK, and Princess Di. Their hero worship is a romance that falters when beloved knights end up unfaithful to their own spouses. People my age aren't amazed by betrayal. We are suspicious of shining armor. Even so, tabloid sales escalate when a Lancelot gives in to temptation—maybe because the jerk who cheats on you somehow becomes more attractive. Other generations have gossiped many of our heroes into philanderer. The presumptuous hero who breaks your heart is the most compelling reason not to get involved in the first place.

45   Seeing your legends discredited is like ending a romance, with someone you loved but ultimately didn't like; however much you longed to trust that person, it just makes more sense not to. Why pine away for an aloof godlet who proves unstable, erratic, and a rotten lover besides? It's sad to give up fantasies but mature to trade them in for healthier relationships grounded in reality.

46   We require a new pantheon: a set of heroes upon whom we can rely, who will not desert us when the winds change, and whom we will not desert. It's unsettling, if not downright depressing, to go through life embarrassed about the identity of one's childhood idols.

47   Maybe we should stick to role models instead. Heroes have become quaint, as old-fashioned as gas-guzzlers—and as unwieldy, requiring too much investment and energy. Role models are more like compact cars, less glam and roomy but easier to handle. They take up less parking space in the imagination. Role models have a certain degree of consciousness about

their job. The cast members of "Beverly Hills, 90210," for example, have acknowledged that they serve as role models for adolescents, and their characters behave accordingly: they refrain from committing major crimes; they overcome inclinations toward substance abuse; they see through adult hypocrisy; and any misdemeanors they do perpetrate are punished. For moral mediators we could do better, but at least the prime-time writing staff is aware of the burden of having teen groupies.

48   Heroes don't have the luxury of staff writers or the opportunity to endorse designer jeans. Hercules can't go on "Nightline" and pledge to stop taking steroids. Prometheus can't get a presidential pardon. Columbus won't have a chance to weep to Barbara Walters that he did-n't mean to endanger leatherback turtles or monk seals or the tribes of the Lucayas. Eliza-beth I never wrote a best-seller about how she did it her way.

> **"Role models are admirable individuals who haven't given up their lives or livelihoods and may even have a few hangups."**

49   Role models can go on talk shows, or even host them. Role models may live next door. While a hero might be a courageous head of state, a saint, a leader of armies, a role model might be someone who put in a three-day presidential bid, your local minister, your boss. They don't need their planes to go down in flames to earn respect. Role models have a job, accomplishment, or hairstyle worth emulating.

50   Rather than encompassing that vast kit and caboodle of ideals, role models can perform a little neat division of labor. One could wish to give orders like Norman Schwarzkopf but perform psychoanalysis like Lucy Van Pelt, to chair a round-table meeting as well as King Arthur but negotiate as well as Queen Esther, to eat like Orson Welles but look like Helen of Troy, and so forth. It was General Schwarzkopf, the most tangible military hero for anyone my age, who vied instead for role-model status by claiming on the cover of his book: *It Doesn't Take a Hero.* With this title he modestly implies that anyone with some smarts and élan could strategize and storm as well as he has.

51   Role models are admirable individuals who haven't given up their lives or livelihoods and may even have a few hangups. They don't have to be prone to excessive self-sacrifice. They don't go on hunger strikes; they diet. They are therefore more likely than heroes to be free for lunch, and they are oftener still alive.

52   Heroism is a living thing for many of my contemporaries. In my informal poll, I not only heard sob stories about the decline of heroes, I also discovered something surprising: the ascent of parents. While the founding fathers may be passe, actual mothers, fathers, grands, and great-grands are undeniably "in." An overwhelming number of those I polled named their household forebearers as those they most admired. By choosing their own

relatives as ideals, people in their twenties have replaced impersonal heroes with the most personal role models of all. Members of my purportedly lost generation have not only realized that it's time to stop believing in Santa Claus, they have chosen to believe instead in their families—the actual tooth fairy, the real Mr. and Mrs. Claus. They have stopped needing the folks from the North Pole, the guys with the wigs, the studs and studettes in tights and capes.

53   In a way it bodes well that Superman and the rest could be killed or reported missing. They were needed to quash the most villainous folks of all: insane communists bearing nuclear weapons, heinous war criminals, monsters named Doomsday. The good news about Superman bleeding to death was that Doomsday died in the struggle.

54   If the good guys are gone, so is the world that divides down the middle into good guys and bad guys. A world without heroes is a rigorous, demanding place, where things don't boil down to black and white but are rich with shades of gray; where faith in lofty, dead personages can be replaced by faith in ourselves and one another; where we must summon the strength to imagine a five-dimensional future in colors not yet invented. My generation grew up to see our world shift, so it's up to us to steer a course between naivete and nihilism, to reshape vintage stories, to create stones of spirit without apologies.

55   I've heard a few. There was one about the woman who taught Shakespeare to inner-city fourth graders in Chicago who were previously thought to be retarded or hopeless. There was a college groundskeeper and night watchman, a black man with a seventh-grade education, who became a contracts expert, wrote poetry and memoirs, and invested his salary so wisely that he bequeathed 450 acres of mountainous parkland to the university when he died. There was the motorcyclist who slid under an eighteen-wheeler at full speed, survived his physical therapy only to wind up in a plane crash, recovered, and as a disfigured quadriplegic started a business, got happily married, and ran for public office; his campaign button bore a caption that said "Send me to Congress and I won't be just another pretty face. . . . "

56   When asked for her heroes, a colleague of mine spoke of her great-grandmother, a woman whose husband left her with three kids in Galicia, near Poland, and went to the United States. He meant to send for her, but the First World War broke out. When she made it to America, her husband soon died, and she supported her family; at one point she even ran a nightclub. According to the great-granddaughter, "When she was ninety she would tell me she was going to volunteer at the hospital. I would ask how and she'd say, 'Oh, I just go over there to read to the old folks.' The 'old folks' were probably seventy. She was a great lady."

57   My grandmother saved her family, too, in the next great war. She did not live to see the age of the fax, but she did see something remarkable in her time, more remarkable even than the emperor riding down the street: she saw him walking down the street. I used to ask her, "Did you really see the emperor Franz Josef walking down the street?"

58   She would say, "Ya. Walking down the street." I would laugh, and though she'd repeat it to amuse me, she did not see what was so funny. To me, the emperor was someone you met in history books, not on the streets of Vienna. He was larger than life, a surprising pedestrian. He was probably just getting some air, but he was also laying the groundwork for my nostalgia of that time when it would be natural for him to take an evening stroll, when those who were larger than life roamed cobblestones.

59   Today, life is larger.

Literacy Connections

1. What do you see as the main idea Jenny Lyn Bader is trying to communicate in her essay on heroes? What is the purpose of her essay?
2. What does Bader have to say about our disillusionment with heroes? What examples does she offer to substantiate her claims?
3. Do you agree with Bader's claim regarding our disillusionment of heroes? If you do, what do you think accounts for this difference in the way many of us think today? If you disagree with Bader, explain your position.
4. Bader states that heroes "don't have to be real. Some of them live in books and legends." Make a quick list of your heroes. Which are real? Which aren't? Does your list include more real or unreal heroes? What do you think might account for that?
5. In the chapter's opening essay, "A Pop Life," Stacey Suver stresses the importance of critically reading the popular culture that surrounds us. How can we critically read the heroes that make up part of that culture? What would such a reading involve?

Before You Read

In the previous essay, "Larger Than Life," Jenny Lyn Bader makes reference to make-believe heroes " . . . who live in books and legends." Before you read the following review of the first installment in the comic book series *Locke & Key: Welcome to Lovecraft*, take a few minutes to think about the make-believe heroes from comic books and graphic novels you're familiar with and the role of comic books and graphic novels in popular culture.

Graphic Novel Review of *Locke & Key* by Joe Hill and Gabriel Rodriguez

Mel Odom

Mel Odom's review of *Locke & Key* was first published on September 26, 2008, on the Web site Blogcritics.org. Odom is the author of more than 100 novels, and on his blog site he describes himself as " . . . a father, a little league coach, a teacher, a friend, and a writer." He teaches writing courses at the University of Oklahoma in Norman and at the Moore-Norman Technology Center in Norman, Oklahoma.

1   I'm harder to scare these days than when I was a kid and horror movies were still black and white and filled with trademark Hollywood monsters. Currently, I've been through a plethora of Dracula, Frankenstein, Wolfman, and ghost movies and their spawn. It takes a lot to scare me these days.

2   Then Hollywood introduced me to *Friday the 13th, Halloween*, and *Nightmare on Elm Street*. George C. Scott's *The Changeling* totally creeped me out, and Tobe Hooper/Steven Spielberg's *Poltergeist* taught me to fear my television. Then I watched adaptations of Thomas Harris' novels, *Red Dragon* and *Silence of the Lambs* and learned to fear serial killers who were really among us.

3   However, I have to admit that somewhere in there I became jaded. I started watching horror movies for special effects and the snappy one-liners that became so popular. I ended up laughing through most of them.

4   Like I said, I'm hard to scare. Of course, I can still scare myself pretty good. Let me curl up at night with a Stephen King book or one of Joseph Delaney's *The Last Apprentice* YA novels, and I can give myself a case of the willies. These books, thankfully, still deliver the sheer, enervating atmosphere necessary to amp up my adrenaline gland.

5   But I found a new fear-inducer in Joe Hill. I discovered him in *Heart-Shaped Box* and got totally weirded out listening to that novel on audiobook. Then I got my hands on the first issue of his comic book series, *Locke & Key*.

6   Imagine a family that falls victim to what appears to be a deranged teenager looking for some payback. That's pretty horrific by today's standards because the news is full of lethal teens—and others. This could happen, so I wasn't immediately getting the spook vibe.

7   The story is harsh and emotional. I felt Ty, Kinsey, and Bodie's pain over losing their father to violence. The way that Joe cut the action between the past and present really upped the suspense and impending feeling of

doom. Gabriel Rodriguez's art is loose and captivating, and he plays with angles that pulled me right into the frames and turned them into movies. I was THERE, inside the story on several occasions. And I wasn't comfortable being there. Especially in the scenes when Bodie was talking to the thing in the wellhouse!

8   As it turns out, though, the teen that planned the murder of Papa Locke wasn't entirely there out of vengeance. He had made a pact with the thing in the wellhouse, and that just spins the whole story on its ear.

9   After their father's murder, the kids end up at the Locke House, a place so riddled with mysteries that Joe says he's got 70 issues plotted out for those bewitched doors, nooks, and crannies already. Personally, I can't wait. I love the puzzles and the mysteries, as well as the fact that THINGS are lurking inside the house and waiting to spring out on unwary victims.

10   Joe and Gabriel have created a whole WORLD of spine-chilling entertainment to come. It's no surprise that Dimension Films has already snapped up the film rights to the property, or that IDW publishing had to reprint the issues several times. I expect they'll have to reprint the new hardcover graphic novel as well, but I didn't take any chances—I've got my copy already.

11   In the various issues, Joe shifts the point of view around from Ty to Bodie to Kinsey, and all of them achieve a distinct voice that bring a different flavor to the emerging story. When I read the graphic novel all at once, the voices didn't quite stand out as much as waiting a month between, but that's only because I was trying to get to the end of the story faster and faster. I'd read the first three issues, then couldn't get my hands on the last three, so I was desperate to know what happened next.

12   The suspense ratchets up like a whipsaw rollercoaster cresting the top of the final plunge leading to a white-knuckled grip (thank God the book is a hardcover or it wouldn't have survived the read!).

13   I couldn't stop reading, and now I can't wait for the next volume in the Locke family's adventures. The old house has a lot of life (and UNLIFE) still waiting to be discovered and feared.

14   Horror fans will love this book because it delivers every delicious thrill and chill a reader could want. And Gabriel's art is absolutely eye-popping: alternately beautiful and then gruesome. *Locke & Key* is a definite, pulse-pounding winner.

Literacy Connections

1. How would you describe the primary audience for whom Mel Odom is writing in his online review of *Locke & Key*? How does this particular envisioned audience affect his writing style?

2. How would you describe the persona Odom creates for himself in his review of *Locke & Key*?
3. If you are a fan of comic books and graphic novels, does Odom's review entice you to read *Locke & Key*? Why or why not? If you are not a fan of comic books and graphic novels, does his review entice you to consider reading this series, even though you usually shy away from this genre? Why or why not?
4. What role do you think comic books and graphic novels play in popular culture? Why are so many readers fans of this genre?
5. How does the writing style Odom uses differ from the style used by Daniel B. Wood in his article "Outpouring over Michael Jackson Unlike Anything Since Princess Di" that appeared earlier in the chapter? How are the writing styles in the two pieces similar?

Before You Read

Following is an interview with Joe Hill, author of the comic book series *Locke & Key*. As you read the interview, think about the review that you just read of the first installment in the series and about how the image you envisioned of Joe Hill as you read the review differs from the image of him you envision as you read the following interview with him.

One fact about Joe Hill that you might find interesting is that he is Stephen King's son—a tidbit of information Hill did his best to keep a secret until he made a name for himself on his own.

Interview with Joe Hill from Graphic Novel Reporter

The interview that follows was first published in June 2009, on the Web site graphicnovelreporter.com, presented by Bookreporter.com.

1   The acclaim for Joe Hill's work continues! His bestselling series *Locke & Key* has just been nominated for two Eisner Awards: Best Limited Series and Best Writer. Now, get to meet Hill yourself in our Behind the Scenes interview.

Do you remember your first comic book or graphic novel? If so, what was it?

2 The first comic book I ever read that cut deep emotionally was the issue of *Spider-Man* in which Gwen Stacy's father was felled by a collapsing chimney. The idea that a good person, a heroic person, could be struck down just because he was standing in the wrong place at the wrong time impressed and moved me. I was also taken with Wendy and Richard Pini's *Elfquest* graphic novels at a very young age. I haven't revisited them in a while, but in memory at least, they strike me as being much riskier and more adult than a lot of the other adventure stuff being done in comic books at that time.

3   It's an interesting, valid question, but I do think that one thing that holds the art form back is the way readers and creators alike fetishize the comic books they read as kids. Most of the stuff I read when I was a little guy was crap. I had the complete run of *Godzilla: King of the Monsters*. I got off on *ROM: Space Knight*. Ninety percent of the comics I read in childhood aren't worth thinking about. The work I care about the most is stuff I've read in the last 10 years, work being published right now, not what I read back when I was wearing Hulk T-shirts to fourth grade.

What do you love about the graphic novel as a format for storytelling?

4 For starters, comics are a hell of a lot of fun to write. I read an article once about a guy who was working as a coder for Rock Star games. And he said he had never imagined he could have a job that made him so happy and left him feeling so fulfilled. He'd roll into work about 11 a.m. and write code until 7 in the evening, then break for pizza and foosball in the rec room, maybe watch a little sports with his buddies. When he felt rested up, he'd go back into his cubicle and code some more until midnight. For him, there was no separation between work and play. And that's kind of how I feel about writing comic books.

5   Also, I think comic books amplify the things I do best—dialogue, action, concepts—while freeing me from the part of writing I fret over the most, the sound and flow of my prose. There's no prose in comics. The pictures are the prose.

Whose work do you admire?

6 Alan Moore and Neil Gaiman are on the short list of my very favorite living writers who aren't actually related to me by blood. Alan Moore and *Swamp Thing* are the reason I write comics . . . which is not to say I think

Swamp Thing is his best work, only that I happened to come across it at just the right time in my life, and it instilled in me some ideas about how character can drive story. As a collection of chilling supernatural tales, *Swamp Thing* is right there with the *Books of Blood*.

7   Among the current crop of writers, I'm very high on Brian K. Vaughan, Ed Brubaker, and Jason Aaron. Warren Ellis's body of work is an abundance of riches. Terry Moore's *Echo* is probably my current favorite monthly. I look at it as the greatest 1980s sci-fi film never made. It's right in the mold of *Starman*, *Back to the Future*, and *The Last Starfighter*. It does it all: action, quiet, believable romance, comedy. I tried to get my wife to read it and she asked what it was about, and I said it was the story of a woman who winds up with a pair of fusion-powered superboobs, and that was about as far as that went. But *Echo* really is all kinds of awesome.

8   As far as artists go, I'll read anything drawn by Tony Harris, Steve Parkhouse, Frank Quitely, Jim Mahfood. Just to start. As a kid, I pretty much had no interest in who wrote what—I bought comics solely based on who drew them. Writers provide the chassis, but artists put together the engine. I've been lucky to work with Gabriel Rodriguez on *Locke & Key*: He's a fuel-injected V12.

Who do you read outside of the graphic novel format?

9   Someone asked me the other day what my five favorite musical acts were, and I said Stones, Beatles, AC/DC, Springsteen, and Steve Earle. And realized I might as well have dropped dead in 1988, because my tastes apparently froze with *Copperhead Road*.

10   I'm sorry to say my reading tastes aren't any more original or edgy. I read a lot of Elmore Leonard, because I think his novels are textbooks on how to write all the things that matter (to me, anyway): character, dialogue, action, the struggle to stay cool under pressure. I love Cormac McCarthy's stern, archaic language and apocalyptic settings; he writes great dialogue too, although that isn't usually noted as one of his strengths. Probably goes without saying I'm a big Stephen King fan.

What kind of reaction do you get when you tell people what you do?

11   My writer friends are always stoked—everyone my age who writes fiction digs that comics are not just an exciting and valid literary form, but also that they're out on the bleeding edge of pop culture. If you look at movies right now, you see a billion-dollar business exploiting yesterday's comics.

If you look at novels, you see a lot of writers wrestling with the outsize and outrageous influence of pop culture on modern life, and comics in particular (*Kavalier & Clay, Fortress of Solitude, Oscar Wao* . . . do I need to say more?).

12   My nonwriter friends are usually amiably puzzled by the comic book thing. The novels they get. And they understand a compulsion to noodle around with short stories. But the appeal of comics is harder to see. Because ultimately comics are still looked at as a little bit of a dodgy, not quite mature form of entertainment. And a lot of them *are* dodgy and immature and ridiculous. Which is why I love them. I'm not one of these dudes who are obsessed with comic books "growing up" and getting respect. I'm not sure I want them to grow up and get respect. I don't want comics to go John Updike on me. I want them to stay scrappy and disreputable.

Do you collect comics? What is the most valuable piece of art, graphic novel, or comic book in your collection?

13   I've got a couple long boxes in the office, and put the comics in bags after I've read 'em. But I'm not a collector in the true sense. I hate seeing a comic in one of those hermetically sealed airtight boxes. Your comics aren't dead bodies and don't need the coffin treatment. To me, a comic with a big fold across the cover and stains from pizza grease on the pages is worth more, because it was read and enjoyed.

14   Probably the most valuable piece of comic art I own, in an emotional sense, is Gabriel Rodriguez's cover to issue #2 of *Locke & Key: Head Games*, which shows Bode's character reimagined as a phrenology diagram.

Is there something you covet adding to your collection?

15   There's a Buscema *Conan* cover I've always wanted, but I wouldn't break the bank to get it. For me, comics are a pure hit of the best high in modern storytelling; I don't need the original issues of, say, *Swamp Thing*, to enjoy it. I don't need the *Absolute* edition either. The inexpensive trade paperbacks are fine. The story is still there, still the same, still good.

Literacy Connections

1. What do we learn about Joe Hill in this interview that we might not learn in an article about the writer? What are the advantages of writing in this genre?

2. When asked about the reaction he receives when he tells people that he writes comics, Hill shares, "My writer friends are always stoked—everyone my age who writes fiction digs that comics are not just an exciting and valid literary form, but also that they're out on the bleeding edge of pop culture." Explore this idea. In what ways are comics ". . . on the bleeding edge of pop culture"?

3. Hill states in the interview: ". . . ultimately comics are still looked at as a little bit of a dodgy, not quite mature form of entertainment. And a lot of them *are* dodgy and immature and ridiculous." What do you think of Hill's claims? Do you agree or disagree with him? Explain your answer.

4. If you had the opportunity to conduct an interview with Joe Hill, what questions would you ask that the *Graphic Novel Reporter* did not ask? What else would you like to know about this writer?

5. How do you think Anthony DeCurtis, author of "I'll Take My Stand: A Defense of Popular Culture" (which appears earlier in the chapter) would respond to someone who claimed that comics are a form of "low culture"? How do you think Hill would respond to the same claim?

Before You Read

Now that you've read a review of Joe Hill's *Locke & Key: Welcome to Lovecraft* and an interview with the author, take time to read the first six pages of the comic. As you read, think about the following statement from the interview:

"As a kid, I pretty much had no interest in who wrote what—I bought comics solely based on who drew them. Writers provide the chassis, but artists put together the engine. I've been lucky to work with Gabriel Rodriguez on *Locke & Key*: He's a fuel-injected V12."

Literacy Connections

1. How would you describe Joe Hill's writing style in these opening pages of *Locke & Key: Welcome to Lovecraft*?

2. How would you describe Gabriel Rodriguez's artwork on these pages?

3. Millions of people are fans of comics and graphic novels, and these publications have an enormous effect on popular culture. What do you see as the appeal of comics and graphic novels such as *Locke & Key: Welcome to Lovecraft*? Why do you think they are so popular?

4. What do you think of the way that many would call "profanity" is used in many contemporary comic books and graphic novels? Is it appropriate? Why or why not?

5. Joe Hill states in the previous interview: "Writers provide the chassis, but artists put together the engine. I've been lucky to work with Gabriel Rodriguez on *Locke & Key*: He's a fuel-injected V12." Do you think that Hill's writing and Rodriguez's artwork complement each other? Why or why not?

Popular Culture Literacy Projects

Popular Culture Literacy Narrative and Reflection

For this assignment, you'll write a composition in which you reflect on particular elements of popular culture that have played a role in shaping who you are. To help you focus your topic, you might choose one area of popular entertainment (such as film, television, contemporary music, books, magazines, or video games) and the role that type of popular culture has played in your life. Or you might write about your fascination with celebrity culture and how particular celebrities have influenced whom you have become.

The writing you do for this essay should go beyond narration. In addition to telling your reader about the popular culture influences that have affected you, you need to reflect on *how* a particular type of popular entertainment or certain celebrities have influenced you, both positively and negatively. For example, you must go beyond telling your reader about the various video games or celebrities you have been obsessed with over the years and also discuss how playing those games or having those celebrities for role models has played a role in shaping your personality and the choices you have made in life.

Popular Culture Analysis Essay

Choose a pop culture event or artifact that interests you and that you would like to carefully analyze. For example, you might choose to analyze and write about a pop culture event such as the transition of Hannah Montana to Miley Cyrus or the changes in the ways the media depicts Tom Cruise from the days of *Risky Business* and *Top Gun* to the emphasis today on his involvement with Scientology. You might analyze a pop culture event such as the annual Cannes Film Festival, MTV Music Awards Ceremony, Super Bowl Halftime Shows, etc. Or maybe you'd like to analyze and write about a pop culture artifact such as a particular kind of toy that is currently popular or perhaps one that has gone through various versions or models over the years—such as Barbie, GI Joe, Mr. Potato Head, Lego, Game Boy, etc. Or perhaps you'd like to analyze a television show that ran for years (such as *The Price Is Right*, *The Simpsons*, *As the World Turns*, *American Idol*, etc.). Be careful to narrow your topic so that you can analyze the event or artifact in the appropriate paper length. In your analysis, consider rhetorical features such as purpose, audience, and context.

Magazine Feature Article

Write an article for a popular culture magazine of your choice, one with which you are familiar and enjoy reading. Take time to carefully look through several editions of the magazine of your choice and analyze its content, style, structure, and audience. Choose a topic that you find engaging—one you truly want to explore—and that would be suitable for publication in the magazine you've chosen. Use the kind of style and structure in your article that is common to the publication for which you are writing. Conduct research as needed to inform your writing, and be sure to give credit in your article to the sources you use.

Television Self-Study

For this project, you'll conduct a self-study in which you keep a record of what you watch on television during a typical week. Keep a journal in which you record the names of the shows and the number of minutes you spend in front of the TV during the week. Make notes as you watch the various TV programs to help you remember what they were about. At the end of the week, analyze the kinds of shows you watched, what they were about, why you watched those particular shows, what you learned from them, and the effect they had on you. Write an essay in which you present your information and analyze it.

Mini-ethnography of a Subculture

For this project, you'll choose a subculture of popular culture, observe it at least five times, take notes, conduct interviews, and write a mini-ethnography in which you analyze the subculture you are observing. You might choose a group to which you already belong, or you might decide to observe and write about a group to which you don't belong. Examples of various subcultures you might analyze and write about include a book club that discusses current best sellers, a group that meets regularly (online, in person, or both) to compete against each other in video games, a group that gets together regularly to play cards, or one that meets regularly to watch reruns of *Seinfeld*, *Friends*, *Sex and the City*, or *Star Trek*, etc. The possibilities go on and on. Choose a group that you find interesting and would like to study.

Group Project: Pop Culture Zine

In a group, you'll create a popular culture zine (a self-published magazine), write the articles for it, and create a published version to either hand in or share online. First, decide on a concept or magazine that would interest the entire group. Perhaps you would like to create a competitor for *Rolling Stone*, *People*, or *Glamour.* As a group, you'll determine your imagined magazine's overall mission/goal/theme, appropriate content, textual style, layout, and audience. Once you have properly formed this analysis, you can choose a topic of interest, conduct the needed research, and write your articles. You'll need to decide how many articles to include and who will write what. For your final draft, your group will compile its articles, determine layout designs, and construct a rhetorically appropriate cover. Although you might write independently, you'll come together to the workshop, discussing how effective the zine's tone, style, and content is. You should add pictures and at least one advertisement. Remember, your material should be mentally engaging, while your layout should be visually appealing.

In addition to submitting your finished magazine, you'll need to give your instructor your drafts, a process memo, and a two- to three-page rhetorical analysis. The rhetorical analysis tells your instructor your group's purpose and audience and outlines your group's editorial decisions and rationale for those decisions. Basically, it's a guide to your magazine: It explains what your group did and why.

8

Situating Academic Literacies

Now that you're a college student, you're probably coming to realize that academic writing is its own kind of literacy, and that each academic field (the natural sciences, the social sciences, the humanities, etc.) has its own ways of thinking, its own genres, and its own conventions.

As composition professor Fiona Glade says in the introductory essay of this chapter, "A college campus is made up of many different discourse communities. As such, there is no single academic discourse." The chapter won't give you a single, easy definition of academic literacies. But it will immerse you in a variety of academic literacies and ask you to critically reflect on your experiences as a college student writing across the curriculum. Part of this critical reflection will mean considering conflicts of race, class, and gender in your entry into academic discourse communities. You'll find that the further along you get in college, the more you'll be asked to think and write like a disciplinary "insider." As Glade says, "Your instructors are asking you to demonstrate that you know how to think like an insider, following the practices of a member of that disciplinary discourse community: therefore, your academic writing should reflect the way that scholars communicate with one another in any given field." The chapter will give you tools to make the transition to academic literacy "insider" and encourage you to add your voice to the ongoing conversations of academic discourse communities.

You'll find selections that will—

- Explore the idea that there is no single set of "rules" for college literacy
- Help you think about what it means to read and write across the college curriculum
- Give you a look at the process that Greg Calabrese, a junior sociology major, went through as he composed a sociology research report
- Help you learn to more effectively adapt to different academic writing situations
- Give you examples of writing outcomes and award-winning student writing from across the curriculum
- Encourage you to think critically about issues of power, race, class, and gender in college literacies.

If you respond to the academic literacy projects at the end of the chapter, you might—

- Analyze college writing assignments
- Interview a college professor
- Discuss the teachers who have influenced you
- Study your own college reading and writing experiences
- Practice conducting academic research
- Analyze an academic discourse community.

Now, let's start thinking about what academic literacy means.

What Are Academic Literacies?

Before You Read

Before you explore the definitions of academic literacies in the essay that follows, use your own experiences with reading and writing assignments in college to come up with a list of features of academic literacies. Be prepared to share this list with the class.

Writing Across the University: Academic Discourse as a Conversation

Fiona Glade

Having earned her Ph.D. at Washington State University, Fiona Glade professes Rhetoric and Composition at California State University, Sacramento.

We should not take lightly the choice of which genres we ask our students to write in. Nor should we keep those choices invisible to students, as though all writing required the same stances, commitments, and goals; as though all texts shared pretty much the same forms and features; as though all literacy were the same. Nor should we ignore students' perceptions of where they are headed and what they feel about the places we point them toward.

—Charles Bazerman: "Life"

1   For many of us, when we began writing for the academic discourse community, we were given a set of rules to follow: the rules that I recall hearing in my own high school classes ran the gamut from stern warning—"*Never* begin a sentence with *and, but,* or *because!*" or "a good essay *always* has five paragraphs"—to gentle encouragement—"write what you *feel*: write towards your *own* truth" and "revision is a writer's best friend." By the time I began college, many years later, I certainly relied on my recollection of those rules, contradictory as they often were, when I needed to make sense of my professors' expectations. This task was made all the more difficult, it seemed to me, by the fact that every professor, every class, wanted something different. For example, while "write what you feel" worked just fine for the personal narrative essays I was assigned in my basic writing class, the five paragraph rule didn't get me a passing grade in my philosophy class. Likewise, while one history professor gave us time to draft, workshop, and revise our writing, another history professor commented only on the grammar errors in my essays. To complicate matters even more, the way in which one professor defined a particular genre was often at odds with the way in which another defined the same genre; in other classes, the persona I selected might be acceptable to one professor yet unacceptable to another.

2   Like the discourse of any community, academic discourse certainly does rely on rules and guidelines. Speaking and writing—but especially writing—are the means by which people in the university engage one another in conversation: writing strategies such as using a shared vocabulary, a commonly understood format, or a specified genre in written communication help writers get their message across in a way that their audience of coworkers will understand more readily. Writing is most often the way in which people in various fields—in college and beyond—have conversations about their field. For example, when I write an article that I'd like to share with other composition professors, I cite sources according to guidelines provided by the American Psychological Association or by the Modern Language Association. Likewise, when I write a course syllabus to share with student colleagues, I use a specific format that includes course goals and a course calendar. These rhetorical choices provide a vehicle for the exchange of knowledge, which is what drives the conversations

of the academy. Charles Bazerman, who participates in the academic discourse community as a professor studying Rhetoric and Composition, reminds us that "Knowledge produced by the academy is cast primarily in written language" (*Shaping* 18); therefore, an understanding of the guidelines or rules—sometimes called the *conventions*—used in any given genre is necessary in order to participate in academic conversations.

3   Certainly, many of us come to college with some assumptions about what those rules are. You may have brought with you some ideas of your own about what constitutes a good essay, or even about the kinds of writing assignments you'll be asked to complete throughout your college career. For instance, the discourse used by those in universities is perceived by some readers to be the absolute epitome of grammatical correctness; however, other audiences may view it as overtly political, or others still as quite dry and boring. In other words, people's assumptions about academic discourse—about what it really is—are extraordinarily varied. Indeed, it is hard to come up with a definition of academic discourse: the task of defining such a complex term could take as long as it takes to get a college degree! We might think of it as a process, much like writing: in order to get to a workable definition, we need to gain a deeper understanding of the college context, of the genres of writing we do in college courses, and of the various audiences for whom we write in college assignments.

4   In fact, a college campus is made up of many different discourse communities. As such, there is no single academic discourse. Perhaps you've found in your own courses that what works well for one piece of academic writing doesn't necessarily work well for another, even when the assignments appear very similar. David Russell, a college professor who teaches and studies writing, explains that "within academia, the conventions (and beyond them the assumptions and methodologies) of the various disciplines are characterized more by their differences than by their similarities" (329). Russell continues by pointing out that "To speak of the academic community as if its members shared a single set of linguistic conventions and traditions of inquiry is to make a categorical mistake" (328). This is significant to an understanding of academic discourses in general because it demonstrates that while there exist enormous differences among academic discourses, there are reasons for those differences.

5   For example, citation guidelines vary greatly among the different academic discourse communities. Instructors will usually require that you use a certain set of citation conventions when they give you a writing assignment; however, correct citation formats are different in each discipline. Writers in the humanities normally follow the guidelines of the Modern Language Association (MLA): the rules for this citation style include a specific format for in-text citation as well as a Works Cited page. On the other

hand, writers in the social sciences often use American Psychology Association format rules, which include a different format for in-text citations, along with a Bibliography. These two different conventions—a Works Cited page and a Bibliography—certainly serve a similar purpose: they inform the audience, who are assumed to be members of that academic or professional discourse community, where the sources were found. However, their different formats exist for a reason: each is indicative of a particular set of concerns shared by the academic discourse community by which it's used. In APA conventions, it's the date of a source that's emphasized: this is because the social science disciplines place higher value on using the most current research available than do the humanities. Still, even though these differences exist within the university, one value that's shared across the disciplines is the importance of citing sources. It's important, then, to understand which citation guidelines your instructors expect you to use, since preferences about citation style reveal far more about the writing for that discipline than meets the eye. In order to be able to participate more fully in the academic discourse community, we need to consider not only *how* to write for each specific context, but also *why* each of those contexts has its own set of rules and guidelines.

Problem-Posing Across the Disciplines

6 In "Banking Concept of Education," Paulo Freire asserts that students are often not encouraged to think for themselves; in the model of education that he describes, while students are learning to participate in a new discourse community by following the genre guidelines of that community, they may have very few opportunities to explore and understand the reasons behind that particular community's rules and guidelines. Freire suggests that one way to fix this is to teach and learn using the "problem-posing" approach. In this model, we learn more about any given topic by generating as many open-ended questions as possible about that issue: as such, Freire's problem-posing approach bears close similarities to the kinds of questions this book teaches writers to ask about purpose, audience, persona, medium, context, and genre.

7   Problem-posing is a strategy that can help a writer figure out the conventions of a discourse community because it fits well into any stage of the writing process. When I was asked recently to co-author a brief article about writing assessment for a faculty newsletter on my campus, I relied on problem-posing at the very beginning of my process. Because my co-author and I were required to keep the article extremely short, we were concerned about including too many long explanations of terminology; at the same time, we were acutely aware that a large majority of our audience, while they may have had some smattering of knowledge of our topic, were

on the whole unfamiliar with—or even hostile towards—best practices in writing assessment. In resolving this difficulty, I problem-posed, coming up with questions such as *When do faculty use writing assessment*? And *How do they talk about it when they use it*? And *How might some of the things my co-author and I know about writing assessment be useful to my faculty colleagues in their own duties*? Answers to these questions, as they led to an increased understanding of our article's audience and context, helped direct our decisions about format, vocabulary, tone, and persona as we drafted the article. More important, these answers helped us negotiate the very tricky question we'd had about the purpose of the article: *How can we use this article to persuade our audience to believe in us enough that we can teach them something about a topic of which they may not be fond*? In this way, problem-posing about audience was useful in helping us learn not only how to understand the expectations and predispositions of our audience, but also how to incorporate a secondary purpose of persuading along with the primary, assigned purpose of informing.

8   Problem-posing is particularly useful in helping us to learn about the academic discourse communities in which we'll participate throughout our college careers because it provides a way to help us read those communities. Different fields of study use writing differently. As context differs, so do genre, medium, and other rhetorical concerns. The purpose of academic discourses is to put writers in relationship with other writers in their field: reading the writings of others is the first step towards participating in the conversation. This kind of reading is a very important part of the writing process: when we read assignments using the lens of rhetorical concerns, we'll see the genre, the purpose, the persona, and so on, of each discipline—those are the categories that constitute the particular version of academic discourse used by a particular discipline. In other words, as newcomers to the university, we can't possibly know how to participate in all of the communities: while you may already be aware of some of the rules that govern the scholarly discourse of Spanish Literature, or some of your class colleagues may have experience using the rules that govern the genres of newspaper or magazine writing, the nature of university learning most often requires that each participant learn how to read a wide range of academic discourse communities.

9   In his research on discourse communities, Bazerman found that he "could not understand what constituted an appropriate text in any discipline without considering the social and intellectual activity which the text was part of" and that he "couldn't see what a text was doing without looking at the worlds in which these texts served as significant activity" (*Shaping* 4). Similarly, Freire, in a book he co-authored with Professor Donaldo Macedo, tells us that "reading the word" cannot be separated from

"reading the world" (16). These arguments are particularly relevant to this chapter on academic discourse because they point to the importance of understanding the rhetorical context of any given text. Clearly, reading and writing are inextricably connected. Freire, Macedo, and Bazerman show us that any newcomer to the university can—and should—learn to read the kinds of writing produced in a particular field. By doing so, we become more than passive consumers of knowledge in that field; rather, we learn how to produce the knowledge in ways that are valued by that particular field: we become participants in the scholarly conversation.

10   Using Freire's problem-posing strategy to read academic discourses is a useful way to learn about the rules and guidelines followed by a particular community. Once you begin to practice reading your writing assignments in this way, problem-posing will help you more clearly to address the expectations behind your assignments. What's even more useful about the problem-posing approach is that it helps writers to uncover a lot of the unspoken, or implicit, expectations that may be lurking in writing assignments in different disciplines. In other words, problem-posing allows writers who are new to academic discourse to participate in their own learning and to assume authority over their own writing choices.

11   Consider, too, that each community produces a variety of texts for a variety of audiences. We need to look beyond the obvious reading materials, such as textbooks, in order to uncover some of the rules and guidelines of academic discourses. What are some of the texts you've come across so far in your college readings? Your teachers may have assigned scholarly articles, technical reports, and case studies, among others. Many of these texts were doubtless written for an audience other than college students. But you have probably also read a plethora of other texts for your courses, including many syllabi, writing assignment sheets, and Web pages. These texts are often written specifically for students; they are, therefore, invaluable when we're learning the rules of a particular academic discourse, because they provide extremely pertinent information about the often unspoken expectations of the conventions that writers in that discourse should follow.

12   Depending on the assumptions you have about academic discourse, the wide range of writing assignments you'll come across in college may surprise you. For example, in the humanities, you may frequently be asked to compose not only informal writings such as journal entries and reading responses, but also much more formal writings such as argumentative essays or critical analyses. You will probably also find a mixture of both formal and information writing assignments in the social sciences. The academic discourse communities of the natural and applied sciences, on the other hand, more often communicate using very formal genres of writing,

such as laboratory reports and technical papers. It is possible, too, that some instructors in different disciplines may give you a writing assignment for a lay audience—an audience consisting of people who are not insiders in the academic discourse community. In problem-posing about ways to write for such an audience, you might consider not only how much your readers know about your discipline, but also their specialized knowledge about a similar discipline. You might also problem-pose about other characteristics of your audience, such as level of formal education, age, and geographical location. This kind of problem-posing will be useful to you in every writing situation, in every new discourse community where you may find yourself.

13   Of course, reading and writing cannot be separated. As we learn to read the conventions of academic discourses, we will almost certainly be tasked with applying them by writing those discourses at the same time. The audience for your college writing tasks will almost certainly vary, not just by discipline, but sometimes even within the same class. For example, in a sociology class you might be asked to write an annotated bibliography for your department's webpage, a service-learning report for your community partner, a book report presentation for your course colleagues, and a research paper for your teacher. Each of these writings certainly encourages your participation in creating knowledge within the specific academic discourse community of sociology; yet each calls for you to use a different genre. If you were to problem-pose about ways to write each of those documents, you might ask questions about the format, audience, and purpose of each one: as you're no doubt aware, you'd certainly come up with very different answers! At the same time, there are characteristics that each of those documents would share, since they're all part of the academic discourse community of sociology: each would need to rely on the most current research in the field, would need to incorporate specific vocabulary and terminology from the field, and would need to adopt the appropriate persona to situate the writer as a participant in the creation of knowledge in that field.

14   This kind of problem-posing will work to help you learn the expectations for any new discipline, whether it is based in the humanities, in the natural and applied sciences, or in the social sciences. Writers in the academic discourse communities of the humanities often write to persuade their readers to consider a new way of reading a text. These writers commonly share the expectation that participants in the discourse will study the word in texts such as works of literature, art, or music to create new knowledge—new ways of thinking—about the world. One example of this would come from a research paper, sometimes also called a critical analysis essay, for a Chinese literature class, for which a college essay would

require an argumentative thesis—one with which the essay's audience could agree or disagree—that is supported through the writer's analysis of literary texts. In another instance, writing a response to a performance for a music appreciation class might require the writer to focus on convincing readers that the work's composer was influenced by a specific social movement. Whatever the assignment, new knowledge is formed in many of humanities' academic discourse communities through participants' articulation of an argument designed to persuade readers to view the word, and therefore the world, in a new way.

15   Writers in the natural and applied sciences, on the other hand, tend to emphasize a primary purpose of informing readers, rather than persuading. These discourse communities share an assumption that an author's neutrality is important; therefore, they emphasize objectivity in their writings. In these disciplines, the purpose is often to inform audiences of new findings. As such, writers adopt an impersonal, objective persona and a neutral tone using passive voice: this is so that readers can, if they wish, replicate the experiments and data. Common genres that you may be asked to write in these disciplines include laboratory reports, reviews of scholarly or technical publications, or reports of your own field observations.

> **". . . the common purpose of a vast majority of your writing assignments . . . will be to demonstrate to your audience . . . that you have learned certain course concepts and terms."**

16   The academic discourse communities in the social sciences bear some similarities to the natural and applied sciences in their shared values. In the social science disciplines, a majority of writing assignments might also ask writers to inform; their purpose is to assume a high level of objectivity in providing recent, useful information to readers in the same discipline. Examples of assignments in the social sciences are a care plan, case notes, and a bibliographic essay.

17   Of course, we might still use our own rhetorical awareness to consider the relative persuasiveness or objectivity of any piece of writing, even in the sciences; however, to do so might well be a secondary purpose for participants in those disciplines. That said, persuasiveness in both the social sciences and the natural and applied sciences is represented in the way that writers maintain credibility within their academic discourse communities. In order to achieve this, it's important that participants not only use disciplinary conventions correctly, but also that they understand the ways of thinking that those conventions reveal, along with the purpose of the writing. This is how writers demonstrate to their readers that they are ready to participate in the conversations of that discourse community.

18   Overall, though, the common purpose of a vast majority of your writing assignments in academic discourses will be to demonstrate to your audience—scholars and professors, student colleagues, or laypeople—that

you have learned certain course concepts and terms. Your teachers will often ask you to engage in critical thinking through writing about course materials; they likely will also want you to demonstrate that you can apply the course content—the word—to your own experience of the world. In one sense, your instructors are asking you to demonstrate that you know how to think like an insider, following the practices of a member of that disciplinary discourse community: therefore, your academic writing should reflect the way that scholars communicate with one another in any given field. These tenets apply across the disciplines: as such, they show new college writers how to read the discourse of any academic community. Every writing assignment calls us to problem-pose about the purpose, audience, and genre: every academic discourse has conventions governing your selections as you respond to these rhetorical concerns.

19   You may encounter situations when the audience, or the purpose, of a particular writing assignment is unspecified. In fact, there are often unspoken assumptions within any given discourse community. For example, when I took my car to have a new clutch installed last week, the mechanic was obviously aware that I am not a member of the discourse community of auto technicians as she listened to my faltering descriptions of the noises my car had been making; moreover, her description a few hours later of the work she had done to fix my car was an acute reminder of my lack of experience and expertise in the vocabulary of that discourse community! And when we chat with our close friends or families, we often use some specific, shared vocabulary or terminology that may not hold the same meaning for people outside our group. In the same way, academic discourse communities are not necessarily always explicit about their assumptions. This can make it difficult for newcomers to read and write the texts of that community. However, the problem-posing approach provides a valuable tool for exploring the values and expectations behind academic discourses. If you are ever uncertain about the purpose or audience of an assignment, consider asking your professor for clarification; in this way, you can set the stage for your own participation in the academic discourse community.

Participation Across the Curriculum

20 One challenge that may prevent us from feeling as though we are full participants in an academic discourse community is that the purpose for writing is almost always decided by someone else, most often by the instructor. This seems to run contradictory to the idea that our own college writing can have real purpose, real authority—that it really can contribute to the making of knowledge in a scholarly discipline. However, full participation in academic discourse consists of a range of activities. Bazerman establishes that disciplinary knowledge is influenced by a variety of sources when he

argues that "Writing is a form of social action; texts help organize social activities and social structure; and reading is a form of social participation" (*Shaping* 10). In other words, it is actually in the acts of writing and reading that the genres of academic discourses are created; these acts compose the genres. It may be difficult, yes, for newcomers to the university to believe that they have the authority to influence academic discourses, especially given the way that those discourses historically have prescribed the ways in which our ideas get onto the page. But as Bazerman points out, the act of writing for and with and in academic discourse communities is, in itself, a form of social action. In other words, no discourse community can exist without its members: readers and writers themselves constitute a discourse community. As you will see from the writers who've contributed to this chapter, any participant can make a valuable contribution to the way an academic discourse community goes about its work. In other words, your own writing work has an influence on those discourse communities. Welcome to the conversation!

Works Cited

Bazerman, Charles. "The Life of Genre, the Life in the Classroom." *Genre and Writing*. Ed. W. Bishop and H. Ostrom. Portsmouth: Boynton/Cook, 1997: 19–26. Print.

—. *Shaping Written Knowledge: The Genre and Activity of the Experimental Article in Science*. Madison: The U of Wisconsin P, 1988. Print.

Freire, Paulo, and Donaldo Macedo. *Literacy: Reading the Word and the World*. Westport: Bergin & Garvey, 1987. Print.

Russell, David. "Rethinking Genre in School and Society: An Activity Theory Analysis." *Written Communication* 14.4 (1997): 504–554. Print.

Villanueva, Victor. "The Politics of Literacy Across the Curriculum." *WAC for the New Millennium: Strategies for Continuing Writing-Across-the-Curriculum Programs*. Ed. S. McLeod et al. Urbana: NCTE, 2001: 163–178. Print.

Literacy Connections

1. In your own words, define *problem-posing*.
2. Because Glade is discussing a complex topic—academic literacies— she draws on scholarly research and uses terms you may not have heard before. Underline any terms or passages in Glade's essay that confused you and discuss them in small groups to try to come to a better understanding of Glade's ideas.
3. In the first paragraph of her essay, Glade discusses "rules" that she was taught for writing, which worked in one class but not in another

class. What is a "rule" of writing you were taught that hasn't worked in one of your college classes? Why didn't the "rule" work?

4. Use Glade's example of problem-posing questions to "problem-pose" with one of the writing assignments you've been given this semester.

5. What advice do you think Glade would have for the student in Lucille McCarthy's "A Stranger in Strange Lands" from the chapter?

Before You Read

Before you read about a sociology major writing a research report for a class in his major, let's find out what you already know about writing and researching in the social sciences. In small groups, come up with a list of everything you know about writing conventions, writing genres, and research methods in social science fields like sociology, psychology, political science, and economics. Be prepared to share the group's list with the class.

Student Case Study: Composing an Academic Research Project

Greg Calabrese was a junior at Albion College when he wrote a research report for Social Psychology, a course for sociology majors. In this case study, we'll look at Calabrese's rough and final drafts of his report and his writing and researching processes in order to get a close look at what it means to write in an academic discipline.

In this case study of Greg Calabrese, we'll look at the composing process of a student engaging in academic research and writing in an upper-division sociology course. In this case study, we'll think about some general features of academic writing and research, but we'll also get a glimpse into what it's like to write and research in an upper-division course in a major. Let's begin by taking a look at the research report assignment Greg was given:

FINAL PAPER AND PRESENTATION (A&S 336—SOCIAL PSYCHOLOGY)

Freeeeeeeeeedom!!!! You're in charge!!!! It's your choice!!!! Do what you want to do!!!!

First, select any topic of interest that is distinctly social psychological [ideally it will be something that interests you so that you will view the paper as a source of education and fun (!) rather than stress]. Second, make sure there are available/obtainable academic sources for your particular topic and that you can conduct some original research on your topic.

NOTE: Your project should either go beyond what was covered in class or address a topic we did not cover.

Sample Topic Ideas

There are limitless possibilities, and the list below is a tiny one not meant to limit your imagination, but rather to offer assistance in your selection process. Please carefully select a topic and stay focused on social psychological *issues as you write.*

Framing and political language (social movements—e.g., pro-choice/life; politicians—e.g., presidential elections; media—e.g., advertising and the use of language similar to the phrases at the top of this handout)

Theoretical debates—e.g., rational choice vs. altruism, core self/personality vs. multiple selves

Social psychology of any major issues or interesting topic (e.g., war in Iraq, militias, homelessness, inequality, intimate violence, peer pressure, social networks, nudists, hypermasculinity, members of racist organizations, cults, revolutions, etc.)

Virtually any sociological topic you can think of has a social psychological component, so please don't hesitate to speak with me about sharpening your idea.

Research Methods

This Project Requires You to Conduct Original Research. *You can do* interviews *with relevant volunteers (see me if you want to do this), pass out* surveys *(see me), do* content analysis *(examine relevant current/historical documents first-hand; see me), or do some* observation *(e.g., attend a political candidate's rally, a protest event, or anywhere you can obtain social psychological data; see me).*

Paper

The paper must be ten (10) pages in length, typed, double-space, Times New Roman 12-point font, one-inch margins, no cover page. You must use no less than five (5) outside academic sources as well as class readings *(can use other sources in addition; e.g., Internet, newspapers, etc., but they must be in addition to five academic sources). A 'References' page should be included at the end with full citation information (i.e., author, title, year, publisher, city, etc.). For examples of how to cite chapters, books, and journal articles properly, look at the 'References' pages after each article in the course reader.*

Greg was glad that he could choose his own topic in the research paper report, and he said that was a common experience for classes in his major:

> When I go about writing a sociology paper I know that I have to have an open mind and be able to think outside the box and think about my arguments from multiple perspectives so that it may appeal to as many people as possible. The one thing that I enjoy most about writing sociology papers is that I can have as much fun with it as I choose. Many times, there are very few restrictions on the topic that you can write on, only basic requirements such as the length of the paper. This becomes truer in the higher level courses taken during junior and senior years of college.

Greg mentioned that he likes it when he can choose his own topic, and, in the case of his research report, he came up with a unique focus: male behavior in bathrooms and locker rooms. When we asked Greg how he came up with such an interesting topic, he said:

> I spent days trying to come up with a topic that I was interested in and one that I would be able to find some kind of research on. I typically spend some time alone either in the library or in my room just going through things that I would want to learn about or that I already have a passing interest in that could turn into something very interesting. This occasion was different. I was having a conversation with a friend about something that led to me choosing the topic that I did. Sometimes the best ideas are ones that come to you at the most unexpected times.

After Greg drafted his research report, he gave himself time to revise it and to get feedback from the teacher:

> Once I write my papers I will usually let it sit for a few days because I am always sure to get papers done at least a week in advance in order to give myself time to get away from it for a few days so that I am better able to edit it when it is not fresh in my mind. But before I edit my draft, I take my paper to the professor if he/she is willing to take a look at it as a draft.

Here's the draft Greg submitted to his teacher followed by his teacher's response:

INTERACTION AT A MINIMUM: MALE BEHAVIOR IN BATHROOMS AND LOCKER ROOMS

Introduction

Seven years. That is how long an average person will spend in a bathroom throughout their entire life. It is hard to imagine spending that much time in a place that is normally viewed as a private and taboo. On the other hand, people do spend 5 years of their lives eating, one third of their lives sleeping, and 8 years in school (without vacation time). The question though, is not how long one will spend in a bathroom throughout their entire life; it is what goes on in that bathroom. Sure there are the routine things such as showering, personal hygiene, and going to the bathroom, but what is it that people, specifically men, do when they are in the restroom or a locker-room? What actions do they take other than the basics? How come there is a set of norms and rules for bathroom conduct? Why are these rules the way that they are? What are the differences in the use of bathrooms by men when they are using public vs. private restrooms? Within these questions there are several themes that one must explore. One is that of the issue of framing. That is, we must consider how we look at a restroom and a locker-room and why we see them that way in which we do. There is the issue of gender in sexuality that is always being brought into question since, as West and Zimmerman argue, gender is something that we "do." Finally there is a difference in the way that many view their private space. Typically, this varies based on social class where the wealthier prefer to have more space in a given area (because they are used to having it) and lower classes are more accustomed to sharing space. All of these issues must be taken into consideration when discussing the social psychology of male bathroom and locker-room interaction.

Literature Review

There have been minimal studies on the interactions of men in bathrooms and locker rooms. Much useful material is a result of similar studies that include both participant observation as well as interviews of people about their ideas of bathroom use but little information focuses on the actual interaction of men in bathrooms and locker rooms. Some psychological research on the topic has been slightly controversial. Back in the 1970s a team of psychologists placed mini cameras in a bathroom to do research on bathroom behaviors. The research has now been deemed unethical and actually concluded very little. The research amounted to finding that there were differences in the amount of time that a man used the bathroom depending on how many people he was sharing the bathroom with. If there were more people, men were more likely to take less time in the bathroom than if there was no one else (Cohen). Some professors use the bathroom as a way to introduce the topic of sociology to their introductory classes. Edgar Burns asks his students which way the toilet paper should hang in a bathroom (away from the wall or towards the wall). Many students defer to the way that the female head of the household says that it should be hung (Burns). I find that this shows that men in these classes, and presumably other men as well, submit to women in their homes as the head of the household.

In yet another class discussion, John Paul offers questions about male bathroom etiquette. He gives his students a diagram similar to the following:

Door   Stall 1   Stall 2   Stall 3

He asks his students which a series of questions about which stall a man should use but changes the scenario every time. A man is expected to stand in the furthest stall if he is alone, alternate stalls when there are two people, and not use the middle stall if there are more than two people. "It is part of the culture of American men's restrooms. Men don't like to give the impression that they are looking at or initiating contact with other men (Paul)." Paul offers this explanation as to why men act in such ways when choosing which stall to use. It is a fact that the stall nearest the door is the one that men use the least because it has the lowest levels of bacteria in almost all of the 51 bathrooms that were studied (Paul). He also claims that "men are expected to do their business quietly, quickly, and independently." Paul also suggests that men do not act much different outside of bathrooms than they do inside of them. He claims that men try to act tough independent both inside and outside of bathrooms.

Yet another study suggests that nudity, even in public restrooms and locker rooms brings morals into question. "When a person willfully exposes himself, we are inclined to question his moral character; when we thing the person has compulsively exposed himself, we are prone to question his mental health (Vivona and Gomillion)." The authors suggest that in public places, those who are less exposed to nudity in bathrooms at home were more likely to react awkwardly in locker room and bathroom situations. The study also concludes that the more that a person is exposed to such occurrences, the more comfortable they become with the idea of seeing another person in the nude (Vivona and Gomillion).

Don Sabo brings up the topic of what men discuss in locker room settings. As children, he claims, men discuss things that they know little or nothing about. Much of the talk is about sex and issues that are related to the topic. Later in school the topic switches to how far others have "gotten" with their girlfriends and talk about each others virginity as well as "jerking off" (Sabo). It is conversations such as these that promote the objectification of women as the author suggests. But what about how it is that men interact? There has been little focus on the interaction and the unspoken norms that exist in male bathrooms and locker rooms. Of course high schools, middle schools, and elementary schools are going to differ from public health clubs, but for purposes of this essay, it is the public restrooms and locker rooms where people of all ages can interact that are the focus.

Methods

For the purpose of this essay, I decided that my research would be two-fold. First, I felt that I would gain a better insight to men's views of how they interact with each other and by themselves if I conducted some form of semi-structured interviews. I chose to interview three college aged men (Alex, David, and Jim), all from a small Midwest college and all who grew up in middle-class families. I asked them a series of questions about their experiences in bathrooms as well as their feelings about certain common occurrences in bathrooms throughout their lives. I also will be discussing what observations I have made in my countless experiences in male bathrooms over the past twenty one years. These observations are intended to supplement my interviews with the three participants as well as add to the discussion of how men interact with each other and by themselves in a restroom or locker-room setting. I feel that it will be interesting to consider not only what interactions are like in a normal bathroom or locker-room, but also to examine these events through a gendered lens to a certain extent.

Discussion

For the past twenty years I have been exposed to male bathrooms and locker rooms. Each has appeared different from another in physical appearance, but much of the same rules of etiquette and interaction remain constant. As Paul discussed, much of male bathroom etiquette can be simply explained by the 1-3-5 rule. That is, men can only use the odd numbered stalls in order to be furthest away from other men. When a man is using the bathroom (read as doing his business) he is looking at the wall or that stall door in front of him. There is no aversion of the eyes or even a whisper of a sound other than that of the flushing toilet. Often, at large sporting events, it is common to use a common toilet in the shape of half of a bath tub. In these restrooms one must never look down or even over at another person even though there are no dividers between people. It is extremely inappropriate to touch another person, even if it is casual contact on the arm because people are so crammed in together. If this is the case, other men will wait until someone has left in order to use the toilet. The case of using stalls is different. It is much more acceptable to use a stall next to someone else. This is only the case because there are doors and walls between people and one can only see another's feet enough to tell that someone is using the stall. As far as interaction goes; men are very unlikely to say anything to or even look at one another if they do not know each other. In fact, from my years of observation, men who do know each other are very unlikely to converse in a public restroom. It is much more likely that they talk if there is no one else in the restroom so as not to break the norm of not talking in a bathroom. Men will typically walk into a bathroom, find the stall or urinal if it is not readily visible, do their business, and either wash their hands or simply walk out. It is normal for a man to wash his hands if he is out to eat or in a place where it is a single or smaller bathroom. Only about half of the men wash their hands in larger bathrooms and especially in bathrooms where the sink is unclean. Large sporting events and concerts are places in which one could make this observation. Where something like not washing one's hands is frowned upon by adults and society as a whole, it is not in such settings.

In a locker room the interaction between men and the overall dynamics of the situation is different. From my experiences, men will walk into the locker room and look for a space where there is either a familiar face or where there is no one at all. Often, locker rooms do not have enough space where either option is available. In these cases, men will try and find someone that is near their age to change near. Each man will do this quietly and typically without acknowledgement of each other. If it is the case that there is a group of people that know each other, they will typically carry on some kind of conversation amongst each other. Many times, the conversation will include the day's events and talk about girls and/or women. I find this holds true even between men of an elderly age but in a much more mature fashion. The older the people are, the less likely the conversation is to be about some form of sexual activity and more about how each others' significant others are doing. The locker room is a safe place for men to discuss such issues because there are obviously no women present to object to what the men are saying and the men do not have to censor themselves. If the men are going to the pool there is one of two options. First, the men will simply walk out onto the deck and go about swimming. Second, the men will shower. Almost always it is the younger men who do not shower and simply walk out to the pool area. Typically, men who are older will use the showers in the nude and then place their swim suits on and walk onto the deck. After a workout the men will re-enter the locker room to either change or shower and change. If men are going to shower they will typically undress and place a towel around their waist until they reach the shower area so as not to expose themselves to the other men who are around. After the shower, the men will dry off using the towel and will then place the towel back around their waists until they reach their locker. At the locker they will drop the towel and dress. If it is the case that two or more men are in a conversation it is not unusual for them to continue their conversation through the shower and their changing. If the men do not shower, the experience is the same as it was on the way in . . . minimal contact with others males while minding one's own business. Of course experiences differ, but these are the prevailing norms in American locker-rooms today.

Additionally, as mentioned earlier, I conducted three interviews with college aged students about their experiences and feelings about interaction among and between males in restrooms and locker-rooms. Their responses were somewhat consistent, but did have some slight differences upon their feelings towards interactions amongst men in bathroom and locker room settings. All three participants acknowledged many of the same observations and behaviors which I have previously discussed. Jim, Alex, and David all claim to use the restroom in the same way that I described in my earlier observations. They all come in, do their business, wash their hands, and leave. They all claimed that they did not use the bathroom if it was dirty and always stayed away from using public bathroom stalls because it was different for them and also not always sanitary.

All three participants claimed that they try to keep a minimal interaction with others in bathrooms and locker rooms. They claimed that it was awkward to look at or talk to others who they do not know in such a private place. Usually their only interactions are with those that they know. David said that he "will joke around with people I know." All three men, when asked, also said that when presented with the urinal scenario that they would use the stall furthest from the door for that reason alone. They felt that they wanted their privacy from those who are standing close outside the door and from those who may come into the bathroom. They all said that they would never use the stall next to a person unless there were no more empty stalls. Alex claimed that it was "rude to use the stall next to someone else if there are empty stalls because it would be an invasion of someone's space."

When asked what they do when they encounter someone who is in the nude in the locker-room all three men has similar responses. Jim claimed that "I try and avoid these men even though I am comfortable with my sexuality, it still makes me uncomfortable." Contrary to what I have observed throughout my life, Alex claimed to take showers in the nude whether he was with people that he knew or not. He claimed that he used to find it weird when he would see people naked in a locker-room but now that he is older he is used to it and is comfortable enough with his body to do such a thing. This is different than most other younger men since younger men only shower with each other in high school and college locker-rooms where showers are mandatory per their coaches' instructions. From my own observations, it is only in these situations that young men and teenagers will shower in the nude. A large majority of men, including my own high school swim team, will wear swim suits in the shower, or refuse to shower in a public locker-room at all.

Analysis

Now that we are aware of the behaviors and actions of men in bathrooms and locker-rooms, we must explore why these behaviors and actions exist and occur. One reason that men limit their interactions within bathroom and locker-room situations is as a result of the way that men view private locales. The way that bathrooms are framed for men is as a private place. As previously discussed, men prefer to use the 1-3-5 rule when using restroom urinals. It is my belief that men use this rule out of fear of their sexuality being called into question. If a man were to choose to stand in stall #2 with someone being in stall #3 and stall #1 was open, the man in stall #3 would most likely give some kind of inquisitive look towards the man breaking the norm. This man may also call into question the sexuality of the man whom has chosen to use the urinal next to his when another is open. Even the unspoken questioning of a man's sexuality is enough of a reason for almost every man to follow this norm. The bathroom is framed as a private place and as a result men want to keep it that way. This is why it is discouraged to invade another man's space by using the urinal next to someone unless it is unavoidable. This is also the reason that men avoid changing in front of other men in locker-rooms. Men want their own space to be able to spread out and also have their private area without wandering eyes watching them.

Symbolic interactionists like to look at people's perspectives, responses, and interpretations of situations. They believe that truth and reality are determined by the context in which they are practiced. In a gym, men will look at each other, talk to each other, help spot one another on a weight bench, and overall, interact with each other. In the locker-room after men use the gym, the context and situation has changed. In the locker-room there is an air of privacy and the definition of the situation has changed. Even though men will still talk to each other in the locker-room, it is at a minimum for fear of making a situation uncomfortable for other men. It is also the reason why David is able to joke around with people that he knows in a bathroom setting as long as there is no one else around. But once someone else enters the restroom or if someone else is already using the restroom, there is no joking between him and his friends. It is the reality of the situation that the locker room and restroom are seen as private places and people are going to act as such by giving others as much space and privacy as they can give. Because the situation changes between the gym, restaurant, or any other situation and the locker room or restroom, so does the interaction between men.

Many men choose not to shower in the locker room or, if they do, will wear their swim suit when they do. Often, the reason for this is because they feel that they are "inadequate" in their own eyes and do not want other men to judge them for their small genitals. Again, it could simply be that men are uncomfortable with the idea of sharing a space with other men while they are completely nude, but I tend to believe that feelings of inadequacy and shame are the reason for this. For men, the size of their genitals is a sensitive topic. If a man does not believe his genitals to be of adequate size he is not going to reveal himself to other men in who he does not know for fear of being judged. Although it has become much less of a fear in recent years, there still exists the notion that there may be men in a locker-room setting that may have homosexual feelings and have some kind of attraction towards other men and for this reason, some men do not wish to expose themselves in a public arena.

References

Abbott, F., & Sabo, D. *Men and intimacy.* USA: The Crossing Press. 16–21.

Burns, E.A. (2003). Bathroom politics: Introducing students to sociological thinking from the bottom up. *Teaching Sociology 31*(1), 110–118. (ERIC Document Reproduction Service No. EJ679284)

Cohen, D. (1978). Behaviors: A watershed in ethnical debate. *The Hastings Center Report 8*, 13.

Lemert, C., & Branaman, A. *The goffman reader.* Malden, MA: Blackwell.

Paul, J. "Flushing" out sociology: Using urinal games and other bathroom customs to teach the sociological perspective. *Electronic Journal of Sociology* (2005), 1–13.

Shove, E. (2003). *Comfort, cleanliness and convenience.* New York, NY: Berg. 93–116.

Vivona, C.M., & Gomillion, M. (1972). Situational morality of bathroom nudity. *The Journal of Sex Research 8*(1), 128–135.

Instructor's Comments

Overall, the draft is in good shape at this stage. Thanks to the topic you've selected and an introduction that immediately engages the reader, the paper is unique and interesting. I've made editing suggestions on your draft, but your writing is generally clear and to the point. I like your integration of ideas from gender theory ("Doing Gender") into this Social Psychology paper and I think you can expand this discussion (more below). Your literature review does a nice job of bringing in both empirical work on bathroom/locker-room behavior and gendered social psychological insights into these findings. I think the strength of a paper like this is its original research, and in this case your interview data. Your observations complement the interview data (more on reorganizing this below). Your analysis section includes some useful ideas about why men fear nudity in public places, including a gendered view that might call into question their sexuality and a generic social psych view about privacy in public places. I think both are useful and can be integrated (again, more below). You explicitly introduce ideas rooted in Symbolic Interactionism (and Erving Goffman) at the end of the paper—you demonstrate a good grasp of these ideas.

I have several suggestions to improve your paper. First and foremost, I think you should introduce your theoretical perspectives earlier and more explicitly. Your literature review section should combine theory as well. Include a longer discussion of "doing gender" as well as a discussion of Symbolic Interactionism (SI). Introduce the basic premises of SI (see the Blumer article we read), and then relate these ideas to your topic and to doing gender. If you plan on incorporating Goffman and the idea of frames, you should introduce this earlier and define and explain what you mean by a frame. Similarly, spend a bit more time introducing and explaining the concept of doing gender, as this will set up your analysis later on in the paper. Following the insights you use about gender, you should replace the term male with men in almost all cases—as you imply with your use of doing gender, men's behavior in bathrooms is about how gender is constructed, performed, and judged by our society, and not a result of some biological drive to cover up their genitals when other dudes are around. I think your data are a bit thin and should be expanded. The three interviews provide some data and quotes, but I think doing a couple more interviews (perhaps with men from different class or cultural backgrounds) will make this paper appear more firmly grounded in empirical research and not simply your recollections of past observations. The observational data is fine and useful, but I think it needs to come second. Use it to complement and fill in the blanks from your interview data, rather than leading with it and using your interview data secondary. You don't need to view these as separate kinds of data/parts to discuss either—instead of discussing these data in separate parts of your results section, you can organize this section by topic, at times (even within the same paragraph where appropriate) discussing interview data and at times discussing observational data. Both are forms of qualitative, ethnographic data. Speaking of which, you have organized your sections based on more of a quantitative approach, separating your results section (you titled this "Discussion") from your discussion/analysis section ("Analysis"). For qualitative research, these two should be integrated into one section ("Results and Discussion") because it makes sense to—in the same paragraph(s)—both share your participants' quotes and analyze them in the context of the theoretical ideas you introduced earlier. With quantitative research, you'd report the numerical findings in one section and then interpret them in the next section. But because you are observing and reporting on interactions (re: processes), it's best to combine the results and discussion sections. As part of your analysis, you'll need to interpret your participants' attitudes and behaviors in the context of SI and doing gender. What is it about privacy, public spaces, gender, nudity, and men's individual experiences that lead them to do and think the things they do? I think you've already begun to answer this, but it should be expanded (particularly your analysis of the importance of gender and sexuality). Then you can have a separate "Conclusion" section, which I think you basically do already beginning on page 9.

Greg read his teacher's comments carefully and revised his report based on his teacher's suggestions. Let's focus on some revisions Greg made to discuss just how extensive the revision process needs to be in successful academic writing. In Chapter 2 of *Everything's a Text*, we talked about the difference between revising and editing. Successful college writers don't just run spell check or clean up their sentences for their revision process. Successful college writers treat revision like Greg does, looking to expand and develop ideas when they revise. Greg added entire paragraphs to his report to flesh out his ideas. For example, in the literature review, he added this paragraph in response to his teacher's suggestion that the literature review needed more sociological theory:

> Erving Goffman suggests that our perceptions matter, but we keep
> re-entering situations that we have already been in and that we are simply

tapping into old frames. He claims that there are such things as rules of interaction (Lemert and Brannaman). It is for this reason that we always are aware of what our actions should be and how interactions should be framed in bathrooms and locker-rooms between men. Since we perceive that the bathroom is a private place, we treat it like one. Since we have been in numerous bathrooms throughout our lives, we know how to act in one. As a result, we are aware of the rules of interaction in these situations and will remain aware of them for the rest of our life and as the rules change and are negotiated. He also has the idea that the whole world is a stage and that we are just playing our roles as people in the play of life. Using this idea, in the bathroom and locker-room we are simply playing a role that has already been written for us and we just keep acting out the parts. It is the same role over and over again, but only the setting changes.

Greg also added more explanation of sociological theory in his concluding paragraph and organized those final thoughts into a section titled "Conclusion," as his teacher suggested. Reread the last two paragraphs of Greg's draft above, and compare it to the final version of his concluding thoughts as follows:

Conclusion

Symbolic interactionists like to look at people's perspectives, responses, and interpretations of situations. They believe that: 1) humans act towards a thing on the basis of the meaning they assign to the thing, 2) meanings are socially derived and there is no absolute meaning because meanings are negotiated between individuals, and 3) the perception and interpretation of social symbols are modified by the individual's thought process. Using a symbolic interactionists perspective one can successfully analyze men's bathroom and locker-room behavior. Men treat and discuss bathrooms and locker-rooms as private areas and the things that are talked about and done in there remain private. There is nothing inherent about what actions take place in a bathroom. Although people are in a locker-room with others of the same sex, we give meaning to the idea of nudity as well as the idea of privacy. We also give meaning to the idea of bathrooms and locker-rooms. They act as a symbol in our society as a place that is private and rarely discussed because individuals have been socialized to treat it that way and because of how these places are framed by the majority of society.

In a gym, men will look at each other, talk to each other, help spot one another on a weight bench, and overall, interact with each other. In the locker-room after men use the gym, the context and situation has changed. In the locker-room there is an air of privacy and the definition of the situation has changed. Even though men will still talk to each other in the locker-room, it is at a minimum for fear of making a situation uncomfortable for other men. It is also the reason why David is able to joke around with people that he knows in a bathroom setting as long as there is no one else around. But once someone else enters the restroom or if someone else is already using the restroom, there is no joking between him and his friends. It is the reality of the situation that the locker-room and restroom are seen as private places and people are going to act as such by giving others as much space and privacy as they can give. Because the situation changes between the gym, restaurant, or any other situation and the locker-room or restroom, so does the interaction between men.

Many men choose not to shower in the locker-room or, if they do, will wear their swim suit when they do. Often, the reason for this is because they feel that they are "inadequate" in their own eyes and do not want other men to judge them for their small genitals. Again, it could simply be that men are uncomfortable with the idea of sharing a space with other men while they are completely nude, but I tend to believe that feelings of inadequacy and shame are the reason for this. For men in the United States and many but not all countries, the size of their genitals is a sensitive topic. If a man does not believe his genitals to be of adequate size he is not going to reveal himself to other men in whom he does not know for fear of being judged. Although it has become much less of a fear in recent years, there still exists the notion that there may be men in a locker-room setting that may have homosexual feelings and have some kind of attraction towards other men and for this reason, some men do not wish to expose themselves in a public arena.

When Greg expanded on Symbolic Interactionism in the first paragraph of his conclusion, he found that he had added so much to that paragraph that he moved the review of how men behave in locker-rooms, gyms, and restrooms to its own paragraph. As you're revising essays for your college classes, you'll find that you'll need to create new paragraphs and move paragraphs around as the content of your essay changes—and sometimes you'll revise the entire focus of your paper. In addition to revising based on suggestions you might get from peers, your teacher, or a tutor at your campus Writing Center, you might also revise based on the conventions of the genre you're composing in. In Greg's case, he came to understand that the genre of the qualitative research report in the sciences combined the results and discussion section but included a separate conclusion.

Academic literacies, and especially the kinds of writing you'll be asked to do in your major, will be challenging and require an intensive writing and revising process. Even though Greg revised the content of his report before submitting it for a grade, the expectations for writing in an academic field are high, and Greg's teacher liked the revisions Greg made but still found places where Greg could have developed his research. Here are the comments Greg received from his teacher on the final draft he submitted for a grade:

The paper has improved in many areas. You've done a good job of analyzing how much interactions change inside and outside of locker-rooms, exposing how highly subjective expectations for behavior are from one situation to the next. Talking while spotting each other on a weight bench—no problem. Talking while showering—probably a problem. And as you point out, gender is key here. All things being equal, women's bathrooms and locker-rooms are not burdened with the same sense of fear, dread, or silence.

You've moved up and explained in greater detail some of your theoretical ideas. I'd still like to see you discuss the basic premises of Symbolic Interaction in your theory section (rather than your Conclusion), and then revisit these ideas as you discuss your interview data. I also think your interview data are a bit thin, given the senior-level course number and expectations. You complement these data with your observations, but still don't lead with or emphasize the interview data enough. Overall, this is a good paper with the potential to be very good.

In academic writing, you're often asked to take on the role of an expert or "insider" on the subject you're writing about, as Greg was in this sociology report, and your audience is often other experts in the academic field. Because of this, you'll be expected to fully develop and explain your arguments, provide substantial evidence from research, and organize your ideas in a way that meets the expectations of whatever genre you're writing in.

In addition to asking Greg about his own writing processes, we asked him to offer some general advice for college reading and writing. Here's what Greg had to say:

Overall, there are several pieces of advice that I have in terms of writing papers. My first is to make sure that you write in an environment that you are comfortable in. Many of my friends have to write or study in the library. Others sometimes write in the basement of my fraternity house with a few other people that are down there. Still others will work in the computer lab that we have set up in our house. Personally, I write in my room at my desk because it is a comfortable place that has distractions that I use every once in a while just to take a short break.

Second, I would recommend that you write when you feel like working on the paper. Typically I will write my papers as soon as they are assigned so that I have as much time as possible to edit them as well as think about them if I lose my drive to write. This allows me to have the most motivation while writing and has resulted in some very good grades at the end of the semesters from my professors. Also, if the professor is open to doing it, I will give them a first draft of my paper so that they can take a look at it and let me know what they think. In the end, you are accomplishing two things by doing this. First, you are giving your draft of a paper to the person who will be grading it and they above anyone will be able to guide your work towards what they would like to see in a finished project. Second, you will show that you have not only an interest in your grade in the class, but also the material that you are covering. In doing this, you will be able to develop a generally positive relationship with your professors. Professors generally remember what it was like being a student and are typically more than willing to help you with any question that you will have so make sure to ask them any question that you have because the only stupid question is the one that wasn't asked.

Finally, make sure to chose a topic (if you are able to do so) that interests you. Not only must the topic interest you, but you should make sure that there is other research that has been done on the topic that you will be able to look at to serve as a guide and part of a literature review. Sometimes topics will have limited sources and are therefore more difficult papers to write because there is generally less information on them in the first place. I have found that writing on topics that are interesting and fun makes the process much more enjoyable than if I am given a topic on which to write on.

As far as reading for college goes, make sure to plan for how much reading you will have for each class. I was always told that the general rule of thumb for class is that you will spend 3 hours of time working outside of class for every hour spent in class. I know students who spend more than that and I know students who spend less than that. Sometimes it depends on the student, but most of the ones who spend less time than they should do not do as well in school as those who spend the 3 hours that they should spend. I also try to find a place to read that I am familiar with and usually won't be distracted in. As I do when I write my papers, I choose to read in my room because I can lock my door and not be bothered for a while and because there is enough room for me to move around if I get anxious or bored. Generally, I will spend Friday evening, Saturday afternoon, and Sunday afternoon doing my reading because most people are not doing anything at that time anyways and it is almost always quiet around campus during those time periods.

Literacy Connections

1. If your class completed the Before You Read for the student case study, review the list of features of writing and researching in the social sciences that the class came up with. Find three examples from Greg's research report that exemplify features of writing and researching that seem to be specific to the social sciences.

2. Describe the research methods Greg uses. What counts as evidence for research in this sociology class?

3. In what ways is your writing process similar to or different than Greg's process, which he describes at the end of the case study? From your perspective, what is the most valuable piece of advice about reading and writing that Greg offers?

4. Based on what you learned from reading this case study, what are some on the features of reading and writing in upper-division classes that you will need to think about as you enter your major?

5. Read Nancy Alkema's research report "The Effects of Parental Neglect Types on Children," which appears later in the chapter. What are features of writing and researching in the social sciences that Alkema's and Calabrese's reports share?

Academic Literacy Readings

Before You Read

Based on your experiences so far in the composition course you're taking (the course you've been assigned this textbook in), what are the most important goals the teacher has for your writing? Think of the goals stated in the class syllabus and assignments, as well as what the teacher has talked about in class and in his or her responses to your writing.

Council of Writing Program Administrators' Outcomes Statement for First-Year Composition

An outcomes statement is a summary of learning goals; in the case of the outcomes statement following, the learning goals are for college composition classes. The Council of Writing Program Administrators is a national organization of people who run college writing programs, and they created the outcomes statement below to give college writing teachers some general guidelines for what students should be able to do by the end of a composition class. These outcomes give you a sense of expectations for college-level writing.

Rhetorical Knowledge

By the end of first year composition, students should:

- Focus on a purpose
- Respond to the needs of different audiences
- Respond appropriately to different kinds of rhetorical situations
- Use conventions of format and structure appropriate to the rhetorical situation
- Adopt appropriate voice, tone, and level of formality
- Understand how genres shape reading and writing
- Write in several genres

Critical Thinking, Reading, and Writing

By the end of first year composition, students should:

- Use writing and reading for inquiry, learning, thinking, and communicating
- Understand a writing assignment as a series of tasks, including finding, evaluating, analyzing, and synthesizing appropriate primary and secondary sources
- Integrate their own ideas with those of others
- Understand the relationships among language, knowledge, and power

Processes

By the end of first year composition, students should:

- Be aware that it usually takes multiple drafts to create and complete a successful text

- Develop flexible strategies for generating, revising, editing, and proof-reading
- Understand writing as an open process that permits writers to use later invention and re-thinking to revise their work
- Understand the collaborative and social aspects of writing processes
- Learn to critique their own and others' works
- Learn to balance the advantages of relying on others with the responsibility of doing their part
- Use a variety of technologies to address a range of audiences

Knowledge of Conventions

By the end of first year composition, students should:

- Learn common formats for different kinds of texts
- Develop knowledge of genre conventions ranging from structure and paragraphing to tone and mechanics
- Practice appropriate means of documenting their work
- Control such surface features as syntax, grammar, punctuation, and spelling

Composing in Electronic Environments

As has become clear over the last twenty years, writing in the 21st-century involves the use of digital technologies for several purposes, from drafting to peer reviewing to editing. Therefore, although the *kinds* of composing processes and texts expected from students vary across programs and institutions, there are nonetheless common expectations.

By the end of first-year composition, students should:

- Use electronic environments for drafting, reviewing, revising, editing, and sharing texts
- Locate, evaluate, organize, and use research material collected from electronic sources, including scholarly library databases; other official databases (e.g., federal government databases); and informal electronic networks and Internet sources
- Understand and exploit the differences in the rhetorical strategies and in the affordances available for both print and electronic composing processes and texts

Faculty in all programs and departments can build on this preparation by helping students learn:

- How to engage in the electronic research and composing processes common in their fields
- How to disseminate texts in both print and electronic forms in their fields

Literacy Connections

1. Circle any terms in the outcomes statement that you are unfamiliar with. In small groups, discuss these terms with your peers to try to come to a better understanding of the terms.
2. Compare and contrast these learning outcomes for First-Year Composition to the learning outcomes in the college courses from across the curriculum that you're currently taking.
3. Discuss whether or not you think these First-Year Writing outcomes will help prepare you for academic literacy across the curriculum. Do you think it's possible for one composition class to prepare you for college writing?
4. Circle all of the outcomes for First-Year Composition that you've already had some experience and practice with in high school or college. Which outcomes do you need the most practice in to help prepare you for academic literacies?
5. Compare and contrast these First-Year Writing outcomes and the writing outcomes statements for departments across disciplines that follow.

Before You Read

Based on your experiences in college so far, how does reading, writing, and researching differ in different classes/academic fields? Give some specific examples.

Writing Outcomes Statements from Across the Curriculum

The following are writing outcomes statements and standards from departments across the curriculum at various colleges: the Department of Natural Sciences at the University of Maine at Farmington, the Philosophy Department at George Mason University, and the Gerontology

Department at California State University, Sacramento. If the Council of Writing Program Administrators' outcomes for First-Year Composition gave you a general sense of the expectations for college writing, these outcomes from different departments will give you a general sense of how writing expectations can vary among different academic discourse communities.

Biology Writing Skills Outcomes: University of Maine at Farmington

A. Students will master, through drafts and revisions, the method of writing used in published papers in their discipline, including both reports of scientific research and review papers.

B. Students will clearly articulate the problem at hand or objective of a study, and then analyze and discuss the available data, drawing conclusions warranted by the evidence.

C. Students will display command of Standard American English in their work.

D. Students will understand the highly structured format of scientific writing used in most peer-reviewed articles, and master this form of communication.

E. Students should be competent in scientific writing and oral communication. Students should understand and be able to apply the scientific method (i.e., to understand procedural knowledge and skills so that one can carry out a scientific study as well as critically analyze the work of others—part of structural biological literacy). This includes the ability to develop hypotheses and make predictions; design experiments to test hypotheses; and critically evaluate results and draw conclusions.

Standards of Good Writing in Philosophy: George Mason University

The following standards were agreed upon by the George Mason philosophy faculty. They are numbered in importance for grading. Students should realize however, that individual instructors are not bound by these standards and may have somewhat different, or additional, expectations for student writing.

1. Essay demonstrates an understanding of the material: The student has correctly grasped a philosophical problem or question, has explained it accurately, and on the basis of a substantially correct

interpretation of any texts involved. Key terms are used correctly. The essay shows evidence of the student's independent thought and is written in her distinctive voice. Quotations are used, when appropriate, to support the writer's analysis, and an explanation is offered for each quotation.

2. Essay has clear and coherent argument: There is a clearly stated thesis and support for this thesis in the body of the paper. Each paragraph contributes to this argument and follows logically from the paragraph before it. The argument presented is persuasive.

3. Essay fulfills assigned task: The essay addresses the entire assigned question or topic, elaborating on important ideas in satisfactory depth, but without bringing in anything extraneous or irrelevant. The introduction of the essay focuses and provides clarity for the paper. Important terms are clearly and accurately defined. Each paragraph conveys a coherent, organized thought.

4. Essay obeys standards for good persuasive writing: the writer shows that he is comfortable using philosophical language, and the prose is clear, not awkward. The structure of the sentences reflects the relationships between/among the ideas discussed.

5. Essay is technically correct: The essay has been carefully and thoughtfully proofread. The argument is written in complete sentences, with punctuation that does not mislead the reader. There are few or no mistakes in spelling, grammar, word choice, and punctuation.

Outcomes for Written and Oral Communication in Gerontology: California State University, Sacramento

The Learner will:

- Write clear, well-organized, grammatically correct and documented papers on age related issues.
- Complete necessary agency reports within written guidelines.
- Orally present information in a professional manner that is clear, organized, concise, correctly documented, and using adult learning principles.
- Demonstrate effective and sensitive verbal and written communication skills with clients, families, agency staff, faculty, and the public to manage and facilitate interdisciplinary interaction and cooperation.
- Operate effectively in agency environments through development and use of communicative and interpersonal skills.

- Collaborate with appropriate individuals and information sources in a timely manner when delivering services in the practice area.

Literacy Connections

1. In what ways do the features of "good writing" differ in these different outcomes statement?
2. In small groups or as a class, use these outcomes as a starting point to come up with a list of features of "good" writing in the natural sciences, the social sciences, and the humanities.
3. Use the previous outcomes statements and your own experiences writing in your college classes and reflect on the ways reading, writing, and researching differ in different academic fields.
4. Based on the previous writing outcomes what writing abilities did you practice in high school that will best prepare you for academic literacies? What writing abilities do you need to work on the most for you to succeed in academic writing?
5. In what ways do these different outcomes statements connect to Fiona Glade's argument about the way writing varies across the curriculum in the opening essay of the chapter?

Before You Read

Write a one-page letter aimed at incoming freshman at your school that describes college writing and gives advice for college writing success. Be prepared to share your letter with the class.

Letter to an Incoming Freshman—
Writing in the Academy

Aaro Lautamo

Aaro Lautamo was a junior at California State University, Sacramento, when he wrote the following letter in response to an assignment in a composition course. The assignment asked students to write a letter aimed at incoming freshmen describing writing in college and offering advice for new college writers. Because you are a new college writer, you are the target audience for Lautamo's letter, and hopefully you can gain something valuable from his advice.

1   As you probably already know, writing is the primary way that academics communicate and share information. Writing at the university level can

be thought of as an extension and diversification of the writing done in high school. High school should have equipped you with all the necessary conventions and techniques to finish any college writing assignment. This does not mean that university level writing is easy or as familiar as the assignments from high school. There is a lot of controversy over how skilled incoming college students are at essential writing skills. Many academics (fellow students/instructors) complain about students that are not proficient writers. As an individual it is best to ignore the politics of academic writing and just continue to develop one's own skills. The major difference in writing at the university level and in high school is in how you must adapt your writing style to the particular demands of a given instructor/assignment. In high school, teachers are very willing to look for what you intended to communicate in your paper. In the academy (i.e., the university) instructors are not always so willing to be charitable to your writing. This means that in order to be successful in the academy your writing must be more than just proficient, it must be properly targeted for the task at hand.

2   The single most important thing to have for your future writing is simply confidence. I do not mean arrogance or excessive ego. I mean you must have the ability to express anything you think or say in the form of written words. If you understand something, you should be able to express that understanding in words. That is what instructors expect at the fundamental level. You should also be able to explain your writing or have your writing explain you. It is crucial that you understand your own points and statements. It is equally important that your written arguments and statements express what you actually mean yourself. There is no single indicator of when your writing is sufficiently developed to write successfully in the academy. The best way to check is to simply analyze the things you say and think through them thoroughly. It is also quite helpful to have a friend or family member read your work and help you develop it. Constructive criticism from someone you trust can be invaluable in the development of your ideas. When you are confident in your writing abilities you can stop worrying about the conventions and about sounding "correct" or "the way you are supposed to" all the time. Indeed, when you get past the mechanics of your own writing and become comfortable with your own literary voice it allows you to become creative and expressive with your use of language and subsequently with your logic and arguments themselves. The reason this self-sufficient aspect of writing is of primary importance is simple: Some instructors will like you, some will not. Some assignments will favor you, some will not. It is important that before you ever assimilate what an instructor or what an assignment demands of you, you must first understand your core writing ability is a separate entity from whatever particular "set of tools" you must use for the task at hand. You must depersonalize from yourself as

the writer and allow yourself to apply your skills to the task at hand as best you can. When you master this ability as a writer you are able to grow and learn from all the writing you do, even when you get a bad grade.

3   There has been somewhat of a fervor over the past few years. Many college systems complain about large numbers of students being incapable writers. There is a hidden premise to the academics that state that modern student writers are not as capable as their predecessors. Namely they seem to suggest a static and unchanging preferred writing standard is valuable and necessary. Standard writing styles and practices may have made sense when pen and paper were the primary conveyance of information. Now we live in the days of email, instant messaging, Internet video, etc. Is it really necessary to retain one single universal writing and information-exchange paradigm that is arbitrarily designated as superior? It is not. Academics that insist that the apparently diminished writing ability of students must somehow be remedied may need to reevaluate the situation. The necessity of the standard essay and writing styles of the last century may not be the permanent fixture academics assumed them to be. That is why, while good writing is important, it is folly to buy into the claims that students are somehow less capable to express themselves in a world of constantly changing information-exchange paradigms. We have no valid perspective from which to make this determination. No one knows what writing skills will be sought after ten, twenty, or thirty years from now. Education should be thought of as intellectual scaffolding that is used to build the future. As such this scaffolding should be adapted to new writing conventions. Education is not meant to edify and preserve the dogmatic structures of academic tradition needlessly. Sadly the latter is how educational institutions often behave. Therefore my advice is to not even bother to humor the "sky is falling" cries of the academic writing world. Just develop your own writing craft the best you can and leave the progress statistics to the statisticians.

4   All that being said, there are useful methods one can use to help craft an essay that accomplishes the assignment at hand. While thesis/support form is the form we are all familiar with it is not necessarily best to strictly apply it in all situations. We can think of the thesis/support form as a particular type of literary scaffolding. It is aptly suited to give the necessary structure to many things we write. However, this scaffold of thesis/support can be over-relied on. In a unique piece of writing this universal scaffolding may not be sufficient to build the idea or paper you intended to. There may be some argument or facet of your topic that simply does not fit in the five paragraph thesis/support form. Part of being a good writer is in knowing when it's okay to take off the training wheels. It is the primary goal of the writer to communicate thoroughly and completely. Structure and form serve to enhance the communication experience by making it faster and more famil-

iar. But, when structure or techniques distort or alter the original intent of a piece of writing it is not a good thing. This means the ideal is simply for you to express a full and complete thought in whatever way it can be most completely expressed. Do not sacrifice content for the sake of structure. Learn to be a good reader of your own writing. Critiquing and reworking is the best way to build a piece of work that is satisfying each time you read it.

5   Ultimately there is no magic bullet in academic writing. You must be prepared to use any fancy trick in your writing should the need arise. Conversely, you must be willing to sterilize your writing and give only simple, boring prose if that is indeed what is asked of you. You are allowed to set your own goals in college writing. You can write to make a point. This is when you are the only credible judge of your piece and you just try to express what you want and accept the grade you are given. You can also write to get a grade. This is when you attempt to adapt your style and content to the particular instructor and assignment at hand. This is a fine method if your GPA is your primary concern. The important thing is to always remember that there is no ultimate authority on writing and how good or bad it is. You have to please your instructors to pass your classes but that does not mean that they or anyone else can accurately or completely evaluate your writing. It is best to use the academy as a place to learn about yourself and the people you interact with. By adapting to the criticisms, fair and unfair alike, you can become a better writer for the rest of your life.

Literacy Connections

1. What do you think is the most important piece of advice Lautamo has for college students?
2. What kinds of writing "formulas" like thesis/support have you been taught? Do you agree with Lautamo that college literacies ask you to move beyond these kinds of writing formulas? Why or why not?
3. To what extent do you agree with Lautamo's assertion that "High school should have equipped you with all the necessary conventions and techniques to finish any college writing assignment"? Explain your response.
4. What is your position on the issue of whether students should adapt their style and content to the instructor and to the assignment to get a good grade or whether they should write in their own voice and style?
5. How does Lautamo's advice compare with Fiona Glade's advice about college writing in the introductory essay to the chapter?

Before You Read

If you were a researcher studying a college junior writing in different classes, what questions would you ask the student?

Excerpts from "A Stranger in Strange Lands: A College Student Writing Across the Curriculum"

*Lucille Parkinson McCarthy**

Lucille Parkinson McCarthy is a writing teacher and researcher whose specialty is the study of writing across the curriculum. She teaches at the University of Maryland, Baltimore County. In "A Stranger in Strange Lands," McCarthy reports on the results of a study of a college junior, Dave Garrison, as he writes in three different classes: first-year composition, Introduction to Poetry, and Cell Biology. "A Stranger in Strange Lands" was published in an academic journal for writing teachers, *Research in the Teaching of English*. Even though the audience for the article is writing teachers, college students can also learn a lot about the way writing expectations differ in different disciplines by reading McCarthy's study.

1   Dave Garrison, a college junior and the focus of the present study, was asked how he would advise incoming freshmen about writing for their college courses. His answer was both homely and familiar.

2   "I'd tell them," he said, "first you've got to figure out what your teachers want. And then you've got to give it to them if you're gonna' get the grade." He paused a moment and added, "And that's not always so easy."

3   No matter how we teachers may feel about Dave's response, it does reflect his sensitivity to school writing as a social affair. Successful students are those who can, in their interactions with teachers during the semester, determine what constitutes appropriate texts in each classroom: the content, structures, language, ways of thinking, and types of evidence required in that discipline and by that teacher. They can then produce such a text. Students who cannot do this, for whatever reason—cultural, intellectual, motivational—are those who fail, deemed incompetent communicators in that particular setting. They are unable to follow what Britton calls the "rules of the game" in each class (1975, p. 76). As students go from one classroom to another they must play a wide range of games, the rules for which Britton points out, include many conventions and presuppositions that are not explicitly articulated.

4   In this article, writing in college is viewed as a process of assessing and adapting to the requirements in unfamiliar academic settings. Specifically,

---

*I am grateful to the participants who made this study possible and to Professors Linda Brodkey, Barbara McDaniel, Susan Lytle, and David Smith whose insights and support were invaluable.

the study examined how students figured out what constituted appropriate texts in their various courses and how they went about producing them. And, further, it examined what characterized the classroom contexts which enhanced or denied students' success in this process. This study was a 21-month project which focused on the writing experiences of one college student, Dave, in three of his courses, Freshman Composition in the spring of his freshman year, and, in his sophomore year, Introduction to Poetry in the fall and Cell Biology in the spring. Dave, a biology/pre-med major, was typical of students at his college in terms of his SAT scores (502 verbal; 515 math), his high school grades, and his white, middle-class family background.

5   As I followed Dave from one classroom writing situation to another, I came to see him, as he made his journey from one discipline to another, as a stranger in strange lands. In each new class Dave believed that the writing he was doing was totally unlike anything he had ever done before. This metaphor of a newcomer in a foreign country proved to be a powerful way of looking at Dave's behaviors as he worked to use the new languages in unfamiliar academic territories. Robert Heinlein's (1961) science fiction novel suggested this metaphor originally. But Heinlein's title is slightly different; his stranger is in a *single* strange land. Dave perceived himself to be in one strange land after another. . . .

Results and Discussion

6 Information from all data sources supports three general conclusions, two concerning Dave's interpretation and production of the required writing tasks and one concerning social factors in the classrooms that influenced him as he wrote. First, although the writing tasks in the three classes were in many ways similar, Dave interpreted them as being totally different from each other and totally different from anything he had ever done before. This was evidenced in the interview, protocol, and text analysis data.

7   Second, certain social factors in Freshman Composition and Cell Biology appeared to foster Dave's writing success in them. Observation and interview data indicated that two unarticulated aspects of the classroom writing contexts influenced his achievement. These social factors were (1) the functions that writing served for Dave in each setting, and (2) the roles that participants and students' texts played there. These social factors were bound up with what Dave ultimately learned from and about writing in each class.

8   Third, Dave exhibited consistent ways of figuring out what constituted appropriate texts in each setting, in his terms, of "figuring out what the teacher wanted." Evidence from the interviews and protocols shows that he typically drew upon six information sources, in a process that was in

large part tacit. These information sources included teacher-provided instructional supports, sources Dave found on his own, and his prior knowledge. . . .

Dave's Interpretation of the Writing Tasks

9 **The Writer's Concerns While Composing.** In spite of the similarities among the writing tasks for the three courses, evidence from several sources shows that Dave interpreted them as being totally different from each other and totally different from anything he had ever done before. Dave's characteristic approach across courses was to focus so fully on the particular new ways of thinking and writing in each setting that commonalities with previous writing were obscured for him. And interwoven with Dave's conviction that the writing for these courses was totally dissimilar was his differing success in them. Though he worked hard in all three courses, he made B's in Freshman Composition, D's and C's in Poetry, and A's in Cell Biology.

10 The protocol data explain in part why the writing for these classes seemed so different to Dave. Dave's chief concerns while composing for each course were very different. His focus in Freshman Composition was on textual coherence. Fifty-four percent of his expressed concerns were for coherence of thesis and subpoints, coherence within paragraphs, and sentence cohesion. By contrast, in Poetry, though Dave did mention thesis and subpoints, his chief concerns were not with coherence, but with the new ways of thinking and writing in that setting. Forty-four percent of his concerns focused on accurately interpreting the poem and properly using quotes. In Cell Biology, yet a new focus of concerns is evident. Seventy-two percent of Dave's concerns deal with the new rules of use in that academic discipline. His chief concerns in Biology were to accurately understand the scientific terms and concepts in the journal article and then to accurately rephrase and connect these in his own text, following the same five-part structure in which the published experiment was reported. It is no wonder that the writing for these classes seemed very different to Dave. As a newcomer in each academic territory, Dave's attention was occupied by the new conventions of interpretation and language use in each community.

11 The same preoccupations controlled his subsequent work on the papers. In each course Dave wrote a second draft, which he then typed. In none of these second drafts did Dave see the task differently or make major changes. He is, in this regard, like the secondary students Applebee (1984) studied who were unable, without teacher assistance, to revise their writing in more than minor ways. And Dave revised none of these papers after the teachers had responded.

12   We can further fill out the pictures of Dave's composing for the three classes by combining the protocol findings with the observation and interview data. In his first protocol session, in April of his freshman year, Dave composed the first draft of his fourth paper for Freshman Composition, an essay in which he chose to analyze the wrongs of abortion. To this session Dave brought an outline of this thesis and subpoints. He told me that he had spent only 30 minutes writing it the night before, but that the topic was one he had though a lot about. As he composed, Dave was most concerned with , and apparently very dependent upon, his outline, commenting on it, glancing at it, or pausing to study it 14 times during the 30 minutes of composing. Dave's next most frequently expressed concerns were for coherence at paragraph and sentence levels, what Dr. Carter referred to as coherence of mid-sized and small parts. These were the new "rules of use" in this setting. Dave told me that in high school he had done some "bits and pieces" of writing and some outlines for history, but that he had never before written essays like this. The total time Dave spent on his abortion essay was five hours.

> "... in high school he had done some 'bits and pieces' of writing and some outlines ..., but ... he had never before written essays like this."

13   In Dave's Poetry protocol session seven months later, in November of his sophomore year, he composed part of the first draft of his third and last paper for that class, a six-page analysis of a poem called "Marriage" by contemporary poet Gregory Corso. To this session he brought two pages of notes and his *Norton Anthology of Poetry* in which he had underlined and written notes in the margins beside the poem. He told me that he had spent four hours (of an eventual total of 11) preparing to write: reading the poem many times and finding a critical essay on it in the library. During his prewriting and composing, Dave's primary concern was to get the right interpretation of the poem, "the true meaning" as he phrased it. And as Dave wrote, he assumed that his professor knew the true meaning, a meaning, Dave said, that "was there, but not there, not just what it says on the surface." Further, Dave knew that he must argue his interpretation, using not his own but the poet's words; this was his second most frequently expressed concern.

14   As Dave composed, he appeared to be as tied to the poem as he had been to his outline in Freshman Composition the semester before. He seemed to be almost *physically* attached to the *Norton Anthology* by his left forefinger as he progressed down the numbers he had marked in the margins. He was, we might say, tied to the concrete material, the "facts" of the poem before him. Dave never got his own essay structure; rather, he worked down the poem, explicating from beginning to end. In the retrospective interview he

said, "I didn't really have to think much about my thesis and subs because they just come naturally now. . . . But anyway it's not like in Comp last year. Here my first paragraph is the introduction with the thesis, and the stanzas are the subpoints." Dave's preoccupation with the poem and the new conventions of interpreting and quoting poetry resulted in a paper that was not an analysis but a summary with some interpretation along the way. His focus on these new rules of use appeared to limit his ability to apply previously learned skills, the thesis-subpoint analytical structure, and kept him working at the more concrete summary level.

15   This domination by the concrete may often characterize newcomers' first steps as they attempt to use language in unfamiliar disciplines (Williams, 1985). Dave's professor, Dr. Forson, seemed to be familiar with this phenomenon when he warned students in his lecture on writing: "You must remember that the poet ordered the poem. *You* order your essay with your own thesis and subtheses. Get away from 'Next. . . . Next'." But if Dave heard this in September, he had forgotten it by November. Dave's experience is consonant with Langer's (1984) finding that students who know more about a subject as they begin to write are likely to choose analysis rather than summary. And these students receive higher scores for writing quality as well.

16   In his writing for Cell Biology the following semester, Dave's concerns were again focused on the new and unfamiliar conventions in this setting. Before writing his last paper, a four-page review of an experiment on glycoprotein reported in *The Journal of Cell Biology,* Dave spent three hours preparing. (He eventually spent a total of eight hours on the review.) He had chosen the article in the library from a list the professor had given to students and had then read the article twice, underlining it, making notes, and looking up the definitions of unfamiliar terms. To the protocol session Dave brought these notes, the article, and a sheet on which he had written what he called "Dr. Kelly's guidelines," the five-part scientific experiment format that Dr. Kelly wanted students to follow: Background, Objectives, Procedures, Results, and Discussion.

17   In his composing aloud, Dave's chief concerns in Biology were, as in Poetry the semester before, with the reading, in this case the journal article. But here, unlike Poetry, Dave said the meaning was "all out on the table." In Poetry he had had to interpret meaning from the poem's connotative language; in Biology, by contrast, he could look up meanings, a situation with which Dave was far more comfortable. But as he composed for Biology, he was just as tied to the journal article as he had been to the poem or to his outline in previous semesters. Dave paused frequently to consult the article, partially covering it at times so that his own paper was physically closer to what he was summarizing at that moment.

18   Dave's first and second most commonly expressed concerns during the Biology protocol session were for rephrasing and connecting parts of the

article and for following Dr. Kelly's guidelines. These were, in essence, concerns for coherence and organization, what Dave was most concerned with in Freshman Composition. But the writing for Biology bore little relation in Dave's mind to what he had done in Freshman Composition. In Biology he was indeed concerned about his organization, but here it was the five-part scientific format he had been given, very different, it seemed to him, than the thesis/subpoint organization he had had to create for his freshman essays. In fact, until I questioned him about it at the end of the semester, Dave never mentioned the freshman thesis/subpoint structure. And the concerns for coherence at paragraph and sentence levels that had been so prominent as he wrote for Freshman Composition were replaced in Biology by his concern for rephrasing the article's already coherent text. In Freshman Composition Dave had talked about trying to get his sentences and paragraphs to "fit" or "flow" together. In Biology, however, he talked about trying to get the article into his own words, about "cutting," "simplifying," and "combining two sentences." Again, it is no wonder that Dave believed that this writing was totally new. It took one of Dave's friends and my prodding during an interview to make Dave see that he had indeed written summaries before. Lots of them. . . .

Social Aspects of the Classrooms that Influenced Dave's Writing

19 Why was Dave's success in writing in these classrooms so different? The answers to this question will illuminate some of the dimensions along which school writing situations differ and thus influence student achievement. It would be a mistake to think that the differing task structure was the only reason that Dave was more successful in Biology and Freshman Composition than he was in Poetry. Assignments are, as I have suggested, only a small part of the classroom interaction, limited written exchanges that reflect the nature of the communication situation created by participants in that setting. Two unarticulated qualities in the contexts for writing in Freshman Composition and Biology appeared to foster Dave's success in those classes. These were (1) the social functions Dave's writing served for him in those classes, and (2) the roles played by participants and by students' texts there.

20 **The Functions Dave Saw His Writing as Accomplishing.** It has been argued that the social functions served by writing must be seen as an intrinsic part of the writing experience (Clark & Florio, 1983; Hymes, 1972a, 1972b; Scribner & Cole, 1981). Evidence from interviews and observations indicate that the writing in Freshman Composition and Biology was for Dave a meaningful social activity, meaningful beyond just getting him through the course. Further, Dave and his teachers in Freshman Composition and Biology mutually understood and valued those functions. This

was not the case in Poetry. The data show a correlation not only between meaningful social functions served by the writing and Dave's success with it, but also between the writing's social meaning and Dave's ability to remember and draw upon it in subsequent semesters.

21   In Freshman Composition Dave's writing served four valuable functions for him. He articulated all of these.

1. Writing to prepare him for future writing in school and career
2. Writing to explore topics of his choice
3. Writing to participate with other students in the classroom
4. Writing to demonstrate academic competence

22   In Biology Dave also saw his writing as serving four valuable functions:

1. Writing to learn the language of Cell Biology, which he saw as necessary to his career
2. Writing to prepare him for his next semester's writing in Immunology
3. Writing to make connections between his classwork and actual work being done by professionals in the field
4. Writing to demonstrate academic competence

Evidence from interviews and observation shows that Dr. Carter and Dr. Kelly saw writing in their classes as serving the same four functions that Dave did.

23   On the other hand, in Poetry, though Dave's professor stated four functions of student writing, Dave saw his writing as serving only one function for him: writing to demonstrate academic competence. Dave, always the compliant student, did say after he had received his disappointing grade in Poetry that the writing in Poetry was probably good for him: "Probably any kind of writing helps you." Though he may well be right, Dave actually saw his writing for Poetry as serving such a limited function—evaluation of his skills in writing poetry criticism for Dr. Forson—that he was not really convinced (and little motivated by the notion) that this writing would serve him in any general way.

24   Dave contended that any writing task was easy or difficult for him according to his interest in it. When I asked him what he meant by interesting, he said, "If it has something to do with my life. Like it could explain something to me or give me an answer that I could use now." Writing must have, in other words, meaningful personal and social functions for Dave if it is to be manageable, "easy," for him. These functions existed for Dave in Freshman Composition and Biology, providing the applications and personal transaction with the material that may be generally required for learning and forging personal knowledge (Dewey, 1949; Polanyi, 1958).

25   Dave's Poetry class, however, served no such personally meaningful functions. Six weeks after the Poetry course was finished, I asked Dave some further questions about his last paper for that course, the discussion of the Corso poem on which he had worked 11 hours. He could remember almost nothing about it. When I asked him to speculate why this was, he said, "I guess it's because I have no need to remember it." By contrast, when I asked Dave in the fall of his junior year if his Cell Biology writing was serving him in his Immunology course as he had expected, he said, "Yes. The teacher went over how to write up our labs, but most of us had the idea anyway from last semester because we'd read those journal articles. We were already exposed to it."

26   Of course the functions of his writing in Biology served Dave better than those in Poetry in part because he was a biology major. The writing for Cell Biology fit into a larger whole: his growing body of knowledge about this field and his professional future. The material in Cell Biology was for Dave a comprehensible part of the discipline of Biology which was in turn a comprehensible part of the sciences. Dave was, with experience, gradually acquiring a coherent sense of the language of the discipline, how biologists think and speak and what it is they talk about. And his understanding of the language of biology was accompanied by an increasing confidence in his own ability to use it. Both of these are probably necessary foundations for later, more abstract and complex uses of the language (Piaget, 1952; Perry, 1970; Williams, 1985).

27   In the required one-semester Poetry class, however, the poems seemed to Dave to be unrelated to each other except for commonly used poetic devices, and his writing about them was unrelated to his own life by anything at all beyond his need to find the "true meaning" and get an acceptable grade. Dave's different relationship to the languages of these disciplines was shown when he said, "In Biology I'm using what I've *learned*. It's just putting what I've learned on paper. But in Poetry, more or less each poem is different, so it's not *taught* to you. You just have to figure it out from that poem itself and hope Dr. Forson likes it." Nor, in Poetry, was Dave ever invited to make personally meaningful connections with the poems. And he never did it on his own, no doubt in part because he was so preoccupied with the new ways of thinking and speaking that he was trying to use.

28   In Freshman Composition the social function of writing that was perhaps most powerful for Dave was writing to participate with other students in the classroom. In his peer writing group Dave, for the first time ever, discussed his writing with others. Here he communicated personal positions and insights to his friends, an influential audience for him. That an important social function was served by these students' work with each other is suggested by their clear memory, a year and a half later, both of their essays and of each others' reactions to them.

29   The four social functions that Dave's writing in freshman Composition accomplished for him enhanced his engagement with and attitude toward the writing he did in that class. This engagement is reflected in Dave's memory not only of his essays and his friends' reactions to them, but also in his memory and use of the ideas and terms from that course. When Dave talked about his writing during his sophomore and junior years, he used the process terms he had learned in Freshman Composition: prewriting, revision, and drafts. He also used other language he had learned as a freshman, speaking at times about his audience's needs, about narrowing his topic, about connecting his sentences, providing more details, and choosing his organizational structure. This is not to say that Dave had mastered these skills in every writing situation nor that he always accurately diagnosed problems in his own work. In fact, we know that he did not. It is to say, however, that Dave did recognize and could talk about some of the things that writing does involve in many situations. Thus, the value of this course for Dave lay not so much in the thesis/subpoint essay structure. Rather, Dave had, as a result of his experiences in Freshman Composition, learned that writing is a process that can be talked about, managed, and controlled.

30   Thus the social functions that writing served for Dave in each class were viewed as an intrinsic part of his writing experiences there. Where these functions were numerous and mutually understood and valued by Dave and his teacher, Dave was more successful in figuring out and producing the required discourse. And then he remembered it longer. In Poetry, where his writing served few personally valued ends, Dave did less well, making a C on the first paper, a D on the second, and a C + on the third. It should be noted, in addition, that grades themselves serve a social function in classrooms: defining attitudes and roles. Dave's low grades in Poetry probably further alienated him from the social communication processes in that classroom community and helped define his role there.

The Roles Played by the Participants and by Students' Texts

31 Other social aspects of these classroom contexts for writing which affected Dave's experiences were the roles played by the people and texts in them. Such roles are tacitly assigned in classroom interaction and create the context in which the student stranger attempts to determine the rules of language use in that territory. Here we will examine (1) Dave's role in relation to the teacher, (2) Dave's role in relation to other students in the class, and (3) the role played by students' texts there.

32 **Dave's Role in Relation to the Teacher.** This is a particularly important role relationship in any classroom because it tacitly shapes the writer-audience relation that students use as they attempt to communicate appropriately. In all three classes Dave was writing for his teachers as pupil to examiner.

However, data from several sources show that there were important variations in the actual "enactments" (Goffman, 1961) of this role-relationship.

33   In Composition, both Dave and his professor played the role of writer. Throughout the semester Dr. Carter talked about what and how she wrote, the long time she spent in prewriting activities, the eight times she typically revised her work, and the strategies she used to understand her audience in various situations. She spoke to students as if she and they were all writers working together, saying such things as "I see some of you write like I do," or "Let's work together to shape this language." And, as we have seen, she structured the course to provide opportunities for students to play the role of writer in their peer groups. She also asked them to describe their writing processes for several of their essays. Dave told me in an interview during his junior year, "In high school I couldn't stand writing, but in Comp I started to change because I knew more what I was doing. I learned that there are steps you can go through, and I learned how to organize a paper." As a freshman, Dave understood for the first time something of what it feels like to be a writer.

34   In Biology both Dave and his teacher, Dr. Kelly, saw Dave as playing the role of newcomer, learning the language needed for initiation into the profession. Dr. Kelly played the complementary role of experienced professional who was training Dave in the ways of speaking in that discipline, ways they both assumed Dave would learn in time.

35   In Poetry, on the other hand, Dave played the role of outsider in relationship to his teacher, the insider who knew the true meanings of poetry. And Dave stayed the outsider, unable ever to fully get the teacher's "true meaning." This outsider/insider relationship between Dave and Dr. Forson was created by a number of factors: (1) Their spoken and written interaction, (2) the few meaningful social functions served for Dave by the writing in that class, (3) the demanding nature of the analytic task, combined with (4) the limited knowledge Dave commanded in that setting, (5) the limited number of effective instructional supports, and (6) the low grades Dave got, which further alienated him from the communication processes in that class. (To the instructional supports provided in Poetry we will return below.) Because, Dave's outsider role was not a pleasant one for him, he seemed increasingly, to separate his thinking from his writing in Poetry, saying several times that he had the right ideas, the teacher just did not like the way he wrote them.

Dave's Role in Relationship to Other Students

36 Students' relationships with each other, like those between students and teachers, are created as students interact within the classroom structures the teacher has set up. These classroom structures grow out of teachers' explicit and tacit notions about writing and learning. What specifically were the relationships among students in Freshman Composition, Biology, and Poetry?

37   In Composition, as we have seen, students shared their writing and responded to each other's work. The classroom structure reflected Dr. Carter's perhaps tacit notion that writing is a social as well as intellectual affair. However, in neither Poetry nor Biology was time built into the class for students to talk with each other about their writing. Dave lamented this as he wrote for Poetry early in his sophomore year, because, he said, he now realized how valuable the small group sessions had been in Freshman Composition the semester before.

38   In Biology, Dave told me students did talk informally about the journal articles they had selected and how they were progressing on their summaries. Dr. Kelly, who circulated during lab, was at times included in these informal talks about writing. And it is no surprise that students discussed their writing in this way in Biology in light of Dr. Kelly's notions about writing. It is, he believes, an essential part of what scientists do. He told me that it often comes as a rude shock to students that the way biologists survive in the field is by writing. He said, "These students are bright, and they can memorize piles of facts, but they're not yet good at writing. They know what science *is,*" he told me, "but they don't know what scientists *do.*" Thus, writing up research results is seen by Dr. Kelly as an integral part of a biologist's lab work. No wonder his students talked about it.

39   In Poetry, however, there was little talk of any kind among students. Classes were primarily lectures where Dr. Forson explicated poems and explained poetic devices. Only occasionally did he call on one of the 22 students for an opinion. This lack of student interaction in Poetry was in line with the image of the writer that Dr. Forson described for students, an image that may be widely shared in literary studies: A person alone with his or her books and thoughts. Dr. Forson did, however, tell students that he himself often got his ideas for writing from listening to himself talk about poems in class. Yet, in conversation with me, he said that he did not want students discussing the poems and their writing with each other because he feared they would not think for themselves. Dave picked up on this idea very clearly. It was not until the fall of his junior year that he admitted to me that he and his girlfriend had worked together on their papers. They had discussed the interpretations of the poems and how they might best write them, but, he told me, they had been careful to choose different poems to write about so that Dr. Forson wouldn't know they had worked together. This absence of student interaction in Poetry may have contributed to the outsider role that Dave played in that class.

40   Throughout this study I was amazed at the amount of talk that goes on all the time outside class among students as they work to figure out the writing requirements in various courses. What Dave's experience in Poetry may suggest is that where student collaboration in writing is not openly accepted, it goes on clandestinely.

41 **The Roles Played by Students' Texts.** What were students' texts called and how were they handled? Interview and observation data show that students' texts were treated quite differently in these three courses, and this affected how Dave saw the assignments, and, perhaps more important, how he saw himself as writer.

42   In Freshman Composition Dave wrote what he referred to as "essays"; in Biology, "reviews"; in Poetry, "papers." This latter term is commonly used, of course, but it is one that Emig (1983, p. 173) says suggests a low status text: "Paper"—as if there were no words on the sheet at all. In Poetry the high status texts, the ones that were discussed and interpreted, were the poems. Students' works were just more or less successful explications of those. Furthermore, in Poetry the one model essay the students read was written by the teacher. Though students were told they should think of their peers as their audience, in fact they never read each other's essays at all. Students' texts were, rather, passed only between student and teacher as in a private conversation.

43   In Biology, student texts enjoyed a higher status. Excellent student reviews were posted and students were encouraged to read them; they were to serve as models. Some student writers were thus defined as competent speakers in this territory, and the message was clear to Dave: This was a language that he too could learn given time and proper training.

44   And in Freshman Composition, of course, student texts were the *objects* studied. The class read good and flawed student texts from former semesters and from their own. This not only helped Dave with his writing, it also dignified student writing and elevated his estimation of his own work. Student texts were not, in short, private affairs between teacher and student; they were the subject matter of this college course.

45   Thus the roles that were enacted by teachers, students, and students' texts were quite different in each classroom and were an integral part of Dave's writing experiences there. The participants' interaction and the social functions that writing serves are important factors working to create the communication situation. And this communication situation, it has been suggested, is the fundamental factor shaping the success of writing instruction (Langer & Applebee, 1984, p. 171).

The Information Sources Dave Drew Upon

46 In a process that was in large part tacit, Dave drew upon six sources for information about what constituted successful writing in Freshman Composition, Poetry, and Biology. These included teacher-provided instructional supports, sources Dave found on his own, and his prior experience. Many of these have been mentioned above. They are summarized in Table 4.

TABLE 4

Information Sources Dave Drew Upon in Assessing Required Discourse

Information Sources	Freshman Composition	Poetry	Cell Biology
What teachers said in class about writing	Constant lectures & exercises about process & products	One lecture General statements to the class about their papers when returning them	Ten minutes giving "guidelines" when returning 1st set of reviews Informal comments in lab
Model texts	Many, including flawed models	One, written by teacher One, written by professional (from library)	The articles being summarized served as models. Posted student reviews
Talk with other students	Frequent groups in class	With friend outside class	Informal, in class
Teacher's written responses to writing	Read responses & revised early essays accordingly	Read. No revision required	Read. No revision required
Dave's prior experience	The extent to which Dave drew upon prior experience is difficult to say. In each class he believed he had no prior experience to draw from. However we know he had had related prior experience.		
Personal talk with teacher	One conference with teacher	None	None

47   Of particular interest are the information sources Dave drew upon (or failed to draw upon) in Poetry, the course in which the writing assignment was the most demanding and in which Dave did least well in assessing and producing the required discourse. The information source that Dr. Forson intended to be most helpful to students, the instructional support on which he spent a great deal of time, was his response to their papers. However his extensive comments did not help Dave a great deal in learning how to communicate in that setting. Dave said that the comments on his first paper did help him some with his second, but he really did not refer to Dr. Forson's responses on the second paper as he wrote the third. Nor did Dave use the comments on the third paper when preparing for the essay question on the final exam. Dr. Forson required no revision in direct response to his comments, and the expected carry-over of his responses from one paper to the next did not occur. Rather, Dave repeated similar mistakes again and again. The assumption that trial and error will improve students' writing across a series of similar tasks did not hold true for Dave's work, in Poetry.

48   Neither was the model text in Poetry, Dr. Forson's analysis of the Herrick poem that he went over in lecture, as useful an information source for Dave as Dr. Forson had hoped it would be. Dave told me that though he had looked at Dr. Forson's model critical essay as he wrote his first paper, it had not helped him a great deal. "Seeing how someone else did it," he said, "is a lot different than doing it yourself." In Freshman Composition and Biology, however, the model texts, both excellent and flawed ones, were more numerous. And in Biology, the model provided by the article Dave was summarizing was virtually inescapable. Model texts are, it seems reasonable, particularly important to newcomers learning the conventions of discourse in a new academic territory.

49   An information source which Dave was not adept at using in any course was direct questioning of the professor, the native-speaker expert in each setting. Dave never voluntarily questioned a teacher, though in October of his sophomore year, when he was doing poorly in Poetry, he did make an attempt to speak with Dr. Forson at his office. But when Dr. Forson was not there, Dave waited only a short time and then left—relieved, he said. He did not return. In Freshman Composition, however, Dave was required to interact with Dr. Carter individually in his mid-semester conference. That interview provided an additional information source upon which Dave could draw as he assessed and adapted to the writing requirements in that class.

Discussion

50 What, then, can be learned from Dave's experiences? First, this study adds to existing research which suggests that school writing is not a monolithic activity or global skill. Rather, the contexts for writing may be so different from one classroom to another, the ways of speaking in them so diverse, the social meanings of writing and the interaction patterns so different, that the courses may be for the student writer like so many foreign countries. These differences were apparent in this study not only in Dave's perceptions of the courses but in his concerns while writing and in his written products.

51   Second, the findings of this study have several implications for our understanding of writing development. This study suggests that writing development is, in part, context-dependent. In each new classroom community, Dave in many ways resembled a beginning language user. He focused on a limited number of new concerns, and he was unable to move beyond concrete ways of thinking and writing, the facts of the matter at hand. Moreover, skills mastered in one situation, such as the thesis-subpoint organization in Freshman Composition, did not, as Dave insisted, automatically transfer to new contexts with differing problems and language and differing amounts of knowledge that he controlled. To better

understand the stages that students progress through in achieving competence in academic speech communities, we need further research.

52   Dave's development across his freshman and sophomore years, where he was repeatedly a newcomer, may also be viewed in terms of his attitude toward writing. Evidence over 21 months shows that his notion of the purpose of school writing changed very little. Though there were, as we have seen, other functions accomplished for Dave by his writing in Freshman Composition and Biology, he always understood the purpose of his school writing as being primarily to satisfy a teacher-examiner's requirements. A change that did occur, however, was Dave's increased understanding of some of the activities that writers actually engage in and an increased confidence in his writing ability. As a freshman, he had told me that he did not like to write and was not very good, but by the fall of his junior year he sounded quite different. Because of a number of successful classroom experiences with writing, and an ability to forget the less successful ones, Dave told me, "Writing is no problem for me. At work, in school, I just do it.". . .

Literacy Connections

1. Because this article was written for an audience of college writing teachers, there were likely some terms and concepts you were unfamiliar with. Choose one of these terms or concepts and conduct an Internet search of the term to get a better understanding. Be prepared to share what you found with the class.

2. Make a list of the aspects of Dave's approaches to writing that McCarthy argues make him effective as a college writer, and another list of the aspects of Dave's approaches to writing that McCarthy argues make him ineffective as a college writer.

3. Compare Dave's college writing experiences to your college writing experiences. To what extent, and in what ways, are your college writing experiences similar to and different than Dave's?

4. McCarthy says, "Writers, like speakers, must use the communication means considered appropriate by members of particular speech or discourse communities. And the writer's work, at the same time, may affect the norms of the community." Can you think of a time when you or another writer's work affected the norms of the community? Talk about what the norms were and how the writer affected the norms.

5. Skim McCarthy's essay and underline places where Dave's teachers discussed their goals and expectations for writing. How do these goals compare to the first-year writing outcomes and the outcomes from across the curriculum from earlier in the chapter?

Student Writing from Across the Curriculum

Before You Read

Make a list of what you think are the features of writing in social science fields such as sociology, education, political science, and economics. Think of features of literacy situations such as tone, style, types of evidence used, common genres, audience, purpose, and so on.

Emotional Disturbances: The Effects of Parental Neglect Types on Children

Nancy Alkema

Nancy Alkema was a student in a child development research methods course at California State University, Sacramento, when she wrote the report, "Emotional Disturbances: The Effects of Parental Neglect Types on Children." Her instructor asked students to write an original research proposal. The assignment required students to "identify an area of interest in child development, conduct a library search to find relevant literature, design a feasible study to test a tangible research question, think about expected results and modes of analysis, and write a research proposal in the style of the discipline (American Psychological Association, APA)." Alkema's report is representative of the kind of writing valued in the social sciences. It was published in *Writing the University*, the online journal of undergraduate student writing at California State University, Sacramento. To view Alkema's cover letter and a cover letter from her instructor, visit www.csus.edu/wac/journal/2009/Alkema.html. The URL for *Writing the University* is www.csus.edu/wac/journal.

Running head: EMOTIONAL DISTURBANCES   1

Emotional Disturbances: The Effects of Parental
Neglect Types on Children

Nancy Alkema

EMOTIONAL DISTURBANCES   2

Abstract

The aim of this current study will be to focus on a silent epidemic, that
because of its often subtle nature goes unnoticed and untreated, yet
creates life-changing problems for the children who experience parental
emotional neglect. This study will attempt to narrow down which types of
neglect are most harmful or most predictive of emotional disturbances.
Neglect types that will be looked at are psychological/emotional, physical,
and cognitive. Some neglectful behavior may fall into two or three of
these categories, and each will be rated in this manner. Participants will be
taken from several juvenile centers across the nation with an equal
amount of males and females who have previously been diagnosed with
emotional disturbances. They will each be interviewed by a highly trained
and experienced juvenile psychologist and monitored by a lie-detector
during the interview. This study will advance the knowledge of parental
neglect on emotional disturbances in children. However, it would be
beneficial for further studies to determine the effects of both neglect and
abuse as separate and combined factors in emotional disturbances.

EMOTIONAL DISTURBANCES   3

Emotional Disturbances: The Effects of Parental

Neglect Types on Children

In working with children with emotional disturbances it is important to understand possible causes of this disorder. Although, there is a vast amount of research on various aspects of emotional disturbances, most of these studies deal with social support systems, while fewer studies investigate the actual causes. There may be some evidence toward biological determinants, as with children with developmental disorders; however, there is more evidence showing an effect between emotional disturbances and parental neglect, most specifically within dysfunctional family systems. The premise behind the current study is consistent with other studies in showing that parental neglect, a form of child abuse, is a significant contributor to emotional disturbances. More specifically, it is important to determine which types of emotional neglect are most harmful in order to understand the problem better. Gender will also be studied to determine whether there is an effect.

The types of emotional neglect that will be looked at are emotional/psychological, cognitive, and physical. Emotional/psychological deals with depriving a child of his or her basic needs that provide support for healthy emotional and psychological growth such as leaving a child feeling anxious, stressed or fearful after experiencing a parental quarrel or fight. Cognitive neglect would be a form of neglect affecting the normal, healthy cognitive growth such as encouraging racism. Physical neglect would be considered as neglectful behaviors that put the child at an increased risk of harm such as ignoring a child's illness, not taking him or her to the doctor or giving medication to relieve pain.

EMOTIONAL DISTURBANCES   4

It is also important to understand the difference between emotional neglect, emotional abuse, and emotional maltreatment. Emotional neglect is considered to be acts of omission concerning the care of a child. It is more narrowly defined as a pervasive problem within the interactions of the relationship. It is distinguished from emotional abuse, which would be acts of commission—deliberate acts. Emotional maltreatment is an inclusive term which includes neglect and abuse (Iwaniec, Larkin, & McSherry, 2007). This term will be used throughout the literature review since that is how it is referred. However, the current study will attempt to single out emotional neglect as an indicator of emotional disturbances.

Iwaniec et al. (2007) also found that the effects of emotional maltreatment are detrimental to the child's development. These acts of maltreatment convey to the child that he or she is worthless, flawed, unloved, unwanted, or endangered. It includes emotional unavailability, unresponsiveness, and withdrawal of attention. An emotional disturbance can be characterized by poor self image, cognitive delays and difficulties, problems with coping, and difficulty forming meaningful relationships, or connecting with others.

Changes in effects can be seen at different stages of development. Children who have been emotionally maltreated have higher aggression, anger, and frustration. Older children and adolescents experience social rejection, dependency, and school difficulties. College students have difficulties with clinical distress and psychological disturbances such as obsessive compulsiveness, depression and anxiety. Symptoms in adults include depression, eating disorders, suicidal ideation, anxiety, low

EMOTIONAL DISTURBANCES 5

self-esteem, interpersonal and sexual problems. They are also more likely than others to have substance abuse problems (Iwaniec, et al. 2007).

Although all forms of maltreatment have an element of emotional harm, (Hart, Binggeli, & Brassard [1998], as seen in Iwaniec et al. 2007), psychological unavailability from parents was seen as the most harmful type of neglect (Egeland & Erickson 1987, as seen in Iwaniec et al. 2007). This type of neglect is defined as punishing positive normal behaviors such as smiling, exploration, discouraging early attachment, damaging self-esteem, and inhibiting the development of interpersonal skills. Consequences linked to psychological maltreatment are problems with verbal and non-verbal communication skills, patience, goal setting, and ego development in regard to confidence and security (Garbarino, 1997, as seen in Iwaniec et al., 2007).

Research also indicates that perceived low parental care and overprotection in childhood are associated with depression and anxiety disorders later in life (Gerlsma et al.1990 as seen in Newcomb, Mineka, Zinbarg, & Griffith, 2007). Further research concluded that child maltreatment presents alarming challenges which interfere with a healthy development of self esteem and depressive symptoms. Physical neglect was positively associated with depressive symptoms, suggesting that children who had experienced physical neglect were at higher risk for depression, compared to those without such experiences (Kim & Ciechetti, 2006).

Another study (Herring, Gray, Taffe, Tonge, Sweeney, & Einfeld, 2006) looked beyond blaming the parents, and concluded that child behavior and emotional problems were significantly positively correlated

EMOTIONAL DISTURBANCES   6

with parent and family distress. While this study was in reference to children with Pervasive Developmental Disorders (PDD), the link between familial stress and the child's emotional problems were significant. Results showed the mothers' stress thermometer at 0.41, and the fathers' stress thermometer at 0.52. These results show significant effects of child behavior and emotional problems on parent outcome. This study did not suggest any evidence that these children were born with an emotional disturbance; instead, it discussed the observable link between parental stress and emotional problems in toddlers. This research suggested that parents of toddlers with PDD had an increased stress level compared to the parents with typical children. It also showed that parental stress and problem behavior are mutually escalating, and that stress contributed to the behavior and not the diagnosis itself, nor was it linked to the severity of the diagnosis (Herring, et al. 2006).

This study showed a link between parental stress and family dysfunction. It suggested that the reduction of the child's behavioral problems has the capability of reducing parental stress, mental health problems and family dysfunctions. The impact of a child's behavior may in fact determine the stress level, as well as the parent's behavior toward that child. However, it could also be speculated that the stress on the parent due to the child's behavior would only uncover dysfunctions already present within the parent, and not cause them. If this idea is correct, then it would also be true that a parent's effect on their child could also uncover dysfunctions already present in the child.

Taking into consideration the difficulties experienced by children due to neglectful parenting, it is imperative to uncover the aspects of this

EMOTIONAL DISTURBANCES 7

problematic family function. These are not moments found throughout childhood that can be overlooked. They are systematic behaviors that can affect the lifespan of the individuals who experience these harmful behaviors. Therefore, further research is crucial. This study is intended to take that closer look into types of neglect and the impact they play on the lives of so many children.

Method

Participants

Participants will be 100 previously diagnosed emotionally disturbed juveniles (50 females and 50 males) between 14 and 17 years old. They will be taken from several juvenile detention centers across the United States. The juveniles will participate on a voluntary basis and will be selected using a simple random design of computer selection. Juveniles will be informed that there will be no early release in exchange for participating in the study and will be given extra T.V. time for completion of the survey. The survey will be conducted by an interviewer who is a highly trained psychologist with background in emotionally disturbed juveniles but will have no previous work experience with the juveniles in this study. A lie detector test will be administered during the interviews to give the study more credibility.

This study will take approximately one year to complete since time is needed to research and contact participants, set up and conduct interviews, and gather and interpret data in a meaningful way.

Procedure

Participants will be interviewed at their respective juvenile centers in the interrogation room or another room allowing little or no disruptions.

EMOTIONAL DISTURBANCES   8

A modified version of the Carers' Emotionally Abusive Behavior
Questionnaire (Iwaniec, et al. 2006) will be used to rate the effect of
different types of neglect on emotional disturbances. The reason for the
modification will be to single out emotional neglect from emotional
abuse, which may be hard to separate, but necessary since acts of neglect
are the central focus of this study.

   The questionnaire will be completed by the interviewer in
response to the answers given by the juveniles during the interview.
The questionnaire consists of 24 questions related to their childhood
memories of being neglected by their parents. In response to each
question, the nominal scale will include the following categories: often,
seldom, almost never, and length of neglect, defined as occasional or
frequent which will help give the background of neglect as well as
separate neglect types into categories. If the length of neglect was less
than a year, or occurred almost never or seldom, it will not considered
as an effect on emotional disturbances. Some neglect types overlap, and
will therefore be scored in more than one group. For example, parental
self-harming behavior would be given a point for emotional neglect, as
well as a point for cognitive neglect, as this act can affect the child's
emotions and cognitive development. The scores will be added and
categories will be compared to find an effect between types of neglect
and emotional disturbances.

EMOTIONAL DISTURBANCES   9

Implications and Limitations

Although this study will increase the understanding of parental neglect on emotional disturbances as it focuses on acts of omission and separates abuse types, there are some limitations which need to be addressed. First of all is that these juveniles may have no memory for some of the neglect which may have happened during their formative years. They may also have suffered memory blocks due to the neglect. There may also be a problem in not looking at the confounding variable of abuse (acts of commission) against the child, which may be the real indicator of, or just an added influence on emotional disturbances. Perception should also be considered as a factor in that these juveniles may perceive neglect to be more serious than it was, or they may have thought that their experiences were normal, especially at a young age when life at home is what they were most familiar with.

One final limitation would be that the juveniles in detention centers do not accurately represent the emotionally disturbed population in the United States, or cross culturally. Nevertheless, this study adds to the knowledge base of understanding of emotional disturbances and may lead to better services to help the families in which these behaviors occur. It is, however, necessary for further studies to look at the comparison of neglect and abuse and how they relate, and differentiate in their effect, both separate and combined, on emotional disturbances.

EMOTIONAL DISTURBANCES   10

References

Armstrong, M.I., Birnie-Lefcovitch, S., & Ungar, M. T. (2005). Pathways between social support, family well-being, quality of parenting, and child resilience: What we know. *Journal of Child and Family Studies, 14*(1), 269–281.

Herring, S., Gray, K., Taffe, J., Tonge, B., Sweeney, D., & Einfeld, S. (2006). Behaviour and emotional problems in toddlers with pervasive developmental disorders and developmental delay: associations with parental mental health and family functioning. *Journal of Intellectual Disability Research, 50*(1), 874–882.

Iwaniec, D., Larkin, E., & McSherry, D. (2007). Emotionally harmful parenting. *Child Care in Practice, 13*(1), 203–220.

Kim, J., & Ciccetti, D. (2006). Longitudinal trajectories of self-system processes and depressive symptoms among maltreated and nonmaltreated children. *Child Development, 77*(2), 624–639.

Newcomb, R.K., Mineka, S., Zinbarg, R. E., & Griffith, J. W. (2007). Perceived family environment and symptoms of emotional disorders: The role of perceived control, attribution style, and attachment. Seacaucus, NJ: *Springer Science + Business Media, LLC.*

Literacy Connections
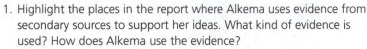

1. Highlight the places in the report where Alkema uses evidence from secondary sources to support her ideas. What kind of evidence is used? How does Alkema use the evidence?
2. The social sciences research report is a genre with some specific conventions of format, style, and tone. How would you describe the conventions of the social sciences research report?
3. Read Alkema's cover letter at www.csus.edu/wac/journal/2009/Alkema.html. How was Alkema's researching and writing process similar to and different from your own processes? In what ways was her process shaped by the literacy context: the purpose, audience, and genre?
4. Find other examples of social science writing in *Writing the University* at www.csus.edu/wac/journal. Create a list of the features of writing in the social sciences, based on your reading. Be prepared to share your list with the class.
5. Compare Alkema's research report to Ashley Nicole Phares' "Mechanistic and Genetic Causes of Depression and the Effect of SSRIs on the Serotonergic Pathway" found later in this chapter. In what ways is Phares' scientific writing different from Alkema's social science writing?

Before You Read
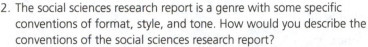

What do you think are the key elements that make writing in humanities fields such as literature, philosophy, music, and art different from writing in the social and natural sciences?

"Constitutionality v. Morality: San Antonio School District v. Rodriguez"

Harshjit Sethi

Harshjit Sethi wrote "Constitutionality v. Morality: *San Antonio School District v. Rodriguez*" in an Introduction to Humanities course at Stanford University. Sethi's essay won an honorable mention for the 2007 Boothe Prize for first-year student writing at Stanford. The prompt Sethi was responding to asked students "to explain which Justice's opinion in *San Antonio v. Rodriguez* is most faithful to the moral logic of *Brown v. Board of Education*." To view more Boothe prize winners, visit bootheprize.stanford.edu/0708/index.html.

Harshjit Sethi

Dr. Jones

English 221

12 Apr. 2007

Constitutionality v. Morality:

San Antonio School District v. Rodriguez

On May 17, 1954, the United States awoke to a radically new educational system—equal and desegregated. *Brown v. Board of Education* was a landmark decision in U.S. judicial history, one which resonated in public schools across the country. The judgment affirmed the 14th Amendment to the Constitution, which guarantees to each citizen "equal protection of the law," and serves as the highest judicial precedent in cases relating to equality in education. Two decades after this historic decision, a case disputing the system of financing public schools in Texas, *San Antonio School District v. Rodriguez,* was brought before the U.S. Supreme Court. Each of the Justices in this case claimed to uphold and further the values of *Brown,* but Justice Marshall's dissent was the most consistent with the moral logic of *Brown.* The plurality decision, however, conformed to the strictest interpretation of the Constitution and was therefore sound on constitutional grounds. This discrepancy between maintaining consistency with the moral principles of *Brown* and with a rigorous interpretation of the Constitution raises fundamental questions about the construal and means of providing education on the "equal terms" to which *Brown* refers. *Brown,* itself, dealt with equality solely in respect to intangible attributes; more essentially, it was concerned with providing parity for people of different races. The present case considers inequality in other, more tangible factors. In assessing these cases, it is essential to consider the disagreement of the conservative and liberal Justices on the question of material inequality for this issue highlights a significant distinction between the liberal premise of maintaining the highest moral standards and the conservative rationale of strict constitutionality.

Brown assumes tremendous importance in the lives of Americans not only because of its prodigious ramifications within the sphere of racial equality in public education, but also because of its moral appeals and the values it upholds. The moral logic of *Brown* encompasses many facets of the lives of ordinary Americans. It stresses the "importance of education to our democratic society" (*Brown* 3), for education is "required for the performance of our most basic responsibilities" and is the "very foundation of good citizenship" (*Brown* 3). It places the onus for public education on state and local governments, emphasizing that "today, perhaps, education is the most important function of state and local governments" (*Brown* 3). Most importantly, it stresses the equality of education for all by claiming that "where the state has undertaken to provide it, [education] is a right which must be made available to all on equal terms" (*Brown* 4). The Court in *Brown* even considered psychological motivations in arriving at a decision, elucidating how a separation of, and distinction between, people of different races "generates a feeling of their inferiority as to their status in the community, that may affect their hearts and minds in a way unlikely ever to be undone" (*Brown* 4). Consequently, the Court reached the unanimous decision that "separate educational facilities are inherently unequal" (*Brown* 4).

The judgment of *Brown,* however, neither explicitly nor tacitly asserts a fundamental right to education. Admittedly, the Court places great importance on education and considers it integral for a responsible and successful member of society. It even stresses the importance of state and local governments providing education. The court stipulates, however, that education is "an opportunity, where the State has undertaken to provide it" (*Brown* 4), thereby granting state governments leeway to decide whether they wish to provide public education. It thus conveys that the Court in *Brown* did not view the right to education as a fundamental right guaranteed by the Constitution, notwithstanding its colossal importance in society.

San Antonio v. Rodriguez considers the same general question of equality in educational facilities. In this case, however, the circumstances and the type of equality demanded by the appellants differed substantially from those in *Brown*. In 1973, the Texas system for funding public elementary and secondary schools drew on federal, state, and local funds. Federal and state funds provided almost half the school budget; the remainder was contributed by local funds, which in turn depended on the amount of taxable property in the district (*San Antonio* 1). Consequently, in more affluent districts, the per pupil expenditure on education was as high as $594 in a particular year, as opposed to some of the poorer districts, which spent only $356 per pupil (*San Antonio* 28). This significant difference in funding created severe inequalities in the educational opportunities provided by different school districts within the state.

Although the plurality accepts this system of inequitable funding, Justice Marshall views the majority's decision as a "retreat from our historic commitment to the equality of educational opportunity" (*San Antonio* 31). The discrepancies in educational expenditure permit schools in affluent districts to hire teachers with college degrees and substantial experience. It also enables them to have a lower student-to-teacher ratio, thereby ensuring certain advantages to students, such as more attention from teachers. Education is therefore not being provided on "equal terms" to all, if equality in this case is interpreted as the access to the same quality of resources for all students. Through his dissent, Marshall conforms to the *Brown* decision of providing education to all on "equal terms," in the most literal sense of the phrase.

The plurality disagrees with Marshall's view, emphasizing that the state, through "the Minimum Foundation Program of Education, provides an 'adequate' education for all the children in the state" (*San Antonio* 7). Although the state and federal funds are distributed almost equally between schools, the disparities caused by local taxation cannot be ignored. The fundamental premise of *Brown* is to provide equality of education for all citizens, not simply to determine whether the education provided by the state is adequate. In segregated schools, where the principle of "separate but equal" (*Brown* 4) could hold, it was assumed that schools were materially equal. However, since these schools discriminated on the basis of race, they were "inherently unequal" (*Brown* 4) and were, consequently, inconsistent with the verdict of the Court in *Brown*. Marshall, in strict adherence to *Brown,* argues that the aim of the state system in financing public education should be to provide completely equal educational facilities, not merely "adequate" ones.

The plurality also draws attention to the "unsettled and disputed question whether the quality of education may be determined by the amount of money expended for it" (*San Antonio* 7). However, in the present scenario of education in the Alamo Heights and Edgewood districts, it is reasonable to conclude that a disparity in the quality of education did exist. Statistics for the 1968/1969 school year revealed that 100% of teachers in Alamo Heights had college degrees, as compared to 80% of teachers in Edgewood, and that 47% of the teachers in Edgewood were on emergency teaching permits, as opposed to 11% in Alamo Heights (*San Antonio* 34). This question is also indirectly answered by Justice Marshall's contention that in issues such as these, "the question of discrimination in educational facilities must be deemed to be an objective one that looks at what the State provides its children, not to what the children are able to do with what they receive" (*San Antonio* 33). In presenting an altogether different perspective on this issue, Justice Marshall stresses the importance of duty and equality for the state.

Recalling the importance *Brown* attaches to education for success in today's society, Marshall contends that "education directly affects the ability to exercise his [a citizen's] First Amendment rights, both as a source and as a receiver of information and ideas" (*San Antonio* 42). Referring to Justice Brennan's opinion in *Abington School Dist. v. Schempp*, [374 U.S. 203, 230 (1963)], Justice Marshall concurs with Brennan that "Americans regard the public schools as the most vital civic institution for the preservation of a democratic system of government" (*San Antonio* 42). By referring to the point of view of other Justices, Marshall not only strengthens his own argument but also demonstrates the traditional importance imparted to education in previous decisions of the Court. This is analogous to the commitment to education asserted in *Brown*, since "these days, it is doubtful that any child may reasonably be expected to succeed in life if he is denied the opportunity of an education" (*Brown* 4).

The plurality counters this opinion by arguing that "the Court has never presumed to possess either the ability or the authority to guarantee to the citizenry the most effective speech or the most informed electorate" (*San Antonio* 10); therefore, even though education is important for the execution of First Amendments rights, the Court has no duty to ensure its provision. However, it is important to note that the appellants in this case seek the opportunity for an equal education and an end to state discrimination on the basis of taxable property, not the best education that the state government could provide. In essence, Justice Marshall argues that the appellants want access to the same educational opportunity, irrespective of its quality. A consequent equalization of educational facilities may result in the lowering of the standards of some schools in affluent districts, since the same amount of tax revenue would be distributed in a manner that ensures an equal expenditure on each pupil of every district. Such a financing program may be contested on moral grounds, because rich parents are being forced to fund the education of other children while their own children would be receiving substantially poorer educational facilities compared with those they currently enjoy. However, since Justice Marshall's contention would result in an egalitarian policy, it would be consistent with the moral logic of *Brown* in providing education on "equal terms to all" (*Brown* 4).

The plurality also believes that "adequate education" (*San Antonio* 7) would be sufficient for the exercise of the fundamental rights accorded by the Constitution; therefore, equality is unnecessary if all citizens acquire enough education to perform basic social and political duties, such as voting and the free exchange of ideas. However, just as the plurality believes that changing the state taxation laws would exceed the Court's jurisdiction, rendering it a "super-legislature" (*San Antonio* 9), so too the Court also lacks authority to define what level, quality, and type of education qualify as "adequate." In a manner similar to Chief Justice Warren in *Brown,* Justice Marshall is also motivated by the psychological effects of the stark inequality of public high schools in *San Antonio.* He argues that the effects of the "inferior education" that "countless children unjustifiably receive 'may affect their minds and hearts in a way unlikely to be ever undone'" (*San Antonio* 31, quoting *Brown* 4), for the "quality of education offered may influence a child's decision to 'enter or remain in school'" [*San Antonio* 42, quoting the decision of *Gaston County v. United States* (395 U.S. 285, 296)]. Coupled with poor facilities and resources, discrimination often promotes a sense of inferiority and social stigma, engendering a general lack of interest in education, which leaves indelible marks on a child's psyche and may influence his decisions about whether to complete schooling and attend college.

While the plurality does not explicitly counter this point, the conservative Court traditionally disregards the psychological effect of laws and judicial decisions on the people. Such factors are often very subjective and influence different people in different ways, arguably nullifying each other. For instance, the Texas system of financing education may displease parents residing in poor districts, whereas the parents in affluent districts would likely support this policy because the money they pay in local taxes is spent exclusively on their children and on other children residing in the district. It is not the duty of the Court to base its decision on such speculations. A conformist to *Brown,* however, would argue that it is essential to consider the psychological effects only on the group that suffers discrimination, for it is they who have been wronged by the policies of the

Sethi 8

state. Likewise, in this case, Marshall is in line with the values of *Brown* by considering only the psychological influences on children in poor districts.

Despite Justice Marshall's adherence to the moral logic of *Brown*, it is the decision of the plurality that is constitutionally correct. The main contention between the majority and the dissenting opinion is whether strict scrutiny applies in this case. The majority agrees that if strict scrutiny were to apply in this case, the Texas system of financing public schools would be considered constitutionally invalid. However, strict scrutiny can only apply to a case in which there exists either discrimination against a suspect class or a denial of a fundamental right, as secured explicitly or implicitly by the Constitution. However, in light of the present case, neither can the class that is suffering discrimination be considered suspect nor can education be deemed an implicit constitutional right.

To be considered a suspect class, a group must meet the following criteria: the group's characteristics must be "immutable," the group must have a "history of discrimination," the group must be "politically impotent," and the group must be "a discrete or insular minority."[1] In the present case, we could describe the disadvantaged group as being composed of all those people who reside in poor districts, which have a relatively low amount of taxable property. It is important to note, here, that members of this group are not necessarily poor; they simply reside within a poor district. The characteristics of this group do not satisfy any of the requirements of the suspect classification: the class described here is the very opposite of "immutable." The poor constitute an "amorphous class" (*San Antonio* 8), since wealth is never stagnant. A simple change of residence would beget a change in categorization. Poor districts may be comprised of persons from different races and socioeconomic strata;

Sethi 9

therefore, there is no basis for asserting the "history of discrimination" or "political impotency" of the group. Depending on the relative definition of "poor districts," any class could qualify as a minority. However, there is no evidence to suggest that people in these districts were in any manner detached from society as a whole. Although the liberal Court may argue that these districts are in fact primarily composed of African Americans or Americans of Hispanic descent, it is possible that a poor district might consist of a white majority. Therefore, since the Court's decision does not directly discriminate against people of those races, which have suffered from a long history of segregation, suspect classification cannot apply.

Education, despite its importance in society today, is not a fundamental right guaranteed either explicitly or implicitly by the Constitution. Even the *Brown* decision, which is perhaps the most famous affirmation of the necessity for education in American society, refers to it merely as an "opportunity" (*Brown* 4) that a state may provide. Like many other facilities and conveniences provided by state and local governments, education is a privilege for the citizens of a state. The conservative Court contends that "if the degree of judicial scrutiny of state legislature fluctuated on the majority's view of the importance of the interest affected, we would have gone far toward making this Court a 'super-legislature'" (*San Antonio* 9), thus emphasizing the importance of judicial restraint.

Our assessment of the constitutional decision is, however, further complicated by the Texas Constitution and the Fourteenth Amendment to the federal Constitution. The Texas Constitution guarantees its citizens the right to an education. According to the Fourteenth Amendment to the Constitution, "No State shall deny to any person within its jurisdiction the equal protection of the laws." Therefore, it is imperative to consider what "equal protection of laws" entails for the conservative and liberal Court and which interpretation is most appropriate in arriving at a decision in this case. The liberal Court strives for equality in every aspect of public education: physical facilities, educational resources, the quality of education imparted, and even intangible factors such as reputation and image. Therefore, any inequality in the features of public education is unacceptable to the liberal Court and is deemed a breach of the "equal protection" clause. Consequently, in *San Antonio*, the dissenting opinion believes that the inequality created by discrepancies in per pupil expenditure and the consequent disparity in tangible educational facilities violates the Fourteenth Amendment. Justice Marshall describes his vision of a "right to every American to an equal start in life" (*San Antonio* 31), referring to the hope that every American would be born to equality; his achievements being solely a result of his own effort and capabilities. Essential to achieving such an equal start in life is equal access, for all, to equitable educational facilities and opportunities. However, in a society where each child is born to a house with a different socio-economic, racial, and cultural profile, and is influenced by a different set of peers, a completely equal start is nearly impossible.

The conservative Court, on the other hand, views "equal protection" of the right to education in a less exacting manner. In *San Antonio*, as long as the state provides public education to all its citizens without discriminating against suspect classes, the system of financing is constitutionally valid. Discrepancies are bound to arise in the tangible and intangible aspects of different schools, and the onus falls upon the state legislature, representing the voice and views of the people, to decide whether to bridge this gap, and how to achieve a greater degree of equality if the people of the state so desire.

The conservative Court contends that "at least where wealth is involved, the Equal Protection Clause does not require absolute equality or precisely equal educational advantages" (*San Antonio* 7). Even if the Texas government were to allocate a fixed and equal amount of educational expenditure per pupil, it is essential to consider whether the State could restrict the local district from contributing toward the education of its children. Should the state prevent local districts from taking any part in the educational process, this would create a less efficient educational system, since the local district is necessarily the most cognizant of its citizens' needs. More importantly, this intervention would infringe on the liberty of citizens by not allowing them to partake in the education of their children. The capacity of parents to contribute financially toward public education in their districts can vary substantially, and eventually the State education system would reach its initial state of inequality. Therefore, the Equal Protection Clause cannot require strict equality in cases relating to wealth, as that would place the clause in opposition to individual liberty—the liberty of individuals to expend their money in the manner they think appropriate. Consequently, the Texas system of financing public schools does not violate the Fourteenth Amendment to the Constitution, and the conservative Court's definition holds.

The case at hand thus draws attention to the discrepancy between morality and constitutionality. The Texas system of financing public education fails on moral grounds due to the wide disparity it creates.

Justice Marshall's dissent upholds the moral logic of *Brown,* aiming to amend the system and thereby deliver to the people of Texas a perfectly egalitarian educational system. However, because the State's financing system does not violate any of the tenets of the Constitution, it remains valid on constitutional grounds. The pronouncement of *Brown* also gestures to this contradiction, because although from a moral perspective "education is the most important duty of state and local governments," constitutionally a citizen has the right to education "only where the state has undertaken to provide it" (*Brown* 6). Because constitutionality is less mutable than morality, which is dependent on individuals and, therefore, on the composition of a jury, an element of objectivity can be introduced in judicial pronouncements only by adhering to the Constitution. Thus, the liberals' hope for a moral system of public education is checked by conservatives' desire to limit the judiciary to the strictest interpretation of the Constitution, demonstrating that in this case recourse to the legislative is the only hope for appellants to obtain an egalitarian system of education on moral grounds. The judiciary will simply uphold the Constitution.

Notes

[1]"Suspect Classification." Wikipedia, the Free Encyclopedia. 7 Nov. 2007. http://en.wikipedia.org/wiki/Suspect_classification

Works Cited

Brown v. Board of Education 347 U.S. 483 US Supreme Court 1954.

San Antonio School District v. Rodriguez 411 U.S. 1 US Supreme Court 1973.

Literacy Connections

1. Sethi's essay is an example of complex academic writing, and you may have had trouble understanding his ideas in places. In small groups, share a place where you struggled to understand Sethi's language or ideas and have the group come up with strategies for reading complex texts.
2. In what ways do you think Sethi's essay is representative of writing in the humanities?
3. Did you find Sethi's essay effective? Why or why not?
4. Find other examples of *Boothe Prize* student writing in the humanities at bootheprize.stanford.edu/0708/index.html. Create a list of the features of writing in the humanities, based on your reading. Be prepared to share your list with the class.
5. Read the "Instructor's Forward" to Sethi's essay by visiting the *Boothe Prize* home page at bootheprize.stanford.edu/0708/index.html and following the link to Sethi's essay. In what ways does the instructor's description of the strengths of Sethi's essay connect to the description of academic literacy in Fiona Glade's opening essay of the chapter?

Before You Read

In small groups, come up with a description of the scientific method. What connections do you think there are between the scientific method and the genres and conventions of writing in the natural sciences?

Mechanistic and Genetic Causes of Depression and the Effect of SSRIs on the Serotonergic Pathway

Ashley Nicole Phares

Ashley Nicole Phares was a student at the University of Alabama when she wrote the scientific report "Mechanistic and Genetic Causes of Depression and the Effect of SSRIs on the Serotonergic Pathway." It was published in the 2008 edition of *JOSHUA: Journal of Science and Health at the University of Alabama* at http://bama.ua.edu/~joshua/. Ashley's work is a reflection of the scientific writing style.

Mechanistic and Genetic Causes of Depression and the Effect
of SSRIs on the Serotonergic Pathway

Ashley Nicole Phares

Mechanistic and Genetic Causes of Depression 2

Introduction

Depression is a very common disorder and up to 20% of the population in the United States suffers from this condition, with twice as many females diagnosed as males (15, 16). Studies have shown that 40–50% of depression risk is genetic, while the other portion consists of non-genetic factors like viral infection, emotional trauma, and stress (16). Diagnosis requires the suffering of a major depressive episode marked by several specific symptoms, including depressed mood and loss of interest (14). The hippocampus is generally considered the prominent site for the generation and treatment of depression, though abnormalities related to the disorder also extended far beyond this region (16). These include two major serotonergic pathways in the brain that are located in the projections ascending from the medial and dorsal raphe and the descending projections from the caudal raphe into the spinal cord (18). Research has established a pathophysiological role of serotonin, also known as 5-hydroxytryptamine (5-HT), in depression (22, 8). In humans, serotonin expressing neurons are highly localized to the spinal cord and brainstem in clusters. In these collections, neurons send out axons whose terminals contain serotonin and innervate many different areas throughout the brain (22). If part of the serotonergic pathway is disrupted, the signaling system will not operate correctly and will therefore likely lead to depression.

But how might this pathway be disrupted? As mentioned previously, genetics play a large role in determining risk for depression (16). If mutations occur in genes coding for elements of the pathway, there is a stronger likelihood for depressive tendencies (16, 3). Yet while

Mechanistic and Genetic Causes of Depression 3

genes predispose many people to depression, others may be affected
by epigenetic mechanisms (21). For instance, long-term alterations
associated with depression are also thought to stem from adverse
experiences early in life (14, 10). Early environmental stressors result
in an enhanced biologic stress mechanism (21). Synergistically, stress
and genetic risk initiate a cascade that disrupts the dynamic
serotonergic system through neurobiological transformations. Other
factors may include high levels of the stress hormone cortisol, or
imbalanced densities of glucocorticoid and/or mineral corticoid
receptors (14). In fact, increased levels of glucocorticoid downregulate
hippocampus 5-HT, and many patients diagnosed with depression
exhibit enlarged adrenal glands. Although it is difficult to reduce the
many emotional and physical symptoms of depression to one
prominent cause, the most widely acknowledged source of this
condition is indeed an imbalance of the neurotransmitter, serotonin.
Solid evidence has shown that low serotonergic activity is directly
linked to major depression disorder (10).

The Mechanics of the Serotonergic Pathway

We know that, when altered, the serotonergic pathway can cause
depression, but what is its normal function and how does it work?
Typically, 5-HT governs autonomic operations, influences learning and
memory, and affects behavior and mood (12). When serotonin is released
by the pre-synaptic cell into the synaptic cleft, it binds to one of its
distinct subtypes of 5-HT receptors, resulting in a signal transduction
cascade. The serotonergic neurotransmission is terminated when 5-HT is

Mechanistic and Genetic Causes of Depression 4

rapidly re-uptaken into the pre-synaptic terminus. The re-uptake is controlled by the serotonin transporter, or SERT (12). [See Figure A]

The brain synthesizes serotonin from the amino acid L-tryptophan. This amino acid comes mainly from the diet and must travel across the blood-brain barrier by active transport in order to reach the brain (18). L-tryptophan metabolism is a highly regulated physiological process (19). Tryptophan hydroxylase (TPH) is the rate-limiting enzyme in the biosynthetic pathway for serotonin. Its role is to convert the tryptophan amino acid into 5-hydroxytryptophan (5-HTP) which in turn is decarboxylated to 5-HT (3). [See Figure B] Levels of serotonin are linked to levels of L-tryptophan, which change with both diet and levels of competing amino acids (18). Pre-cursor loading and increased intake of tryptophan can increase serotonin concentrations (9). Tryptophan depletion leads to decreased levels of 5-HT and often depression (18).

Serotonin receptors are the targets for the 5-HT neurotransmitter and are primarily located on the surface of the post-synaptic terminal

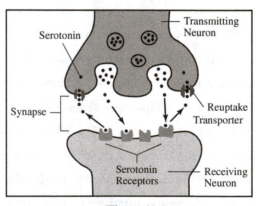

(Figure A)

Mechanistic and Genetic Causes of Depression 5

(Figure B)

(11). Research has established that there are at least seven distinct receptor families, each with multiple subtypes (18). These include 5-HT1A, 5-HT1D, 5-HT3, and most importantly, 5-HT2A, 5-HT2B, and 5-HT2C which each affect a distinct neural system (22, 13). Direct-acting agonists and antagonists often show selective affinity for a specific family and subtype of receptor (9). Perhaps the most studied subtype of receptors is the 5-HT2C (11). This subtype is widely distributed throughout the brain and is considered a member of the class A G-protein-coupled receptor homodimers which act in intracellular signaling pathways (11, 20). It couples to G alpha q, phospholipase D, and arachidonic acid metabolism. 5-HT2C receptors function as homodimers, regardless as to whether they are in the active or inactive conformation. These two

Mechanistic and Genetic Causes of Depression 6

conformations result from receptor isoforms produced by RNA editing (11). 5-HT also acts on some pre-synaptic receptors, such as 5-HT1B/1D and 5-HT1A, which act in a negative feedback mechanism. When bound by a neurotransmitter, they inhibit firing rates, therefore decreasing the amount of serotonin released into the synaptic cleft (18).

The serotonin transporter mediates the re-uptake of the neurotransmitter from the synaptic cleft, back to the pre-synaptic nerve terminal (12). It is found on serotonin neuron processes, nerve terminals, and also platelets and its density varies according to location (3). The SERT is an integral membrane protein that belongs to the $Na+/Cl-$ dependant family that transports metabolites and neurotransmitters, as well as moves monoamines and amino acids through the lipid bi-layer (12). The human serotonin transporter is a twelve membrane-spanning protein that is affectively a neuronal uptake pump for 5-HT (22). Many different mechanisms, such as protein kinase C triggered internalization, control SERT activity. It has been found that with prolonged administration of serotonin re-uptake inhibitors, adaptive changes in SERT mRNA and protein levels occur (12). Each of these parts of the serotonergic pathway are integral to the working system and if altered, will likely result in an increased risk for depression.

Genetic Mutations to the Serotonergic Pathway Components

Evidence of genetic causation comes from observation of a link between depression and family history, twin comparisons, and twin adoption studies (3). Also, as stated before, epidemiological studies have shown that 40–50% of depression risk is derived from genetic

Mechanistic and Genetic Causes of Depression 7

variation (16). Since each of the components of the 5-HT pathway are so essential for correct function, if any mutations occur in genes coding for a part of the serotonergic system, problems are bound to occur (3). Thus, genes related to this system are prime targets for investigation in the search for the causes of depression (3, 15). Polymorphisms in these genes can contribute to altered forms, or isoforms, that display different levels of wildtype functionality (3).

Worthy of study are the polymorphisms of the serotonin biosynthetic enzyme, tryptophan hydroxylase, or TPH. Since alteration in 5-HT neurotransmission is implicated in depression, it makes sense to look at this important member of serotonin's synthetic pathway. The TPH gene is located on chromosome 11 and two polymorphisms in intron seven have been detected, which are in a tight linkage disequilibrium. These consist of A to C substitutions in either nucleotide 779 or 218. Less TPH is not apparent in the dorsal raphe nucleus of depressed suicide victims, which predicts that this enzyme protein may be altered in the isoforms so as to have less activity (3).

Altered levels of 5-HT receptors are often reported in depression (1). For example, a reduced number of serotonin receptors has been observed in the post-mortem hippocampus of depressed suicides (10). This eludes that genes coding for the 5-HT receptors are also prime targets for study (2, 3). Two polymorphisms for the 5-HT1B receptor have been detected at nucleotides 129 and 161. These involve silent mutations of a C to a T and a G to a C respectively. These polymorphisms were found at similar frequencies in normal and depressed patients, but exhibit a lower level of binding in the latter. Studies have also detected an uncommon

Mechanistic and Genetic Causes of Depression 8

substitution of a phenylalanine residue for a cysteine (3). Polymorphisms have additionally been found in genes coding for 5-HT2C receptors. Recent studies have shown that life stress increases production of 5-HT2C receptor isoforms, which have reduced 5-HT sensitivity. Moreover, genetics and life stress early on are synergistic in producing more of these receptor isoforms (5). Two prominent polymorphisms have been seen in the 5-HT2A receptor gene. In one, a T is changed to a C at nucleotide 102 and in the other, an A is replaced by a G at 1438. Other less frequent polymorphisms of 5-HT2A were observed as well (3). However, strong evidence showing that alterations in this subtype result in increased risk for depression have not been shown (15).

The human gene for the serotonin transporter is located on chromosome 17. It has been found that less 5-HTT expression and binding may result from a 44 bp insertion/deletion in the 5' regulatory region adjacent to the promoter. It appears that this polymorphism results in a decreased number of binding sites (3). There is mounting evidence that single nucleotide and simple repeat sequence polymorphisms in coding and regulatory genes of the serotonergic pathway can result in a significant difference in the functionality of the system (7). Mutations associated with the genes coding for components of the 5-HT pathway, no matter how small, are certainly worthy of investigation for the role they likely play in the increased risk for depression.

The Effect of SSRIs on the Serotonergic Pathway

Much research has been done in order to find mechanisms to treat the causes and symptoms of depression. One of the major solutions to

Mechanistic and Genetic Causes of Depression 9

this search has been the discovery and implementation of selective serotonin reuptake inhibitors (SSRIs). SSRIs were developed to target and inhibit the serotonin transporter, or neuronal uptake pump. This mechanism involves altering the 5-HT system in order to increase the level of neurotransmitter in the synaptic cleft (22, 23). [See Figure C] Inhibition of the transporter yields an increase of serotonin in the synapse, and therefore an increased activation of the presynaptic inhibitory receptors. Over the period of about three weeks, the negative feedback mechanism achieves a therapeutic effect (18).

Imipramine was the first compound shown to block the reuptake of serotonin by the transporters and since then citalopram, fluvoxamine, fluoxetine, paroxetine, sertraline, duloxetine, and others have been added

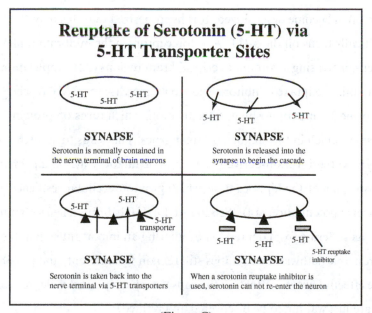

(Figure C)

Mechanistic and Genetic Causes of Depression 10

to that list (22, 7, 17). SSRIs have common serotonin agonists that meditate their effects. As far as affecting the uptake pump, SSRIs have proven to be selective. They affect particular receptors that in turn affect a multitude of particular neural systems; hence, no SSRI works exactly the same (22). Selective serotonin reuptake inhibitors vary in elimination half-life, selectivity for serotonin ratios, and affinity for the 5-HT receptor (18). In order to be effective, regular levels of serotonin must still be available. This was shown by administering depletion of tryptophan, the precursor of serotonin, and observing the effects of the SSRIs. Without adequate serotonin being produced, the SSRIs had no positive effect (4, 18). In fact, serotonin depletion leads to reoccurrence of symptoms in up to 80% of patients (22).

With continuous exposure to SSRIs, postsynaptic receptors in the brain often become desensitized. It is hypothesized that this may specifically focus on the 5-HT1A autoreceptors in the midbrain raphe nucleus, increasing serotonin in critical brain regions (22). Application of monoamine reuptake inhibitors leads to an increase in cAMP (cyclic adenosine 3-5 monophosphatase) activation, which turns on protein kinase A, which in turn regulates target genes. This leads to an increase in BDNF synthesis (brain-derived neurotrophic factor) which is a primary neurotrophin of the hippocampus which promotes cellular resilience and long-term potentiation (14). [See Figure D] SSRIs bring relief for many patients suffering from depression by altering an important step in the serotonergic pathway. Possibilities still remain for different, and possibly more effective, ways of treating the causes and symptoms of depression that are just waiting to be discovered and refined.

Mechanistic and Genetic Causes of Depression 11

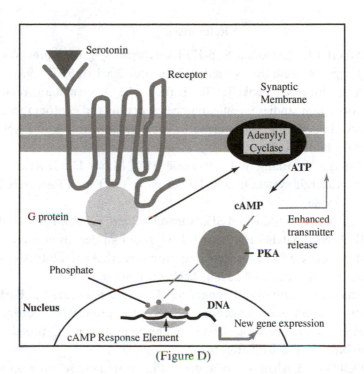

(Figure D)

Conclusion

Depression is a common disorder that plagues a large percentage of the population. One of the main causes of this condition has been linked to alterations in the serotonergic pathway for neurotransmission. Negative outcomes often occur when mechanistic and genetic changes produce a change in the 5-HT system, resulting in an increased risk for depression. Through increased understanding of the serotonin pathway and the genetics governing its components and function, treatments such as SSRIs, can and will continue to be developed and perfected in order to treat the causes and symptoms of depression.

Mechanistic and Genetic Causes of Depression 12

References

1. Albert PR, Lemonde S. 5-HT1A receptors, gene repression, and depression: guilt by association. Neurosci. 2004;10(6):575–93.
2. Anguelova M, Benkelfat C, Turecki, G. A systematic review of association studies investigating genes coding for serotonin receptors and the serotonin transporter: I. Affective disorders. Mol Psychiatry. 2003; 8(6):574–91.
3. Arango V, Huang Y, Underwood MD, Mann JJ. Genetics of the serotonergic system in suicidal behavior. J of Psych Research. 2003; 37:375–86.
4. Argyropoulos SV, Hood SD, Adrover M, Bell CJ, Rich AS, Nash JR, Rich NC, Witchel HJ, Nutt DJ. Tryptophan depletion reverses the therapeutic effect of selective serotonin reuptake inhibitors in social anxiety disorder. Biol Psych. 2004;56(7):503–9.
5. Bhansali P, Dunning J, Singer SE, David L, Schmauss C. Early life stress alters adult serotonin 2C receptor pre-mRNA editing and expression of the alpha subunit of the heterotrimeric G-protein Gq. J of Neurosci. 2007;27(6):1467–73.
6. Dell'Osso B, Allen A, Hollander E. Fluvoxamine: a selective serotonin re-uptake inhibitor for the treatment of obsessive compulsive disorder. Expert Opin Pharmacother. 2005;6(15):2727–40.
7. D'Souza UM, Craig IW. Functional polymorphisms in dopamine and serotonin pathway genes. Hum Mutat. 2006;27(1):1–13.
8. Freeman SL, Glatzle J, Robin CS, Valdellon M, Sternini C, Sharp JW, Raybould H.E. Ligand-induced 5-HT3 receptor internalization in enteric neurons in rat ileum. Gastroent. 2006;131(1):97–107.
9. Fuller RW. Role of serotonin in therapy of depression and related disorders. J Clin Psych. 1991;52 Suppl:52–7.
10. Graeff FG, Guimaraes FS, De Andrade TGCS, Deakin JFW. Role of 5-HT in stress, anxiety, and depression. Pharm Biochem and Behavior. 1996;54(1):129–41.
11. Herrick-Davis K, Grinde E, Weaver BA. Serotonin 5-HT2C receptor homodimerization is not regulated by agonist or inverse agonist treatment. European J of Pharm. 2006;568:45–53.

Mechanistic and Genetic Causes of Depression 13

12. Jess U, El Far O, Kirsch J, Betz H. Interaction of the C-terminal region of the rat serotonin transporter with MacMARCKS modulates 5-HT uptake regulation by protein kinase C. Biochem and Biophys Research Communications. 2002;294:272–279.

13. Leysen JE. 5-HT2 receptors. Curr Drug Targets CNS Neurol Disord. 2004;3(1):11–26.

14. Maletic V, Robinson M, Oakes T, Iyenger S, Ball SG, Russell J. Neurobiology of depression: an integrated view of key findings. Int J Clin Prac. 2007;61(12):2030–40.

15. Minov C, Baghai TC, Schule C, Zwanger P, Schwartz MJ, Zill P, Rupprecht R, Bondy B. Serotonin-2A-receptor and transporter polymorphisms: lack of association in patients with major depression. Neurosci Letters. 2001;303:119–122.

16. Nestler EJ, Barrot M, DiLeone RJ, Eisch AJ, Gold SJ, Monteggia LM. Neurobiol of depression. Neuron. 2002;34:13–25.

17. Norman TR. Prospects for the treatment of depression. Aust N Z J Psychiatry. 2005;40(5):394–401.

18. Nutt DJ, Forshall S, Bell C, Rich A, Sandford J, Nash J, Argyropoulos S. Mechanisms of action of selective serotonin reuptake inhibitors in the treatment of psychiatric disorders. Eur. Neuro-Psychopharm. 1999;9 Suppl.3:S81–86.

19. Ruddick JP, Evans AK, Nutt DJ, Lightman SL, Rook GA, Lowry CA. Tryptophan metabolism in the central nervous system: medical implications. Expert Rev Mol Med. 2006;8(20):1–27.

20. Serretti A, Artioli P, De Ronchi D. The 5-HT2C receptor as a target for mood disorders. Expert Opin Ther Targets. 2004;8(1):15–23.

21. Shelton RC. The molecular neurobiology of depression. Psychiatr Clin North Am. 2007;30(1):1–11.

22. Vaswani M, Linda FK, Ramesh S. Role of selective serotonin reuptake inhibitors in psychiatric disorders: a comprehensive review. Progress in Neuro-Psychopharm & Bio Psych. 2003;27:85–102.

23. Weizman A, Weizman R. Serotonin transporter polymorphism and response to SSRIs in major depression and relevance to anxiety disorders and substance abuse. Pharmacogenomics. 2000;1(3):35–41.

Literacy Connections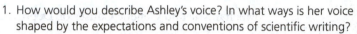

1. How would you describe Ashley's voice? In what ways is her voice shaped by the expectations and conventions of scientific writing?
2. Based on Ashley's writing style and content, how would you describe her audience?
3. Browse through other examples of student writing in *JOSHUA* at bootheprize.stanford.edu/0708/index.html. Create a list of the features of scientific writing, based on your reading. Be prepared to share your list with the class.
4. What do you think are the strengths and the weaknesses of scientific writing?
5. Compare all three examples of student writing in the chapter and create a list of general features of academic literacy that all three examples reflect. Be prepared to share this list with the class.

Academic Literacy Projects

College Writing Assignments Analysis

The purpose of this project is to get you thinking about the nature of academic literacies by analyzing writing assignments at your college. In a portfolio, you'll collect three different writing assignments from three different classes and do a rhetorical analysis of each assignment. Consider rhetorical factors like purpose, audience, persona, genre, and context. Also include a reflection letter talking about all three assignments: Are there some general features of academic literacy found across the three assignments? How do the assignments differ, and are differences connected to the academic field of the assignments? Based on these assignments, what skills do you personally need to practice to be a successful academic writer, and what skills are you already strong in? To gather the three assignments, you can use examples from your own classes, examples from your peers' classes, or find examples on your school's Web site search engine (for example, you could enter the term "writing assignment" or "writing assignments").

Professor Interview Paper

In this project, you're going to interview a college professor and ask him or her about literacy expectations. Your teacher might divide the class and ask each person to interview someone in a different academic field, or your teacher might ask you to interview a professor in a major you're interested in knowing more about. Brainstorm some possible questions about the teacher's reading and writing expectations ahead of time, either individually, in small groups, or as a class. Then choose four or five questions to ask. Make sure you arrange the interview as soon as possible—remember that professors are busy and may not be able to meet with you right away. When you contact the professor you'd like to interview, explain the purpose of the interview and ask what times would be most convenient for the professor to meet, rather than giving him or her a time (allow at least a half an hour for the interview). At the interview, take notes but also bring a voice recording device if possible. Write a transcript of the interview, summarizing your questions and the professor's answers, and also write a reflection on the interview discussing what you learned about academic literacies (or the specific literacy expectations in a major) from doing the interview.

Academic Literacy Influences: Writing about Teachers

The purpose of this project is to reflect on which teacher or teachers had the biggest effect on shaping your literacy history. This might be a teacher or teachers who helped you improve as a reader and writer, or a teacher or teachers who had a negative influence, or both. Use a narrative form to tell the stories of the teacher or teachers you choose, and be sure to both narrate your experiences in vivid detail and also reflect on the significance of your experiences and how the teachers influenced you, either in positive or negative ways. Your teacher might choose to have the class share their stories, either by reading them aloud, collecting them in a book, publishing them online, etc.

Academic Literacy Case Study

In this project, you'll use a research method that's common in the social sciences—a case study. A case study is a methodical and in-depth study of one "case" of a topic—one example. In this project the "topic" is academic literacies and the "case" is you. You'll study your own experiences as an academic reader and writer and write up the results of your investigation of your own academic literacies. In order to research your own academic literacy experiences, you'll need to analyze your college reading and writing assignments, reflect on and evaluate your reading and writing processes, closely analyze rough and final drafts of your college writing, and consider connections and conflicts between your experiences of reading and writing in college and your experiences reading and writing outside of college (for example, at home or in the various communities you belong to). Think of a logical way to organize the report of your research for your readers. For example, you might have different sections with different headings, like "Background," "Research Methods," "Analysis," and "Results."

Joining a Conversation: Academic Research Project

In this project, you'll have a chance to practice one of the most valuable skills for college literacies: academic research. Choose one of the student academic writing journals below, and write an academic researched argument for possible submission and publication in the journal. In order to get a sense of the conventions of the journal you might submit your essay to, before you begin writing your researched argument, do a two- to three-page rhetorical analysis of the journal, considering the purposes, audiences, genres, personas, conventions, etc., of essays in the journal you've chosen. The kind of argument you make, the way you structure your essay, your writing style, and the number and types of outside sources you use for evidence will depend on the conventions of writing for the journal you submit to. Also include a one- to two-page process memo reflecting on your writing and researching process, discussing what you learned about academic literacies by engaging in academic research and evaluating the strengths and weaknesses of your researched essay.

Here are some college writing journals and writing contests that accept submissions from undergraduate students in any region:

Pittsburgh Undergraduate Review: http://136.142.181.181/~pur/
Lethbridge Undergraduate Review: www.lurj.org/
Neo-Vox International Student Online Magazine: www.neo-vox.org/
Teen Ink Magazine: www.teenink.com/index.php
The Nation student writing contest: www.thenation.com/student/
The Atlantic student writing contest: www.theatlantic.com/a/contest.
  mhtml
Public Writing: http://scholarlyexchange.org/ojs/index.php/PW/index

You can also check to see whether your college has an undergraduate writing or researching journal, or you may choose to publish the results of your research online in the form of a Web site or a *Wikipedia* entry.

Group Project: Academic Discourse Community Analysis

In this project, the class will form small groups and each group will write a collaborative essay analyzing an academic discourse community. The group will observe the community, conduct interviews with community members, and analyze literacy documents used and produced by the community in order to investigate and report on the academic reading, writing, and researching conventions of the community. The community could be broad (for example, a department or an area of focus within a department) or narrow (for example, a class or a discussion group). When the group writes up the results of their analysis, they might choose to organize the essay using the style of the qualitative report in the social sciences discussed in the student case study in this chapter (an introduction section, a research methods section, a results and discussion section, and a conclusion section). To help you focus your analysis, you might consider the following questions:

- What purposes do texts serve in the community?
- What kinds of texts does the community value?
- What research methods are used by the community?
- What specialized terms do community members use?
- What are some common genres used in the community, and what are the conventions of those genres?
- What kinds of personas do writers in the community take on?
- How is power/authority distributed in the community?

9

Situating Civic Literacies

An important aspect of learning to compose is exercising your rights as a citizen and engaging in civic discourse. When you write an e-mail to your local congressperson, create a petition about a public issue, share your political opinions in a blog, support a charity through *mycause.com*, or give a speech at a student government meeting, you're engaging in civic literacy. In her introductory  essay in this chapter, Professor Catherine Gabor defines *civic literacy* as the "ability to use writing as power in public, political, and community-based situations." Because civic literacy contexts involve public audiences and a variety of stakeholders, Gabor argues that "the collaborative nature of making knowledge is even more obvious with civic literacy." Often teachers emphasize civic literacy contexts by asking you to engage in service learning projects, which typically involve some kind of collaboration. Service learning writing projects involve writing *about* a community outside the classroom, writing *for* a community outside of the classroom, or writing *with* a community outside of the classroom.

In this civic literacies chapter, you'll find selections that will—

- Introduce you to the history and importance of civic contexts and genres of literacy
- Define different categories of civic literacies
- Give you a look at the process that Rani Marcos, a junior English major, went through as he composed a report for a city program in a professional writing class

- Encourage you to engage with important debates about the nature of civic literacy in America
- Encourage you to think about your own definition of what makes for a literate citizen in America.

If you respond to the civic literacy projects at the end of the chapter, you might—

- Analyze media
- Compose a campus newspaper editorial
- Create a public service ad campaign
- Explore your own position on what it means to be a literate citizen in America
- Write with the community in a service learning project
- Create a parody newspaper such as *The Onion*.

Now, let's explore the variety of civic literacies.

What Are Civic Literacies?

Before You Read

Make a list of all of the kinds of composing you've done for a civic audience outside of school in the last year (for example, composing an editorial, a blog, a speech, a brochure, a flier, a Web site, etc.). What were the primary purposes for your composing? Who were the primary audiences? What genres have you composed in?

Writing as Public Power: Civic Literacies

Catherine Gabor

Catherine Gabor is an Assistant Professor of Rhetoric and Composition in the Department of English and Comparative Literature at San Jose State University. From 2007 to 2009, she served as California Campus Compact–Carnegie Foundation Service Learning for Political Engagement Program Fellow. This fellowship dovetails with her ongoing teaching and research interests in civic literacy and service-learning, as well as writing in electronic environments.

1   You might think it strange for textbook in a writing class to have a chapter on civic literacy. "Doesn't that belong in a civics textbook or a

political science class?" you might ask. The duties of citizenship and the study of composition actually have been linked since their inception in ancient Greece (in the Western tradition). But the connection is not just a dry factoid from history—people have used speech and writing to exercise their rights throughout history and continue to do so today. "Fine," you might be thinking, "but I still don't get what it has to do with my college writing class." At the end of his book on the history of college writing instruction, James Berlin claims that composition classes should:

1. teach students the expectations of college-level writing;

2. serve as pre-professional training (that is, get students ready for future jobs);

3. prepare students to exercise their rights and responsibilities as citizens (*Rhetoric and Reality* 189).

Along with Berlin, many educators believe that college composition classes must train students to use writing for citizenship right along with the other goals of the class.

2   If we now understand why civic literacy is included in writing instruction, then let's take a more detailed look at what it is and how it is used in and out of the classroom. Throughout this book we have talked about "literacy" as knowledge of and ability to use writing in a variety of contexts—academic, personal, popular, etc. Civic literacy is no different: it is the understanding of and ability to use writing as power in public, political, and community-based situations. We have also talked about literacy and writing as ways of making knowledge. When you write a paper for your composition class, you are not simply repeating facts you have heard in a lecture; you are creating new knowledge by presenting your ideas in this particular assignment, using the words and quotes that you have chosen. Civic literacy also gives rise to making knowledge. You may have learned that all knowledge is created in collaboration. While you are the author of your paper and you do bring ideas and words together in a unique way in a specific paper, you are relying on past conversations, lectures, things you have read and written before. In other words, no one writes or creates meaning in a vacuum. The collaborative nature of making knowledge is even more obvious with civic literacy, which you use to negotiate the ideas of many stakeholders in public issues and create community-based documents.

3   How do you think most people respond to the question: "What is the most powerful way to get what you want?" While violence may come to mind, writing is equally—if not more—powerful. In the wake of World War II, two rhetoricians named Lucie Olbrects-Tyteca and Chaim Perleman wrote a long book that urged people to use writing and speaking

instead of war to settle differences. They had seen the cost of using violence and strove to show their fellow human beings another path: civic rhetoric. These authors argue that if more people know how to use writing and rhetoric to ease conflicts, inspire others, and solve public problems, then perhaps violence will become a less common reaction. This chapter provides historical examples and activities for you that are meant to illustrate civic literacy.

4   As I mentioned earlier in this chapter, rhetoric (persuasive writing and speech) and democracy were born together in the history of Western civilization. Historian of rhetoric George Kennedy explains, "Democratic government was emerging in Athens and some cities, based on the assumption that all citizens had an equal right and duty to participate in their own government. To do so effectively, they needed to be able to speak in public" (vii). He points out that access to participation is a right; this is an idea that most Americans today would agree with, as would many residents of the United States who seek to become citizens and enjoy such rights. However, we might not all think of civic literacy as a "duty," but the ancient Greeks did. For hundreds of years, active participation in civic life through writing and speaking was the norm for the average citizen (keep in mind, citizenship was limited to middle-class men in most societies). These days, though, most young adults do not consider enacting public literacy as one of their duties. Recently, American scholar Ann Colby and her colleagues conducted a study of college students to find out why civic engagement was on the decline in that age group. Their study points to two significant results:

- young adults do not feel like they have the skills to engage in civic debate;
- young adults do not feel like they have access to the civic or political system.

In other words, even if college students knew how to compose civic documents and speeches, they feel like there is no place for them in the system. Just like many people do not vote because they feel their vote will not make any difference, the college students in Colby's study said that they felt like civic discourse was closed off to them and reserved for professional politicians.

5   Following Colby's research, Nicholas Longo launched his own study, asking: "If college students are not politically engaged, then what do they do?" The answer, in short, is that they volunteer in their communities. Many of the students he talked to said they liked to work on a local level where they could easily make changes and see the results of their efforts. Longo asks readers of his study: is this political engagement or not? People will answer that question differently. I believe that volunteering locally is certainly a form of civic engagement, but it is only a form of civic literacy if the volunteers are using writing or rhetoric (including visual

rhetoric). Serving breakfast in a homeless shelter or tutoring children after school are both excellent examples of getting involved in one's community. However, writing a letter to the editor about the problems in local schools or speaking at a city council meeting against closure of a homeless shelter involves civic literacy: the use of words and rhetorical symbols to persuade an audience to act a certain way regarding an issue of public concern.

6   The term "rhetoric" has been used quite a bit in this textbook. Over the years, many people have offered definitions of rhetoric. Those of us interested in civic literacy usually like Aristotle's ideas about rhetoric. He noted that logic can be used to explain the facts, but that rhetoric is needed to debate "the probable." In other words, when there is not one clear "right" answer, people need to use rhetoric to hash out what the best course of action will be. If a building is on fire, we do not need to debate what to do—we use our logic to tell us to get water and put out the fire. However, if a historical building is in the path of a much-needed freeway route, we use rhetoric to debate and discuss the ideas of all of the stakeholders and come to a decision about the best way to proceed at that given time: tear down the building in favor of freeway construction or preserve the building and spend extra money to reroute the freeway (or some other solution that people can be persuaded of).

7   For many centuries public literacy and civic literacy were considered the same thing because the only people who had a public voice were citizens and the only people granted citizenship tended to be a homogenous group of middle-class men. However, in the 21st century public literacy and public discourse include much more than civic discourse. As you can see in Chapter 7: "Situating Popular Culture," there are many forms of writing that are disseminated to the public (primarily through the Internet) that are not aimed at addressing concerns of specific communities or governments—many of them are simply meant as entertainment. However, as we will see later in this chapter, humor and entertainment can be used as civic discourse.

8   What does civic literacy look like when it is used in the real world (as opposed to what it looks like when it is described in a textbook)? We might think of an important speech like "The Gettysburg Address" as a prime example of civic literacy. While I certainly would not question Abraham Lincoln's rhetorical skills or his ability to move an audience, I discount his speech a bit because it was made while he was a sitting president. We tend to think of civic literacy as used by common people, not by those in power. "The Declaration of Independence" might qualify a little better as an act of civic literacy because Thomas Jefferson was not president when he wrote it. It further qualifies because he was trying to use his persuasive language to settle a public, political problem without violence. Even closer

to the kind of civic rhetoric you may produce is college student Rani Marcos's paper in the student case study in this chapter. Rani worked with three other students to study homelessness and alcoholism in his city. Based on researching statistics, attending city meetings, talking with police, attorneys, business owners, and homeless people, Rani and his classmates wrote a report for the City Manager's Office advising them on how to best spend public funds allocated for the homeless. Rani is a "regular" college student just like you who had no special knowledge of homelessness or city funding structures when he started this project. When interviewed about his experience with civic literacy, Rani said, "I believe writing is one of the most effective forms . . . to be politically active and a lot of decisions are made because of writing . . . not just [from] those officials but [from] citizens like us." In his class, he learned how to read public documents as well as techniques for identifying stakeholders in the problem, interviewing people, and, ultimately, rhetorical strategies for persuading a public audience. In the next section of this chapter, you can learn more about the kinds of community-based projects that teach and tap into civic literacy.

Locations of Civic Literacy

9 Currently, there are many manifestations of civic literacy in writing class assignments. Part of this is due to the fact that the terms *civic* and *literacy* are both "slippery" and therefore get interpreted and enacted in a variety of ways. Another reason there are so many kinds of assignments and activities that fall under "civic literacy" is because a lot of things qualify as using knowledge of writing as a citizen. Teachers and students can exercise these literacies in a range of assignments, from fairly traditional research to out-of-the-classroom service to letters to the editor. In this chapter, we will look at the different ways to learn about and express civic literacy.

Civic Rhetoric

10 Some assignments may ask you to identify and analyze civic literacy. The ability to understand how arguments are structured and presented can be considered a skill of citizenship—it certainly makes you a more savvy consumer of political and civic messages. For example, you might be asked to bring in examples that you find in your neighborhood that qualify as civic rhetoric. You could find a flyer letting you know about an on-campus forum to talk about the quality of cafeteria food or dorm conditions. Perhaps you will download a *YouTube* or thetruth.com video urging you to stop smoking. Maybe you will be downtown and record a protest or sidewalk speaker on your cell phone. Once you have some examples of public

literacies you can analyze who they target, how they work, and what they hope to accomplish; in doing this, you could learn the names of common rhetorical terms. As another exercise, you might respond with a counter-argument or suggest improvements to make the discourse better.

Community-Based Research

11 Instead of looking at one piece of discourse and analyzing the rhetoric used, you might be asked to identify a current civic issue and gather documents from many stakeholders in order to present a fuller picture of all of the people using civic literacy about a certain issue. This kind of research would probably involve a combination of reading newspapers, government documents, Internet sites, and perhaps conducting interviews. The Internet is an increasingly common place for people to exercise their civic literacy. From political blogs to grass-roots organizations' listservs to chat rooms dedicated to specific policies, regular citizens use the Internet to express their ideas, learn about other people's positions, and—sometimes—engage in debate. As technology gets more sophisticated, more websites will be set up to receive comments from viewers, so passive readers can become active citizens by typing in their own ideas and responses. For an assignment like this, you might choose to focus on something that affects you directly, like local road conditions, or you might research a concern that is thousands of miles away from you, like the women's peace movement in Israel and Palestine. In an article about the women's peace movement, researcher Sibylle Gruber says, "Supporters of virtual communities have argued that cyberspace moves beyond the restrictions of face-to-face communities and creates opportunities for communication that do not exist in 'real' space" (79). She shows how Israeli women and Palestinian women who are separated by physical walls and military checkpoints can collaborate to plan simultaneous peace marches. While you may enjoy the benefits of the Internet's ability to bring you into communication with fans of your favorite band or *MySpace* friends across the country, you could look at the Internet differently in our research: as a venue for civic literacy, for example.

Political and Civic Engagement

12 College professors, students, administrators, and politicians argue about the place of political engagement in education. Writing teachers who want to emphasize civic literacy often design assignments that encompass both civic engagement and political engagement, terms that overlap quite a bit. You may start with one of the assignments described above and then be asked to insert your own voice into the civic sphere. Is this civic engage-

ment? Political engagement? Both? Neither? This book is not designed to answer that question for you—perhaps that very question will be an essay prompt or class discussion topic. If you do get an assignment to create rather than just analyze or report on civic literacy, there are many forms your text could take (and your professor may have some guidelines for the form, length, medium, etc.). The baseline requirement would be, of course, that your rhetoric (written, spoken, visual) be aimed at an audience that can take action on an issue of concern to you.

13   In 2007 and 2008, a group of faculty in California came together to study the best way to infuse education with civic and political engagement (the group was sponsored by the Carnegie Foundation and California Campus Compact using a Serve and Learn Grant from the federal government). One of the activities they came up with was this survey. Try answering the questions below—your answers will help you clarify your own definition of civic engagement and civic literacy as well as give you some idea what other people think qualifies. After you and your classmates finish this exercise, you may be asked to get up and move around your classroom, standing at one end if you scored an item with a "1" and standing at the other side of the room if you scored it a "5." This exercise might generate a class discussion, a homework assignment, a short essay, or all three.

14   Put a number next to each item. For the ratings, use a scale that runs from 1 to 5, with 1 representing clearly apolitical civic engagement, 5 clearly political engagement, using the intermediate numbers to represent cases that fall between those two extremes.

Volunteering for a candidate in a local, state, or national election

Leading an interracial dialogue on neighborhood crime prevention

Signing a petition calling upon your local university to provide a living wage for all its workers

Reading a daily newspaper and accessing other media to keep up with current events

Writing and submitting an editorial on campaign finance reform to campus and local papers

Leaving your car at home and biking or walking to school/work every day

Tutoring children from a local school

Attending a public debate about tensions between national security and civil rights

Serving on a jury

Organizing a grassroots campaign to stop domestic violence

Giving money to the Red Cross or other charities for relief to victims of Hurricane Katrina

Getting your friends to write letters to state legislators opposing increases in school tuition

Boycotting products that are known to be produced in sweatshops

Service Learning

15 Service Learning is a method of teaching that requires students to give something tangible to the local community while learning the academic content of the course. Service-learning courses and assignments are found across the curriculum in every major and in quite a few General Education courses. In composition courses, service learning has three common forms, all of which relate to civic literacy. Writing professor Tom Deans named the three ways to do service learning in a writing class:

- by writing about the community
- by writing for the community
- by writing with the community

Writing About

16 A service-learning class that asks you to write about the community usually requires you to engage in some form of service outside the classroom and write about it. The service experience will be very similar to volunteer experience you may have done that meets a local need. What are some

volunteer activities you have done in the past? Did your high school require some community service? Have you participated in your sorority's or fraternity's philanthropic activities? Are you a member of a religious group that does community outreach? If you said "yes" to any of these, then you have already done service, but what about the learning part? That comes in when you write about your service, when you make knowledge about your lived experience through your writing. You might keep a journal or field notes in which you reflect on your experience and what you are learning. Or, your teacher might ask you to research the underlying causes of the community problem that your service work seeks to address. In any combination, these kinds of writing assignments constitute writing about the community and will help you become a more knowledgeable citizen.

Writing For

17 In service-learning assignments that use the "writing for" model, the writing itself is the service. In other words, a local community organization might not be able to afford the time or person power to produce much needed documents, such as press releases, organizational histories, interviews of their clients, or written materials to support grant applications. Your role would be to use your civic literacy and produce rhetoric that would reach a public audience and hope to influence local decision-makers. In some cases, the decision-makers may be your own classmates. For example, if a local environmental group is trying to get more people to take public transportation and you are helping them create flyers to promote a "No Driving Day," your classmates are part of the target audience because they live and drive in the local area. Some "writing for" projects take all semester, and some are much smaller and can be done in the same amount of time as writing a traditional essay. No matter how long or short the project, you will practice using civic literacy.

Writing With

18 In this case, you would work with local stakeholders on a specific issue, coming together to exercise your civic literacy by planning and publicizing an event or writing a document for a target audience (or creating a website to bring attention to a matter of concern). This may sound a lot like the "writing for" model, but the big difference is collaborative authorship. While one or two people may write the final product, many voices may be included in brainstorming and drafting the document. Linda Flower, a well-known writing teacher who uses service learning, came up with an idea called "rivaling hypotheses." What this fancy term refers to is the process of getting as many diverse ideas on the table from as many stakeholders as pos-

sible before even deciding on a main claim, let alone writing the document. In Pittsburgh, Pennsylvania, Flower works with a local literacy center to produce documents that address issues that plague the community. For example, one semester, the participants decided to look at the curfew for people under 18. She brought together people ranging from police officers to city council members to high school dropouts to local sports fans in order to gather as many perspectives as possible. At one brainstorming session, the participants watched a skit about police officers stopping two teenagers out after curfew. The police in the room saw the skit as an example of good law enforcement; the teens in the room saw the skit as harassment and possible racial profiling. Without listening to rival hypotheses, the authors could not have written a full report on the curfew, nor could they have suggested ideas that would appeal to all of the parties involved.

". . . college students across the nation are getting more education in how to use civic literacy and beginning to have an impact in the public sphere."

19   You may be given the option to pick one of these three models in order to fulfill an assignment. In that case, you should consider your interests and the needs of the community partner you want to help; you will be able to practice your budding civic literacy whichever you chose.

20   When you started this chapter, you may have seen *civic literacy* as a topic far removed from your life, as something that only history teachers or political candidates are interested in. Now, you may see that using words to impact public, civic, or political life is a real option for you: college students across the nation are getting more education in how to use civic literacy and beginning to have an impact in the public sphere. As college student Rani Marcos said after completing the civic literacy project featured in this chapter: "[I]f you just rally and march they know what you are rallying and marching about, but there is no conversation . . . Other people can't see the reasons why you're claiming this side, and through writing you're able to express those reasons; you're able to persuade people who have the power to change."

Works Cited

Berlin, James. *Rhetoric and Reality: Writing Instruction in American Colleges, 1900–1985.* Carbondale and Edwardsville: Southern Illinois U P, 1987. Print.

Colby, Ann, Elizabeth Beaumont, Thomas Erlich, and Josh Corngold. *Educating for Democracy: Preparing Undergraduates for Responsible Political Engagement.* San Francisco: Jossey-Bass, 2007. Print.

Deans, Tom. *Writing Partnerships: Service-Learning in Composition*. Urbana: NCTE, 2000. Print.

Flower, Linda, Elenore Long, and Lorraine Higgins. *Learning to Rival: A Literate Practice for Intercultural Inquiry*. Mahwah: Lawrence Erlbaum, 2000. Print.

Gruber, Sibylle. "The Rhetorics of Three Women Activist Groups on the Web: Building and Transforming Communities." *Alternative Rhetorics: Challenges to the Rhetorical Tradition*. Ed. Laura Gray-Rosendale and Sibylle Gruber. Albany: SUNY P, 2001. 77–92. Print.

Kennedy, George. "Prooemion." Aristotle. *On Rhetoric: A Theory of Civic Discourse*. Trans. George Kennedy. New York: Oxford U P 1991. Print.

Longo, Nicholas V. "The New Student Politics: Listening to the Political Voice of Students." *The Journal of Public Affairs* 7.1 (2004): 61–74. Print.

Perleman, Chiam, and Lucie Olbrects-Tyteca. *The New Rhetoric: A Treatise on Argumentation*. South Bend: U of Notre Dame P, 1969. Print.

Literacy Connections

1. How does Gabor differentiate between civic discourse and public discourse? Based on Gabor's definition, create a list of five examples of civic discourse and five examples of public discourse.
2. How does Gabor define *service learning*? What are the three types of service learning, and how do they differ?
3. Do you feel "closed off" from public discourse like the students in Ann Colby's survey? What kinds of public discourse do you have the power and access to participate in?
4. Find an example of a work of civic literacy and bring it into class. In small groups, choose one example and do a group rhetorical analysis of the example you choose. Consider rhetorical features such as purpose, audience, medium, genre, persona, and context. Be prepared to discuss your analysis with the class.
5. As you read the selections from the chapter, keep track of the ways each author defines civic literacy, and compare those definitions to Gabor's.

Before You Read

Think of a time when you wrote something for an audience other than for a teacher. What aspects of your audience did you need to keep in mind as you composed? How did writing for the audience affect your composing processes?

Student Case Study: Composing a Service Learning Project

In this case study, we'll look at the composing process of a student engaging in research and writing with the community. Rani Marcos was a junior at California State University, Sacramento, when he was asked to complete a group service-learning project for Professional Writing. This case study of Rani's project will provide you with a concrete example of civic literacy and service learning.

Rani Marcos was a junior at California State University, Sacramento, when he completed a group service-learning project for a professional writing course. In this case study of Rani's writing, we'll focus on the primary writing project for the course, a report for the Sacramento City Manager's office. Even though Rani completed his project in a class, his primary audience was Sacramento legislators. This emphasis on writing for a civic audience, and not just for the teacher, is clear from the teacher's learning objectives:

LEARNING OBJECTIVES

By the end of the semester, students will:
- *Demonstrate an understanding of a range of professional rhetorical situations and the cultural conditions that guide responses;*
- *Recognize and produce various professional genres (letter, proposal, project plan, progress report, etc.);*
- *Articulate their knowledge about the role of writing in public policy making and implementation;*
- *Critically analyze professional writing tools and technologies;*
- *Be able to explain the relationship(s) between words and images in print and electronic texts;*
- *Communicate with versatility and awareness of professional document design, style, tone, format, and organization;*
- *Produce polished documents and presentations.*

The major assignment was to work in groups to produce a document for a community partner. Here's the assignment from the syllabus:

Service-Learning Writing Project: In groups, draft, write, and revise approximately 5,000 words (in print and/or electronically) for a local organization. Depending on the specific needs of the community partners, the writing may be one long document or several shorter documents. At the culmination of this project, you will give a formal presentation to the class and the community partners.

Rani chose to work on a report for the City of Sacramento's SIP program, a sobriety program for the homeless. This report was submitted to the City Manager's office to help them make decisions about how best to use public funds to help the homeless. Audience plays a crucial role in civic literacy contexts, and Rani told us that the audience shaped the style of the report and the use of visuals:

> *Our primary audience . . . is the legislators in the city of Sacramento and other officials who can create change. They are busy professionals who have limited time reading reports. Therefore, we made sure our writings are succinct with visuals for shorter yet effective information . . . Being an English major, it is tempting to use creative and eloquent words. However, this is not necessary for this kind of writing; in fact, it could hinder our purpose. We focused on being short and straight to the point.*

In addition to asking him about the role that his audience played in composing the report, we asked Rani about the role of genre. Rani said that the City Manager's office didn't give him a specific format to follow, but they did provide examples of the kind of report they were looking for. Rani told us that

> *Cassandra Jennings, the assistant city manager, did provide us a report of the San Diego SIP, which inspired us to create an in-depth and clear analysis report.*

Whether you're writing a book review on *Amazon.com*, a literature review for a sociology class, or a report for a government agency like Rani was asked to write, it's always helpful to seek out examples of the genre you're composing in.

Let's look at Rani and his group's initial rough draft of the report:

Of Sacramento County:
Addressing the Homeless
Serial Inebriate
Population

WHAT IS THE SERIAL INEBRIATE PROGRAM?

What is the Serial Inebriate Program?

- The Serial Inebriate Program (SIP) is a court-mandated alternative to the Sacramento County Jail.

What is the purpose of the SIP?

- The overall goal of the SIP is to curve the recidivism rates amongst the Sacramento homeless serial inebriate population, reducing the exhaust of various public safety net services. For example: Sacramento police (SPD), fire (SFD), ambulance, and hospital services due to penal code violations involving alcohol; therefore, saving the City and County of Sacramento and taxpayers unnecessary spending of money.

Who are the serial inebriates?

- Homeless individuals who have violated any city penal code while intoxicated; for example, PC 647(f).

Where is the SIP? Who directs the program?

- The SIP is operated by the Volunteers of America (VOA) at its facility where there are also two other programs: the Comprehensive Alcohol Treatment Center (CATC, also known as the 600 Club) and a long-term care facility, Residential Treatment Center (RTC, also known as the 700 Club).

When did the SIP begin in Sacramento? Why was it implemented?

- The SIP began in May 2006 after much distress of local community partners: Downtown Sacramento Partnership, representing Downtown merchants, SPD, District Attorney (DA)'s Office, and the VOA. It was implemented to relieve Downtown Sacramento of the homeless serial inebriate population.

WHY DID THE SIP ARISE?

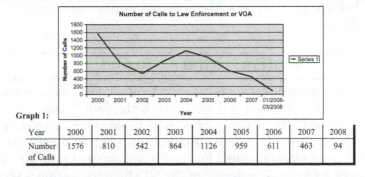

Graph 1:

Year	2000	2001	2002	2003	2004	2005	2006	2007	2008
Number of Calls	1576	810	542	864	1126	959	611	463	94

Result: Due to the exhaust of resources through the DSP and SPD alone, the transportation of this population to the VOA was not enough to keep them off the streets. NOTE: Graph does not include other public services.
Source: Downtown Sacramento Partnership Wagon Calls (2000–03/2008)

KEY TERMS AND DEFINITIONS

Court-Mandated—The SIP is one such as this where a homeless serial inebriate goes before a judge for sentencing and is sentenced to the SIP.

Community Partners—Individuals and organizations in collaboration to meet the goals of the SIP.

Public (Safety Net) Services—Including, but not limited to: police, fire, ambulance, hospital, jail, and social services.

Serial Inebriate—Homeless individual who has a history with alcohol abuse.

KEY ROLES IN THE SIP

City of Sacramento: Help fund services for homeless population, as well as homeless serial inebriates.

County of Sacramento: Responsibility for the homeless population and services implemented for their care.

DA: District Attorney, also known as a Community Prosecutor who works with the DSP and the VOA in addressing the homeless serial inebriate individuals to offer them the SIP as an alternative to County Jail. In the matter of the SIP, Rita Spillane is the Community Prosecutor who is consistently handling the SIP cases, so that when going through the court system, there is consistency.

DSP: Downtown Sacramento Partnership. Main liaison between Downtown businesses and merchants and social services to reduce homelessness.

SPD: Sacramento Police Department. Involved in arrest of homeless serial inebriates or driving to VOA facility.

VOA: Volunteers of America. The non-profit organization taking the SIP under its roof.

WHO IS ELIGIBLE FOR SIP?

An eligible participant of the SIP is an individual who has been arrested, booked and/or incarcerated at the Sacramento County Jail, or has been accepted at the CATC twenty, five or more times within a twelve month period. When brought before a judge, a participant must have been arrested for an alcohol-related incident when arrested prior to arraignment in order to be considered for the SIP; thereby, having a sentence court-mandated. There are three main conditions of when a person will be arrested, booked and/or incarcerated in such a case:

1. he was under the influence of liquor or drugs
2. was jeopardizing his or others' safety
3. was obstructing a public walkway
(Section 647 (f) of California penal Code).

Those not accepted into the SIP: violent offenders, those with Department of Motor Vehicle (DMV) issues and who have pending cases involving victim restitution.

There is no limit to how many times a person may enroll in the program. *(County of Sacramento, California, Department of Human Services, 2006)*

SERIAL INEBRIATES AT A GLANCE

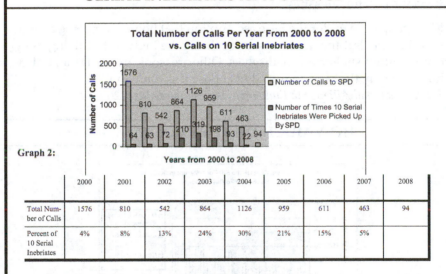

Graph 2:

	2000	2001	2002	2003	2004	2005	2006	2007	2008
Total Number of Calls	1576	810	542	864	1126	959	611	463	94
Percent of 10 Serial Inebriates	4%	8%	13%	24%	30%	21%	15%	5%	

Result: Since the DSP has been keeping records of the calls made to the SPD in regards to the homeless serial inebriates, starting in 2000, with only ten serial inebriates taken into account, it is clear to see that with the consideration that a few are responsible for occupying more than half of services; yet, only ten amongst many others are taken into consideration here. Moreover, since the SIP's implementation in 2006, the numbers made a drastic jump from current years.
Source: DSP and DA (2008).

Real Serial Inebriates

Six interviews were conducted by the Quatre SIP Team in the month of March 2008 to find that these people really needed help. They had an addiction that they knew was the cause of all their woes: alcohol. Most of these participants came from families, had a home, and reaped the rewards of having a job; yet, their one downfall took the best of their lives. Now, years later, they suffer not only from the loss of a life never to be repeated, but from various disabilities caused by drinking and living on the streets: fights with others, falling and hurting themselves, lack of personal care due to no health care and/or poor diet, and various other reasons. In Sacramento County, 74% of all homeless people have one disability, 54% of all homeless have a drug or alcohol disability, and 28% have a mental disability
Source: Individual SIP Participants and Sacramento County, Homeless in Sacramento County Report (2007).

Reasons for Homelessness

Most people are under the false assumption that homeless people choose that lifestyle, but the main reason for this is the high cost of living; they cannot afford shelter for themselves. Other reasons are: drugs and alcohol, no family ties, and some might choose this route in life.
Source: National Alliance to End Homelessness, Explainer (2007)

HOW MUCH DO THEY COST?

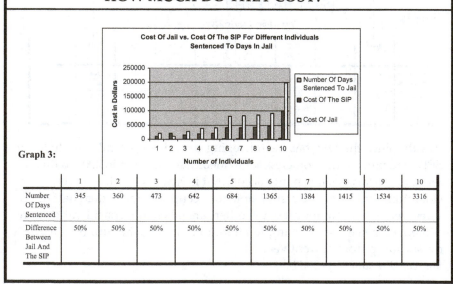

Graph 3:

	1	2	3	4	5	6	7	8	9	10
Number Of Days Sentenced	345	360	473	642	684	1365	1384	1415	1534	3316
Difference Between Jail And The SIP	50%	50%	50%	50%	50%	50%	50%	50%	50%	50%

Result: With the implementation and application of the SIP, the cost per individual, even for the same amount of time sentenced to jail, the County of Sacramento would be spending less on these individuals for those number of days. NOTE: The multiplier here was $30 per day in the SIP, and $60 per day in County Jail; a rough estimate offered by Community Prosecutor.
Source: Community Prosecutor Data (2008)

There are various other services that are occupied by the homeless that cost the City and County of Sacramento taxpayers' dollars: the police, fire, ambulance, emergency rooms and other social services. In an eighteen-month period, 227 homeless serial inebriates tally up about $6 million in health care costs. The costs for police, ambulance and fire is still unknown, but will add a lot more to the figure previously mentioned. An example of this is one chronic offender had been taken to detox 212 times while another tallied up a hospital bill equaling $187,000 in two years.
Source: San Diego County, Turning Lives Around (2003)

Most serial inebriates have been comfortable with the "Revolving Door Method" of using police, fire, ambulance, emergency rooms, detox, and jails. Most of these offenders have been picked up by police or arrested more than the required twenty five times for the SIP. The numbers and days sentenced to jail are astonishing. There has been a clear indication that the criminal justice system is not the answer for such conditions, but can be a motivational force for change. One officer noted that as a police officer, he never thought that he would also be a social worker, helping to curve the recidivism population of homelessness, but he enjoyed it. Such new job descriptions play a vital role in bringing about change in this arena. Even the DSP is an example of how roles can change, being a liaison between the businesses Downtown, and advocating on behalf of the homeless.
Source: (Can't find it right now, but will).

WHAT ARE THE PUBLIC ASPECTS OF THE SIP?

EQUITY

- **Homeless individuals** are afforded an opportunity of receiving help for their addictions and disabilities due to their chronic condition and alcohol addiction. They also have the opportunity to meet their health care needs, and work towards autonomy in a housing unit upon completion of the SIP; a major incentive.

Result: Fairness and equal opportunity for individuals.
Source: (I don't have right now, but will).

<u>FUNDING</u>

- **Taxpayers** pay taxes to the federal and state governments who in return distribute funds to states, cities and counties.
- **City and County of Sacramento** help fund various programs for different social needs, although Sacramento County is responsible for the homeless population.
- **Private Contributions** by private individuals and/or organizations help the SIP cause.

Source: (I don't have right now, but will).

<u>ROLE OF GOVERNMENT</u>

- **Federal Government** is responsible in the greater sense to the homeless population.
- **Sacramento County** is responsible for the homeless population.

Result: The SIP helps the County fulfill its duty to providing for them.

Source: (Will follow next time, promise).

PRIVATE ASPECTS OF THE SIP?

<u>DOWNTOWN SACRAMENTO</u>

- Businesses, through the DSP, pay for services that include working towards solutions for the homeless problem in Sacramento.
- DSP is also a private organization that makes a profit, which makes it very unique to this multi-faceted relationship between private business and social services.

Source: DSP (2008)

OUTCOMES IN SACRAMENTO COUNTY

How many people have gone through the SIP?

- Since its implementation in May 2006, 104 individuals have gone through the SIP.

Of those 104, how many of them completed the program?

- The pass rate is a remarkable 87.5% from May 2006 to February 2008.

How much does the SIP cost?

- There are no additional costs relating to the SIP, since VGA began the program at its facility. The $1.4 million contributed by the city, and other funds cover the SIP as well at the VOA facility.

Is the SIP utilized in any other part of Sacramento?

- No, the only SIP in existence in Sacramento is at the VOA facility.

What happens after the SIP?

- Proposals and work have been done to expand the program to include housing after completion of the program, in which funds would be needed. Just last month, March 2008, Sutter Health has funded Self Help Housing with $91,000.00 to cover costs of two case managers for eight serial inebriates from the SIP.

  Source: (Will do later, promise).

UNINTENDED CONSEQUENCES

Table 1: Unintended Consequences of the SIP

Unintended Consequence:	Result:
1. A housing element for the SIP graduates.	After the SIP, considering that individuals can return many more times, the cycle of homelessness, exhaustion of public safety net services and the "Revolving Door Method" continues because they have no place to go.
2. Lack of record keeping.	Lack of information may be due to a variety of reasons. Different places, although community partners, have varied data.
3. SIP participants stay longer after graduation.	No real incentive or motivation for individuals to excel.

CONCLUSION

The SIP makes it possible for individuals to acknowledge and treat their alcohol addiction, as well as their disability/ies in a place that fosters their needs and addresses their addiction(s), such as the VOA. The SIP saves people money because these individuals, about 1,600 of them in Sacramento, are in one facility that does not cost extra money, versus going through the criminal justice system or feeding on various public safety nets.

Businesses in Downtown, and Downtown specifically, can be relieved of the mishaps going on in front of merchants' place of business, and Downtown can grow and prosper, which will be beneficial for Sacramento County as a whole.

As with anything in life, everything has its tradeoffs, but from where I stand, the biggest benefit of the SIP is many, and many people will benefit years to come, not just the homeless serial inebriates.

REFERENCES

(Sources cited, of course).

Authored by California State University, Sacramento, Professional Writing Students:

<u>Quatre SIP</u>

- Loselea Naufahu
- Rani Marcos
- Lorraine Powell
- Peter Schwarck

KEY ISSUES TO BE CONSIDERED

- Fact: The SIP creates equity and affords opportunity to individuals who would otherwise not receive treatment or a window of chance to make change. This equity is created at the benefit of public money.

Should government take a more active role in funding the SIP? And to find a better means of expanding the program as to not allow for more "Revolving Door Methods"?

- Fact: The DSP receives funds from the Downtown businesses associated with the costs of serial inebriates.

Should the private industry be responsible for funding what is a public issue? Is it not government's responsibility, the county's responsibility? Is it a private or public issue? To what extent should private business be involved in social affairs?

- Fact: The SIP is only a small portion of the bigger fight against homelessness.

Are the findings relating to the SIP enough to warrant attention and intervention?

- Fact: Little is known about the success of the SIP.

If this is so, and records are lacking in reliability as well, how sure can the community partners be that the results will be an accurate judgment of the program?

Rani mentioned that he and his group got a lot of feedback on this initial draft:

SIP's final draft went through copious revisions. We are fortunate to have one of our group members to have some experience in public policy and service learning; thus, we focused less on the format and concentrated more on its contents. In our revision, we each had a copy of the very first draft and utilized the Internet to see and make comments, as well as implementing the discussed changes.

After revisions within our group, we asked our professor to be our test reader, reading the report as if she has no further knowledge about our work. We recognized that although we know what we'd like to express and illustrate, our audience might not perceive the same.

Finally, we also asked our community partners to review our draft. Despite their busy schedule, they managed to view it. We valued their feedbacks because they know more about the SIP and they are the people who will use our report. Before finalizing the draft, they saw some errors with our statistics and citation. They are minor details but extremely important for a consistent and credible final draft.

Rani and his group didn't just write a single draft—they got feedback on the content and mechanics of their writing from within the group and from the teacher and community partner. Experienced composers know that the more feedback they can get, the better the final draft will be. Rani and his group's final draft reflects the significant revisions they made based on the feedback they received:

Addressing the Homeless Serial
Inebriate
Population In Sacramento County
April 25, 2008

WHAT IS THE SERIAL INEBRIATE PROGRAM?

What is the Serial Inebriate Program?

- The Serial Inebriate Program (SIP) is a 90-day court-mandated alternative to the Sacramento County Jail.

What is the purpose of the SIP?

- The overall goal of the SIP is to curb the recidivism rates for the Sacramento serial inebriate population, reducing the expense of various public safety net services, including police, fire, ambulance, and hospital.

Who are the serial inebriates?

- Individuals (predominantly homeless) who have been arrested or admitted to the Volunteers of America (VOA) facility while intoxicated 25 times or more in the previous 12 months.

Where is the SIP? Who directs the program?

- The SIP is operated by the (VOA) at its facility at 700 North 5th Street in Sacramento.

When did the SIP begin in Sacramento? Why was it implemented?

- The SIP began in May 2006. It was implemented to relieve Downtown Sacramento of the homeless serial inebriate population.

SIP REDUCES VISIBLE INEBRIATES AND SAVES MONEY

Graph 1 below illustrates that in the beginning of 2007, the Downtown Sacramento Partnership (DSP) saw a substantial decline in calls to law enforcement compared to prior years, and it continues to maintain lower numbers than figures in the past eight years. The graph only indicates the participation of the SPD and the VGA; other public services are not included.

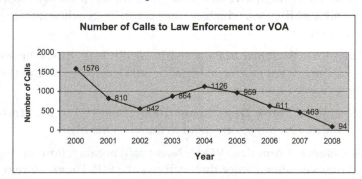

Number of Calls to Law Enforcement or VOA

Graph 1:

This has resulted in a significant decline in wagon calls that transport serial inebriates either to law enforcement or the VOA. This chart shows a steep decline in calls after SIP's implementation in 2006. Expenses in prior years for transportation of offenders alone was exorbitant.
Source: Downtown Sacramento Partnership Wagon Calls (2000–03/2008)

KEY TERMS AND DEFINITIONS

Court-Mandated—Judge sentencing of serial inebriate to jail time or SIP (in lieu of jail).

Community Partners—A partnership between the DA, DSP, VOA and SPD to meet the goals of the SIP.

Penal Code (PC) 647(f)—Most frequent offense by serial inebriates, being drunk in public.

Public (Safety Net) Services—Including, but not limited to: police, fire, ambulance, hospital, jail, and social services.

Serial Inebriate—Individual who has been arrested or transported to VOA 25 or more times in one year.

KEY ROLES IN THE SIP

City of Sacramento: Helps fund services for homeless population, including homeless serial inebriates.

County of Sacramento: Responsible for the homeless population and services implemented for their care.

District Attorney (DA): Also known as a Community Prosecutor, works with the DSP and the VOA in addressing the serial inebriates to offer them the SIP as an alternative to County Jail. The Community Prosecutor handles all the SIP cases, which ensures consistency when going through the court system.

Downtown Sacramento Partnership (DSP): Main liaison between Downtown businesses and social/public services to reduce serial inebriate offenses and homelessness.

Sacramento Police Department (SPD): Involved in the arrests of serial inebriates, also transports them to the VGA facility.

Volunteers of America (VOA): Non-profit organization serving as a alcohol detoxification center that includes the SIP. There are two other programs at this facility: the Comprehensive Alcohol Treatment Center (CATC) and a long-term care facility, Residential Treatment Center (RTC).

WHO IS ELIGIBLE FOR SIP?

An eligible participant is an individual who has a history of penal code violations involving alcohol that results in arrests and/or admission into the CATC 25 times or more within a 12 month period. When arraigned before a judge, a court-mandated discretionary amount of jail time or 90 days in the SIP is offered to the potential SIP participant. There are 3 main conditions required for an inebriated person to be arrested under PC 647(f):

1. under the influence of liquor or drugs
2. jeopardizing one's own or others' safety
3. obstructing a public walkway

Source: Section 647 (f) of California Penal Code

Those not accepted into the SIP: violent offenders, those with Department of Motor Vehicle (DMV) issues and who have pending cases involving victim restitution.

There is no limit to how many times a person may be admitted in the SIP. *Source: County of Sacramento, California, Department of Human Services (2006)*

SERIAL INEBRIATES AT A GLANCE

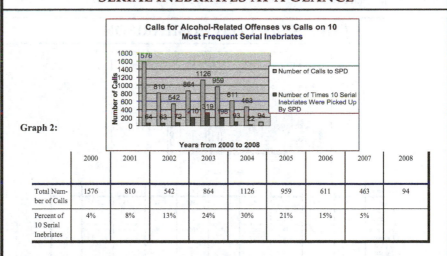

Graph 2:

Calls for Alcohol-Related Offenses vs Calls on 10 Most Frequent Serial Inebriates

☐ Number of Calls to SPD
■ Number of Times 10 Serial Inebriates Were Picked Up By SPD

Years from 2000 to 2008

	2000	2001	2002	2003	2004	2005	2006	2007	2008
Total Number of Calls	1576	810	542	864	1126	959	611	463	94
Percent of 10 Serial Inebriates	4%	8%	13%	24%	30%	21%	15%	5%	

The chart above shows DSP's record of the calls made to the SPD for homeless serial inebriates, starting in 2000. The red bars show the impact of ten serial inebriates. These ten offenders were responsible for the consumption of more than half of services used. Notice that the start of the program in 2006 shows a dramatic reduction in calls.
Source: DSP and DA (2008)

Actual Serial Inebriates

The Quatre SIP Team conducted interviews of obliging SIP participants in March 2008 (see Appendix A: Real Serial Inebriates). We found that most of these participants had families, homes and jobs at one time; yet, their alcoholism (sometimes coupled with drug abuse) devastated their lives. After years of abuse, they suffer lot only from the loss of a happy family life, but from various disabilities caused by drinking and living on the streets. Damage is caused by, but not limited to: being victimized (beaten, robbed, and/or raped), fighting with others, falling and hurting themselves, lack of health care, and a poor diet. Most serial inebriates are homeless and in Sacramento County, 74% of all homeless people have one disability, 54% of all homeless have a drug or alcohol disability, and 28% have a mental disability.
Source: Individual SIP Participants and Sacramento County, Homeless in Sacramento County Report (2007).

Reasons for Homelessness

Homelessness is often assumed to be a lifestyle choice, but the main reason is the high cost of living. Some individuals cannot afford shelter for themselves. Other reasons are: drugs and alcohol, no family ties or a breakdown of family ties due to substance abuse.
Source: National Alliance to End Homelessness, Explainer (2007).

JAIL VS. SIP: COST COMPARISON

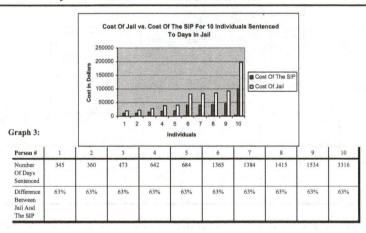

Graph 3:

Person #	1	2	3	4	5	6	7	8	9	10
Number Of Days Sentenced	345	360	473	642	684	1365	1384	1415	1534	3316
Difference Between Jail And The SIP	63%	63%	63%	63%	63%	63%	63%	63%	63%	63%

Result: The cost of the SIP is roughly one-third the cost of incarceration over the same number of days.
NOTE: The multiplier here was $28 per day in the SIP, and $76 per day in County Jail.
Source: Community Prosecutor and VOA Data (2008)

OTHER COMMUNITY SERVICES: COST COMPARISON

There are other services that are utilized by the homeless that cost taxpayers' dollars: police, fire, ambulance, emergency rooms and other social services. In an 18 month period, 227 homeless serial inebriates tallied up approximately $6 million in health care costs. The costs for police, ambulance and fire is still unknown, but will increase this figure. For example one chronic offender was taken to detox 212 times while another tallied up a hospital bill equaling $187,000 in two years. In Sacramento, one serial inebriate's 24-hour hospital stay cost $3,770; another's 4 to 8 hours cost $2,767.94; and another's couple of hours in order to sober up before being transported to jail cost $1,143.58.
Source: San Diego County, Turning Lives Around (2003), and Community Prosecutor (2008)

Most serial inebriates have been comfortable with the "Revolving Door Method" of using police, fire, ambulance, emergency rooms, detox, and jails. Most of these offenders have been picked up by police or arrested more than the required twenty-five times for the SIP. There has been a clear indication that the criminal justice system is not the answer for such conditions, but can be a motivational force for change.
Source: National Alliance to End Homelessness, Fact Checker (2007)

PUBLIC ASPECTS OF THE SIP

EQUITY

- **Homeless individuals** are afforded the opportunity of receiving help for their addictions and disabilities due to their chronic poor living conditions and substance abuse. They also have the opportunity to meet their health care needs, and work towards autonomy in a housing unit upon completion of the SIP, a major incentive.

- **Result:** Fairness and equal opportunity for individuals.

FUNDING

- **Taxpayers** pay taxes to the federal and state governments who in return distribute funds to states, cities and counties.

- **City and County of Sacramento** help fund various programs for different social needs, although Sacramento County is responsible for the homeless population.

- **Private Contributions** are given by private individuals and/or organizations to help the SIP cause.

- **Result:** The SIP helps the County fulfill its duty to provide for the homeless population.

PRIVATE ASPECTS OF THE SIP

DOWNTOWN SACRAMENTO

- Businesses, through the DSP, pay for services that include working towards solutions for the serial inebriate and homeless issues in Sacramento.
- DSP is also a private organization that makes a profit, which makes it very unique to this multi-faceted relationship between private business and social/public services.

Source: DSP (2008)

OUTCOMES IN SACRAMENTO COUNTY

How many people have gone through the SIP?

- Since its implementation in May 2006, 30 individuals have gone through the SIP.

Of those 30, how many of them completed the program?

- The completion rate is a remarkable 87.5% from May 2006 to February 2008.

What is the fiscal impact of the SIP?

- The $1.4 million contributed by the County, City, and other donated funds cover the SIP along with the other programs at the VOA facility. There are no additional costs relating to the SIP.

Is the SIP operated in other areas of Sacramento County?

- No, the only SIP in existence in Sacramento is at the VOA facility.

What happens after the SIP?

- Proposals and work have been initiated, to expand the program to include housing after completion of the SIP. In March 2008, Sutter Health funded Self Help Housing with $91,000.00 to cover the costs of two case managers for eight serial inebriates from the SIP.

Source: (Will do later, promise).

UNEXPECTED ISSUES

Table 1: Unanticipated Issues of the SIP

Problem:	Result:	Possible Solution:
Unmet Housing Needs for SIP graduates	Serial Inebriates have no place to go after the SIP. Many return to the streets or the SIP for lack of alternatives.	Obtain housing funds for SIP graduates with minimal counseling support to help maintain sobriety and develop life skills.
Lack of Comprehensive Record Keeping	Not all data is available for examination. There may be unknown issues that need attention.	Increase data gathering
SIP participants stay at the VOA after graduation.	There is no real incentive or motivation for individuals to excel. SIP housing may be more expensive than basic housing program.	Set up a direct link between successful completion of the SIP program and follow-up housing.

CONCLUSION

The SIP makes it possible for individuals to acknowledge and treat their alcohol addiction, as well as their disabilities, in a place that fosters their needs and addresses their addiction, such as the VOA facility. The SIP saves money because these individuals are in one facility that costs roughly one-third the price of jail. The serial inebriates are no longer going through the criminal justice system or using various public safety nets (such as emergency medical services) in as high a percentage, which saves public funds.

Due to the SIP, businesses in Downtown can be relieved of the penal code violations going on in front of their businesses, and Downtown can grow and prosper. The SIP will be beneficial for Sacramento County as a whole, as well as the homeless serial inebriates.

KEY ISSUES TO BE CONSIDERED

- Fact: The SIP creates equity and affords opportunity to individuals who would not otherwise receive treatment or a chance to make changes in their lives. This equity is created at the benefit of public funds.

Should government expand the funding of the SIP? This in order to insure a better means of increasing the program for all qualified individuals to avoid the default of the expensive "Revolving Door Methods."

- Fact: The Downtown Sacramento Partnership (DSP) receives funds from the Downtown businesses associated with the costs of serial inebriates.

Is it a private or a public issue? Should private industry be responsible for funding what is a public issue? Should it be the government's responsibility? To what extent should private business be involved in social affairs?

- Fact: The SIP is only a small portion of the bigger fight against homelessness.

Are the findings relating to the SIP enough to warrant attention and intervention? Should the SIP be expanded? Should a housing program for the SIP graduates be implemented?

- Fact: More data and information would be helpful for assessing the program.

Because of a deficiency of data, how sure can the community partners be that the results will be an accurate judgment of the program?

- Fact: Housing is needed for reformed serial inebriates, with supportive counseling to keep them on the right track.

Will supportive housing keep reformed serial inebriates from returning to homelessness and substance abuse?

REFERENCES

"CATC and SIP Evaluation Needs." 17 Jan. 2008.
"County of Sacramento California." 11 Apr. 2006.
Dunford, James V., et al. Impact of the San Diego Serial Inebriate Program on Use of Emergency Medical Resources. 2006.
Executive Summary. Sacramento City and County Ten-Year Plan to End Chronic Homelessness 2006–2016. 5 Dec. 2005. 23 Mar. 2008.

"The First Year." 2007 Progress Report for Sacramento's Ten-Year Plan to End Chronic Homelessness. 2007.

Greene, Jan, Serial Inebriate Programs: What to do About Homeless Alcoholics in the Emergency Department. 22 May 2007. 05 Apr. 2008. http://www.sciencedirect.com/science?_ob=ArticleURL.

"Impact of a Multi-Disciplinary Serial Inebriate Program (SIP) on Emergency Care Services in San Diego." 5 June 2001. 02 Apr. 2008.

"Interagency Council on Homelessness." 13 Apr. 2008.

Irby, Clenton. Group meeting with community partners at VOA facility. 11 Mar. 2008

Leavenworth, Stuart. Rousting the homeless embarrasses our community. 11 Nov. 2007. 28 Mar 2008. http://www.sacbee.eom/ l10/v-print/story/482019.html.

Loofbourrow, Ryan. Group meeting. 25 Mar. 2008.

National Alliance to End Homelessness. June 2007. 11 Apr. 2008. http://www.ich.gov/innovations/index.html.

—Explainer, Sept. 2007.

—Fact Checker. Mar. 2007.

"Prevention: Diversion From Criminal Justice. 2008.

Serial Inebriates. Personal interviews by Quatre SIP Team. 02–03 Apr. 2008.

Spillane, Rita. Group meeting. 01 Apr. 2008.

"Ten Year Plan to End Chronic Homelessness." 2006. 27 Mar. 2008. http://www.communitycouncil.org/level-3/homeless-plan.html.

Authored by California State University, Sacramento, Professional Writing Students:

Quatre SIP:

- Rani Marcos
- Loselea Naufahu
- Lorraine Powell
- Peter Schwarck

Appendix A: Real Serial Inebriates

The following stories are taken from interviews with serial inebriates enrolled in the SIP. All interviewees were given pseudonyms to protect their privacy.

SPOTLIGHT ON SOBRIETY; A COMPREHENSIVE STORY OF ONE MAN'S LIFE

Joe has been homeless for many years; the serial inebriate program, detox and jail have been his only refuge. He saw some gruesome things living on the streets. He saw a homeless friend hanging from a tree. She had committed suicide. But the defining event for him was when he found his drinking buddy frozen on the sidewalk. He had passed out drunk and died of hypothermia. Joe realized then that he could have easily been the one who was too drunk to know he was freezing to death.

Joe is a sleepy, heavy-set, forty-eight-year-old, who grew up in Elk Grove. He comes from a large family. He says, "My Hispanic father had a macho attitude, he was proud that I could drink beer at age five."

In the early part of his life he was successful, both working on motorcycles and working as a "lead man" on a carpentry crew for Embassy Suites. He considered his job running a crew of carpenters stressful, because he was required to hire, fire, and run the crew, while living at different locations. Since the company paid for the crew to sleep in their suites, there was an opportunity for them to party together after work. Joe says there was lots of drinking and he started using cocaine and other drugs.

Joe became a motorcycle mechanic and started using methamphetamine and seconol as well as the cocaine and alcohol. By now, he had a bad back and medicated himself with the drugs and alcohol. He had a work hard/play hard life and made lots of money. He says he once came home on a Christmas Eve with $50,000 in his pocket and loaded with presents for his family. But there are holes in his memory, he cannot remember if he was too hard on his four kids or not hard enough, though he remembers yelling at them.

His younger brother died at age twenty-one from a heart attack, which Joe witnessed in the front yard of his mother's home. Shortly afterwards his father and grandmother died and his girlfriend left. He fell into despair, not caring if he lived or died. Alcohol took over, a substance that Joe considers more addictive to him than the drugs—even methamphetamine.

He is subject to panic attacks and hallucinations. He says he sometimes hears his dead brother beckoning to him, calling, "Come on Joe—it's ok." Or he sees a pair of red cat eyes staring in the distance and then hears a low growling that amplifies to the snarl of a tiger right in the same room. The sound of gunshots in the distance or a car backfiring make him hit the floor, like a post-traumatic stress disorder victim.

Joe is determined to stop drinking. He describes the terrors of detoxifying his body as a process of waking up screaming for booze, having delirious tremors and feeling like a "nervous jack-in-the-box." Although he has gone through the process in civil protective custody many times, longer-term residential treatment has been his best alternative. Because he is a long-time serial inebriate, he is well acquainted with the district attorney, and taking her advice, he enrolled in the SIP program. He then willingly signed up for a second 90-day commitment to the SIP program.

Diagnosed with bipolar disorder; he suffers from paranoia and schizophrenia. He takes medication to correct a chemical imbalance in his brain. According to the counselors in the SIP program where he currently resides, Joe must be given his medications on a strict schedule to manage his condition and to avoid pill hoarding and subsequent self-over-medication.

He says he did not grasp the concept of being clean and sober on his first 90-day commitment at SIP. He says it takes a while to normalize to the new feeling of being sober and aware and look at the life he had been medicating himself from. He feels comfortable learning from the staff at the VOA where he is learning to be nice and patient and take one day at a time. He enjoys the Bible study and the Alcohol and Narcotics Anonymous meetings, and struggles with the group counseling, where he is forced to look at his life in a very structured, honest way. Although he would love getting an apartment and being godfather to his older brother's twins, this is not a viable option. Joe requires constant supervision.

SHERYL'S STORY

Sheryl spent time in an orphanage and then lived in many different foster homes in Los Angeles. Her birth mother, who she describes as, "a wicked witch," died just three years ago.

She says she lived on the Sacramento streets for seven years. She had a spot on the sidewalk on Alhambra Boulevard, right across the street from the AmPm MiniMart. She would spread out her sleeping bag, line up her stuffed animals and sleep with one eye open. Robbed many times by other homeless people, she survived by panhandling and by the charity of local churches and programs such as Loaves and Fishes. Infrequently, she spent the night in a single occupancy hotel.

She shared her life sometimes with a boyfriend, but he had a drug problem as well as an alcohol addiction. The crack cocaine he used made him unstable and, like others on the streets, sometimes desperate for money. She estimates that she averaged two or three fights a month with other homeless people, as well as abuse from her boyfriend.

Sheryl says God delivered her from alcoholism by the help of her Christian faith. She enjoys the Bible study the SIP program holds every day and finds the Alcoholics Anonymous helpful. She does not think she needs the skills counseling or the limited placement in housing for recovering substance abusers. She hopes to return to Los Angeles. She considers the SIP a better environment compared with jail where the inmates can simply lay around.

DON'S STORY

Don joined the air force in 1981. He worked on F-16s and F-17s as a mechanic for many years. After his service, he worked in a family owned machine shop. Then he learned carpentry and worked as a skilled cabinetmaker. He was also a social drinker without any alcohol abuse problems.

Next, he took a job as a security guard in the Arden area of Sacramento, patrolling an apartment complex on the graveyard shift. He also hooked up with a woman, who as he says, "drove him to drinking."

The change was gradual at first; he started out only drinking on the weekends, but progressed to where he was drinking everyday. He and his friends were bad influences on each other. They began to play drinking games to see who could drink the most. Don says he was teased about being hen-pecked and tried to show off by outdoing his friends in the alcohol consumption department. Soon he was drinking all day, every day.

Don has been through the 90 day SIP program three times. He says he prefers it to jail, where he is, "mostly just locked up." He likes the counseling in the SIP program, and is on a list waiting for supportive housing. He wants to return to his carpentry work and believes it is best to work on day shift since the graveyard shift is where he first got into alcohol abuse.

Some of the changes Rani and his group made were small, "local" changes, like changing the title or correcting some mechanical errors. Other changes were larger, "global" changes, like adding cost comparisons of jail versus other community services and adding an appendix of serial inebriate stories. Rani and his group didn't make these big changes just to try to fill up more space and make the report longer. Each change was based on appealing to their audience and making the report more persuasive. For example, Rani said that he added the appendix of SIP participants "to provide a human face and discover the root of the conflict that affects them and the public."

Rani said that writing for a civic audience outside the classroom was challenging, but it was also rewarding:

> *Writing for a public audience seems to have more pressure on students than writing for a teacher. On top of obtaining a good grade, our report is based on real-world experience and viewed and utilized by real-world professionals. I've personally experienced more support, especially from teachers, fellow students, and of course, our community partners. At the same time, I felt more independent and influential, working only with three other students and our community partners towards making a better change in our community and hopefully in others. When writing travels outside a classroom, it becomes more meaningful and powerful, encouraging me, personally, to do better and work harder.*

Literacy Connections

1. How did the target audience affect Rani and his group's composing processes and the final product?
2. Based on Rani and his group's final product, what are some features of the genre of the report the group was asked to write?
3. In her learning outcomes, Rani's teacher talks about document design. What design elements did Rani's group incorporate in the report? Do you think the design is effective? Why or why not?
4. Evaluate Rani and his group's report. Given the literacy context, is the report effective? Why or why not?
5. In what ways does this service learning project exemplify Catherine Gabor's definitions of *civic literacy* in the introductory essay of the chapter?

Civic Literacy Readings

Before You Read

To get you thinking about issues of civic engagement discussed in the reading that follows, in a five-minute freewrite, discuss whether or not you think it's important that students get involved to make things better for society and why or why not. Discuss your answer with the class.

Excerpt from *Millennials Talk Politics: A Study of College Students' Civic Engagement*

The Center for Information and Research on Civic Learning and Engagement

The Center for Information and Research on Civic Learning and Engagement (CIRCLE) conducts research on the civic and political engagement of young Americans. The following excerpt is from a study of 386 college students who were asked to discuss their civic and political attitudes and experiences. The study found that today's college students (the "Millennials") are more engaged with civic literacy than the previous generation ("Generation X"), but they are also skeptical of formal political parties. You can find out more about CIRCLE at their Web site, www.civicyouth.org. To view the entire report that this reading is excerpted from, visit www.civicyouth.org/?page_id=250.

1. Today's College Students are More Engaged than Generation X Was

THE IMPETUS FOR this project was to learn from college students how civic and political attitudes and experiences have changed (if at all) since the early 1990s, when there was evidence of deep alienation from the political system.

We found that students live in a different world from those who attended college in the early nineties. Students communicate differently today and have many new opportunities. Millennials are more involved in both civic and political life than their predecessors, and this may be the result of their increased likeliness to see political engagement as important. Yet we also found significant differences of experience among the Millennial as a generation.

From the 1990s to Today

In 1993, The Charles F. Kettering Foundation published *College Students Talk Politics,* a national study conducted by Richard C. Harwood and John A. Creighton of the Harwood Group. The authors conducted focus groups on ten American campuses from 1991 to 1992 and found, among other things, that students considered politics "irrelevant" to their lives. According to the report, many college students equated citizenship with individual rights, not with responsibilities for collective action. Students drew "tenuous" connections (if any) between citizenship and politics and saw little purpose in actively participating in the political system. These findings were consistent with contemporary news reports about "Generation X," then the predominant group in college, which depicted them as individualistic, cynical, and alienated.

In 2006 and 2007, we interviewed college students, the majority of whom belong to the Millennial Generation (born after 1985). We designed our methodology to produce a comparable sample and our findings are substantially different from the 1993 study.

Today's students are eager to get out into their communities and put their acquired talents and abilities to work. One Minnesota student says,

"You sit in a classroom and you read your dusty books with your dusty professors about dusty things, and then you don't learn anything about what you can do with it, and then you go into the community and all of a sudden you're like, wow, this is who I am and this is where my skills can go."

In the survey that accompanied the focus groups, we ask whether it is the respondents' choice or their responsibility to "get involved to make things better for society." Only 22 percent say that it is simply a choice. Furthermore, 92 percent of the students in our sample believe that "people working together as a group" can make "some" or "a lot" of difference in solving the problems they see in their community. This is not much different from the 85 percent of college students who gave the same answer in our national survey in 2006.[1]

The students in our focus groups do not write off politics as irrelevant or unchangeable. By a ratio of almost eight to one, they say that government policies are relevant to the issues that concern them. In the words of a Maryland student: "If individuals themselves don't take it upon themselves to do something about issues that are actually about policy change, then nothing is going to be done."

Many students in our focus groups see politics as a vehicle for change, albeit an inefficient and difficult one. Many of these college students want to be involved and consider it important to participate, although often they do not know how to engage or doubt their ability to have a great deal of impact.

The Historical Context

During the 1990s, many observers became alarmed about decreases in political engagement among youth. Surveys showed that between 1972 and 1992, there were substantial

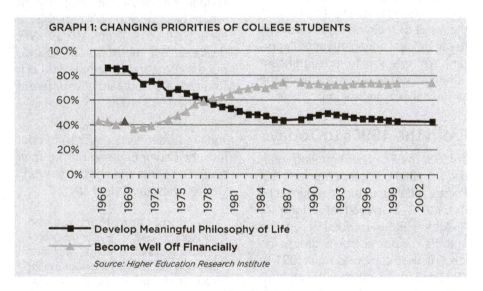

GRAPH 1: CHANGING PRIORITIES OF COLLEGE STUDENTS

■ Develop Meaningful Philosophy of Life

▲ Become Well Off Financially

Source: Higher Education Research Institute

[1]Lopez, M.H., Levine, P., Both, D., Kicsa, A. Kirby. E.H. & Marcelo. K.B. (October 2006). *The 2006 Civic and Political Health of the Nation: A Detailed Look at How Youth Participate in Politics and Communities.* College Park. MD: CIRCLE (www.civicyouth.org).

declines in the proportion of college students who discussed politics,[2] considered it important to keep up with current affairs,[3] voted,[4] read a newspaper,[5] and trusted other human beings.[6]

Values had changed, too. In the late 1960s, when the Higher Education Research Institute began surveying incoming college freshmen, most said that "developing a meaningful philosophy of life" was a top priority, whereas they ranked "becoming well off financially" much lower. By 1992, those two priorities had switched. Either because of declining idealism or an increased sense of economic risk and vulnerability, members of Generation X appeared focused on getting ahead as individuals, not developing personal philosophies or participating as citizens. To the extent that they engaged civically, it was often through individual acts of service, not political organizing or engagement with large institutions.

As the 1990s progressed, two further developments became evident. First, it turned out that 1992 had been a peak in youth voter turnout. The turnout rate of young college students fell to 48 percent in the presidential election of 2000, down one third compared to the 1970s. Meanwhile, volunteering increased substantially, until almost four out of five American high school seniors reported volunteering—a rate substantially higher than in previous decades.[7]

Nicholas Longo and Ross Meyer wrote that the trends in voting and volunteering split apart during the 1990s like the blades of a pair of open scissors.[8] Perhaps students turned to service in retreat from major political institutions, reflecting the individualism—and the alienation from large-scale politics—that the Harwood report had already detected in 1992. Or perhaps young people volunteered because opportunities for service and service-learning were rapidly expanding during the 1990s, whereas little effort was made to recruit them into politics.

In any event, by the early 2000s, volunteering had become commonplace, but connections to formal politics remained tenuous. By 2000, when youth voter turnout reached its lowest point for presidential

[2]Pryor, J.H., Hurtado, S., Saenz, V.B., Santos, J. L., & Korn, W.S. (2007). *The American Freshman: Forty Year Trends*. Los Angeles: Higher Education Research Institute, UCLA.

[3] Ibid

[4] Lopez. M.H., Kirby, E.H., Sagoff, J. & Kolaczkowski, J.P. (July 2005). *CIRCLE Fact Sheet: Electoral Engagement Among Non-College Attending Youth*. College Park, MD: CIRCLE (www.civicyouth.org).

[5]General Social Survey analyzed by CIRCLE.

[6]DDB Needham surveys analyzed by CIRCLE.

[7]Monitoring the Future survey of high school seniors, analyzed by CIRCLE. See also DDB Life Style Surveys, analyzed for the youth population in National Conference on Citizenship, Broken Engagement:

[8]Longo, N.V. & Meyer, R.P. (May 2006). *CIRCLE Working Paper 46: College Students and Politics: A Literature Review*. College Park, MD: CIRCLE (www.civicyouth.org).

elections,[9] only 28 percent of incoming college freshmen considered it important to keep up with public affairs.[10] But then, as a result of deliberate organizing by civic organizations or a more intense political environment—or both—the tide seemed to turn. Youth voter turnout rose substantially in 2004 and again in 2006, despite modest increases among older voters. Young people reported rising interest in the news and public affairs. As seen in Graph 2, the gap between volunteering and voting narrowed, largely because voting rose (along with interest in the news and political discussions).

These changes in civic behavior are also reflected in our focus groups. It is not that today's college students are fully engaged with the political system; they do not feel adequately informed or able to make a difference as individuals. For the most part, however, these students are aware of the importance of policy and politics, conscious that it is desirable to be informed and engaged, and fairly optimistic about the power of collective actions.

Why The Differences?

Although our focus groups cannot explain the reasons for the significant changes in college students' civic attitudes since the 1990s, we can speculate about two major causes. One is a shift in the political environment. The

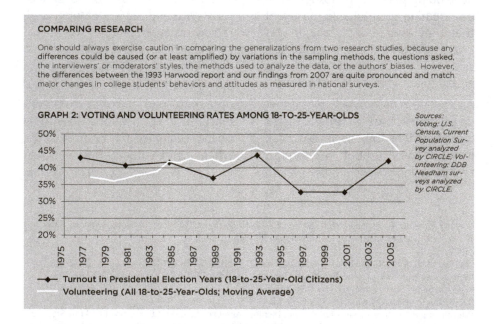

COMPARING RESEARCH

One should always exercise caution in comparing the generalizations from two research studies, because any differences could be caused (or at least amplified) by variations in the sampling methods, the questions asked, the interviewers' or moderators' styles, the methods used to analyze the data, or the authors' biases. However, the differences between the 1993 Harwood report and our findings from 2007 are quite pronounced and match major changes in college students' behaviors and attitudes as measured in national surveys.

GRAPH 2: VOTING AND VOLUNTEERING RATES AMONG 18-TO-25-YEAR-OLDS

Sources: Voting: U.S. Census, Current Population Survey analyzed by CIRCLE; Volunteering: DDB Needham surveys analyzed by CIRCLE.

◆ Turnout in Presidential Election Years (18-to-25-Year-Old Citizens)
— Volunteering (All 18-to-25-Year-Olds; Moving Average)

[9]Lopez et al. (2005).
[10]Pryor, J.H., Hurtado, S., Saenz, V.B., Santos, J. L., & Korn, W. S. (2007). *The American Freshman: Forty Year Trends:* Los Angeles: Higher Education Research Institute. UCLA.

Millennials have come of age at a time of closely contested national elections, ideological polarization, terrorist attacks, and war. The parties and other groups are making deliberate efforts to mobilize young people to vote and to participate in other ways. The major news events and political outreach efforts have no doubt caught college students' attention and made them aware that politics matters and that they ought to form opinions about it. Their opinions are in flux, as shown by the ambivalence of many of their answers in our focus groups. But they are trying to pay attention and are actively learning.

Second, the institutional environment has changed. Schools, colleges, and government agencies built an impressive infrastructure to support voluntary service during the 1990s, a decade when youth volunteering rates rose. Although some volunteering pro-grams were episodic and individualistic, a significant proportion of the community service work of the 1990s involved teamwork and group reflection on social issues. Then around 2000, many of the organizations that were concerned about youth civic engagement broadened their attention from volunteering or community service to politics, and indicators of youth political engagement—such as voting—began to increase.

We cannot conclude that deliberate civic programs between 1993 and 2007 were directly responsible for a greater degree of civic and political engagement in the Millennial Generation. However, it is clear that today's college students, compared to college students from Generation X, have more structured opportunities to engage in community service and are presented with more messages about the importance of civic participation.

Literacy Connections

1. Make a list of the major findings of the CIRCLE study.
2. How does CIRCLE define *civic engagement* in this study?
3. As a class, conduct your own research study of college students' civic engagement. Design a survey with questions about civic engagement, distribute the survey to college students, and tabulate and discuss the results.
4. Read the full report of *Millennials Talk Politics* at www.civicyouth.org/?page_id=250, and write a 1–2 page personal response to the report, discussing connections or disconnections between the report and your own experiences and attitudes about civic engagement.
5. Compare the findings of this study by CIRCLE to the research on student civic engagement cited by Catherine Gabor in the opening essay of the chapter, and locate your own experiences within the discussion.

Before You Read

Make a list of ten books that you think all Americans should read. Then, get into small groups and compare your lists. Were there any books that all group members listed? How much did each group member's list depend on his or her personal or cultural preferences and background?

Excerpt from *Cultural Literacy: What Every American Needs to Know*

E. D. Hirsch

E. D. Hirsch's book *Cultural Literacy* became a best-seller when it was published in 1987. Hirsch's arguments about the things every American should know were controversial, and he was criticized for promoting a limited and static view of language and civic knowledge. Hirsch's arguments present a different point of view than most of the readings in this chapter and in *Everything's a Text*, because Hirsch feels that there is a standard way of writing and speaking and a set of texts that every American should be familiar with as part of their civic literacy.

1   Why is literacy so important in the modern world? Some of the reasons, like the need to fill out forms or get a good job, are so obvious that they needn't be discussed. But the chief reason is broader. The complex undertakings of modern life depend on the cooperation of many people with different specialties in different places. Where communications fail, so do the undertakings. (That is the moral of the story of the Tower of Babel.) The function of national literacy is to foster effective nationwide communications. Our chief instrument of communication over time and space is the standard national language, which is sustained by national literacy. Mature literacy alone enables the tower to be built, the business to be well managed, and the airplane to fly without crashing. All nationwide communications, whether by telephone, radio, TV, or writing are fundamentally dependent upon literacy, for the essence of literacy is not simply reading and writing but also the effective use of the standard literate language. In Spain and most of Latin America the literate language is standard written Spanish. In Japan it is standard written Japanese. In our country it is standard written English.

2   Linguists have used the term "standard written English" to describe both our written and spoken language, because they want to remind us that standard spoken English is based upon forms that have been fixed in

dictionaries and grammars and are adhered to in books, magazines, and newspapers. Although standard written English has no intrinsic superiority to other languages and dialects, its stable written forms have now standardized the oral forms of the language spoken by educated Americans. The chief function of literacy is to make us masters of this standard instrument of knowledge and communication, thereby enabling us to give and receive complex information orally and in writing over time and space. Advancing technology, with its constant need for fast and complex communications, has made literacy ever more essential to commerce and domestic life. The literate language is more, not less, central in our society now than it was in the days before television and the silicon chip.

3   The recently rediscovered insight that literacy is more than a skill is based upon knowledge that all of us unconsciously have about language. We know instinctively that to understand what somebody is saying, we must understand more than the surface meanings of words; we have to understand the context as well. The need for background information applies all the more to reading and writing. To grasp the words on a page we have to know a lot of information that isn't set down on the page.

4   Consider the implications of the following experiment described in an article in *Scientific American*. A researcher goes to Harvard Square in Cambridge, Massachusetts, with a tape recorder hidden in his coat pocket. Putting a copy of the *Boston Globe* under his arm, he pretends to be a native. He says to passers-by, "How do you get to Central Square?" The passers-by, thinking they are addressing a fellow Bostonian, don't even break their stride when they give their replies, which consist of a few words like "First stop on the subway."

5   The next day the researcher goes to the same spot, but this time he presents himself as a tourist, obviously unfamiliar with the city. "I'm from out of town," he says. "Can you tell me how to get to Central Square?" This time the tapes show that people's answers are much longer and more rudimentary. A typical one goes, "Yes, well you go down on the subway. You can see the entrance over there, and when you get downstairs you buy a token, put it in the slot, and you go over to the side that says Quincy. You take the train headed for Quincy, but you get off very soon, just the first stop is Central Square, and be sure you get off there. You'll know it because there's a big sign on the wall. It says Central Square." And so on.

6   Passers-by were intuitively aware that communication between strangers requires an estimate of how much relevant information can be taken for granted in the other person. If they can take a lot for granted, their communications can be short and efficient, subtle and complex. But if strangers share very little knowledge, their communications must be long and relatively rudimentary.

7   In order to put in perspective the importance of background knowledge in language, I want to connect the lack of it with our recent lack of success in teaching mature literacy to all students. The most broadly based evidence about our teaching of literacy comes from the National Assessment of Educational Progress (NAEP). This nationwide measurement, mandated by Congress, shows that between 1970 and 1980 seventeen-year-olds declined in their ability to understand written materials, and the decline was especially striking in the top group, those able to read at an "advanced" level. Although these scores have now begun to rise, they remain alarmingly low. Still more precise quantitative data have come from the scores of the verbal Scholastic Aptitude Test (SAT). According to John B. Carroll, a distinguished psychometrician, the verbal SAT is essentially a test of "advanced vocabulary knowledge," which makes it a fairly sensitive instrument for measuring levels of literacy. It is well known that verbal SAT scores have declined dramatically in the past fifteen years, and though recent reports have shown them rising again, it is from a very low base. Moreover, performance on the verbal SAT has been slipping steadily *at the top*. Ever fewer numbers of our best and brightest students are making high scores on the test.

8   Before the College Board disclosed the full statistics in 1984, antialarmists could argue that the fall in average verbal scores could be explained by the rise in the number of disadvantaged students taking the SATs. That argument can no longer be made. It's now clear that not only our disadvantaged but also our best educated and most talented young people are showing diminished verbal skills. To be precise, out of a constant pool of about a million test takers each year, 56 percent more students scored above 600 in 1972 than did so in 1984. More startling yet, the percentage drop was even greater for those scoring above 650—73 percent.

9   In the mid 1980s American business leaders have become alarmed by the lack of communication skills in the young people they employ. Recently, top executives of some large U.S. companies, including CBS and Exxon, met to discuss the fact that their younger middle-level executives could no longer communicate their ideas effectively in speech or writing. This group of companies has made a grant to the American Academy of Arts and Sciences to analyze the causes of this growing problem. They want to know why, despite breathtaking advances in the technology of communication, the effectiveness of business communication has been slipping, to the detriment of our competitiveness in the world. The figures from NAEP surveys and the scores on the verbal SAT are solid evidence that literacy has been declining in this country just when our need for effective literacy has been sharply rising.

10   I now want to juxtapose some evidence for another kind of educational decline, one that is related to the drop in literacy. During the period 1970–1985, the amount of shared knowledge that we have been able to take for granted in communicating with our fellow citizens has also been declining. More and more of our young people don't know things we used to assume they knew.

11   A side effect of the diminution in shared information has been a noticeable increase in the number of articles in such publications as *Newsweek* and the *Wall Street Journal* about the surprising ignorance of the young. My son John, who recently taught Latin in high school and eighth grade, often told me of experiences which indicate that these articles are not exaggerated. In one of his classes he mentioned to his students that Latin, the language they were studying, is a dead language that is no longer spoken. After his pupils had struggled for several weeks with Latin grammar and vocabulary, this news was hard for some of them to accept. One girl raised her hand to challenge my son's claim. "What do they speak in Latin America?" she demanded.

12   At least she had heard of Latin America. Another day my son asked his Latin class if they knew the name of an epic poem by Homer. One pupil shot up his hand and eagerly said, "The Alamo!" Was it just a slip for *The Iliad?* No, he didn't know what the Alamo was, either. To judge from other stories about information gaps in the young, many American schoolchildren are less well informed than this pupil. The following, by Benjamin J. Stein, is an excerpt from one of the most evocative recent accounts of youthful ignorance.

> *I spend a lot of time with teenagers. Besides employing three of them part-time, I frequently conduct focus groups at Los Angeles area high schools to learn about teenagers' attitudes towards movies or television shows or nuclear arms or politicians. . . .*
>
> *I have not yet found one single student in Los Angeles, in either college or high school, who could tell me the years when World War II was fought. Nor have I found one who could tell me the years when World War I was fought. Nor have I found one who knew when the American Civil War was fought. . . .*
>
> *A few have known how many U.S. senators California has, but none has known how many Nevada or Oregon has. ("Really? Even though they're so small?") . . . Only two could tell me where Chicago is, even in the vaguest terms. (My particular favorite geography lesson was the junior at the University of California at Los Angeles who thought that Toronto must be in Italy. My second-favorite geography lesson is the junior at USC, a pre-law student, who thought that Washington, D.C. was in Washington State.). . .*
>
> *Only two could even approximately identify Thomas Jefferson. Only one could place the date of the Declaration of Independence. None could name even one of the first ten amendments to the Constitution or connect them with the Bill of Rights. . . .*

On and on it went. On and on it goes. I have mixed up episodes of ignorance of facts with ignorance of concepts because it seems to me that there is a connection. . . . The kids I saw (and there may be lots of others who are different) are not mentally prepared to continue the society because they basically do not understand the society well enough to value it.

13 My son assures me that his pupils are not ignorant. They know a great deal. Like every other human group they share a tremendous amount of knowledge among themselves, much of it learned in school. The trouble is that, from the standpoint of their literacy and their ability to communicate with others in our culture, what they know is ephemeral and narrowly confined to their own generation. Many young people strikingly lack the information that writers of American books and newspapers have traditionally taken for granted among their readers from all generations. For reasons explained in this book, our children's lack of intergenerational information is a serious problem for the nation. The decline of literacy and the decline of shared knowledge are closely related, interdependent facts.

Literacy Connections

1. Reread and annotate Hirsch's text, underlining places where he defines or describes *literacy*. How is Hirsch's definition and view of literacy different than the definitions of literacy presented in Chapter 1 of *Everything's a Text*?
2. In your own words, write a paragraph that summarizes how Hirsch defines *standard written English*.
3. Hirsch argues, "The function of national literacy is to foster effective nationwide communications. Our chief instrument of communication over time and space is the standard national language. . . ." To what extent do you agree or disagree with Hirsch's argument?
4. Hirsch focuses on the disadvantages of a lack of shared knowledge among diverse groups that are trying to communicate. Can you think of advantages of a diversity of backgrounds and viewpoints in civic literacy situations?
5. In the reading that follows, Eugene Provenzo lists eight questions that he feels conservatives like E. D. Hirsch need to answer. Choose one of these questions and imagine Hirsch's response. Take on Hirsch's persona in your response.

Before You Read

Think of a time when you were silenced because your language or literacy wasn't valued or respected, or a time when your language or literacy was privileged and you used that privilege to silence someone else. Write for five minutes about the time you chose, and be prepared to share your experience with the class.

Excerpt from *Critical Literacy: What Every American Ought to Know*

Eugene Provenzo

E. D. Hirsch's *Cultural Literacy: What Every American Needs to Know* caused such a strong reaction from Eugene Provenzo that he wrote a book in response to Hirsch's. *Critical Literacy* challenges Hirsch's ideas about a standard language and common set of texts that all Americans should be familiar with. Provenzo explores many of the concepts of language diversity and multiple kinds of literacies we've been discussing in *Everything's a Text*, with a focus on the importance of critical literacy.

1   I would maintain that there are a large number of questions that educational and cultural conservatives like E. D. Hirsch, Jr., need to answer. In most instances they are questions that have been raised in different contexts by a wide range of critical educational and cultural theorists. They are questions that repeat many of the issues already described in this work, and also challenge Hirsch's assumptions.

2   *What constitutes really useful knowledge? Whose interest does it serve? What kinds of social relations does it structure and at what price?*

3   This is among the most fundamental questions that Hirsch and his fellow conservatives fail to address. Hirsch assumes that there is a fundamental core of knowledge that is the foundation of American culture. He believes that this core knowledge is largely self-evident and defines what it is to be an American. As he explains, there is a need for an "anthropological model of education" since

> . . . all human communities are founded on specific shared information. Americans are different from Germans, who are in turn different from Japanese, because each group possesses specifically different cultural knowledge. In an anthropological perspective, the basic goal of education in a human community is acculturation, the transmission to children of the specific information shared by the adults of the group or polls.

4   In a highly diverse and multicultural society such as the United States, it is not enough to assume that there is a set and defined culture that all people know. The tradition of competing groups and the struggle for equal representation in American culture makes it different from many other more traditional or homogenous cultures.

5   Ask an African American, a Chicano, a lesbian, or any of the other many disenfranchised individuals if a consensus about what it is to be an American has ever "reigned." Ask a successful female corporate leader,

lawyer, or university president, whether such a consensus existed. Ask the same question of someone from a minority religion.

6   The reality is that American culture has been defined as much by conflicts as consensus. We are a nation that was born in revolution and that has rebelled over different interpretations of the culture ranging from the Civil War to the civil rights movement. One of our greatest virtues as a nation has been to engage in dialogue and discussion, as well as compromise.

7   As a result, it can be argued that the most useful knowledge that educated Americans can have concerns the problems and unresolved issues that we face and the democratic principles on which our nation was founded. Such an approach certainly includes knowing key facts and information, but also emphasizes the idea of learners and citizens being engaged in critical discussions and dialogues about the nature and purpose of a democracy. Examples of questions that need to be addressed in such a model would include: Why have certain groups historically had privileges over others? How has this worked out in terms of race, gender, and ethnicity? How has this contributed to structural inequality in our culture? What problems are evident in our culture as a result of inequality? How can inequality best be addressed?

7   Asking questions of the type outlined above requires the foundation of fundamental background knowledge—knowledge that allows the individual to understand the "patterns which connect" and the forces that have shaped our history and culture. Thus knowledge of the history of slavery, racial discrimination, and ethnic and gender discrimination would be critical. Hirsch's notion that "a human group must have effective communications to function effectively" is obvious. Such communication is predicated, however, on much more than a common foundation of information or "shared culture." Instead it may be based on the sharing of conflicting and sometimes contradictory models that are discussed, debated, and negotiated. Hirsch, by arguing that "Only by accumulating shared symbols, and the shared information that the symbols represent, can we learn to communicate effectively with one another in our national community" leaves out the critical elements of dialogue and exchange.

8   Dialogue, discussion, and debate, with a sound foundation in historical facts and truth, have a much greater potential to lead us to the ideals of a democratic culture and society than a transmission model of education that selects what "every educated American needs to know." Hirsch fails to recognize that the American culture may, in fact, be defined by the debate over what our culture is and what it represents.

9   *What and whose knowledge will be included in a national curriculum?*

10   In reference to any curriculum, Kristen Buras asks "What and whose knowledge is to be included or excluded? Who will decide?" To a large

extent, one's inclusion in the curriculum of any school or culture is a reflection of social and political power. Representation and inclusion does not take place unless one has power. This has been a reality of American history, which can be demonstrated by any careful examination of the experience of groups as diverse as African Americans, women, immigrants, and ethnic minorities. National curricula will exclude their history and specific cultural issues, as a means of maintaining power and the status quo.

11 *What is literacy? What does it mean to be literate?*

12 Literacy is defined by Hirsch within a relatively narrow range of traditions and experiences. Despite his declarations to the contrary, Hirsch leaves out much that is essential to alternative views of American culture and society (see the alternative list of 5,000 items "literate Americans ought to know" later in this book). Historical literacy needs to be much more than the list of the victors. As Todd Gitlin explains, "You don't know American history unless you know the victims as well as the victors."

13 Cultural literacy and the meaning of what it is to be literate are far more sophisticated and complex than anything put forward by Hirsch. If we are to be culturally literate, we must understand who we are as a people and a nation. Historically we have been a federation of states with significant independence and autonomy. Central control has been relatively weak. Our country was settled by "refugees, adventurers, conquered peoples, and slaves—in sum, by peoples, not by a singular people claiming a common root."

14 Cultural literacy is defined by knowledge of the complexity and diversity of the American people. It is a literacy refined in the dialogue that is the essence of the democratic process, and that we should pursue as an essential element of education, whether at the K–12 or university level. Such a model assumes that multiple and competing literacies are at work in American culture. These literacies compete with each other for attention and represent an ongoing process of dialogue and exchange. As Henry Giroux and Stanley Aronowitz explain:

> To acknowledge different forms of literacy is not to suggest that they should all be given equal weight. On the contrary, it is to argue that their differences are to be weighed against the capacity they have for enabling people to locate themselves in their own histories while simultaneously establishing the conditions for them to function as part of a wider democratic culture. This represents a form of literacy that is not merely epistemological, but also deeply political and eminently pedagogical.

15 According to Giroux and Aronowitz, literacy is political since it is a means by which people can be empowered and disempowered. It is pedagogical because it "always involves social relations in which learning takes place; power legitimates a particular view of the world, and privilege, a specific rendering of knowledge."

16   *How does school knowledge enable those who have been generally excluded from schools to speak and act with dignity?*

17   School knowledge that emphasizes a largely transmission model by definition largely precludes the idea of a dialogue and alternative or competing ideas. This does not mean that the knowledge being conveyed is not valid or important. It simply means that it should be subject to *interpretation, contextualization* and *critical interrogation.* Thus Columbus's "discovery of the New World" needs to be critically examined. Whose "New World" was discovered? Was it an "Old World" for the native pre-Columbian populations who occupied North and South American? Was it a discovery, or a conquest, or perhaps even a genocide?

> **"The creation of any cultural canon is by definition selective. Whose history gets chosen is largely a function of power."**

18   Questions such as those listed above explain in part why in 1992 the 500th anniversary celebration of Columbus's discovery of "the New World" was not particularly well received, as compared to the celebrations held 100 years earlier.

19   *What are the basics and why are we teaching them?*

20   The educational philosopher Madeline Grumet makes the interesting point that "If the basics were basic, we imagine, they would be felt in the community. They would be measured in the gait of its people and weighed in the lightness of sorrow." Hirsch assumes that there are basics and they must be taught. In and of itself, this is not a problem. Failing to recognize the fact that there is a selection process involved that "ranks some issues as essential and others as not" is a problem.

21   One thinks back to the early 1980s and the AIDS epidemic in the United States. Raising questions about and curing the disease was less of an issue when its threat seemed to be limited to the gay community. When the disease began to spread into the general population, all of a sudden its identification and cure became a much more "basic" problem.

22   Grumet summarizes the issue over the basics in the following way:

> The basics in all their generic and reductive splendor are meaningless to me when promulgated without reference to persons, places, or times. Basic to whom? Basic to what?

23   These are again some of the fundamental and obvious questions Hirsch fails to answer: What basic core knowledge is being selected? And for what purpose?

24   *Who speaks in a culture? Whose voice is heard?*

25   The creation of any cultural canon is by definition selective. Whose history gets chosen is largely a function of power. It is no accident that until

the 1960s, women's history and literature were largely ignored in university curricula across the country. As women increasingly gained political and social power, they increasingly were able to change the nature of the canon. As James J. O'Donnell argues: "So whoever 'we' are, our version of western civilization is selective in the extreme."

26   *How can a democracy be sustained without an ethic of criticism?*

27   Kristen L. Buras in her review essay of Hirsch's *The Schools We Need and Why We Don't Have Them* asks "how a democracy can be maintained without an ethic of criticism?" She maintains that consensus is essential to Hirsch's theory of schooling. The problem is that consensus—no matter how well-meaning—has the potential to be highly restrictive and undemocratic. Hirsch argues that, "in a large diverse nation, the common school is the only institution available for creating a school-based culture that, like a common language, enables everyone to communicate in a common sphere."

28   As a result Hirsch argues for the creation of a national curriculum—one he has been implementing since 1986 as part of the Core Knowledge Foundation. The problem with a national curriculum is who decides on the content of the curriculum? Buras, drawing on the work of R. W. Connell, refers to the idea of "curricular justice." What about the possibility of the development of a national curriculum from the perspective of social and cultural groups who have been politically disenfranchised? What if a national curriculum was written from the perspective of race relations, gay rights, women's rights? What would be the meaning and content of a national curriculum from the perspective of Native Americans?

29   I suspect that such an approach would be inconceivable to Hirsch. Equally, I believe that Hirsch would have great difficulty in understanding the essentially undemocratic nature of his efforts.

30   *Can there be a shared meaning or commonality in what it means to be an American?*

31   This is a difficult question. There is a distinct problem in American culture in the way we have lumped everyone together for the convenience of categorizing and naming people. We have "blacks" who are described by their skin color as being the same, while failing to recognize the profound social, cultural, and economic differences between them. What does a working class or poor black woman in her late 50s from rural Georgia have in common with a teenage "black" immigrant male from Somalia? What do "Latinos," including Colombians, Puerto Ricans, Argentineans, Mexicans, and Cubans hold in common? What about communities based on sexual orientation, and so on?

32   Our diversity as Americans is a reality that binds us together—perhaps as no other single factor. The debate over culture, the dialogue it engenders and requires, is what defines us. Cultural literacy cannot be a static and conservative phenomenon of the type conceived by Hirsch, but instead must be an active and engaged process—one requiring constant reinterpretation and negotiation. We must go beyond our labels and avoid isolating ourselves from one another as we negotiate who and what we are as a people.

33   Although it would be comforting to tell a single story about the progress and advancement of the American people, the reality is that there is no single story, except that there are many stories, many dialogues, and many outcomes. The United States is a plurality. Its language and culture is far more dynamic and varied than the limited model of cultural literacy put forward by Hirsch and like-minded critics. The anxiety we have about our culture and who we are is understandable. It is also probably inevitable. American culture, with its different religions, languages, geographies, and its commitment to equality and the dream of human perfectibility, cannot be so easily pigeonholed and categorized as Hirsch would like. It is our curse and challenge as a people, our blessing and our future.

Literacy Connections

1. In your own words, summarize Provenzo's definitions of *cultural literacy*. In what ways is Provenzo's definition of *cultural literacy* different from Hirsch's?
2. Now that you've read Hirsch's and Provenzo's excerpts, come up with your own definition of *cultural literacy*.
3. Describe a moment in American history where one group's literacy has been privileged over another's in civic discourse. What effect has that historical moment had on current civic discourse in America?
4. Provenzo argues that "there are many stories" about what it means to be an American. Tell a story from your own experiences about what it means to be an American, focusing on civic literacy.
5. How does Provenzo's notion of "critical literacy" connect to the definitions of *literacy* we discussed in Chapter 1?

Do an Internet search for "Guerilla Girls." As you browse for information, take some notes about who the Guerilla Girls are, what their purpose is, who their audience is, and how they make use of civic literacies.

Guerrilla Girls Posters

The Guerrilla Girls are a feminist art group who use "guerrilla advertising" to make political statements about issues of gender and racial discrimination. The Guerrilla Girls use a variety of genres to participate in civic literacies: books, posters, billboards, art, and ads. To keep their identity secret, members of the group wear guerrilla masks and assume the names of deceased female artists. You can find out more about the Guerrilla Girls at their Web site, www.guerrillagirls.com.

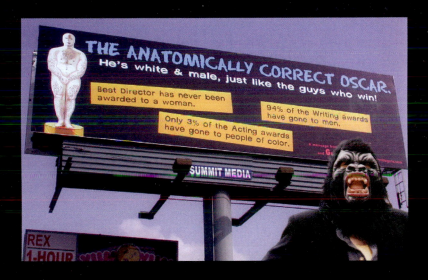

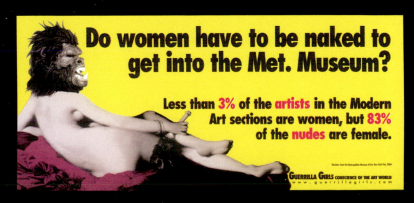

THE U.S. HOMELAND TERRO ALERT SYSTEM
FOR WOMEN

SEVERE
PRESIDENT CLAIMS WOMEN DO HAVE RIGHTS: CAN JOIN ARMY, FIGHT UNPROVOKED WAR, KILL INNOCENT PEOPLE

HIGH
PRESIDENT DECLARES ABSTINENCE HIS FAVORITE FORM OF BIRTH CONTROL AND THE ANSWER TO AIDS EPIDEMIC

ELEVATED
PRESIDENT'S ECONOMIC POLICIES RESULT IN LARGEST JOB LOSSES FOR WOMEN IN 40 YEARS

GUARDED
PRESIDENT APPOINTS MAN TO FEDERAL DRUG ADMINISTRATION WHO BELIEVES PRAYER IS THE BEST TREATMENT FOR PMS

LOW
PRESIDENT RIDES AROUND ON HORSE, CLEARS BRUSH ON RANCH

Notwithstanding the multilingual history of the United States, the role of English as our common language has never seriously been questioned. Research has shown that newcomers to America continue to learn English at rates comparable to previous generations of immigrants. All levels of government should adequately fund programs to teach English to any resident who desires to learn it. Nonetheless, promoting our common language need not, and should not, come at the cost of violating the rights of linguistic minorities.

Literacy Connections

1. In your own words, summarize the main arguments of the position statement.
2. Make a list of the benefits of multilingualism. Then make a list of the disadvantages. Use this list to help you explore the rest of the Literacy Connection questions.
3. The Linguistic Society of America argues, "Where linguistic discord does arise . . . it is generally the result of majority attempts to disadvantage or suppress a minority linguistic community, or it reflects underlying racial or religious conflicts." To what degree is this true or not true in America? Give specific examples to help you explore this question.
4. Do you think bilingualism is perceived as a strength or a handicap in civic discourse in America? Explain and support your position.
5. In what ways do the views of the Linguistic Society of America conflict with E. D. Hirsch's views in the excerpt from *Cultural Literacy*?

Before You Read

Visit the Web site of U.S. English at www.us-english.org/ and browse the site. Then, answer the following questions: What are the goals of U.S. English? What do they mean by "Official English"? According to U.S. English, in what ways is "Official English" different from "English Only"?

Excerpt from the U.S. English Web Site

The following bulleted list of "facts and figures" is from the Web site of U.S. English at www.us-english.org/. According to their Web site, U.S. English is "the nation's oldest, largest citizens' action group dedicated to preserving the unifying role of the English language in the United States. Founded in 1983 by the late Senator S.I. Hayakawa, an immigrant himself, U.S. English now has 1.8 million members nationwide." The U.S. English Web site presents a different view of the relationship between English and civic literacy in America than the Linguistic Society of America's Statement on Language Rights.

7. Multilingualism also presents our nation with many benefits and opportunities. For example, bilingual individuals can use their language skills to promote our business interests abroad. Their linguistic competence strengthens our foreign diplomatic missions and national defense. And they can better teach the rest of us to speak other languages.

8. Moreover, people who speak a language in addition to English provide a role model for other Americans. Our national record on learning other languages is notoriously poor. A knowledge of foreign languages is necessary not just for immediate practical purposes, but also because it gives people the sense of international community that America requires if it is to compete successfully in a global economy.

9. Furthermore, different languages allow different ways of expressing experiences, thoughts, and aesthetics. America's art and culture are greatly enriched by the presence of diverse languages among its citizens.

10. To remedy our policies towards the languages of Native Americans and to encourage acquisition or retention of languages other than English by all Americans, the Linguistic Society of America urges our nation to protect and promote the linguistic rights of its people. At a minimum, all residents of the United States should be guaranteed the following linguistic rights:

    A. To be allowed to express themselves, publicly or privately, in the language of their choice.

    B. To maintain their native language and, should they so desire, to pass it on to their children.

    C. When their facility in English is inadequate, to be provided a qualified interpreter in any proceeding in which the government endeavors to deprive them of life, liberty or property. Moreover, where there is a substantial linguistic minority in a community, interpretation ought to be provided by courts and other state agencies in any matter that significantly affects the public.

    D. To have their children educated in a manner that affirmatively acknowledges their native language abilities as well as ensures their acquisition of English. Children can learn only when they understand their teachers. As a consequence, some use of children's native language in the classroom is often desirable if they are to be educated successfully.

    E. To conduct business in the language of their choice.

    F. To use their preferred language for private conversations in the workplace.

    G. To have the opportunity to learn to speak, read and write English.

2. The territory that now constitutes the United States was home to hundreds of languages before the advent of European settlers. These indigenous languages belonged to several language families. Each native language is or was a fully developed system of communication with rich structures and expressive power. Many past and present members of the Society have devoted their professional lives to documenting and analyzing the native languages of the United States.

3. Unfortunately, most of the indigenous languages of the United States are severely threatened. All too often their eradication was deliberate government policy. In other cases, these languages have suffered from biased or uninformed views that they are mere "dialects" with simple grammatical structures and limited vocabularies. The decline of America's indigenous languages has been closely linked to the loss of much of the culture of their speakers.

4. Because of this history, the Society believes that the government and people of the United States have a special obligation to enable indigenous peoples to retain their languages and cultures. The Society strongly supports the federal recognition of this obligation, as expressed in the Native American Languages Act. The Society urges federal, state and local governments to continue to affirmatively implement the policies of the Act by enacting legislation, appropriating more adequate funding, and monitoring the progress made under the Act.

5. The United States is also home to numerous immigrant languages other than English. The arrival of some of these languages, such as Dutch, French, German, and Spanish, predates the founding of our nation. Many others have arrived more recently. The substantial number of residents of the United States who speak languages other than English presents us with both challenges and opportunities.

6. The challenges of multilingualism are well known: incorporating linguistic minorities into our economic life, teaching them English so they can participate more fully in our society, and properly educating their children. Unfortunately, in the process of incorporating immigrants and their offspring into American life, bilingualism is often wrongly regarded as a "handicap" or "language barrier." Of course, inability to speak English often functions as a barrier to economic advancement in the United States. But to be bilingual—to speak both English and another language—should be encouraged, not stigmatized. There is no convincing evidence that bilingualism by itself impedes cognitive or educational development. On the contrary, there is evidence that it may actually enhance certain types of intelligence.

Before You Read

To help you better understand the social contexts of the following readings on "English Only" and language rights, search the Internet for information about the following terms that you'll find in the readings:

Indigenous language   LEP
Linguistic community   Bilingualism
Dialect   Monolingual
English Only

Statement on Language Rights

Linguistic Society of America

Professional organizations like the Linguistic Society of America often write position statements on important civic issues. Their Position Statement on Language Rights argues for a view of civic literacy that connects with the multiple literacies theme of this book.

The Linguistic Society of America was founded in 1924 to advance the scientific study of language. The Society's present membership of approximately 7000 persons and institutions includes a great proportion of the leading experts on language in the United States, as well as many from abroad. Many of the Society's members have experience with, or expertise in, bilingualism and multilingualism. Despite increasing interest in these topics, public debate is all too often based on misconceptions about language. In this Statement, the Society addresses some of these misconceptions and urges the protection of basic linguistic rights.

1. The vast majority of the world's nations are at least bilingual, and most are multilingual, even if one ignores the impact of modern migrations. Countries in which all residents natively speak the same language are a small exception, certainly not the rule. Even nations like France, Germany and the United Kingdom have important linguistic minorities within their borders. Furthermore, where diverse linguistic communities exist in one country, they have generally managed to coexist peacefully. Finland, Singapore, and Switzerland are only three examples. Where linguistic discord does arise, as it has with various degrees of intensity in Belgium, Canada, and Sri Lanka, it is generally the result of majority attempts to disadvantage or suppress a minority linguistic community, or it reflects underlying racial or religious conflicts. Multilingualism by itself is rarely an important cause of civil discord.

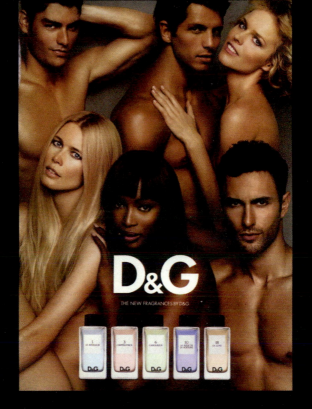

Literacy Connections

1. Do a close visual analysis of one of the magazine ads, considering the ways the ad uses images to influence its audience.
2. In what ways does each ad reflect its time period?
3. In what ways do you think advertisements aimed at men differ from advertisements aimed at women? Whom do the advertisements above seem to be aimed at?
4. Find an advertisement aimed at women from a magazine or Web site. Make a copy of the ad and bring it to class. In small groups, share the ads you found. Make a list of adjectives that describe the way women are portrayed in the ads, and choose one ad to discuss with the class.
5. What connections do you see between Catherine Gabor's definitions of civic literacy and the images from these advertisements?

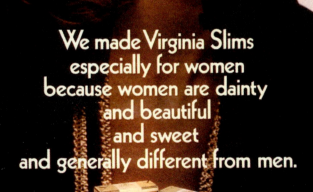

We made Virginia Slims
especially for women
because women are dainty
and beautiful
and sweet
and generally different from men.

Regular or Menthol

You've come a long way, baby.

For You, Too!

STAR-LIKE GLAMOUR TODAY
...A LOVELIER SKIN TOMORROW

Capture that thrilling look of star-like glamour right now . . . in less than a minute . . . with "Pan-Cake" make-up, the famous glamorizing make-up, originated by *Max Factor Hollywood*. It creates a smooth, flawless, beautiful new complexion, helps hide tiny skin faults, and instantly gives you that alluring look of glamour that screen stars always have . . . that you have always wanted. Try it.

DOROTHY LAMOUR
Star of PARAMOUNT'S
"ROAD TO RIO"

PAN-CAKE
BRAND
MAKE-UP

Complete Your Make-up in Colour Harmony with *Max Factor Hollywood* Face Powder, Rouge and Lipstick.

MAX FACTOR
'Cosmetics of
the Stars' are
obtainable
from your local
Chemist, Hair-
dresser & Store

Max Factor
HOLLYWOOD & LONDON

Think of a commercial, billboard, or magazine ad that reflects attitudes about gender in the United States. Describe the ad you're thinking of and why it's a reflection of cultural beliefs about gender.

Images of Women from Magazine Ads Past and Present

The following magazine ads are from the 1920s, 1930s, 1970s, and 2000s. Each of these ads targets a female audience and appeared in magazines with a primarily female readership. As examples of civic literacy, these magazine ads can help you think about the ways in which civic literacies can influence our perception of gender and how those perceptions change over time.

MISS BLOSSOM.

Pure Ivory, (so painters knew,)
Brought out the beauties when they drew
The fine-arched brow and dainty dress
That marked the style of loveliness
Which seems so quaint to me and you.

Now, altered fashions quite eschew
The empire waist and high-heeled shoe,
Yet modern beauties need no less,
Pure Ivory.

So May, whose skin is like the hue
Of orchard sprays when spring steals through—
Her hand, and hair and summer dress
So soft their touch seems a caress—
Finds Ivory her dependence, too—
Pure Ivory Soap.

IT FLOATS

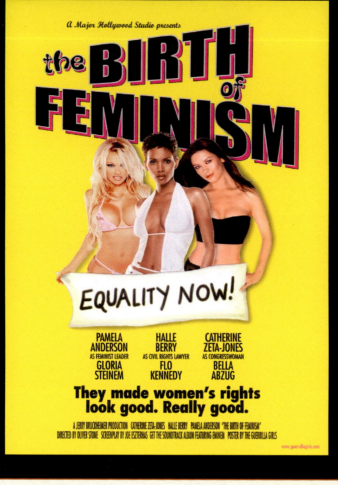

Literacy Connections

1. Write a one- to two-page visual analysis of the four posters, discussing the ways the Guerilla Girls use color and imagery to help persuade readers of their messages.
2. In what ways does the medium the Guerilla Girls communicate in affect the way their messages are communicated?
3. Make a list of other examples of posters as civic literacy. Choose one of your examples and describe the poster and how it makes civic literacy arguments.
4. Create your own poster in the style of the Guerilla Girls and share it with the class.
5. In what ways do the Guerilla Girls posters connect to and work against the images of women from magazine ads?

Facts and Figures

- 92 percent of the world's countries have at least one official language. (Source: *2002 World Almanac*, 2001 U.S. Bureau of the Census Estimates)

- English is the sole official language in 31 nations. An additional 20 nations recognize English as one of two or more official languages. (Source: *2002 World Almanac*, 2001 U.S. Bureau of the Census Estimates)

- In 2000, 21.3 million U.S. residents (8.1 percent of the U.S. population) met the definition of limited English proficient set by the U.S. Census, meaning that they spoke English "less than very well." Of these, 11.0 million, or 4.2 percent spoke English "not well" or "not at all." (Source: Census 2000)

- The number of Americans who do speak English "not at all" jumped from 1.22 million in 1980 to 3.37 million in 2000, a 176 percent increase over 20 years. (Source: U.S. Census)

- California leads the nation in the number of limited English proficient persons, with 6.3 million, or one-fifth of the population of the Golden State. Texas is second with 2.7 million, followed by New York, Florida and Illinois. New Jersey, Arizona, Massachusetts, Georgia and Pennsylvania round out the top 10. (Source: U.S. Census)

- Since 1980, the number of U.S. residents who are limited English proficient has more than doubled, from 10.2 million to 21.3 million. In 1980, fewer than 1-in-20 Americans struggled with English. Now, nearly 1-in-12 do. (Source: U.S. Census)

- In 2000, 11.9 million U.S. residents lived in linguistically isolated households, meaning that no one in the household spoke English at home or spoke English "very well." This figure is up 54 percent from 7.7 million in 1990. In all, more than 1-in-25 households in the United States is linguistically isolated. (Source: Census 2000)

- There are 322 languages spoken at home in the United States. Behind English, the most common languages are Spanish, French, Chinese, German, Tagalog, Vietnamese, Italian, Korean and Russian. (Source: Census 2000)

- California has the most languages spoken at home of any state with 207. New York is second with 169, followed by Washington, Texas and Oregon. Pennsylvania, Florida, Illinois, New Jersey and Arizona round out the top 10 states. (Source: Census 2000)

- English proficiency rates among immigrants vary widely by ancestry. More than 80 percent of the immigrants from several ancestry groups speak English "very well," including Egyptians (90.4 percent), Lebanese (89.5), Pakistanis (87.7), Romanians (86.5), Iranians (86.1), Thais (83.0) and Argentineans (81.6). Other ancestry groups lag far behind the overall average of 71.4 percent English proficient, including Cambodians (65.7), Vietnamese (64.4), Hondurans (53.5), Guatemalans (52.8) and Mexicans (49.9). (Source: Census 2000)

- In 1999, the average employed immigrant who spoke English very well earned $40,741, more than double the $16,345 earned by immigrants who did not speak English at all. The increasing scale of English proficiency and earnings was recorded at every education level from less than high school through master's degree and beyond. (Source: Educational Testing Services, *A Human Capital Concern: The Literary Proficiency of U.S. Immigrants*, March 2004)

- The ability to understand English was so crucial to immigrant success that foreign-born workers with moderate-to-high levels English proficiency had higher earnings than native-born workers with the same degree of English proficiency. More important, data from the National Adult Literacy Survey found that immigrants with a low degree of English proficiency earned one-half of what those with a medium degree of proficiency earned and less than one-third of highly English proficient immigrants. (Source: Educational Testing Services, *A Human Capital Concern: The Literary Proficiency of U.S. Immigrants*, March 2004)

- Immigrants who speak English "not well" or "not at all" have median weekly earnings approximately 57 percent of those of U.S. born workers. The weekly earnings of immigrants who speak another language at home, but speak English "very well" or "well" are nearly 90 percent of those of U.S. born workers. Immigrants who speak English at home are best off, with median weekly earnings 20 percent higher than U.S. born workers. (Source: U.S. Department of Labor, How Do Immigrants Fare in the U.S. Labor Market?, *Monthly Labor Review*, December 1992)

- The U.S. Department of Education found that those with limited English proficiency are less likely to be employed, less likely to be employed continuously, tend to work in the least desirable sectors and earn less than those who speak English. Annual earnings by non-English proficient adults were approximately half of the total population surveyed. (Source: U.S. Department of Education, National Center for Education Statistics; English Literacy and Language Minorities in the United States, August 2001)

- The Tomas Rivera Policy Institute found that, "far and away, the most commonly cited obstacle to gaining college knowledge was the language barrier." While 96 percent of the Latino parents surveyed in the nation's three largest cities expected their children to go to college, nearly two-thirds missed at least half of the questions on a "mini-test of college knowledge." (Source: Tomas Rivera Policy Institute, *College Knowledge*, April 2002)

- Effective English language instruction is an essential antipoverty tool for working immigrant families. Poverty and the need for public benefits, such as food stamps, are more closely related to limited English proficiency than with citizenship or legal status. (Source: Urban Institute, *Immigrant Well-Being in New York and Los Angeles*, August 2002)

- The Canadian Government spends $260 million annually to do government business in both of the nation's official languages. This figure was 0.16% of the Canadian federal budget. If the U.S. was to spend 0.16% of the federal budget to do government business in two languages, the cost would be $3.8 billion. (Source: Office of the Commissioner of Official Languages, Canada)

- The Canadian Government spends $24 per Canadian resident per year to do government business in both of the nation's official languages. If the U.S. was to spend $24 per person per year on government multilingualism, the cost would be $5.7 billion. (Source: Office of the Commissioner of Official Languages, Canada)

- There are 25 nations and 20 official languages in the European Union, yielding 380 translation combinations. (Source: European Commission)

- In June 2004, facing a backlog of 60,000 pages awaiting translation, European Union officials were asked to limit their documents to 15 pages to avoid further burdening the system. The average document size prior to this request was 32 pages. (Source: European Commission)

- There are 1,800 translators, representing eight percent of the entire staff, at the European Commission. (Source: European Commission)

- In 2004, the cost of translation and interpretation at the European Commission was $720 million. It is estimated that by 2007, the cost will have risen to $1.06 billion. (Source: European Commission)

- The cost of multilingual ballots and translations represented one-eighth of Los Angeles County's $16 million expense in the Nov. 2004 general election. (Source: European Commission)

- The City of San Francisco must spend $350,000 for each language that a document is translated into under the city's bilingual government ordinance. (Source: Janet Ng, Asian Week.com, June 2001)

- The total annual cost for the California Department of Motor Vehicles (DMV) to provide language services is $2.2 million. (Source: U.S. Office of Management and Budget, Report to Congress: Assessment of the Total Benefits and Costs of Implementing Executive Order No. 13166: Improving Access to Services for Persons with Limited English Proficiency, March 14, 2002)

- Of the 3,600 Chinese ballots prepared for the Sept. 2002 primary election in King County, Wash., only 24 (or 0.67 percent) were used. (Source: Warren Cornwall, Bilingual voter turnout low: Only 24 Chinese ballots returned in primary, *Seattle Times*, October 9, 2002)

- The total cost of providing multilingual services for the Immigration and Naturalization Service would be between $114 million and $150 million annually. (Source: U.S. Office of Management and Budget, Report to Congress: Assessment of the Total Benefits and Costs on Implementing Executive Order No. 13166: Improving Access to Services for Person with Limited English Proficiency, March 14, 2002)

- It costs $1.86 million annually to prepare written translations for food stamp recipients nationwide. The cost for oral translations skyrocket to $21 million nationally per year. (Source: U.S. Office of Management and Budget, Report to Congress: Assessment of the Total Benefits and Costs of Implementing Executive Order No. 13166: Improving Access to Services for Person with Limited English Proficiency, March 14, 2002)

- 79 percent of Americans, and 81 percent of first and second generation Americans favor making English the official language of the United States. Majority support for official English was recorded among every subgroup, including age, gender, race, and political affiliation. (Source: Zogby International, June 2005)

- A 2001 Gallup poll found that 96 percent of Americans believe that it is essential/important that immigrants living in the United States learn to speak English. (Source: Gallup Poll, 2001)

- 85 percent of Americans believe it is very hard or somewhat hard for immigrants to get a good job or do well in this country without learning English. (Source: Gallup Poll, 2001)

- Nearly two-in-three foreign born adults say that the United States should expect all immigrants to learn English. (Source: Public Agenda survey of 1,002 foreign born adults, 2002)

- 68 percent of Hispanics say that the goal of bilingual education programs should be to make sure that students learn English well. (Source: The Latino Coalition survey of 1,000 Hispanic adults, 2002)

- Three-in-four foreign born adults believe that schools should teach English to immigrant students as quickly as possible, even if it means that they need to catch up in other subjects. (Source: The Latino Coalition survey of 1,000 Hispanic adults, 2002)

- Nearly 90 percent of Latinos believe that adult Latino immigrants need to learn English in order to succeed in the United States. (Source: Pew Hispanic Center/Kaiser Family Foundation survey of 2,929 Hispanic adults, 2002)

- 86 percent of Americans call the ability to speak and understand English an absolutely essential or very important obligation for all Americans. (Source: National Opinion Research Center survey of 2,904 adults, 1996)

Literacy Connections

1. Choose the three statistics in the Facts and Figures list that you felt were the most persuasive. Why did you find them persuasive?
2. Based on the persona and the statistics presented in the Facts and Figures list, whom do you think the primary audience is? Explain your answer.
3. Consider the assertion that "the most commonly cited obstacle to gaining college knowledge was the language barrier." What are some "language barriers" you face in college? What "language barriers" do you face outside of college in your experiences with civic discourses?
4. The U.S. English Web site states that 68 percent of Hispanics say that the primary goal of bilingual education should be to make sure that students learn English well. What are some other goals that you think bilingual education should have? Do you agree that making sure students learn English well should be the primary goal of bilingual education?
5. Contrast these "Facts and Figures" from U.S. English with the Linguistic Society of America Position Statement on Language Rights. Where do you position yourself in the debate?

Before You Read

Think of a time that you didn't have access to something because of a language or cultural barrier. What were your emotions? How did you respond to this lack of access?

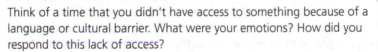

Executive Order 13166: Improving Access to Services for Persons with Limited English Proficiency

President Bill Clinton

President Clinton signed Executive Order 13166 into law in 2000. The goal of the Executive Order is to increase access to government services for citizens who are Limited English Proficient (LEP). In addition to cam-

paigning to make English the official language of the United States,
English Only groups such as U.S. English are working to overturn this
Executive Order. The genre of the "Executive Order," which is a way for
the president to help agencies manage government duties, is an example of a civic discourse genre.

1   By the authority vested in me as President by the Constitution and the
laws of the United States of America, and to improve access to federally
conducted and federally assisted programs and activities for persons who,
as a result of national origin, are limited in their English proficiency (LEP),
it is hereby ordered as follows:

Section 1. Goals.

2 The Federal Government provides and funds an array of services that can
be made accessible to otherwise eligible persons who are not proficient in
the English language. The Federal Government is committed to improving
the accessibility of these services to eligible LEP persons, a goal that reinforces its equally important commitment to promoting programs and activities designed to help individuals learn English. To this end, each Federal
agency shall examine the services it provides and develop and implement
a system by which LEP persons can meaningfully access those services consistent with, and without unduly burdening, the fundamental mission of
the agency. Each Federal agency shall also work to ensure that recipients
of Federal financial assistance (recipients) provide meaningful access to
their LEP applicants and beneficiaries. To assist the agencies with this
endeavor, the Department of Justice has today issued a general guidance
document (LEP Guidance), which sets forth the compliance standards that
recipients must follow to ensure that the programs and activities they normally provide in English are accessible to LEP persons and thus do not discriminate on the basis of national origin in violation of title VI of the Civil
Rights Act of 1964, as amended, and its implementing regulations. As
described in the LEP Guidance, recipients must take reasonable steps to
ensure meaningful access to their programs and activities by LEP persons.

Sec. 2. Federally Conducted Programs and Activities.

3 Each Federal agency shall prepare a plan to improve access to its federally
conducted programs and activities by eligible LEP persons. Each plan shall
be consistent with the standards set forth in the LEP Guidance, and shall
include the steps the agency will take to ensure that eligible LEP persons
can meaningfully access the agency's programs and activities. Agencies
shall develop and begin to implement these plans within 120 days of the

date of this order, and shall send copies of their plans to the Department of Justice, which shall serve as the central repository of the agencies' plans.

Sec. 3. Federally Assisted Programs and Activities.

4 Each agency providing Federal financial assistance shall draft title VI guidance specifically tailored to its recipients that is consistent with the LEP Guidance issued by the Department of Justice. This agency-specific guidance shall detail how the general standards established in the LEP Guidance will be applied to the agency's recipients. The agency-specific guidance shall take into account the types of services provided by the recipients, the individuals served by the recipients, and other factors set out in the LEP Guidance. Agencies that already have developed title VI guidance that the Department of Justice determines is consistent with the LEP Guidance shall examine their existing guidance, as well as their programs and activities, to determine if additional guidance is necessary to comply with this order. The Department of Justice shall consult with the agencies in creating their guidance and, within 120 days of the date of this order, each agency shall submit its specific guidance to the Department of Justice for review and approval. Following approval by the Department of Justice, each agency shall publish its guidance document in the Federal Register for public comment.

Sec. 4. Consultations.

5 In carrying out this order, agencies shall ensure that stakeholders, such as LEP persons and their representative organizations, recipients, and other appropriate individuals or entities, have an adequate opportunity to provide input. Agencies will evaluate the particular needs of the LEP persons they and their recipients serve and the burdens of compliance on the agency and its recipients. This input from stakeholders will assist the agencies in developing an approach to ensuring meaningful access by LEP persons that is practical and effective, fiscally responsible, responsive to the particular circumstances of each agency, and can be readily implemented.

Sec. 5. Judicial Review.

6 This order is intended only to improve the internal management of the executive branch and does not create any right or benefit, substantive or procedural, enforceable at law or equity by a party against the United States, its agencies, its officers or employees, or any person.

WILLIAM J. CLINTON
THE WHITE HOUSE,
August 11, 2000.

Literacy Connections

1. How would you describe the tone and style of the genre of the Executive Order? In what ways ara the tone and style appropriate for the purpose, audience, and context?

2. How does President Clinton justify the Executive Order?

3. If you were the President of the United States, would you support this Executive Order or would you overturn it? Explain your position.

4. Do an Internet search for "Executive Order 13166" and write a summary of the arguments made both for and against the order. To what extent do you agree or disagree with the arguments you've found?

5. Write a script for a talk show with the theme of "The English Only Debate" and include President Clinton, a representative from the Linguistic Society of America, and a representative from U.S. English as guests. In your script, have your three guests debate the issues surrounding English Only.

Civic Literacy Projects

Political Media Analysis

In this project, you'll do a rhetorical analysis of an artifact from the media that focuses on politics—for example, the Opinion section of a newspaper, a news show or cable news network, a political blog, a speech from a political figure, etc. Examine the rhetorical features of the artifact such as purpose, audience, medium, persona, genre, and context. If your artifact includes sound and/or images, you will need to consider oral and visual rhetoric. When you consider the context of the artifact you analyze, discuss the ways that the artifact reflects or influences civic literacy.

Campus Newspaper Letter to the Editor

In this project, you'll write to a civic audience beyond the classroom in a common civic literacy genre: the editorial. Read through several editions of your campus newspaper (online or in print) and choose an article you'd like to respond to. Then, write a letter to the editor, following the format prescribed by the editor of your campus newspaper. E-mail or mail the letter to the editor, following the instructions described in the newspaper. Also give a copy to your teacher, along with a one- to two-page process memo describing the ways that writing for a civic audience was different from writing for the audience of the teacher.

Public Service Ad Campaign

This project will give you a chance to create your own public service ad campaign for an audience beyond the classroom. Think of a public issue you are interested in researching and creating an ad campaign for. It could be a campus issue, such as course fees or binge drinking or student diversity, or a broader local or national issue. Write a one- to two-page audience analysis in which you discuss the characteristics of your target audience. Then, create a flier or poster ad campaign aimed at your target audience that combines both words and images. You'll most likely need to conduct research to learn more about the issue. Create at least three kinds of fliers or posters, and make enough copies to post them around campus or the community (be careful to post them only in areas that are not "off-limits" for posting). Your teacher might ask you to present your campaign to the class and discuss the rhetorical choices you made as you created your campaign, and/or to reflect on your campaign and your composing processes in a process memo.

Cultural Literacy Position Paper

In this project, you'll enter the conversation between Hirsch and Provenzo and discuss your position on cultural literacy. Reread the excerpts from Hirsch and Provenzo and underline their central arguments. Then, choose one of these arguments and enter the conversation, giving your own position on the issue in response to Hirsch and Provenzo. To support your position you might use evidence from the readings, your own experiences, or evidence from outside research. Don't feel as though you need to take one side or another in the debate—you might have a more nuanced argument that takes into consideration a variety of viewpoints. You can choose the genre of the text you create. It could be an academic essay, an editorial, a Web site, a script of a news show, a documentary, etc.

Writing with the Community: Service Learning

In this project, your teacher will help you connect with a nonprofit community service agency to complete a service learning project like the one from the case study of Rani in the chapter. Because service learning projects are often complex and extensive, your teacher might ask you to work in groups. Like Rani from the case study, you'll want to share drafts of your project with your peers, your teacher, and with the service agency you are connected with. Include with your final draft of the project any rough drafts and a two- to three-page process letter in which you explore the following questions:

- How was writing for the community similar to and different than writing for a classroom audience?
- How did the public audience shape the final product and the revisions you made?
- What genre did you compose in, and how did the genre shape your composing process and the rhetorical choices you made?
- If you had more time, what revisions would you make?

Group Project: Parody Newspaper

In this project, the class will form groups of three to five people, and each group will create its own print or online parody newspaper. For an example of a parody newspaper, browse *The Onion* at www.theonion.com/content/index. Group members may write articles individually or collaboratively, and the newspaper could include images (and even sound and video, if you choose to publish it online). Although each group member should participate in writing articles, it might be helpful to give each member a role (for example, "editor," "scheduler," "researcher," "publisher" etc.).

Credits

Text Credits

Academy of American Poets: "A Brief Guide to Slam Poetry," online at http://www.poets.org/viewmedia.php/prmMID/5672. Reprinted by permission of The Academy of American Poets.

Accawi, Anwar: "The Telephone" from *The Boy from the Tower of the Moon* by Anwar Accawi, first published by Beacon Press, Boston. © Anwar Accawi, © Éditions Autrement, Paris, 2010. Reprinted by permission of Éditions Autrement.

Alexie, Sherman: "Superman and Me" by Sherman Alexie, originally published in the Los Angeles Times, April 19, 1998. Copyright © 1998 Sherman Alexie. Reprinted by permission of Nancy Stauffer Associates. All rights reserved.

Alkema, Nancy: "The Effects of Parental Neglect on Types of Children" by Nancy Alkema, from *Writing the University*, Vol. 1, 2009. Reprinted by permission of the author.

Anderson, Dustin: "Surfing, Searching, and Social Networking: Redefining Digital Literacy with Facebook and Wikipedia" by Dustin Anderson. Reprinted by permission of the author.

Anzaldúa, Gloria: From *Borderlands/La Frontera: The New Mestiza* by Gloria Anzaldúa. Copyright © 1987, 1999, 2007 by Gloria Anzaldúa. Reprinted by permission of Aunt Lute Books. www.auntlute.com.

ASPCA: Homepage, www.aspca.org, copyright © 2010, The American Society for the Prevention of Cruelty to Animals (ASPCA). All Rights Reserved. Reprinted with permission.

Bachrach, Dustin: "10 Necessary Mac Apps for the College Student," posted at http://dbachrach.com/blog/2007/09/10-necessary-mac-apps-for-the-college-student/. Reprinted by permission of the author.

Bachrach, Dustin: Icons for Show Yourself, Todos, and Digg Update are used by permission of Dustin Bachrach.

Bader, Jenny Lyn: "Larger Than Life" by Jenny Lyn Bader. Copyright © 1994 by Jenny Lyn Bader, from *Next: Young American Writers on the New Generation*, edited by Eric Lieu. Used by permission of the author and W.W. Norton and Company, Inc.

Bang, Molly: From *Picture This: How Pictures Work* by Molly Bang. Copyright © 2000 by Molly Bang. Reprinted by permission of Chronicle Books LLC, San Francisco. Visit ChronicleBooks.com.

Barry, Lynda: "Two Questions" by Lynda Barry. Copyright © 2004 by Lynda Barry. Originally published in McSweeney's Quarterly Concern and used courtesy of Darhansoff, Verrill, Feldman Literary Agents.

Beals, Ellen Wade: "Between the Sheets" by Ellen Wade Beals. Reprinted by permission of the author.

Davidson, Alexis: "Oral Literacies–Finding Your Voice" by Alexis Davidson. Reprinted by permission of the author.

DeCurtis, Anthony: "I'll Take My Stand: A Defense of Popular Culture" from *Rocking My Life Away: Writing About Music and Other Matters* by Anthony DeCurtis, © 1998. Reprinted by permission of the author.

Dumka, Allison: "Mascot ban about abuse, not political correctness" by Allison Dumka, published in the Arizona Daily Wildcat, March 1, 2007. Republished with permission form the Arizona Daily Wildcat.

Eppler, Martin: "A Periodic Table of Visualization Methods" by Martin J. Eppler, posted at www.visual-literacy.org/periodic_table/periodic_table.html. Reprinted by permission of the author.

Etresoft: EtreTask icon used with permission from Etresoft.

Gabor, Catherine: "Writing as Public Power: Civic Literacies" by Catherine Gabor. Reprinted by permission of the author.

Gee, James Paul: From *What Video Games Have to Teach Us About Learning and Literacy* by James Paul Gee. Published 2003 by Palgrave MacMillan. Copyright © James Paul Gee, 2003. Reproduced with permission of Palgrave MacMillan.

George Mason University: "Standards of Good Writing in Philosophy" by Faculty of the Department of Philosophy, George Mason University. Reprinted by permission.

Giang, Alexandra: "Not for Sale" by Alexandra Giang. Reprinted by permission of the author.

Glade, Fiona: "Writing Across the University: Academic Discourse as a Conversation" by Fiona Glade. Reprinted by permission of the author.

Gooden, Jasmine: From "Musings of a College Student," online at http://musingsfacollegestudent.net/wordpress/?p=37. Reprinted by permission of the author.

Granger, Cameron: "Pictures in America: It Isn't Just About How Many Words They're Worth" by Cameron Granger, published in *e-Vision,* the online publication of James Madison University's School of Writing, Rhetoric and Technical Communication, Vol. Six, Spring/Fall 2005. Reprinted by permission.

Greenpeace: "Green my Apple" screenshot at http://www.greenpeace.org/apple/ is used by permission of Greenpeace.

Haflidason, Almar: Online movie review of *Trainspotting* (1996) is reprinted by permission of Almar Haflidason.

Hall, Peter: "Living the Virtual Life: A Second Life" by Peter Hall. Reprinted by permission of the author.

Hamilton, Amy Hodges: "What I Got to Do with It? Personal Literacies in the Writing Classroom" by Amy Hodges Hamilton. Reprinted by permission of the author.

HBO: "About the show: Russell Simmons presents *Def Poetry*," press release from HBO. Used by permission of Home Box Office, Inc.

Henderson, Amanda: "Flying Cars and Endless Playlists" by Amanda Henderson. Reprinted by permission of the author.

Hirata, Satoshi: Reprinted from *Behavioural Processes*, Vol. 75, Issue 1, Satoshi Hirata, "A note on the responses of chimpanpanzees (Pan troglodytes) to live self-images on television monitors," pp. 85-90, copyright ©2007 Elsevier B.V., with permission from Elsevier.

McDonough, Yona Zeldis: "Sex and the Single Doll" from *The Barbie Chronicles* by Yona Zeldis McDonough. Originally published as "What Barbie Really Taught Me" in the New York Times, Jan. 25, 1998. Copyright © 1998 The New York Times Company. Reprinted by permission.

Melzer, Scott: Instructor comments by Scott Melzer, from "Student Case Study: Composing an Academic Research Project" by Greg Calabrese. Reprinted by permission of Scott Melzer.

NCTE: From "The Defiinition of 21st Century Literacies," adopted by the National Council of Teachers of English (NCTE) Executive Committee, Feb. 15, 2008 (http://www.ncte.org/governance/literacies).

O'Malley, Jennifer: "ENC1102 Class blog," at http://enc1102fall2009.wordpress.com/ is reprinted by permission of the author.

Odom, Mel: Graphic Novel Review of "Locke & Key" by Joe Hill and Gabriel Rodriguez, review by Mel Odom. Originally published September 26, 2008 on Blogcritics.org. Reprinted by permission.

Online Review of The *Twilight* Saga: *New Moon* is reprinted by permission.

Osborne, Cheryl: "Outcomes for Written and Oral Communication in Gerontology," by Dr. Cheryl Osborne, posted online at Department of Gerontology, California State University Sacramento website. Reprinted by permission.

Phares, Ashley Nicole: "Mechanistic and Genetic Causes of Depression and the Effect of SSRIs on the Serotonergic Pathway" by Ashley Nicole Phares, published in *JOSHUA: Journal of Science and Health, University of Alabama*, Vol. 5, May 2008. Reprinted by permission.

Pitcher, Gopi: Student Case Study, "Composing a Digital Slideshow" by Gopi Pitcher. Reprinted by permission of the author.

Provenzo Jr., Eugene: This selection was originally published in *Critical Literacy: What Every American Ought to Know* by Eugene Provenzo, Jr. (Paradigm Publishers, 2005) and has been reprinted with the consent of the publisher.

Quindlen, Anna: "Public and Private: Barbie at 35" by Anna Quindlen, originally published in The New York Times, Sept. 10, 1994. Copyright © 1994 by Anna Quindlen. Reprinted by permission of International Creative Management, Inc.

Ritchie, Donald A.: From "An Oral History of Our Time" from *Doing Oral History: A Practical Guide, 2e* by Donald A. Ritchie. Copyright © 2003 by Donald A. Ritchie. Reprinted by permission of Oxford University Press, Inc.

Rogers, Ray: Interview with Beck (Hansen) by Ray Rogers, *Interview Magazine*, 1996. Reprinted by permission of Brant Publications, Inc.

Sethi, Harshjit: "Constitutionality v. Morality: San Antonio School District v. Rodriguez" by Harshjit Sethi. Reprinted by permission of the author.

Shacked Software, LLC: Flickpad icon is used by permission of Shacked Software, LLC.

Sia, Beau: "An Open Letter to the Entertainment Industry" by Beau Sia. Reprinted by permission of the author.

Smith, Dante: From "Dollar Day," words and music by Dante Smith (Mos Def, pseud.) Published by EMI Blackwood Music, Inc., and No Mistakes Allowed Publishing. All rights reserved. Used by permission.

Photo Credits

p. 1 (both): Photos taken by author; **p. 8:** The William J. Clinton Presidential Library; **p. 13:** © Getty Images; **p. 23:** © Cynthia Hart Designer/Corbis; **p. 24:** © GL Archive/Alamy; **p. 25:** Image courtesy of The Advertising Archives; **p. 27 (both):** Photos taken by author; **p. 30:** © Miramax Films/courtesy Everett Collection; **p. 39:** The National Highway Traffic Safety Administration (NHTSA); **pp. 46–47:** M. C. Escher's "High and Low" © 2010 The M. C. Escher Company—Hollard. All rights reserved. www.mcescher.com; **p. 62 (left):** © ICP-UK/Alamy; **p. 62 (right):** Photo taken by author; **p. 135 (both):** Photos taken by author; **p. 195 (top):** Photo taken by Donald Sullivan; **p. 195 (bottom):** Photo taken by Jerry Walsh; **p. 209 (both):** Photos taken by author; **p. 214:** Courtesy of Tina Griffin; **p. 221 (top left):** © Eric Miller/Reuters/Landov; **p. 221 (top right):** SunnyS/Fotolia; **p. 221 (bottom left):** © Danny Moloshok/Reuters/Landov; **p. 221 (bottom right):** © G Bill Greene/Boston Globe /Landov; **p. 225 (top):** © Ted Soqui/Corbis; **p. 225 (bottom left):** © Culver Pictures/The Art Archive; **p. 225 (bottom right):** © Hulton Archive/Getty Images; **p. 255 (left):** © Getty Images; **p. 255 (right):** © Stephen Mcsweeny/Shutterstock; **p. 256:** © General Motors Corp. Used with permission, GM Media Archives; **p. 264 (both):** Photos taken by author; **p. 333 (left):** Photo taken by author; **p. 333 (right):** © Fred Prouser/Reuters/Landov; **pp. 388–393:** © 2010 Joe Hill, Gabriel Rodriguez and IDW Publishing. Used with permission; **p. 398 (left):** Photo taken by author; **p. 398 (right):** © Laurence Gough/Shutterstock; **p. 488 (left):** Photo taken by author; **p. 488 (right):** © Media Bakery/Alamy; **p. 502 (top left):** © Sauber/plainpicture/Corbis; **p. 502 (top right):** © Prentice Hall, Inc.; **p. 502 (center):** © Prentice Hall, Inc.; **p. 502 (bottom left):** © Jérôme Sessini/Sygma/Corbis; **p. 502 (bottom right):** © Prentice Hall, Inc.

Inserts:

Chapter 5

p. 3: Image Courtesy of Pest Control Office; **p. 4 (both):** © AFP/Getty Images; **p. 5:** © omen514.com; **p. 6:** © Edward Hopper, "Nighthawks". 1942. Oil on Canvas. 40" x 60". Friends of American Art. Photography © 2010 The Art Institute of Chicago. All Rights Reserved. **p. 7 (top):** © The Phillips Collection, Washington, D.C.; **p. 7 (bottom):** © Francis G. Mayer/Corbis.

Chapter 7

p. 2: Courtesy of *OK! Magazine;* **p. 3:** Courtesy *JET Magazine.* All rights reserved.; **p. 4:** ©Vanity Fair/Conde Nast Publications; **p. 6** (top): © www.Beepstock.com/Robinbeckham/Alamy; **p. 6 (bottom):** © Topham/The Image Works; **p. 7 (both):** © Scott Houston/Sygma/Corbis; **p. 8:** © Marty Lederhandler/AP Images.

Chapter 9

p. 1-3 (all): Copyright © by Guerrilla Girls, Inc. Courtesy www.guerrillagirls.com; **p. 4:** © North Wind Picture Archives/Alamy; **p. 5-8 (all):** Image courtesy of The Advertising Archives.

Index